PERSUASION

RECEPTION AND RESPONSIBILITY

PERSUASION

RECEPTION AND RESPONSIBILITY

SIXTH EDITION

CHARLES U. LARSON

Northern Illinois University

Wadsworth Publishing Company
Belmont, California
A Division of Wadsworth, Inc.

To Mary, without whom, ...

Communications Editor: Holly Allen
Development Editor: Maggie Murray
Editorial Assistant: Katherine Hartlove
Production: Del Mar Associates
Print Buyer: Randy Hurst
Permissions Editor: Robert Kauser
Designer: Stuart Paterson/Image House
Copy Editor: Andrea Olshevsky
Technical Illustrator: Salinda Tyson
Cover Design and Illustration: John Odam
Compositor: Thompson Type

This book is printed on acid-free paper that meets Environmental Protection Agency standards for recycled paper.

1 2 3 4 5 6 7 8 9 10 — 96 95 94 93 92

Library of Congress Cataloging in Publication Data

Larson, Charles U.
    Persuasion : reception and responsibility / Charles U. Larson. —
6th ed.
      p.   cm.
    Includes bibliographical references and index.
    ISBN 0-534-14982-0
    1. Persuasion (Psychology)   I. Title.
BF637.P4L36   1991
302.2'4 — dc20   91-11823
                                    CIP

CONTENTS

Chapter 3

APPROACHES TO PERSUASION RESEARCH: THE ROOTS OF RESEARCH IN PERSUASION   54

Chapter 4

THE MAKING, USE, AND MISUSE OF SYMBOLS   95

Chapter 5

TOOLS FOR ANALYZING LANGUAGE AND OTHER SYMBOLS   112

PART

APPLICATIONS OF PERSUASIVE PREMISES   258

Chapter 10

THE PERSUASIVE CAMPAIGN OR MOVEMENT   260

Chapter 11

BECOMING A PERSUADER   296

Chapter 12

MODERN MEDIA AND PERSUASION   319

Chapter 13

THE TECHNIQUES OF PROPAGANDA   349

Chapter 14

THE USE OF PERSUASIVE PREMISES IN ADVERTISING   370

PREFACE

When I wrote the first edition of *Persuasion: Reception and Responsibility* in 1973, I never expected to write a sixth edition. I wrote the book then because I was concerned about the degree to which the speech communication field had neglected the role of the receiver in the persuasion process. This neglect seemed particularly dangerous in light of the times in which we were living. The United States was on the verge of a national nervous breakdown over Vietnam, racism, sexism, political assassination, and corruption in high places; a counterculture promoted free sex, free drugs, communal living, rejection of traditional values, and splitting of the generations. The public was vulnerable to almost overwhelming amounts of all kinds of persuasion, from both the far left and the far right. Much of the persuasion came from the federal government and was made even more potent because of newly developing technologies in mass communication.

Published in the midst of these events, the first edition of *Persuasion: Reception and Responsibility* received a warm welcome. In 1973, most college students were idealistic baby boomers who refused to trust anyone over thirty (which was fine with me since I was still a few years away from that age bracket). They believed that the sheer moral force of their collective wills could change the course of history. (And perhaps it did — they toppled two presidents, advanced the rights of women and minorities, and brought government under increasing scrutiny.) They — and their professors, my colleagues in the discipline — were ready for a book that was receiver-oriented and that encouraged critical reception and acceptance/rejection of persuasive messages, judged from a perspective of what we called "ethical behavior."

With each revision of the book since then, I have tried to respond to the communication/persuasion *milieu* that I believed was (or soon would be) facing the generation of students who would be using the book — just as I tried to respond to the needs of an anti-war generation of student receivers that first time around. This sixth edition has been no exception.

CHANGES IN THE SIXTH EDITION

Many changes have occurred in the world of persuasion since the fifth edition was published in 1989: a savings and loan scandal that may exceed $165 billion in losses that you and I will have to pay for as citizens; the apparent bankruptcy and collapse of Leninist-Marxism and the accompanying fall of various Soviet Bloc governments; new and more vigorous concern for the environment; and Operation Desert Storm and its effects on world-wide foreign policy, to name a few. These and other events are reflected in new examples, visuals, and discussion throughout the book.

Another change is the addition of two new chapters: Chapter 5 is "Tools for Analyzing Language and Other Symbols" and Chapter 9 is "Nonverbal Messages in Persuasion." Although some elements in these chapters were included in previous editions, they were always considered in a secondary position. The tools for analyzing language were discussed with a chapter on the human imperative to use symbols and language, and non-verbal elements of persuasion were touched on briefly in conjunction with the chapter on "Cultural Premises in Persuasion." By giving each of these topics chapter status, I have been able to deal with them more fully.

Finally, some chapters have undergone major revisions to bring them up to date with contemporary research. The best example is the chapter on "Content Premises in Persuasion," which takes into account several major reviews of current research into evidence and reasoning. Also included is a new focus in the chapter on the explanatory power of the "Elaboration Likelihood Model" of persuasion.

These changes, together with other strengths of previous editions (for example, the chapters on ethics, propaganda, advertising, campaigns, and the mass media) make this sixth edition not only responsive to current events and theories but, I believe, anticipatory of the persuasion barrage facing receivers of the 1990s and beyond. In any case, its focus on the receiver, or consumer, of persuasion is still the central thrust of the book and one that many say make it unique in the marketplace.

ACKNOWLEDGMENTS

No book ever reaches print without the help of many talented and sharing persons: colleagues, students, editors, and critics, all of whom deserve thanks. First and foremost, I thank the graduate and undergraduate students who keep challenging my sometimes old-fashioned and limited view of persuasion; I have learned as much from them as they have from me. I would also like to thank those who formally critiqued the manuscript while in progress: Richard Armstrong, Wichita State University; James Dillard, University of Wisconsin, Madison; Steve Duck, University of Iowa; Bruce Gronbeck, University of Iowa; Virginia Katz, University of Minnesota, Duluth; Heidi Much, Wright State University; and Fred Rogers, California State University, Long Beach. You have all offered valuable advice and continue to lead me to new sources of and perspectives on persuasion.

Finally, the sixth edition would not have been possible without the staff at Wadsworth: Becky Hayden, who first recognized the need for a receiver-oriented textbook in persuasion; Kris Clerkin and Peggy Randall, who kept me on task and on schedule; and all the other Wadsworth staffers and freelancers who helped make this sixth edition possible. Most especially, though, I offer thanks to you teachers and students who have used earlier editions and who will use this edition. I welcome your suggestions and advice for further revisions, and I hope that, in some way, this book will help make us all critical receivers of the persuasion of the next millenium.

PART

I

THEORETICAL PREMISES

The 1990s were ushered in with a breathtaking set of megachanges. Consider a few of them: the collapse and final bankruptcy of over seventy years of Marxist/Leninist socialism in Eastern Europe and the Soviet Union; the end of the cold war; huge federal deficits; a massive savings and loan industry scandal that will cost us and our children thousands of dollars each; more soldiers stationed in Saudi Arabia than were in Vietnam; political elections à la bash and smear, complete with innuendo and name-calling; and the worsening of the AIDS and drug epidemics, to name but a few. Underlying all of this change is a constant — the permanent presence of persuasion from all sides. Persuasion has been a common denominator in the arenas of economics, politics, religion, business, and interpersonal relations ever since humans began to interact. Never before, however, has it had such great potential as a tool for affecting our daily lives, as a means to many ends — both good and not so good — and as a presence in nearly every moment of our waking lives. Our world today and the world we will face as we approach the millenium rest on the power of various kinds of persuasion.

As you read and use this book to study persuasion, I hope you will change in important ways. We live in a world in which persuasive messages of various types continually compete for our attention and favor. What's more, the exciting times in which we live depend heavily on successful persuasion, whether in rebuilding Eastern Europe and other Soviet Bloc nations or in electing a new President of the United States. On less global levels, persuasion affects consumer behavior, interpersonal behavior, and intrapersonal behavior — self-persuasion. Most of the time, we do not send persuasive messages; instead, we are predominantly in the role of the persuadee, or receiver and consumer, of persuasive messages. The goal of this book and class is to make you more critical and responsible consumers of persuasion.

In some ways, we are already critical receivers, but we can improve our reception skills; that is what this book should teach you to do. You will need to identify how critical a receiver you are presently: How easily are you persuaded? How does persuasion work on you? What tactics are most effective with you? With others? Which are least effective? Part I investigates these questions and establishes a perspective for you. Part II is a search for fundamental persuasive premises that can sway most receivers. These are the foundations on which persuaders build their arguments. We need to understand how and why persuaders appeal to these premises. Why do we respond to certain psychological appeals and not to others? Why are some lines of reasoning more convincing than others? Why do persuadees in some cultures respond to certain appeals and not to others? These are the questions Part II will try to answer. Finally, Part III explores some of the contexts in which persuasion operates — campaigns, public speeches, interpersonal persuasion, some parts of the mass media, propaganda, and advertising.

Chapter 1 looks at the degree to which persuasion dominates our lives. We will examine several definitions of persuasion, ranging from those rooted in ancient Greece to those derived from our contemporary media age. We will discuss a useful model suggested by Hugh Rank, a scholar of persuasion and propaganda. The model was an outgrowth of Rank's work with the National Council of Teachers of English (NCTE) and their concern over the increase in "doublespeak," the attempt to use words to confuse and mislead an audience. In Chapter 2, Richard L. Johannesen provides a variety of approaches to the ethical issues that arise whenever persuasion occurs. Keep in mind that these approaches and issues involve both persuaders and persuadees — senders and receivers, advertisers and consumers, politicians and their constituents, governments and citizens.

Chapter 3 looks at a variety of theories that explain how persuasion operates from different perspectives. This summary of theories is intended to whet your appetites for more in-depth study of these perspectives. Consider Chapter 3 as a table of appetizers or hors d'oeuvres at a banquet — as a sampler of views for you to try. Chapter 4 examines the raw material of persuasion — human symbolic behavior — especially as it occurs in language. Part I concludes with Chapter 5, which describes and demonstrates several alternative ways receivers can analyze, interpret, decode, and finally critique persuasive language. It is not important that you find one approach that you prefer, but that you consider the various alternatives.

Part I sets the stage for a deeper investigation of persuasion and its applications. Exploration of this field can be traced back to Aristotle and his study of persuasion in the Greek democracy. He knew that by establishing common ground, persuaders could get audiences to identify with them. Thus, it was the persuader's task to find areas of common beliefs and preferences. Aristotle believed that having identified this common ground, persuaders could develop arguments in which the audience participates by providing a part of the argument — usually a widely held major premise. He called these participative arguments *enthymemes*, or abbreviated syllogisms. Thus our search in Part II for those premises that seem persuasive to large numbers of persuadees reflects Aristotle's teaching.

When you finish this book and course, I hope you will find that you have changed from a somewhat uncritical persuadee to a responsible and analytical receiver, ready to face the persuasion blitz of the 1990s and beyond.

■

CHAPTER 1

Persuasion in Today's World

▼

CHANGE AND STABILITY IN A TECHNOLOGICAL AGE

It has been nearly twenty years since the first edition of *Persuasion: Reception and Responsibility* was published. Naturally, the world is quite a different place from what it was in the midst of the Vietnam war, with its angry demonstrations and revolutionary rhetoric. Yet some things remain constant, especially in regard to the dynamics of persuasion.

Change

Consider just a few of the changes that we have experienced during the past two decades. We came close to impeaching a president; we abandoned a major war in Vietnam; the Democratic party faded from dominance; the national debt passed $1 trillion; the stock market took its biggest tumble in history; and the age of the personal computer dawned. We have also incorporated a host of technological innovations into our daily lives: video cameras and recorders, cable and satellite television options, new telephone systems, and automatic teller machines among them. On the political/economic front, we were each billed several thousand dollars to bail out the savings and loan industry; America found itself unable to dictate its will in Latin America, Europe, the Middle East, or anywhere else; and, most dramatically, we watched as Marxist/Leninist socialism crumbled from within.

Stability

At the same time, some things remain the same. We are still faced with processing more persuasion than ever. People still respond to persuasive appeals from advertisers, politicians, and ideologues; we still esteem traditional institutions and values such as the family, success, and education; and we still play politics on campus, on the job, in our organizations, and in our families. Unfortunately, we also continue to face an energy crisis, and we continue to foul our environment. And

although it is still difficult to move the average citizen to political action, advocates still try to persuade us to demilitarize the U.S. economy, to vote for certain candidates, and to buy thousands of products.

PERSUASION IN AN INFORMATION AGE

In one way or another, everything we've just cited has in one way or another been related to persuasion. The impeachment hearings of the Watergate era persuaded Americans that deception was practiced in the highest office in the land. During the past decade we have been persuaded that the United States is no longer the world's number one economic power, and we have been persuaded that we cannot live without items such as automated teller (ATM) cards, plastic credit, color television, and personal computers.

As voters we need to be persuaded to support candidates and, as consumers, to buy products. Whether as individuals, corporations, or governments, we need to be persuaded to do our part in saving and restoring the environment. For these and many other reasons, it is more important than ever to train ourselves to become responsible and critical receivers of persuasion. Let's consider just a few of the areas in which we need to become better persuadees. *Advertising Age* magazine estimates that the average American is exposed to over 5000 persuasive messages a day. These messages appear in many formats. A prime example is the television spot, with its high-tech artistry utilizing computer graphics and digital sound. At the same time as these ads gain in sophistication, they are also shrinking in duration. Whereas 30- and 60-second spots were long the staples of television advertising, the 15-second spot, the 10-second reinforcement spot, and soon 7½-second spots will dominate television advertising.[1] Other formats containing persuasive messages include newspaper or magazine advertisements in all their artistic and nonartistic forms, billboards and signs along the roadside, radio spots, t-shirts with product names imprinted on them, and so on. Even the packaging of the various products we use is persuasive in nature, as are the "shelf talkers" in the supermarkets and the coupons or rebate forms that accompany products today. Most recently there has been a deluge of direct-marketing messages, ranging from catalogs and direct-mail appeals to telephone solicitation and direct-response television ads, to television "auctions" and channels devoted solely to people who shop at home. Perhaps the most aggravating of all is telephone solicitation — one of the fastest-growing modes of direct marketing. And I have only begun to list what we face each day.

Furthermore, as you read these words, newer and more sophisticated forms of advertising are being devised. For example, computer billboards and networks are now exploited by persuaders, and interfaces between home computers, electronic mail, and computer-generated graphics and filing systems make it possible for individuals to receive their own personalized "newspaper," which includes only subjects of interest to them.

Although the thought of receiving totally individualized information and services is widely appealing, little serious consideration has been given to the implications of this kind of deep segmentation. Primary among these is the fact that we must divulge much of our individual and group identity — demographics, interests, age, political and sexual preferences, religion, income, media habits, and a host of other "private" information needed to create these individualized products.

In fact, in the eyes of the advertising industry, this relinquishing of intimate data has already been achieved. **Brand scanning**, for instance, is advertising's newest tool for analyzing consumers and designing ads to persuade them. In brand scanning, consumers are given either an electronic scanning "wand" or a "consumer card," similar to a credit card, which is presented at the cash register where the actual purchases are recorded and compared with the information the consumer has volunteered (television viewing habits and demographic and psychographic information, for example). In the electronic-wand method, the consumer passes the wand scanner over the UPC

(Universal Product Code) of the product as it is put into the cupboard, and the same individualized set of data is collected and compared. For the first time, advertisers have a direct link between advertising exposure and actual product purchase. And what do we guinea pig consumers get in return for giving away large chunks of our private selves? The answer is: a small discount on our groceries in one system and the chance to enter a sweepstakes in the other.

Thus the intimate details of our lives are becoming increasingly available to marketers who want to sell us everything from politicians to beer. Some of the sources from which marketers obtain personal data include census information, sold to advertisers by our federal government; and demographic and biographical information drawn from driver's license bureaus, hunting and fishing licenses, tax departments, and highway patrol records, sold regularly by state governments. It's very easy, for example, to identify households with incomes of $70,000 in which both parents are college graduates and in which there is at least one sixteen-year-old son who has blue eyes and blond hair and intends to go to college. Each time we fill out a product-warranty questionnaire, we give away information that is also sold to marketers. We are rapidly losing our privacy and our individuality as we are "packaged" into market segments or potential consumer groups.

PERSUASION IN A TECHNOLOGICAL WORLD

Today, more than ever before in human history, persuasion pervades our everyday lives. We are in the midst of what Alvin Toffler calls "the third wave" of great change experienced by humanity — the technological revolution.[2] Although persuasion was useful in instituting change in the first two "waves" of great innovation — the agricultural wave and the industrial wave — it will be essential in inducing people to try, accept, and finally adopt the many new ways of thinking, believing, and behaving that go hand-in-hand with the worldwide shift to the technological age. We are seeing but the first vague dimensions of only a few of the changes that will be facing us. Children no longer take their parents' word as law—they need to be motivated to avoid drugs, to take core subjects at school, to turn down the volume of their Walkmen to avoid damage to their hearing. Our government has discovered that it must make increasing use of persuasion to convince the citizenry to conserve energy, to "find themselves" in the Army, to use nine-digit zip codes, or to be honest when filling out their income tax reports. Social institutions, such as churches, fraternal groups, and community organizations, are finding it more necessary than ever to use persuasion to gain or even to maintain membership levels and financial support for their projects. Even in the world of marketing, brand loyalty or price competitiveness no longer can be relied on to sell a product. Instead, marketers must convince consumers that the product will add excitement to life—that it will make consumers more successful, sexier, or more secure. In education, we find persuasion becoming more important in motivating students to achieve, to listen, and to participate. All of these persuaders vie for our attention and for our loyalties and support.

We could go on and on. Clearly, persuasion pervades our world. Clearly, too, in such a world we need training in persuasion: not only in how to persuade others but in how to—and how not to—be persuaded.

Of course, you could decide to simply reject all the persuasion directed at you. But, if you reject all persuasion by politicians, how will you know for whom to vote? If you reject all advertising, how will you compare brands or learn about new products? If you reject the persuasion of your teachers, how will you know on what courses to focus or in which area to major? Perhaps you could personally investigate the record of every politician on the ballot or personally test every detergent or motor oil or ski wax on the market. Maybe you could even take one of every kind of course and evaluate its career possibilities. But if you did, you would have little time for anything else!

The world around us tells us that we need to be persuaded, if only to reduce our alternatives before making choices. At the same time, we need

to be prepared for the many potent and perhaps mistaken—even negative—things our persuasion world can do to us. Noted communications expert Neil Postman called attention to just one aspect of persuasion and its potency in shaping our values: the television commercial. According to Postman, by the time you're twenty you're likely to have seen about a *million* commercials.[3] That averages out to a thousand a week. That figure may seem too high—and it does conflict with some other reports—but it averages out to 180 commercials a day, or twenty to twenty-five for each of the seven to eight hours the average American spends in front of the TV set each day.

Imagine what we would think if a Big Brother–type propaganda artist were pumping persuasion down our throats that often every week. Some would call us robots. What impressions do we get from these commercials? Here is Postman's analysis:

> This makes the TV commercial the most voluminous information source in the education of youth. . . . A commercial teaches a child three interesting things. The first is that all problems are resolvable. The second is that all problems are resolvable fast. And the third is that all problems are resolvable fast through the agency of some technology. It may be a drug. It may be a detergent. It may be an airplane or some piece of machinery. . . .
>
> The essential message is that the problems that beset people—whether it is lack of self-confidence or boredom or even money problems—are entirely solvable if only we will allow ourselves to be ministered to by a technology.[4]

How often have we been affected by this very simple little belief or value? How often have we bought that bottle of Obsession or Ban, or those Hanes stockings, because we subconsciously believe that they will make us more attractive to the opposite sex and give us a successful lovelife? Or help us land a job or impress a teacher? How many of us believe that the atmosphere will be saved by technology or that some little old scientist in Lake Wobegon, Minnesota, will invent a tablet that will convert water to gasoline, thus saving us from the energy shortage? At one time or another, every one of us has fallen for a pitch like this.

One of the purposes of this book is to make us at least aware of what is happening to us in this persuasion world. The title of this book, *Persuasion: Reception and Responsibility*, suggests the direction we will take. Our focus is on the training of *persuadees* — those on the receiving end of all the persuasion. We need to learn to be critical, to observe and judge the persuasion coming at us.

Of course, persuasion is not a recent discovery, and it would have been good in past times for people to have been aware of the persuasion going on around them. If they had been, perhaps many tyrants of history might not have risen to power; wars might have been avoided; diseases might have been cured; and shortages might not have occurred. But in a technological age in which the means through which persuasion can be designed and disseminated are extremely sophisticated, being an aware and cautious persuadee is more essential than ever. The National Council of Teachers of English (NCTE) recognized this need when it instituted its regular conferences on "doublespeak" and when it began to announce an annual "doublespeak award," to be given to the persuader(s) whose language was most "grossly unfactual, deceptive, evasive, confusing, or self-contradictory."

DOUBLESPEAK IN A PERSUASION-FILLED WORLD

Even in a persuasion-riddled world such as ours, you would not need defensive training if all persuaders stayed out in the open and talked straight. Too many, however, speak in doublespeak. **Doublespeak** is the opposite of language: It tries to *not communicate*; it tries to conceal the truth and to confuse. The word is related to a term coined by George Orwell for his chilling description of the world he anticipated in his novel *1984*, where it was called "newspeak" and was used to shift meanings for words and concepts in order to confuse the citizenry. For example, "war" meant

"peace" and "freedom" meant "slavery." Although Orwell's frightening depiction of his future has not come to pass, enough of it has come true to make us all take a second look at the doublespeak of our times. Consider the "peacekeeping" missions the United States has engaged in around the world: naval escorts in the Persian Gulf, "freedom" fighters in Central America, the "heroism" of Ollie North, and hundreds of thousands of troops in Saudi Arabia. In his first term as president, Ronald Reagan spoke of using what he called "income enhancement" by the government to help hold down the national debt and large deficits. Although he steadfastly resisted the notion that "income enhancement" was really a new name for taxes, that is, in fact, what it was. A similar pattern of doublespeak was seen in the early years of the Bush administration. Bush called on voters to read his lips when he promised "No new taxes" during his presidency. However, when budget costs soared, he had to "soften" his position. The terms *income enhancement* and *softening* on a position to resist tax increases represent a kind of linguistic "camouflage" that is typical of contemporary politicians, advertisers, and promoters. In the Middle East war, citizen casualties were "camouflaged" by terming them "collateral damage."

Of course, doublespeak isn't confined to the world of politics. A real-estate ad that notes the house is "convenient to the interstate" probably means that you will hear cars whoosh by day and night. College administrators who refer to "stricter admission standards" when they mean rising enrollments are using doublespeak, as are used-car dealers who refer to a junker as a "good work car." You can identify numerous examples of doublespeak once you get started. One of the most humorous, which received the 1980 NCTE award for doublespeak from a foreign source, was made by General Joao Baptista Figueiredo, the president of Brazil. He told reporters, "I intend to open this country to democracy, and anyone who is against that I will jail; I will crush!"[5]

Unfortunately, doublespeak seems to be on the increase; the average American eighteen-year-old has seen 20,000 hours of television and views scores of commercials per week.[6] In short, we are rapidly becoming numbed by doublespeak. Advertisers can even tell us the obvious — "V.O. is V.O." — and get results.

DEFINING PERSUASION — FROM ARISTOTLE TO BURKE

Let us begin our study of the persuasion process by looking at how it has been defined at various times and by various experts.

The field of modern communication can trace its roots to the ancient Greeks, who were the first to systematize the use of persuasion, calling it "rhetoric." They studied it in their schools, using it in their courts and in implementing the first democracies in the Greek city-states. Primary among the ancient theorists was Aristotle, who defined rhetoric as "the faculty of observing in any given case, the available means of persuasion." According to Aristotle, persuasion was made up of *artistic* and *inartistic* proofs, both of which we will explore in more depth in Chapter 3. Persuasion, according to Aristotle, could be based on a source's credibility (or *ethos*), emotional appeals (or *pathos*), and/or logical appeals (or *logos*).[7] He also thought that persuasion was most effective when it was based on a *common ground* between persuader and persuadee. This common ground permitted persuaders to make certain assumptions about the audience and its beliefs. Knowing these beliefs, the persuader could use the *enthymeme*, a form of argument in which the first or major premise in the proof remains unstated by the persuader and, instead, is provided by the audience. The task of the persuader, then, was to identify common ground, those first or major premises held by the audience, and to use them in enthymematic arguments. (We will explore this concept in more depth in Chapter 3.)

Roman students of persuasion added specific advice on what a persuasive speech ought to include. The Roman orator Cicero identified five elements of persuasive speaking: inventing or discovering evidence and arguments, organizing them, styling them artistically, memorizing them, and finally delivering them skillfully. Another Ro-

man theorist, Quintilian, added that a persuader had to be a "good man" as well as a good speaker.

Those early definitions clearly focused on the sources of messages and on persuaders' skill and art in building a speech. Later students of persuasion reflected the changes that have come with a mass-media world. In *Persuasion: A Means of Social Control* (1952), Winston Brembeck and William Howell, two communication professors, described persuasion as "the conscious attempt to modify thought and action by manipulating the motives of men toward predetermined ends."[8] In their definition, we see a notable shift from the use of logic toward the internal motives of the audience. By the time Brembeck and Howell wrote their second edition, in the 1970s, they had changed their definition of persuasion to "communication intended to influence choice."[9] In the mid-1960s, Wallace Fotheringham, another communication professor, defined persuasion as "that body of effects in receivers"[10] that had been caused by a persuader's message. Here the focus is almost entirely on the receiver, who actually determines whether persuasion has occurred. By this standard, even unintended messages, such as gossip overheard on a bus, could be persuasive if they caused changes in their receivers' attitudes, beliefs, or actions.

Kenneth Burke, literary critic and theorist, defines persuasion as the artful use of the "resources of ambiguity." Burke believed that the degree to which persuadees feel that they are being spoken to in their "own language" is critical to creating a sense of **identification** — a concept close to Aristotle's "common ground."[11] In Burke's theory, when true identification occurs, the persuaders of the world try to act, believe, and talk like the audience. Figure 1.1 thus demonstrates not only common ground but identification as well. It does this by using specific verbal and nonverbal cues. In other words, the ad speaks the language of the targeted readers.

In the first edition of this book, persuasion was defined as "a process" that changes attitudes, beliefs, opinions, or behaviors.[12] In that definition, the *process* of persuasion gets the attention. Persuasion occurs only through cooperation between

source and receiver. Following Burke's lead, persuasion is defined here as *the co-creation of a state of identification or alignment between a source and a receiver that results from the use of symbols*. Once you identify with the kind of world a huckster wants you to like — say, *Marlboro Country* — persuasion has occurred. You may never smoke, but you have been changed. The world of Marlboro Country has become attractive to you. Maybe you'll respond to the appeal of the attitude and begin to value ruggedness and individualism, or perhaps you'll try to emulate the Marlboro Man's dress and demeanor, or perhaps you'll vote for a candidate who projects a "Marlboro" image. You have been aligned with or identified by a certain set of values and a specific lifestyle. Here, the focus of persuasion is not on the source, the message, or the receiver. It is on *all* of them equally. They all *cooperate* to make a persuasive process. The idea of **co-creation** means that what is inside the receiver is just as important as the source's intent or the content of the message. In one sense, *all* persuasion is **self-persuasion** — we are rarely persuaded unless we *participate* in the process. This is what the ancients meant when they referred to finding "common ground." I will be persuasive to the extent that you see me as having common ground — shared values, goals, interests, and experiences — with you.

The words "co-created" and "self-persuasion" are central. Persuasion is the result of the combined efforts of source and receiver. Even in cases of terrorism and hostage-taking, some hostages begin to identify with their captors and may even embrace the terrorists' cause. Patty Hearst, who actually participated in a robbery with her captors,

is one such example. Thus, even in coercive situations, persuasion may be operating, and the role of the receiver is absolutely critical to the success or failure of any persuasive act.

CRITERIA FOR RESPONSIBLE PERSUASION

How does this cooperative persuasion happen? What makes it work? Although persuasion can occur under the most unlikely circumstances (in the midst of an emotional argument, during a riot, and even in a concentration camp), three circumstances seem to increase the chances that responsible receivers can be rationally and ethically persuaded.

First, persuasion is most likely to occur in a responsible and fair way *if both sides have an equal opportunity to persuade and if each has approximately equivalent ability and access to the media of communication*. If a gag rule is imposed on the proponents of one side of a question while advocates of the other side have freedom to persuade, then receivers will get a one-sided and biased view of the issue. A good case in point was the outlawing of Solidarity, the Polish labor union that so threatened the government that it finally imposed martial law to enforce the gagging of the union. Solidarity's chief spokesperson, Lech Walesa, was even held under house arrest for many months to prevent the union side of the debate from being articulated. Yet, the persuasive message of Solidarity continued to win the day, culminating in the formal acceptance of the group by the communist government. Ultimately, when the communist leadership was overthrown, many of Solidarity's leaders were elected to high political office. Even in communist China, where pro-democracy student demonstrators were arrested, sometimes even executed, the pro-democracy persuasion was not silenced.

Second, *there should be a revelation of agendas*. Each side should notify the audience of its true aims and goals and say how it intends to go about achieving them. Candidates ought to admit that they intend to attack their opponents' credibility by linking them with a scandal or with wasteful spending, for example. Auto manufacturers ought to notify potential customers that they are trying to get them to buy cars by appealing to their need for status. Of course, if we receivers knew the hidden agendas of many persuaders, we would quickly be put on guard against their appeals; thus, in many cases, this criterion is met only partially. But even having a hint of the real goal of a persuader can make us more responsible receivers, so it is useful to try to determine a persuader's intentions before acting on his or her advice.

Third, and most important, is *the presence of critical receivers* — receivers who test the assertions and evidence presented to them. They look for information from all sides in a debate, and withhold final judgment until all the data are in. If we have such a set of receivers, the first two criteria need be met only minimally, and responsible persuasion can still occur. Even though the Solidarity Union was gagged, and even though the government obscured its real agenda, the presence of large numbers of critical and responsible receivers in the Polish populace made it impossible for the dissent to be smothered.

Because the receiver is central to persuasion, it's a good idea for each of us to study the process of persuasion from that point of view. We need to watch ourselves being persuaded, and try to see why and how it happens so that we can be more conscious of our changes. Our knowledge will allow us to be more critical and therefore more effective in rejecting persuasive messages when appropriate — and in accepting others when it seems wise to do so.

THE SMCR MODEL OF PERSUASION

The simplest model of communication, and the one most widely referred to, is the **SMCR model** (Figure 1.2), suggested by Claude Shannon and Warren Weaver in 1949 and modified since that time by others such as David Berlo.[13] The model contains four essential elements:

A **source** (S), who or which is the encoder of the message. The code may be verbal, nonverbal, visual, musical, or in some other modality.

A **message** (M), which is meant to convey the source's meaning through any of the codes.

A **channel** (C), which carries the message and which may have distracting noise.

A **receiver** (R), who decodes the message, trying to sift out channel noise and adding his or her own interpretation.

To illustrate the components of the SMCR model, let's suppose that your young niece or nephew is watching an ad for a "complete set of Mutant Ninja Turtles" and is promised by the advertiser that owning the set can practically guarantee instant popularity and acceptance by his or her peers. You want the child to be a more discriminating consumer, so you point out that the sponsor is actually interested in profit, not peer popularity. In this case, you are explaining a *source-related* aspect of persuasion. Then you alert your young friend to the doublespeak going on in the ad — the

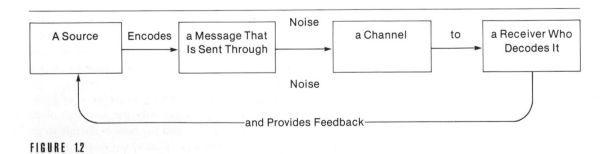

FIGURE 1.2

The SMCR model.

product "virtually guarantees" popularity. You ask what the word *virtually* means in this advertising claim and by doing so focus attention on the *message* itself and not the motives of the persuader. Finally you point out that clever camera work and skillful editing have made the Ninjas seem almost alive, when in reality they are composed of flimsy plastic. Now you have focused on the persuasive impact of the medium of transmitting the message, or on the *channel*. Then you might ask your young friend whether there is some internal or unstated reason he or she wants to be popular, thus focusing on the *receiver* element of this model.

These elements are also part of the persuasive process that is the focus of our definition of persuasion. Being prepared for persuasion involves being critical of all four elements. We must be alert to the motives of the source, whether they are obvious or disguised. We must pay attention to the message — its symbols and its meaning. It is also a good idea to think about the channel, or medium, being used to send the message — what kinds of effects does it have? Finally, we need to be aware of our own role in persuasion — what are we adding?

One of our goals is to explore various tools that we can use to try to determine a source's **motives**. Language choice, for example, can tip us off to source intent. The ideas the source thinks will be persuasive to the audience are often expressed in the words the source chooses, the metaphors the source uses, and even the kinds of sentences in the message. Are they questions? Exclamations? Short and punchy? Long and soothing?

For example, several years ago the Schick razor company came out with a "cosmetic" razor called "Personal Touch." What do the words *cosmetic, personal,* and *touch* tell you about the Schick company's view of its potential customers? Is it aiming at a "macho" man? A business tycoon? A sports enthusiast? Or is it aiming at women who feel they deserve special attention and haven't been getting it lately? Analyzing the source has two benefits. First, it alerts us to the persuasion being aimed at us. Second, it tells us things about the source that can help us when the source becomes our per-

suadee. In a way, sources tip us off to their *own* persuasive weaknesses. If you hear a friend trying to persuade you by using statistics, for instance, you can pretty safely bet that statistics will be a big help when you are trying to persuade that person of something. Of course, we may misinterpret or read too much into a source's words. But if we stay alert, at least we won't be dumbly led around by the nose.

Another of our goals is to explore tools that allow us to analyze the **message** and what it is intended to say. We will look at the organization of the message, its style, and the appeals it makes. You will learn to look at the evidence contained in the message and at how it relates to the persuasive goal. You may want to look at the nonverbal as well as the verbal elements in the message to see which of these codes has what kinds of effects.

For example, consider the wording of an ad placed in newspapers across the country by the International Fund for Animal Welfare (IFAW), which was opposing the yearly harvest of the harp seal in Canada — a highly emotional issue because the young seals are clubbed to death as they emerge onto the ice floe and are helpless to defend themselves or to escape (see Figure 1.3):

Do You Really Know What Can Go into a Simple Fish Sandwich?

Fish caught by Canadian Fishermen who also kill the baby seals. Your purchase of a McDonald's or Burger King Fish Sandwich could help buy the boats, hard wooden clubs, and guns used by the seal hunters as they turn from fishing to the cruelty of killing adult and baby seals.

The words were accompanied by a picture of a baby seal next to a fish sandwich and another smaller picture of a seal hunter about to club a baby seal. By looking at the impact of the pictures and words such as "hard wooden club" (which create a brutal image) or "what can go into," the receiver can be alerted to investigate more fully. Such an investigation might reveal that only a few Canadian fishermen are also seal hunters, that clubbing the seals is actually the least painful,

Do you really know what can go into a simple fish sandwich?

Fish caught by Canadian Fishermen who also kill the baby seals. Your purchase of a McDonald's or Burger King Fish Sandwich could help buy the boats, hard wooden clubs, and guns used by the seal hunters as they turn from fishing to the cruelty of killing adult and baby seals.

If you made a pledge today not to buy fish sandwiches from McDonald's or Burger King unless you were assured by the companies that no Canadian fish was used...your decision would save the seals. Canadian fishermen would have to stop sealing since they are totally dependent on their fish sales, with seal hunting a tiny sideline in comparison.

Canadian Globe and Mail of 13 March 1984, had this to say of IFAW's call for a worldwide boycott of Canadian fish: *"...But what really has the officials spooked is the U.S. market. (There) The International Fund for*

Animal Welfare (IFAW), which spearheads the anti-sealing protest worldwide, has started pressing U.S. purchasers not to take Canadian fish. The U.S. market is worth $1-billion a year to Canadian fishermen and the fast-food business in the United States is about a fifth of that market. Canada fears that, if one U.S. fast-food chain caves in to the protestors, all will surrender"

Over 15,000 seals, mostly babies just 2-4 weeks old, have been clubbed or shot over the last 28 days...and yet the Canadian Minister of Fisheries says there is no baby seal hunt.

You have it in your hands to save the baby seals today.

Please write or telephone one or both of the companies listed below and seek an assurance that they will not purchase Canadian fish until the Canadian Government passes a law banning the seal hunt forever.

Mr Fred L Turner,
Chairman of the Board,
McDonald's Corporation,
McDonald's Plaza, Oak Brook, Illinois,
IL 60521
Tel: 312/887-3200

Mr J Jeffrey Campbell, Chairman,
Burger King Corporation,
7360 North Kendall Drive,
Miami,
Florida FL 33156
Tel: 305/596-7277

SAVE THE SEALS
NO ⊘
TO CANADIAN FISH

To the International Fund for Animal Welfare
I'll put animals first ... I'll do my part to help you fight the baby seal hunters.
Enclosed is my tax-exempt contribution to IFAW in the amount of:
☐ $10   ☐ $15   ☐ $25   ☐ $35   ☐ $50   ☐ $100   ☐ $500   Other $_____
We need hundreds of gifts this size to save the baby seals forever.
Name_____
(please print)
Address_____
_____ Zip Code_____

International Fund for Animal Welfare
169 Main Street, Yarmouth Port,
Massachusetts 02675 U.S.A.
Our financial statement is available to contributors.
IFAW

Our boycott campaign needs your support. We cannot succeed without your funds, to carry our boycott to every community in America.
A copy of the last financial report filed with the Department of State may be obtained by writing to: N.Y. State Department of State, Office of Charities Registration, Albany, N.Y. 12231 or IFAW.

FIGURE 1.3

Ad encouraging people to boycott fish sandwiches in order to stop the killing of harp seals. (Used by permission of IFAW.)

most humane means of killing them (a claim made by the hunters), that the flesh of the seal is not used in the fishwich as the picture suggests, or that other attempts at boycotting the seal furs were largely unsuccessful. By looking at the message carefully, receivers can be alerted to get other sides of the story or can identify places where the full story is not given or even where the argument is deceptive, as in the suggestion that the baby seal may be part of your next Whaler sandwich from Burger King.

A third goal is to train ourselves to be alert to

the kinds of effects that various **channels** have on persuasion. Does the influence of TV, for example, make a message more or less effective? Has TV made us more vulnerable to certain message types? What are the effects of other media, such as radio and billboards? Are certain kinds of ballyhoo more useful or persuasive than others? Why do some media use certain techniques and others use different ones?

For example, during his years as president, Ronald Reagan used controlled (that is, without a question-answer session by reporters) radio presentations nearly every week. Why? What was it about this form of radio speech that was so attractive? How do radio messages differ from live news conferences? By looking at the persuasive effects of this element in the SMCR model, receivers can begin to understand how a persuasive message works — what its goals are.

Finally, you need to look at yourself, the **receiver** in the persuasive transaction, to determine what kinds of motives, biases, and perspectives *you* bring to the persuasive situation. What fascinations, needs, and desires do each of us bring to the world of persuasion? The answer, of course, is continually being sought by persuaders, whether they are politicians, ideologues, advertisers, propagandists, or even our co-workers, friends, and colleagues. Knowing even a part of the answer can make us more critical and responsible receivers.

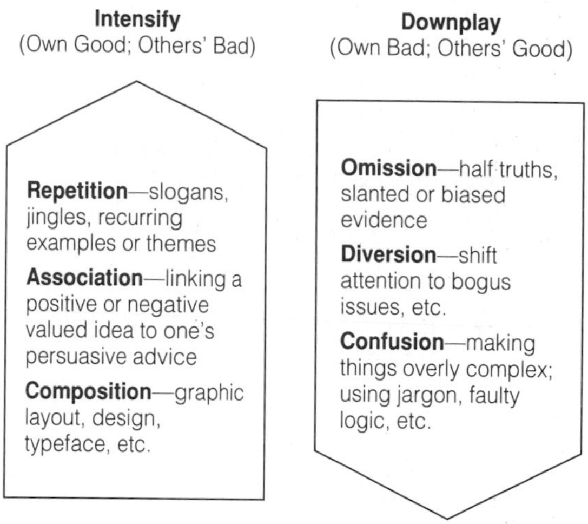

RANK'S MODEL OF PERSUASION

As part of the National Council of Teachers of English (NCTE) Project on Doublespeak, several persons were asked to suggest ways of teaching people to be critical receivers of persuasion. In 1976, Hugh Rank, a researcher on the project, put the challenge this way:

These kids are growing up in a propaganda blitz unparalleled in human history. . . . Will the advertisers and political persuaders of 1980 or 1984 be less sophisticated, less informed, less funded than they are today? . . . Schools should shift their emphasis in order to train the larger segment of our population in a new kind of literacy so that more citizens can recognize the more sophisticated techniques and patterns of persuasion.[14]

Rank outlined a model of persuasion that could help teach people to be critical receivers. He called it the **intensify/downplay schema** and tried to keep it as simple as possible. It can serve as a good overall model for you.

Intensify (Own Good; Others' Bad)

Repetition—slogans, jingles, recurring examples or themes
Association—linking a positive or negative valued idea to one's persuasive advice
Composition—graphic layout, design, typeface, etc.

Downplay (Own Bad; Others' Good)

Omission—half truths, slanted or biased evidence
Diversion—shift attention to bogus issues, etc.
Confusion—making things overly complex; using jargon, faulty logic, etc.

FIGURE 1.4

The intensify/downplay schema. (Adapted by permission of Hugh Rank.)

The basic idea behind Rank's model is that persuaders usually use two major tactics to achieve their goals. They either *intensify* certain aspects of their product, candidate, or ideology, or they *downplay* certain aspects. Often they do both. Like a magician, they want to draw attention away from some things and toward others in order to pull off the illusion. Rank depicted his model and the major ways of intensifying or downplaying as shown in Figures 1.4 and 1.8.

On the strategic level of Rank's model, persuaders can choose to

1. intensify their own good points.
2. intensify the weak points of the opposition.
3. downplay their own bad or weak points.
4. downplay the good points of the opposition.

On the tactical level, persuaders can use **repetition, association,** and **composition** to intensify their own good points or the bad points of the opposition. They can also use **omission, diver-**

sion, and **confusion** to downplay their own bad points or the good points of the opposition.

Persuasive strategy, then, is the overall step-by-step program for making one's case or reaching one's goal. Strategy relies on tactics, which are the specific kinds of arguments or points one tries to make. Thus if a candidate wants to persuade voters to support her (her goal), she can try to make them feel good about her candidacy (her strategy of intensifying her own good), which she will accomplish by associating herself with forthright stands on issues; by repeating her campaign slogan on signs, buttons, bumperstickers, and advertisements; and by using the state capitol building in the background of all her ads and photos (her tactics of association, repetition, and composition). Let's explore the strategies and tactics of the Rank model in more depth.

Intensification

The first strategy in the Rank model is intensification. Within this strategy are the two substrategies of intensifying either one's own strong or good points or the weak or bad points of the opposition. The advertisement in Figure 1.5 tries to accomplish an overall goal (sale of a product) by using a strategy (intensifying one's own good points and the other's bad points), using the tactic of associating the product with certain positive features and feelings while associating the competition with certain negative ones.

Basic to all of us is the desire to look good in the eyes of the world. Some of the tactics that can be used to intensify our own good points and the other's bad points (making us look good by comparison) are *repetition, association,* and *composition.*

Repetition One way we can intensify good or bad points about a product, person, or candidate is by repeating them over and over. Consider a series of Bud Lite TV ads, popular several years back. The basic format of these ads was to have the central character—a naive but good-natured and attractive young male—enter the bar and say "Gimme

a Lite," whereupon he was faced with one of a variety of "lights" he didn't intend: a flaming hoop with trained animals jumping through it, a blowtorch, a lighted wand like that of *Star Wars* fame, or even an old-fashioned railroad lantern. His response was always the same, too—"I mean a Bud Lite," whereupon he was served the sponsor's product.

The harp seal ad repeatedly intensifies the bad aspects of the seal hunt through its brutal images and language and through the helpless- and innocent-looking baby seal. It also repeatedly puts you, the reader, into the story. Using an appeal called *putting it up to you*, which is frequently used in sales, the IFAW puts the responsibility for the continued hunt on the reader. Notice the words "your purchase," "if you made a pledge today," "you have it in your hands to save the baby seals today." This repetition intensifies IFAW's good possibilities if only each individual reader would make a commitment.

Association Another tactic for intensification suggested by the Rank model is association, which relies on a three-part process: (1) a cause, product, or candidate is linked (2) to something already liked or disliked by (3) the audience; thus, the cause, product, or candidate picks up or is identified with the thing liked or disliked. In the harp seal ad, the hunters are associated with cruelty and brutality. When we first see the ad, most of us are shocked by the thought that baby-seal meat might be mixed into the fish sandwich. The sandwich is pictured next to the seal, and the clubbing scene provides the negative association. Some of the minor details drive home the point and may even nauseate the reader—15,000 seals clubbed to death in twenty-eight days, the guns, the hard wooden clubs, and the thought of eating baby seal with mayonnaise and lettuce on a sesame seed bun effectively add to the negative associations.

Persuaders engage in careful audience analysis to identify the fears, wants, and biases of their target audience. They then mesh their goals with this set of alignments. For example, politicians know that we have fears about nuclear power, so

While the masses seek solace in overstuffed chairs, BMW offers a slightly more compelling form of therapy.

Analysis of the open road.

It's found in the heady form of the new K75RT, the first luxury tourer in the 750cc class. A motorcycle as unrepressed as it is responsive.

Let others debate fine points of Freudian theory. At BMW, we engineer our philosophies into finely sculpted riding machines.

We don't mean to suggest we can cure paranoia or banish childhood demons. But our high powered psyche-tour can restore youthful ardor to urban captives.

Like all BMW motorcycles, the highly-balanced, 3-cylinder K75RT employs a drive shaft like those in cars. And it offers options like full touring saddlebags and an AM-FM radio cassette player.

So instead of weekly visits to a shrink, dissolve stress with a single trip to your authorized BMW motorcycle dealer. There you can see the K75RT and other inspired forms of coping such as the basic K75, starting at a most modest $5,990.*

Then ask about the sanest feature to grace any motorcycle. Free riding school for new buyers.**

Further rationalization is provided by our three-year, unlimited mile, limited warranty that's three times more reassuring than most other motorcycle warranties. Because it's three times longer.***

And the feeling of security that comes with our BMW Motorcycle Roadside Assistance Plan is assured with your purchase of any new BMW.****

So follow the same advice any good doctor might prescribe.

Just sit back. Relax.

And change gears for a while.

CHEAPER THAN A PSYCHIATRIST.

WORTH THE OBSESSION.

FIGURE 1.5

(Reprinted by permission of BMW of North America)

they tie these fears to their own cause by stating that, if elected, they would put a freeze on all building of new nuclear power plants. An advertiser might associate a product — a certain kind of athletic shoe — with a well-known professional athlete who uses them. The ad might also associate the shoes with everyday people who are athletic — joggers, tennis players, or, as Nike did, even with a person in a wheelchair. This set of associations intensifies the good aspects of the shoe and demonstrates that one doesn't have to be an athlete to benefit from its features.

Composition The third and final tactic of intensification is composition, which means emphasizing one's own good characteristics or the other's bad characteristics by changing the physical makeup of the message. This change is frequently accomplished in nonverbal ways and can take several forms. For example, the makeup of the printed word can be altered, as in changing "U.S.A." to "U.$.A." or "America" to "Amerika," to send messages on several levels. The makeup, or composition, of a candidate's publicity photo can be manipulated. For example, by using the device of a low camera angle, a candidate can be made to look larger than he or she really is. The low angle also tells us to look up to the candidate. The layout of an advertisement can also be used for purposes of intensification. Notice how the composition of the Ultima II ad in Figure 1.6 draws your attention first to the woman's lips and then to the product and product name in the lower right-hand corner.

Composition is also used by persuaders who create comparison and contrast in the media. Marshall McLuhan called this technique the "brushing of information against information."[15] One bit of information about a candidate for political office is pictured against some dramatic setting — say, the Vietnam War Memorial in Washington, D.C. Perhaps music on the sound-track is a muted version of "Oh Beautiful, For Spacious Skies," and a voice-over talks about the candidate's determination to avoid losing more American lives in an intensified war in Central America. The camera zooms back to show the true size of the memorial as the muted sounds now swell, and the words "Senator Jones — A Man Who Cares. Keep Our Beautiful America Out of War — Vote November 3rd as if Your Lives Depended on It" crawl up the screen and the ad closes with the disclaimer "This ad was sponsored by 'Thousands of Citizens for Senator Jones.'" The background, the camera work, the voice-over, the music, and the printed words on the screen all "compose" a certain meaning. Shift any of these elements of composition, and you shift the meaning of the ad in some way. If the background had been the U.S. Capitol building, we would lose the impact of the potential loss of human life. If the music were shifted to the national anthem, another slight shift in meaning would be evident, and the words about keeping "Beautiful America" out of war would make less sense. So the brushing of information against other information creates sophisticated nuances of meaning through the tactics of intensification — in this case, both association and composition are central to the creation of meaning.

As noted earlier, juxtaposing the baby seal with the fishwich in the harp seal ad creates a dramatic effect — an innocent victim becomes part of your fishburger. Of course, as we read on we find that this is not the case, but the initial association and the headline make the point emphatically enough to gross out the average McDonald's or Burger King customer. In the lower right-hand corner of the ad, the "Save the Seals" logo also uses composition by superimposing the killing of a seal with the words "NØ to Canadian Fish." Further, the letter "Ø" with the slash through it looks like the international highway sign that we frequently see warning us not to turn left or right onto a one-way street or not to park in a certain place. The composition of both the logo and picture, as well as the altering of the print, tie negative feelings to Canadian fish.

As you can see, by using Rank's model for intensification as a starting place in becoming a critical receiver, we can gain insights into how a particular piece of persuasion works. We can do the same thing with the other component of the Rank model — downplaying.

(Reprinted by permission of Charles Revson, Inc.)

Downplaying

Sometimes persuaders do not want to intensify or call attention to something (their own shortcomings, for example), because this would defeat their persuasive purpose. Likewise, it would not be useful to advertise the strong points of your competition. What the persuader does is to *downplay* his or her own bad points and the competitor's good points.

For example, in 1990, President Bush reversed his position on the need to enact new taxes — something he had promised not to do during the 1988 election campaign. (Remember his phrase, "Read my lips. No new taxes"?) His opponent, Michael Dukakis, had predicted that an increase was inevitable, and had accused Bush of double-speaking on the tax issue. When it became clear that the tax increase *was* inevitable, Bush downplayed his broken campaign promises (his own bad attributes) and failed to mention Dukakis's accuracy in predicting the necessity of raising taxes (the other's good attributes). In another case of downplaying, both Ford and General Motors initially downplayed Chrysler Corporation's innovative use of the "5 year or 50,000 mile warranty" (the other's good), since Ford and GM were offering only "12 months or 12,000 miles." Later, they offered even better warranties (6 years or 60,000 miles, for example) and downplayed the fact that their warranties were really "me too" offers (own bad) that had been forced on them by Chrysler's pre-emptive strategy. Let's look now at the specific tactics of downplaying: *omission, diversion,* and *confusion*.

Omission Omission is simply the leaving out of critical information to avoid highlighting one's own shortcomings. For example, the Claussen company intensifies its own good when it advertises that its pickles are refrigerated rather than cooked and are therefore much crisper than Vlasic pickles, its major competition. However, Claussen *omits* to tell the consumers that in order to extend the pickles' shelf life, their product is relatively higher in sodium than Vlasic pickles (their own bad) and that refrigeration isn't necessary for Vlasic pickles (other's good). On the political front, in the 1988 presidential election, vice-president Dan Quayle omitted telling that he had used family connections to avoid service in Vietnam, while Michael Dukakis omitted information about his wife Kitty's drug and alcohol problems.

Diversion Diversion, another downplaying tactic, consists of shifting attention away from another's good points or one's own bad points. For example, while he was enmeshed in the Watergate web, Richard Nixon attempted to divert attention away from the scandal by focusing attention on the oil crisis. The Middle East crisis also served as a handy diversionary issue from the uncomfortable budgetary problems of 1990 for the Bush administration and the Congress as well. Following product tampering and the resulting deaths of several persons, the McNeil Consumer Products Company, makers of Tylenol, focused attention on its efforts to prevent such tragedies in the future, thus diverting attention from its initial carelessness regarding product control. And we all can recall instances of interpersonal communication with a parent, sibling, teacher, or friend in which we tried to divert the discussion and attention away from an embarrassing or distressing topic.

Humor can also be used to divert attention. For instance, President Franklin Roosevelt used humor to divert attention from criticism of his ordering a warship to pick up his dog Fala. The Republicans charged that the dog was being pampered at public expense. Roosevelt replied, "I don't resent the attacks, but Fala does resent them." The comment diverted attention *away from* the extravagance of sending a warship to fetch a dog and *onto* the pettiness of the criticisms.

Other tactics for diverting attention cited by Rank include setting up a "straw man" to draw fire or criticism, such as blaming the umpire for losing the baseball game when it was really the manager's fault, or focusing on an unrelated or false issue, or "red herring," as Richard Nixon did in his famous Checkers speech, in which he diverted criticism from his use of secret campaign funds to the issue of whether he would return the gift of a cocker spaniel.

Another tactic is to use emotional appeals that rely on an opponent's personality or appearance, sometimes called the *ad hominem* argument. In this argument, the persuader diverts attention from the real issue by attacking the personality or character of his or her opponent. A politician might divert attention away from an opponent's years of government experience by attacking the opponent's wealthy background or her lack of involvement in community affairs. The *ad hominem* argument, or attack on the personality, is one of the more frequently used logical fallacies in diverting attention away from one's own shortcomings and onto the shortcomings of one's opponents. It is also an unethical tactic.

Finally, "splitting hairs" in certain arguments or debates can divert attention from the major issues of the debate and can consume valuable time that could have been spent on serious discussion of substantive issues. A recent example on my campus was "hairsplitting" over the words "due process," used in a small section of one of ten articles that were debated during a major revision of the university's constitution. "Do these words mean we will guarantee *only* those rights to be heard and to face one's accusers which we are legally required to guarantee?" asked the hairsplitter. "Or are we as a university going to say that we will guarantee much more than that?—I would hope so. Then what will the phrase 'due process' mean in practice? Can anyone tell me?" And of course the myriad answers to the nit-picking question consumed a full half-hour of a meeting that was supposed to be limited to three hours to discuss all ten articles.

Confusion A final tactic for downplaying one's own weak points or the competition's strengths is to create *confusion*. This can be accomplished by introducing jargon, overdetailed information, contradictory information, and so on. An insurance salesperson recently suckered me into listening to his pitch for an evening by promising a computer analysis of my protection status that would cover estate protection, too. The pitch claimed that I needed insurance even after my children were grown and independent because of es-

tate taxes that might follow the death of both my wife and myself. Such pitches always focus on the large amount of money the beneficiaries will collect. The fact that the purchaser must die before anyone collects is a point insurance salespeople are trained never to mention.

Consider the advertisement for a Canon A-1 camera shown in Figure 1.7. Note that the headline confuses through the use of jargon. What in blazes does "hexa-photo-cybernetic" mean? By looking more closely, you see that the Canon A-1 has six supposed advantages. That explains *hexa* (as in hexagon). Then we see that it has several automatic devices to match shutter speed with lens opening, which is usually called "automatic exposure." This involves some mathematical programming of the apparatus and, moreover, the settings are digitally displayed. So the word *cybernetic* can be honestly used. And *photo* simply relates to camera. Nevertheless, "hexa-photo-cybernetic" is pseudoscientific ad lingo intended to impress if not to confuse. The ad omits mentioning that many cameras in the same price range have similar features, and Canon is not alone among cameras in having some kind of automatic exposure sensors. Although Canon's having all the automatic features on a single camera was unique at the time the ad was featured, the invented term "hexa-photo-cybernetic" is confusing, especially if it is intended for photographers interested in automatic features—they tend to be amateurs who prefer the camera to do the work while they merely point and shoot.

Another device for downplaying one's own weaknesses or the competition's strengths through confusion is the use of *faulty logic*. "She's Beautiful! She's Engaged! She Uses Earth Balsam Hand Creme!" is one example. The supposed logical flow is that because "she" uses the hand cream, she is beautiful, and because she is beautiful, she met and won the man of her dreams and is now engaged. Not even fairly naive consumers are likely to buy this whole "package," but the idea that the hand cream will make the user more attractive to men is fairly likely to stick.

Rank cites a number of other ways to confuse, including *being inconsistent, contradicting,* and

hexa·photo·cybernetic
The Possibilities are Endless.

Shutter-Priority *1000 5.6*

FIGURE 1.7

How is Rank's *confusion* used here? (Used by permission of Canon U.S.A., Inc.)

talking in circles — "V.O. is V.O." or "So Advanced, It's Simple."

SELF-PROTECTION: A METHOD

In his discussion of doublespeak, Rank offers some general advice on how to detect the flaws of persuaders who use various tactics to intensify or downplay: "When they intensify, downplay." That is, when we recognize a propaganda blitz, we should be cool, detached, and skeptically alert not only to the inflated puffery of advertising with its dreams and promises, but also to intensified attack propaganda, the threats and exploitation of fears by a demagogue or government agent, elected or appointed. Rank also says, "When they downplay, intensify." A way to do this systematically is to divide a sheet of paper into quarters, as shown in Figure 1.8, and then enter the kinds of downplaying and intensifying being practiced. Simply by seeing these, the persuadee can become more alert to what kind of manipulation is going on.

Let's try this technique with a brief example. Consider the ad for Smirnoff vodka shown in Figure 1.9. First let's look at the intensification used in the ad. Remember that the persuader may intensify by repeating, by using association, and by manipulating the composition of the message.

Notice the *repetition* of the product name in the ad. (This is also *intensification* of the product's own good, because consumer folklore includes the belief that the only true or authentic vodka must be Russian — and the name Smirnoff does seem Russian.) Then, the ad uses *association* in its copy. Smirnoff vodka is associated with "Europe's elite," with "proper food," with a "delicious evening," with being "impeccable," with being "memorable," and with fine crystal. So association is used to intensify the own-good aspect of the message. *Composition* is used to intensify in several ways. Look at how the picture is organized: The wine glasses are untouched, whereas the highball glasses are in people's hands and clearly have been sampled. *Word choice* is used to intensify — another example of composition. The ad also intensifies the opposition's bad points: The wine just sat there. Wine can ruin your palate. Again, word choice intensifies the "badness" of wine. Wine is made to seem disreputable because it "plays with your palate," because it is "forceful."

Now, does the persuader *downplay* anything? Vodka can be potent, especially if you drink it like water during a dinner party. That fact is omitted. Instead we are told that it "leaves you breathless" — no one can smell that you've been drink-

Intensify Own Good	Intensify Others' Bad
1.	1.
2.	2.
Downplay Own Bad	Downplay Others' Good
1.	1.
2.	2.
3.	3.

FIGURE 1.8

Intensify/downplay scorecard. (By permission of Hugh Rank.)

The wine sat there and the Smirnoff flowed. Amusing.

But not terribly surprising. Smirnoff (a long-time member of Europe's elite) had found its way to the dinner table. The Smirnoff Bullshot (with bouillon and lime wedge) tastily complemented proper food, and the Smirnoff Spritzer (soda water and a twist) didn't take over the way the more forceful wines play with your palate. It was a delicious evening. Impeccable. Crystal clear. Memorable.

Smirnoff
leaves you breathless®

ing. There is some faulty logic here as well. Why is it amusing that while the Smirnoff flowed, the wine only "sat there"? Why is that "not surprising"? With all these allusions, the ad *confuses* the reader. By identifying the many tactics at work, persuadees can become alert to and critical of the persuasive messages that come their way.

We will discuss a number of other tools of analysis as we proceed, but Rank's intensify/downplay tool is a useful general one to employ at first. You will want to try it with a variety of persuasive messages that you encounter. In future chapters, we will discuss the role of language as it is used to persuade. We will also look at how our own internal motives and drives can be exploited by those who wish to persuade us. Our preferences for certain kinds of logic can be used by the persuader who designs the message. Cultural premises that are trained into us from birth are the bases for many persuasive appeals. Finally, we are also affected by the way we respond to the different media used in persuasion.

REVIEW AND CONCLUSION

If you are now more alert to the possible ways you are being manipulated, you are well on your way to becoming a critical receiver. You are ready to arm yourself with some of the tools of analysis that make wise consumers, and there is a bonus for learning them. In learning how you are persuaded and in exploring the tactics that other persuaders use, you can become a more skillful persuader yourself. Seeing what works, in what circumstances, with what kinds of people, will be useful as you prepare to become a persuader. Skillful consumers of messages learn to be more effective producers of messages. As we move ahead, it will be useful to apply the tools of persuasion on your

FIGURE 1.9

Intensification and downplaying in a persuasive message. (Courtesy Ste. Pierre Smirnoff, a division of Heublein.)

own or through using the study questions and exercises outlined at the end of each chapter.

It is also useful to examine the ways in which you are persuaded on the interpersonal level. Every day you make decisions in nonpublic settings. You decide to heed or reject your parents' advice on the basis of your interpersonal communication with them. They try to persuade you to major in a certain field, to seek a summer job, or to continue or cease dating a certain person. Rank's model can be helpful here too. Identify what your parents intensify and downplay. You can do the same thing with other interpersonal relationships in which persuasion is used — between roommates, friends, or colleagues, or with your boss. You can also see whether identification or alignment is occurring between you and the other individuals, and spot the kinds of symbols that lead to or discourage identification. Critical analysis of interpersonal persuasion can help you make decisions and improve your critical reception skills in many situations. We are persuaded daily in the public arena through advertisements, speeches, radio or television programs, and newspaper or magazine articles; we need to remember that significant persuasion also frequently takes place in our personal lives.

QUESTIONS FOR FURTHER THOUGHT

1. If you or someone you know recently made a major purchase (for example, an auto, a stereo component, or a word processor), identify the context in which you or your friend was persuaded. Where did the persuasion take place? In the showroom? Through a television ad? Interpersonally, such as in discussing the purchase with a friend? What kinds of appeals were made? What characteristics were intensified? Downplayed? Discuss all aspects of persuasion that influenced your choice.

2. Much persuasion occurs in interpersonal contexts. Examine one of your interpersonal

relationships, such as that between you and your parents, your boyfriend or girlfriend, your roommate, an athletic teammate, or a fellow member of an organization or church. Describe how, when, and where persuasion has been used in the relationship. What characteristics about yourself have you intensified? Downplayed? What characteristics has the other person intensified? Downplayed? Has repetition been used? Association? Omission?

3. Beginning with the definition of *persuasion* offered in Chapter 1, p. 11, attempt to create a model that reflects all of the important elements of the definition. (Note: You might begin with a model such as that offered by David K. Berlo in *The Process of Communication* and elaborate on it or make appropriate adaptations.)

4. Identify three different types of persuasion you have seen recently (such as advertisements, speeches, persuasive appeals in discussions with others), and analyze each according to the definition offered in this chapter. What are the symbols? What is the persuader's intent? What does the persuasion say about the persuadee's probable frame of reference?

5. What are the tactics of intensification? How do they work? Give examples of their use on television, in print, on radio, by politicians, and by advertisers.

6. What are the tactics of downplay? How do they work? Give examples of their use on television, in print, on radio, by politicians, and by advertisers.

7. What is a "propaganda blitz"? Identify one that is presently going on in media coverage of an event or in regard to some political issue. Give an example of one that has been or is now being used on your campus; for example, a fraternity or sorority rush or a series of investigative news articles on increased student fees.

8. Identify some current examples of the strategies of intensification and downplaying being

used by the Soviet Union as it continues to struggle for a sound economic system?

9. Listen to the sports interviews on the evening news. Note some examples of intensification and downplaying used by coaches and players as they analyze their past wins and losses or as they predict their future prospects.

10. Where are the various tactics of intensification and downplaying being used in regard to environmental issues?

NOTES

1. *The Today Show*, Monday, November 10, 1986. NBC, News Transcript, pp. 36–38.

2. Alvin Toffler, *The Third Wave* (New York: Bantam, 1980).

3. Neil Postman, Interview, *U.S. News and World Report*, January 19, 1981, p. 43. (David Burmeister, who is cited in Chapter 10, reports the number as being around 350,000.)

4. *Ibid.*, p. 43.

5. *Ford's Insider: 1981* (Knoxville, TN: 13–30 Corporation, 1981), p. 5.

6. For a more complete breakdown on how these hours are divided on a daily and weekly basis, see A. C. Neilsen, *The 1990 Nielsen Report on Television* (Northbrook, IL: Nielsen Media Research, 1990).

7. Aristotle, *The Rhetoric*, in *The Works of Aristotle*, translated by R. Robert (Oxford: Clarendon Press, 1924), section 1355b.

8. Winston L. Brembeck and William S. Howell, *Persuasion: A Means of Social Control* (Englewood Cliffs, NJ: Prentice-Hall, 1952), p. 24.

9. Brembeck and Howell, *op. cit.* (2d ed., 1976), p. 19.

10. Wallace C. Fotheringham, *Perspectives on Persuasion* (Boston: Allyn and Bacon, 1966), p. 7.

11. Kenneth Burke, *A Grammar of Motives* (Berkeley: University of California Press, 1970), Introduction.

12. Charles U. Larson, *Persuasion: Reception and Responsibility* (Belmont, CA: Wadsworth, 1973), p. 10.

13. Claude E. Shannon and Warren Weaver, *The Mathematical Theory of Communication* (Urbana: University of Illinois Press, 1949). See also David K. Berlo, *The Process of Communication* (New York: Holt, Rinehart & Winston, 1960).

14. Hugh Rank, "Teaching about Public Persuasion," in *Teaching about Doublespeak*, ed. Daniel Dieterich (Urbana, IL: National Council of Teachers of English, 1976), Chapter 1. The discussion of the intensify/downplay model in this chapter is based on this study.

15. Marshall McLuhan, *Understanding Media: The Extensions of Man* (New York: Signet Books, 1964).

Perspectives on Ethics in Persuasion

Richard L. Johannesen
Northern Illinois University

"What Ever Happened to Ethics?" asked the cover study of *Time* (May 25, 1987, pp. 14–29). "A Nation of Liars?" inquired a lengthy article in *U.S. News and World Report* (February 23, 1987, pp. 54–60). As the decade of the 1980s unfolded, evidence mounted of citizen concern with the decline of ethical behavior, especially among persons in positions of significant public or private responsibility. A February 1987 poll by *U.S. News and World Report* and the Cable News Network showed that more than half of those surveyed believed that people were less honest then than ten years earlier. And seven out of ten of those surveyed were dissatisfied with current standards of honesty—the highest figure since the peak of the Watergate scandal in 1973. According to *Time*: "Large sections of the nation's ethical roofing have been sagging badly, from the White House to churches, schools, industries, medical centers, law firms, and stock brokerages." *Time* concluded: "Ethics, often dismissed as a prissy Sunday School word, now is at the center of a new national debate."

Beyond a continuing focus on the ethics of political communication, public concern has risen about the ethics of communicators in business and other organizational settings. In one survey of 671 managers, almost 25 percent said that high ethics could hinder a successful career; bending the rules was necessary for survival (*Wall Street Journal*, September 8, 1987). A *Gallup Report* poll (August 1985) found that standards of honesty and ethics were rated as a combined low/very low for the following: business executives—18 percent; lawyers—30 percent; realtors—31 percent; insurance salespersons—38 percent; advertising practitioners—39 percent. When asked by the *Wall Street Journal* (July 14, 1987) if he would hire Lt. Col. Oliver North, a central figure in the illegal sale of arms to Iran and diversion of government funds to the Nicaraguan Contras, the president of a public relations firm said he would: "If he's lying, he's lying very well, which would make him a highly excellent PR guy."

Imagine that you are an audience member listening to a speaker—call him Mr. Bronson. His aim is to persuade you to contribute money to the cancer research program of a major medical research center. Suppose that, with one exception, all the evidence, reasoning, and motivational appeals he employs are valid and above ethical suspicion. However, at one point in his speech, Mr. Bronson *consciously* chooses to use a set of *false* statistics to scare you into believing that, during your lifetime, there is a much greater probability of your getting some form of cancer than there actually is.

To promote analysis of the ethics of this hypothetical persuasive situation, consider these issues. If you, or the society at large, view Mr. Bronson's persuasive end, or goal, as worthwhile, does the worth of his end justify his use of false statistics as one means to achieve that end? Does the fact that he consciously chose to use false statistics make a difference in your evaluation? If he used the false statistics out of ignorance or out of failure to check his sources, how might your ethical judgment be altered? Should he be condemned as an unethical person, as an unethical speaker, or, in this instance, for use of a specific unethical technique?

Carefully consider the standards, and the reasons behind those standards, that you would employ to make your ethical judgment of Mr. Bronson. Are the standards purely pragmatic? In other words, should he avoid the false statistics because he might get caught? Are they societal in origin? If he gets caught, his credibility as a representative would be weakened with this and future audiences. Or his getting caught might weaken the credibility of other cancer society representatives. Should he be ethically criticized for violating an implied agreement between you and him? You might not expect a representative of a famous research institute to use questionable techniques and thus you would be especially vulnerable. Finally, should Mr. Bronson's conscious use of false statistics be considered unethical because you are denied accurate, relevant information you need to make an intelligent decision on a public issue?

As receivers and senders of persuasion, we have the responsibility to uphold appropriate ethical standards for persuasion, to encourage freedom of inquiry and expression, and to promote the health of public debate as crucial to democratic decision making. To achieve these goals, we must understand their complexity and recognize the difficulty of achieving them.

In this chapter, I do not intend to argue my own case for the merit of any one particular ethical perspective or set of criteria as *the best one*. Rather, I view my role here, as I do in the classroom, as one of providing information, examples, and insights and of raising questions for discussion. The purpose is to stimulate you to make reasoned choices among ethical options in developing your own position or judgment.[1]

Ethical issues focus on value judgments concerning degrees of right and wrong, goodness and badness, in human conduct. Persuasion, as one type of human behavior, always contains *potential* ethical issues because

1. it involves one person, or a group of people, attempting to influence other people by altering their beliefs, attitudes, values, and overt actions.
2. it involves conscious choices among ends sought and rhetorical means used to achieve the ends.
3. it necessarily involves a potential judge (any or all of the receivers, the persuader, or an independent observer).

As receivers and senders of persuasion, how you evaluate the ethics of a persuasive instance will differ, depending on the ethical standards you are using. You may even choose to ignore ethical judgment entirely. Several justifications are often used to avoid direct analysis and resolution of ethical issues in persuasion:

1. Everyone knows this appeal or tactic obviously is unethical, so there is nothing to talk about.
2. Only success matters, so ethics are irrelevant to persuasion.
3. After all, ethical judgments are only matters of our individual personal opinion, so there are no final answers.

Nevertheless, potential ethical questions are there, regardless of how they are answered.

Whether you wish it or not, consumers of persuasion generally will judge your effort, formally or informally, in part by their relevant ethical criteria. If for none other than the pragmatic reason of enhancing chances of success, you would do well to consider the ethical standards held by your audience.

ETHICAL RESPONSIBILITY

As persuaders, your ethical responsibilities may stem from a status or position you have earned or have been granted, from commitments (promises, pledges, agreements) you have made, or from subsequent consequences (effects) of your communication on others. Responsibility includes the elements of fulfilling duties and obligations, of being accountable to other individuals and groups, of being accountable as evaluated by agreed upon standards, and of being accountable to your own conscience. But an essential element of responsible communication, for both sender and receiver, is exercise of thoughtful and deliberate judgment. That is, the responsible communicator carefully analyzes claims, soundly assesses probable consequences, and conscientiously weighs relevant values. In a sense, a responsible communicator is *response-able*. She or he exercises the ability to respond (is responsive) to the needs and communication of others in sensitive, thoughtful, fitting ways.[2]

Whether persuaders seem *intentionally and knowingly* to use particular content or techniques is a factor that most of us take into account in judging degree of communication ethicality. If a dubious communication behavior seems to stem more from accident, from an unintentional slip of the tongue, or even from ignorance, often we are less harsh in our ethical assessment. For most of us, it is the intentional use of ethically questionable tactics that merits our harshest condemnation.

In contrast, it might be contended that, in argumentative and persuasive situations, communicators have an ethical obligation to double-check the soundness of their evidence and reasoning before they present it to others; sloppy preparation is not an adequate excuse to lessen the harshness of our ethical judgment. A similar view might be advanced concerning elected or appointed government officials. If they use obscure or jargon-laden language that clouds the accurate and clear representation of ideas, even if it is not intended to deceive or hide, they are ethically irresponsible. Such officials, according to this view, should be obligated to communicate clearly and accurately with citizens in fulfillment of their governmental duties. As a related question we can ask, does *sincerity* of intent release a persuader from ethical responsibility concerning means and effects? Could we say that *if* Adolf Hitler's fellow Germans judged him to be sincere, they should not have assessed the ethics of his persuasion? In such cases, evaluations are probably best carried out if we appraise sincerity and ethicality separately. For example, a persuader sincere in intent may use an unethical strategy.

What are the ethics of audience adaptation? Most persuaders seek to secure some kind of response from receivers. To what degree is it ethical for them to alter their ideas and proposals in order to adapt to the needs, capacities, desires, and expectations of an audience? To secure acceptance, some persuaders adapt to an audience to the extent of so changing their ideas that the idea is no longer really theirs. These persuaders merely say what the audience wants them to say, regardless of their

FIGURE 2.1

own convictions. On the other hand, some measure of adaptation in language choice, supporting materials, organization, and message transmission to reflect the specific nature of the audience is a crucial part of successful communication. No ironclad rule can be set down here. Persuaders must decide the ethical balance point between their idea in its pure form and that idea modified to achieve maximum impact with the audience.

In light of what has just been said concerning responsibility, intention, sincerity, and adaptation to an audience, develop your own judgment about the ethicality of the following example. Consider the description in *Newsweek* magazine of 1984 presidential candidate Walter Mondale's habit of telling widely varied interest groups that *each* group's specific interests are "at the very core of my being." Commented *Newsweek*: "In a single three-week period, Mondale used this same phrase to express his commitment to civil rights, his concern for quality education, and his fidelity to upholding 'the rights of unions.' Some joke that the core of his being must be very large, divided into small wedges or rentable on short notice."[3]

RESPONSIBILITIES OF RECEIVERS

Receivers of persuasive messages evaluate them according to standards they perceive as relevant. For example: Is the message interesting and directly related to my concerns? Am I clearly understanding the message as intended by the persuader? What is the persuader's purpose? Do I perceive the persuader as a credible source on this subject (expert, competent, trustworthy, experienced, sincere, honest, concerned)? Has the persuader presented sufficient evidence and reasoning for me to accept the message as reasonable (workable, practical, efficient, and so forth)?

As a receiver, do I see a legitimate connection between the persuader's message and my related needs, motives, and goals? Is the persuader's message consistent with my related beliefs and attitudes? Is the message consistent with my relevant values, my conceptions of the good or desirable?

As a receiver, do I think that the nonverbal elements of the persuader's message reinforce or conflict with the verbal aspects? How do I perceive the persuader's view of my personal worth and abilities? What role does the persuader's message play in some larger, continuous campaign of persuasion? To what degree are the persuader's techniques, appeals, arguments, and purpose ethical?

What are your ethical responsibilities as a receiver or respondent in persuasion? An answer to this question stems in part from the image we hold of the persuasion process. Receivers bear little responsibility if audience members are viewed as inert, passive, defenseless receptacles, as mindless blotters uncritically accepting ideas and arguments. In contrast, persuasion can be viewed as a transaction in which both persuaders and persuadees bear mutual responsibility to participate actively in the process. This image of persuadees as active participants suggests several responsibilities, perhaps captured by two phrases: reasoned skepticism and appropriate feedback.

Reasoned skepticism includes a number of elements. It represents a balanced position between the undesirable extremes of being too open-minded, too gullible, on the one hand, and being too closed-minded, too dogmatic, on the other. Persistent doubtfulness describes one aspect. You are not simply an unthinking blotter "soaking up" ideas and arguments. Rather, you exercise your capacities actively to search for meaning, to analyze and synthesize, and to judge soundness and worth. You do something to and with the information you receive: You process, interpret, and evaluate it. Also, you inform yourself about issues being discussed; and you tolerate, even seek out, divergent and controversial viewpoints, the better to assess what is being presented.

As receivers of persuasion, we must realize that accurate understanding of a persuader's message may be hindered by our attempt to impose our own ethical standards on that persuader. Our immediate "gut-level" ethical judgments may cause us to distort the intended meaning. Only after reaching an accurate understanding of the persuader's ideas can we reasonably evaluate the ethics of his or her persuasive strategies or purposes.

In this era of public distrust of the truthfulness of public communication, reasoned skepticism also requires that we combat the automatic assumption that most public communication is untrustworthy. Just because a communication is of a certain type or comes from a certain source (government, candidate, news media, advertiser), it must not automatically, without evaluation, be rejected as tainted or untruthful. Clearly, we must always exercise caution in acceptance and care in evaluation, as emphasized throughout this book. Using the best evidence available to us, we may arrive at our best judgment. However, to condemn a message as untruthful or unethical solely because it stems from a suspect source and before directly assessing it is to exhibit decision-making behavior detrimental to our political, social, and economic system. Rejection of the message, if such be the judgment, must come after, not before, our evaluation of it. As with a defendant in the courtroom, public communication must be presumed ethically innocent until we, or experts we acknowledge, have proved it guilty. However, when techniques of persuasion do weaken or undermine the confidence and trust necessary for intelligent public decision making, they can be condemned as unethical.

As an active participant in the persuasion process, it is also necessary to provide **appropriate feedback** to persuaders. Your response, in most situations, should be an honest and accurate reflection of your true comprehension, belief, feeling, or judgment. Otherwise, persuaders are denied the relevant and accurate information they need to make decisions. Your response might be verbal or nonverbal, oral or written, immediate or delayed. A response of understanding, puzzlement, agreement, or disagreement could be reflected through your facial expression, gestures, posture, inquiries, statements during a question-answer period, and letters to editors or advertisers. In some cases, because of your special expertise on a subject, you even may have the obligation to respond, to provide feedback, while other receivers remain silent. You need to decide whether the degree and type of your feedback are appropriate for the subject, audience, and occasion of the persuasion. For instance, to interrupt with questions, or even to heckle, might be appropriate in a few situations but irresponsible in many others.

Disagreement and conflict sometimes occur in intimate and informal interpersonal settings. In such situations, when at least one participant may be emotionally vulnerable, individual personalities often affect each other in direct and powerful ways. When you as a receiver in such a situation decide to respond by expressing strong disagreement, there are some "unfair" tactics of verbal conflict you may want to avoid because they are irresponsible.[4] Avoid monopolizing the talk with the intent of preventing others from expressing their position. Avoid entrapment, in which you lure someone into saying something that you intend to use later to embarrass or hurt them. Avoid verbally "hitting below the belt" by taking unfair advantage of what you know to be the other person's special psychological vulnerability. Avoid stockpiling or accumulating numerous grievances so that you can overwhelm others by dumping the complaints on them all at once. Finally, avoid dragging in numerous irrelevant or trivial issues and arguments in order to pile up an advantage.

SOME ETHICAL PERSPECTIVES

We will briefly explain six major ethical perspectives as potential viewpoints for analyzing ethical issues in persuasion. As categories, these perspectives are not exhaustive, mutually exclusive, or given in any order of precedence.

As receivers of persuasion, we can employ one or a combination of such perspectives to evaluate the ethical level of a persuader's use of language (such as metaphors, ambiguity, and what Richart M. Weaver labels "God terms" and "Devil terms") or of evidence and reasoning (such as what Stephen Toulmin calls data, warrant, backing, reservation, qualifier, and claim). We also can use them to assess the ethics of psychological techniques, such as appeals to needs and values, the stimulation and resolution of dissonance and imbalance, or the appeal to widely held cultural images and myths. The persuasive tactics of campaigns and social movements also can (indeed must) be subjected to ethical scrutiny.

Religious Perspectives

Religious perspectives stem from the moral guidelines and the "thou shalt nots" embodied in the ideology and sacred literature of various religions. For instance, the Bible warns against lying, slander, and bearing false witness. Taoist religion stresses empathy and insight, rather than reason and logic, as roads to truth. Citing facts and demonstrating logical conclusions are minimized in Taoism in favor of feeling and intuition. These and other religiously derived criteria could be used to assess the ethics of persuasion.

Human Nature Perspectives

These perspectives probe the *essence* of human nature by asking what makes a human fundamentally human. Unique characteristics of human nature that distinguish us from "lower" forms of life are identified. Such characteristics then can be used as standards for judging the ethics of persuasion. Among some of the suggested characteristics are capacity to reason, capacity to create and use symbols, capacity for mutual appreciative understanding, and capacity to make value judgments. The assumption is that uniquely human attributes should be promoted, thereby promoting fulfillment of maximum individual potential. A determination could be made of the degree to which a persuader's appeals and techniques either foster or undermine the development of a fundamental human characteristic. A technique that *de*humanizes, that makes a person less than human, would be unethical. Whatever the political, religious, or cultural context, a person would be assumed to possess certain uniquely human attributes worthy of promotion through communication.

Political Perspectives

The implicit or explicit values and procedures accepted as crucial to the health and growth of a particular political-governmental system are the focus of political perspectives. Once these essential values are identified for that political system, they can be used for evaluating the ethics of persuasive means and ends within that system. The assumption is that public communication should foster achievement of these values; persuasive techniques that retard, subvert, or circumvent these basic political values would be condemned as unethical. Different political systems usually embody differing values leading to differing ethical judgments. Within the context of American representative democracy, for example, various analysts pinpoint values and procedures they deem fundamental to healthy functioning of our political system, and, thus, values that can guide ethical scrutiny of persuasion therein. Such values and procedures include enhancement of citizen capacity to reach rational decisions, access to channels of public communication, access to relevant and accurate information on public issues, maximization of freedom of choice, toleration of dissent, honesty in presenting motivations and consequences, and thoroughness and accuracy in presenting evidence and alternatives.

Situational Perspectives

To make ethical judgments, situational perspectives focus *regularly* and *primarily* on the elements of the specific persuasive situation at hand. Virtually all perspectives (those mentioned here and others) make some allowances, on occasion, for the modified application of ethical criteria in special circumstances. However, an extreme situational perspective *routinely* makes judgments *only* in light of *each different context*. Criteria from broad political, human nature, religious, or other perspectives are minimized; absolute and universal standards are avoided. Among the concrete contextual factors relevant to making a purely situational ethical evaluation are:

1. Role or function of the persuader for the audience
2. Expectations held by receivers concerning such matters as appropriateness and reasonableness

3. Degree of receiver awareness of the persuader's techniques
4. Goals and values held by receivers
5. Degree of urgency for implementation of the persuader's proposal
6. Ethical standards for communication held by receivers

From an extreme situational perspective, for instance, it might be argued that an acknowledged leader in a time of clear crisis has a responsibility to rally support and thus could employ so-called emotional appeals that circumvent human processes of rational, reflective decision making. Or it might be argued that a persuader may ethically employ techniques such as innuendo, guilt by association, and unfounded name-calling as long as the receivers both recognize and approve of those methods.

Legal Perspectives

Legal perspectives would take the general position that illegal communication behavior also is unethical. That which is not specifically illegal is viewed as ethical. Such an approach certainly has the advantage of allowing simple ethical decisions; we would need only to measure persuasive techniques against current laws and regulations to determine whether a technique is ethical. We might, for example, turn for ethical guidance to the regulations governing advertising set forth by the Federal Trade Commission or the Federal Communications Commission. Or we might use Supreme Court criteria or state legislation defining obscenity, pornography, or libel to judge whether a particular message is unethical on those grounds. However, we also must consider to what degree legal perspectives lead to oversimplified, superficial judgments of complex persuasive situations.

Dialogical Perspectives

Dialogical perspectives emerge from current scholarship on the nature of communication as dialogue rather than as monologue.[5] Such perspectives contend that the attitudes toward each other among participants in a communication situation are an index of the ethical level of that communication. Some attitudes are held to be more fully human, humane, and facilitative of personal self-fulfillment than are other attitudes.

Communication as *dialogue* is characterized by such attitudes as honesty, concern for the welfare and improvement of others, trust, genuineness, open-mindedness, equality, mutual respect, empathy, humility, directness, lack of pretense, non-manipulative intent, sincerity, encouragement of free expression, and acceptance of others as individuals with intrinsic worth regardless of differences over belief or behavior. Communication as *monologue*, in contrast, is marked by such qualities as deception, superiority, exploitation, dogmatism, domination, insincerity, pretense, personal self-display, self-aggrandizement, judgmentalism that stifles free expression, coercion, possessiveness, condescension, self-defensiveness, and viewing others as objects to be manipulated. In the case of persuasion, then, the techniques and presentation of the persuader would be scrutinized to determine the degree to which they reveal an ethical dialogical attitude or an unethical monological attitude toward receivers.

With the above six ethical perspectives (religious, human nature, political, situational, legal, dialogical), we can confront a variety of questions that underscore difficult issues relevant to ethical problems in persuasion. As receivers constantly bombarded with a variety of verbal and nonverbal persuasive messages, we continually face resolution of one or another of these fundamental issues.

ETHICS, PROPAGANDA, AND THE DEMAGOGUE

Is propaganda unethical? The answer to this question in part depends on how propaganda is defined. As Larson will emphasize in a later chapter, numerous, often widely divergent, definitions abound. Originally, the term "propaganda" was associated with the efforts of the Roman Catholic church to persuade people to accept the church's doctrine. Such efforts were institutionalized in

1622 by Pope Gregory XV when he created the Sacred Congregation for Propagating the Faith. The word "propaganda" soon came to designate not only institutions seeking to propagate a doctrine but also the doctrine itself and the communication techniques employed.

Today one cluster of definitions of propaganda presents a *neutral* position toward the ethical nature of propaganda. A definition combining the key elements of such neutral views might be: Propaganda is a *campaign* of *mass* persuasion. According to this view, propaganda represents an organized, continuous effort to persuade a mass audience, primarily using the mass media.[6] Propaganda thus would include advertising and public relations efforts; national political election campaigns; the persuasive campaigns of some social reform movements; and the organized efforts of national governments to win friends abroad, maintain domestic morale, and undermine an opponent's morale both in "hot" and "cold" war. Such a view stresses communication channels and audiences and categorizes propaganda as one species of persuasion. Just as persuasion may be sound or unsound, ethical or unethical, so too may propaganda.

Another cluster of definitions takes a *negative* stance toward the ethical nature of propaganda. Definitions in this cluster probably typify the view held by many average American citizens. A definition combining the key elements of such negative views might be: Propaganda is the intentional use of suggestion, irrelevant emotional appeals, and pseudoproof to circumvent human rational decision-making processes.[7] Such a view stresses communication techniques and sees propaganda as *inherently* unethical.

Are the traditional propaganda devices always to be viewed as unethical? Later Larson will describe the traditional list: name-calling, glittering generality, transfer, testimonial, plain folks, card stacking, and bandwagon. Such a list, however, does not constitute a sure-fire guide, a "handy-dandy" checklist, for exposing unethical persuasion. The ethics of at least some of these techniques depends on how they are employed in a given context.

The *plain folks* technique stresses humble origins and modest backgrounds shared by the communicator and audience. The persuader emphasizes to the audience, although usually not in these words, that "we're all just plain folks." In his whistle-stop speeches to predominantly rural, Republican audiences during the 1948 presidential campaign, Democrat Harry Truman typically used the plain folks appeal to establish common ground in introductions to his speeches. He used the device to accomplish one of the purposes of the introductory segment of most speeches — namely, establishment of rapport; he did not rely on it for proof in the main body of his speeches. If a politician relied primarily on the plain folks appeal as pseudoproof in *justifying* the policy he or she advocated, such usage could be condemned as unethical. Furthermore, Truman really was the kind of person who could legitimately capitalize on his actual plain folks background. A politician of a more privileged and patrician background, such as Edward Kennedy, could be condemned for using an unethical technique *if* he were to appeal to farmers and factory workers by saying "you and I are just plain folks."

Today the label "demagogue" is frequently used to render a negative ethical judgment of a communicator. Too often, the label is only vaguely defined; the criteria we are to use to evaluate a person as a demagogue are unspecified. In ancient Greece, a demagogue simply was a leader or orator who championed the cause of the common people.

In the following journalistic description of a former governor from the South, what characteristics are suggested as marks of a demagogue? To what extent should we agree with them as appropriate criteria for judging a demagogue?

> He is the quintessential demagogue, combining the missionary zeal of a Barry Goldwater, the raw pursuit of power of a Kennedy, the expansive populism of a Huey Long, the chameleon-like adaptability of a Nixon, and the disarmingly blunt, or somewhat crude, appeal of an Archie Bunker.[8]

You now are invited to consider the following five characteristics collectively as possible appropriate guides for determining to what degree a persuader merits the label "demagogue."[9]

1. A demagogue wields popular or mass leadership over an extensive number of people.
2. A demagogue exerts primary influence through the medium of the spoken word — through public speaking — whether directly to an audience or by means of radio or television.
3. A demagogue relies heavily on propaganda defined in the negative sense of intentional use of suggestion, irrelevant emotional appeals, and pseudoproof to circumvent human rational decision-making processes.
4. A demagogue capitalizes on the availability of a major contemporary social issue or problem.
5. A demagogue is hypocritical; the social cause serves as a front or persuasive leverage point whereas the actual primary motive is selfish interest and personal gain.

Several cautions are in order in applying these guidelines. A persuader may reflect each of these characteristics to a greater or lesser degree and only in certain instances. A persuader might fulfill only several of these criteria (such as items 1, 2, and 4) and yet not be called a demagogue; characteristics 3 and 5 seem to be central to a conception of a demagogue. How easily and accurately can we usually determine a persuader's *actual* motivations? Should we limit the notion of a demagogue solely to the political arena?

ETHICAL STANDARDS FOR POLITICAL PERSUASION

Directly or indirectly, we daily are exposed to political and governmental persuasion in varied forms. The president appeals on national television for public support of a diplomatic treaty. A senator argues in Congress against ratification of a treaty. A government bureaucrat announces a new regulation and presents reasons to justify it. A federal official contends that information requested by a citizen-action group cannot be revealed for national security reasons. At any given moment, somewhere, a national, state, or local politician is

campaigning for election. At a city council meeting, a citizen protests a proposed property-tax rate increase. What ethical criteria should we apply to judge the many kinds of political-governmental persuasion? We will consider a number of potential sets of criteria in the hope that among them you will find ones especially useful in your own life.

Traditional American textbook discussions of the ethics of persuasion, rhetoric, and argument often include lists of standards suggested for evaluating the ethicality of an instance of persuasion. Such criteria often are rooted, implicitly if not explicitly, in what we earlier in this chapter described as a political perspective for judging the ethics of persuasion. The criteria usually stem from a commitment to values and procedures deemed essential to the health and growth of the American political-governmental system of representative democracy. Obviously, other cultures and other governmental systems may embrace basic values that lead to quite different ethical standards for persuasion.

What follows is my synthesis and adaptation of a number of such typical traditional lists of ethical criteria for persuasion.[10] Within the context of our own society, the following criteria are not necessarily the only or best ones possible; they are suggested as general guidelines rather than inflexible rules, and they may stimulate discussion on the complexity of judging the ethics of persuasion. Consider, for example, under what circumstances there may be justifiable exceptions to some of these criteria. Also bear in mind that one difficulty in applying these criteria in concrete situations stems from differing standards and meanings people may have for such key terms as *distort, falsify, rational, reasonable, conceal, misrepresent, irrelevant,* and *deceive.*

1. Do not use false, fabricated, misrepresented, distorted, or irrelevant evidence to support arguments or claims.
2. Do not intentionally use specious, unsupported, or illogical reasoning.
3. Do not represent yourself as informed or as an "expert" on a subject when you are not.

4. Do not use irrelevant appeals to divert attention or scrutiny from the issue at hand. Among the appeals that commonly serve such a purpose are: "smear" attacks on an opponent's character, appeals to hatred and bigotry, innuendo, and God terms or Devil terms that cause intense but unreflective positive or negative reactions.

5. Do not ask your audience to link your idea or proposal to emotion-laden values, motives, or goals to which it actually is not related.

6. Do not deceive your audience by concealing your real purpose, self-interest, the group you represent, or your position as an advocate of a viewpoint.

7. Do not distort, hide, or misrepresent the number, scope, intensity, or undesirable features of consequences or effects.

8. Do not use "emotional appeals" that lack a supporting basis of evidence or reasoning, or that would not be accepted if the audience had time and opportunity to examine the subject themselves.

9. Do not oversimplify complex, gradation-laden situations into simplistic two-valued, either/or, polar views or choices.

10. Do not pretend certainty where tentativeness and degrees of probability would be more accurate.

11. Do not advocate something in which you do not believe yourself.

Some guidelines for evaluating the ethical responsibility of governmental communication have been developed by Dennis Gouran.[11]

1. The deliberate falsification of information released to the public, especially under circumstances involving the general welfare, is inappropriate and irresponsible.

2. The classification of government documents for the purpose of deceiving or otherwise keeping the public uninformed on matters affecting private citizens' well-being is inappropriate and irresponsible.

3. The deliberate use of official news sources for the purpose of obscuring embarrassing and deceitful governmental acts is inappropriate and irresponsible.

4. Criticism of the press for the purpose of assuring that governmental acts are viewed only in favorable terms is inappropriate and irresponsible.

5. Deliberate attempts by governmental agents to suppress or otherwise interfere with an individual's legitimate exercise of free expression within the limits defined by our courts are inappropriate and irresponsible.

6. Overt and covert governmental acts designed to misrepresent a political candidate's, or any other citizen's, character or position or to violate said individual's rights are inappropriate and irresponsible.

7. Language employed by governmental figures for the purpose of deliberately obscuring the activity or idea it represents is inappropriate and irresponsible.

For the 1976 presidential campaign, Common Cause, a national citizens' lobbying group, proposed a set of standards that, even today, easily might aid in assessing the ethics of any political candidate's campaign. According to their criteria, an ethical candidate exhibits the following behavior:

1. Engages in unrehearsed communication with voters, including participation in open hearings and forums with other candidates on the same platform, where the public is given opportunities to express their concerns, ask questions, and follow up on their questions

2. Holds press conferences at least monthly throughout the campaign, and in every state where contesting a primary, at which reporters and broadcasters are freely permitted to ask questions and follow-up questions

3. Discusses issues that are high on the list of people's concerns, as evidenced, for example, by national public opinion polls; clarifies alternatives and trade-offs in a way that sets forth the real choices involved for the nation; and makes clear to the American people what

choices he or she would make if elected to office

4. Makes public all information relating to a given poll if releasing or leaking any part of a campaign poll (including when and where the poll was conducted, by whom, a description of the sample of the population polled, as well as all questions and responses)

5. Allows interviews by a broad spectrum of TV, radio, and newspaper reporters, including single-interviewer formats that provide maximum opportunity for in-depth questions

6. Takes full public responsibility for all aspects of his or her campaign, including responsibility for campaign finance activities, campaign practices of staff, and campaign statements of principal spokespersons

7. Makes public a statement of personal financial holdings, including assets and debts, sources of income, honoraria, gifts, and other financial transactions over $1000, covering candidate, spouse, and dependent children

8. Does not use taxpayer-supported services of any public office now held — such as staff, transportation, or free mailing privileges — for campaign purposes, except as required for personal security reasons

9. Uses only advertising that stresses the record and viewpoint on issues of the candidates

Frequently, political candidates are condemned for stressing "image" over "issues" in their campaigns. Traditionally, so-called image-oriented campaigns are viewed as ethically suspect. However, a contrasting view should be considered.[12] Some scholars argue that issues and stands on issues are too transitory and too complex for voters to make dependable judgments. For example, an issue vital today often fades quickly, to be replaced by one unforeseen during the campaign. Or issues may have to be created if none loom large in the public mind at the inflexible time when the campaign occurs. Instead, suggest some scholars, voters should assess the basic dimensions of the candidate's image (personal qualities) as a better basis for evaluations. In the long run, the key ques-

tions would be: Does the candidate's past record demonstrate strength of character, decisiveness of action, openness to relevant information and alternative viewpoints, thoroughness in studying a problem, respect for the intelligence of others, and the ability to lead through public and private communication?

During the 1980s, political analysts in the mass media often criticized President Ronald Reagan for misstating and misusing examples, statistics, and illustrative stories. They charged he did this not just on rare occasions, but with routine frequency in his news conferences, informal comments, and sometimes in speeches. Following are instances from Reagan's public communication during that period.[13] You are encouraged to make your own assessment of their ethicality by bringing to bear our previous discussions concerning intention, sincerity, responsibility, the "political perspective," and suggested standards for political persuasion.

On April 15, 1982, President Reagan explained his views on gun control in part by mentioning a British law under which a "criminal with a gun, even if he was arrested for burglary, was tried for first-degree murder and hanged if found guilty." A *New York Times* search failed to locate such a law. The White House Deputy Press Secretary Larry Speakes defended Reagan's use of the example by saying, "It made the point, didn't it?"

During a speech on June 15, 1982, President Reagan quoted Justice Oliver Wendell Holmes as having said, "Keep the government poor and remain free." An expert on Holmes was unaware of anything in Holmes's writing that resembled the statement. Later an official in the White House speechwriting office explained, "Holmes never said anything point-blank exactly like that . . . we're still trying to track it down."

Early in 1982, to illustrate abuse of federal programs for the needy, President Reagan recounted a story of wealthy children taking advantage of a school-lunch program somewhere in upstate New York. When asked for more details at his February 18, 1982, news conference, the president was unable to identify the source of the information or to verify its validity. He explained, "I simply re-

counted it as having been told to me by someone. . . . I know that it was up in New York
someplace."

ETHICAL STANDARDS FOR COMMERCIAL ADVERTISING

Consumers, academic experts, and advertisers
themselves clearly do not agree on any one set of
ethical standards as appropriate for assessing commercial advertising. Here we will simply survey
some of the widely varied criteria that have been
suggested. Among them you may find guidelines
that will aid your own assessments.

Using a kind of religious perspective, John
McMillan contends that the first responsibility of
an advertiser is not to either business or society
but rather to God and principles higher than
self, society, or business.[14] Thus, advertisers are
responsible to multiple neighbors—to owners,
employees, clients, customers, and the general
public. Second, they have a responsibility for objective truth. Third, they are responsible for preparing advertising messages with a sense of
respect for their audience. Finally, argues Mc-
Millan, advertisers are responsible for seeking
product improvements.

Several writers on the ethics of advertising suggest the applicability of perspectives rooted in the
essence of human nature. Thomas Garrett contends that a person becomes more truly human in
proportion as his or her behavior becomes more
conscious and reflective.[15] Because of the human
capacity for reason and because of the equally distinctive fact of human dependence on other people
for development of potential, Garrett suggests
there are several ethical obligations. As humans,
we are obliged, among other things, to behave
rationally ourselves, to help others behave rationally, and to provide truthful information. Suggestive advertising, in Garrett's view, is that which
seeks to bypass human powers of reason or to
some degree render them inoperative. Such advertising is unethical not just because it uses emotional appeal, Garrett believes, but because it

demeans a fundamental human attribute and makes
people less than human.

Clarence Walton observes that some critics employ a philosophical model that identifies three
components of human nature as vital elements to
be considered in evaluating the ethics of marketing
practices: (1) human capability for rational judgment, (2) human capacity for exercising free options among defined alternatives, and (3) human
motivation to serve primarily selfish interests or to
serve the welfare of others.[16] By extending the
implications of such a framework, advertising and
marketing tactics could be judged by the degree to
which they undermine the human capacity for rational decision, constrict free choice among alternatives, and foster largely selfish interests.

Theodore Levitt uses a human nature position
to *defend* advertising techniques often viewed by
others as ethically suspect. While admitting that
the line between distortion and falsehood is difficult to establish, his central argument is that
"embellishment and distortion are among advertising's legitimate and socially desirable purposes;
and that illegitimacy in advertising consists only
of falsification with larcenous intent."[17] Levitt
grounds his defense in a "pervasive, . . . *universal*, characteristic of human nature—the human
audience *demands* symbolic interpretation of
everything it sees and knows. If it doesn't get it, it
will return a verdict of 'no interest.'"[18] Because
Levitt sees humans essentially as symbolizers, as
converters of raw sensory experience through
symbolic interpretation to satisfy needs, he can
justify "legitimate" embellishment and distortion.
He contends:

> Many of the so-called distortions of advertis-
> ing, product design, and packaging may be
> viewed as a paradigm of the many responses
> that man makes to the conditions of survival in
> the environment. Without distortion, embel-
> lishment, and elaboration, life would be drab,
> dull, anguished, and at its existential worst.[19]

Sometimes advertisers adopt what we earlier in
this chapter called legal perspectives, in which
ethicality is equated with legality. However, Har-

old Williams observes, concerning the ethics of advertising:

> What is legal and what is ethical are not synonymous, and neither are what is legal and what is honest. We tend to resort to legality often as our guideline. This is in effect what happens often when we turn to the lawyers for confirmation that a course of action is an appropriate one.
>
> We must recognize that we are getting a legal opinion, but not necessarily an ethical or moral one. The public, the public advocates, and many of the legislative and administrative authorities recognize it even if we do not.[20]

Typically, commercial advertising has been viewed as persuasion that argues a case or demonstrates a claim concerning the actual nature or merits of a product. To such attempts at arguing the quality of a product, many of the traditional ethical standards for "truthfulness" and "rationality" have been applied. For instance, are the evidence and the reasoning supporting the claim clear, accurate, relevant, and sufficient in quantity? Are the emotional and motivational appeals directly relevant to the product? The techniques that Larson will discuss as "weasel words" and as "deceptive claims" might be judged unethical according to this standard of truthfulness.

The American Association of Advertising Agencies, in a code of ethics revised in 1962, went beyond simple obedience to the laws and regulations governing advertising to broaden and extend "the ethical application of high ethical standards." As you read the following standards, consider their degree of adequacy, the degree to which they still are relevant and appropriate today, and the extent to which they presently are followed by advertisers. Association members agree to avoid intentionally producing advertising that contains[21]

1. false or misleading statements or exaggerations, visual or verbal.
2. testimonials that do not reflect the real choice of a competent witness.
3. price claims that are misleading.
4. comparisons that unfairly disparage a competitive product or service.
5. claims insufficiently supported or that distort the true meaning or practicable application of statements made by professional or scientific authority.
6. statements, suggestions, or pictures offensive to public decency.

What if ethical standards of truthfulness and rationality are *irrelevant* to most commercial advertising? What if the primary purpose of most ads is *not* to prove a claim? Then what ethical standards we apply may stem from whatever alternative view of the nature and purpose of advertising we do hold. Some advertisements function primarily to capture and sustain consumer attention, to announce a product, to create consumer awareness of the name of a product.[22] What ethical criteria are most appropriate for such attention-getting ads?

Lawrence W. Rosenfield views commercial advertising as a type of poetic game.[23] Here, techniques of making the commonplace significant, of esthetically pleasing structure, of connotation, and of ambiguity all combine to invite consumers to participate in a recreational, emotionally satisfying experience. If there is such a thing as commercial "advertising-as-poetic," what ethical standards should we use to judge this kind of poetry?

Finally, consider Tony Schwartz's resonance theory of electronic media persuasion, which Larson will discuss later.[24] As part of his view, he argues that because our conceptions of truth, honesty, and clarity are products of our print-oriented culture, they are appropriate in judging the content of printed messages. In contrast, he contends that the "question of truth is largely irrelevant when dealing with electronic media content."[25] In assessing the ethics of advertising by means of electronic media, Schwartz thinks that the Federal Trade Commission should focus not on truth and clarity of content but on effects of the advertisement on receivers. He laments, however, that at present "we have no generally agreed-upon social values and/or rules that can be readily applied in judging whether the effects of electronic communication are beneficial, acceptable, or harmful."[26] Schwartz summarizes his argument by concluding that

> truth is a print ethic, not a standard for ethical behavior in electronic communication. In addition, the influence of electronic media on print advertising (particularly the substitution of photographic techniques for copy to achieve an effect) raises the question of whether truth is any longer an issue in magazine or newspaper ads.[27]

THE ETHICS OF SUBLIMINAL PERSUASION

In a later chapter, Larson describes the nature and some possible uses of subliminal persuasion. Such persuasion involves words or pictures flashed on a movie or television screen so rapidly, played on an audio channel so softly, or disguised in a magazine ad so skillfully that viewers or listeners do not consciously recognize them. However, the subliminal messages, it is claimed, are absorbed subconsciously by the receivers. Larson also notes that use of such techniques might raise ethical issues.

In the late 1950s, at the federal and state levels, a number of bills were introduced to make illegal the use of subliminal techniques in commercial or political advertisements. None of these bills ever became state or federal law. In January 1974, the Federal Communications Commission did issue a Public Notice warning broadcasters that because such subliminal perception techniques were intentionally deceptive, they were contrary to the obligation of stations to serve the public interest; revocation of a broadcast license might result from using them. Both the Television Code and the Radio Code of the National Association of Broadcasters voluntarily pledge member stations not to use any techniques that attempt to convey information "by transmitting messages below the threshold of normal awareness."

In the 1980s, companies started marketing subliminal self-persuasion programs for voluntary self-improvement. One of these firms offered for sale a series of audiocassettes containing subliminal suggestions to help a person lose weight, stop smoking, and improve memory. Another firm advertised videocassettes for home television that included subliminal messages on such topics as stress control, alcohol control, career motivation, golf expertise, and sexual confidence. This latter company emphasized the voluntary nature of using its programs and the fact that viewers could replay the videotapes in slow motion if they wished to see the messages consciously.

What judgments might be made concerning the ethicality of subliminal persuasion?[28] From the human nature perspective described earlier in this chapter, the unique capacities for conscious value judgment and for rational processing of information could be stressed for protection. In addition, the right of privacy of an individual's mental processes might justify declaring that use of subliminal techniques in situations of involuntary and unconscious exposure is ethically irresponsible. An individual should have the freedom, in the view of Olivia Goodkin and Maureen Phillips, "to choose the time, circumstances, and extent to which his attitudes, beliefs, behavior, and opinions are to be influenced and shaped by another."[29] Thus, because hidden use of subliminal persuasion circumvents and undermines capacities and freedoms that are essential to human self-fulfillment, it could be condemned as unethical.

Negative ethical judgments of subliminal persuasion also might grow from one version of the political perspective described earlier. The values fundamental to the health of American representative democracy as a system of self-government could provide standards for ethical assessment. Essential to this democratic system is the development of a person's ability to be consciously aware of her or his own mental activities, "to question their validity, to judge them critically, to alter or correct them."[30] Franklyn Haiman sees promotion of our capacity to reason logically as a value necessary for adequate functioning of our system of representative democracy. The ethical standard advocated by Haiman is the degree of rationality, the degree of conscious free choice, reflected in and promoted by any specific persuasive technique or appeal. Condemned as unethical in Haiman's view (especially in political campaigning, governmental communication, and commercial advertising) are techniques that influence the receiver "by short-circuiting his conscious thought processes and planting suggestions or exerting pressures on the periphery of his consciousness which are intended to produce automatic, nonreflective behavior."[31] Unannounced use of subliminal persuasion would particularly warrant ethical condemnation because it attempts to circumvent the human mind and reason and to elicit nonreflective, semiconscious, or unconscious responses.

From the previously discussed legal perspective, society's negative ethical judgments of subliminal persuasion could be formalized by making specific types of subliminal techniques illegal. Haiman sees "no First Amendment barrier to outlawing" subliminal stimuli when used on unconsenting persons.[32] Goodkin and Phillips reject as legal remedies, on the one hand, the total prohibition of the manufacture, sale, and use of subliminal persuasion devices, or, on the other hand, regulation restricting uses to those deemed beneficial to society. Instead they advocate laws requiring disclosure of any public or private use of subliminal techniques and disclosure of the content subliminally transmitted.[33]

THE ETHICS OF INTENTIONAL AMBIGUITY AND VAGUENESS

"Language that is of doubtful or uncertain meaning" might be a typical definition of ambiguous language. **Ambiguous** language legitimately is open to two or more interpretations. **Vague** language lacks definiteness, explicitness, or preciseness of meaning. Clear communication of intended meaning usually is one major aim of an ethical communicator, whether that person seeks to enhance receiver understanding or seeks to influence belief, attitude, or action. Textbooks on oral and written communication typically warn against ambiguity and vagueness; often they directly or indirectly take the position that intentional ambiguity

is an unethical communication tactic. For example, later in this book Larson discusses ambiguity as a functional device of style, as a stylistic technique that often is successful while ethically questionable.

Most people probably would agree that intentional ambiguity is unethical in situations where accurate instruction or efficient transmission of precise information is the acknowledged purpose. Even in most so-called persuasive communication situations, intentional ambiguity would be ethically suspect. However, in some situations communicators may believe that the intentional creation of ambiguity or vagueness is necessary, accepted, expected as normal, and even ethically justified. Such might be the case, for example, in religious discourse, in some advertising, in some legal discourse, in labor-management bargaining, in political campaigning, or in international diplomatic negotiations.

We can itemize a number of specific purposes for which communicators might believe that intentional ambiguity is ethically justified: (1) to heighten receiver attention through puzzlement; (2) to allow flexibility in interpretation of legal concepts; (3) to use ambiguity on secondary issues to allow for precise understanding and agreement on the primary issue; (4) to promote maximum receiver psychological participation in the communication transaction by letting receivers create their own relevant meanings; (5) to promote maximum latitude for revision of a position in later dealings with opponents or with constituents by avoiding being "locked in" to a single absolute stance.

In political communication, whether during campaigns or by government officials, several circumstances might be used to justify intentional ambiguity ethically. First, a president or presidential candidate often must communicate to multiple audiences through a single message via a mass medium such as television or radio. Different parts of the message may appeal to specific audiences, and intentional ambiguity in some message elements avoids offending any of the audiences. Lewis Froman describes a second circumstance: A candidate "cannot take stands on specific issues because he doesn't know what the specific choices will be until he is faced with the necessity for concrete decision. Also, specific commitments would be too binding in a political process that depends upon negotiation and compromise."[34] Third, groups of voters increasingly make decisions about whether to support or oppose a candidate on the basis of that candidate's stand on a single issue of paramount importance to those groups. The candidate's position on a variety of other public issues often is ignored or dismissed. "Single-issue politics" is the phrase frequently used to characterize this trend. A candidate intentionally may be ambiguous on one emotion-packed issue in order to get a fair hearing for his or her stands on many other issues.

In his *Law Dictionary for Non-Lawyers*, Daniel Oran warns against use of vague language but also notes: "Some legal words have a 'built-in' vagueness. They are used when the writer or speaker does not want to be pinned down. For example, when a law talks about '*reasonable* speed' or '*due care*,' it is deliberately imprecise about the meaning of the words because it wants the amount of speed allowed or care required to be decided situation by situation, rather than by an exact formula."[35]

In some advertising, intentional ambiguity seems to be understood as such by consumers and even accepted by them. Consider the possible ethical implications of the Noxzema shaving cream advertisement that urged (accompanied by a beautiful woman watching a man shave in rhythm with strip-tease music):"Take it off. Take it *all* off." Or what about the "sexy" woman in the after-shave cologne advertisement who says, "All my men wear English Leather, or they wear *nothing at all*."

THE ETHICS OF NONVERBAL COMMUNICATION

Nonverbal factors play an important role in the persuasion process. In a magazine advertisement, for example, the use of certain colors, pictures, layout patterns, and typefaces all influence how the words in the advertisement are received. Later

in this book, Larson provides examples of what he terms nonverbal "bias" in photo selection, camera angle and movement, and editing in news presentation. In *The Importance of Lying*, Arnold Ludwig underscores the ethical implications of some dimensions of nonverbal communication:

> Lies are not only found in verbal statements. When a person nods affirmatively in response to something he does not believe or when he feigns attention to a conversation he finds boring, he is equally guilty of lying. . . . A false shrug of the shoulders, the seductive batting of eyelashes, an eyewink, or a smile may all be employed as nonverbal forms of deception.[36]

Silence, too, may carry ethical implications. If to be responsible in fulfillment of our role or position demands that we speak out on a subject, to remain silent may be judged unethical. On the other hand, if the only way that we successfully can persuade others on a subject is to employ unethical communication techniques or appeals, the ethical decision probably would be to remain silent.

Spiro T. Agnew, when vice-president of the United States, catalogued numerous nonverbal elements of television news broadcasts that he believed carried ethical implications: facial expressions, sarcastic tone of voice, raised eyebrow, and vocal inflection.[37] In the context of contemporary American political campaigns, Dan Nimmo questions the ethicality of electronically induced voice compression in radio or television advertisements for candidates. "A slow-talking, drawling Southerner can be made to speak at the rate of a clipped-worded New Englander. A hesitant, shy-sounding speaker becomes decisive and assured."[38]

In *Harper's* magazine, Earl Shorris condemns as unethical the nonverbal tactics of the *New York Times* in opposing Bella Abzug as a candidate for mayor of New York City:

> The *Times*, having announced its preference for almost anyone but Mrs. Abzug in the mayoral election, published a vicious photograph of her taken the night of her winning the endorsement of the New Democratic Coalition.

In the photograph, printed on page 1, Mrs. Abzug sits alone on a stage under the New Democratic Coalition banner. There are three empty chairs to her right and five empty chairs to her left. In this forlorn scene the camera literally looks up Mrs. Abzug's dress to show the heavy calves and thighs of an overweight woman in her middle years.

While the editorial judgment may be right, in that Bella Abzug is probably not the best choice or even a good choice for mayor of New York, the photograph is an example of journalism at its lowest.[39]

Do the ethical standards commonly applied to verbal persuasion apply equally as appropriately to nonverbal elements in persuasion? Should there be a special ethic for nonverbal persuasion in place of, or in addition to, the ethical criteria for assessing human use of language to persuade? For instance, what ethical standards should govern eye contact, facial expression, tone of voice, or gestures? How should the ethics of silence be judged?

THE ETHICS OF RACIST/SEXIST LANGUAGE

In *The Language of Oppression*, Haig Bosmajian demonstrates how names, labels, definitions, and stereotypes have been employed to degrade, dehumanize, and suppress Jews, blacks, Native Americans, and women. His goal is to expose the "decadence in our language, the inhumane uses of language," that have been used "to justify the unjustifiable, to make palatable the unpalatable, to make reasonable the unreasonable, to make decent the indecent." Bosmajian reminds us: "Our identities, who and what we are, how others see us, are greatly affected by the names we are called and the words with which we are labelled. The names, labels, and phrases employed to 'identify' a people may in the end determine their survival."[40]

"Every language reflects the prejudices of the society in which it evolved. Since English, through most of its history, evolved in a white, Anglo-Saxon, patriarchal society, no one should be surprised that its vocabulary and grammar frequently reflect attitudes that exclude or demean minorities and women."[41] Such is the fundamental position of Casey Miller and Kate Swift, authors of *The Handbook of Nonsexist Writing*. Conventional English usage, they believe, "often obscures the actions, the contributions, and sometimes the very presence of women." Because such language usage is misleading and inaccurate, they see ethical implications in it. "In this respect, continuing to use English in ways that have become misleading is no different from misusing data, whether the misuse is inadvertent or planned."[42]

To what degree is the use of racist/sexist language unethical and by what standards? At the least, racist/sexist terms place people in artificial and irrelevant categories. At worst, such terms intentionally demean and "put down" other people through embodying unfair negative value judgments concerning traits, capacities, and accomplishments. What are the ethical implications, for instance, of calling a Jewish person a "kike," a black person a "nigger" or "boy," an Italian person a "wop," an Asiatic person a "gook" or "slant-eye," or a thirty-year-old woman a "girl" or "chick"? Here is one possible answer: "In the war in Southeast Asia, our military fostered a linguistic environment in which the Vietnamese people were called such names as *slopes, dink, slant, gook*, and *zip*; those names made it much easier to despise, to fear, to kill them. When we call women in our own society by the names of *gash, slut, dyke, bitch*, or *girl*, we — men and women alike — have put ourselves in a position to demean and abuse them."[43]

Within a particular political perspective, we might value access to the relevant and accurate information needed to make reasonable decisions on public issues. Racist/sexist language, however, by reinforcing stereotypes, conveys inaccurate depictions of people, dismisses taking serious account of people, or even makes them invisible for purposes of the decision. Such language denies us access to necessary accurate information and thus is ethically suspect. From human nature perspectives, such language is ethically suspect because it dehumanizes by undermining and circumventing the uniquely human capacity for rational thought or for using symbols. From a dialogical perspective, racist/sexist language is ethically suspect because it reflects a superior, exploitative, inhumane attitude toward others, thus hindering equal opportunity for self-fulfillment for some people relevant to the communication situation.

ETHICAL STANDARDS FOR INTERPERSONAL COMMUNICATION

As Larson discusses later in this book, varying degrees of persuasion are attempted in two-person and small-group settings. One difficulty in assessing the ethics of persuasion in such interpersonal situations is that most standards for ethical persuasion are intended specifically for public persuasion. Are these ethical standards for public communication also applicable to private, face-to-face communication? Or are ethical standards needed that apply uniquely and most appropriately to interpersonal communication? Here are several sets of ethical guidelines that have been proposed for interpersonal communication.

John Condon explores a wide array of ethical issues that typically emerge in interpersonal communication settings: candor, social harmony, accuracy, deception, consistency of word and act, keeping confidences, and blocking communication. In discussing these ethical themes, Condon stresses that any particular theme may come into conflict with other themes and that we may have to choose one over the other in a given situation. Although Condon does not formulate specific ethical criteria, perhaps we can restate some of his views in the form of potential guidelines that we may want to consider.[44]

1. Be candid and frank in sharing personal beliefs and feelings. Ideally, "we would like *no* to mean *no*, we would like a person who does not understand to say so, and a person who disagrees to express that disagreement directly."

2. In groups or cultures in which interdependence is valued over individualism, keeping social relationships harmonious may be more ethical than speaking our minds.

3. Communicate information accurately, with minimal loss or distortion of intended meaning.

4. Avoid intentional deception, which generally is unethical.

5. Make verbal and nonverbal cues, words and actions, consistent in the meanings they communicate.

6. Avoid intentionally blocking the communication process — such as by cutting off persons before they have made their point, changing the subject when the other person obviously has more to say, or nonverbally distracting others from the intended subject — because this is usually unethical.

Central to both public and interpersonal communication is a minimal level of trust among participants. Kim Giffin and Richard Barnes offer an ethic of interpersonal trust based on a particular view of human nature. They assume that although humans are essentially good by nature, there are realistic limits and constricting circumstances that most of the time limit achievement of ideal human potential.[45] An ethic that increases our trust in each other is desirable because our trust of others tends to stimulate their trust of us, because our own self-image can be improved, and because our psychological health is nurtured. On the other hand, Giffin and Barnes do recognize the dangers of trusting people. Others may use our trust to deceive us, and continued exposure to broken trust breeds alienation from others and declining self-confidence.

Giffin and Barnes present three ethical guidelines for trust in interpersonal communication.[46] First, we should attempt actively to extend our trust of those around us as widely as possible. This is desirable most of the time for most people. Second, "our trust of others should be tentative." Our trust should be offered a little at a time and we should clarify to others "what we are risking, what we are counting on them to do or be, and what we expect to achieve." Third, trust should not only be given but it also should be earned. "An act of trust is unethical unless the trusted person is trustworthy — it takes two to trust one."

Ernest Bormann suggests ethical standards for task-oriented small-group discussions. These ethical guidelines are rooted in a political perspective based on values central to American representative democracy. In summary and paraphrased form, they are:[47]

1. Participants should be allowed to make up their own minds without being coerced, duped, or manipulated.

2. Participants should be encouraged to grow and to develop their own potential.

3. Sound reasoning and relevant value judgments should be encouraged.

4. Conflicts and disagreements that focus on participants as persons rather than on ideas or information should be avoided.

5. Participants should not manipulate group members solely or primarily for their own selfish ends.

6. When in the advisor role, participants should present information honestly, fairly, and accurately. They should reveal their sources. They should allow others to scrutinize their evidence and arguments. They should not lie, because lying breaks the trust necessary for participants to assess information.

7. With respect to external groups or individuals, participants within the group should be committed to defending true statements of fact, praiseworthy value statements, and sound advice.

8. Participants should communicate with each other as they would want others to communicate with them.

9. Communication practices in the group should be judged within a framework of all relevant values and ethical criteria, not solely or primarily by the worth of the end or goal to be reached. Gandhi's ethical touchstone is sound:

"Evil means, even for a good end, produce evil results."

ETHICS AND PERSONAL CHARACTER

Ethical persuasion is not simply a series of careful and reflective decisions, instance by instance, to persuade in ethically responsible ways. Deliberate application of ethical rules is sometimes impossible. Pressure for a decision may be so great or a deadline so near that there is insufficient time for careful deliberation. We may be unsure what ethical criteria are relevant or how they apply. The situation may seem so unique that applicable criteria do not readily come to mind. In such times of crisis or uncertainty, our decision concerning ethical persuasion stems less from deliberation than from our formed "character." Furthermore, our ethical character influences the terms with which we describe a situation and whether we believe the situation contains ethical implications.[48]

Consider the nature of moral character as described by ethicists Richard DeGeorge and Karen Lebacqz. According to DeGeorge:

> As human beings develop, they tend to adopt patterns of actions, and dispositions to act in certain ways. These dispositions, when viewed collectively, are sometimes called character. A person who habitually tends to act as he morally should has a good character. If he resists strong temptation, he has a strong character. If he habitually acts immorally, he has a morally bad character. If despite good intentions he frequently succumbs to temptation, he has a weak character. Because character is formed by conscious actions, in general people are morally responsible for their characters as well as for their individual actions.[49]

And Lebacqz believes: "Indeed, when we act, we not only *do* something, we also shape our own character. Our choices about what to do are also choices about whom to be. A single lie does not necessarily make us a liar; but a series of lies may. And so each choice about what to *do* is also a choice about whom to *be* — or, more accurately, whom to become."[50]

In Judeo-Christian or Western cultures, good moral character usually is associated with habitual embodiment of such virtues as courage, temperance, wisdom, justice, fairness, generosity, gentleness, patience, truthfulness, and trustworthiness. Other cultures may praise additional or different virtues that they believe constitute good ethical character. Instilled in us as habitual dispositions to act, these virtues guide the ethics of our communication behavior when careful or clear deliberation is not possible.

During 1987, intense news media scrutiny of presidential primary candidates focused on the "character issue" and the search for significant "character flaws." Democratic candidate Gary Hart temporarily withdrew from the race after allegations of a pattern of sexual indiscretion in his private life. Republican candidate Pat Robertson denied any pattern of deception to the numerous exaggerated, misleading, or erroneous statements about himself in his résumé, speeches, and books.[51]

The withdrawal of Democratic Senator Joseph Biden from the presidential primary race clearly illustrates the relation of moral character and communication ethics. A pattern of *plagiarism* was a major issue of communication ethics in Biden's case. Plagiarism stems from the Latin word for kidnapper. It involves a communicator who uses another person's words and ideas without properly acknowledging their source and who presents those words or ideas as his or her own. Plagiarism may take various forms, such as repeating almost word-for-word another's sentences, "repeating someone else's particularly apt phrase without appropriate acknowledgment, paraphrasing another person's argument as your own, and presenting another's line of thinking in the development of an idea as though it were your own."[52]

The press revealed that in campaign speeches Biden often presented as his own, without acknowledgment, various phrases, sentences, and long passages from speeches by John F. Kennedy, Robert Kennedy, and Hubert Humphrey. On two occasions Biden plagiarized a lengthy segment from a speech by British Labour party leader Neil Kinnock. In this case, however, Biden also inaccurately presented, as his own, parts of Kinnock's life history. Biden falsely claimed that his ancestors were coal miners and that he was the first in his family to attend college. In addition, evidence surfaced that, while a first-year law student, Biden had plagiarized word-for-word five pages from a law journal article. Although not a matter of plagiarism, a final element in Biden's flawed character emphasized by the news media involved his false claims in an informal interview with a small group of New Hampshire voters. Biden claimed that as an undergraduate he graduated with three degrees and was given an award as the outstanding political science student. Further, he claimed that he attended law school on a full academic scholarship and won an international moot-court competition. In fact, none of these claims were true.[53]

What defenses and excuses were offered by Biden and his aides? Aides pointed out that on some occasions Biden had credited Kinnock and Robert Kennedy as sources. Biden contended that the episodes of plagiarism, past and present, stemmed from ignorance, stupidity, or inattention to detail rather than from intentional deceptiveness. Concerning the plagiarism from Kinnock's speech by Biden at the Iowa State Fair, an aide explained: "He's under a huge amount of pressure. He didn't even know what he said. He was just on automatic pilot."[54] To what degree, if at all, should any of these defenses justify Biden's communication or soften our ethical judgments? Especially consider our earlier discussion in this chapter of conscious intent of the persuader as an element influencing ethical assessment.

Biden's case illustrates patterns or habits of communication that the news media interpreted as a serious character flaw. Lack of judgment to restrain impulses, falsification of facts, and inflation of his intellectual and communication abilities became the elements of Biden's doubtful ethical character.[55] Columnist Stephen Chapman suggests three reasons why media scrutiny of the character issue was so intense on the 1988 presidential candidates. First, voters are imposing increasingly higher ethical standards. Second, "personal integrity is one of the few matters that lend themselves to firsthand judgments by the voters. Most voters may feel unable to judge whether a politician is right about the defense appropriations bill. But they are able to consider evidence about a politician's ethics and reach a verdict, since they make similar evaluations about people every day." Third, voters "tend to vote for general themes, trusting candidates to apply them in specific cases. A politician who creates doubt about his personal honesty doesn't merely sow fear that he will steal from the petty cash. He creates doubt that his concrete policies will match his applause lines."[56]

In *The Virtuous Journalist*, Stephen Klaidman and Tom Beauchamp contend that citizens "should expect good character in our national leaders, and the same expectations are justified for anyone in whom we regularly place trust."[57] The *Wall Street Journal* surveyed dozens of top executives of American companies to see whether they would hire Lt. Col. Oliver North (of the Iran-Contra scandal) if he applied for a job. Many executives enthusiastically said they would hire him, but some would place restrictions on his responsibilities. Among those who would refuse to hire him, one especially pinpointed the issue of character, saying "it is a real character flaw when someone is willing to lie, cheat, and steal to accomplish the end of his superiors. That flaw will ultimately hurt the company. It's a character flaw that I would find unacceptable despite the strengths of his loyalty. The integrity flaw outweighs any other."[58] Admittedly, the news media (or anyone) may at times be overzealous and focus on trivial or irrelevant character traits. But in general the emphasis on moral character in evaluating presidential candidates is central "to what the electorate seems to value most in its presidents — authenticity and honesty."[59]

To aid in assessing the ethical character of any person in a position of responsibility or any person who seeks a position of trust, we can modify guidelines suggested by journalists. Is it probable that the recent or current ethically suspect com-

munication behavior will continue? Does it seem to be habitual? Even if a particular incident seems minor in itself, does it "fit into a familiar pattern that illuminates more serious shortcomings?" If the person does something inconsistent with his or her public image, "is it a small miscue or a sign of hypocrisy?"[60]

IMPROVING ETHICAL JUDGMENT

One purpose of this book is to make us more discerning receivers and consumers of communication by encouraging ethical judgments of communication that are specifically focused and carefully considered. In making judgments of the ethics of our own communication and the communication to which we are exposed, our aim should be specific rather than vague assessments, and carefully considered rather than reflex-response "gut level" reactions.

The following framework of questions is offered as a means of making more systematic and firmly grounded judgments of communication ethics.[61] At the same time, we should bear in mind philosopher Stephen Toulmin's observation that "moral reasoning is so complex, and has to cover such a variety of types of situations, that no one logical test . . . can be expected to meet every case."[62] In underscoring the complexity of making ethical judgments, in *The Virtuous Journalist*, Klaidman and Beauchamp reject the "false premise that the world is a tidy place of truth and falsity, right and wrong, without the ragged edges of uncertainty and risk." Rather, they argue: "Making moral judgments and handling moral dilemmas require the balancing of often ill-defined competing claims, usually in untidy circumstances."[63]

1. Can I *specify exactly* what ethical criteria, standards, or perspectives are being applied by me or others? What is the concrete grounding of the ethical judgment?

2. Can I justify the *reasonableness and relevancy* of these standards for this particular case?

Why are these the most appropriate ethical criteria among the potential ones? Why do these take *priority* (at least temporarily) over other relevant ones?

3. Can I indicate clearly in what respects the communication being evaluated *succeeds or fails in measuring up* to the standards? What judgment is justified in this case about the *degree* of ethicality? Is the most appropriate judgment a specifically targeted and narrowly focused one rather than a broad, generalized, and encompassing one?

4. In this case, to whom *is ethical responsibility owed* — to which individuals, groups, organizations, or professions? In what ways and to what extent? Which responsibilities take precedence over others? What is the communicator's responsibility to herself or himself and to society at large? Are the ones to whom primary responsibilities are owed the ones who most appropriately should decide the ethics of this case?

5. *How do I feel about myself* after this ethical choice? Can I continue to "live with myself" in good conscience? Would I want my parents or spouse to know of this choice?

6. Can the ethicality of this communication be justified as a *coherent reflection of the communicator's personal character*? To what degree is the choice ethically "out of character"?

7. If called upon *in public to justify* the ethics of my communication, how adequately could I do so? What generally accepted reasons or rationale could I appropriately offer?

8. *Are there precedents* or *similar previous cases* to which I can turn for ethical guidance? Are there significant aspects of this instance that set it apart from all others?

9. How thoroughly have *alternatives been explored* before settling on this particular choice? Might this choice be less ethical than some of the workable but hastily rejected or ignored alternatives? If the only avenue to successful achievement of the communicator's goal requires use of unethical communication techniques, is there a realistic choice (at least temporarily) of *refraining* from communication — of not communicating at all?

REVIEW AND CONCLUSION

The process of persuasion demands that you make choices about the methods and content you will use in influencing receivers to accept the alternative you advocate. These choices involve issues of desirability and of personal and societal good. What ethical standards will you use in making or judging these choices among techniques, contents, and purposes? What should be the ethical responsibility of a persuader in contemporary American society?

Obviously, answers to these questions have not been clearly or universally established. However, the questions are ones we must face squarely. In this chapter, we have explored some perspectives, issues, and examples useful in evaluating the ethics of persuasion. Our interest in the nature and effectiveness of persuasive techniques must not overshadow our concern for the ethical use of such techniques. We must examine not only *how* to, but also *whether* to, use persuasive techniques. The issue of "whether to" is both one of audience adaptation and one of ethics. We should formulate meaningful ethical guidelines, not inflexible rules, for our own persuasive behavior and for use in evaluating the persuasion to which we are exposed.

QUESTIONS FOR FURTHER THOUGHT

1. What standards do *you* believe are most appropriate for judging the ethics of political-governmental persuasion?

2. What ethical standards do *you* think should be used to evaluate commercial advertising?

3. When might intentional use of ambiguity be ethically justified?

4. To what degree is use of racist/sexist language unethical? Why?

5. What standards should be used to assess the ethicality of nonverbal elements of persuasion?

6. What should be the role of personal character in ethical persuasion?

NOTES

1. For a much more extensive exploration of the perspectives, standards, and issues discussed in this chapter and identification of relevant resource materials, see Richard L. Johannesen, *Ethics in Human Communication*, 3rd ed. (Prospect Heights, IL: Waveland Press, 1990). The present chapter, in whole or in part, may not be reproduced without written permission from the publisher and from the author. My personal view of ethical persuasion is rooted in the political perspective of American representative democracy and in Martin Buber's conception of dialogue.

2. This discussion of responsibility is based on J. Roland Pennock, "The Problem of Responsibility," in *Nomos III: Responsibility*, ed. Carl J. Friedrich (New York: Liberal Arts Press, 1960), pp. 3–27; Ludwig Freund, "Responsibility—Definitions, Distinctions, and Applications in Various Contexts," in *Ibid.*, pp. 28–42; H. Richard Niebuhr, *The Responsible Self* (New York: Harper and Row, 1963), pp. 47–89, 151–154; Edmund L. Pincoffs, "On Being Responsible for What One Says," paper presented at Speech Communication Association convention, Houston, December 1975.

3. Walter Shapiro, "Liftoff for Campaign 1984," *Newsweek*, October 3, 1983, p. 32.

4. Raymond S. Ross and Mark G. Ross, *Relating and Interacting* (Englewood Cliffs, NJ: Prentice-Hall, 1982), pp. 77, 138–141.

5. For a general analysis of communication as dialogue and monologue, see Richard L. Johannesen, "The Emerging Concept of Communication as Dialogue," *Quarterly Journal of Speech* 57:373–382, 1971. See also Maurice S. Friedmann, *Martin Buber: The Life of Dialogue* (New York: Harper Torchbooks, 1960).

6. For example, see Terrence H. Qualter, *Propa-ganda and Psychological Warfare* (New York: Random House, 1962), Chapter 1; Paul Kecskemeti, "Propaganda," in *Handbook of Communication*, eds. Ithiel de Sola Pool, Wilbur Schramm, Frederick W. Frey, Nathan Maccoby, and Edwin B. Parker (Chicago: Rand McNally, 1973), pp. 844–870.

7. For example, see W. H. Werkmeister, *An Introduction to Critical Thinking*, rev. ed. (Lincoln, NB: Johnson, 1957), Chapter 4; Stuart Chase, *Guides to Straight Thinking* (New York: Harper and Row, 1956), Chapters 20 and 21.

8. Stephen Lesher, "The New Image of George Wallace," *Chicago Tribune*, January 2, 1972, section 1A, p. 1.

9. The basic formulation from which these guidelines have been adapted first was suggested to me by Professor William Conboy of the University of Kansas. These five characteristics generally are compatible with the standard scholarly attempts to define a demagogue. For instance, Reinhard Luthin, *American Demagogues*, reprinted ed. (Gloucester, MA: Peter Smith, 1959), pp. ix, 3, 302–319; Barnet Baskerville, "Joseph McCarthy: Briefcase Demagogue," in *The Rhetoric of the Speaker*, ed. Haig A. Bosmajian (New York: D.C. Heath, 1967), p. 64.

10. For example, see the following sources: E. Christian Buehler and Wil A. Linkugel, *Speech Communication for the Contemporary Student*, 3d ed. (New York: Harper and Row, 1975), pp. 30–36; Robert T. Oliver, *The Psychology of Persuasive Speech*, 2d ed. (New York: Longmans, Green, 1857), pp. 20–34; Wayne Minnick, *The Art of Persuasion*, 2d ed. (Boston: Houghton Mifflin, 1968), pp. 278–287; Henry Ewbank and J. Jeffery Auer, *Discussion and Debate*, 2d ed. (New York: Appleton-Century-Crofts, 1951), pp. 255–258; Wayne Thompson, *The Process of Persuasion* (New York: Harper and Row, 1975), Chapter 12; Bert E. Bradley, *Fundamentals of Speech Communication*, 5th ed. (Dubuque, IA: William C. Brown, 1988), pp. 23–31; Thomas R. Nilsen, *Ethics of Speech Communication*, 2d ed. (Indianapolis: Bobbs-Merrill, 1974); Karl R. Wallace, "An Ethical Basis of Communication," *Speech Teacher* 4:1–9, 1955.

11. For a detailed discussion of the guidelines, see Dennis Gouran, "Guidelines for the Analysis of Responsibility in Governmental Communication," in *Teaching about Doublespeak*, ed. Daniel Dieter-

ich (Urbana, IL: National Council of Teachers of English, 1976), pp. 20–31.

12. For example, see Dan F. Hahn and Ruth M. Gonchar, "Political Myth: The Image and the Issue," *Today's Speech* 20:57–65, 1972; James David Barber, *The Presidential Character: Predicting Performance in the White House*, 3rd ed. (Englewood Cliffs, NJ: Prentice-Hall, 1985), Chapter 1.

13. For detailed analysis and complete documentation of these three instances, and others, see Richard L. Johannesen, "An Ethical Assessment of the Reagan Rhetoric: 1981–1982," in *Political Communication Yearbook 1984*, eds. Keith R. Sanders, Lynda Lee Kaid, and Dan Nimmo (Carbondale, IL: Southern Illinois University Press, 1985); see also Mark Green and Gail MacColl, *There He Goes Again: Ronald Reagan's Reign of Error*, expanded and updated ed. (New York: Pantheon, 1987).

14. John E. McMillan, "Ethics and Advertising," in *Speaking of Advertising*, eds. John S. Wright and Daniel S. Warner (New York: McGraw-Hill, 1963), pp. 453–458.

15. Thomas M. Garrett, *An Introduction to Some Ethical Problems of Modern American Advertising* (Rome: Gregorian University Press, 1961), pp. 39–47.

16. Clarence C. Walton, "Ethical Theory, Societal Expectations and Marketing Practices," in *Speaking of Advertising*, eds. John S. Wright and Daniel S. Warner (New York: McGraw-Hill, 1963), pp. 359–373.

17. Theodore Levitt, "The Morality (?) of Advertising," in *Advertising's Role in Society*, eds. John S. Wright and John E. Mertes (St. Paul, MN: West, 1974), p. 279.

18. *Ibid.*, p. 284.

19. *Ibid.*, p. 285.

20. Harold M. Williams, "What Do We Do Now, Boss? Marketing and Advertising," *Vital Speeches of the Day* 40:285–288, 1974.

21. *1974/75 Roster and Organization of the American Association of Advertising Agencies* (New York: AAAA, 1974), p. 16.

22. For example, see Lawrence W. Rosenfield, Laurie Schultz Hayes, and Thomas S. Frentz, *The Communicative Experience* (Boston: Allyn and Bacon, 1976), pp. 310–312, 324.

23. *Ibid.*, pp. 254–283.

24. Tony Schwartz, *The Responsive Chord* (Garden City, NY: Anchor Books, 1974), pp. 1–8, 23–25, 92–97. See also Rosenfield et al., pp. 313–323.

25. *Ibid.*, p. 19.

26. *Ibid.*, p. 22.

27. *Ibid.*, p. 22.

28. A comprehensive discussion of the history, effectiveness, legality, and ethics of subliminal techniques is Olivia Goodkin and Maureen Ann Phillips, "The Subconscious Taken Captive: A Social, Ethical, and Legal Analysis of Subliminal Communication Technology," *Southern California Law Review* 54:1077–1140, 1981.

29. *Ibid.*, p. 1104.

30. Nathaniel Branden, "Free Will, Moral Responsibility, and the Law," *Southern California Law Review* 42:264–291, 1969.

31. Franklyn S. Haiman, "Democratic Ethics and the Hidden Persuaders," *Quarterly Journal of Speech* 44:385–392, 1958.

32. Franklyn S. Haiman, *Speech and Law in a Free Society* (Chicago: University of Chicago Press, 1981), Chapter 11.

33. Goodkin and Phillips, *op. cit.*

34. Lewis A. Froman, Jr., "A Realistic Approach to Campaign Strategies and Tactics," in *The Electoral Process*, eds. M. Kent Jennings and L. Harmon Zeigler (Englewood Cliffs, NJ: Prentice-Hall, 1966), p. 9.

35. Daniel Oran, *Law Dictionary for Non-Lawyers* (St. Paul, MN: West, 1975), pp. 330–331.

36. Arnold M. Ludwig, *The Importance of Lying* (Springfield, IL: Charles C Thomas, 1965), p. 5.

37. Spiro T. Agnew, "Television News Coverage," *Vital Speeches of the Day*, December 1, 1969, pp. 98–101.

38. Dan Nimmo, "Ethical Issues in Political Campaign Communication," *Communication* 6:187–206, 1981.

39. Earl Shorris, "The Fourth Estate," *Harper's*, October 1977, p. 106.

40. Haig Bosmajian, *The Language of Oppression*, reprinted ed. (Lanham, MD: University Press of America, 1983), pp. 1–10. Also see J. Dan Rothwell, *Telling It Like It Isn't: Language Misuse and Malpractice* (Englewood Cliffs, NJ: Spectrum Books, 1982), Chapters 5 and 6.

41. Casey Miller and Kate Swift, *The Handbook of*

Nonsexist Writing (New York: Barnes and Noble, 1981), pp. 3–8. Also see Susan Mura and Beth Waggenspack, "Linguistic Sexism," in *The Rhetoric of Western Thought*, 3d ed., eds. James L. Golden et al. (Dubuque, IA: Kendall-Hunt, 1983), pp. 251–260.

42. *Ibid.*, p. 8.

43. Richard W. Bailey, "George Orwell and the English Language," in *The Future of Nineteen Eighty-Four*, ed. Ejner J. Jensen (Ann Arbor, MI: University of Michigan Press, 1984), pp. 42–43.

44. John C. Condon, *Interpersonal Communication* (New York: Macmillan, 1977), Chapter 8.

45. Kim Giffin and Richard E. Barnes, *Trusting Me, Trusting You* (Columbus, OH: Charles E. Merrill, 1976), Chapter 7.

46. *Ibid.*, p. 67.

47. Ernest G. Bormann, *Discussion and Group Methods*, 2d ed. (New York: Harper and Row, 1975), Chapter 3.

48. Karen Lebacqz, *Professional Ethics* (Nashville, TN: Abingdon Press, 1985), pp. 77–91; Stephen Klaidman and Tom L. Beauchamp, *The Virtuous Journalist* (New York: Oxford University Press, 1987), pp. 17–20; Stanley Hauerwas, *Truthfulness and Tragedy* (Notre Dame, IN: University of Notre Dame Press, 1977), pp. 20, 29.

49. Richard DeGeorge, *Business Ethics*, 2d ed. (New York: Macmillan, 1986), p. 89.

50. Lebacqz, *op. cit.*, p. 83.

51. Jonathan Alter, "A Change of Hart," *Newsweek*, December 28, 1987, pp. 12–16; Garry Wills, "Hart's Guilt Trick," *Newsweek*, December 28, 1987, pp. 17–18; T. R. Reid, "Rewriting the Book on Pat Robertson," *Washington Post National Weekly Edition*, October 15, 1987, p. 15.

52. Joseph Gibaldi and Walter S. Achtert, *MLA Handbook for Writers of Research Papers*, 2d ed. (New York: Modern Language Association, 1984), pp. 19–23.

53. "Biden's Borrowings Become an Issue," *Chicago Tribune*, September 16, 1987, sec. 1, p. 4; Mickey Kaus, "Biden's Belly Flop," *Newsweek*, September 28, 1987, pp. 23–24; Jon Margolis, "Biden

Threatened by Accusations of Plagiarism in His Speeches," *Chicago Tribune*, September 17, 1987, sec. 1, p. 3; Jon Margolis, "For Biden, as for Hart, It's the Stupidity That Hurts," *Chicago Tribune*, September 22, 1987, sec. 1, p. 15; "Biden Was Eloquent—If Not Original," *Chicago Tribune*, September 12, 1987, sec. 1, pp. 1–2.

54. Jon Margolis, "Biden on Quote Furor: I've Done Some Dumb Things," *Chicago Tribune*, September 18, 1987, sec. 1, p. 3; Raymond Coffey, "Biden's Borrowed Eloquence Beats the Real Thing," *Chicago Tribune*, September 18, 1987, sec. 1, p. 23.

55. David S. Broder, "The Latest Departed Candidate," *Indianapolis News*, September 25, 1987, p. A-7; Mickey Kaus, "Biden's Belly Flop," *Newsweek*, September 28, 1987, pp. 23–24.

56. Stephen Chapman, "How Seriously Has Joe Biden Hurt His Presidential Effort?" *Chicago Tribune*, September 20, 1987, sec. 4, p. 3.

57. Klaidman and Beauchamp, *op. cit.*, p. 17.

58. "Oliver North, Businessman? Many Bosses Say That He's Their Kind of Employee," *Wall Street Journal*, July 14, 1987, Eastern edition, sec. 2, p. 35.

59. Paul Taylor, "Our People-Magazined Race for the Presidency," *Washington Post National Weekly Edition*, November 2, 1987, p. 23; also see Broder, "Latest Departed Candidate."

60. Jonathan Alter, "The Search for Personal Flaws," *Newsweek*, October 19, 1987, p. 79.

61. For some of these questions I have freely adapted the discussions of H. Eugene Goodwin, *Groping for Ethics in Journalism*, 2nd ed. (Ames, IA: Iowa State University Press, 1987), pp. 14–15; Christians, et al., *Media Ethics*, 2nd ed., pp. 17–20; C. Perelman and L. Olbrechts-Tyteca, *The New Rhetoric*, trans. John Wilkinson and Purcell Weaver (Notre Dame, IN: University of Notre Dame Press, 1969), pp. 25, 483.

62. Stephen Toulmin, *An Examination of the Place of Reason in Ethics* (England: Cambridge University Press, 1950), p. 148.

63. Klaidman and Beauchamp, *op. cit.*, p. 20.

Approaches to Persuasion Research: The Roots of Research in Persuasion

ARISTOTLE AND PROOF
Ethos — Charisma and Credibility
Pathos and the Virtues
Logos and Topoi or "Places of Argument"

CONTEMPORARY PERSPECTIVES ON PERSUASION

"SINGLE-SHOT" ATTITUDE CHANGE
Source
Message
Channel
Receiver

CONSISTENCY THEORIES
Balance Theory
Congruency Theory
Cognitive Dissonance Theory
Rokeach's Belief Hierarchy

LEARNING THEORY
Skinnerian Behaviorism
Social Learning Theory

SOCIAL JUDGMENT–INVOLVEMENT THEORY

MASS-MEDIA EFFECTS THEORIES
The Experience Pool
Receiver Selectivity
How We Use Media
Mass Media as Cultural Texts
The Marxist Approach to Mass Media

PERSONAL CONSTRUCT THEORY

REVIEW AND CONCLUSION

QUESTIONS FOR FURTHER THOUGHT

As noted in the preceding chapters, there exist certain patterns of permanence and change in the world of persuasion. These patterns also appear in the established and emerging research on persuasion. You will be able to observe them throughout this chapter as we explore persuasion research from Aristotle (whom we met briefly in Chapter 1) to contemporary persuasion research occurring in college and university departments, advertising agencies, public relations (PR) firms, government, and elsewhere. To cite just a few, studies focus on attitude change, message retention, motivation research, color psychology, perception, and language preferences.

I hope that this brief overview will give you a sense of how broad and pervasive research in persuasion is. Additionally, the research cited may give you a few clues or ideas in the search for the widely held major premises in what Aristotle called the *enthymeme* — a truncated syllogism in which the audience or persuadee supplies the major premise while the persuader provides the minor premise that leads to the audience-drawn conclusion. As noted in Chapters 1 and 2, human beings have been trying to explain how and why persuasion works, and to define its ethics and its values as well as its dangers, since the time of Aristotle. The age-old questions concerning the ethical and unethical uses of persuasion have become even more central to modern life in a highly sophisticated technocracy such as ours and will continue to be raised as we approach the twenty-first century. Such questions probably will be increasingly difficult to answer because of the awesome power(s) of various new and old technologies for human communication.

We begin our study of contemporary persuasion by returning to the roots of persuasion research — to the height of Greek civilization and its dominance of the known world. This was the time of Alexander the Great, when persuasion was essential to every citizen because each man had to represent himself and his interests before the Greek courts to settle matters of property, guilt or innocence, inheritance, and other legal issues.[1] Further, the Greek city-states had a long history of democratic forms of government in which each person had the right to speak his mind on the issues of the day. Greek philosophers attempted to describe what happened when persuasion occurred and to address the issues of ethical and unethical means of persuasion. As you will see, Aristotle was the first of these students of the power of persuasion, and much of what he said on the subject is as true and vital in today's complex society as it was thousands of years ago.

Later, after Greece had been conquered by the Romans, Greek interests in persuasion were continued by Roman philosophers such as Cicero, Quintilian, and Seneca. What has been said of the timeless nature of much of Aristotle's work can be said of the Romans as well. Except for the Middle or Dark Ages, when the study of persuasion was largely reserved to the church, people have been interested in persuasion for the same reason Aristotle had — that is, because persuasion is such a central part of everyday life, particularly in a democracy. And the ethical issues have not changed much either. These ancient resources should serve to set the stage for our contemporary attempts to study the power of persuasion.

Across the centuries, various theories or explanations of persuasion have been suggested, and in this discussion we will look at some of them. Keep in mind that our central focus in Parts I and II is on the search for "first premises," or the common ground on which persuasion is built. As we trace this search since Aristotle's time, you will find that things haven't changed much across the centuries. What *has* changed is how we perceive first premises. In Aristotle's day, the habits of Greek democracy may have determined the nature of important first premises. Today, the stresses and emerging habits of a developing technological world may determine which first premises are important. The process by which we are persuaded, however, has remained amazingly constant. Remember that our focus is on the receiver in these relationships and on how our abilities to create and manipulate symbols can make persuasion succeed or fail. Our study of theories of persuasion aptly begins with Aristotle.

ARISTOTLE AND PROOF

Aristotle developed his theory by observing many persuaders at work in Athens—in the law courts, the government, and the marketplace. He was a remarkable person. His father had been the court physician to Philip, the King of Macedonia, so Aristotle was destined to receive the finest education. He studied for twenty years with Plato and was then selected by Philip's son, Alexander the Great, to be what we might call the secretary of education. Not only did Aristotle develop schools using the methods of Platonic dialogue, but he also set 1000 men to work to catalog everything known about the world at that time. Aristotle was thus the first great librarian and researcher of Greece. He also wrote up the findings of his 1000 researchers in over 400 books covering a variety of topics, including the all-important work on which today's persuasion theory is based. In his *Rhetoric*, considered by some to be the single most important work on the study of speechmaking, Aristotle focused on what he called the *artistic proofs* or *appeals* that a persuader could create or manipulate.[2] Inartistic proofs are those that are not under the control of the persuader (for example, situational factors such as the place where the persuasion occurs or the speaker's height or physical attractiveness). Recall from Chapter 1 that Aristotle identified three major types of artistic proof, which he called *ethos, pathos,* and *logos*. He identified "topoi"—topics or places where one might find logical persuasive appeals. Also, emotional appeals were identified as the "virtues" that the Greek citizenry valued. Because these lessons from ancient times still apply in today's complex world of persuasion, it is useful to explore them more closely before looking at how contemporary theorists have dealt with the age-old problem of persuading the citizenry in the age of electronic technology.

Ethos—Charisma and Credibility

Ethos, the first element in Aristotle's theory of persuasion, had several dimensions. Before actually making a persuasive presentation, all persons are perceived in some way by their audience. Even if a persuader is totally unknown to the audience, audience members will draw certain conclusions about him or her based on what they see—the speaker's body type, height, complexion, how the speaker moves or dresses, whether he or she is well groomed or disheveled, and a host of other nonverbal messages. In cases where the persuader is known, he or she has a reputation, for example, for honesty, knowledge, experience, a sense of humor, and so forth. All of these qualities, which were apparent to the audience before the actual presentation, were labeled "reputation" by Aristotle. Then additional characteristics became apparent as the speech is being given that add to or detract from the effectiveness of the message—for example, vocal quality, cleverness of argument, word choice, eye contact, gestures, and so on. More recently, researchers have added other dimensions—sincerity, trustworthiness, expertise, and dynamism or potency. Taken together they might be what we call "credibility" or "charisma."

In today's world we often hear of a persuader's charisma or credibility, which fits into Aristotle's conception of the reputation dimension of ethos. Today, however, this is a much more artistic kind of proof than it was in Aristotle's day. Press releases, image consultants, flattering photography, and a host of other devices can develop a speaker's "ethos" to an audience. To give you a contemporary example—one in which the persuader's "image" may have been a detriment to his development—consider Jesse White, the actor who played the "Lonely Maytag Repairman" on TV ads for the product. He had become so recognized as that character that he found it difficult to get other roles, not only as an actor in serious television drama, but even as a spokesperson for other products. People saw him on the screen and said, "He's not a crook! He's just the Maytag repairman!"

More recently, the various shifts in Mikhail Gorbachev's credibility accompanied media focus on the massive changes he instituted throughout Russia and its satellite states, demonstrating the power of the media to alter a person's credibility. Early in Gorbachev's years of control of the Soviet

Union, most Americans would not have had much faith in his truthfulness. However, as events unfolded, he was perceived to be increasingly believable and to be honestly trying to change things. Of course, the fact that Gorbachev is a masterful and charismatic communicator who exudes sincerity, integrity, and humility is a key factor in the credibility mix as well.

As mentioned earlier, the second dimension of persuasion using one's ethos relates to what occurs during the speech. It includes how smoothly the persuader delivers the message, how he or she uses gestures, eye contact, and vocal variations, and so on. Clearly, these are artistic proofs—the speaker controls them. For example, a persuader might use powerful language and figures of speech, smoothly articulating the carefully chosen and rehearsed words and all the while working in strategically planned gestures and variations in tone, volume, and rate of delivery. The speaker might make a point of using eye contact to touch on various areas of the audience and might make direct eye contact with the television cameras. All of these and other artistic proofs make up a person's *image, charisma,* or *ethos.* Whether the persuaders are politicians, corporations, or organizations, they all can have an image or ethos, and it is based on their reputation as well as the delivery of their message.

At times, one element in ethos may outperform the others. For instance, in the early 1990s, Tommy Lasorda was a spokesperson for Ultra Slim-Fast. He was not a diet expert, so the expertise factor did not have a bearing on his value as a user of Ultra Slim-Fast. However, Lasorda *had* lost a lot of weight using the product, and his weight loss was very noticeable. In this case, physical appearance was the critical factor in his credibility. Sometimes a person's reputation might be the critical factor—surely the scandals involving various televangelists damaged the credibility of many other evangelists. Or consider the credibility of billionaire Donald Trump, who could not for a time meet the interest payments on his debt. How credible do you think he was at that time in the eyes of potential lenders? Thus credibility is a shifting quality that sometimes depends on circumstances as well as on the traditional elements of sincerity, expertise, and dynamism.

Pathos and the Virtues

Pathos relates to the emotions. It includes appeals to the passions or the will. Persuasion aimed at our fears of nuclear annihilation, for example, utilizes pathos. So do messages aimed at our emotional attachments to our families. Bell Telephone recognizes this with its slogans "Reach Out, Reach Out and Touch Someone" and "Just call."

In today's terms, Aristotle's appeals to pathos are psychological appeals; they rely on the receiver's emotions. In using such appeals, persuaders assess the emotional state of their audience and design artistic appeals to those states. Knowing that the audience feels helpless in the face of events, a persuader can succeed by reassuring them of the value of their individual roles and perhaps by giving them some outlet for individual action. Sometimes these outlets stem from deep-seated values called "virtues" by Aristotle.

The following list describes several of the *virtues* cited by Aristotle as pathos, or appeals to the emotions. As you consider them, try to think of contemporary examples for each.

1. *Justice* involves respect for laws, people's right to have what belongs to them, tolerance, and related attributes. This virtue, or the lack of it, is often the topic of the evening news as one scandal or another is featured or when an injustice is exposed.

2. *Prudence* relates to how one gives advice or demonstrates good judgment. On the tennis scene, for example, John McEnroe seems to lack prudence, or good judgment, whereas on the basketball court, a seemingly humble athlete such as Michael Jordan is thought of as having good judgment—as being prudent.

3. *Generosity* involves not only giving money to good causes but having an unselfish attitude at home, at work, in one's community, in government, or in international relations. The word *self*less*ness* sums it up. Our contemporary society seems woefully lacking in this virtue.

Our technological society has fragmented people into isolated units who are "looking out for Number One."[3] Fortunately, following the self-indulgence and greed that characterized the 1980s, the 1990s seem to be a time for a resurgence of this ancient virtue, as demonstrated in the current concern for the environment, caring for others, and a growing sense of community.[4]

4. *Courage* is a virtue that is quite obvious in today's world. To Aristotle it meant doing what you think is right, even under pressure — not backing away from unpopular issues or positions. A recent example might be Boris Yeltsin, a Soviet populist who criticized the Gorbachev reforms as being too little, too late. As *Newsweek* put it, "He has a clear sense of what is wrong with his country. He is brave enough or cracked enough to speak his mind."[5] Whistleblowers (people who call attention to the illegal or unethical business practices of their employers) also exemplify courage.

5. *Temperance* was associated by Aristotle with qualities such as self-restraint and moderation in all areas of human conduct, not just in eating or drinking. The temperant person was in control of his or her emotions and desires. Such people weren't self-indulgent in their opinions, nor were they likely to be excessive in giving advice. They were open-minded and willing to consider all sides of a situation and tried to be empathic with the other person's point of view.

6. *Magnanimity* was felt by Aristotle to be a willingness to forgive and forget, a desire to seek ways to better the world, and the ability to rise above pettiness. The ability to be as gracious in losing as in winning is a sign of magnanimity.

7. *Gentleness* was an important virtue in Aristotle's day. Contemporary American culture doesn't seem to regard gentleness as a "manly" virtue. We do, however, respond to the kind of warmth exuded by Bill Cosby, who projects a gentle image, and we look for

politicians who are at once resolute and empathic.

8. *Magnificence* is the ability to recognize and be committed to the better qualities in human beings and to encourage them in oneself and in others through persuasion. History abounds with examples of magnificent persuaders — Washington, Madison, Henry, Lincoln, Churchill, Franklin Roosevelt, Martin Luther King, Jr., and others. Their magnificence came from the ability to encourage the best in themselves and others.

9. *Wisdom* was never really defined by Aristotle, but it is obvious that he conceived it to be more than just knowledge or intelligence. He seems to have associated it with good judgment, character, and experience.[6]

It is easy to see how many of these virtues were tied not only to emotional persuasion but to ethos as well. Of course, some appeals can be emotional but not virtuous — appeals to anger, hatred, and greed, for example. The boundaries of ethos, pathos, and logos are not always so clear and distinct as they might have been in ancient Greece and Rome.

Logos and Topoi or "Places of Argument"

Logos appeals to the intellect, or to the rational side of humans. It relies on the audience's ability to process information (such as statistical data, examples, or testimony) in logical ways to arrive at some conclusion. The persuader has to be able to predict how the audience will do this and thus has to assess their information-processing and conclusion-drawing patterns. Aristotle and other ancients most frequently combined information syllogistically.

Syllogisms begin with a major premise such as:

The chemical PCB is dangerous to humans.

This major premise is then associated with a minor premise:

Cattle raised near chemical plants absorb PCB.

Which leads to the conclusion:

> Cattle raised near chemical plants are dangerous to humans.

(Note that a second minor premise has been assumed—that eating cattle that have PCB in their flesh will expose humans to PCB.) Of course, the persuader would then offer a course of action for consumers, such as identifying the origin of the meat they eat or perhaps avoiding beef altogether. In any case, to use this kind of proof, the persuader predicts how the audience logically will assemble the information.

Clearly, being able to identify these patterns of information processing and being able to design arguments and use evidence effectively is an artistic proof. You can find logical appeals operating daily in your lives. Your parents, for example, might use data about the cost of tuition, living in a dormitory, and travel to and from college to persuade you to attend one school as opposed to another. Politicians use statistics and examples to persuade you to believe in a certain view or to vote in a certain way. Advertisers use graphs and tables to persuade you to smoke their cigarette, drive their make of car, or add a new appliance to your home. In each of these cases, the persuader is betting that you will process the information logically and predictably. In these cases, there has been a co-creation of meaning using the syllogistic form of reasoning.

Aristotle advised persuaders to use *enthymemes*, syllogistic arguments in which the major premise is already believed by the audience and thus does not need to be stated. For example, knowing that the audience already believes that PCB is a danger to health, the persuader can take a shortcut and focus on proving that cattle raised near chemical plants absorb PCB. Much of contemporary marketing research attempts to identify the major premises held by audiences so that persuaders can shape their appeals to them. For example, the beer industry knows that a large portion of its potential market holds the major premise that "Being slim is good." Using this building block, it can design appeals that emphasize that the new low-alcohol beer has fewer calories than does tra-

ditional beer—a minor premise that might be stated: "Low-alcohol beer helps you keep slim." The conclusion that the low-alcohol beers are good comes from the audience and not the persuader—there has thus been a *co-creation of meaning or identification*.

Consider the cartoon in Figure 3.1. There is obviously a hidden premise that causes the reaction in the last panel—probably something like "People do not like to be forced to pay for the mistakes of the government." By stating the minor premise ("Every man, woman, and child will have to pay over $1000 for the savings and loan scandal."), the cartoonist persuades the reader to co-create the conclusion: "This is an important issue."

As previously pointed out, the ancient concept of the enthymeme remains a foundation of persuasion. This is especially true when enthymemes are coupled with audience involvement—the co-creation of proof or meaning. This shared creation forms what Aristotle called "common ground," areas where major premises can be assumed to be shared by persuader and persuadee.[7] Aristotle thought that a good way to find such "common ground," or places where identification could occur, was to categorize the "topoi"—places or topics of argument. Persuaders had to hunt for these places and try to determine whether they would work for a particular audience. Let's look at a few of these places as Aristotle saw them. Again, you probably will find them remarkably contemporary.

1. *Arguments as to degree, or "more or less."* Is it more or less just to demand life imprisonment or the death sentence for convicted criminals? Will it profit me more or less to sell my inventory at reduced rates rather than to store it? Will candidate A be more or less trustworthy than candidate B? Are Guess jeans more or less durable than Levis? Are they more or less fashionable than Levis? Is durability more or less important than style or brand name? Is there more or less pollution in our streams today?

2. *Arguments of possibility versus impossibility.* Is it possible for Third World countries to live

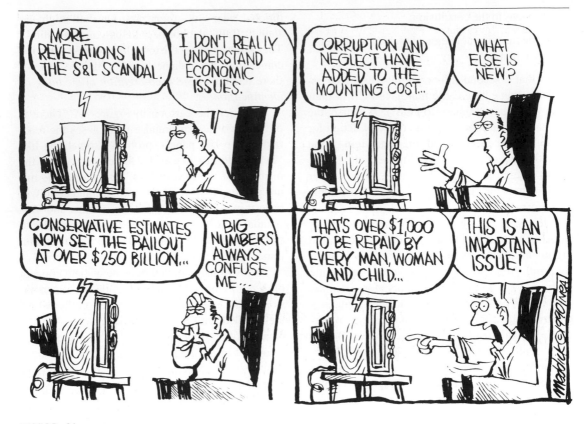

FIGURE 3.1

A hidden premise. (Reprinted by permission of NEA, Inc.)

in ecologically sound ways? Will the Japanese continue to dominate the electronics industries in the 1990s? Will people adopt and use the new technology? All these questions reflect the *topoi* of possibility versus impossibility.

3. *Past fact: Has an event really occurred?* This topoi is very important in the courts, where it must be proved that a crime actually occurred. In slander cases, for example, it must be demonstrated as past fact that

   a. the statement made was truly slanderous.
   b. the person who made the statement knew that it was false.
   c. the person also maliciously intended to slander the plaintiff.

   d. the statement resulted in real damage to the plaintiff.

4. *Future fact: Is something likely to occur in the future?* This *topoi* differs from the argument of possibility versus impossibility in that it focuses on certainties, not probabilities. Will the IRS continue to audit only a small number of tax returns or will improved technology and simplified tax laws lead to more audits? The likelihood of something occurring in the future serves as the major premise in enthymemes focusing on "future fact."

5. *Size and magnifying or minifying.* Is AIDS a major or a minor problem for you? Is the choice of candidate A important, or won't it

make a difference who wins? Is front-wheel drive a major or minor improvement? Will "Colors de Benneton" make a major or minor improvement in your sex appeal? Will having a car on campus make for a major or minor improvement in your social life?

As you can see from these examples, they too overlap with the emotional parts of human experience and also depend on the ethos of the speaker, candidate, sponsor, or persuader. Once again, however, these ancient descriptions of what is or is not likely to persuade seem remarkably contemporary. In fact, we could argue that most contemporary persuasion research is derived from the work of Aristotle in some way or another. Aristotle and his 1000 researchers were trying to discover patterns in nature and in human behavior. The topoi and the virtues are examples of the kinds of "rules" they were describing for their time. The fact that their rules correspond to many of those of the theorists using "the rules perspective" is a powerful argument for the validity of Aristotelean theory about persuasion.

CONTEMPORARY PERSPECTIVES ON PERSUASION

The following overview of more-contemporary theoretical perspectives on persuasion should help you to see how today's researchers try to identify and explain the effects and uses of the major premises held by audiences. Sometimes, the major premise is a need to receive social approval or to identify with a certain reference group. At other times, the audience's major premise is the need to feel internally consistent. Finally, the premise may be a shift in attitudes or values or the degree to which one trusts a given persuader.

We can mark the beginning of these contemporary perspectives and approaches with the end of World War II. Perhaps this interest emerged then because the years before and during the war showed the awesome power of persuasion, particularly when conveyed to the masses via the new electronic media. Charismatic leaders such as Hitler, Mussolini, Roosevelt, and Churchill had demonstrated how entire societies could be powerfully manipulated through skillful persuasion. The same kind of mass persuasion was happening in the everyday marketplace as well. In politics, religion, and commerce, the effective persuader was reaching mass audiences in unprecedented numbers and kinds, made possible by the new media of the postwar years. In the social sciences—especially in psychology and sociology—researchers were trying to explain, predict and ultimately control human behavior in terms as scientific as those used by physicists, and with a similar degree of accuracy. Much of this activity focused on persuasion and on what variables seemed most effective in getting people to change their behavior—voting and purchasing behavior in particular.

Communications researcher Stephen Littlejohn has observed that this body of research focused on three major questions:[8]

1. *What kind of behavioral changes do receivers exhibit that can be linked to persuasive messages?* Research focusing on receiver behavior investigates such variables as how receivers' attitudes influence their behavior. The critical feature in this research is its emphasis on the word *behavior.* If you can't identify a behavioral change, whether in political, purchasing, or communication behavior, you can't infer that persuasion has occurred. These changes are particularly hard to demonstrate, so researchers sometimes try to measure persuasive effects using other variables.

2. *What are the processes that lead to change in people that can be tied to persuasive messages?* In other words, what processes within individuals cause them to respond to persuasion?

3. *How much does the receiver of persuasion have to do with determining how, when, and under what conditions change will take place?* This is a rather recent focus. In the 1950s and 1960s, receivers were thought of as passive reactors to persuasion; they added nothing to the process. Research into consumer behavior, however, has shown that the audience often is

critically involved in determining the effects of persuasion. Do they ignore or focus on certain evidence or examples? Do they trust certain kinds of persuaders more than others? Do they add their own examples to a persuasive idea? These and other questions relating to the receiver are the focus of recent research. They too reflect some of Aristotle's concerns about the nature of reputation in ethos or the passions and will in pathos.

All of these questions reflect on *changes* in receivers. Another kind of persuasion *reinforces* existing behavior, attitudes, or beliefs. Although largely neglected by contemporary researchers, it is now emerging as a focus for research into brand loyalty, party affiliation, religious zealotry, and other areas in which reinforcement is critical.

A number of research perspectives, models, or theories have been tested in order to get at the questions posed by Littlejohn. We will explore several of them.

1. *"Single-shot" attitude change models.* These theories have a long research history, dating back to the 1950s and the rise of the scientific method in the social sciences. Researchers operating from this perspective assume that persuasion is a process in which the persuadee's initial attitudes toward a topic can be changed by a single "shot" of some persuasion variable such as evidence, organization, delivery, visual aids, or others. It is assumed that once the attitude has changed, the persuadee will alter his or her behavior accordingly. The research conducted from this perspective usually uses the experimental method.

2. *Consistency theories.* These are similar to attitude change theories in that they, too, are *quasi-scientific* — they use the experimental method to discover patterns or rules of change. Consistency theories predict that behavior will change as a result of inconsistencies perceived by the receiver. The inconsistencies may be between attitudes held by the receiver and new information introduced by the persuader, or between the receiver's existing attitudes and his or her behavior. A classic case is the person who wishes to be healthy, believes smoking to be unhealthy, and yet continues to smoke. Another might be the inconsistency a receiver notes between his or her attitudes and those of important others (persons or groups). Consistency theories predict that because humans gravitate away from inconsistency, they will alter their behavior so as to bring it in line with new input or information; conversely, they will alter the new information or input to bring it in line with existing behaviors. The consistency approach has led to a large body of research and subsequent theory.

3. *Learning theories.* There are a variety of learning theories ranging from Pavlov's classical conditioning to B. F. Skinner's schedules-of-reinforcement theory. We will focus on Skinner's work, since it seems to have had such an impact on more recent theories. Skinner's theory revolves around the idea that responses of laboratory animals (and presumably people as well) are geared to the kinds of reinforcement they get for certain behaviors. In other words, given the proper administration of positive or negative *reinforcers*, patterns of behavior can be established or *learned*. Thus, the audience is "persuaded" to repeat the desired behavior — be it purchasing, voting, joining, marching, or ignoring. In pure Skinnerian behaviorism, only the *stimulus* and *response* are important. That is, there are no unobservable "mental events" used as explanations for behavioral changes — no internal mechanisms such as motives, drives, desires, attitudes, and so on. Behavioral change can be explained only by the stimulus-response relationship. For example, suppose someone fails to get a soda from a vending machine and responds by attacking it. Skinnerian psychologists would describe this as a response to a particular stimulus. Other explanations might refer to the person's anger at not getting the product, but Skinnerians do not speak of *anger* as an emotion but rather as a set of observable behaviors, such as kicking or shouting.

4. *Social judgment and social learning theories.* Although these theories also rely on the experimental method, they primarily are interested in what *internal and unobservable* pressures are affecting the persuadees. Like attitude change and consistency theories, social judgment and social learning theories take into account unobservable variables such as attitudes, feelings of psychological "dis-ease," or the way our feelings compare to the feelings of those with whom we meet and discuss topics and issues. Social judgment theory explains persuasion as the result of individuals comparing persuasive messages with their internal *anchors*, or reference points. These anchors are related to and strengthened by one's social affiliation or ego-involvement. Thus, if hunters hear a message about stricter gun control, they will compare it with their internal beliefs about gun ownership, gun licensing, and so on. Because hunters have made a symbolic social commitment to gun ownership by taking to the field with other hunters or by joining the National Rifle Association (NRA), they will have more ego-involvement with the gun-control issue than would a nonhunter who has made no such social statement. Therefore, it is more likely that hunters will reject the strict gun-control message, especially if it is radically divergent from their internal anchors. In addition, other anchors are likely to influence each hunter, and the ultimate result is that hunters will or will not alter their attitudes — and presumably their behavior — as a result of their social judgments. Applying this approach to a political candidate, for example, we would compare our feelings about Gary Hart's indiscretion with model Donna Rice to the feelings others have about the same incident. Persuasion is thus explicable in terms of the receiver's social or public commitments, among other things.

5. *Mass-media effects theories.* These explanations for persuasion are diverse and are often at odds with one another. However, several common threads run through them (some of which we will examine in more detail in later chapters). One recurring theme is that, in our mass-media culture, people come to depend on information that is directed toward them by the mass media. This media dependence has several persuasive results. First, it creates a common pool of information that is used to justify decisions by large groups of people to buy, to elect, to join, to reject, and so on. Second, media dependence makes each of us vulnerable to (1) propaganda, (2) the distortion of reality, and (3) direction of our attention to certain topics or decisions and away from others. Finally, media dependence alters the way we think about the world and the importance we attach to various issues.

Another recurring theme, which seems almost contradictory to the dependency issue, is that the individual receiver, especially when he or she engages in interpersonal communication with others about mass-mediated information, is an active participant in the persuasive process. In other words, we can choose to be persuaded or not to be persuaded by selectively exposing ourselves to media persuasion and by comparing our evaluations of the information with those of other people.

A third common theme is that mass-mediated persuasion is so pervasive and universal that we are in danger of being overwhelmed by it. In fact, important issues are being raised about the potential effects of today's media in depersonalizing the individual by separating him or her from the rest of society. For example, you probably wouldn't try to converse with or even greet someone who is walking across campus wearing earphones, nor would you try to carry on a conversation while watching television. And the home computer has created endless ways of isolating the individual from family and friends. I can't talk to my teenage daughters when they are "on" the computer. They simply ignore me or perhaps don't even "hear" my voice. I am bombarded with much more information than I can possibly process — all of it forcing me to be without other human interaction. This sense of isolation and dehumanization is bound to make us anxious about the future, vulnerable to propaganda, and without a "sense of place" as Joshua Meyrowitz so aptly put it.[9] We will delve into some of these mass-media effects theories in more depth in a later chapter.

6. *Personal construct theory.* This theory postulates that we change our attitudes on the basis of our own private constructions of the world. Each of us is a "scientist" who puts together "personal constructs" about our lives. These constructs shape our responses to persuasion. If we find our constructs to be useful in living,

we keep them. Conversely, if they are misleading, we alter or replace them. For example, consider the cartoon in Figure 3.2. The psychiatrist is obviously suggesting that there are major differences between a world constructed using Bart Simpson as a model and one constructed using Homer Simpson as a model.

There are other contemporary approaches to the study of persuasion, but these six should give you a good feel for and a fairly broad perspective concerning contemporary persuasion research.

FIGURE   3.2

How would constructs using a Bart Simpson model differ from those based on Homer as a model? (*Berry's World* reprinted by permission of NEA, Inc.)

Let us now turn to each of the approaches in more depth.

"SINGLE-SHOT" ATTITUDE CHANGE

"Single-shot attitude change research grew out of an ambitious research project conducted in the late 1940s and 1950s by the Yale Communication and Attitude Change Program headed by psychologist Carl Hovland.[10] This theory posits that actions by humans have certain constraints, or harnesses. Primary among these constraints are attitudes, with which we act in accordance most of the time. In other words, our attitudes control our behavior. If we have a negative attitude toward littering, it compels us to act in certain ways — to pick up the litter of others, to put our own litter away, to teach our children not to litter, or perhaps to chide litterbugs. Thus, if persuaders want to alter the behaviors of their target audience, they must change those audience attitudes that are either preventing the desired behavior or are causing the undesirable behavior. The question for the research then becomes: "What factors in the persuasive process are most important in changing people's attitudes?"

Because the Yale studies were rooted in learning theory and information processing, the researchers assumed that people would change their attitudes if they were provided with sufficient reinforcement for the change. In other words, you have to motivate people to process information that will change their existing attitudes and hence the actions that flow from those attitudes. The researchers maintained that persuasion depends on a chain of five characteristics:

1. *Attention*. If persuadees do not attend to a message, they cannot be persuaded by it.
2. *Comprehension*. If persuadees do not understand or comprehend a message, they cannot be persuaded by it.
3. *Acceptance*. If persuadees reject the message after attending to and comprehending it, they will not be persuaded.

4. *Retention*. Most of the time, persuadees have to withhold action for some time after comprehending and accepting the mesage. They therefore must retain or remember the message and its advice until the time comes to act on it.
5. *Action*. The specific behavioral change or action requested in the message must be in accordance with the accepted and retained appeals. The Yale approach assumes people act in logical ways that are consistent with the argument of the persuader.

Although each of these elements in the persuasive process was seen as important to the success or failure of a message, most of the researchers who conducted studies in the Yale tradition focused on the third step, the *acceptance* stage. In other words, they tried to discover what factors most powerfully led to acccptance or rejection of a message. We will now use the model described in Chapter 1 to summarize the findings of the Yale approach regarding the source, message, channel, and receiver.

Source

The **source** was an important factor in the acceptance stage in two ways: first was the source's *credibility* or *believability*, which we touched on in our discussion of ethos; second was the source's *attractiveness* to the receiver. Much of the early credibility research relied on the Aristotelean notion of *reputation*. In source-varied studies, the same message frequently was attributed to persuaders having various kinds of reputations. So a message about smoking and lung cancer, for example, was attributed either to a college sophomore or to a doctor from the surgeon general's office. Not surprisingly, there was more attitude change when the audience believed the message was coming from the doctor than when they thought it was coming from the student. However, after the passage of time, this "reputation" effect on credibility declined in what Hovland and his colleagues called a "sleeper effect." People forgot the source, and a few weeks after they heard the message there was little difference between those who thought they had heard it from a doctor and those who believed it came from a sophomore. Reputation affected the immediate acceptance or rejection of a message but had little or no effect on *retention*. The immediate effect was probably a result of audience respect for the expertise of the source. Other source studies focused on questions such as whether the height of a source led to more or less attitude change, whether the rate of delivery had effects, whether eye contact had effects, and so on. As we walk across campus, we probably pass many people we don't know. Yet we make judgments about them based on their appearance, their dress, or even the way they walk. These judgments are similar to those made by an audience when they consider a persuader's message. Researchers found that perceived height *is* a factor in source attractiveness; taller persuaders were rated as more believable and more trustworthy than shorter ones. Also, if persuaders delivered their messages in halting or introverted ways, they had less effect on attitudes than did those who delivered their speech in smooth and extroverted ways. Gender also influenced acceptance; attractive but same-sex persuaders were rated as having less credibility than did attractive but opposite-sex persuaders.

An important factor in determining attractiveness or likability in a source seems to be the degree to which the source is similar to ourselves. Most of us probably think of ourselves as nice, likable persons — we don't see ourselves as boastful, snobbish, or conceited. When we perceive persuaders to be any of these, we probably reject their messages. However, when we hear humble and down-to-earth persuaders, as we perceive ourselves to be, we find them more believable and attractive than we do persons unlike us. That is probably why we believe the testimonials of Michael Jordan for Wheaties. In spite of his highly successful career, he is still a humble, down-to-earth person. So credibility as a source variable seems to be related to attractiveness and likability. But there are other dimensions to source credibility — honesty, for example.

In an interesting field study, Timothy Brock found that persuaders whose experiences were similar to those of receivers were believed more than persuaders who, despite their expertise, were not seen as having had similar experiences. The study was conducted in a paint store in Ohio. Certain salespeople emphasized that they were well informed about the paint products but that their experiences were different from those of their customers. Other salespersons emphasized experiences similar to the customer's in selecting and using paint but confessed to general lack of expertise in the paint field. At the end of the test period, the second set of sales staff had sold significantly more paint than the "experts," whom customers saw as being different from "themselves."[11]

The overall conclusion of the Yale studies on credibility is that sometimes reputation is a critical factor and sometimes it interacts with attractiveness, similarity, or other variables. Although the source is an important element in effecting attitude change, the specific attributes of the source that cause attitude change vary from situation to situation and from time to time.

Message

Another factor in persuasion is the nature of the **message**. For example, researchers have studied such variables as the order of presentation of the message — should the most important piece of evidence be presented first or last?[12] Once again, the considerable body of research on this question has not produced any clear-cut conclusions. Sometimes it is better to place the most controversial or important piece of evidence first in the message; at other times it is better to present it later. One important finding, however, that relates to the thrust of this book, is that receivers play an important part in determining whether particular evidence affects their attitudes. When the evidence is in line with the receiver's beliefs, it will be accepted and will cause a greater shift in attitudes than when it runs counter to the receiver's beliefs.[13] Of course, that makes perfect sense — we all like to hear, and we remember, things that confirm our beliefs. Politicians know this well and mirror back to audiences what the latter already believe and know. This was confirmed in a study that found that local politicians used interpersonal communication with constituents as the basis for their public speeches. Their conversations with voters served as ghostwriters for them—they repeated the voters' words and ideas in their own public speeches in the district.[14]

Another aspect of the message is whether the persuader presents one side or two sides of a particular topic. Hovland and his colleagues studied whether a message given to American soldiers just after the defeat of Germany regarding the continued war against Japan was more believable if only one side was presented (that the war against Japan would probably last another two years), or if the two-sided message (the government's two-year prediction and another more optimistic prediction) was more persuasive.[15] The results were inconclusive. With soldiers who were more educated and with those who opposed the government's position, the two-sided message worked best, whereas with soldiers who were less educated and with those who supported the government position, the one-sided argument was more believable. Many studies like Hovland's have used different topics, and their conclusions are that two-sided messages seem to be most effective in the long run, especially with people who are opposed to your side of the story.

The issue of using appeals to fear in the message has also received research attention. The overall conclusion is that the use of moderate fear appeals seems to produce the most enduring and significant changes in attitudes and behavior. For example, receivers quit smoking more often when given moderately frightening reasons for doing so (for example, "You run a risk of contracting lung cancer, heart disease, or emphysema and dying at a young age if you smoke") than when given highly frightening reasons (for example, "You will die a painful and horrible death smothering slowly from emphysema or cancer and the pain will be intense, as these pictures of cancerous lung tissue show"). High-fear appeals seem to produce a "boomerang effect"—the persuadees reject the message because it is too frightening.[16]

Other aspects of messages, such as amount of evidence, use of visual aids, and so on, have also been studied. The results are not conclusive, suggesting that change is caused by myriad variables in the source and the message.

Channel

The **channel** has been studied in several ways. An obvious approach is to compare the effects of an identical message transmitted over different channels—the print medium versus the audiovisual medium, for instance. Usually, messages presented via the audiovisual medium result in greater attitude change than do those on the audio channel alone, and messages on the audio channel in turn produce greater acceptance and attitude change than do printed versions of the same message—*as long as the message is simple*. Once a certain level of complexity is reached, the written channel is most effective.[17]

An interesting aspect of the channel effect in attitude change is *noise*. In the Berlo model, noise interferes with the decoding of the message. In noise studies, an attempt is made to distract the receivers. The distractions can be caused by showing one thing visually (on a screen, for instance) while telling another thing in the auditory channel. In the short run, such distractions accompany more attitude change when the topics run counter to the original attitudes of the receivers and correlate with less attitude change when the message is in agreement with initial attitudes. The short-term change associated with the distraction quickly fades, however.[18] Again, it is interesting to note that it is the receiver who makes the difference. If the message resonates with the receiver, one result occurs; if it clashes with the receiver's position, another result occurs. All of which brings us to the last, and most important, element in the Berlo model—the receiver of the persuasive message.

Receiver

Although numerous attitude-change studies explore the various aspects of the **receiver** that may affect persuasion, they tend to cluster around two central issues: *personality variables*, such as self-esteem, confidence, anxiety, or ego-defensiveness, and the degree to which the receiver is *ego-involved* with or committed to the issue at hand. Generally speaking, high self-esteem makes us willing and able to comprehend and weigh messages, but it also makes us somewhat immune to persuasion. Low self-esteem makes people vulnerable to being influenced and to shifting their attitudes but not as willing or able to comprehend, retain, or analyze complex arguments and evidence. This makes sense. If you feel uncertain of yourself, you turn to others for direction, just as you do if you feel worried or anxious. Your lack of self-confidence makes you vulnerable to persuasion but also leads you away from coming to grips with opposing views, complex evidence, or lengthy arguments. Perhaps this is why Eric Hoffer found that many mass movements were populated by "social misfits" — persons with low self-esteem who found in the movement the certainty that their personal lives lacked.[19] On the other hand, high self-esteem gives you the confidence to risk analyzing opposing views or entering into arguments. This, conversely, makes you less vulnerable to persuaders. Your willingness to analyze the issues and perhaps to counter them — even if only in your own mind — leads to a reduced likelihood

that you will be influenced by any persuader who comes along. After all, you are sure enough of your own position to debate the points the opposition brings up.

Self-esteem seems to work hand-in-hand with one's degree of ego-involvement with a topic. If you are deeply involved in some issue — say a nuclear freeze — not only will you devote time and resources to the issue but you will be able to remember and produce many counterarguments to an opponent and supporting data for your position. In a study conducted by the author regarding six separate local campus issues ranging from budget cuts to bulldozing the last remaining half-acre of Illinois prairie land on the campus, high commitment to the issue (for example, a willingness to lobby legislators personally or to padlock oneself to trees to obstruct oncoming bulldozers) led to a higher overall level of communication related to the topic (usually argument and evidence) and to a greater variety of it in vocabulary, imagery, and so on. Again, this makes sense. When faced with opposition to a topic with which we are highly ego-involved, we are likely to try to defend our position. Further, because of our commitment, we probably have been exposed to a greater variety of arguments and bits of evidence than have persons who are less ego-involved. Naturally, we will have

FIGURE 3.3

Here the receiver is determining "meaning." Does the cartoon "resonate" with your experiences, and how does that affect the credibility of the U.S. Postal Service? (*Frank and Ernest* reprinted by permission of NEA, Inc.)

more persuasive ammunition than does the un-committed or uninvolved persuadee. However, when the persuasion is consistent with our posi-tion, we process this information efficiently and respond with greater attitude change than do those having less involvement.

As communication researchers Stephen Little-john and Mary John Smith both point out, the Yale approach to the study of persuasion and the atti-tude change research that flowed from it for over thirty years provide lots of "What?" answers, a few "How?" answers, but rarely any "Why?" an-swers to the many questions raised about persua-sion. Although the studies assume a set of *causal* relationships between variables and subsequent shifts in attitude, they are able to demonstrate only *correlations*. Littlejohn notes that the studies are little more than a "modern day empirical elabora-tion of Aristotelean theory" and criticizes them as "overly linear, ignoring interaction and feed-back."[20] Smith criticizes them for assuming cau-sality, for inappropriateness, and for focusing on what people "do with" messages instead of what messages "do to" people.[21] Another problem is potentially more critical to any of the theories involving attitudes than these: the inability of researchers, regardless of their perspective, to demonstrate consistently attitude shift and subse-quent behavioral change. Apparently, attitudes are not the only constraint on behavior—or perhaps they interact in varied and unpredictable ways with myriad other variables. As we will see, this prob-lem will resurface with both the consistency theories and the social judgment–involvement theories.

For example, in a recent incident at a nearby high school, a highly committed student began posting leaflets announcing a nuclear-freeze rally. When a teacher demanded to know who had given him permission to post the leaflets, the student responded, "God and the Constitution." Not to be outdone, the now-committed teacher ordered the student to the office, where he was asked his name. He replied "Leon Trotsky" (a famous early com-munist who was found with a pickax in his skull in Mexico, where he had fled from Lenin). They punched the name into the computer and of course found no record of a Leon Trotsky. Later escala-

tions in the affair finally led the by-now highly committed principal to give two ten-day suspen-sions to the student, who had leaked the story to the local papers. This led to a good deal of deri-sion for the school officials, who didn't know who Trotsky was. Social psychologist Martin Fishbein's work helps to explain such cases. His explanation relates to the ways belief operates in the real world. Fishbein claims that there are at least two di-mensions of belief.[22] He calls one a *belief in* something—you or I have a belief in peaceful demonstrations as a reasonable means to protest a governmental policy, such as reinstating the draft. A second kind of belief is called *belief about* some-thing—you or I believe that drafting young people into the army is forced servitude and is hence un-constitutional. When taken together, these two kinds of beliefs lead to an attitude—we have a positive attitude toward flag burners who oppose the draft. There might be other beliefs in the mix as well: a belief that individual rights supercede the rights of the state; a belief that the flag is only a symbol, not the essence of the nation; or a belief that the draft is a drain on human resources that could go to the betterment of all people. It isn't strange that researchers found it difficult to consis-tently demonstrate attitude-behavior relationships, because attitudes involve a complex set of beliefs. Values are even more complex. When I value free enterprise, I base my value on many attitudes—attitudes toward profit, capitalism, laws of supply and demand, and competition. Just as each attitude is made up of a complex set of beliefs, each value is made up of a complex set of attitudes.

Fishbein also suggested measuring the effects of various persuasive variables on the persuadee's behavioral intentions and not on their attitudes. Instead of asking people to rate their attitude to-ward "recycling," for example, Fishbein would ask them to rate their intensions to actually *en-gage in* recycling. Following this initial response, the persuasion variable—say evidence—is intro-duced. After hearing about how many thousands of years it takes for a plastic bleach bottle to de-compose, how much longer present landfills would last with recycling, how much usable material could be recycled, what it would be worth, and other evidence about the issue, the subjects would again rate their intentions to recycle. Not only did this approach focus on a less fickle measure, but it seemed to be better at predicting actual behavior.

Social psychologists Richard Petty and John Cacioppo have also moved beyond the early outlines of the Yale studies and have suggested what they call their **Elaboration Likelihood Theory**.[23] They argue that human beings exhibit one or more kinds of reactions to information: They can *cognitively* know and understand it; they can *affectively*, or emotionally, feel about it, and they can *exhibit behavior* toward it.

There are two critical concepts in the Elaboration Likelihood model. There is the *thought process* (how much thinking goes into making decisions based on persuasion) and, more important, there is our *involvement with the topic or decision* — in other words, how likely it is that the decision will impact our lives. High-involvement issues or decisions are processed centrally, whereas low-involvement decisions are processed peripherally. Persuasion in the central-processing route, ". . . occurred as a result of a person's careful and thoughtful considerations of the true merits of the information presented."[24] Persuasion in the peripheral processing route ". . . occurred as the result of some simple cue in the persuasion context (for example, an attractive source)."[25]

To simplify the case, let's say that people can either think "a little" or "a lot" about a topic, depending on their motivation and their ability to process information. If the decision to be made is complex and personally involving — which kind of car should we buy, for example — then "a lot" of careful thinking will go on. Price won't be the only thing we consider and compare. We might compare wheelbase length, engine size, safety features, the warranty, consumer reports on each vehicle, and other complex factors. Our thinking will involve reasoning, scrutiny of evidence, and an evaluation of our transportation needs, to name a few. This information will be centrally processed. If, on the other hand, the decision to be made is trivial — the difference between two different kinds of household bleach, for example — we are not likely to think "a lot" about the decision. After all, most brands are about the same, so

price, packaging, who endorses which product, or some other minor element may be the major factor in our decision. We don't really have a personal stake in the decision. This issue or decision will follow the peripheral-processing path. Petty and Cacioppo also believed that people want to hold correct attitudes and are willing to process information about the attitudes and change them as a result. In other words, even if they hold a belief that flag burning is OK, they are willing to hear arguments against that position. Petty and Cacioppo also believed that variables could affect the direction and number of one's attitudes and could enhance or reduce argument strength. In other words, if an attractive or highly credible source is against flag burning, that factor could increase or decrease the weight you might give to the Supreme Court's decision that flag burning is not prohibited by the Constitution. Petty and Cacioppo further postulated that increased scrutiny of attitudes lessens the impact of peripheral cues, and vice versa. That is, as you investigate the flag-burning issue, it is more and more unlikely that a source's appearance will have an effect on you. Finally, the researchers believed that attitudes could be affected by bias. In other words, if you are already biased against the Supreme Court, this bias could affect your attitude toward their decision on flag burning.[26] One can readily understand how truly complex are the apparently simple elements in the theory underlying the Yale studies. For example, when I travel, I don't need to stay in anything fancier than a Motel 6, where the "rooms are about $24, and they always leave a light on for you." My spouse, on the other hand, feels that I should stop when it's convenient and hang the price. This imbalance has created some ticklish situations, as when I suggest that there'll be a Motel 6 at the next exit as my wife is yawning and getting irritable. This, in turn, makes me feel tense, since it would be more comfortable if we agreed. I try to reduce the tension by cleverly pointing out the popular opinion that "Really, you just need the motel room for a night's sleep, not a central headquarters for everyday life." If I am lucky, there is a Motel 6 at the next exit, and it is acceptable. If, on the other hand, there is no Motel 6 and I have to register in another motel where rates exceed $24, I experience different kinds of tensions, or feelings of "dis-ease," and have to reduce them as well. I usually do this by thinking that at least I have pleased my spouse or that the motel *is* somewhat nicer than a Motel 6, and besides, they serve a free continental breakfast. Tension reduction can be explained by the various consistency theories.

CONSISTENCY THEORIES

Consistency theories of persuasion rest on the assumption that human beings don't like inconsistency. As noted earlier, the inconsistency may be between two sets of information—the one you have in your hand and the one a persuader introduces—or between your behavior and a set of information that a persuader presents to you—as when a smoker continues the habit in the face of evidence showing the unhealthy effects of smoking. The inconsistency might also be between your behavior and the behavior that is expected of you by another person in a given situation. For example, a boss may expect certain behavior from employees (being prompt, respecting and maintaining equipment, or taking pride in work done) and may experience inconsistency when the employee doesn't exhibit the expected behavior. Given any of these inconsistencies, the employer will try to resolve them, according to consistency theory, through employee counseling or perhaps dismissal.

Balance Theory

The earliest consistency theory was that proposed by Fritz Heider[27] and later elaborated by Theodore Newcomb,[28] who applied it to the simplest form of human communication—one person communicating interpersonally with another person about a single topic. In this extremely simple situation, inconsistencies may arise—you may hold a certain belief or opinion about the topic, and the other person may hold a slightly different position.

Such disagreements are common in most interpersonal relationships. You have probably experienced this type of recurring but never-resolved argument frequently. It makes us uncomfortable, and it is this discomfort that provides the human dynamics for the Heider-Newcomb explanation of **balance theory**. Remember that the model reduces human interaction to its simplest or most elementary instance—one person talking to another person about a single topic or idea. And remember that when tensions arise either between or inside individuals, human beings try to reduce these tensions, either through self-persuasion or by trying to persuade others. Here is where balance theory can offer strategies for interpersonal and public persuasion.

Let's look at how such instances of balance or imbalance might be diagrammed. Attitudes between the two persons (the persuader and the persuadee) can be represented by positive signs (+) or by negative signs (−). Thus, the two persons could like (+) or dislike (−) one another. They could agree that the idea they are dealing with has bad (−) or good (+) values. They might disagree with one another, so that one feels good (+) toward the topic whereas the other feels bad (−) toward it. Notice in Figure 3.4 that both the receiver and the source have good feelings about one another. Because they agree on the topic and relate positively toward each other, they have a feeling of comfort—in Heider's word, *balance*.

There are three ways in which a person can feel this balance:

1. The source and receiver can have a negative attitude toward the object or idea and a positive attitudinal set toward one another, as in Figure 3.4. (You and I can both dislike politics and like one another, so we experience comfort and balance.)
2. The source and receiver can have a positive attitude toward the object or idea and can have good feelings toward one another. (You and I can like the same idea or object and like one another, thus experiencing comfort and balance.)
3. The source and receiver can disagree about the idea or object and can dislike one another. (You and I are not alike and we dislike one

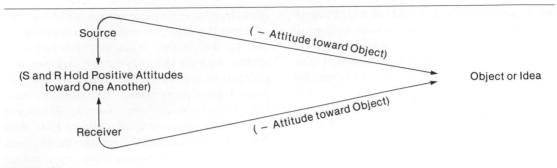

FIGURE 3.4

The Heider-Newcomb model of balance.

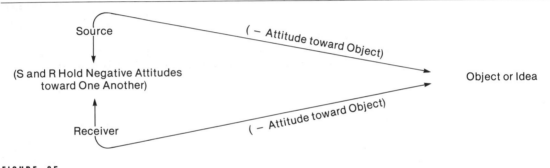

FIGURE 3.5

The Heider-Newcomb model of imbalance.

another, so it is comforting to know that we disagree about the values of certain things or ideas.)

It is nice to know that those we respect and like have the same values and ideas as we do. It is also nice to know that those fools we dislike don't agree with us.

The persuader who tries to strengthen preexisting beliefs in an audience can do so by creating a *balanced*, or comfortable, situation for the receiver. As persuadees, we need to be aware of this strategy. When a persuader deals with you on a face-to-face basis and tells you what you already know or believe (for example, that living in a suburb is bad, that the price of food is skyrocketing,

that you are a wise person), you ought to realize that creating balance is the strategy.

Suppose that the persuader wants to *change* beliefs and attitudes. It would be foolish to try to create balance for the persuadees. Instead, the persuader will try to throw our view of the world out of whack by creating imbalance, in which our beliefs are shaken. Consider Figure 3.5. In this situation, someone I do not respect dislikes the same things I dislike. I am bound to feel uncomfortable, or in a state of imbalance, in such a case. How can I agree with such an idiot?

If you assume that I think my mother-in-law is an idiot, the model would fit that example only if she and I agreed about allowances. Given that situation, I would either have to alter my opinion of my mother-in-law or my opinion about allowances to achieve balance. Thus, to persuade persons to change their minds, persuaders need to create imbalance. The sense of inconsistency forces the receiver to shift evaluations to achieve balance and thus psychological comfort.

There are probably only two ways in which imbalance in persuasive situations can be created:

1. If the source and receiver favor one another but disagree about an object or idea, the receiver will experience imbalance.
2. If the source and receiver disfavor one another but agree on attitudes toward an object or idea, the receiver will experience imbalance.

Again, a principle we already know is operating. We want the world to live up to our expectations of it. If it does not, we experience imbalance; if it does, we experience balance.

Persuaders who want to get receivers to change their minds about an idea or object can create feelings of psychological imbalance, or discomfort. When persuaders destroy your beliefs (for example, they prove that joining a fraternity or some other group will detract from your social life, not add to it), you ought to realize that they are creating imbalance for you. They want to change your opinion by relying on your need for psychological balance, or comfort.

Congruency Theory

Another approach to the consistency idea is **congruency theory**, proposed by Charles Osgood and Percy Tannenbaum.[29] This approach doesn't necessarily involve two persons; it may involve two sets of information or two concepts on which a judgment needs to be made by a single observer. If the two are similar or congruent, there is no problem. If, however, they are not congruent, Osgood and Tannenbaum predict that the observer will experience pressure to change his or her judgment of one of the cases.

Take, for example, the institution of marriage. It involves several separate and complex components — love for the other person, sexual attractiveness, intellectual compatibility, altering one's

lifestyle, adjusting to another person's idiosyncrasies, and the implications of choosing a mate for life, to name a few. When one does choose a spouse, he or she may question the wisdom of this choice from time to time, resulting in feelings of incongruency. According to researchers, this is especially so in the first year of marriage. Take some time to identify your feelings about getting married and all that it implies, and then consider the following facts:

1. 38.8 percent of newlyweds report having at least one major fight a week, and a third of those fights last several hours. Sound like a lot of fun?
2. The favorite means of aggression during these fights are screaming — 42 percent, storming out of the house — 15 percent, and violence against property — 8.4 percent.
3. 41 percent find marriage to be tougher than expected, and over half think that their marriage won't last.[30]

These facts may not match up with your preconceived ideas of marriage and hence may cause feelings of incongruity for you. You are thus faced with the problem of finding some way to restore your congruity: You may change your entire opinion of marriage, you may alter some aspects, such as your belief that marriage is typified by bliss, or you may dismiss the research findings altogether.

Cognitive Dissonance Theory

A problem for both balance theory and congruency theory relates to the degree of difference between the two people or the two instances to be judged. In other words, although both theories account for *qualitative* differences between judgments, neither deals with *quantitative* differences. At first glance, this may seem to be a minor problem, but when you consider the differences that might exist between persons or between concepts in regard to controversial topics such as abortion or school prayer, you can begin to sense the need to take into account how far persons are from one another on a topic or how incongruous two sets of evidence are. The **cognitive dissonance theory,** first suggested by Leon Festinger, addresses this problem of quantitative as well as qualitative differences between persons and ideas.[31] Littlejohn has labeled Festinger's theory "one of the most important theories in the history of social psychology"[32] because of the tremendous quantity of research and analysis that has been spurred on by the theory and its critics.

An important difference between Festinger's cognitive dissonance theory and the balance and congruency theories is that whereas the earlier theories predict a change in attitudes, judgments, or evaluations, dissonance theory predicts that when two things do not follow from one another we will experience psychological tension, which we will try to *reduce* in some way. **Tension reduction** involves more than change. Notice that the idea of tension reduction indicates that the tension has a *quantitative* as well as a *qualitative* dimension. In other words, we can change our evaluations or judgments a little, a moderate amount, a lot, or not at all. Another feature of dissonance theory is that the tension is produced by dissonance within an individual's *psychological* system. Balance and congruity theories rely more on *logical* inconsistencies than on *psychological* ones. However, our attitudes and opinions are made up of how we feel about different ideas and how that relates to our prior experience and our idiosyncracies, how we feel at a particular moment, and so on — individual differences. Dissonance theory allows us to take those things into consideration. Let us examine its major tenets in more detail.

Festinger defines dissonance as a feeling resulting from the existence of two nonfitting pieces of knowledge about the world: "Considering the two alone, the obverse of one element would follow from the other." **Consonance**, Festinger's pair term for balance, exists when "considering a pair of elements either one [of which] does follow from the other." The degree to which one of these elements may or may not follow from one another can vary, which is not true in congruency or balance theory. Although I may greatly dislike door-to-door sales representatives as a group, my weak positive feelings toward a certain salesperson may create only slight feelings of dissonance or imbalance.

As in balance theory, there are times when things fit, or "go together." This is *consonance*, from the Latin "to sound together, harmonize, agree." Festinger says that any two beliefs can be shown as two parallel lines (see Figure 3.6). The solid line shows belief A, and the X on the line marks a position on that belief. The broken line represents other information about A. The Y on this line represents our position on the new information, which we might call belief B. The distance between these two points — X and Y — is the amount of *dissonance* we feel when the two beliefs are not congruent. We feel psychic discomfort — the world is not acting as it should — as a result of the dissonant cognitions. The dissonance must be reduced, providing the basis for many actions. Some persons change dissonant cognitions by moving their beliefs closer to one another. Others rationalize the problem away by discrediting the source of the cognitions. Others escape from feelings of dissonance by the process of selective perception, selective retention, or selective exposure; in other words, they choose to forget or not to receive/perceive or not to be exposed to the information.

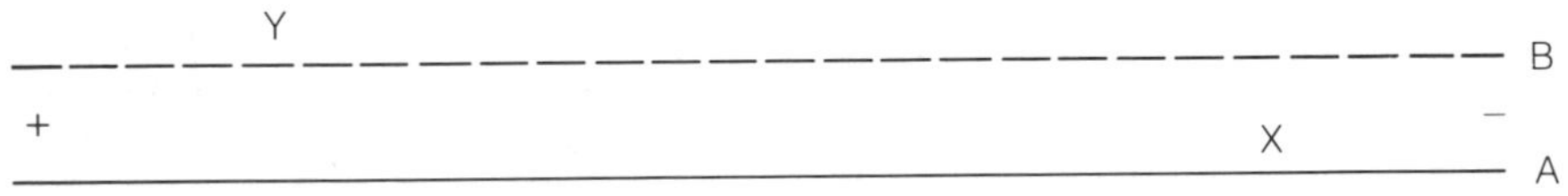

FIGURE 3.6

Festinger's model of dissonance.

A good friend of mine is in the coin-operated game business, and as a result attends coin-operated trade shows around the country. She reported on the case of a colleague who was able to earn over $100,000 per year with a minimal investment. Of course I wanted to know how he did it. She explained that he went to sleazy bars and gas stations in Wisconsin and bought about a hundred antiquated coin-operated condom vending machines from the men's restrooms in these bars and service stations. He had them reconditioned and then installed them in women's restrooms in classy Chicago restaurants, resorts, and upscale bars. He reported profits of over $1000 per month from each machine, which demonstrates how fearful people are of contracting AIDS (Acquired Immune Deficiency Syndrome) and other sexually transmitted diseases (STDs).

In the past, men were the major purchasers of condoms, using them as birth control devices. But today a new sense of "dis-ease" is filling everyone who is sexually active, and most intelligent persons know that the major causes of infection by the AIDS virus are unsafe sex practices, the sharing of needles among intravenous drug users, and, to some degree, blood transfusions or accidental exposure of one's blood to the blood of AIDS carriers. (Incidentally, that's why dentists and their assistants recently have begun wearing rubber gloves — people's gums often bleed when being examined or worked on, and the unprotected dentist or assistant might accidentally expose a small wound on his or her hands to AIDS-infected blood.)

Under Festinger's theory, intelligent, sexually active women fear infection from the AIDS virus as a result of all the media attention given to the epidemic recently. These women once used other methods of birth control, but these methods give no protection against the AIDS virus. As a result, the women are feeling dissonance about their sexual activity. What can they do to reduce these feelings of psychological "dis-ease"? There are a variety of options:

1. They may devalue their initial beliefs about the most appropriate methods of birth control.

2. They may devalue the AIDS information by telling themselves that this news blitz is just a scare tactic dreamed up to cut down on the promiscuity of the younger generation.

3. They may selectively perceive the information, telling themselves that their sexual partners are not likely carriers of the AIDS virus. This process is called *selective perception*.

4. They may try to forget the frightening information about AIDS. This process, called *selective retention*, means remembering or forgetting what you want to.

5. They may try to rationalize the problem away by telling themselves that a cure for AIDS is just around the corner.

6. They may begin protecting themselves against AIDS, which seems to be the case, according to the report by the coin-operated condom vending machine operator.

7. They may do more than one of the above.

Let us suppose that you are considering entering some aspect of the dental profession. After reading the information about the potential for contracting AIDS in this profession, might you be feeling dissonant? How could you reduce these feelings?

Although Festinger does not deal deeply in his book with the notion of consonance, it seems clear that we seek it. We listen to the candidate of our choice but more often than not avoid listening to the person we will not vote for. A good deal of research shows that we seek information that fits with our beliefs and avoid data that conflict with our beliefs. Conservative people read conservative newspapers; liberal people read liberal newspapers. It's another way of saying "birds of a feather flock together." This is probably why people try so hard to avoid political or religious arguments. You really can't persuade anyone on such matters, it seems, so you just change the topic to something more neutral.

For example, let's suppose that you have decided to major in computer sciences, even though you have never been very good in mathematics. You find that not only are your classes tough and time-consuming but they are boring to boot. You now go to the computer lab center and hear fellow students around the vending machines complaining about how hard their classes are. They talk about how much time they spend debugging programs, and so on. You will probably think something like "Whew! Then it's not just me." You add some conversation to the effect that "Yeah, and some of it isn't the most interesting stuff in the world either." You are seeking that final bit of consonant information. Much to your delight, those gathered there come back with sentences like "You said it!" or "That's the understatement of the year, but at least we'll make big bucks when we graduate." You experience consonance, especially because it was the attractive job opportunities that lured you into the field anyway. With such confirmation, there is no need to resolve any inconsistency or psychic discomfort.

Experiences like this are common; we find information confirming our position, and that makes our belief stronger. There are many actions we can take as a result of feelings of consonance:

1. We can revalue our initial beliefs, making them stronger in all likelihood — "It really *was* a good idea to major in computer sciences."
2. We can revalue the source of the information input. "Boy! Those other computer science students are really sharp and on the ball. They'll go far in this world."
3. We may perceive the information as stronger than it actually is and focus on the strongest parts of it.
4. We may remember the most positive parts of the information and choose to highlight those that best support our belief — the high salaries, maybe.
5. We may seek more supporting information by going to the placement office, for instance, and copying down the starting salaries of computer science graduates.
6. We may do several of the above.

The tactic of creating consonance, then, is used to strengthen attitudes, to gird existing cognitions, and to increase one's source of credibility. Consonance probably is used as frequently in persuasion as is dissonance, for we often want to reinforce people's opinions, attitudes, beliefs, or behaviors.

Unfortunately, Festinger's theory and the myriad resulting research studies focus mainly on those cases in which dissonance arises or in which an alteration in opinion, attitude, belief, or behavior is desired. Another shortcoming of the theory is that it, like its predecessors, oversimplifies the human situation. Nonetheless, we know a great deal more about persuasion today as a result of the many studies spawned by Festinger's theory. Most important, Festinger's work places emphasis on what the receiver does with the persuasion aimed at him or her. It is the receiver's internal state and psychological mechanisms that determine the outcome of persuasive appeals at least as much as does the source's skill at designing and delivering the message. As Figure 3.7 illustrates, Moses seems to know the internal state of the children of Israel better than Jehovah does. As a result, Moses offers advice on message design.

Rokeach's Belief Hierarchy

The receiver has also been the emphasis of investigations by social psychologist Milton Rokeach.[33] His theory deals with the idea of inconsistency as well as with its quality and quantity, but he goes much further in addressing the complexity of human attitudes, beliefs, and behavior changes. Rokeach speculates that attitudes, beliefs, and values are interwoven and ranked in various hierarchies into a single belief system that receivers bring to the persuasive situation. Like the layers of an onion, some are at the core, or center, of the system, whereas others are at the periphery. The outer layers are much easier to alter than are the ones at the center, and, as we get closer and closer to the core, change becomes nearly impossible. Rokeach postulates five levels of belief:

1. *Primitive beliefs* (*unanimous consensus*). These lie at the core of the system and come from our direct experience of the world. We find consensus about them from our peers. An example might be that the sun rises in the east

FIGURE 3.7

What kind of imbalance, incongruity, or dissonance is Moses feeling in this cartoon? Why? (*Frank and Ernest* reprinted by permission of NEA, Inc.)

or that we are a certain age or that fire is hot and thus burns us. These beliefs rarely change and are almost axiomatic.

2. *Primitive beliefs* (*zero consensus*). These are also learned by direct experience but are private and sometimes idiosyncratic. They are personal, and we don't get direct outside confirmation. An example might be a belief that you are basically a certain kind of person — lazy, energetic, selfish, or generous. Another might relate to your perceptions of how others feel about you, such as "most people like me." These beliefs also rarely change.

3. *Authority beliefs*. These are sometimes controversial and depend on our interchange with others — usually our parents or peers. "Honesty is the best policy" or "the Christian philosophy is the most humane" are examples. These beliefs are changeable, but only with much experience or persuasion.

4. *Derived beliefs*. These we develop from our interchanges with sources we trust, but in a secondhand fashion instead of directly. Examples might be beliefs we develop from books, news reports, or persons whose credibility is high (editors, political leaders, or perhaps religious leaders). These are easier to change than any of the deeper beliefs.

5. *Inconsequential beliefs*. These relate to individual preferences and tastes and are relatively easy to change because we don't have to alter our self-identity to change them. "I prefer living where there is a change of seasons" is an example.

According to Rokeach, these beliefs cluster to form attitudes, which then predispose people to behave in certain ways. There can be hundreds of thousands of beliefs in each person's attitude system, and they interact with one another and cluster to produce a whole host of attitudes, which fall into two major classes — (1) attitudes toward objects and (2) attitudes toward situations. Any time we have a decision to make or are faced with new information, these two types of attitudes come into play. For example, I might despise a certain person or activity or type of food, but I might behave politely toward that person, engage in that activity, or eat that food in one social situation — and do the opposite in another. Notice again that the *receiver* is at the heart of any persuasive situation, and it is the receiver's attitudes toward objects and situations that determine any outcome. You can especially appreciate this in the interpersonal realm, as when you try to persuade a roommate to go to a bar on a weeknight or when you try to persuade a parent to let you live off campus. The other persons' evaluations of the topic or situation are critical.

For Rokeach, beliefs and attitudes may *predispose* us to action, but values *guide* us to action and are therefore the most important element in the belief-attitude-value triad. He identified two types of values — **terminal values**, which are life goals (for example, a comfortable life, a sense of accomplishment, world peace, true friendship, or wisdom), and **instrumental values**, which are types of behavior that help us get to the life goals (for example, acting ambitious, independent, broadminded, controlled, or cheerful). These values, taken together with our attitudes and beliefs, result in what Rokeach called our *self-concept*. We all want to be satisfied with our self-concept, and we work hard to achieve this sense of well-being. Although shifts in beliefs or attitudes might result in short-term changes in behavior, only when inconsistency, incongruence, or dissonance is great enough to lead us to question our self-concept can lasting and important change take place.[34] That is, for persuasion to occur in a significant and enduring way, a receiver's self-concept needs to be confronted with some kind of inconsistency.

LEARNING THEORY

Some researchers define *persuasion* as a specialized kind of learning. We *learn* to believe in a certain religion. We *learn* to set certain goals for ourselves. We *learn* to behave in a certain way and to vary our behavior according to the situation. Of course there are many learning theories — too many to review here — but most contemporary ones are rooted in the behavioral tradition. Typically, these approaches to human behavior and persuasion rely on experimental proof. Their goal is to predict and ultimately to control behavior through such methods as conditioning.

Skinnerian Behaviorism

The name most identified with the word "behaviorism" is of course B. F. Skinner, and although this book is not a psychology textbook and this course is not a psychology course, much of Skinner's work is applicable to the study of persuasion. For example, Skinner identified what he called **schedules of reinforcement**. This refers to how frequently and for what kind of behavior positive or negative stimuli (or what most of us call rewards or punishments) are presented. If a positive stimulus (or reinforcer) is presented for every instance of a specified behavior, the schedule is a *continuous* one. We all behave in conformity with such schedules in our everyday lives. Vending machines are good examples of continuous reinforcement, unless they are not functioning properly.

Another kind of schedule is the *ratio schedule*, in which the reinforcer is presented only after the required behavior has occurred a specified number of times. Again, we all have behaved in accordance with ratio schedules at various times in our everyday lives. Piecework is an example; practicing a musical instrument is another; doing math homework problems is another. For each of these examples, the required behavior is elicited a certain number of times and then a reinforcement occurs — pay, praise, or a grade. Soft drink companies have run contests in which the customer is required to peel off a seal under the bottletop. Beneath the seal is a symbol, word, or number identifying the value of that particular top. Initially, the companies distributed many tops worth small monetary prizes — 10¢, 25¢, and 50¢. In a sense, these early bottletops are examples of continuous reinforcers. The customer always gets something — either money or tops that help spell out the words in a $1000 slogan: "Pepsi Over Coke," for example. Later, though, the buyer gets letters that he or she already has. It may be that the buyer has to go through a whole eight-pack before getting a top that has monetary value or a needed letter. But the customer is "hooked" by the early continuous reinforcement and so goes on peeling seals even when the system has shifted to a ratio schedule.

An *interval schedule* occurs when reinforcement (or reward) is given only after the recipient has been behaving in the desired way for a specified period of time. Payday is an example of an interval schedule; final grades are another; graduation is another. Regarding persuasion, this kind of schedule has certain disadvantages. One of them is that we all have a tendency to drag our heels at the start of an interval and slack off in the middle of it. You know how it is at the beginning of the semester or term. Only when the end of the interval approaches does behavior pick up. Then papers get written, workers show up on time, projects get finished. At many industrial plants, absenteeism is highest on Mondays and lowest on Fridays or paydays.

The most powerful kind of reinforcement schedule is called *random intermittent*. Here, there is no way to predict how long it will take or how many times a required behavior must be completed before reinforcement will occur. This is how parents train children to behave, to be polite, to use the toilet, and so on. It is also the way many jobs operate. You may get praise from the boss today and next week and then not again for six weeks. Most advertisements are based on random intermittent reinforcement. Gentlemen don't *always* prefer the woman in the Hanes pantyhose. In fact, the woman can't really determine analytically when or even if the glances she gets on the bus, in the park, or at the opera are because of her attractive legs. The Hanes advertisements show the Hanes women being noticed by men in public places. On the bus, any woman will find that some men will look at her when she gets on — if only because the seats face toward the front. It is also likely that at least some men in any public place will look at a woman, so the promise from Hanes is intermittently met. In the ads, when the Hanes woman is noticed, the other women are wearing slacks or their legs can't be seen. In that situation, the uncovered Hanes legs are more likely to attract attention than the potentially equally attractive legs hidden by the slacks. Again the "preferential" glances of the males are intermittent, and the ad lives up to its promise — at least from time to time.

None of this is very complicated when you think of it. You and I knew these things before we ever read about B. F. Skinner and his theories. He merely systematized and labeled the process of reinforcement. But his work was extremely important because it helped people in a wide variety of contexts to determine analytically whether they were appropriately reinforcing others — children, workers, voters, customers, and so on. For example, Skinner worked with the Emery Air Freight company to increase employee productivity and accuracy. Giving verbal rewards to the employees for answering the phone within two rings, for routing deliveries efficiently, and for packaging items efficiently, Skinner was able to get extremely significant improvements in a short time. We could say that he used praise to "persuade" the workers to improve.

One task for persuaders, then, is to analyze the target audience to determine what patterns of reinforcement will work best with them. Let's look to the world of advertising for some examples of how schedules of reinforcement are used or appealed to in order to persuade. Consider the ad for Chivas Regal scotch in Figure 3.8. The six panels depict a repeated gesture — the giving and receiving of Chivas on special occasions. The advertisers have even custom-wrapped the Chivas and surrounded it with appropriate symbols. The wrapping for the bon-voyage party includes shipside streamers, and the "new home" Chivas is wrapped in a blueprint. The ad is intended not for the person getting the Chivas but for the person who gives it. Everyone knows the good feelings one gets for bringing the perfect gift, and the reward for being considered thoughtful and clever by others. That is the positive reinforcer.

In the world of politics, the persuader's task is to determine the voter's pattern of reinforcement. This is why candidates engage in so much polling: to determine whether their stimuli — speeches, ads, position papers, and so forth — are making a difference with the voters. It is also why they have their pollsters ask for statements — to get verbal responses from the voters. Frequently these statements are later crafted into the candidates' speeches and ads. Of course, a candidate can also be caught in a pattern of negative stimuli, as in the case of Joseph Biden (Chapter 2), which causes his or her place in the polls to go down.

You can see, then, that patterns of reinforcement can have various effects. As receivers/voters, we need to evaluate the reinforcements

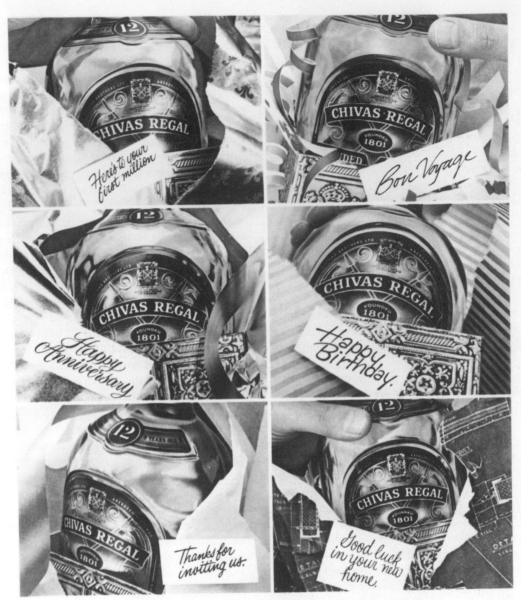

Why wait for Christmas?

12 YEARS OLD WORLDWIDE • BLENDED SCOTCH WHISKY • 86 PROOF • GENERAL WINE & SPIRITS CO., NEW YORK, N.Y.

FIGURE 3.8

What reward does this ad imply that *purchasers* of Chivas Regal will receive? What is the reward for the *recipients*?

politicians offer us. Are the campaign promises positive or negative stimuli? What will we have to do to get the positive reinforcements and to avoid the negative ones? Will the reinforcements be given regularly or irregularly? Are the reinforcements generalized (for example, reduced taxes or inflation)? Or are they secondary (for example, "If you work and vote for me, you can have prestige, you'll be able to tell interesting stories about the campaign, and you'll be participating in the political process in a very real way.")? Are we considering joining, donating, purchasing, or becoming active because we want a specific reinforcement such as a patronage job, valuable experience, and so forth? Or are we participating or purchasing for more generalized secondary reinforcements — status, social prestige, admiration, seduction, or love? Unlike the theories discussed earlier, traditional learning theory places less emphasis on the receiver than on the source. In fact, Skinner would not admit to the testing of any **black-box constructs**. By this he meant mental states such as drives, motives, instincts, attitudes, values, or beliefs. All of these were unknowable to Skinner because they were all internal in a person's mind and body — they were inside the black box. For him, correlation of the subject's behavior with the researcher's manipulation of the environment was the only real observation that could be recorded. A Skinnerian psychologist thus might study whether the color of a room was correlated with more or fewer purchases of a particular product. Their explanations of behavior thus relate to things outside the persuadee, such as room color, rather than internal things, such as mood.

Social Learning Theory

Social learning theory, as explained by Albert Bandura, is not so restrictive, and does permit concept that are inside the black box to explain how change occurs.[35] Bandura doesn't believe that humans are mere automatons responding to changes in their environments; rather, there is continuous interaction between a person's internal state and the social reinforcements that follow from the person's behavior with others. Thus we learn how to behave from our social interactions.

When we perceive that a certain behavior is not socially rewarding or perhaps even leads to social punishment, we learn, or are persuaded, to continue the behavior or to cease it. The reinforcers come from two major sources — external information, in the form of direct or vicarious experience, and internally developed, self-reinforcing systems, such as our self-concept.

From the external world, we may get direct reward or punishment for our behavior and as a result discover a social rule and behave accordingly. You have no doubt discovered that certain behaviors in the classroom are socially unacceptable. For example, although it is socially acceptable to speak up in class and engage in the discussion, it is not acceptable *always* to offer a comment or *always* to stop by the instructor's desk at the end of the class to offer your analysis of the session. That behavior is usually perceived as apple polishing. From early experiences in school, we may have learned that being the teacher's pet is socially unrewarding. Unfortunately, some people never seem to learn this. Almost every semester, I find that there is one overly talkative, precocious student who simply can't resist making comments or asking questions all the time. It takes only a few class sessions to identify the student, and I usually have to caution him or her against monopolizing discussion time, to the relief of the rest of the class. Most of the social rules we follow are learned through direct experience, and, although many of them are formed in our early years, we continue to discover new social rules throughout our lives.

Another external source through which we learn acceptable social behavior is **role playing**. We all do this every day — we imagine ourselves in the position of some other person or in some other situation. In this safe context — the imaginary role — we can try simple behavioral alternatives without risk. We can imagine, for example, what the other persons will say or do in response to us. You have probably used this technique unconsciously. Researchers use it more deliberately to persuade people — or rather, to let people persuade themselves. In some experiments, people who smoke have been asked to imagine themselves as cancer patients and then verbalize their feelings when they learn of the disease or of a setback in treatment. In smoking clinics, smokers are asked to attend the funeral of someone of approximately their age and to imagine themselves in the casket surrounded by their bereaved friends and family. They visit cancer wards in hospitals and imagine being the patient. Not surprisingly, the research results show behavior alteration ranging from quitting to drastically cutting down cigarette consumption. The changes also seem to endure; follow-up studies indicate that the end-of-study rates of cigarette consumption or even quitting remain stable many months later. In many companies, management personnel are asked to role play the person they may have to fire the next week or the person with whom they will have a performance appraisal interview. In these uses of the technique, we learn or persuade ourselves to behave in socially acceptable ways. Role playing can be acted out as well as imagined.

A final external source of reinforcement identified by Bandura is the use of **role models**. Certain behaviors have predictable consequences. For example, we are told by the advertisement that we will make others happy if we "Reach Out and Touch Someone" with long-distance phone calls. Of course, grandma and grandpa are always home, happy, and healthy when they get the call—in the ad; in real life, this is not always the case. However, the message of the ad is that calling grandma is socially acceptable behavior—the caller in the ad is a role model. We also get many examples of acceptable behavior from our family and peers. We model our behavior after theirs and in so doing persuade ourselves to value that kind of behavior. As we will see in a later chapter, many of these models come to us through the mass media and can persuade large groups to behave in similar ways.

Role models also seem to be more important at some times in our lives and less important at other times. Junior high school seems to be a time when peer role models heavily influence behavior. Try to recall your junior high years. Whom did you try to model yourself after? What behaviors were socially acceptable? Unacceptable? In polling my classes, I find that although most students can identify their modeling behavior in those years,

few recall the experience with any fondness. This is perhaps a result of the tremendous peer pressure during early adolescence. Other critical periods seem to be early childhood, early adulthood, the much-talked-about "mid-life crisis" at age thirty-five or forty, and retirement. During each of these periods, we persuade ourselves to alter our behavior in conformity to, or sometimes in defiance of, socially approved patterns.

The second major source of reinforcements comes from within each person. These internal (given by the self) reinforcements develop early and continue to develop and shift throughout life. They are closely tied to one's self-concept. For example, one thing I value about myself is that I am blunt. I don't like people who beat around the bush when discussing an issue. Although my bluntness is sometimes positively and sometimes negatively reinforced by external sources, the most powerful reinforcer for bluntness is my own evaluation of whether it is generally a good thing to be blunt. In fact, I interpret the reactions of others to my bluntness as being positive—sometimes people thank me for getting all the cards on the table or for telling it like it is. But even when I get negative external reinforcement or hostile responses from others, I tell myself that it was worth it to cut through all the baloney.

Persons with low self-esteem give themselves little internal self-reinforcement for their actions; persons with high self-esteem give themselves lots of self-reinforcement. Of course, if I run into repeated negative external reinforcement and maybe even censure, I may shift my behavior and correspondingly alter my internal reward systems. In any case, this approach to learning theory as an explanation of persuasive effects also has a major focus on the role of the receiver.

SOCIAL JUDGMENT– INVOLVEMENT THEORY

Social judgment–involvement theory is another receiver-based explanation for persuasion. Originated by Muzafer Sherif and his colleagues, the theory has two key concepts, both of which are internally based in the receiver.[36] The first of these — *anchor points* — are internal reference points that each of us has inside. We use them when we make judgments about people, issues, events, products, and so on. When faced with the need to make a judgment, we turn to our internal reference points and compare the information regarding the judgment with those anchor points that are relevant. For example, suppose you were asked to support a proposition, put out by your student association or student government, condemning your school because it accepted a gift of $10,000 in South African gold-mine stock. In making your judgment concerning whether to support the proposition, you may have several internal reference points. You may have seen a documentary on racism in South Africa. You may have known a white South African foreign-exchange student with whom you have discussed the situation in South Africa. You may have a position in regard to universities or colleges accepting *any* kind of stock, because it is usually given for tax purposes. Social judgment–involvement theory predicts that you will compare the proposition with all of these anchors before making a judgment. In other words, you make your judgment only *in reference to your anchors*. They are the touchstones on which you base your judgments.

You will be able to accept the student proposition fairly easily if it is close to your already established anchor points, but you will not accept the proposition if it is distant from them. In the former case, the proposition falls within your **latitude of acceptance**, whereas in the latter it falls into your **latitude of rejection**. One's latitude of acceptance can accommodate several positions that vary in intensity. You might accept not only a resolution condemning the school officials for accepting a gift but also an even stronger one that demands that the gift be returned or that the stock be sold and the funds used to offer scholarships to South African blacks. You might even be willing to support a statement that demands the resignation of the school official who made the deal. All of these could fall within your latitude of acceptance.

Conversely, perhaps the proposition goes well beyond your initial anchor points. Then you will

likely find it too radical to accept: It is thus in your latitude of rejection. Maybe your anchor points include one that holds that any questioning of external funding by extralegal groups such as the student association is not only unwise but dangerous to boot. In this case, the proposition, regardless of how it is stated, falls into your latitude of rejection. No matter how hard the group tries to persuade you, you find it impossible to accept the very idea of issuing such a statement. They could soften it, changing the wording from "*condemns* the officials for accepting the gift" to "*questions* the officials . . ." and this would make no difference to you. The theory predicts that when a statement or position falls into your latitude of rejection, you will almost automatically throw it out as unfair, biased, lunatic, or worse.

Between the latitude of acceptance and the latitude of rejection is the **latitude of noncommitment**. Here lie the positions about which you do not feel all that strongly. For example, suppose the board of regents issues a statement questioning or even condemning the school officials for taking the South African stock. Here, your internal anchor about extralegal groups is irrelevant; the governing board has a legal right to question administrative decisions. You might not find this idea close enough to your own position regarding South Africa to fall within your latitude of acceptance and not far away enough to fall into your latitude of rejection. You might ignore the issue or wait to see what develops. In this area, you do not have strong enough attitudes to decide either way; you neither accept nor reject the position.

Put another way, receivers are extremely vulnerable to persuasion within their latitude of acceptance, almost immune from persuasion in their latitude of rejection, and open to persuasion and objective about issues in their latitude of noncommitment. For some of us, the latitude of acceptance on a given issue is wide, whereas for others it is narrow. The same is true of the latitudes of rejection and noncommitment — they vary from issue to issue and from person to person. It is critical that persuaders know what are audiences' latitudes of acceptance, rejection, and noncommitment in order to shape messages that have a chance of changing audiences' attitudes, beliefs, or behavior.

The second important concept Sherif and his followers dealt with was that of *ego-involvement* with the issue. Ego-involvement, as defined by Sherif and his fellow researchers, is an attitude about which persuadees feel strongly and that they incorporate as part of themselves. This closely relates to the idea of self-concept suggested by Rokeach. If people's involvement is particularly strong, they may even label themselves with the position, as in "I'm a gay libber," "I'm a feminist," or "I'm an environmentalist." Sometimes our involvement is not all that strong. We may just be willing to join groups or make public statements on behalf of the environmentalist position, for example.

Sherif thought that such social affiliation with like thinkers was a critical factor in determining the degree of ego-involvement a person had in a given issue. This may be a shortcoming of the theory, but, whatever the degree of involvement, it will lead to message distortion and hence to judgmental distortion. Highly involved persons see things as either pro or con — there is no middle ground for them. Less-involved persons do not polarize as much, and for them there are probably shades of gray and areas where they can see both sides of the story. Highly involved persons may judge an issue as so close to their anchors that they incorporate the position as their own. Sherif calls this **assimilation**, or minimizing the difference between one's anchors and the new information. Highly involved persons also compare and distort positions that diverge from their own; they see a greater discrepancy than there really is. This is called the **contrast effect**. It is usually impossible to change highly ego-involved persons and, for this reason, most persuasion is aimed not at them but at persons with low to moderate involvement.

Again, we see that the receiver is central in the explanation of persuasive effects in social judgment–involvement theory. An important difference here, however, is that social commitments to or identifications with a particular peer group enter in and are especially important if the receiver has become highly involved in the issue by making a social and perhaps public commitment to the issue.

MASS-MEDIA EFFECTS THEORIES

Although we will be looking at the mass media, especially electronic media, in detail in a later chapter, several common threads run through the literature on the effects of mass media and offer another explanation for persuasion. The common themes in **mass-media effects theories** are: (1) that by sharing a common pool of experience, we become vulnerable to distortion and propaganda, (2) that we are selective about the media messages we expose ourselves to, and (3) that mass-mediated messages have become so pervasive that we are on the verge of being overwhelmed by them.

The Experience Pool

Technological determinism theory partially explains contemporary persuasion. It maintains that the technology of any given era is the major determinant of the cultural patterns of that era. The late Marshall McLuhan was a controversial technological determinist. As he put it, "the message of any medium or technology is the change of scale or pace or pattern that it introduces into human affairs,"[37] or, in briefer terms, "the medium is the message."[38] In our era, the dominant technology of our times is electronic communication, including television, radio, telephones, tape recorders, phonographs, and computers, to name a few. These media provide us with access to a huge pool of common information and experience. To get a feeling for the range of information and experience we all share, consider the similar if not identical answers we would probably get to the following questions were we to interview a hundred people on any downtown street:

1. What NFL running back holds the all-time record for yards gained rushing?
2. Who is Arnie Becker's secretary on L.A. Law?

3. Who spins "The Wheel of Fortune"?

4. What is the major product sold at the Golden Arches?

5. What is Dolly Parton's most noticeable physical feature?

6. Who turned the economic fortunes of Chrysler around and what car did he earlier pioneer while at Ford?

7. What are at least two meanings of *macintosh*?

8. Which realtors wear the gold-colored smocks?

9. What film and actor brought great attention to Australia?

10. Who are Bartels and Jaymes?

11. What technique was used to create "The California Raisins"?

12. What happened to the Berlin Wall in 1989?

13. What president of Panama is now in jail charged with drug-related crimes?

14. What is an "Infinity"?

15. What television family features a trouble-making child named Bart?

16. The death of what movie star centered national attention on AIDS?

17. Who will have to pay for the savings and loan scandal, and how much will they have to pay?

18. What character did Madonna portray in the movie "Dick Tracy"?

19. Why would it be humorous for the Democratic party to serve quail at a fundraiser?

20. What black leader was released from prison in South Africa after many years, and what effect did his release have?

These are just a few of the many questions we could ask, but they demonstrate how much we all share and from a variety of contexts, all due to the mass media. But what does that have to do with persuasion? Given the persuasive importance of the concept of common ground, or identification, since the time of Aristotle, we can readily imagine how some of this pool of common knowledge and experience could be used to create enthymemes. Bart Simpson, for example, becomes such an effective emblem of rebellion that some school systems outlaw the wearing of any Bart Simpson paraphernalia (t-shirts, buttons, hats, and so on). References to the Berlin Wall become commonplace in political speeches. Marxism is seen as an unworkable economic system, and the Soviet Union is in crisis, with many of its affiliated republics declaring independence. Madonna endorses a certain line of cosmetics. Because of the power and pervasiveness of electronic media, receivers become vulnerable to mass persuasion through appeals to shared information and experience.[39] Each of us is part of a mass target for advertisers, politicians, religious spokespersons, demagogues, and other persuaders.

Our electronic technology not only provides us with this vast store of cultural icons, it also shapes the way we think about things — even abstract things. Communication researcher James Carey has pointed out that with the invention of the telegraph and later the wireless, *time* became a critical factor in human affairs.[40] Desperados had to cut the telegraph lines as they left town to give them more *time* for their getaway. As we all know from scores of spy movies, agents transmitted critical information in *time* for the government to prepare for an attack. Because the telegraph made it easy for commodity buyers to almost instantly know prices paid for wheat in faraway Kansas, the margin for profit between purchase and sales of the wheat shrank so drastically that it was necessary to invent what we know of today as the "futures market." In it you buy wheat not yet planted, you sell it before it is harvested, you never take physical charge of a product that you will never see, yet you may have invested thousands of dollars! What a remarkable change in thinking about time. The use of the telephone sped things up even more, and, to this day, telephones are not permitted on the floor of the major stock and commodity exchanges, to provide a thin sliver of *time* for the traders — which means the margin between profit and loss. A student impressed on me how immensely important this tiny edge can be when he recounted how, in his job as a runner for the

Chicago Board of Trade, he had one day been cautioned not to stop for anything on his trip to the trading floor with a sell order. His message to sell the commodity at a certain price involved over forty boxcars of a precious metal. One minute's delay might have meant millions of dollars of extra profit or additional loss. Another student, who was involved in the business-forms industry, told how a late delivery of a supply of billing forms to a major credit-card company meant a loss to the company of $65,000 per day from interest on the float — the money in essence lent to the purchaser during the *time* it takes to send a bill and receive a payment.

Of course, time isn't the only concept affected by our electronic technology. Only a few years ago, my children went to something called "computer camp," and now we own two PCs (personal computers) and are shopping for replacements. I save money on my long-distance calls by telephoning a computer that relays my call by satellite to another computer in the city I'm calling. We throw away a credit-card size calculator that we purchased a few years ago for $10, which is capable of doing the computations that only cumbersome, slow, and expensive desktop models costing over $1400 could do just fifteen years ago. Why throw it away? Not because it doesn't work, but because a replacement battery for it costs more than a new, solar-powered calculator. It is estimated that, for the foreseeable future, the cost of home and other computers will be halved every three years, whereas their capabilities will double.[41] One expert notes that if the automobile industry had maintained the same rate of change as that of the computer industry, the Rolls Royce would now cost about $2.50 and would get over 1000 miles per gallon of gas.[42] It's mindboggling to imagine the many ways in which what McLuhan called the "change of scale, pace, or pattern" has affected our culture in the past five years, and that mindboggle is dwarfed if we try to imagine the next five. All the changes of scale, pace, and pattern influence us as persuadees, shifting the ways we are affected by messages and, probably, increasing our vulnerabilities.

Receiver Selectivity

Running almost counter to the pervasive effects posited by the technological determinists is a well-documented trend on the part of receivers to engage in individual, nonmass selectivity. Thus, although electronic media dominate our era, the total number of books read per capita has dropped dramatically, and the number of persons who rely on newspapers or news weeklies for their information has also dropped, it is also true that people are becoming increasingly selective in choosing which media — electronic or print — to patronize.[43] Thus, although fewer persons read newspapers, the number of different newspapers being published has increased. One trip to your local newsstand will confirm this. You can find a periodical publication for almost any narrow interest you can imagine — a publication for those interested in monsters; for those who like to shoot muzzle-loading, black-powder shotguns and rifles; for those who jog; for those who grow only amaryllis bulbs; and so on. The same increase in options is occurring in the electronic media, especially with the growth of cable TV, dish-satellite antennae, videotaped programs or movies, and so on. All of these have led to the term **narrowcasting**, which refers to the design of electronic messages (especially in television) for specific clusters of people who have certain interests, hobbies, or activities. Thus, although our technology is increasingly altering the scale, pace, and pattern of our lives, it is also providing us with more alternatives to choose from, making us unique and at the same time part of a mass.

How We Use Media

An undeveloped theoretical approach to the persuasive effects of mass media is known as **uses and gratification theory**. It is centered in the receiver of communication, maintaining that "the audience is actively utilizing media contents rather than being passively acted upon by the media."[44] Until its introduction, there had been little focus on the role of the receiver in mass communication research or theory. For the most part, it was assumed that receivers were message sponges who merely absorbed media messages until they were motivated to act and then went out and purchased, voted, or joined in accord with the various media pitches.

Simply put, the theory assumes that the receivers have various needs, ranging from low-order basic needs, such as food, shelter, or sex, to high-order, complex needs, such as self-identity. There are many ways in which to meet those needs, and the receiver makes a choice as to how to meet them. Some of these choices—in fact many of them—involve using the mass media. As a result, a particular mass medium competes with other mediated and nonmediated methods of gratifying needs.

For example, suppose I need to perceive myself as "sports-minded." So I develop an interest in outdoor sports such as hunting and fishing as well as spectator sports such as football or baseball. There are several ways I can meet this high-order self-identity need. I could watch Monday Night Football and focus on the halftime review of Sunday's games so I will be able to fill in the football pool at work and not look like an idiot. Or I could read the sports section of the newspaper, again focusing on the details, reviews, and commentaries on the weekend's games. This will also allow me to fill in the football pool and look good, and I can still make it to my meeting at the YMCA. Well and good, as long as it is Monday night. But suppose it is Sunday afternoon and my hunting or fishing partner calls up and suggests going out to the fields or lake for several hours. Now my self-identity needs can be met in either mediated or nonmediated ways: I can go out and maybe bag my limit or catch a lunker and be able to brag about it at work and also enjoy the companionship of my friend today. As for the football pool? Well it's just a dollar, and I can choose the same picks as my morning paper and still appear to be informed. My self-image (and I hope others' image of me) will now include not only being a knowledgeable fan of pro football but being an active outdoor-sports enthusiast as well. Note that, in this example, not

only do media compete with nonmedia activities to meet the receiver's needs, they also compete with one another.

From a persuasive point of view, the media must compete with one another to capture my time so that they can insert their advertising appeals between the pages of the sports section or throughout the broadcast of the halftime show on Monday Night Football. One of the major effects of the 1983 football strike was that previously hooked viewers and readers discovered other means to gratify their needs. As a result, when the strike was over and the season resumed, pro-football viewership and readership dropped off and has not as yet returned to pre-1983 levels. Some former viewers are now bowling, jogging, or enjoying their own games of touch football. Others are watching college games. Still others are working on repair projects on Sunday afternoons or have gotten involved in some other nonsport activity that competes to gratify their needs.

Jay Blumler, one of the originators of and foremost theorists in the uses and gratifications approach, has outlined four kinds of needs that motivate people to turn to media.[45] The first he calls **surveillance**, the need to keep track of our environment. We look to media to find out what's happening that might be of use to us. Even though you may think your college newspaper is worthless, you probably still glance over it regularly to find out what is going on. You notice not only campus and local news and sports, but some of the advertisements, announcements from organizations on campus, and the personals column.

The second kind of need is **curiosity**, the need to discover new and previously unknown information. We frequently see appeals to this need in sensationalist publications like the *National Enquirer*. Sensational headlines like "Test Tube Baby Put Up for Adoption!" or "Rock Star Has Incurable Disease!" or "Head Transplant Succeeds!" are designed to tickle our *need to know* and get us to buy the paper. Most frequently, the story doesn't live up to the promise of the headline, but apparently that doesn't matter to the curious readers, because the *Enquirer* has the world's largest circulation. Of course, there are less dramatic examples of curiosity at work. Many people are unable to let the phone ring without answering it. In fact, at least one bank robber answered the phone and was interviewed by a reporter in the midst of a robbery, thus risking capture. Curiosity lies at the heart of this kind of behavior.

A third kind of need identified by Blumler is **diversion**. We need relief from our day-in-and-day-out routines and use media to escape. The need for escape is met in many different mediated and nonmediated ways, such as reading intrigue novels, watching a TV show, or going to a movie. This powerful need to check out of the here-and-now and into the there-and-then frequently is most easily met by media, especially electronic media.

Finally, Blumler identifies the need for **personal identity**, which is closely related to Rokeach's self-concept. Media help us to identify who we are, through our reading, listening, or viewing. Blumler and his colleagues found a fascinating difference between the print and electronic media. Apparently, persons who are sure of themselves and who are outgoing, social, and interactive tend to get a sense of who they are through reading, whereas less socially interactive and perhaps less self-assured persons rely on viewing to get a sense of who they are or to find a substitute for social activities.[46] This sense of identity may come from role models we see on television, from political views written in newspapers, or from a certain type of music that we listen to and identify with our own lifestyle. Country-and-western fans, for example, are likely to have different personal identities than do opera fans.

The uses and gratifications approach to mass-media persuasion also places the consumer or receiver at the center of the persuasive act. Receivers can and do select and choose from the mediated and nonmediated alternatives for meeting their surveillance, curiosity, diversion, and personal-identity needs; their selections may make the difference between the profit and loss, victory and defeat, or success and failure of a persuader.

We could go into other approaches to mass-media persuasion, but technological determinism and uses and gratifications provide good examples of the variations among theoretical explanations for persuasive effects. In some theories, the media effects are immense enough to affect culture. In others, the receiver is central to any persuasive effect, and mass media are only peripheral alternatives in a large set of potential persuasive message sources.

Mass Media as Cultural Texts

In recent years, scholars have begun to examine communication events (speeches, interviews, news broadcasts, interpersonal interactions, works of literature, and films, to name a few) as "texts" that are meant to be "read" by audiences and analysts. Without getting involved in theoretical determinants of what does and does not constitute a text, let us assume that mass-media messages are in fact "texts" that can be read and interpreted.

Imagine that you are a cultural anthropologist 5000 years from now and you happen upon a time capsule containing a huge collection of television commercials from the last decade of the twentieth century. You find a way to view these curious ribbons of videotape and try to draw some conclusions about what life was like way back then. What did people do for a living? What did they believe in? What kinds of values did they have? How did they relate to one another?

One conclusion you would likely reach is that twentieth-century people were powerfully influenced by and tied to the automobile. There seems to have been two levels at which this influence occurred. First, there is the utility level. Apparently you couldn't have lived in the twentieth century without an automobile. On a second level, local dealers seem to have taken great pride in using insincere "hard sells." They must have been convinced that they themselves had great media appeal. In spite of their transparent insincerity, they repeatedly went on the air as their own spokespersons instead of using famous athletes or entertainers, indicating their belief that consumers were incredibly gullible.

There would also be many other cultural details discernible in the ads (color and style preferences, physical characteristics of the vehicles, lucky outcomes that came about because one owned this or that car, and so on). And you have just touched a tiny tip of the iceberg, for there are many other categories of commercials. For example, twentieth-century people must have been incredibly filthy: Witness the numerous ads for laundry detergents, foot disinfectants, room and personal deodorants, antidandruff shampoos, toothpastes, mouthwashes, douches, toilet paper, and so on. All in all, the newfound commercials would serve as a set of texts that illuminate the nature of twentieth-century America at least as well as the ancient written texts of Biblical times indicate what culture was like in 500 B.C.

This recent approach to mass-media messages as "cultural texts" is fascinating and has identified a great number of significant patterns in our culture, such as our compulsion to consume products, energy, and various raw materials. This compulsion draws fire from various critics, among them the Marxists.

The Marxist Approach to Mass Media

Another interpretation of the function of mass media has been advanced by Marxist critics of our society. Such critics would find the hypothetical repository of television advertisements to be a goldmine for demonstrating another function of mass media: to support and continue the prevailing ideology. Clearly, the ads encourage consumption on the part of the masses, and it can be argued that this leads to an endless cycle of "working to earn money to buy things so that the masses must continue to work to earn money to buy. . . ." Marxist critics would identify news reporting as the undergirding of the prevailing political and economic ideology. They would argue that the mass media depict terrorists as outlaws, whereas a perfectly valid argument could be made for the position that terrorists represent the proletariat and that terrorism is merely a strategy to dramatically state an opposing ideology.

Marxists would also condemn audience studies as mere tools of the capitalistic superstructure to manipulate the proletariat. To Marxist critics, the mass media in general serve to communicate a view of reality that supports the status quo. Naturally, such critiques are controversial; however, they may be useful if only to alert us to potential persuasive strategies that we as receivers may face.

Although still in its infancy, mass-media criticism is likely to grow into an important means of defining our culture and of identifying ways in which consumers are lured into purchasing products. From the point of view of persuasion, these mass-media "texts" certainly must indicate the kinds of first premises that operate in convincing enthymemes. They demonstrate what kinds of appeals stand a chance of being successful and what strategies and tactics persuaders will use to convince us to buy their products, vote for a certain candidate, or support a given cause. The study of media messages as texts can do a lot to inform persuadees.

PERSONAL CONSTRUCT THEORY

As noted earlier, this approach to persuasion theory is far less scientific than many others we have looked at.[47] Its major tenets include the belief that although people can be induced to behave in very predictable ways, they do so for a variety of reasons. Researchers working from this perspective are interested in *the reasons* people give for changing their minds or altering their behavior. They believe that the variety of reasons given for acting in a certain way is attributable to the fact that each of us, acting as our own private "research scientist," begins in childhood to develop many "constructs." These constructs almost always differ from person to person, because not all of us have the same set of experiences on which to base our constructs. Furthermore, these constructs are arranged hierarchically, with some being more important than others. Also, constructs change as we grow and develop from childhood to adolescence to early adulthood to middle age to retirement and to old age. As a result, there are probably as many reasons for believing or behaving as there are individuals. What do researchers look for when using the constructivist perspective, and what methods do they use?

One aspect of persuasion constructivists look for is the degree of sophistication in communication strategy used by persuaders. Another is the degree to which persuaders adapt to and analyze audiences. Audience adaptation and audience analysis are inherently constructivist because it is assumed that each audience and each member of the audience has a somewhat unique set of constructs. But since they share some of the same concepts, the persuader has to seek out the common sets of audience constructs that will motivate the audience members as individuals *and* as a group. This sounds a lot like Aristotle's ideas on "common ground" or the notion of "co-creating meaning" between persuader and persuadee discussed in Chapter 1.

One of the assumptions associated with this approach is that the higher or more sophisticated one's constructs have developed, the more sophisticated is the audience adaptation and strategy development. For example, in an experiment by Ruth Clark and Jesse Delia,[48] children were asked to develop strategies to induce a stranger to take a homeless puppy. The least sophisticated approach was simply to request the stranger to keep the puppy, offering no further persuasive arguments. The second level of sophistication involved not only the puppy but the child. Here, the child asked the stranger to take the stray because it would make the child happy if the dog had a good home. Notice that the child's message included at least one reason for taking the pup. In the third level of sophistication, the child asked the stranger to take the puppy, adding that it wouldn't cost much to feed. Such a strategy implies audience analysis because it anticipates a potential objection on the part of the stranger. In the most sophisticated level of persuasion, audience awareness was most obvious. Here the child asked the stranger to take the puppy home, but also described the benefits the stranger would derive from having a fine watchdog. This is a far more sophisticated persuasive message than the mere request to take the puppy or any of the other levels of sophistication, as shown by its audience awareness and subsequent development of a persuasive strategy.

A far more sophisticated and costly "real-world" piece of constructivist marketing research is the development of the "I've got a secret—in the refrigerator" campaign for Arm and Hammer baking soda. Although the researchers probably would never have labeled their research "constructivist," they nonetheless operated from that perspective in that they tried to identify constructs

INSTEAD OF MIDDLE AGE, I CALL IT "YOUTH, THE SEQUEL".

THAVES 9-18
© 1987 by NEA, Inc.

FIGURE 3.9

Here is an example of the altering and adapting of a construct — middle age — to fit the emotional needs of a particular audience — the baby boomers — the first of whom reached age 40 in 1986 and the last of whom will reach age 40 in 2004. (*Frank and Ernest* reprinted by permission of NEA, Inc.)

about baking soda and its uses in the minds of consumers. At the time of the study, the major uses for the product were: as an antacid, for brushing teeth, for eliminating acid from automobile battery terminals, for bathing and cleaning — especially refrigerators — and as a leavening agent, mainly for chocolate chip cookies. Even though Arm and Hammer had a 97 percent share of the market, they wanted to stimulate further customer usage. After all, one box could make about 400 batches of chocolate chip cookies, and because baking soda has a long shelf life, not much of it was being used, even though almost everyone had a box in the house.

Using a research technique called "focus-group interviews," the researchers asked small groups of homemakers to discuss their uses of and attitudes toward baking soda. After repeatedly analyzing many such groups, the researchers discovered a sophisticated concept in the minds of many of the homemakers. The concept was that of "refrigerator guilt," caused by not cleaning the refrigerator as often as they remembered their mothers doing it once a month. The busy homemakers were lucky to get at the job twice a year, always finding several withered vegetables, dried up cheese, and a few unidentifiable and disgusting substances.

The campaign designed with this concept in mind, promoted putting a box of baking soda in the refrigerator to absorb odors and keep it smelling sweet. For years the idea had been listed on the Arm and Hammer box as one of the uses for the product, but now it was being marketed from the *consumers'* perspective based on the "refrigerator guilt" construct. The initial ads sometimes featured two homemakers discussing how busy they were and how one seemed to have such a clean refrigerator. She finally admitted that "I've got a secret — in the refrigerator," and the TV viewer would be shown the box inside the refrigerator with vapors — presumably the bad odors — being sucked into it. The second homemaker was duly impressed, vowing to go out and buy the product right away. Later spots needed only to use the slogan and the video showing the vapors getting sucked into the Arm and Hammer box. These were reinforced with print ads depicting the same story.

The approach was so successful that Arm and Hammer had to postpone a nationwide campaign using it, because their market tests in California showed that they would never be able to meet the increased nationwide demand without building new factories. A year later, with the new factories in operation, the nationwide rollout took place and was a phenomenal success. And today most of us have a box of Arm and Hammer in the refrigerator and one in the freeze, and we pour it down the garbage disposal every two months to "sweeten" the drain. The chocolate chip cookie factor now accounts for only a minuscule slice of annual sales.

The critical factor here was the identification of the reason(s) *why consumers purchased the product and how they used it*. That approach is focused on the construct(s) in the consumers' minds and hence is a piece of constructivist research. Market researchers using such constructivist approaches (even though they don't call them that) are becoming more and more sophisticated at identifying our vulnerabilities to clever persuasion.[49]

REVIEW AND CONCLUSION

There are a variety of possible explanations for persuasion. This survey of just a small portion of possible explanations should give you a feel for the complexity of the study of persuasion. An important development in the past decade of persuasion research has been the increasing focus on the centrality of the receiver in the process of persuasion, as our review of perspectives demonstrates. Whether you find one theory or explanation more satisfactory or fascinating than another is not particularly important. What *is* important is that you as a receiver attempt to find some explanation for what happens to you when you are persuaded.

QUESTIONS FOR FURTHER THOUGHT

1. What was the major focus of the attitude researchers, as exemplified by Hovland and his associates?

2. What is the latitude of acceptance? How does it work? What is the latitude of rejection? The latitude of noncommitment? What is ego-involvement as defined by Sherif? What does it do to information that runs counter to one's position?

3. How does learning theory relate to persuasion?

4. Explain the following from the perspective of social learning theory as postulated by Bandura: external sources of reinforcement, self-reinforcement, role playing, and role modeling.

5. What is meant by a "behavioral intention" as used by Fishbein? Give some examples. How do behavioral intentions relate to attitudes? To behaviors? What is the difference between a belief *in* something and a belief *about* something?

6. What are the three dimensions or ways in which human beings exhibit reactions to information as presented in persuasive messages? What is the difference between the central- and peripheral-processing routes in Likelihood Elaboration Theory?

7. What are the primitive beliefs according to Rokeach's perspectives? What are authority beliefs? Give examples. What is the difference between one's attitude toward an object or a topic and one's attitude toward a situation? What is the difference between terminal and instrumental values? Which is strongest: a belief, an attitude, or a value? Which is easiest to change?

8. What are some shortcomings of the Heider-Newcomb balance theory? How does congruency theory go beyond balance theory? How does dissonance theory go beyond both the balance and congruency models?

9. What are the virtues, and how do they relate to both ethos and pathos? Can you identify any of these virtues in our nation's leaders? In professional athletes? In film or television characters?

10. How did the "refrigerator guilt" construct affect the average American homemaker?

What did Arm and Hammer do to exploit this construct? How might this be related to the consistency theories discussed in this chapter?

11. What are "topoi"? How do they work? Can you identify any ways in which today's political leaders use them? Are they apparent in any television spots you have seen recently? In any of the catalogs and other direct-mail pieces you have received? In any print ads?

12. What is the significance of having a "common experience pool," and how does it relate to the Aristotelean concept of the enthymeme?

13. What is the "uses and gratifications" explanation of the functions of mass media. How might this apply to political persuasion during election times? How might it apply to advertising? How might the mass-media function of determining a personal identity relate to political persuasion and advertising?

14. Explain the phrase "mass-media messages are texts."

15. If you were a cultural anthropologist examining the repository of television spots from the 1990s, what kinds of values (beyond the fixation on the automobile and cleanliness) might you identify as typical of consumers in the last decade of the twentieth century?

16. How do Marxist critics view the mass media? Do you agree with their assessment? If so, why? If not, why not?

NOTES

1. I use the word "man" here instead of "man or woman" because women were not permitted to argue to Greek courts or to speak before the governing bodies of the day. The same applies to the use of "he," "him," and "his."

2. Aristotle, *Rhetoric*, trans. W. Rhys Roberts (New York: Modern Library, 1954); see also Lester Thonssen and A. Craig Baird, *Speech Criticism* (New York: Ronald Press, 1948), p. 57.

3. For an in-depth discussion of this tendency away from the virtues espoused by Aristotle, which is still recognized by many contemporary social critics, see Charles U. Larson and Christine Oravec, "*A Prairie Home Companion* and the Fabrication of Community," *Critical Studies in Mass Communication* 4 (September 1987), pp. 221–244 and the editor's note that prefaces the article.

4. For an excellent discussion of how this sense of isolation and fragmentation has been observed, see the work of Robert Bellah and his colleagues in *Habits of the Heart: Individualism and Commitment in American Life* (Berkeley: University of California Press, 1985) and M. Scott Peck's *The Different Drum: Community Making and Peace* (New York: Simon & Schuster, 1987).

5. "Yeltsin's Challenge," *Newsweek*, June 11, 1990, p. 20.

6. All references to the virtues and the topics are drawn from Lane Cooper, *The Rhetoric of Aristotle: An Expanded Translation* (New York: Appleton-Century-Crofts, 1960).

7. This is only a partial explanation of the enthymeme and deals with only one of its forms. For further elaboration, see Lloyd Bitzer's insightful article, "Aristotle's Enthymeme Revisited," *Speech Monographs* 45:399–408, 1959.

8. Stephen Littlejohn, *Theories of Human Communication*, 2d ed. (Belmont, CA: Wadsworth, 1983), p. 306.

9. Joshua Meyrowitz, *No Sense of Place: The Impact of Electronic Media on Social Behavior* (New York: Oxford University Press, 1985).

10. Carl I. Hovland, Irving L. Janis, and Harold H. Kelley, *Communication and Persuasion* (New Haven, CT: Yale University Press, 1953). For an excellent review of the Yale studies, see Chapter 9 of Mary John Smith, *Persuasion and Human Action* (Belmont, CA: Wadsworth, 1982), pp. 213–240.

11. Timothy C. Brock, "Communicator-Recipient Similarity and Decision Change," *Journal of Personality and Social Psychology* 23:650–654, 1965.

12. See, for example, Carl Hovland, ed., *The Order of Presentation in Persuasion* (New Haven, CT: Yale University Press, 1959). See also Martin F. Kaplan, "Context Effects in Impression Formation: The Weighted Average versus the Meaning-Change Formation," *Journal of Personality and Social Psychology* 19:92–99, 1971; Norman Anderson, "Primacy Effects in Personality Impression Formation Using a Generalized Order Effect Paradigm," *Journal of Personality and Social Psychology* 2:1–9, 1965.

13. See, for example, John T. Cacioppo and Richard E. Petty's two articles "Effects of Message Repetition and Position on Cognitive Response, Recall and Persuasion" and "Attitudes and Cognitive Responses: An Electrophysical Approach," both in *Journal of Personality and Social Psychology* 37 (1979), pp. 97–109 and 2181–2199.

14. Roger Wimmer, "A Descriptive Field Study of the Campaign of Ray A. "Dutch" Scott for Senator from the 37th District," unpub. M.A. thesis, Northern Illinois University, 1973.

15. Carl I. Hovland, Arthur A. Lumsdaine, and Fred D. Sheffield, "The Effects of Presenting 'One Side' versus 'Both Sides' in Changing Opinions on a Controversial Subject," in *Experiments on Mass Communication* (Princeton: Princeton University Press, 1949), pp. 201–227.

16. For a good explanation of the boomerang effect, see W. J. McGuire, "Personality and Attitude Change," in *Psychological Foundation of Attitudes*, eds. A. G. Greenwald, T. C. Brock, and T. M. Ostrum (New York: Academic Press, 1968), pp. 171–196.

17. Shelly Chaiken and Alice H. Eagly, "Communication Modality as a Determinant of Message Persuasiveness and Message Comprehensibility," *Journal of Personality and Social Psychology* 34:605–614, 1976.

18. William A. Watts and Lewis E. Holt, "Persistence of Opinion Change Induced by Forewarning and Distraction," *Journal of Personality and Social Psychology* 37:779–789, 1979.

19. Eric Hoffer, *The True Believer* (New York: Perennial Library, 1966); see especially Part II: "The Potential Converts."

20. Littlejohn, *op. cit.* p. 114.

21. Smith, *op. cit.* pp. 236–237.

22. Martin Fishbein and Icek Ajzen, *Belief, Attitude, Intention, and Behavior* (Reading, Mass.: Addison-Wesley, 1975).

23. Richard E. Petty and John T. Cacioppo, *Communication and Persuasion* (New York: Springer Verlag, 1986).

24. *Ibid.*, p. 3.

25. *Ibid.*

26. *Ibid.*, p. 5.

27. Fritz Heider, "Attitudes and Cognitive Organization," *Journal of Psychology* 21:107–112, 1946. Heider later elaborated on this work, applying it to interpersonal communication and relations in *The Psychology of Interpersonal Relations* (New York: Wiley and Sons, 1958).

28. Theodore Newcomb, "An Approach to the Study of Communicative Acts," *Psychological Review* 60:393–404, 1953.

29. Charles Osgood and Percy Tannenbaum, "The Principle of Congruity in the Prediction of Attitude Change," *Psychological Review* 62:42–55, 1955.

30. "Marital Ballistics," *Playboy* 37, April 1990, p. 15.

31. Leon Festinger, *A Theory of Cognitive Dissonance* (Stanford, CA: Stanford University Press, 1962). See also Shel Feldman, ed., *Cognitive Consistency* (New York: Academic Press, 1966); J. S. Brehm and A. R. Cohen, *Explorations in Cognitive Dissonance* (New York: Wiley and Sons, 1962).

32. Littlejohn, *op. cit.*, p. 149.

33. Milton Rokeach, *Beliefs, Attitudes, and Values: A Theory of Organization and Change* (San Francisco: Jossey-Bass, 1968); see also Milton Rokeach, *The Nature of Human Values* (New York: Free Press, 1973).

34. Rokeach, *The Nature of Human Values*, pp. 220–224.

35. Albert Bandura, *Social Learning Theory* (Englewood Cliffs, NJ: Prentice-Hall, 1977).

36. Muzafer Sherif, Carolyn Sherif, and Roger Nebergall, *Attitude and Attitude Change: The Social Judgment–Involvement Approach* (Philadelphia: W. B. Saunders, 1965); Carolyn Sherif and Muzafer Sherif, *Attitude, Ego-Involvement, and Change* (New York: Wiley and Sons, 1967).

37. Marshall McLuhan, *Understanding Media: The Extensions of Man* (New York: Signet Books, 1964), p. 24.

38. *Ibid.*, Chapter 1.

39. Present estimates are that we have over 120,000,000 television sets in America—over 97 percent of American homes have one, and nearly 50 percent have two or more sets. See *Broadcasting Yearbook: 1984* (Washington, DC: Broadcasting Publishing, 1984), p. A2.

40. James Carey, "The Telegraph and Its Effects," lecture delivered at Northern Illinois University, Spring, 1982.

41. *Direct Marketing Magazine* 47:42, 1984.

42. Wilson P. Dizard, Jr., *The Coming Information Age: Overview of Technology, Economics, and Politics* (N.Y.: Longman Inc., 1975).

43. Tony Schwartz, *The Responsive Chord* (Garden City, NY: Anchor Press/Doubleday, 1973). In this regard, it is also shocking to note that illiteracy in the United States is close to 33 percent; see Jonathon Kozol, *Illiterate America* (New York: Doubleday, 1985).

44. Elihu Katz, Jay Blumler, and Michael Gurevitch, "Uses of Mass Communication by the Individual," in *Mass Communication Research: Major Issues and Future Directions*, eds. W. D. Phillips and Frederick Yu (New York: Praeger Books, 1974), pp. 11–35. For an excellent critique of this theory, see David L. Swanson, "Political Communication Research and the Uses and Gratifications Model: A Critique," *Communication Research* 6: 37–53, 1979.

45. Jay Blumler, "The Role of Theory in Uses and Gratifications Studies," *Communication Research* 6:9–34, 1979; see also Jay Blumler, *The Uses of Mass Communication* (Beverly Hills, CA: Sage Publications, 1974).

46. Blumler, *The Uses of Mass Communication*.

47. For a good review of constructivist research, see Jesse G. Delia, Barbara J. O'Keefe, and Daniel J. O'Keefe, "The Constructivist Approach to Communication," in *Human Communication Theory*, ed. F. E. X. Dance (New York: Harper & Row, 1982).

48. Ruth Anne Clark and Jesse G. Delia, "The Development of Functional Persuasive Skills in Childhood and Early Adolescence," *Childhood Development* 47:1008–1014, 1986.

49. Jack Honomichil, *Marketing Research People: Their Behind the Scenes Stories* (Chicago: Crain Books, 1984), pp. 5–22.

The Making, Use, and Misuse of Symbols

Throughout history, the uniquely human ability to create symbols has made possible major cultural advances. Before the development of the spoken word, humans were not much different from beasts, but the ability to make use of symbols for communication enabled humans to live cooperatively. Tribes, for example, were formed using the communicative power of symbols. Communication also facilitated the specialization of labor, as some tribe members assumed the duties of hunting while others made tools or weapons, farmed small plots, wove, or sewed clothing. As in the opening of Pandora's box, however, the use of symbols to communicate also allowed humans to engage in less constructive behaviors, such as teasing, aggravating, breaking promises, deceiving, scolding, demeaning, and lying. And with the development of the written word and movable type, people found that treaties could be both made and broken, legal contracts could destructively bind people for years, and laws could be used for evil as well as good. Language theorist Kenneth Burke describes human beings as "symbol making, symbol using, and symbol misusing" creatures who can do much good and much harm with these abilities; in fact, our words are frequently symbolic acts. When we say "I could just sock that person," we have symbolically done just that.[1]

This ability to use symbols — verbal, pictorial, gestural, musical, or nonverbal — lies at the heart of persuasion and so deserves our attention. As receivers, we need to get to the bottom of persuasive meanings, and carefully analyzing the symbols used or misused by persuaders can help us get there. For instance, picture a television advertisement for Michelob beer. Now, try to identify some of the verbal symbols (that is, those that employ spoken or written language). First there are the song lyrics — "Weekends Were Made for Michelob," which call up a mental picture of a time of companionship and enjoyment. The lyrics also associate the product with the kind of free and exciting lifestyle that the truly "in" people are supposed to have. Superimposed on these aural symbols might be written other verbal symbols, such as the word "Michelob" or the slogan

"Weekends Were Made for Michelob," which reinforces the images presented aurally (and, of course, in pictures). In addition, the entire message (for example, the colorful sunsets, the clothing worn by the actors, and the musical score) can symbolically build and reinforce the brewer's persuasive message.

By examining the various kinds of symbols used in persuasion, we can

1. discover the persuader's use or misuse of symbols.
2. discover the persuader's stylistic preferences and what they may reveal about his or her motives.
3. anticipate, using the knowledge gained from points 1 and 2, the kinds of messages likely to come from this source in the future. In addition, we can predict how that persuader might, in turn, be persuaded.

How is it that a careful examination of a persuader's symbols can reveal so much? The answer is that making symbols is a creative act, and, as such, is ego-involving, thus revealing a good deal about the persuader's modes of expression.

LANGUAGE AND ITS ROOTS

Eloquent persuasion is unique and fresh. It strikes us as having caught the moment; it may even prophesy the future. The speech made by Martin Luther King, Jr., the night before he was killed had elements of prophecy. He said that God had allowed him "to go up to the mountain," that he had "seen the promised land," and that he doubted that he would get there with his followers. He concluded, "And I am happy tonight! I'm not fearing any man! Mine eyes have seen the glory of the coming of the Lord!" Although the words were drawn from the Old Testament and Julia Ward Howe's *Battle Hymn of the Republic*, King's use of them was unique in the context of the movement he was leading. After his assassination, they seemed prophetic.

When we think about persuasion, then, we are

inevitably faced with the artistic process of making word symbols. These are symbolic *acts* — like the assassination of a president or pope, which express rejection of authority, outrage at capitalism or Catholicism, or some other objection. But these are not the usual stuff of persuasion — language is.

Where did language come from? How did humans discover that they could speak, and why did this ability progress from the use of simple to complex symbols? Some think that the development of human speech parallels the progression from the babbling of infancy to the use of words and then sentences.[2] Others explain the development of language by tracing it to certain stages in the development of the brain and its many cells. By the time a child reaches age two, the brain is ready to learn language. The two-year-old talks almost nonstop, sometimes making mistakes, sometimes being cute, and sometimes adding new and different words. In her book, *Philosophy in a New Key*, Susanne K. Langer argues that it is neither use of tools nor language that makes humans unique among the beasts. Rather, she suggests, one aspect of behavior that only humans display is the ability to make symbols.

Even the earliest cave dwellings show this impulse. Long before we had spoken language, we made symbols. Sometimes they were in the form of paintings; sometimes they were charms or amulets to bring luck in the hunt or to ward off evil spirits. We know that the power of these symbols in certain primitive cultures was sufficient to kill. If a voodoo spell was cast over someone using a doll-like image of the person and then the doll was "killed," the real person frequently died, because he or she believed that the doll — the symbol — carried the real person's spirit.

Today we find many groups responding to symbols in ways nearly as dramatic. Some people make a point of wearing pins that symbolically convert them from one kind of person to another. Or they might use a bumper sticker to do the same thing. One pin/bumper sticker campaign used by environmentalists bears the statement "I Love My Mother," followed by a picture of the Earth. The words capture our attention, and they make us puz-

zle a little bit to decipher the "Mother Earth" reference. Gun lobbyists wear buttons claiming that "Guns Don't Kill! People Do!" The act of making any statement is a symbolic act that is ego-involving for the language user; those who display bumper stickers will likely show up to vote for a politician, cheer for a team, buy a product, or support a cause.

Language can also be misused, as we discovered in our discussion of euphemism as a form of doublespeak. For example, in the 1980s, aid sent to the Contra rebels in El Salvador was initially called "nonmilitary" and "humanitarian," in order to forestall criticism. Later, when jeeps, spare parts for weapons, and military advisors were sent, the aid was termed "nonlethal," because in and of itself, it wasn't lethal. Of course, the spare parts *did* make previously useless weapons lethal, and the jeeps *did* transport lethal soldiers to killing raids, but the misuse of the word "nonlethal" made things seem not so deadly. Misuse of language is not always so treacherous. For example, *Newsweek* regularly carries a feature called "Buzzwords," which describes the names people in various occupations use to describe their clients. Telephone operators, for example, use the terms *captive customer* (for prison inmates who make collect calls), *Gods* (for self-important persons who insist on getting unlisted numbers), and *TUIs* (for drunks who use the phone).[3] Movers refer to odds and ends as *chowder*, because they just toss them together in one box. *Lumpers* are the muscle men who actually move the stuff into or out of the truck.[4] The symbols and language used in advertising also frequently border on misuse. Market researchers decided to use the words "Recipe for Success," for example, to assure working women who use Crisco that they are indeed "cooks" and not just "microwavers" who merely thaw and reheat meals.[5] Consider the language in the ad for GM in Figure 4.1. GM doesn't just "buy just any seats," they "design them" because they use "Human Factors Engineering" and they "think it's worth it."

The receiver of persuasive messages can learn a lot about a persuader's motives by paying careful

We don't buy just any seats. We design them.

GM begins with detailed studies of the human body. Biomedical research. The kind of comprehensive investigation of anatomy da Vinci undertook in the 1500s.

As a leader in the field of Human Factors Engineering, we design interiors scientifically to minimize the possible distractions from your driving.

It may take us two years and countless clay models to arrive at a more comfortable, durable seat for new GM cars and trucks. But we think it's worth it.

And we believe old Leonardo would have thought so, too.

We believe in taking the extra time, giving the extra effort and paying attention to every detail. That's what it takes to provide the quality that leads more people to buy GM cars and trucks than any other kind. And why GM owners are the most loyal on the road.

That's the GM commitment to excellence.

Chevrolet • Pontiac • Oldsmobile • Buick • Cadillac • GMC Truck

Leonardo da Vinci gave us a great idea for bucket seats.

Let's get it together. Buckle up.

Nobody sweats the details like GM.

attention not only to the whole message but also to its particular words. Consider the language used by Hitler and other German Nazis of the 1930s in referring to the Jews: *vermin, sludge, garbage, lice, sewage, insects*, and *bloodsuckers*. Those words were red flags signaling Hitler's march toward an "ultimate solution" — concentration camps and gas chambers. If more Europeans of Jewish heritage had listened carefully to Hitler's *words*, they might have fled in time to avoid the fate of six million Jews who were ultimately treated exactly like vermin or lice — by extermination. Isn't that what we're supposed to do with rats? Hitler's words helped the S.S. Corps to feel like dutiful soldiers when they methodically rounded up and killed the Jews, wove their hair into rug pads, pried out their gold teeth, and rendered their bodies into soap.

Even in less dramatic settings, we find that words create emotional responses and can demean people. Consider the term "lady doctor." What is the person using those words implying? That the doctor is not as good as a male physician? That the doctor is in the business only for the fun or sport if it? Why does the use of "lady" carry so much meaning and emotional response? I'm sure you can guess the reason. Consider the response reported by a speaker at a meeting of department store employees who objected to being referred to as "clerks" and demanded that they be called "salespersons." What is it about the first word that they thought so demeaning? Why was the second name better? This example shows how careful word usage can persuade as well as outrage. The world of marketing provides many examples.

Product names often reveal producers' attitudes toward their customers, or even toward the public in general. Oster Corporation has a "food crafter" instead of a "food chopper." This choice of words tells us that Oster is taking a gourmet approach. (*Chopping* sounds like work. *Crafting?* Now, that's art.) In the status-and-power-conscious

FIGURE 4.1

What does the language of this ad imply about GM? (Used by permission of General Motors Corporation.)

1950s and 1960s, cigarettes had "classy" names such as Viceroy, Pall Mall, Marlboro, and Benson and Hedges. If you were status-minded, those were brands for you. Quite a different attitude is suggested by the names of brands more recently introduced — Fact, True, Merit, Vantage, and More. These suggest an honest, open, and "up-front" audience. Virginia Slims, on the other hand, made a fortune from feminist smokers. How nonsexist was their appeal?

Similar plays to perceived public attitudes occur in the names given to cars. Before the oil crisis of the nineties and the advent of the conservation movement, automakers used names like Roadmaster, Continental, Charger, Impala, Delta 88, or Thunderbird to symbolize speed, luxury, and — especially — power. Then in the years of the energy shortage and energy consciousness — 1974 to 1984 — cars got names like Rabbit, Aries, Horizon, or Colt, to suggest faster and lighter images. Once the price of gasoline stabilized in the eighties, and there was a glut of oil on the market with OPEC unable to control the production and export of its member nations, there was a return to status and power consciousness. Now cars were called names like LeBaron, Taurus (the bull), and Sable, and expensive foreign makes like the BMW, Mercedes, Volvo, and the Sterling were becoming status symbols for the upwardly mobile baby boomers who had been promoted a few rungs up the organization ladder. What will the turmoil in the Middle East in the 1990s bring?

By understanding the many ways in which language can be manipulated, persuadees can look beyond the surface to delve deeper into the meaning of the message and motives of the source. Persuaders, on the other hand, can analyze receivers and craft their words and phrases to appeal to them. They can "listen" to their audience for clues to what receivers need and want to hear.

How can we learn to identify the uses and misuses of symbols, especially in the language used by politicians, advertisers, employers, customers, and other persuaders? One way is to investigate how language scholars view the power and use of words. An early and useful approach to language use is the general semantics approach.

THE SEMANTIC APPROACH TO LANGUAGE USE

Beginning in 1933 with the landmark work *Science and Sanity*, by Count Alfred Korzybski,[6] scholars called **general semanticists** began a careful and systematic study of the use and meaning of language. Their purpose was to improve understanding about human communication problems and to encourage careful and precise uses of language. They wanted to train people to be very specific about sending and receiving words in or-

der to avoid such pitfalls as the stereotyping typical of Fascist propaganda in Europe and the United States. Hitler, Franco, and Mussolini had risen swiftly to prominence and had gained enough early public support to institute dangerous regimes. The general semanticists believed that an effective way to prevent such dictatorships is to teach people to be aware that the appeals of demagogues reflect "the map [inner perception] and not the territory [reality]."

Everything changes, the semanticists reasoned. Even when based on the observed traits of an in-

Berry's World

© 1988 by NEA, Inc.

"I'm a value-free yuppie. You're a value-free yuppie. Let's do something that calls for some MORAL RELATIVISM!"

FIGURE 4.2

What is your map for "Yuppie"? What is the actual territory for today's "Yuppie"? (*Berry's World* reprinted by permission of NEA, Inc.)

dividual, stereotypes are unreliable, simply because no member of a class or group is exactly like any other member. As Korzybski suggested, *the map is not the territory*. In other words, the internal perceptions or conceptions of persons, groups, things, and ideas we carry around in our heads are likely to be different from the real persons, groups, things, and ideas. Our faulty concepts usually are expressed through language; we create and use words to convey them.

Asa Baber, a regular columnist for *Playboy* magazine, was undoubtedly creating a map when he produced *The Real Man's Dictionary*.[7] In it, he made, used, and distorted some language symbols. For example, the word *schmuckette* was illustrated with a picture of Roseanne Barr and defined as "a really gross broad who bashes men a lot and then claims she's for equal rights." A *femfascist* was defined as "a woman (or a man) who glories in the excesses of feminism and likes trashing men." After coming up with such definitions, or "maps," Baber and others then act as if they were the real group, person, or idea, thus making the map into the "territory," a mistake Korzybski believed to be potentially dangerous. Korzybski believed that we all carry thousands of maps around in our heads that represent nonexistent territories, or at least unreal terrritories. To demonstrate this concept for yourself, write down the name of a food you have never eaten, a place you have never been, and an experience you have never had. Associated with these names are maps for unknown territories. For example, you may think that fried brains (the food, not the drug-induced type) are slimy and gooshy, when in reality they feel like scrambled eggs. What is your map for skydiving? Hang gliding? Being a rock star? How do these maps match up with the real territories? In some aspects, the territory will agree with your map, which is probably a result of the *media exposure* you have had to other countries, foods, and activities. But in most cases, your maps will be very different from the territories as they really are. Our mental and word maps represent a real problem in communication, especially in persuasion. Just as persuaders have to discover the common ground of ideas in order to persuade you to adopt their point of view, they also have to identify the maps you carry around in your head. Then they must either play on those maps, using your misperceptions to their advantage, or they must try to get you to correct your faulty maps. Only then can they persuade you to buy, join, or change your behavior. Our faulty maps frequently are expressed through langauge; we create and use words to express our maps. We react to them as if they are true representations of the territories we imagine. To the semanticists, this "signal response" was a frequent cause of misunderstanding and faulty communication.

The Signal Response

Reacting to a word or other symbolic act as if it were the real thing is what semanticists called a **signal response**. Signal responses are emotionally triggered reactions to symbolic acts (including language use) as if the actual act were being committed. In recent times people have responded to the burning of the American flag as if the values — indeed the very honor of the country itself — were being destroyed. The Congressional debate over a proposed amendment to ban flag burning was nearly evenly divided between those who felt that flag burning (the "map") was equivalent to destroying the country and those who felt that the "territory" (the ideas behind the flag — the Constitution, the Bill of Rights, freedom of expression, and so on) were more important than the flag itself. Those who opposed flag burning often exhibited violent *signal responses*, such as physically attacking flag burners. The semanticist approach to language is to train senders and receivers to be continually alert to the difference between signals (signs that accompany and indicate something, such as thunder indicating rain) and symbols that stand for something (for example, the word *hate*, which merely stands for the concept of hatred). Semanticists isolate meaning in concrete terms. For example, suppose I tell you that "College students are conservative, selfish, and lazy." Probably your response will be negative because

FIGURE 4.3

What would a semanticist think of this cartoon? The words *reproach* and *beneath contempt* might be likely to prompt a signal response? Why? (*Frank and Ernest* reprinted by permission of NEA, Inc.)

of the potential negative connotations of the word *conservative* and because of the clear negativity of the words *selfish* and *lazy*. I certainly would not be establishing much common ground with you either, so probably my persuasive attempts would be doomed. One of the problems is that the words *college students* imply that I mean *all* college students are conservative, selfish, and lazy. If you were face-to-face with me, you might respond with a similar sentence relating to left-wing, ivory-tower, egghead professors and how much money they make for how little work they actually do, and we would be off on an argument. Neither of us would be *communicating with* one another but instead would be *communicating at* one another. Persuasion by either side would be nearly impossible. Semanticists would advise both of us to use what they call **extensional devices**, techniques for getting outside of the emotional connotations that often accompany words.[8] These devices were suggested by Korzybski as ways to avoid misunderstandings and to be more specific and concrete. Using extensional devices helps us avoid making signal responses — responding to the words *conservative* and *lazy* as if they were the territory and not just an idosyncratic map in my head.

One extensional device I could use to modify my language would be to identify the specific college students I have in mind. This is called **indexing**. In this case I would alter my statement to something like "College students who have everything paid for by their parents are conservative, selfish, and lazy." That would calm down some of you — at least a little — because you probably know fellow students who get everything paid for, including lots of extras you don't get. But I still would not be as clear as I could be, according to the semanticists.

They would further urge me to use an extensional device called **dating**, or letting you know the time frame of my judgment about college students. Using dating, I would alter my sentence further by saying something like "College students of the nineties who have everything paid for by their parents are conservative, selfish, and lazy." That would cool you down more, unless, of course, you are a college student whose expenses are paid for by their parents. Here is where the extensional device semanticists call **Etc.** comes into play. This device is meant to indicate that I can never tell the *whole story* about any person, event, place, or thing. Using this device, I would alter my sentence to something like "College students who have everything paid for by their parents are conservative, selfish, and lazy, *among other things*." Now I have suggested that conservativism, selfishness, and laziness aren't the students' only attributes. For example, they also might be "societally concerned about environmental issues," "concerned about honesty," or any of a number of other positive attributes.

Finally, Korzybski and his colleagues advised using an extensional device they called **quotation marks**, a way to indicate that I am using those flag words in a particular way — my way — which isn't necessarily your way. For example, my meaning of the word "selfish" might relate to the students' unwillingness to help other students succeed in class. Or it could mean their unwillingness to get involved in volunteer experiences for the good of the community, or any one of a number of meanings that wouldn't necessarily match your meaning for the word "selfish." Now my sentence might read "College students of the nineties who have everything paid for by their parents are 'conservative,' 'selfish,' and 'lazy,' among other things." Now how would you react to the sentence? You probably would probe for my meanings for the emotional words, or you might even agree with me if your meanings for those words were similar to mine.

The end result of using extensional devices is to make the "maps" in our heads more closely resemble the "territory" to which we are referring. It would be wise for persuaders to design careful, specific, and concrete extensional messages, especially when using emotionally charged words or abstract words for which there can be many meanings — but frequently they don't. Abstract words such as *power, democracy, freedom, morals*, and *truth* are particularly vulnerable to misunderstanding. And as pointed out earlier, frequently unethical persuaders intentionally use abstract or emotionally charged language to achieve their purposes. As a result, as ethical persuadees or receivers, it is our task to remember the map/territory distinction and use the extensional devices as we listen for the uses and misuses of symbols in interpersonal communication (such as gossip), public communication (as in sermons and speeches), and, most important, in mass communication (such as advertising). We must remember that as receivers, we too have "response-ability."

Advertising as a Map

Of all the forms of persuasion to which we are exposed each day, none has the potential for more map/territory misunderstanding than contemporary advertising. Its overwhelming abundance alone makes this likely. It comes to us via television and radio spots, newspaper and magazine ads, direct mail, catalogs, billboards, the "shelf talkers" at the supermarket, packaging of all kinds, and on brochures, matchbooks, balloons, t-shirts, and a host of other media too numerous to mention. For example, "spots" are now inserted into rental videotapes; there is talk of using videotape cases as advertising space for local fast-food franchises, delivery services, and other products; and computer networks use their "bulletin boards" for personal "advertising."

Someone once defined an advertising executive as a person who comes to work in the morning to find a molehill on his or her desk and who has to turn it into a mountain by quitting time. In other words, the goal of most advertising is to exaggerate the benefits of a product, candidate, service, idea, or organization and to avoid mentioning the shortcomings of that product, person, or idea.

Advertisements are really "maps" for whatever is being promoted. For example, consider Figure 4.4. In recent years, with the increase in two-wage-earner families, sewing one's own clothing has decreased, and buying ready-to-wear clothes has increased — especially clothes purchased via catalogs.

In an attempt to counteract the decrease in home sewing, the American Home Sewing Association launched a campaign to promote sewing and to give it a new image. No longer was sewing promoted as a way to save money, as Figure 4.4 demonstrates. The ads/maps conveyed the message that sewing is "wild," "sexy," and "provocative" — words that one wouldn't necessarily associate with this activity. Notice too what else the ads do: They use wild, sexy, and provocative models wearing relatively wild, sexy, and provocative outfits. Further, the detailed copy promises that sewing will make you "a master of fashion, not a slave to it"; it will make you "one of a kind,

FIGURE 4.4a

Is sewing really sexy?

FIGURE 4.4b

Or provocative?

not one of the crowd"; and if you sew a miniskirt that's "drop dead short," you can be "as daring as you dare." To top it off and get you into a fabric store and back into sewing, they are willing to give you a designer hatbox with $15 worth of sewing accessories for only $9.95. Wow! What an offer!

Now is the time to remind yourself of the reality of sewing — the true "territory": Sewing is frequently frustrating (if a seam doesn't come out just so), time consuming (especially if you are going to create the outfits worn by the models), and some-

times boring. And of course the same could be said for the subjects of thousands of other ads that inundate us during the course of our daily lives.

THE PSYCHOLINGUISTIC APPROACH TO LANGUAGE USE

As its name implies, the **psycholinguistic approach** to language combines two major avenues of investigation into human behavior. These are

SEWING IS...

WILD

Sewing makes you one of a kind...a master of fashion, not a slave to it. That's the magic of sewing. For everything you want, visit your fabric store and bring home an original! DESIGNER HATBOX OFFER! SAVE UP TO $40! Designer hatbox with sewing notions—regular $50 value...only $9.95 with $10 purchase at your participating fabric stores.

American Home Sewing Association
1375 Broadway, New York, N.Y. 10018

FIGURE 4.4c

Or wild? Or are these words maps for nonexistent territory?
(Used by permission of American Home Sewing Association.)

the *psychological approach*, whereby we try to discover or sense human motivation, and the *linguistic approach*, whereby we try to discover patterns in language use. These ideally lead us to a pattern or a set of rules to explain why people communicate in certain ways.

The combining of these two approaches came about following the rise of the behavioral and social sciences in the 1950s. Language use was treated as an indicator of what is going on in the psyche. An interesting example of how such research and study is done is the work of Charles Osgood, a noted language researcher.[9] Osgood wanted to find out whether there were any differences in the linguistic styles used in two kinds of suicide notes — those written by people who were asked to construct an imaginary suicide note and those written by people who actually had attempted suicide. He found that although most of the pretend suicide notes contained similarities to the real suicide notes, certain language or stylistic features in the real notes were different. These included the proportion of certain parts of speech (nouns and adjectives were used more frequently than verbs and adverbs in the real notes, for example), and the organization or disorganization of the words. The sentences in the authentic suicide notes were shorter, and they contained more errors and explosive segments. The point is that the writers' psychological states were reflected in their verbal styles. This offers support for the basic premise of psycholinguistics: Our underlying, or subconscious, motives, fears, or intentions can be reflected outwardly in our use of words.

Other theorists look carefully at the sentence structure people use, or the phrases they repeat. Most of us do this kind of language analysis almost unconsciously. That is why comedians who imitate actors, politicians, and other public figures can impress audiences with their mimicry. They combine language patterns with nonverbal gestures and facial expressions typical of the person they are imitating.

The following curious letter was actually sent to the chairperson of my department several years ago. (I have removed the name of its author and other identifying information.) Read it and then, for practice, try to determine what the writer was like. For example, on the basis of language and style used, see whether you think the person was a male or a female. Did he or she come from an urban or a rural background? Would this person be likely to pledge a fraternity or sorority? How bright is the author? What kinds of entertainment would he or she prefer? What kinds of books? What kinds of clothing? What political beliefs?

Although you won't be able to approach style with the same scientific precision that Osgood used as he analyzed the real and bogus suicide notes, you will be training yourself to pick up hints of motives, attitudes, and intentions that are scattered through a persuader's style. The writer of the letter is asking to be exempted from taking the basic speech fundamentals course.

Dear Professor Jones,

I am interested in directives as to how one may proficiency out of the speech requirement. Having been advised to seek counsel from you "specifically" — I sincerely hope you will not be displeased with my enthusiasm by asking this indulgence. There is a basis for my pursuing this inquisition as I am an adept speaker with substantiating merits. I will be overburdened with more difficult courses this fall — at least they will be concomitant with my educational objectives in the fields of Fine Arts and Languages. It would be a ludicrous exercise in futility to be mired in an unfecund speech course when I have already distinguished myself in that arena. I maintained an "A" average in an elite "advanced" speech course in High School. I am quite noted for my bursts of oratory and my verbal dexterity in the public "reality" — quite a different platform than the pseudo realism of the college environs. There is a small matter of age — I shall be twenty-two this fall. I am four years older than the average college freshman. I am afraid that I would dissipate with boredom, if confined with a bunch of teenagers. Surely you can advise something that would be a more palatable alternative?

Yours sincerely,

P.S. Please do not misconstrue this "inquiry" as the enterprise of an arrogant student, but one who will be *so* immersed in serious intellectual pursuits that the "speech" requirement will be *too* nonsensical and burdensome.

If ever a student needed to know about communication, it was this person.[10] But what does the language usage here tell you about the writer of the letter? She uses sixty-four-dollar words — perhaps a clue to insecurity — but she seems unsure about her choice of words: Several times she puts words into quotation marks. She says that she is pursuing an "inquisition" when she means an "inquiry." (An inquisition is a tribunal for suppressing religious heresy.) She says she has "substantiating merits" when she probably means that she has "substantial reasons" for being excused from the course.

Now, whether your analysis was accurate or not, it is clear that we all make judgments about others on the basis of their use of language — especially their stylistic choices. A problem with doing so, however, is that we can make mistakes like those you probably made in regard to that student's letter. It's easy to misassess others, because we seldom go about our analysis very systematically.

Some of the tools we will look at should help you become more systematic as you listen to the language used by others and attempt to identify their motives, and as you select your own language in persuading others. The right selection can make the difference between success and failure. Even the choice of the definite article versus the indefinite article can make a great difference. For example, psychologist Elizabeth Loftus studied the difference between trial witnesses who were asked "Did you see *the* broken headlight?" instead of "Did you see *a* broken headlight?" Those asked the first question responded with more certainty than those asked the second, and they were "twice as likely to remember a broken headlight even when there was none."[11] (Saying "*the* broken headlight" implies that one existed.) Another researcher who looked at language choice in the courtroom found that witnesses who used a tentative style (words such as "I think" or "maybe" or "it seems that") or who used intensifiers (words such as "very close friends" instead of "close friends") were seen as less competent, believable, and intelligent than speakers who used a more powerful style.[12]

LANGUAGE AND POWER

As you can see from the preceding discussion, language can change people's perceptions of reality and even their motivations for buying products, voting, joining, or supporting ideological causes.

Language also has the ability to *empower*. A simple example: A person labeled a "college junior" has "power" over a "college freshman," because the freshman has to wait to register for classes until the demands by upperclassmen have been met. What's more, juniors can speak with more authority than freshmen, at least about campus affairs. The use of language to *name* or to define also confers power in companies, where "salaried employees" are more powerful than "hourly workers," where those with "seniority" have more power than those without it, and where some departments, such as "marketing," have more power than others, such as "personnel." President Bush gained power over Michael Dukakis in the 1988 election by saying that he was not a "big spender" who would raise taxes. Bush also charged that Dukakis was a poor steward of the environment, had raised taxes, and had run an unsuccessful prisoner furlough program, which then resulted in more crime. These examples show how the power of language to assign a name or definition can be persuasive.

According to communication scholar Andrew A. King, our culture also has a set of myths about how language use can result in shifts in perceived power. For example, powerful people supposedly speak more slowly than powerless persons, talk more in groups than do powerless persons, and take more turns at talking. One's vocabulary and dialect can also empower.[13] Thus, as we analyze persuasive appeals, we need to examine not only the type of language being used but how it is being used as well.

Language can also be a tool of power when it is used to *characterize* or to define the terms of an issue. In this instance, certain ideas, persons, or institutions can be downplayed and even terminated by language uses. For example, characterizing a public relations staff as "latter-day appendages" can negatively affect their futures. Calling a certain service a "frill" can negate it. Declaring that the seniority system is "antiquated" can diminish its power. Claiming that certain data are valid only in a specific circumstance reduces the power of evidence. If, for example, a corporate polluter claims that evidence of an increase in sulfur dioxide in the air is only a ten-year trend, he invalidates the evidence. Name-calling, or the *ad hominem* argument, is another way to characterize an opponent so as to reduce his or her power. For example, calling a politician "soft on crime," a "Johnny-come-lately," or "unethical" can reduce the candidate's power.

On the other hand, language can mythologize a speaker and hence give him or her power. Characterizing a senator as the "pioneer" or "guiding light" of the reform movement empowers him or her. Products are characterized as being "first" with front wheel drive, or described as "biodegradable" or made with "natural" ingredients. These characterizations create credibility and power. In 1990, the Florida courts tried to ban the rap group "2 Live Crew" by characterizing their album "As Nasty as They Wanna Be" as obscene. This tactic, however, failed to reduce the group's power and actually increased the album's sales.[14] Thus another aspect to consider when examining persuasive language is how it is used to *characterize* persons, practices, products, ideas or institutions.

Combining the power of language with emotion-evoking visual images can also empower, as is seen in advertising. King notes that advertising is able to create power by merging verbal texts or language and images:

> Advertising works through merger. It forges a connection between the external world of affairs and the private world of wishes and fantasies. The act of purchase becomes the means of operationalizing one's values, expresses one's personal aesthetic, enacts one's deepest beliefs, asserts one's identity. Raw desire, need for belongingness, and fear of loss are its levers of persuasion.[15]

Notice how the ads for "Obsession" perfume, for example, merge language and imagery to empower a product and its users. The product name — "Obsession" — signifies passion. The visual imagery includes perfectly proportioned nude men and women posed as Greek gods and goddesses. The word merged with the images empowers the product to promise a certain life-style.

Calvin Klein forbids reprinting of the "Obsession" ads in other publications (such as textbooks) and thus further empowers the ads by making them scarce. According to King, the visual in successful advertising (in this case the sensuous scenes and the Calvin Klein models) is

> implicit, mythic, and energizing. It evokes childhood, the haunted past, racial memory, buried ideals, nameless fears, unrealized aspirations and dreams. Its emotional tug is stinging sharp and at the same time deep as the roots of the race.[16]

On the other hand, the verbal language of the ad (in this case the name of the product and the words "For Men" or "For Women") is

> hot and specific. It is a vector of force, channeling and directing the image into a resolution, an explicit and limited act.[17]

This merging of the specific language and the vague promise of the visual create great appeal and persuasive power.

There are other ways in which language can empower or, conversely, disempower products, candidates, and ideas. As receivers, we need to explore the issue of language and power as we try to identify the persuasive strategies and tactics persuaders use to move us to action and change.

THE SEMIOTIC APPROACH TO LANGUAGE AND MEANING

Another approach to the study of language and meaning is **semiotics**, or, as Arthur Asa Berger puts it in his book *Signs in Comtemporary Society*, "the 'science of signs' and of the codes used to understand them."[18] The word "sign" means one thing to semioticians and another to semanticists. To the semiotician, a sign is a larger category and contains both sign(al)s and symbols as they are used in language and as other conveyors of meaning (for example, color, surroundings, clothing, and many others — frequently nonverbal). In order to distinguish the two ways of using these words,

we will follow the approach of the semiologists and use "signifier" and "signified" instead. Thus the word "running" as a *signifier* can refer to various *signified* things — running for political office, water running in a stream, a nose running, running a footrace, getting your car running, running a nylon stocking, and others.

According to semiologists, the only way we can understand how a word is being used is to see it not only in a sentence but also from the perspective of the culture or subculture in which it is used. The receiver or communication analyst therefore investigates context, nonverbal aspects of the word, and other culturally imposed patterns.

For example, the first time I went to visit relatives in Sweden, I tried to call them long-distance from Copenhagen to tell them when I would be arriving. I made my request of the operator and then heard the Swedish operator "take over" the call from the Danish operator with the words "ett ögonblick," which I correctly translated as "one eyeblink." At first thought, the words seemed nonsensical. Then I recalled that an operator in America might say "just a minute" or "one moment" or something similar. I was bound for a moment by my culturally imposed set(s) for deciphering meaning.

Semiology takes culture into account as well as many other patterns that affect meaning. One such pattern is what semioticians call "the code," or the way of discovering or translating meaning. A simple code is the use of black and white hats in old cowboy movies to indicate who is the good guy and who is the bad guy. Recall in old movies the filmic code of pages being blown off a calendar to indicate the passage of time. A third example of a code might be the type of cup a person uses for his coffee at the dorm or on the job. What meanings are conveyed by drinking out of mugs as opposed to styrofoam cups or fine china? Each type of cup is a signifier, and each coffee drinker, consciously or unconsciously, on purpose or by accident, is conveying a different kind of message. Yet words aren't even involved. In a semiotic approach to the study of meaning, we try to "read" each message from several perspectives: from the words that are or are not spoken, from the context in which or from which they are spoken, and from the other signifiers included in and with the message — visuals, colors, tone of voice, and so on.

The semiotician approaches any communication event as if it were a "text" to be "read" by the receiver/analyst. Berger and others use an interesting analogy in explaining this approach at uncovering meaning. He likens the semiotic receiver to the famous detective Sherlock Holmes, who "reads" an event, a room, or a piece of evidence analytically, often uncovering meaning from the smallest detail.[19] Berger's example comes from one of Holmes's most famous cases, "The Blue Carbuncle," in which Holmes deduces that the owner of a hat lost at the scene of a crime is "highly intellectual," "fairly well off within the past three years although he has now fallen upon evil days. He had foresight, but has less now than formerly." The hat owner has also had a "moral retrogression — probably drink," and though his wife has ceased to love him, he still retains some self-respect. Furthermore, according to Holmes, the owner of the hat is a person "who leads a sedentary life, goes out little, is out of training entirely, is middle-aged, has grizzled hair which he has had cut within the last few days and which he anoints with lime cream" and, finally, he has not yet put gas lights in his home.

Poor old Dr. Watson is baffled as to how his companion can "get" these meanings "out of the hat." As ever, Holmes explains how "elementary" his conclusions are: Because the hat is large, "a man with so large a brain must have something in it." Though of the best quality, the hat is three years old, indicating that the man hasn't had the money to buy a new one, implying the decline of his fortunes. He had special ordered a "hat securer" installed, so he must have had foresight, but because it has been broken and not repaired, there has been "moral retrogression," according to Holmes. The hair ends on the band indicate a recent haircut. The hat smells of lime cream; it has house dust, not street dust, on it, indicating the man doesn't go out much and that his wife has stopped loving him (if she loved him, she would

dust his hat). Finally, the hatband is sweaty, indicating that the owner is out of shape, and a wax spot on the hat indicates that the owner uses candlelight, not gas lights.

In this case, Holmes is semiotically analyzing the hat by observing the many details an ordinary person would overlook. He sees "structure" where there apparently is none by observing and relating signifiers and searching for a pattern. The responsible receiver of persuasive messages needs to act likewise whenever possible.

This is especially so for the future, because more and more marketing and advertising research is being conducted from a semiological approach, according to Curt Suplee of the *Washington Post*.[20] He quotes advertising/design celebrity George Lois as saying, "When advertising is great advertising, it fastens on the myths, signs, and symbols of our common experience and becomes, quite literally, a benefit of the product. . . . As a result of great advertising, food tastes better, clothes feel snugger, cars ride smoother. The stuff of semiotics becomes the magic of advertising."[21] Sounds a lot like Aristotle's "common ground" or the "co-creation of meaning" noted in Chapter 1, doesn't it?

Here is a description of a semiotically designed ad created by the Webb and Ethey ad agency for the Perpetual American Bank, which had a big recognition problem in the Washington, D.C. area: "An oddly modern-faced caveman is running across a barren rockscape. He is breathing hard, glancing around as if fearing pursuit. Finally he comes to a ledge and leaps . . . to become a snugly space-suited astronaut floating above the earth." The voice-over for these actions says, "You don't need a bank that keeps pace. You need a bank that sets it. Perpetual. What your bank is going to be."[22] Now see if you can semiotically "read" the meaning in that ad. Compare your reading with what its designers have to say about it in this explanation by account executive Mark McMullen: In order to suggest that the bank is forward looking and pace setting, "we show early man — by analogy the viewer and his 'primitive' banking system — and the various things he has to react to.

Then we show him taking a literal leap of faith" into the future with Perpetual as his bank. Did it work? How many of you can recall the sponsor's name and that this ad was an ad for a bank? Why is that?[23]

REVIEW AND CONCLUSION

The goal of Chapter 4 was to give you a deeper understanding of symbol making, symbol using, and symbol mis-using. Perhaps you now realize how much you can discover when you begin to critically analyze persuasive symbols, both verbal and nonverbal. It takes some time and care to discover a "code," a "map," or a "signifier," and as a responsible receiver you need tools of analysis. Chapter 5 will try to give you such tools so you will be able to identify and decode the various kinds of persuasive symbols and messages you encounter each day.

QUESTIONS FOR FURTHER THOUGHT

1. Why is symbol making such a powerful human activity? Give several examples of how symbols create high involvement in people.

2. What is meant by Burke's phrase "symbol misusing"? Give some examples of the misuse of symbols.

3. What is the difference between a "map" and a "territory" according to the general semanticists? What is an example of one of your food maps? One of your geographic maps? One of your experience maps?

4. What is a "signal response"? Give several examples.

5. What are the extensional devices recommended by general semanticists? What purpose do these devices serve? Give examples.

6. What is the psycholinguistic approach to the study of language symbols? Give some examples of how it is used.

7. How can language empower people, products, and ideological causes? Give several examples of each kind of empowerment.

8. How can language destroy or disempower people, products, or ideological causes? Give examples.

NOTES

1. Kenneth Burke, *Language as Symbolic Action* (Berkeley: University of California Press, 1986).

2. Susanne K. Langer, *Philosophy in a New Key* (New York: New American Library, 1951).

3. "Periscope" *Newsweek*, June 4, 1990, p. 8.

4. "Periscope" *Newsweek*, July 2, 1990, p. 6.

5. "You Are What You Buy," *Newsweek*, June 4, 1990, p. 60.

6. Alfred Korzybski, *Science and Sanity* (Lakeville, CT: The Non-Aristotelean Library, 1947).

7. Asa Baber, "Men," *Playboy*, April 1990, p. 40.

8. Robert Potter, *Making Sense* (New York: Globe, 1974).

9. Charles Osgood, "Some Effects of Encoding upon Style of Encoding," in *Style in Language*, ed. T. A. Sebeok (Cambridge: MIT Press, 1960).

10. To determine how right or wrong you might be about the student who wrote this letter, here is what we do know about *her*. Yes — the writer was female. She lived on a farm, as the letter gave a rural route box number in a nearby farming community. And the student never attended NIU.

11. As quoted in Lori B. Andrews, "Exhibit A: Language," *Psychology Today*, February 1984, p. 30.

12. *Ibid.*, p. 31.

13. Andrew A. King, *Power and Communication* (Prospect Heights: Waveland Press, 1987). pp. 15–16.

14. "The Importance of Being Nasty," *Newsweek*, July 2, 1990.

15. King, *op. cit.*, pp. 80-81.

16. *Ibid.*, p. 81.

17. *Ibid.*

18. Arthur Asa Berger, *Signs in Contemporary Society* (New York: Longman and Sons, 1984). p. ix.

19. *Ibid*., pp. 16–18. See also Thomas A. Sebeok and Jean Umiker-Sebeok, "You Know My Method: A Juxtaposition of Charles S. Pierce and Sherlock Holmes," *Semiotica* 26:3–4, 1979, and Arthur Asa Berger, *Media Analysis Techniques* (Beverly Hills, CA: Sage Publications, 1982), especially Chapter 1.

20. Curt Suplee, "Semiotics: In Search of More Perfect Persuasion," *Washington Post*, January 18, 1987, "Outposts" sec., pp. 1–3.

21. *Ibid*., p. 3.

22. *Ibid*.

23. *Ibid*.

CHAPTER

5

Tools for Analyzing Language and Other Symbols

SYMBOLIC EXPRESSION AND PERSUASIVE LANGUAGE

Having gained some perspective on the making, using, and misusing of symbols, we can now turn to ways in which we can critically process and analyze persuasive symbols. We begin our introduction to the tools of analysis by looking at several dimensions of language. In Figure 5.1, language is represented as a cube containing all the various qualities that words and sentences can carry to and elicit from the listener. There are several dimensions along which certain types of meaning can be charted. One dimension charts the possible meanings that a word or a series of words can have: the **semantic dimension**. Another charts the purposes the words serve in the sen-

tence: the **functional dimension**. For example, certain words name things, others connect ideas, some activate, and still others are used by speakers or writers to devalue their opponents. In the third dimension, the **thematic dimension**, combinations that result from word choice and give us the texture or the feel of the phrase are charted. For example, most people derive a soft, slithery, smooth association from the slogan "Feel Black Velvet."

Consider this line of copy from a magazine advertisement: "Sudden Tan from Coppertone tans on touch for a tan that lasts for days."[1] On the *functional dimension*, the words "Sudden Tan" name a product. *Semantically*, however, much more is involved. The word *sudden* indicates that the tan is almost instantaneous, and indeed this is a major advantage of the product — it dyes your skin on contact to look tanned. The ad's headline is reinforced by the semantic meaning of the word *sudden*, as is the photo over which the words are printed. The headline is "Got a Minute? Get a Tan." The photo shows before-and-after pictures of an attractive blonde woman who has been (presumably) dyed tan by the product.

On a *textural*, or *thematic*, level, the words that name the product do even more. The word *sudden* sounds or feels like the word *sun*, so the product name sounds like the word *suntan*. The *s* and *t* sounds are repeated in the line of copy, reinforcing the notion of suntan. Try to describe how the message would make you feel if the meanings of the words disappeared and only their sounds remained.

Here are some more examples of the thematic, or textural, qualities language can have: The Presto Corporation named its new corn popper The Big Poppa! in the hope that our minds would establish a thematic link with the sounds of popping corn while we chuckle at the takeoff on the familiar "Big Daddy" cliché and the popper/poppa play on words. A well-established cleaning product suggests that it will save you work — Lestoil is its name. A product associated with the energy shortage is the Kero-Sun heater, which burns kerosene and warms your house like the sun. You can have a Soup-erb Supper with a package

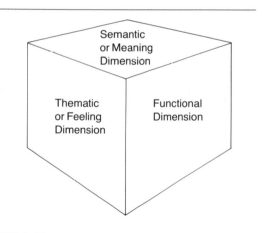

FIGURE 5.1

This figure is based on a description of a model for meaning suggested by Charles E. Osgood, George J. Suci, and Percy H. Tannenbaum in *The Measurement of Meaning* (Urbana, IL: University of Illinois Press, 1957). They suggest that semantic meaning for any word or concept can be located by charting it in "semantic space" using the *semantic differential*, a tool whereby receivers respond to a word, phrase, or concept along several polar scales. Each end of the scale represents an adjectival description (for example, good/bad or heavy/light). The cube here expands such charting to include two other attributes/functions and the "feel," or *motif*, of words. An investigator could add other axes to chart the sexual, aggressive, dialectical, or other qualities of a particular symbol.

of Hamburger Helper's beef-vegetable soup. And then there is the product that will make every woman Smooth, Soft, and Sexy.

The Functional Dimension: What Do the Words Do?

Words have jobs. We traditionally group these jobs into grammatical classes — nouns, verbs, adjectives, adverbs, prepositions, conjunctions, interjections, and so on. We all have memorized some of the definitions of these — for example, "A noun is the name of a person, place, thing, or idea." It would be impossible for us to diagram all the sentences we hear, but diagraming might show a preferred pattern of sentence structure or a tendency to use certain words or word classes more frequently than others. Such preferred patterns are normal for most speakers but tell us little about the source. We need a way to answer the question "What are the words doing *in this message*?" On this level, we are interested in the *form* of the message, not the *content*. Consider the following example: "Some Leaders Are Born Women." The sentence does a surprise syntactical (functional) reversal on the old chestnut "Some Men Are Born Leaders." The functional aspects of the message are in reverse order. The substitution of words is a semantic shift that also catches our attention. In this example, then, we are looking at what words can do (*functional meaning*).

Persuaders want their messages to perform at least three jobs:

1. Identify, or locate, an issue or topic.
2. Assign a cause or a cure for a problem associated with the issue.
3. Motivate the audience to take action.

These three functions — identification, assignment of cause or cure, and motivation — are served by language, or words. Look at them as you are being persuaded. Where is the persuader taking you? How is the issue located? What words assign cause? What motivational technique is being used?

Return for a moment to the research on language use in the courtroom to see how much influence the functional dimension can have. In the trial of a physician charged with manslaughter in a case involving a late abortion, the defense attorney repeatedly used passive verbs or verbs as nouns to blunt the accusations. For example, the attorney referred to previous attempts to abort the fetus by saying, "after two unsuccessful attempts." The prosecutor used active verbs and identifying nouns, saying, "they tried twice . . . they were unsuccessful," to focus the blame directly on the doctor.[2] In the one case, the function of the words was to blunt the accusation; in the other, to focus the blame on the doctor and mother. The functional dimension has powerful persuasive potential; if nothing else, it can simply shift our focus.

The Semantic Dimension: What Do the Words Mean?

The semantic dimension focuses on the various shadings of meaning that can be given to certain words. For example, in the same abortion case, the defense succeeded in getting a favorable ruling censoring the use of the words "baby boy" and "human being" and having the word "fetus" substituted throughout the trial. What is the difference in the meaning or connotation of these words? The defense attorney said, "the word 'fetus' mitigates the connotation of aliveness for the 'baby/fetus' in question, thereby distancing the defendant from wrongdoing."[3] Clearly, choosing the word with the proper semantic meaning can be critical for the persuader, and persuadees need to focus on why certain words have been chosen whereas others have not.

Word selection can provide a clue about the source's underlying intentions and, perhaps, believability. For example, mock jurors rated witnesses who used hypercorrect speech as less convincing, less competent, and less intelligent than witnesses who chose less formal words and phrases.[4]

The meaning of a specific word may be critical. In the trial of John Hinckley for his attempted assassination of Ronald Reagan, the jury became confused by the word "poetry" and requested that a dictionary be sent into the deliberation room. The defense had claimed that Hinckley's "bizarre poetry" was evidence of his insanity, thus justifying the request for a verdict of not guilty by reason of insanity. The prosecutor had argued, on the other hand, that all poetry is fiction and that Hinckley's poems just happened to be some "eccentric fiction." Notice the critical difference the two adjectives make. If the poetry is "bizarre," we get a sense of its author living in a fantasy world divorced from reality — perhaps a world of insanity. However, if the poetry is merely "eccentric," its author may be a little odd, but he is certainly not insane. Further, even if the poetry was bizarre, if all poetry is fiction anyway, as a prosecution psychologist had argued, Hinckley still could have been sane when he fired the shots. The jury thought the dilemma could be resolved by a dictionary definition of "poetry." Interestingly, the judge in the trial refused to let the jury have a dictionary sent to them.[5] Although we do not know exactly what happened during the deliberations, the jury's questions and request for the dictionary certainly testify to the importance of the meaning dimension, or the semantic aspect, of language used in persuasion. In all likelihood, there was a lot of discussion in the jury's deliberations on the different shades of meaning between the words "bizarre" and "eccentric."

You may want to experiment with how words can be used and how subtle differences in meaning can occur due to word choice and the semantic dimension of language.

The Thematic Dimension: How Do the Words Feel?

A third question we can ask is: "What unites the words used *in this message*?" "What underlying theme do they suggest?" Answers to these questions depend on the textural qualities of language — the flavors or "feel" of the words used.

Richard Weaver, in *The Ethics of Rhetoric*, noted that style is a process of accumulation.[6] We discover a persuader's style only after listening to it over time. Winston Churchill was one of the best-known persuaders of the first half of the twentieth century. One of the thematic devices of his persuasion was to cast light-dark images, or pictures related to day and night.[7] He always described the Nazis as thugs or "gangsters" engaging in monstrous acts in dark places; on the other hand, he described the English as bright, sturdy, and capable.

More recently, during the 1988 presidential primary campaigns, we witnessed an ironic reversal of events regarding candidate style. Bush's Iowa caucus campaign manager had attacked Senator Robert Dole's wife, Elizabeth, over her financial dealings and a blind trust set up while she served in the Reagan cabinet. In response to questions about the criticisms, Bush said, "There should never be a criticism of somebody's wife. . . . If there were, I would totally apologize here. She's a friend."[8] Then in a highly publicized news interview with Dan Rather in which Bush criticized Rather's earlier walk off the news set, he again let slip an unseemly comment when he said that Rather "makes Leslie Stahl [anchor of CBS's *Face the Nation*] look like a pussy!"[9] The comment was recorded on tape and was leaked like a reference to vice-presidential candidate Geraldine Ferraro had been just four years earlier. What does this say about Bush's verbal style? Might it be a reliable indication of his attitude toward women? Bush was forced to apologize to numerous women's groups, explaining he had only meant that Stahl was as harmless as "a pussy cat."[10] Interestingly enough, Bush was the big loser in the Iowa caucuses a few weeks later.

These examples should alert you to one of the abilities you already have, an ability based on your years as a language user. Because you are a regular language user — sending and receiving — you have had to learn to be a somewhat critical listener. All we need to do to improve your abilities is to provide you with some tools to make your various analyses more systematic. Consider the language used in each of the following presidential campaign slogans or catch-phrases:

1960: The New Frontier (John F. Kennedy)

1964: A Great Society (Lyndon B. Johnson)

1968: Bring Us Together *and* Nixon's the One
       (Richard M. Nixon)

1972: Re-Elect the President (Richard M.
       Nixon)

1976: Leadership — For a Change (Jimmy
       Carter)
       I'm Feeling Good about America
       (Gerald Ford)

1980: Together — A New Beginning (Ronald
       Reagan)

1984: Leadership — That Works (Ronald
       Reagan)

1988: Experienced Leadership: For America's
       Future (George Bush)

How would you go about interpreting each of these slogans, considering what they seem to mean? The problem is to choose a method of analysis that allows you to proceed objectively. You should experiment with several methods and then work out your own. Your goal is to take apart the persuasion directed at you and to look behind the words for some indication of what the persuader is like.

Return to the presidential slogans. Offhand, what can we say about them? Well, we can first describe their structure and form — the functional dimension. Kennedy used a three-word descriptive phrase: a definite article, "the," an adjective, "new," and a noun, "frontier." Johnson also had a three-word descriptive phrase containing an article, an adjective, and a noun. It differs from the Kennedy slogan in that its article is indefinite (the word "a" denotes one of several, whereas the word "the" refers to the only one). One 1968 Nixon slogan has self-centered qualities — "Nixon's the One." The other 1968 Nixon phrase is not descriptive — it is imperative (it gives an order for action, not a description of a situation). It begins with a verb, "bring," followed by a pronoun, "us," and ends with an adverb, "together." Nixon followed this pattern again in 1972: The word order is imperative — "Re-Elect the President." This imperative too shows an obsession with the self. This time there is no collective pronoun, and the order has shifted direction. In 1968, it was an order from the people to the candidate.

By 1972, the order is from the candidate to the people. The 1972 slogan provides a tip-off to Nixon's attitude and motivation: He *is* the president and the people are beneath him, subject to his commands. Moreover, there is no longer a candidate to be elected or defeated; instead, there is an office to be verified. The candidate has become the office and has ceased to have an individual personality. The Ford slogan is the longest; it describes a personal feeling. The winning slogan for that year (Carter's) was "Leadership — For a Change."

Reagan's 1980 slogan "Together — A New Beginning," is similar in its structure to the 1976 Carter/Mondale slogan: "Leadership — For a Change." Both slogans operate from a cause-effect perspective. The cause is first stated — either "Leadership" or "Together." These words stand as complete thoughts in themselves, as indicated by the use of the dash. Then the effects these causes will have are described, again in a kind of single thought. In the Reagan slogan, the cause (togetherness) will produce "A New Beginning," which carries several possible meanings. In some ways, the phrase suggests going back to square one and getting the engine of state back on track.

Consider the following description of an ad from the 1988 election campaign — a positive "image ad" on behalf of George Bush titled "The Future."

The ad begins with a black screen. The words "The Future" dissolve onto the screen, which then dissolves to a little girl running in slow motion in a meadow. She has golden curls and blue eyes. There is heroic music playing with the visuals. The camera freezes as the little girl's eye catches the sunlight. The camera is using a starburst filter, which gives the effect of a five-pointed star of light coming from the little girl's eyes. The voice of George Bush is heard giving his acceptance speech. He begins, "I want a kinder gentler America" as the starburst dissolves to convention hall and the cheering crowds. Suddenly, there are many bursts of light as the filter picks up all of the flashbulbs going off. The announcer's voice says, "It is the President who defines the character of America." The screen now dissolves to Bush at the speaker's podium waving at the cheering crowds. As his face dissolves to a typical kitchen scene, Bush says, "I'm a quiet man, but I hear the quiet people others don't . . . ," and we see Bush in the kitchen scooping corn on the cob from a canning kettle. Bush continues, ". . . the ones who raise the families, pay the taxes . . . ," as the kitchen scene dissolves to a picnic. Bush is seated on the ground eating a hot dog. Children are running up and hugging him. Bush's voice continues, ". . . who meet the mortgage, (pause) and I am moved." The screen has again dissolved back to the convention hall and Bush at the podium. As Bush waves to the crowd, the announcer's voice says, "The President—the heart, the soul, the conscience of the nation," and the screen dissolves back to the original meadow with the little girl being swept up into Bush's arms. She is his granddaughter. He picks her up and lifts her to the blue sky above as the screen dissolves to the words "George Bush—Experienced Leadership for America's Future." Fade to black.

Notice the ad's cyclical nature—it ends where it began—Bush's parallel use of the common person, and the description of the President as "heart, soul, and conscience." The purpose of the message is to get people to feel good about voting for George Bush. The strategy is to show heartwarming and confident shots of the candidate and to let the audience hear and see what kind of person he is. The tactics include all of the symbols—verbal and nonverbal—that are used in the spot. The title, printed on the screen, symbolizes the overall campaign theme of "Experienced Leadership for America's Future." The starbursts and the effect of many rays of light create excitement and a bright outlook on the future. Bush's words about the quiet voices he hears symbolize his promise to be a caring president whose administration will be responsive to the people. The little granddaughter at the start and end of the commercial is the future personified. As Bush lifts her up to the sky, he

symbolically lifts the future of the country. The thematic feeling of the entire ad is uplifting, with the words, music, and visual images working together to provide the thematic texture for "The Future."

We can identify other verbal and nonverbal symbols, acting alone and interacting with one another, to develop the overall meaning of the ad. Even if our interpretation of the ad doesn't match that of the ad's creators, the process of identifying the symbols and trying to interpret what they mean is a positive step in preparing us for responsible reception of persuasion. It can alert us to the uses and misuses of persuasive symbols.

USING SYMBOLIC EXPRESSION

In the case of the campaign ads, we have admittedly been doing amateur psychoanalysis on the basis of the candidates' words. However, given the power of persuasion in our times (remember that if you're eighteen, you've spent whole years of your life watching TV), it is better to be overly skeptical about the persuasion we encounter than to discover painfully and too late that candidates meant all that their slogans implied. Given the power of symbols to motivate peoples and cultures, it is wise to look for the motives the symbols carry.

For example, the kinds of symbols people use and respond to can affect their health. People who use expressions such as "I can't stomach it" or "I'm fed up" or "It's been eating away at me now for a year" have more stomach ulcers than others. The symbols (stomach words) become reality (ulcers) for these people.[11] Symbolic days, such as birthdays, can also have dramatic effects. In nursing homes, more persons die during the two months after their birthday than die during the two months before. Thomas Jefferson and John Adams both died in 1826, precisely on the fourth of July, a date of tremendous significance for both of them.[12] Jefferson is even reported to have awakened from a deathlike coma on July third to ask his doctor if it was the fourth yet.

Some people die soon after the death of a loved one—and from the same disease. In other words, symbolic sympathy pains can become real. In the mid-1970s, Dr. Arnold Mandel, a psychiatrist, reported on an in-depth study of a pro-football team. Hired to try to find out why the team was losing, he found instead that the various players symbolically acted out their on-the-field roles while they were off the field. Wide receivers were narcissistic and always groomed themselves carefully, whereas defensive linemen and linebackers — the destroy boys — had the most run-ins with the law for bar-room brawling and unpaid parking tickets. Quarterbacks saw themselves as saviors of the team on the field and were most likely to hold strong religious beliefs. [13]

Not only do symbols deeply affect individuals but they also serve as a kind of psychological cement for holding a society or culture together. The central symbol for the Oglala Sioux Indians was a sacred hoop representing the four seasons of the Earth and the four directions from which weather might come. In the center of the hoop were crossed thongs that symbolized the sacred tree of life and the crossroads of life. Shortly after the hoop was broken during the Wounded Knee massacre of 1890, the tribe disintegrated. An Oglala wise man named Black Elk explained the symbolic power of the circle for his tribe:

> You have noticed that everything an Indian does is in a circle, and that is because the Power of the World always works in circles, and everything tries to be round. In the old days when we were a strong and happy people, all our power came to us from the sacred hoop of the nation and so long as the hoop was unbroken the people flourished. . . . Everything the Power of the World does is done in a circle. The Sky is round and I have heard that the Earth is round like a ball and so are all the stars. The Wind, in its greatest power, whirls. Birds make their nests in circles, for theirs is the same religion as ours. The sun comes forth and goes down again in a circle. The moon does the same, and both are round. Even the seasons form a great circle in their changing and always come back again to

where they were. The life of a man is a circle from childhood to childhood and so it is in everything where power moves. Our tipis were round like the nests of birds and these were always set in a circle, the nation's hoop, a nest of many nests where the Great Spirit meant for us to hatch our children. [14]

Black Elk believed that the Sioux had lost all their power or medicine when the whites forced the Indians out of their traditional round tepees and into the square houses on the reservation.

What symbols serve as the cultural cement for our way of life? A good place to identify some of the central symbols in our culture is in advertisements. Consider the language and images in Figure 5.2. The word *comfortable* is used three times in the ad. Other value–oriented words or phrases in the ad include *peace, Close to people you value, family, economy, mastered, the art of comfortable living, the unusual*, and *simply treasure the moment*. The ad's visual symbols reinforce the language symbols. The room is comfortable looking — it is a place where you can be warm and relaxed. People read, sip coffee, enjoy good art and classy furniture, and pet their cat in this room. Of course, this is only a brief examination of a single ad, but if further study of other ads confirmed or repeated these values, we could be pretty sure our analysis was valid. Let's consider just a few product slogans. Vantage cigarettes have "The Taste of Success." American Airlines promises to be "Something Special in the Air." The Buick Regal is "World Class" and is "The New Symbol for Quality in America." Hotel Nikko promises "To sustain you," "To refresh you," and "To renew you." The promises add up to Nikko's slogan — "Simply everything . . . simply." Mazda promises a "Minimum Investment" and a "Maximum Yield," because "Mazda — It Just Feels Right." And Realty World gives you "Something

FIGURE 5.2

(Reprinted by permission of Northern Illinois Gas Co.)

The art of comfortable living.

It's a moment, now and then, of peace.

Being warm. Close to the people you value most.

Do you, at these rare times, reflect on what gas heat means to your family?

No. But the fact is, nearly 100% of Northern Illinois homeowners have clean-burning natural gas heating systems fueled by Northern Illinois Gas. And that keeps their homes and their families comfortable.

There is economy, too. A high-efficiency gas furnace can save you over $400 a year compared to an electric heating system.

Clearly, you have mastered the art of comfortable living.

With Northern Illinois Gas providing the energy, you do the unusual.

Simply treasure the moment.

To find out more, call Pat Manning at 1-800-34-NIGAS.

NORTHERN ILLINOIS GAS
*PROVIDING YOU THE ENERGY
TO PERFORM.*

to Believe In" because they are "The Results People."

We can also look to political rhetoric to find symbolic evidence of our cultural values. Since the breakup of the communist world, two important words used by politicians are "freedom" and "equality." As columnist David Broder noted, "Words are important symbols, and . . . 'freedom' and 'equality' have defined the twin guideposts of American Democracy."[15] The words have the thematic qualities to stir patriotic emotions. Interestingly, however, they are not rated the same by all persons. As several sociological researchers have noted, "Socialists rank both words high, while persons with Fascist tendencies rank both low; Communists rank 'equality' high but 'freedom' low and Conservatives rate 'freedom' high but 'equality' low."[16] Broder followed up on his hunches about these two words by counting their frequency in several presidential speeches. He found that Reagan used forms of the word "freedom" forty-four times but forms of "equality" or "equal rights" only twice in the same speeches.[17] What do these thematic word choices tell us? What do they reveal about their users?

It is easy to see that the power of symbols in their semantic and thematic dimensions is considerable. Not only can they reveal motives but they can also affect our self-image and express our cultural ideals and national character. As we turn to examine the functional dimension and how we can take it into account in analyzing the persuasion aimed at us, let's keep this power of the semantic and thematic dimensions in mind. Remember that the cube diagram in Figure 5.1 demonstrates that no single word can be charted in semantic space without referring to all of its various dimensions.

TOOLS FOR THE FUNCTIONAL DIMENSION

We will now consider three functional tools: (1) the "rhetorical aspect of grammatical categories" suggested by philosopher Richard Weaver,

(2) the ways in which word arrangement, or syntax, affects persuasion, and (3) how ambiguity helps in persuasion.

Grammatical Categories

Sentence Structure Weaver said that the grammatical form used by persuaders may indicate their intentions. He argues that sentence structure, for example, may reflect a person's method of using information and of coming to conclusions. The person who uses simple sentences does not see a complex world. As Weaver puts it, such a person "sees the world as a conglomerate of things . . . [and] seeks to present certain things as eminent against a background of matter uniform or flat."[18] The simple sentence sets the subject off from the verb and object; it sees *causes* that *act* to have *effects* on *objects*. When a persuader uses this form, the persuadee ought to look at what is being highlighted, at what affects what, and how action occurs. For example, during the 1988 presidential primary campaigns, television actor Bill Cosby endorsed the Reverend Jesse Jackson in several 10- and 30-second commercials focused on a simple sentence. The words "Bill Cosby for Jesse Jackson" were superimposed over a simply dressed (shirt and sweater) Cosby pictured from the chest up. Cosby said, "Vote for somebody you really want to vote for. Vote for Jesse Jackson."[19] What is featured in the first sentence? That's right—the voter. And in the second sentence the focus is on the candidate. In other words, the voter is in the foreground in the first sentence, and Jesse Jackson is in the foreground in the second sentence.

Complex Sentences The complex sentence features a more complex world—several causes and several effects at the same time. Weaver says that it "is the utterance of a reflective mind" that tries "to express some sort of hierarchy."[20] Persuaders who use complex sentences express basic principles and relationships, with the independent clauses more important than the dependent clauses. For example, consider the following paragraphs from an advertisement run by the Mobil Oil Company in its campaign to get the public to influence Congress to grant more offshore oil leases to the major producers:

> Economic obstacles: It defies all logic to raise the price of already discovered oil through taxes, while denying the oil companies a share of the resulting revenues. The producers will be forced to sell oil from existing wells at far below its replacement cost. Ignored is the fact that today's petroleum exploration and development is growing ever more costly because of the need to explore in remote frontier areas like Alaska or in deep water offshore, and to resort to expensive recovery methods to squeeze more oil from reservoirs. How long could any businessman stay in business if he must sell his inventory at prices substantially lower than he will have to pay to restock? We believe that the social and economic consequences of development are being grossly overestimated by many in Washington and that, as subsequent messages in this series will point out, the social and economic consequences of nondevelopment are being grossly underestimated.[21]

Examine each complex sentence. Look at the first sentence. The clause stating the principle is independent — it can stand alone. The dependent clause (". . . while denying . . .") states the minor message elements. The independent material is higher on the source's ladder of values than the dependent material. That is, it is probably more important to Mobil corporate management that people realize the undesirability of imposing taxes to raise prices on oil already discovered than that profits be questioned. Most people realize that Mobil has a vested interest in getting a share of profits from high-priced oil.

Remember what Weaver said about the use of the simple sentence to depict "the world as a conglomerate" in which certain facts are highlighted against a flat background? Note what Mobil does in the second paragraph: With one exception, all the sentences are simple. The tactic is to rattle off

a series of assertions as if they were absolute truths. This rat-tat-tat style is convincing.

Compound Sentences Weaver says that the compound sentence sets things either in balance (for example, "He ran, and he ran fast") or in opposition (for example, "He ran, but she walked"). It expresses some kind of tension — whether resolved or unresolved. Weaver says it "conveys that completeness and symmetry which the world ought to have, and which we manage to get, in some measure, into our most satisfactory explanations of it."[22] Persuaders who use compound sentences see the world divided into polar opposites or similarities — totally against one another or in concert with one another. The union leader, for example, says, "You are either against us, or you are with us!" and thus oversimplifies a complex world by using a compound sentence.

For example, consider the following sentences from a *New York Times* story about the revitalized Ku Klux Klan. Notice the difference in sentence structure between the paragraphs written by reporter Wendell Rawls and the sentence quoted from an FBI agent.

> *Cullman Ala., Sept. 26. Hidden in the hills of Northern Alabama, a small contingent of Ku Klux Klansmen, and a woman, are training to become commandos prepared to provide security at Klan rallies and to kill black people in "the race war that's coming," their leader says. . . . FBI officials in Birmingham acknowledge that they are watching the activities of this Klan group. "Of all the Klan groups, this is the most unpredictable" an agent said, "and I guess that would make them potentially the most dangerous."*[23]

The reporter used the complex sentence, thus setting up a hierarchy of importance to be attached to the various parts of his sentence. The independent elements contain the heart of the story — that KKK members are training to kill blacks. The less important parts are dependent and rank lower on the hierarchy of importance. Later in the story a Mr. Hadley, who is the Imperial Klaliff or vice-president of the Klan group, is also quoted. Note that he uses the simple sentence.

> The 35-year-old sheet metal worker said he is not active in the unit because he is recovering from back surgery and is receiving a disability pension. "I have a lot of time to think and plan for the white race," he said.[24]

The world is indeed simple to Mr. Hadley, and he sees himself and his group as the cause of many future actions that he believes will benefit his race. So in this example we can see all three kinds of sentences operating, and we can speculate about the kinds of persons who frame these sentences.

Word Choice and Function Weaver also had some observations about types of words. For example, nouns, because they are thought of as words for things and as labels for naming, are often reacted to *as if they were the things they name*. They "express things whose being is completed, not whose being is in process, or whose being depends upon some other being."[25] Thus, when someone calls his or her enemy a pig, he or she makes the enemy into an object—a thing. It is easy to spit on a pig. The pig is an object; the police officer is a person with a family and feelings. One of the functions of a noun is to label something as we want it to be. Looking at persuaders' nouns may clue us as to their perceptions of things. They may also reveal what the persuader intends to do about those things. When persuaders reduce persons to things or objects, they do it for a reason: They indicate their desire to deal with people as things, not as people.

The function of adjectives is to add to the noun, to make it special. To Weaver, adjectives are second-class citizens. He called them "question begging" and said that they showed an uncertain persuader. If you have to modify a noun, Weaver would say you are not certain about the noun. In Weaver's opinion, the only adjectives that are not uncertain are *dialectical* (good and bad, hot and cold, light and dark). Examining adjectives used by persuaders may reveal what the persuaders are uncertain about, and what they see in opposition to what.

Adverbs, to Weaver, are words of *judgment*. Unlike adjectives, they represent a community judgment—one with which others can agree and which reflects what the persuader thinks the audience believes. For example, adverbs such as "surely," "certainly," or "probably" suggest agreement. When persuaders say, "Surely we all know and believe that thus-and-such is so," they suggest that the audience agrees with them.

For example, an advertisement for the Ford Escort promised that the car had "Sure-Footed Handling" and a "Smooth Comfortable Ride." Why did the advertiser choose these question-begging adjectives? Could the choice be related to customer fears about the effects of front-wheel drive? In any case, the adjectives suggest some uncertainty about how customers will evaluate the Escort's ride and maneuverability.

An interesting footnote on word choice comes from research done by the Family Television Research Program at Yale University. The researchers there found that children who are heavy TV watchers (defined as those who watch three hours of TV per day or more) are affected in four ways in their language use:

1. They use fewer adjectives.
2. They use shorter sentences.
3. They use fewer adverbs.
4. They use simpler sentences.

Conversely, children who are light TV watchers (defined as those who watched one hour per day or less) use more advanced vocabularies and speak in more complete sentences than do the heavy TV watchers.[26]

Syntax as an Analytical Tool

In contrast to using grammatical categories and sentence types to analyze persuaders' messages, we can look at **syntax**, the way in which words are ordered within sentences. For example, persuaders can choose to emphasize emotional or surprising words by placing them at or near the beginning of a sentence, or they can position such words at the end of the sentence, where they might have more dramatic and lasting effect. Suppose a persuader says, "There is no greater hypocrite than an animal rights advocate who opposes the use of animals in the research laboratory and who then eats meat for dinner every night." *Hypocrisy* is the theme, or topic, of the sentence, but we have to wait until the last clause to find out that eating meat every night is the hypocritical behavior being referred to. The sentence is dramatic, and its syntax builds the listener's curiosity regarding hypocrisy. If, on the other hand, the persuader had elaborated and explained the source of the hypocrisy by saying ". . . and who then eats meat for dinner every night as if the hog, steer, lamb, calf, or chicken didn't face the same fate as the animals used for scientific research," not only would the drama of the sentence have been greatly reduced but the cause of the hypocrisy would have been obscured as well.

Word order, or syntax, can also tell us something about an author. Consider the following sentence from an editorial by Robert Shrum of *New Times* magazine. Shrum was lamenting the swing to conservatism that seemed to be occurring in the late 1980s. "The House has approved the neutron bomb, the ultimate weapon of a dehumanized capitalism: it will kill people but leave the real property standing.[27] The first clause stands as an indictment of the House of Representatives. The second phrase elaborates the indictment, expanding on it in highly accusatory terms. The last clause explains his indictment. It gives us his reasoning for making the judgment. The order of the argument reveals that the author is a deductive thinker waiting until the conclusion to offer his specific pieces of evidence. He tends to move from the general to the specific.

Ambiguity as a Functional Device

Another stylistic element is the degree to which words are specific or ambiguous. It would appear that the most effective persuasion ought to be the simplest. Yet if you consider the fact that no two people ever see the world in exactly the same way, the simplest might *not* be the best. Perhaps an ambiguous message would be better. Let us sup-

pose that I was trying to persuade you to buy a certain kind of automobile. If I told you the reason why *I* thought you should buy the car, I might antagonize you. I would never be able to touch the key strings of motivation that might cause you to make the purchase. For example, suppose I described the car as dependable and sturdy in construction. If the key motivation for you is sex appeal — how the car symbolizes potent sexuality, for example — I would lose the sale. Dependability and sturdiness seem more tied to vehicles like tractors, Jeeps, or family station wagons than to sexy sports models or hatchbacks. A better strategy would be to be less specific, to let you "sell yourself" on the sexy body style, color, or interior design. In other words, by being ambiguous I allow you to enter into the persuasive process. I let you define the terms (and a good salesperson listens carefully to customers and reinforces their statements). Furthermore, if the message is ambiguous enough, the same strategy will work with diverse sets of people. Most politicians are judged by media reporters as being fuzzy on the issues at one time or another. Perhaps they are just being ambiguous in hope of persuading as many of their constituents as possible and alienating as few as possible. Although this may not result in the most intelligent votes or in the best person being elected, it probably does result in more winning and less losing for the skillful politician — which gives us another reason why we should strive to be responsible persuadees.

TOOLS FOR THE SEMANTIC DIMENSION

Ambiguity of Meaning

In contrast to its function of avoiding specificity, ambiguity has another function: to encourage persuadees to "fill in" their own private meanings for words. Thus ambiguity can provide a semantic "escape hatch" for the persuader who wants to please everyone. There are several ways in which persuaders can create persuasive messages. One way is *semantically*: The persuader carefully chooses words that can be interpreted in many ways, often in contradictory ways, depending on the receivers. For example, a politician favors "responsibility in taxation and the education of our youngsters." Those who think teachers are underpaid and need substantial raises might hear this as a call for *spending* tax dollars. Those who hold a reverse view could as easily interpret the statement as saying that educational spending needs to be *cut*. There are other possible interpretations as

well. The key word, the one that increases the ambiguity, is *responsibility*. It sets up the rest of the sentence. Thus, not only can ambiguity operate on the functional level, it can also operate semantically, as we will see.

Take the words *fiscal responsibility*, which were in vogue during the budget-cutting 1980s. Many politicians claimed that they were "for fiscal responsibility" — but what did that mean? To some politicians, responsibility meant cutting corporate taxes to allow capital investments in machinery to

THE FAR SIDE   By GARY LARSON

"Hang him, you idiots! Hang him! . . . 'String-him-up' is a figure of speech!"

FIGURE 5.3

Ambiguity in the semantic dimension of language can be the basis for puns and other forms of humor.

modernize industry. They thought that American industry was becoming old-fashioned and was being outpaced by the Japanese. To them, it would be irresponsible *not* to encourage corporate tax cuts. To others, fiscal responsibility meant that the government would have to run in the black — no more deficit spending. Still others believed that fiscal responsibility meant controlling the growth of the money supply. Some politicans likely embraced all these definitions. Besides, which of them would dare take a position *opposing* "responsibility"? The words *fiscal responsibility* derived their persuasive power not from their specificity but from their ambiguity, which allowed many interpretations. In this sense, the words were rich with meaning.

Ambiguity can be created by *juxtaposing or combining words or phrases in startling ways or by presenting issues in a new light*. For example, the term *born again* became familiar in the 1980s and was persuasive to many people. *Born again* refers to people who claim to have been converted to Christianity, although they were members of Christian denominations before their conversion. The term *born again* suggests that the earlier beliefs are forgotten or incorrect and that the conversion causes them to be revitalized and re-created. The term became a code word among such believers, along with other phrases such as "having a personal relationship with the Lord" or "preaching in the flesh." Some members of this born-again movement decided that they needed to assert their beliefs in the political arena and endorsed certain candidates, such as Pat Robertson, on the basis of the candidates' stands on religious issues. Some born-again lobbyists labeled their political group the *moral majority*, creating highly persuasive and intentional ambiguity. The term was ambiguous first because the group did not constitute a majority but actually a minority. The phrase had perhaps been borrowed from Richard Nixon, who invented a "silent majority" during his years as president. One could identify *that* majority by its silence. In the same manner, the term *moral majority* not only falsely implies that the group has majority standing but that, because most people try to behave morally (at least in public), almost

anyone sitting next to you or working with you could be a member. This ambiguous term had great persuasive appeal.

Media preachers created what political researchers Dan Nimmo and James Combs call "The Electronic Church."[28] *Moral Decay* became another highly persuasive and also ambiguous term. We respond to "moral decay" in the same way we respond to tooth decay.

Let's examine the term *neoconservative* (which to those in the know means a group of former liberals and/or Democrats who have become more conservative vis-à-vis certain issues but want to identify themselves as distinct from mainstream Republicans). Why is this term persuasive? Who are the neoconservatives? Are they young or old? Rich or poor? Good or bad? What do they stand for? How difficult would it be for you or me to masquerade as one? If you try to answer these questions, you will see why the term is powerful: It is ambiguous enough to include almost anyone who wants to declare himself a new conservative. On the other hand, if the term were to develop negative connotations in the public eye, it is ambiguous enough to be used as a smear label. This is the power and danger of the persuasive use of ambiguity.

How can we defend ourselves against ambiguous language? The semanticists advise using more specific and concrete elaborations on any ambiguous term. The semioticians advise us to seek the full meanings in persuasive "texts" by delving into various verbal and nonverbal "signifiers" to determine what is really being "signified." Using both the semantic and the semiotic approaches, you can reduce ambiguity in language.

Examining the denotations and connotations of persuasive symbols is another tool for studying the semantic dimension of language. **Denotation** refers to a word's explicit dictionary definition and nothing more, whereas **connotation** includes the many other meanings attached to various words. A good way to remember which is which is to recall that the Latin prefix *de* means "a loss of" or "a doing away with," (as in the word *demerit*, which means a loss of or a doing away with merit). Thus *denotation* is a loss of or a doing away with extra meanings or "notations." Connotation, on the other hand contains the Latin prefix *con*, which means "with," (as in "chili *con* carne," chili beans *with* meat). Thus *connotation* means "with" extra meanings, or "notations."

For instance, consider the word *depression*. The explicit dictionary definition, which is not overly descriptive, is: "A state of feeling sad." But the second definition given in the dictionary adds some connotations to the word. In the case of *depression*, this includes the symptoms that characterize depression: "sadness, inactivity, difficulty in thinking and concentration, a significant increase or decrease in appetite and time spent sleeping, feelings of dejection and hopelessness, and sometimes suicidal tendencies."[29] This definition has taken us far beyond "feelings of sadness." Each individual has his or her own idiosyncratic connotations for a word, depending on the individual's experiences with it. Best-selling author William Styron, for example, described his experience with depression as "suffering a pain he couldn't dislodge" and finding that everything around him related to suicide: The attic rafters were a place to hang himself; his garage was a good place to asphyxiate himself; his bathtub was a good place to slit his wrists.[30] Cases of mistaken connotation can sometimes be embarrassing. For example, vice-president Quayle was quite impressed with Congresswoman Claudine Schneider at a reception they were attending at the Belgian embassy — she spoke fluent French to the Belgians. At the conclusion of the speech, Quayle said, "I was recently on a tour of Latin America, and the only regret I have was that I didn't study Latin harder in school so I could converse with those people.[31]

There are other tools for approaching the semantic dimension of language. Among the more useful is the dramatistic approach suggested by philosopher and literary critic Kenneth Burke.

Kenneth Burke and Ambiguity

Kenneth Burke, in his book *A Grammar of Motives*, notes that persuasion is really a process of coming to identify with the persuader's position.

The persuader gets the audience to identify by achieving common ground, by adopting beliefs similar to those of the audience, by using terms similar to those used by the audience, or even by dressing in clothes like those worn by the audience. In a sense, the persuader and the persuadee appear to be cut from the same cloth. The title of Burke's book gives a clue to his purpose: He wants to present a set of terms, or a "grammar," for identifying the audience's motives and thus establishing common ground. Burke's device, the **dramatistic pentad**, is a tool for analyzing language usage and also for developing a persuasive language strategy on the semantic level. Burke believes that when we communicate, we choose words because of their dramatic potential, and that different individuals find some elements in the drama more potent than others. Some, for example, may believe that great people affect the outcome of events; when persuading, such persons give examples of individual effort winning the day. Burke describes their persuasion as based on the *agent*, or actor. For other persons, the *scene*, or setting, may be the motivating element; they choose scenic words and phrases to persuade. Let us look at Burke's pentad in more detail.

The Dramatistic Pentad Burke's basic premise is that human beings see the world in terms of drama. He identifies five universal elements of drama that he says include all of the possible parts of dramatic action: scene, act, agent, agency, and purpose. According to Burke, different people focus on different elements, depending on which element seems to correspond most closely with their view of the world:

1. *Scene* (the place where action occurs). Persons who focus on the scene are *materialists*. They believe that changing the scene or environment will change people. They would support urban renewal, for example.

2. *Act* (the action that occurs). Persons who focus on the act are *realists*. They process and record information and believe that a mixture of causes directs human affairs. They support the status quo.

3. *Agent* (the actor who acts out the action or plot). Persons who focus on the agent are *idealists*. They believe that people control their own destiny. Persuaders who focus on the agent would support self-help programs.

4. *Agency* (the tool actors use to accomplish their ends). Persons who focus on the agency are *pragmatists*. They search for the most speedy and immediately practical solutions. They might support gas rationing, for example.

5. *Purpose* (the reason why people do what they do). Persons who focus on purpose are *mystics*. They believe a power or focus beyond them directs human destiny. They would support religious or patriotic plans.

These five terms can be used to develop a persuasive strategy. For example, if you were trying to get a date for a rock concert, you might feature the *scene*, describing the stage, sounds, costumes, lighting, exciting colors, and other scenic elements. An alternative strategy would be to focus on the *act*, describing the kinds of music and the interactions between the performers and the audience. You might also choose to focus on the *agent* element. Here, you would describe the rock musicians, their reputations, and their appearance. If you chose to feature *agency*, you might mention the sound system, the unique instruments, and special effects such as explosions on stage. Finally, you could feature *purpose* by telling your prospective date that "To be really 'in,' you shouldn't miss attending a live rock concert, and you might meet other interesting people from the audience."

The most inclusive of the dramatic elements is *scene*. Burke notes that the scene must be the "proper container" for the action that is occurring or that is about to occur. If there is some kind of imbalance between scene and act in what he calls the **scene-act ratio**, high drama — tragic, comic, or melodramatic — is likely to occur. In *Hamlet*, for example, the dramatic tension created in the scene-act ratio comes from the fact that Hamlet's mother has married his uncle following the mysterious death of Hamlet's father, the king. Worse, the marriage followed the funeral by less than one month, hardly the proper act for a scene in which

mourning for a deceased king should be occurring. Hamlet is disturbed by this imbalance in the scene-act ratio, and curses his mother and uncle in a soliloquy, saying, "She married. O, most wicked speed, to post with such dexterity to incestuous sheets!" Later, Hamlet teases his friend Horatio, asking whether he had visited court for the funeral or the wedding. Hamlet expresses his anger ironically in these bitter words, which reflect his reaction to the imbalance of the scene-act ratio: "Thrift, thrift, Horatio! The funeral baked meats did coldly furnish the marriage tables." We can almost hear him ready to use more damning language, yelling "Whore! Slut." The same imbalance can lead to comedy, as when a silent movie shows a pompous man in a tuxedo walking down the street and then cuts to a ragamuffin Charlie Chaplin dropping a banana skin on the walk. We know what is about to happen — there soon will be a funny pratfall.

In political persuasion, we frequently hear the scene-act ratio used as candidates declare that their program is "right for the times" or that their opponent's approach is "out of sync" with the rest of the country. For example, in a race for state's attorney in my county, an irate voter who felt that he'd been neglected by the incumbent dumped a load of horse manure on the local courthouse steps and another load on the state capitol steps. The incongruity between the act and the scene drew wide attention from not only local but also national media. The incumbent, who was favored to win, lost reelection by a wide margin.

We also frequently see the persuasive power of the scene-act ratio in advertisements. For example, in Figure 5.4, the scene — the state of Alaska — offers tourists great fishing with the words "if you like your fish wild" and "twelve native species, all of them pugnacious." It adds that Alaska has "two oceans, two seas, and hundreds of bays," thereby furthering the scene-act balance — after all, where but in the largest state would you expect the biggest fight with a fish?

Scene can also interact with the other elements of the pentad. In the **scene-agent ratio**, balance or imbalance again can indicate potent persuasion or high drama — comedy, tragedy, or melodrama. In

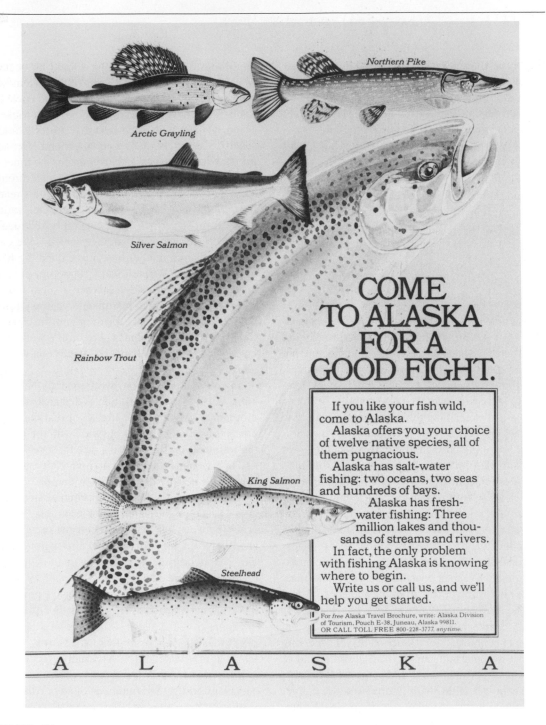

How are the scene and the act balanced in this ad?
(Used by permission of the Alaska Division of
Tourism.)

the film *Psycho*, one of Alfred Hitchcock's masterpieces, viewers instinctively note a scene-agent imbalance when Anthony Perkins tells Janet Leigh that he has stuffed all the taxidermic specimens in the office of the Bates Motel. The imbalance is intensified when we see him peek at her through the secret peephole in the eye of one the specimens. The imbalance here draws our attention to the strong possibility of danger, and we may even whisper "Don't stay at this motel—find another one down the road!" The tension caused by the scene-agent imbalance is increased when we hear Perkins and his "mother" arguing at the Victorian house near the motel—again we want to tell Leigh to "close and lock the bathroom door whenever you take a shower." Her murder is later "discovered" by Perkins, who is shocked at the scene-agent disparity of someone as kind as his "mother" stabbing a young girl to death. Hitchcock uses scene-agent tension throughout the rest of the film as well as in his other films to keep the audience on the edges of their seats.

In cigarette ads, we see the scene-agent ratio used when Camel and Vantage smokers are always depicted in the foreground of an exciting scene—an undersea diving rig, a film studio, a whitewater raft run, a mountain, or a raft on the Amazon. Throughout these and other examples of the scene-agent ratio, the consistency or discrepancy between the two elements can be potent raw material for persuasion.

The **act-agent ratio** can often be seen in the world of politics. For example, during the stormy months following the incredible political changes in Eastern Europe, Mikhail Gorbachev's political future was simultaneously under attack. *Newsweek* magazine featured Boris Yeltsin, one of Gorbachev's challengers, on its cover—a clear agent focus. The accompanying headline read, "After the Summit—The Yeltsin Challenge." Not only was the agent the focus of the photo, but his potential actions were the central issue posed by the headline.[32]

The ad in Figure 5.5 features the agency—Goodyear tires—against a "great outdoors" scene. Notice that the agent is barely visible, that the tire is at the center of the ad, and that the purpose is mentioned in the headline "For All That Rolls In The Great Outdoors." The **scene-purpose ratio** is often demonstrated in political advertising. For example, the Capitol Building (scene) is featured, and the headline declares, "Here Is Where We Decide the Future!"

Burke and Key Terms   Each term of the pentad can interact with any other one, forming what Burke calls the *ratios*, of which there are ten: scene/act, scene/agent, scene/agency, scene/purpose, act/agent, act/agency, act/purpose, agent/agency, agent/purpose, and agency/purpose. As noted, these ratios represent places where dramatic tension can possibly develop. The assassination of a priest at prayer in church demonstrates a high degree of dramatic tension because of the imbalance in the scene/act ratio—the church being a holy place and, therefore, an especially inappropriate place for assassination. As you examine the persuasion aimed at you, try to determine how the mismatching of dramatic elements creates dramatic tension. Using the ten ratios and a small sample of a source's persuasive language, you should also be able to determine the sources **key term(s)**. Identifying a persuader's key terms is useful because it tips you off as to what to expect from that persuader in the future. If the persuader seems to see a problem and its solution as by-products of a scene, he or she will probably analyze future problems through the scenic lens. And in trying to persuade this person, you will be most successful if you couch your arguments in similar scenic language. Consider the following:

> Over the past few years, the image of politics that has taken shape for me is that of an immense journey—the panorama of an endless wagon train, an enormous trek, a multitudinous processing of people larger and more confused than any of the primitive folk migrations.
>
> There—ahead—lies the crest of the ridge, and beyond it perhaps the plateau or the sunlit valley—or danger. The procession stretches

For All That Rolls In The Great Outdoors.

Before that next big bass expedition, have a Goodyear Retailer check your tires. All your tires. Including those on your light truck, on the trailer you tow...even on the ATV.

Goodyear's the logical place to go for this kind of service, because we have a great tire for just about anything that rolls in the Great Outdoors.

That's Goodyear Wrangler Radials for your light truck. And Goodyear specialty tires for your other outdoor vehicles. For more details, see the attached card.

GOODYEAR

NOBODY FITS YOU LIKE GOODYEAR

out for endless miles, making its way up the tangled slopes through strange new country. . . .

Up there, at the head of the advance column, the leaders quarrel bitterly among themselves, as do the people behind. From their heights they have a wider view of the horizon.[33]

The scenic quality of the quotation is clear. The author has a vision of a setting and a background. What is important is the panorama — the view from the ridge — the scene. The author sees the setting as powerful, drawing people and leaders forward, forcing them onward, even in ignorance of what lies ahead.

Other persons may see the world as being controlled or motivated by an agent. For example, psychologist and psychiatric therapist Martin P. Seligman has proposed what he calls "a theory of helplessness"[34] to explain a variety of psychiatric disorders. Seligman developed this theory by observing how people attach blame when tragic or even just unfortunate things happen to them. Seligman notes:

Evidence is mounting that stressful life events such as bereavement and school and family pressures lead to increased vulnerability to infection and disease. But not everyone reacts in the same way. Some fight against stresses while others see them as uncontrollable and react with helplessness and passivity. . . . People with a poor explanatory style are more likely to go on and have bad health than those with an optimistic outlook.[35]

Seligman and his colleagues developed a research technique called CAVE (Content Analysis of Verbatim Explanations), which uses people's words to predict subsequent behavior. They applied the technique to a variety of situations and persons and found that the way an agent explains

events frequently determines subsequent events. For example, they analyzed the newspaper quotations of Baseball Hall of Famers from 1900 to 1950 and found that those with optimistic explanatory styles ("Nothing but the breaks of the game beat me") outlived those with pessimistic or helpless explanatory styles ("My aim is still good, but I know I haven't got the stuff I used to have").[36] Seligman's theory certainly puts the agent at the center of explanation and motivation. Interestingly enough, Seligman's explanation of his own behavior in following the researcher role as opposed to the therapist role reflects his belief in the power of the agent. "As a therapist, . . . I might help 200 or 300 people during my life, but I think I can make a better contribution by trying to uncover general laws of psychology that might help many many more people."[37]

The same sort of analysis can be carried out with the act and the agency as keys. A persuader who is convinced that means are more important than ends might be an agency-oriented persuader. Phone company persuaders often focus on means (long distance) over scenes (home). For example, they advertise that "Long Distance Is the Next Best Thing to Being There." Or they urge you to "Reach Out and Touch Someone," combining the idea of transcending distance with the appeal of touching a loved one. An act-oriented persuader would probably describe an action that has taken place and then imply that another action can remedy or improve the situation. Take, for instance, this ad copy: "Overdone by the sun? When the sun burns you up and makes you sizzle, when you're overdone by the sun, stop sunburn pain fast with Solarcaine."

Burke's dramatistic pentad can be used in various ways: to discover the persuasive focus and hence the underlying beliefs or key elements of an advocate, or to discover and to label a persuader's characteristic symbols and rituals. When we look at what persuaders say and at how they use language (what kinds of words they use frequently), their view of the world and their view of human motivation become clear. Burke described such analysis, when done with literature, in terms of

FIGURE 5.5

(Reprinted by permission of The Goodyear Tire & Rubber Company.)

using **associational clusters**. The word or symbol clusters serve as benchmarks to the persuader's own beliefs and agenda for following through on those beliefs. As receivers, we need to isolate such clusters whenever possible before responding to the persuasive appeals that surround them. If we agree with the persuader's clusters or key terms and see the world as the persuader does, we can follow his or her advice. If we find that the persuader's view doesn't match up with our own, we can reject, question, or investigate it further, depending on circumstances.

TOOLS FOR THE THEMATIC DIMENSION

As noted earlier in this chapter, the thematic dimension of language is that quality in certain words or sets of words that gives them a texture or "feel." Although the words do have a semantic meaning and a syntactical function, their most important persuasive aspect is their ability to set a mood, develop a feeling, or generate a tone or theme for the persuasion; hence the term "thematic." For example, Lincoln set the theme for his famous Gettysburg Address with his words

> Fourscore and seven years ago our fathers brought forth on this continent a new nation, conceived in liberty and dedicated to the proposition that all men are created equal.

How far less stirring the speech would have been if he had said:

> Eighty-seven years ago the signers of the Declaration of Independence started a new country designed to assure us of freedom and equality.

The two sentences have nearly equivalent semantic and functional meanings; the obvious difference between them lies in their tone.

Thematic differences sometimes come from repeated sounds, as in the words from an ad for a ski resort at Stratton, Vermont: "Stratton's Special! Lifts, Lodging, and Lunch." The repetition and alliteration used here involves the letters "s" and

"l." They make the Stratton message easy to remember. The *l* sound repeated three times is like "la, la, la." The repetition of the "ssss" sound also sets a mood for a sexy cigarette called Satin — "Smooth, Silky, Satin Cigarettes."

Parallel sentence structure can also set a mood and can almost become a refrain. For example, a Windsor Canadian whiskey ad pictures three couples gathered around a kitchen stove watching the host and hostess whip up their favorite recipe. They are all happy and enjoy sampling tastes of the dish being prepared. The ad copy reads "As easy as an old recipe. As warm as a kitchen get-together. As enjoyable as a favorite story. That's a taste of what Windsor is all about." The repeated comparisons serve to set a comfortable mood, and the semantic dimension of the words used in the comparisons creates a positive motif.

Thematic differences can also come from the metaphors persuaders create or from the use of **onomatopoeia** (words that sound like their meaning, such as "swish," "swoosh," "burp," "rustle," or "clap"). We will now look at several tools of the thematic dimension of language use: the choice of motifs and metaphors; the development of God, Devil, and charismatic terms; and the differences between the pragmatic and unifying styles of persuasion.

Metaphorical Style

Persuaders can convey a great deal of their message by setting the mood for the persuadees. They can depict a setting appropriate for the message by repeatedly using certain sounds and images. Michael Osborne studied the use of *archetypal metaphors* (universal and primal images consistent within and even across cultures), in particular the light-dark comparison.[38] He maintains that, traditionally, we identify light with the sun, warmth, growth, comfort, and so on; we associate dark with mystery, night, cold, and other uncomfortable and troubling things. Osborne points out that persuaders often use repeated references to this dichotomy. John F. Kennedy, in his inaugural address, used this archetypal metaphor when he talked about passing a torch from one generation to another and predicted that the light from this symbolic torch could illuminate the world for freedom; the light was viewed as good, warm, friendly, and virtuous. Elsewhere, the world was filled with darkness and poverty.

There are other archetypal metaphors. For example, the power of the sea and the life-giving power of water may explain the holy or magical powers traditionally ascribed to water (as in the fountain of youth or baptism). Mircea Eliade is convinced that there is an archetypal metaphor of "the center."[39] In his view, we repeatedly look for a central point—a symbolic navel for our world. For some groups, it is a specific place (Mecca for Moslems, Munich for Nazis, Jerusalem for Jews and Christians).

Most such archetypal metaphors relate to life experiences that all people—primitive as well as modern—can relate to. The light-dark metaphor probably emerged eons ago from a fear of the unseen dangers that lurked in the darkness of night and the lessening of fears that came with light. The "power of water" metaphor probably relates to water's cleansing abilities as well as its life-giving and life-sustaining powers. What are some other universal experiences that humans share from culture to culture and from age to age? When you discover them, you will see that they are often used in advertising and political persuasion, and that perhaps you may also use them in your interpersonal encounters as you try to persuade others.

Sensory Language and the Thematic Dimension

Two courtroom communication experts, Stephanie L. Swanson and David Wenner, maintain that the most effective lawyers rely on sensory words, words relating to the senses.[40] They speculate that jurors can be categorized as:

1. auditorily dependent; that is, relating best to words that are tied to sound.
2. visually dependent; that is, relating best to words that are tied to sight.
3. kinesthetically dependent; that is, relating best to words that are tied to the sense of touch.

For example, an attorney might ask three witnesses to describe an automobile accident. The auditorily dependent witness might answer by saying, "I was walking down Oak Street *listening* to my Walkman, when I *heard* the screech of brakes, and then there was a sickening *sound of crashing* glass and metal, and someone screamed." The visually dependent witness might say, "I *saw* this brown Mazda coming around the corner practically on two wheels. Then he must have hit the brakes, because it *looked* like the car slid sideways toward me, and then I *saw* the front end of the Mazda *make a mess* of the little GEO." The kinesthetically dependent witness might say, "I had this *feeling* that something was about to happen, and when it did I *felt* frightened and helpless and I *cringed* as the cars crumpled up like scrap paper." Swanson and Wenner advise attorneys to "listen closely to the sensory language used by your clients . . . try to respond in kind—matching the sensory language of the other person."[41] They advise them to carefully listen to the kinds of words used by prospective jurors during the *voire dire* process and then try to shape trial testimony and courtroom appeals along those lines. They also advise them to "tailor your language to your listeners' primary sensory channel. You can 'paint a picture' for a visual person, 'orchestrate the testimony' for an auditory person, and 'touch the heart' of the kinesthetic individual. By using sensory language, you let the jurors feel that your discourse is directed toward them individually."[42]

Thus, in trying to identify a persuader's use of the thematic dimension of language, another aspect to explore is the sensory language used in the persuasion.

God, Devil, and Charismatic Terms

Another thematic or textural characteristic of style often used in persuasion is the development of **families of terms**. Persuaders, like the rest of us, like to see the world as divided into neat categories. They use these categories to try to persuade others and are often successful. One of these category sets is made up of *God terms* and *Devil terms*, as noted by Richard Weaver.[43] Weaver said that terms or labels are really only parts of propositions. However, they are often linked with other terms or labels to shape a message or a persuasive argument. He defines "God term" as an expression "about which all other expressions are ranked as subordinate and serving dominations and powers. Its force imparts to the others their lesser degree of force. . . ."[44] Weaver sees a God term as an unchallenged term that demands sacrifice or obedience in its name. He uses three terms as examples of God terms: *progress, fact,* and *science.* Although these were God terms for the 1950s when Weaver wrote, their force has changed. We do not now attach high positive values to "progress"—counterterms have identified it with waste, war, pollution, and a series of other ills. Science, too, has lost some of its credibility, for science has produced, along with constructive marvels, nuclear weapons and technology that may destroy the Earth through pollution.

During the 1970s, a "counterculture," triggered by the Vietnam War, developed across the country. This movement had its God and Devil terms, also. It was good to be an "individual," to "do your own thing," and to have an "alternative life-style." The seventies became identified as the "me decade," and this reflection of self-centeredness lasted well into the eighties, ending perhaps with the stock market crash of 1987 and the realization that AIDS was going to reach epidemic proportions. The first *Newsweek* issue of 1988 declared, "The 80s Are Over: Greed Goes Out of Style." The magazine went on, in an extensive article, to describe the "God terms" of the "me generation/decade," as symbolized by nouvelle cuisine, running and aerobics, Madonna's *Material Girl*, BMW's "Ultimate Driving Machine," cocaine, Rambo, expensive vacations, television evangelism, free love (until AIDS), and *Lifestyles of the Rich and Famous* with its "aptly named" host Robin Leach.[45]

What will be the God and Devil terms of the 1990s? Based on a poll and the counsel of persons who specialize in spotting trends, the same issue of *Newsweek* predicted that God terms will include "the family," "security," "marriage" (in 1986 the

divorce rate dropped for the first time in fifteen years), and "altruism." The "aging baby boomers are thinking longingly of settling down and taking a nice nap."[46]

What are the God and Devil terms of your subculture or other subcultures? Explore them, for they will alert you to potential persuasive appeals you might use. More important, they are most likely being used on you day in and day out.

Weaver points out that the connotations of certain negative terms can sometimes be reversed, making the terms neutral or even positive.[47] Take, for example, the expression "wasted" or "getting wasted," which in the early 1980s often referred to getting drunk or doped up. Its use during the 1970s referred to killing Viet Cong or others perceived to be the enemy during the Vietnam War. During the election campaign of 1988, George Bush turned an earlier God term—the word *liberal*—into a Devil term by calling it "the 'L' word." Other Devil terms for the 1990s include "polluter," "waste," and "exploitation."

Weaver also described **charismatic terms**—"terms of considerable potency whose referents it is virtually impossible to discover. . . . Their meaning seems inexplicable unless we accept the hypothesis that their content proceeds out of a popular will that they *shall* mean something."[48] His example is the word *freedom*, which has no apparent concrete referent but which seems, even thirty-five years after Weaver used it, to have considerable potency for many people. For example, in the early 1980s, the Solidarity Union movement drew tens of millions of members and attracted worldwide attention and admiration. The word *solidarity* was soon picked up and used in other countries because of its charisma. Even when martial law was declared, Solidarity's leaders jailed, and the movement outlawed, the union continued to flourish in Poland, and the word *solidarity* retained its charismatic quality there and elsewhere. In fact, it became a kind of universal name for the drive to speak up and be free. In the United States, the old union organizers' song *Solidarity Forever* was sung, and "solidarity" was seen on posters even at nonunion activities. In Chicago, home of so many Polish immigrants, local radio and television stations had the word printed on buttons so people could show their support for the movement. When the communist government of Poland was finally forced to come to terms with Solidarity and several members of the previously outlawed union were elected to office, the word became legitimized and lost some of its charismatic qualities. In fact, political infighting within the union in early 1990 caused some members to harshly criticize the movement and its leadership.

The use of God terms, Devil terms, and charismatic terms is not limited to political or ideological persuasion. In marketing products, advertisers need to identify the God, Devil, and charismatic terms of their target market. An interesting example is No Nonsense Fashions, a manufacturer of pantyhose. The company discovered a previously unknown secret market segment in the mid-1980s: men. It seems that after pro-football players began wearing pantyhose during cold-weather games, other men began experimenting with them as a substitute for bulky long underwear. A considerable number of outdoorsmen, construction workers, police officers, mail carriers, motorcyclists, and firefighters were secretly wearing pantyhose because of their light weight, warmth, and support. However, the word "pantyhose" was a Devil term to these men, so they were sending their wives and girlfriends to buy the pantyhose instead of going themselves. The problem was to identify a term that could be either a God term or a charismatic term to this male segment of the pantyhose market and then to develop further product features from the name. During a creativity-training session reported in *Psychology Today*, several attempts to identify a God or charismatic term as a name for male pantyhose were promising — "Jox Sox," for instance, or "Power Hose." The most promising was "Mach-Hose."[49] What others might there be? Product alterations that fit in with the macho product name included putting odor-absorbing footpads in the hose, adding a velcro fly, making the hose in macho colors like "forest green" or "fireman's red," and offering them in "six-packs" or through "male order" catalogs.

Clearly, other inducements could be added — making the pantyhose in camouflage, for instance, or offering price-off coupons on the hose with each sale of men's work or outdoor boots. The idea of identifying the God or charismatic terms, however, provided the breakthrough.

Another persuasive arena in which to discover God, Devil, and charismatic terms is the interpersonal realm that we share with our friends, spouses, parents, or co-workers. What are the God and Devil terms of your parents, for example? What are those of your teachers? Your boss? Your friends? Identifying such terms can be useful in persuasion. We can also identify charismatic terms of value in appealing to large numbers of people and not just one market or one target. What are some of the charismatic terms operating in the world of mass persuasion today? Look to the advertising in major mass-media appeals. It can tip you off as to what terms the market researchers believe have charismatic qualities. Tune your ear to the words chosen by political leaders and candidates. Do any of these terms seem to carry charismatic persuasive power? In all likelihood, these terms, or variants of them, will be persuasive in the interpersonal context as well. By listening for such God, Devil, and charismatic terms, you train your receiving skills and gain the added advantage of knowing which thematic qualities to work into your own persuasive attempts. Let us turn now to two different styles that also have thematic meanings associated with them.

Pragmatic and Unifying Styles

A final characteristic that builds a thematic wholeness or gives a texture to persuasion is the reliance of a persuader on one of two kinds of styles — the **pragmatic style** or the **unifying style**.[50] These styles can be thought of as signifying two separate strategies; however, persuaders can use the tactics of either strategy, or they can combine the two extremes.

Pragmatic persuaders usually find it necessary to convince listeners who do not necessarily support their position. As a result, they must try to change minds as opposed to reinforcing beliefs, and they must choose appropriate tactics. *Unifying persuaders* are in a much more comfortable position. They talk to people who, in large measure, already believe what is going to be said. They do not need to change minds; they need only reinforce beliefs — to whip up enthusiasm and dedication or to give encouragement. These two styles demonstrate two opposing situations, and they describe the problems facing the persuader in these situations. The problems for pragmatic persuaders are practical — they must change opinion before they can expect action. Unifying persuaders can be much more idealistic — they usually can afford to be more bombastic without offending the audience. These persuaders can be more emotional and less objective than the persuader faced with a questioning audience. What are the stylistic devices of these extremes?

The unifying persuader can afford to be idealistic and to focus on the then-and-there — on the past or on the future — when things were ideal or when they can become ideal. The position of unifying persuaders is that things look better in the future, particularly if we compare them with the present. Because the audience will fill in the blanks, language choice can be abstract. It is usually poetic and filled with imagery that excites the audience's imagination. Although there may be little that is intellectually stimulating (or that requires careful logical examination) about what unifying persuaders say, there is much that is emotionally stimulating. The words and images offered by such persuaders are precisely the words listeners believe *they* would have said if they were talking. The unifying persuader is thus the mouthpiece or sounding board for the entire group, providing them with the cues, but not the details, of the message. The audience can participate with the persuaders in the creation of the message; in fact, audiences sometimes participate actively by yelling encouragement to unifying persuaders or by repeating shibboleths to underscore their words — "right on" or "Amen, brother" or "tell it like it is."

Pragmatic persuaders, because they must win an audience, cannot afford to take the risk of appealing to abstract ideals. They must be concrete, focusing on facts instead of images, emphasizing what cannot be disputed or interpreted so easily. They do not try to depict an ideal situation in subjective there-and-then terms. Instead, they have to focus on real aspects of immediate problems familiar to the audience — problems of the here-and-now that are realistic, not idealistic. Their orientation is to the present instead of the future. Because pragmatic persuaders are forced to be concrete and realistic, their language is concrete and prosaic. Lofty thoughts are of little value, especially if they are expressed in equally lofty words. These persuaders tend to focus on facts and statistics instead of imagery.

Clearly, these two extremes are not an either/or proposition — persuaders may, on occasion, use the tactics of both perspectives. When they do, they are probably responding to their audience's level of doubt or acceptance. In the following excerpt, the author is using the pragmatic style. Note the use of here-and-now references, the down-to-earth prosaic language, and concrete examples and references.

My team won the World Series. You thought we couldn't but we knew we would and we did and what did your team do? Now we're heading down to spring training looking even better than before, and your team that looked pitiful then looks even less hot now. . . . Your lead-off guy had a bad infection in January and now he gets dizzy at the first sign of stress and falls down in a heap. Sad. Your cleanup guy spent the winter cleaning his plate. He had to buy new clothes in a size they don't sell at regular stores. . . . Tough beans. Your big left-hander tried hypnosis to stop smoking and while in a trancelike state discovered he hated his mother for tying his tiny right hand behind his back and making him eat and draw and tinkle with his left. So he's right-handed now, a little awkward but gradually learning to point with it and wave goodbye. . . . We're No. 1. We knew it first and now you know it too. You thought we were quiet and modest in the Midwest but that's because you're dumb, as dumb as a stump, dumber than dirt. . . . We're the best, so beat it, Charley or we'll shell ya like a pea pod, dunk ya like a donut.[51]

The author and humorist, Garrison Keillor, is midwestern born and bred. Note his use of "here-and-now" references, his concrete (though hypothetical) examples, and his use of prosaic, everyday language, and colloquialisms. Keillor is facing an audience that views his persuasive purpose — to demonstrate the positivity of midwestern values — as suspect. He needs to win them over, and he probably does, by using the pragmatic approach.

Now let's look at an example of a unifying persuader whose topic is the audience's and his own use of words:

Because I have come to believe that I am the words I speak, and that speak me, the nature of my words, and the voice that speaks them, is starting to bother me. Somewhere along the way I used up some words and discarded others. . . . Perhaps I shouldn't even say "I used up" or "I discarded," because together we are creating a way of speaking that uses some words and not others and a way of saying them and not others. . . . We seem to like words with sharp edges better than soft ones. We write more easily about power than compassion. . . . What I am puzzling over is . . . "tone," . . . that suggests something about who we are and how we live. . . . Our ways of speaking . . . may also hide a longing, beyond the injuries of patriarchy, racism and class, for something we can't name, something those old songs called "grace." It's a small but rich word that suggests among other meanings, *assistance, virtue, blessing, kindness, mercy, privilege, reprieve, ease of movement, charm,* and *fitness or proportion of expression.*

Sometimes I imagine a cultural critic of some future age . . . trying to figure out who these people were, how they carried themselves and what they believed. . . . The critic, I hope, would discover in our writings traces of a world where there seemed to be, in Jackson Lear's phrase, "no place of grace" but

where we nonetheless still found ways to fill up the old word with some of its meanings.[52]

Many, if not most, of this writer's (David Eason) audience would agree with him, so he can use the unifying style with its many there-and-then references, its poetic style and language, and its emotional and sometimes abstract images to reinforce and activate what the audience already believes.

In all likelihood, both Keillor and Eason have used both the pragmatic and the unifying styles. These two styles are a function of the audience and its needs and not of the speaker. We can learn something about persuaders by observing which style they choose for which kinds of audiences. Persuadees can gain insight into how they are being seen by the persuader by identifying the style of the message.

Semiotics as a Tool for Decoding Persuasion

We have briefly referred to the emerging field of semiotics as a way to study meaning. Although the origin of this approach to the study of meaning goes back to the work of Charles Morris and Charles Pierce in the late 1940s and 1950s, its most important contemporary theorist is Umberto Eco, an Italian semiotician better known for his best-selling novels *The Name of the Rose* and *Foucault's Pendulum*, both of which address the subject of meaning in unusual ways. Like other semioticians, Eco believes that the process of "signification" (or the giving of meaning to a "sign") involves four elements: (1) the objects or conditions that exist in the world, (2) the signs that are available to represent these objects or conditions, (3) a set of choices among signs, or a *repertoire* of responses we can have or give to signs, and (4) a set of rules of correspondence that we use to encode and decode the signs we make and interpret.[53]

It is this final characteristic that most directly addresses the goal of this course. The discovery of the various codes used by persuaders and understood by persuadees characterizes *cooperatively* created meanings. In other words, we participate in our own persuasion by "agreeing with" the code(s) persuaders use. Most important, we can become critical consumers of persuasion by continually striving to discover and reveal these codes.[54] The work of semiotician and former circus owner and ringmaster Paul Buissac offers some fascinating examples.[55] The following brief semiotic analysis of the circus act should demonstrate this idea of an easily discernible code that is understood by "children of all ages," around the world.

Wild animal, tightrope, and trapeze acts never occur back to back in the circus, Buissac tells us; they are always interspersed with clown acts, small animal acts, magic acts, or the like. If a daring act is canceled, the entire order of acts needs to be altered because of audience expectations, the need for tension reduction, and to communicate that the world is alternately serious and comedic.

According to Buissac, "Death-defying acts also have a code — usually a five-step sequence." First, there is the introduction of the act by the ringmaster (a godlike figure able to control not only the dangers but the chaos of the circus). This introduction, with its music, lights, and revelation of dazzling and daring costumes, is followed by "the warm-up," in which minor qualifying tests occur: The animal trainer, dressed as a big-game hunter, gets all the animals to their proper positions; the trapeze artist, with his beautiful assistants, can easily swing out and switch trapeze bars in mid-air; the tightrope walker dances across the rope with ease. Then comes the major tests or tricks: getting the tiger to dance with the lion, double trapeze switches, and walking the wire blindfolded. Having passed these tests, the circus performer then attempts the "glorifying," or "death-defying," test. It is always accompanied by the ringmaster's request for absolute silence and, ironically, by the band breaking the critical silence with a nerve-tingling drum-roll. Then comes the feat itself: The animal tamer puts his head into the lion's mouth; the trapeze artist holds up a pair of beautiful assistants with his teeth, demonstrating his

amazing strength; and the tightrope walker puts a passenger on his shoulders and rides a bicycle backward and blindfolded across the high wire. Frequently there is a close call: An unruly tiger tries to interfere with the "head-in-the-mouth" trick; there is a near miss on the trapeze, a stumble on the high wire, and so on. Once the glorifying test is passed, the ringmaster calls for applause as the act exits and then returns for a curtain call. This sequence is a "code" we all understand.

More subtle examples of codes are frequently found in advertising. For example, consider the ad for Bostonian shoes in Figure 5.6. What codes are operating in this ad? Some are rather obvious, but others are more subtle. In fact, some codes in the ad are embedded within other codes. The most obvious code is that the ad is trying to sell a product. However, what kind of product is not so clear; finding out requires more detailed decoding, but we soon discover that the product is men's shoes. Another less-obvious code is that the product is an up-scale one, as indicated by the composition and copy of the ad and by the price of the shoes — $105. The ad is understated; there is little actual ad copy. Finally, the photography is distinctively "fine-art" in its composition.

Within these codes is an even more subtle code — one that is only implied, never directly stated. This code signifies the life-style that goes with the product, of which the shoes are merely an emblem. What do we see in this photograph? Clearly, it is the "morning after" a very satisfying night of lovemaking (notice the coffee cups and pastries on the bed, the negligé on the well-rumpled bedding, the indentations on both pillows). The life-style includes a fine home (notice

FIGURE 5.6

What messages are implied by the "code" of physical objects in this ad (theater tickets, rumpled bedclothes, articles of clothing that seem to have been hurriedly discarded, an empty cocktail glass, and so on)? (Reprinted by permission of the Bostonian Shoe Company.)

Perfectly fitting and proper. This day. Every day.

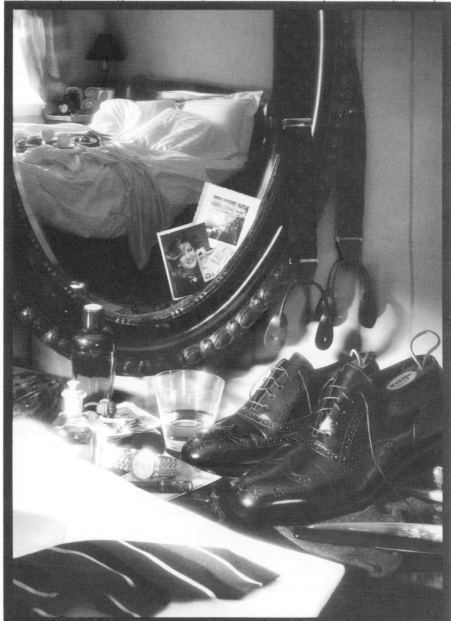

Every decision should be as clear-cut as your choice of Bostonian. These wingtips are trimmer, more richly detailed. And more comfortable. With cushioned innersoles and glove-soft leather linings. About $105. For nearby stores, call 1-800-444-2624.

perfectly fitting and proper

BOSTONIAN

since 1899.

the expensive furniture and the framed photographs on the nightstand in the upper left corner). This life-style includes expensive accessories (a Rolex watch and a Mont Blanc pen are on the dresser), stylish suspenders, theater tickets, a beautiful wife in the picture under the tickets, and being physically attractive (note the snapshot of him, bare chested and muscular). It is clear that this ad carries a lot of meaning and that this meaning is "signified" by the verbal and nonverbal symbols being used (or perhaps misused), depending on one's perspective.

Although analyses like these may be intriguing, they are difficult to carry out without some kind of methodology. The fields of theoretic semiotics and applied semiotics (for example, advertising and image and political consulting) are rapidly expanding, and you as a receiver need a simplified way to pin down these uses (or misuses) of symbols. A methodology for doing this kind of semiotic analysis has been developed by communication scholar Arthur Asa Berger, whom we met briefly in Chapter 4.[56] Berger provides a fairly simple checklist for doing such an analysis (my students find it useful). First, consider the pieces of persuasion aimed at you as if they are "texts" to be read, and then put on your Sherlock Holmes hat and start looking for clues. According to Berger (and adapted for you), here are some steps you might take:

A. Isolate and analyze the important signs in your text.
 1. What are the important signifiers?
 2. What do they signify?
 3. Is there a system that unifies them?
 4. What codes can be found (for example, symbols of status, colors, music)?
 5. Are ideological or sociological issues being addressed?
 6. How are they conveyed or hinted at?
B. Identify the central structure, theme, or model of the text.
 1. What forces are in opposition?
 2. What forces are teamed with one another?
 3. Do the oppositions or teams have psycho-

logical or sociological meanings? What are they?
C. What is the narrative structure of the text? (That is, if a "story" is being told, what are its elements?)
 1. How does the sequential arrangement of events affect meaning? What changes in meaning would result if they were altered?
 2. Are there any "formulaic" aspects to the text (for example, hard work leads to success, justice prevails, honesty gets its reward)?
D. Does the medium being used affect the text? How?
 1. Use of shots, camera angles, editing, dissolves, and so on.
 2. Use of lighting, color, music, sound, special effects, and so on.
 3. Paper quality, typefaces, graphics, colors, and so on.
 4. How do the speaker's words, gestures, and facial expressions affect meaning?
E. How does the application of semiological theory alter the original meaning you might have ascribed to the text? (You may want to do further reading in semiotics to answer this question effectively).

Of course, this discussion of the semiotic approach to language and meaning is brief and necessarily simplified. Nonetheless, it should give you another tool to discover the important first premises that emerge from our language preferences and the images that are molded from them.

FIGURE 5.7

Using the semiotic approach to uncovering meaning as outlined by Berger, uncover the meaning of this ad/text. Note that the woman has "lost" items from her pockets — a passport, the keys to an Audi, credit cards, a picture of herself drawn by her child, jewelry, aspirin, a champagne cork, a $100 bill, and other items. What do they signify? How old is this woman? Is she sentimental? Stressed? Busy? (Used by permission.)

WHAT DO YOU CALL A WOMAN WHO'S MADE IT TO THE TOP?

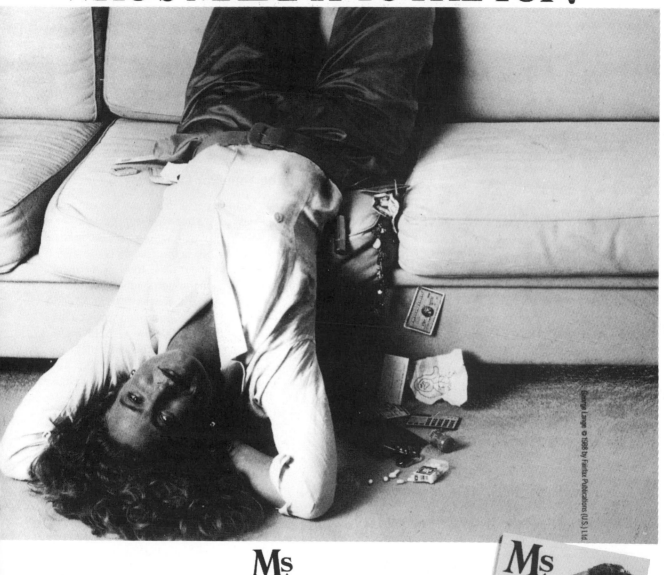

Ms.

She's a better prospect than ever. Because we've turned the old *Ms.* upside down to reflect how women are living today. And you're going to love the results.

The new *Ms.* is witty and bold, with a large-size format that's full of surprises. Whether it's money, politics, business, technology, clothing trends, humor, or late-breaking news—if it's up-to-the-minute, it's part of the new *Ms.*

So if you want to reach the top women consumers in America, reach for the phone. And call Linda Lucht, Advertising Director, *Ms. Magazine*, One Times Square, New York, N.Y. 10036. Tel: (212) 704-8581.

The new Ms. As impressive as the woman who reads it.

Gender and Style

In an article titled "He: This is an okay (lovely) analysis (emotional investigation) of our words (deepest corridors of meaning)," language critic and English professor Edwin Bruell considers how gender affects our use of language and style.[57] As you may have guessed from the way the title of the article is written, the words inside the parentheses represent the feminine mode of expression, and the words outside the parentheses represent the masculine mode of expression. As Bruell notes, "There seems to be a form of poverty in America that is strictly a masculine phenomenon: poverty of expression."[58] He goes on to point out some differences between male and female word choice. For example, women can characterize clothing, dolls, furniture, or sunsets with words like *lovely, darling, sweet, adorable,* or *cute,* whereas men rarely use such words. Men may perhaps use the word *lovely* to express their assessment of a new dress on their spouse or another woman, but they would never use it to describe the new suit of clothes on another man. Bruell claims that "men shy away from all such usages because they passionately fear being labeled sissified. Their superlatives are likely to be far less flowery."[59] Instead they tend to limit their superlatives to words like *fine, great, good,* and occasionally *grand* if they are talking about a sports event. Also, according to Bruell, "Women will speak of 'fragrance' and 'scent' and 'aromatic, seductive' concoctions. A man will speak of 'smell' . . . and . . . a shutout defeat just 'stinks.'" To men, locker room jokes are *dirty stories*, but at cocktail parties, women listen to the same stories but label them risqué party stories. An orderly desk is *tidy* to a woman, but it is *neat and organized* to a man. An attractive, well-dressed, and carefully groomed woman may be described as *dainty* or *fetching* by another woman, but she will be *nice, okay,* or *swell* to a man. Bruell recounts an encounter with a female confidant who exclaimed, "How cunning they are! How positively ravishing!" which he thought referred to stereotypes that "frighten me (no, make that 'scare the ---- out of me')." Actually she was rhapsodizing about her first view of a set of burly tag-team wrestlers.[60]

So, language choices can reveal much information about persuaders: their cultural heritage, their political inclinations, their philosophy, the nature of their audiences, their gender, and a host of other kinds of meanings and interpretations. It becomes essential, therefore, for critical and ethical receivers of messages to look beyond the substance of the message for deeper indications of the persuader's attitudes and world view as well as his or her potential future actions. How do we go about this?

Tuning Your Ear for Clues

Aware and critical persuadees tune their ears to the various clues to style and motives. What are some ways in which you can tune your ear? Using some of the tools described in this chapter is one way. If you have thought about these tools, if the theory about self-revelation through symbols has sparked your imagination, or if you have tried to apply these tools to the persuasion around you, you have already started the tuning process. Applying the study questions at the end of this and other chapters is another good way to continue. There are at least three other strategies you might use to make yourself more critical of style and to "read" or "psych out" persuaders:

1. *Role play the persuader.* Assume that you are the persuader or a member of a group with a persuasive cause. How would you shape the persuasion you wish to present? For example, if you favor high salaries for ballplayers, how would you frame a pragmatic message for half-hearted believers, those who are neutral, or others who are only moderately opposed? You might mention the shortness of most players' careers (hence they receive a low overall salary across a lifetime, despite high yearly salaries). You might compare ballplayers to entertainers, who make several million dollars per year for relatively little actual work time. You might cite overall profits made by ballclubs and the rather meager retirement programs in pro sports. If your audience happened to be the Association of Professional Baseball Players, you could afford to

bypass the numbers and use highly emotional and abstract language to motivate the audience. You might create images of club owners as filthy-rich bloodsuckers who mindlessly use up the best years of an athlete's life as strip-miners ravage the landscape. Your language would probably be there-and-then — referring to new goals of the group or past abuses. Your style would show your view of the audience.

2. *Restate a persuasive message in various ways.* Instead of pretending to be a ghostwriter for the persuader, just try to restate what the persuader has said in several different ways. Ask yourself what the options are (as we did sketchily with the presidential slogans earlier in this chapter). Then try to determine how these alternatives will change the intent of the message and its final effects. This process should lead you to draw some conclusions about the persuader's intent. You might determine the persuader's pentadic emphasis and then restate the persuasion from the viewpoint of the other four elements of the dramatic pentad.

    For example, take the following slogan for Grand Marnier Liqueur: "There Are Still Places on Earth Where Grand Marnier Isn't Offered after Dinner." The slogan is printed on a photo of a deserted island. The appeal is scenic. An agent-oriented version of this slogan might be "People with a Taste for the Good Things of Life Offer Grand Marnier." A purpose-oriented version might read something like: "When You Want to Finish the Conference, Offer Grand Marnier." An agency-oriented version might say, "From a Secret Triple-Orange Recipe," stressing the method of production. The act might be emphasized by saying, "Do the Right Thing Now — Offer Grand Marnier." Of course, each slogan would accompany appropriate visuals.

3. *Attend to language features in discourse.* Don't allow yourself passively to buy into any persuasive advice that is being hawked. Instead, get into the habit of looking at a message's style. Analyze messages on billboards and in TV commercials, the language used by your parents when they try to persuade you, the wording on packages you purchase, or the phrases used in discussions between you and friends, enemies, or salespersons. In other words, start listening not only to *ideas* — the thrust of the messages aimed at you — but to *words*, the packaging of those ideas. Try it on me. What kind of words do I use? Why? What do you think I'm like? How does my style differ from that of Richard Johannesen (see Chapter 2)? From that of other textbook writers? From the way you would have said it? Focusing on these features in as many situations as possible will give you an intriguing pastime in which to operate as an amateur psychoanalyst. Further, you will develop an ear for stylistic tip-offs, a skill that will prove valuable in your interpersonal relations: It allows you to predict and respond to the communication of others.

REVIEW AND CONCLUSION

There are several ways to become a responsible receiver of persuasion that relate to the language a particular persuader chooses. We can gain general insight by looking at the semantic connotations of the words chosen. We can look at word order, or syntax, and at how frequently various parts of speech are chosen. The degree of ambiguity used by the persuader is often revealing, as in a dramatistic analysis such as that suggested by Burke. The motifs and metaphors chosen by a persuader often reveal motive. And persuadees can "psych out" the persuader by looking at the God, Devil, and charismatic terms used, as well as the choice of pragmatic versus unifying style. Finally, we can apply the semiotic approach to the interpretation of persuasive messages — identify as many of the signifiers in a persuasive message as possible. Then we can try to determine what is being signified and whether there is an overall theme or thrust to the message we are examining.

All these critical devices are enhanced by role playing, restating, and developing awareness of the words and style as well as the ideas used in a persuasive message, whether a speech, a TV documentary, a film, a political slogan, a social movement, a package designed to sell a product, or a friend's request.

QUESTIONS FOR FURTHER THOUGHT

1. Transcribe the lyrics of a popular song. Now analyze them according to the functional tools presented in this chapter. Is there a preference for a certain word type? A certain sentence structure? Is the message ambiguous or concrete? Explain.

2. Describe several semantic tools. What do you think is the pentadic perspective of the author of this book? Why? What do you think is the pentadic favorite of your instructor?

3. Describe the tools for a thematic or textural analysis of language and use some of them to analyze the persuasion occurring in a recent political campaign. What do these analyses tell you about the candidate?

4. What are the God terms of your parents? What are their Devil terms? Shape a request for something from your parents, expressed in their God terms. Now do the same thing using their Devil terms. Try them on your parents as an experiment. Which is more effective? Why?

5. How does a unifying persuader differ from a pragmatic one? Find examples of each type of persuader in your class, in persuasive attempts of the past, or in defenders of some persuasive issue being discussed in your community. Are there other differences between these two types? What are they?

6. What are the differences between *semantics* and *semiotics*? Which is more objective? When might it be appropriate to use each approach? How do you use semantics and semiotics to both analyze and create persuasive messages?

7. What is the difference between a text and a symbol? What is the difference between a signifier and the signified?

8. How does gender affect how we use language? Can you give examples beyond those cited in Chapter 5?

NOTES

1. *House and Garden*, June 1977, p. 31.
2. Lori B. Andrews, "Exhibit A: Language," *Psychology Today*, February 1984, p. 30.
3. *Ibid.*
4. *Ibid.*, p. 32.
5. *Ibid.*
6. Richard Weaver, *The Ethics of Rhetoric* (Chicago: Henry Regnery, 1953).
7. Michael Osborne, "Archetypal Metaphors in Rhetoric: The Light-Dark Family," *Quarterly Journal of Speech*, April 1967, pp. 115–126.
8. Michael Tackett, "Iowa Caucus Maze Puts 1988 Show on the Road," *Chicago Tribune*, February 8, 1988, p. 2.
9. "The Great TV Shout-Out," *Newsweek*, February 8, 1988.
10. *Ibid.*, p. 21.
11. "Fed Up? It May Lead to an Ulcer," *Chicago Daily News*, November 24, 1972, p. 30. For a more detailed discussion, see Howard Lewis and Martha Lewis, *Psychosomatics: How Your Emotions Can Damage Your Health* (New York: Viking Press, 1972).
12. Peter Koenig, "Death Doth Defer," *Psychology Today*, November 1972, p. 83.
13. "Psychiatric Study of Pro-Football," *Saturday Review/World*, October 5, 1974, pp. 12–16; and "A Psychiatrist Looks at Pro-Football," *Reader's Digest*, January 1975, pp. 89–92.
14. Black Elk, *Touch the Earth*, ed. T. C. McLuhan (New York: Outerbridge and Dienstfrey, 1971), p. 42.
15. As quoted in Sandra J. Ball-Rokeach and Milton Rokeach, "The Great American Values Test," *Psychology Today*, November 1984, p. 41.
16. *Ibid.*
17. *Ibid.*

18. Weaver, *op. cit.*, p. 120. For a discussion of the Platonic idealism and political conservatism underlying Weaver's conception of rhetoric, see Richard L. Johannesen, Rennard Strickland, and Ralph T. Eubanks, "Richard M. Weaver on the Nature of Rhetoric," in *Contemporary Theories of Rhetoric*, ed. Johannesen (New York: Harper & Row, 1971), pp. 180–195.

19. Stephen W. Colford, "Cosby Goes to Bat for Jackson," *Advertising Age*, February 8, 1988, p. 1.

20. Weaver, *op. cit.*, p. 121.

21. *1977 Mobil Current Energy Series #3* (New York: Mobil Oil Corporation, 1977), reprinted in the *Chicago Tribune*, July 28, 1977, sec. 1, p. 8.

22. Weaver, *op. cit.*, p. 127.

23. Wendell Rawls, Jr., "Klan Group in Alabama Training for 'Race War,'" *New York Times*, September 28, 1980.

24. *Ibid.*

25. Weaver, *op. cit.*, p. 128.

26. Marilyn Preston, "On TV," *Chicago Tribune*, May 14, 1981, sec. 1, p. 15. The researchers did frequency counts of the usage in the normal everyday speech of various children and correlated this with hours of television watched per day.

27. Robert Shrum, "Party Lines," *New Times*, July 22, 1977, p. 4.

28. Dan Nimmo and James Combs, *Mediated Political Realities* (New York: Longman and Sons, 1984), pp. 184–187.

29. *Webster's Ninth New Collegiate Dictionary*, (Springfield, Mass.: Merriam-Webster, Inc., 1987), p. 431.

30. Dannye Romine, "Styron's Choice," *The Chicago Tribune*, July 3, 1989, sec. 5, pp. 1–2.

31. "A New Quayle Tale," *The Chicago Tribune*, April 26, 1989, sec. 1, p. 20.

32. *Newsweek*, June 11, 1990, cover.

33. Theodore H. White, *The Making of the President: 1964* (New York: Atheneum, 1966), p. v.

34. As quoted in Robert J. Trotter, "Stop Blaming Yourself," *Psychology Today*, February 1987, pp. 31–39.

35. *Ibid.*, p. 37.

36. *Ibid.*, pp. 36 and 37.

37. *Ibid.*, p. 32.

38. Michael Osborne, *op. cit.*

39. Mircea Eliade, *The Myth of the Eternal Return* (Princeton, NJ: Princeton University Press, 1971).

40. Stephanie L. Swanson and David Wenner, "Sensory language in the courtroom," *Trial Diplomacy Journal*, Winter 1981, pp. 37–43.

41. *Ibid.*, pp. 38–39.

42. *Ibid.*, p. 42.

43. Weaver, *op. cit.*, pp. 211, 212, 214.

44. *Ibid.*, p. 211.
    Newsweek, January 4, 1988, cover page.

45. Bill Barol, "The Eighties Are Over," *Newsweek*, January 4, 1988, pp. 40–48.

46. *Ibid.*, p. 48.

47. Weaver, *op. cit.*, pp. 224–226.

48. Weaver, *op. cit.*, p. 230.

49. Berkeley Rice, "Imagination to Go," *Psychology Today*, May 1984, pp. 50–51.

50. For examples of speeches illustrating these styles, see Wil Linkugel, Ron R. Allen, and Richard L. Johannesen (eds.), *Contemporary American Speeches* (Prospect Heights, IL: Waveland Press, 1988).

51. Garrison Keillor, "Three New Twins Join Club in Spring," *The New Yorker*, February 22, 1988, pp. 32–33.

52. David L. Eason, "Editor's Note," *Critical Studies in Mass Communication*, September 1987, pp. v and vi.

53. Umberto Eco, *Semiotics and the Philosophy of Language* (London: Macmillan Press Ltd., 1984).

54. Umberto Eco, *The Role of the Reader* (Bloomington: Indiana University Press, 1979).

55. Paul Buissac, *Circus and Culture: A Semiotic Approach* (Bloomington: Indiana University Press, 1976).

56. Arthur Asa Berger, *Signs in Contemporary Society* (New York: Longman and Sons, 1984), and Arthur Asa Berger, *Media Analysis Techniques* (Beverly Hills: Sage Publications, 1982), especially Chapter 1.

57. Edwin Bruell, "He: This is an okay (lovely) analysis (emotional investigation) of our words (deepest corridors of meaning)," *Chicago Tribune*, December 31, 1986, sec. 7, p. 12.

58. *Ibid.*

59. *Ibid.*

60. *Ibid.*

PART

II

IDENTIFYING PERSUASIVE FIRST PREMISES

As we saw in Part I, there are many ways to define, explain, and interpret persuasive messages and the symbols used to convey them. And we noted that the critical question of ethics enters into every persuasive decision we make, whether as receivers or as persuaders. As we continue our study, it will help you to return to what we learned in Part I about the foundations of persuasion theory, the many theoretical explanations of persuasive phenomena, and the various means of analyzing the verbal and nonverbal symbols used in persuasive language, regardless of their source.

Underlying all means to analytically process the symbols of persuasion is the ancient Aristotelean concept of the *enthymeme*, which was briefly discussed in Chapter 3, where we examined Aristotle's triad of "available means of persuasion," or ethos, pathos, and logos. The enthymeme will serve as the analytical metaphor or organizational device for Part II. It might be useful to think of Part II as a search for sources used by persuaders as major premises in enthymemes: They are felt or held to be true by large numbers of persons.

Aristotle thought that the most effective arguments used syllogistic (Aristotelean) logic. Syllogisms usually include: (1) a *major premise*, which asserts some condition in the world (that the continued destruction of the ozone layer must be stopped); (2) a *minor premise*, which asserts a sec-

ond condition or a particular case that relates to the major premise (the use of aerosol sprays adds to the continued destruction of the ozone layer); and (3) a *conclusion*, which flows from the major and minor premises (the use of aerosol sprays must be stopped). The *enthymeme* carries this one step further: It assumes that since the audience already believes the major premise to be true, the persuader can take a shortcut by stating or proving only the minor premise. Thus the enthymeme allows receivers to participate in their own persuasion, making it more potent and likely to lead to action.

In Part II, we will do what many persuaders do. They identify those major premises that audiences believe and those minor premises that audiences can be convinced of in order to prompt the desired conclusion. We will look at certain major categories of premises that audiences believe: We will hunt for major premises.

The first category of major premise is the *process premise*, which is covered in Chapter 6. Process premises rely on psychological factors that operate in nearly all persuadees. Persuaders can tie their product, candidate, or idea to these process premises, which are used as the major premises in enthymemic arguments that have wide appeal.

In Chapter 7, we will look at the second category of major premises: *content premises*. Their persuasiveness lies in the audience's belief in the truth or validity of the argument.

For example, if the audience believes that history repeats itself and that as a result we can avoid the mistakes of the past, then the persuader merely has to draw a convincing analogy between the past and the present. This is precisely what happened when Iraq invaded its neighbor Kuwait in the summer of 1990, taking foreigners as hostages and inflicting brutal treatment on Kuwait's citizenry. The invasion bore a striking resemblance to Hitler's 1938 invasion of his neighbor Austria. Iraq's leader, Saddam Hussein, also reminded people of Hitler in his complete dictatorship over the people of Iraq. President Bush used this analogy to muster world opinion against Hussein. The analogy was so convincing that the United Nations passed a number of resolutions condemning the invasion and authorizing a massive trade embargo against Iraq. What's more, troops were sent to the Kuwaiti border to force Iraq to leave, and the U.N. even voted to authorize the use of military force if necessary. It was the first time the U.N. had voted such extreme measures with such unity. The audience supplied the logically based major, or content, premise and drew the desired conclusion: Stop Hussein now and avoid a repeat of World War II.

You have probably noticed that there is considerable similarity between process premises and content premises. Process premises rely on *psychological* or *emotional* needs, whereas content premises rely on *logical* or *rational* patterns. We have been trained in these patterns of inference since early childhood; they have been reinforced throughout our lives. When we tell two-year-old children that if they continue to cry they will have to go without television or a particular toy, we are using "If . . . then . . ." reasoning, for instance.

The third major category of process premises, discussed in Chapter 8, is the *cultural premise*. This kind of premise relies on patterns of behavior or beliefs that are almost articles of faith for audiences and that have been passed on to them by their culture or society. For example, Americans learn that when faced with a problem they should seek a solution to it, perhaps by establishing a task force or swallowing a pill. This seems so obvious that we are dumbstruck to discover that people from some other cultures prefer to accept the inevitable when faced with a problem. Problem solving is a culturally transmitted pattern for us. Knowing that, the persuader can motivate us to take actions by portraying the actions as solutions. Even if we don't perceive that there is a problem, and thus are not searching for solutions, the clever persuader can create a problem and sell us a cure. Cultural premises consist of the myths and values our society holds dear.

In Chapter 9, we will explore *nonverbal premises*, which are similar to cultural premises in that they vary from culture to culture as well as from subculture to subculture. These nonverbal premises can sometimes be more potent than sophisticated verbal premises. Often, nonverbal premises result in the ultimate success or failure of persuasion.

As you read Part II, think of yourself as searching for major premises that you and an audience hold in common. By identifying these major premises you can not only become a more skillful persuader but also, and more important, you can evaluate more effectively the persuasion aimed at you.

CHAPTER 6

Process Premises: The Tools of Motivation

One of the less predictable kinds of persuasive premises relates to human emotions, attitudes, and beliefs. For our purposes, we will call them **process premises**. Persuaders use process premises to appeal to the emotions or passions, and such premises frequently rely on the less rational side of human nature. Historical examples of the use of emotional appeals include Mark Antony's funeral oration in *The Tragedy of Julius Caesar*, Patrick Henry's "Give Me Liberty or Give Me Death" speech, and Abraham Lincoln's "Second Inaugural Address." Franklin Roosevelt used emotional appeals in the midst of the Great Depression to assure the country that it had "nothing to fear but fear itself." Winston Churchill made masterful use of emotional appeals in his attempts to inspire the English to fight on after the fall of France and the disastrous retreat at Dunkirk. While London was being bombed to rubble, Churchill vowed to fight the Germans in the streets and hills or if necessary from the countries of the Empire. The phrases he used are classics of the art of persuasion:

> We shall not flag or fail. We shall go on to the end. We shall fight in France, we shall fight on the seas and oceans, we shall fight with growing confidence and growing strength in the air, we shall defend our island, whatever the cost may be, we shall fight on the beaches, we shall fight on the landing grounds, we shall fight in the fields and in the streets, we shall fight in the hills; we shall never surrender.[1]

We know from Churchill's diaries that he himself doubted that what he called for was possible. Nonetheless, his emotional speeches bolstered English resolve to endure until the United States entered the war.

More recently, we have observed the process premise operating in the eloquent and moving "I Have a Dream" speech by Reverend Martin Luther King, Jr. King knew that his audience already desired — in fact fervently wished for — racial equality. This was the major unstated process premise. His minor premises were specific examples of what equality could be like. In the late 1980s and early 1990s, process premises appealing to attitudes and beliefs were used to bring about

the collapse of communist governments in Poland, East Germany, Czechoslovakia, Hungary, Romania, and Bulgaria, and these kinds of appeals will certainly be used in the next decade as those countries try to forge new forms of government. In these appeals, the major premise is that a free marketplace is good. Minor premises such as the desirability of private ownership of property were used to lead audiences to the conclusion that communism was bankrupt. And of course emotional appeals that rely on emotions and psychological processes are evident in other persuasive arenas such as interpersonal persuasion between spouses, parents and children, siblings, lovers, and bosses and employees. Psychological appeals are seen in business, marketing, advertising, sales promotion, and ideological advocacy on behalf of emotionally loaded issues such as right to life, prochoice, flag burning, and others.

THE CLASSICAL VIEW OF EMOTIONAL APPEALS

As we have already noted, the systematic study of persuasion began with the Greeks and Romans, who categorized **emotional** or **nonlogical appeals** into several types. One kind of emotional appeal entails the use of figures of speech, highly charged words, and other elements of *style* to appeal to the passions or the will. This use of emotional style might appeal to the audience's sense of rage, their desire for justice, their inherent greed or hatred, their need for love and friendship, or a host of other emotional or nonlogical needs.

Another kind of nonlogical process premise is the argument derived from or based on authority or tradition (called the *ad vere cundium* argument by the ancients). This appeal relies on our inherent emotional response to persons of authority or to the way things have always been done. For example, in their advertising, some corporations cite a date of origin or the number of years the product has been available or how long the company has been in business. There is not much that is logical about this type of appeal — after all, being in business a long time might indicate only that the firm is conservative and old-fashioned. We respond to the appeal because of our fear of fly-by-night operations or because we feel more secure about products that have a record of performance. For example, if you were promoting a new kind of automobile—say, the Skoda from Czechoslovakia—it would be better to compare its performance to that of the Volkswagen (which has been around and successful for about fifty years) rather than to that of the Yugo (which was a flop as a new make in the American auto market).

The ancients also believed that the type of technique used in delivering messages could enhance these appeals, making them even stronger. Outraged or bombastic delivery, for instance, could stir up the audience. Weeping or crying out during the speech might also awaken the audience's emotions. Speaking softly might force audience attention and hint of inside knowledge that the speaker could share with the audience. Recently we have seen sensational persuaders such as Morton Downy, Jr., and Geraldo Rivera appeal to the baser emotions. These all relate to needs that process premises address.

In sum, we can identify three major types of process premises. One type of process premise addresses the individual's own set of needs, some of which relate to physical survival (for example, the need for food, air, or water), and some of which relate to the enhancement of our sense of well-being (for example, health insurance). A second type of process premise appeals to the set of opinions, attitudes, beliefs, and behavioral tendencies held by all persuadees. The third type of process premise addresses our desire to live in a predictable world—one that avoids inconsistencies (a need that is becoming increasingly difficult to fulfill in our rapidly expanding technocracy). Let's explore these process premises in more detail.

NEEDS: THE FIRST PROCESS PREMISE

Each of us has a set of individual **needs**. Some of them are critical to us—we can't live without them; others are not critical—we can easily get along without them. Not everyone's priorities are identical, but our needs resemble one another's enough that various theories of motivation can identify those that typify audiences. Some theories identify needs that are physiologically based, such as our needs for the staples of survival and physical security, which go back to mankind's very beginnings. Other theories focus on less concrete needs, ones that, although not directly related to survival, lend themselves to our overall sense of well-being (success on the job, or the need for religious belief, for example). Without them or some substitute, we feel frustrated, anxious, afraid, or even angry. These needs are hard to measure (unlike physiological needs—we know just how many minutes or hours one can live without food, water, or air), so we infer them from patterns of behavior that people exhibit. For instance, because people seem concerned about making a good impression on others, we infer that they have a need to be recognized.

Knowing that the audience has a need for recognition, a persuader can design appeals to this need to sell products such as designer jeans, sporty automobiles, or homes of distinction. Such products become symbolic representations of the fulfillment of our need to be recognized. For the most part, persuasion in today's changing world is aimed at promoting or selling symbolic ways to meet our physiological and emotional needs. Although there *are* some products (such as self-improvement courses) that really can help you make a better impression on the boss, your parents, your peers, or that special someone, for the most part what we buy and support doesn't have a direct effect. We buy and use Binaca breath spray not because it ensures that we will make a better impression but because we hope it will prevent us from having bad breath; we think that avoiding bad breath will help us make the special impression.

Our needs make us vulnerable to persuasion, and effective persuaders successfully determine our needs. If they analyze our needs incorrectly, persuasion can boomerang. For example, a well-known luggage manufacturer once spent thousands of dollars to produce an impressive and clever TV ad. The spot opened with luggage being handled roughly as it was loaded into the cargo bay of a huge airliner. (The central piece of luggage was made by the sponsor). The plane was next seen in flight and we were shown a slight problem: someone had failed to latch the cargo bay door. As the plane banked, our star piece of luggage fell out of the now-open bay door. The camera followed the suitcase as it fell 30,000 feet and landed with a huge thud on some rocks. Then the case was opened to reveal the undamaged contents. Now, that ought to be a pretty convincing ad. However, airing of the commercial was followed by a tremendous drop in sales. Why? Using in-depth interviews, researchers found that most people, even regular airline travelers, fear a plane crash. They resented the implication that their luggage would survive them in the event of a crash and so rejected that brand.

In the late 1950s, some of the motivation research done on behalf of advertisers was chronicled by author and critic Vance Packard in a book titled *The Hidden Persuaders.*[2] It was promoted with sentences like these:

In this book you'll discover a world of psychology professors turned merchandisers. You'll learn how they operate, what they know about you and your neighbors, and how they are using that knowledge to sell you cake mixes, cigarettes, soaps and even ideas.[3]

Packard reported that a majority of the hundred largest ad firms in the country had been using a psychoanalytic approach. He noted that other professional persuaders—public relations executives, fund-raisers, politicians, and others—were turning to psychological theorists to discover customers' motives. They then tied their products, candidates, and causes to these motives. Packard quotes one ad executive as saying:

Motivation research . . . seeks to learn what motivates people in making choices. It employs techniques designed to reach the subconscious mind because preferences generally are determined by factors of which the individual is not conscious. . . . Actually in the buying situation the consumer acts emotionally and compulsively, unconsciously reacting to im-

ages and designs which in the sub-conscious are associated with the product.[4]

Another advertiser gave some examples of how the research was used:

The cosmetic manufacturers are not selling lanolin; they are selling hope. . . . We no longer buy oranges, we buy vitality. We do not buy just an auto; we buy prestige.[5]

Clearly, psychology had entered the field of advertising. According to Packard, market researchers operating from this perspective had three assumptions about people. First, they assumed that people don't always know what they want when they make a purchase. Second, they assumed that one cannot rely on what people say about what they like and dislike. Finally, they assumed that people do not act logically or rationally. Packard gave several examples of how these assumptions operate. For instance, motivation researchers wondered what made people buy laundry detergent. Purchasers *said* they bought it because of its cleaning power. A sample group of consumers were given three boxes of detergent. They were asked to test the three types and report back. Actually, the three boxes contained the same detergent—only the color of the boxes was different. The test group reported that the detergent in the yellow box was too harsh. The one in the blue box was too weak; it left clothes gray after washing. But the stuff in the yellow and blue box was great.

The psychoanalytic approach to marketing most closely reflects the symbolistic tradition of psychology. Indeed, much of the in-depth research that Packard describes is like psychoanalysis. The researchers used in-depth interviews that encouraged customers to describe the fears, pleasures, nightmares, fantasies, and lusts they associated with the product or the ad for it. Other researchers used complex psychological tests like the Minnesota Multiphasic Personality Inventory (MMPI). Still others used projective tests in which people completed sentences about the product or described the "real meaning" behind cartoon vignettes related to the product. The trend continues, more than thirty years after Packard first described it. In fact, the "hidden persuaders" are using increasingly sophisticated methods to fight against the new technologies for meeting or "skipping" commercials by "zapping" them with a fast-forward remote control.

> Advertisers aren't about to take this lying down. Desperate to keep you tuned to their pitches, they're trying some new tricks. If that's news to you, it may be because these new techniques are manipulating you in ways you're not aware of. "Many of these commercials have more impact on the subconscious level," charges New York University media professor Neil Postman. Perhaps more disturbing, ad agencies often enlist psychologists and neurophysiologists to make sure the pitches have the desired effect.[6]

We will discuss the various kinds of techniques advertisers use to outwit "clutter" in chapters that deal with advertising and mass media. But for right now, the important thing is that you become aware of persuaders' reactions to such persuadee defenses as "zapping."

In his research, Packard found eight "compelling needs" that were frequently used in selling products via the motivation research approach.[7] We will see that the marketing folks still use them today, although probably with more sophistication.

Packard's Eight "Hidden Needs"

The hidden needs that Packard described were discovered using the depth interview or the projective test. Once the needs were determined to be "compelling," merchandisers designed their ads to promise that the product or service would provide some degree of real or symbolic fulfillment of the compelling need (see Figure 6.1). You can almost imagine Freud himself as the director of a Madison Avenue ad agency think-tank, probing ever deeper into the consumer's subconscious, looking for the "hot" buttons that will turn people on to products and avoiding the "cold" ones that will turn them against a product. In spite of the time that has passed since Packard did his work, we still see

pitches in advertising, politics, propaganda, and elsewhere aimed at his eight "hidden needs," which we will now discuss.

Need for Emotional Security We are living in one of the most insecure eras in human history. Terrorism seems unstoppable. Our environment is becoming more and more polluted with potentially deadly wastes. The protective ozone layer surrounding our planet is disintegrating. The world economy is delicately poised on the edge of disaster. AIDS will change the demographic structure of many countries — in some places in Africa, over half the population is infected. Our national debt appears to be so out of control that even with tax increases and budget cuts we may still face financial disaster. On the world scene, no one knows what will replace the bankruptcy of Marxism in Eastern Europe and the Soviet Union. Ours is a very insecure and unpredictable world. Little wonder that we search for substitute symbols of security: deodorants that promise social security, health-related products and services, home ownership, job security, and retirement planning — all of which serve as minor premises in enthymemes that begin with the major premise "Security or permanence is good," and which lead us to buy the product, adopt the service, or support the cause. At a time when we need permanence, we face unpredictable change, and that makes us vulnerable to persuasion aimed at assuring or reassuring us of some semblance of security.

Need for Reassurance of Worth We live in a highly competitive and impersonal society in which it is easy to feel like mere cogs in a machine. Packard noted that people need to feel valued for what they do. Housewives, factory workers, and public service workers need to feel that they are accomplishing something of value, are needed by their families and organizations, and are appreciated by others. In other words, people need to feel that they make a difference. This need forms the basis of many persuasive appeals by volunteer organizations; self-help tapes promoting self-esteem; and companies selling products that purportedly help us to be better parents (Bactine),

"GREAT PARTY! WHO DID YOUR DEMOGRAPHICS?"

FIGURE 8.1

Apparently, being a successful hostess is considered a "compelling need" by some people. The humor of the cartoon underscores the degree to which hidden persuaders in the form of various advertising technologies (for example, demographic analysis) are

perceived in our culture. (*Freeze Frame* cartoon from *Advertising Age*, December 28, 1987. Copyright Crain Communications, Inc. Reprinted by permission of Crain Communications and Bill Whitehead.)

better spouses ("Remember her with flowers"), and more successful at work (matchbook advertisements for career training).

As a nation, we need to feel assured of our worth in the world. At a time when skepticism is "in," when people don't seem to really communicate with one another, many people believe that "they no longer live in a world of friends and neighbors and families, but in a world of associates, clients, and customers who will look them in the eye, smile — and lie like a rug."[8]

This skeptical outlook was carefully chronicled in a best-selling study of American society titled

Habits of the Heart: Individualism and Commitment in American Life. Robert Bellah and his coauthors set out to study the degree to which contemporary middle-class individuals felt commitment to things other than themselves. They interviewed over 200 persons in depth. Their findings are disturbing. Most of the interviewees found reassurance of worth in material things. In a section titled "The Poverty of Affluence," Bellah and his colleagues concluded that most contemporary Americans see themselves in a race for material goods, prestige, power, and influence. And in this race they separate themselves from others and find

FIGURE 6.2

Who is getting the ego gratification here — Hagar, because his wife is concerned for his well-being, or his wife, because he does a rare thing by confessing his need for her? How has the cartoonist made this clear? (*Hagar the Horrible* © 1988 King Features Syndicate, Inc. Reprinted by permission.)

little emotional security in "the lonely crowd." Small wonder that we have become a "culture of consumption," seeking in the ownership of material goods the self-worth we can only find from being committed to and relating with others in our personal and public lives.[9]

Need for Ego Gratification Packard found that many of the consumers he studied not only needed to be reassured of their basic worth but also needed their egos "stroked" as if they were really special — a step beyond mere self-worth. This need for ego gratification can come from a variety of sources: friends, co-workers, neighbors, parents, groups, institutions, and, most important, from ourselves. Packard refers to a heavy–road-equipment manufacturer who increased sales by featuring drivers rather than machines in magazine ads. Operators have major say-so in purchase decisions; that is, when contractors buy heavy equipment, they ask those who operate the machines for their opinions. Persuaders often identify a group whose members feel they have been put down for some time — teachers, police, or social workers, for instance. It is easy to sell products, ideas, or candidates by hooking into the out-group's ego needs in personal ways that appeal to an individual's self-perception.[10] For example, for years the traditional family was out of style as divorce rates soared and couples chose to live together instead of getting married. Those who remained committed to the ideal of the traditional family and its associated values felt like outcasts. This was the perfect time for a persuasive "pro-family" appeal, and that is precisely what happened on both sides in the 1988 election campaign. Both George Bush and Michael Dukakis promised to restore the family to its prior place of respect.

Ego-gratification needs are potent. A good example of an ad based on this need is shown in Figure 6.3. Note that the ad copy stresses the importance Hyatt places on the individual — in this case a woman executive, whose needs have been largely overlooked by the hotel industry until recently. Hyatt offers her thoughtful extras — skirt hangers, shampoo, and even hair dryers in the room. She must be pretty special to have a large hotel chain go out of its way to provide her with such amenities.

FIGURE 6.3

Hyatt promises to fulfill the need for ego gratification. (Used by permission of Hyatt Corporation.)

COMFORTABLY HYATT.

In an unfamiliar city, it's important to find a truly comfortable hotel. That's why so many frequent travelers find their way to Hyatt.

For women, as for all our guests, our comforts are many. A room with the location you prefer. A thoughtful, professional staff with a gift for anticipating your next request. The small touches are never overlooked. Like imported soap, shampoo, skirt hangers, even hair dryers in many rooms. And our sunny atrium lounges are wonderful places to brighten your spirits throughout the day.

For us the greatest comfort is to see so many guests return, again and again. A comfortable touch of Hyatt. Don't you **WISH YOU WERE HERE**℠

TAMPA
Hyatt Regency Tampa is downtown, 5 miles from airport, with health club, indoor whirlpool, outdoor pool.

HOUSTON
In the very heart of exciting Houston, walk to business through climate-controlled tunnel system.

VANCOUVER
On Discovery Square, overlooking Vancouver Harbor and convenient to business district.

BALTIMORE
Overlooking the Inner Harbor, the spectacular Hyatt Regency Baltimore is connected to Harborplace.

NORTHWEST CHICAGO
The Hyatt in Chicago's suburban Schaumburg is at Woodfield Mall near O'Hare.

HYATT ⌗ HOTELS

For reservations, call your travel planner or 800 228 9000. © 1984 Hyatt Hotels Corp.

Need for Creative Outlets In our modern technocracy, few products can be identified with a single artisan. Before the rise of industrialism, around the turn of the century, this was not the case. For example, craftsmen such as cabinetmakers created a piece of furniture from beginning to end—it was their unique product. The same applied to bakers, cobblers, farmers, and the housewives who did the weaving, knitting, sewing, and cooking. But with the advent of mass production and Henry Ford's invention of the assembly line, more and more people became only a part of the production cycle—cogs in the wheel. They had less and less that they could point to as their own unique product, and they felt less and less "creative" in many ways. Packard identified a need for substitute ways for expressing one's own unique creativity: paint by numbers, jewelry making, macramé, or gourmet cooking, to name a few.

In today's quickly evolving technocracy, the opportunity for creative outlets is further reduced as more and more workers work in service occupations instead of the manufacturing sector, in which the actual construction of products occurs. This trend, unfortunately, is likely to continue beyond the year 2000. Even a book such as this one is not the end result of individual work and creativity—critics review a preliminary book proposal and suggest alterations; it is most likely written on a word processor; editors alter the second and third drafts for style and mechanics; a designer selects the page size, typeface, paper, and cover design; and typesetters use computers to set the type for final production. Most advertising, news releases, public relations efforts, film and television programming, political speaking, and other familiar forms of persuasion are also the product of many hands.

In a modern technocracy, more and more of the work formerly done by individuals is now being done by technology—robots, computers, word processors, food processors, microwave ovens, and so on. And the outlook for the future indicates the trend to be growing, not lessening. Yet people still seem to need to demonstrate their own handicraft skills. Given this need, macramé, gourmet-cooking classes, bonsai gardens, home-improve-ment tools, and other hobby-type activities are bound to succeed. Even with prepared foods, from which the art of cooking has been almost totally removed, creativity still sells. Hamburger Helper leaves room for you, the cook, to add your own touch. Noodles Romanoff makes you a chef worthy of the Czar. Even Old El Paso taco dinner reminds you of all the creative toppings you can put on a taco shell.

Need for Love Objects People whose children have grown up need to replace the child love object—a situation called the empty-nest syndrome. For some, the replacement is a pet; for others it is a child met through the organization Foster Grandparents. Persuaders understand this need and strive to meet it in a variety of ways. Television producers, for example, provide us with childlike entertainment personalities such as Gary Coleman and Fred Savage of "The Wonder Years." The recent popularity of professional wrestling among the young reflects a need for harmless villains and unbelievable heroes. The trend masks another market segment, however: elderly widows for whom the wrestlers are substitute love (and perhaps hate) objects.

Many persons have pets as love objects. Advertisements for pet food respond to pet lovers' emotions forcefully. Tender Vittles, for instance, comes in an individual pouch so kitty can have fresh moist food every day. Even the name of the product humanizes pets and reinforces the owner's feelings of love. "Tender Vittles" suggests that the food is like our own and is certainly of the highest quality. "Chuck Wagon" suggests that the pup will get the ranch flavor of the Old West.

Need for a Sense of Power If you have ever driven a motorcycle on the open road, you know what it is like to feel powerful. We Americans, perhaps more than members of any other culture, seem to be programmed to chase potency and power and also to gratify our need for these symbolically. The bigger the engine, the better. Snowmobiles and dune buggies are marketed by the sense of power they give. Almost any automotive product will feature the phrase "heavy-duty" to convince you that you are getting a powerful replacement part. Although some of our politicians are short or have slight builds, the big powerful types seem to win more frequently.

Consider the ad for Jeep Cherokee (Figure 6.4), which the manufacturer reminds us is "Leaner and Meaner," gets better mileage, and has "More Horsepower Per Pound . . . this is Jeep Ruggedness. Jeep Power. Jeep Agility." Whether the product is a double-triggered chain saw or a garden tractor, power is the emphasis. An owner of a tow-truck business noticed that over half his calls come from owners of 4-wheel-drive vehicles—the very vehicles that are supposed to be able to go through anything and never get stuck. That, apparently, is the problem. The owners of these vehicles satisfy their power needs by finding impossibly tough terrain through which to take their vehicles—or at least they attempt to get through. Often, they get bogged down and have to call for a tow. I have since verified this phenomenon with other tow-truck firms.

Need for Roots One of the predominant features of our times is increasing mobility. If you are employed by any large firm, chances are you will have to move several times during your career. During the ten years following college graduation, the average American will move at least a dozen times, and several of the moves will involve crossing county borders; at least one will involve a move across a state line. IBM moved its young executives so frequently that the company was jokingly referred to by employees as "**I**'ve **B**een **M**oved." When you do move, especially if it is some distance from home, there are several "pieces of home" you can bring with you to keep you from getting too lonely. One is brand loyalty; college students have one of the strongest levels of brand loyalty. If you have ever moved to another state, you will have noticed how disconcerting it is to not find familiar supermarket chains or your favorite service-station chain. Advertisers make appeals to these feelings.

This need for roots and brand loyalty also helps explain the concept of "line extension" in the development of new products. Because brand names

are a part of home we can take with us, we will feel more comfortable, for example, buying Florsheim shoes if that brand is a familiar one. Similarly, we feel more at home buying the new Quaker Oats Squares rather than another brand because of the familiar old-fashioned face of the Quaker promising "An honest taste from an honest face." He is an emblem of our youth and our roots.

Thus brand names are portable—we can take them to a new home to remind us of our roots. Nabisco, for example, recently increased its nationwide shelf space by twenty miles by using line extension for "New Stars," an eighteen-item cookie and cracker product. The old and familiar name of the manufacturer helped to establish the credibility of the new product.[11] The need for roots can be appealed to using emotional ties to "home" too. The Lane furniture company, for example, offers the newlyweds a Lane Cedar Chest to "take part of home with you" when you marry or move off to that new job.

We see the appeal in ads for the "old-fashioned," whether apple pies, Heartland Cereal, or stockbrokers who earn their money "the old-fashioned way." We've already noted the appeal politicians make to the value of family. It is surprising how many politicians manage to hold their marriages together just until they win an election.

With increasing mobility, traditional roots are torn up, and replacements are needed. And this trend of increasing mobility and fragmentation of our lives probably will continue into the future. As a result, the need for roots that Packard described many years ago is still with us and is still an important touchstone. It is a responsive chord that advertisers, politicians, and ideologues will continue to use in their many persuasive appeals to us.

Need for Immortality None of us believe in our own mortality. We like to think that life will go on and on in much the same way as at present. Packard suggests that the fear of dying and the need to believe in an ongoing influence on the lives of others underlies many kinds of psychological appeals. The breadwinner is made to feel that in buying insurance, for instance, he or she buys "life after death" in the form of financial control over

the family. The buyer can help the kids go to college even if he or she isn't there.

Other products make similar appeals to the fear of death. Dannon yogurt ran a series of ads featuring people from the Ukraine who reportedly lived well past one hundred years, supposedly because they ate yogurt. Promise margarine will keep you healthy longer because "Promise is at the heart of eating right." And Nivea's Visage face cream keeps your skin "firmer, healthier, and younger" for only pennies a day. As the ad executive noted in an earlier quote, we aren't buying lanolin (or Polly Bergen's Secret Turtle Oil), we are buying hope — hope for a chunk of immortality and youth.

This need for immortality seems particularly relevant in our modern technocracy. Perhaps people now feel even more helpless to control their lives than they did when Packard conducted his research. In the last decades of the twentieth century, many of us do feel, as Ralph Waldo Emerson did, that "Things are in the saddle, / And ride mankind."

As a critical consumer of persuasion, it behooves you to make yourself more aware of the pitches you will encounter. Let's look at another way to identify the needs that are appealed to by clever persuaders.

Maslow's Pyramid of Needs

Abraham Maslow, a well-known psychologist, offered a starting point for examining major need levels.[12] He noted that people have various kinds of needs that emerge, subside, and then re-emerge.

In Maslow's pyramid of needs, the lower levels represent the stronger needs and the higher levels represent the weaker needs (Figure 6.5). Remember that the pyramid is only a model and that the lines between needs are not as distinct as the picture suggests. Also note that higher needs are not *superior* to lower ones. They are just different and,

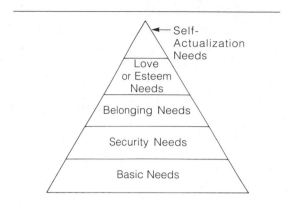

FIGURE 6.5

Maslow's pyramid of needs.

in all likelihood, weaker and less likely to emerge until stronger needs are met. Recall that the metaphor used in Chapter 3 to describe the individual's beliefs was that of peeling an onion until one got down to the core, or primitive, beliefs, on which there was unanimous agreement (for example, the sun rises in the east). In Maslow's pyramid of needs, the core of the onion is the base of the pyramid — these are needs or beliefs about which there is unanimous agreement. As we move up the pyramid or out from the core we find needs or beliefs on which there may not be unanimous agreement and on which individuals may place varying degrees of value. So there is an upward or outward dynamic in Maslow's hierarchy of needs — as more powerful needs are met, less potent needs emerge. As time passes the earlier needs emerge again as they are or are not met. For example, the need for food or water emerges and then recedes as we eat or drink. Maslow argued that these needs have a **prepotency** — that is, they are tied together so that weaker needs, such as ones for self-respect, emerge only after stronger needs, like ones for food, have been filled. We probably could not persuade our dehydrated desert wanderer to clean up a little before going to the well. We had better fulfill the need for H_2O first. Our need to slake thirst is prepotent; until it is fulfilled, it is impossible for us to consider other ideas.

FIGURE 6.4

How many appeals to the need for power can you find in this ad? (Used by permission of Jeep Corporation.)

This concept is similar to Rokeach's belief hierarchy, which we discussed in Chapter 3.

Basic Needs On the bottom level are the strongest needs we have — basic needs. These are the physiological needs of each human being. We need regular access to air, food, water, sex, sleep, and elimination of wastes. Until these needs are met, we cannot concern ourselves with other, higher needs. The basic needs are too strong to be forgotten in favor of other needs. At the same time, they can be used to motivate behavior. The person who is starving can be motivated to do all sorts of unusual things to secure food, ranging from stealing it to eating insects. And we know that the need for air can cause drowning swimmers to panic and drown not only themselves but their rescuers as well.

Security Needs The second level of Maslow's pyramid contains our needs for security. There are several ways one might look at these needs. We may want to feel secure in our ability to satisfy basic needs. If we feel that our job may end shortly, we have a strong need to obtain income security. We may want to get another, more secure job. Or we might want to save money for hard times. This is one kind of security. At the same time, we might look at this need level in another light. Let us suppose that we have job security — our boss assures us that we will be the last to be let go. We still may feel insecure because of the rising crime rates in our neighborhood. We might take drastic action to ward off thieves, such as installing a burglar alarm system, or sleeping with a loaded pistol under the pillow. Even when we feel secure about our home, we still may feel insecure about world politics. We may feel that our country needs more missiles or antimissile missiles. A person may have social insecurity and as a result spend money on self-improvement classes, deodorant, hair transplants, and mouthwash.

We can recognize the insecurity of Alvin Toffler's emerging "Third Wave" of technology as reason enough for pretty powerful motivation.[13] Those who are not technically trained to meet the requirements of the computer age realistically fear falling by the wayside. Global competition has eaten into the market share of U.S. industries, leaving thousands unemployed. Many analysts explained several election results as related to fears of economic displacement and the resulting loss of jobs. According to Maslow's model, the fear emerged in response to current economic conditions. In other words, this need for security emerges and reemerges as various threats to our security become evident and must be met. Once the need is met, it redefines itself and thus is always present to some degree.

More recently, the awesome changes occurring in previously communist European countries have introduced a new source of insecurity, for if free-market economic and democratic political reforms fail, these countries will be ripe for revolution. Revolution is always unpredictable and hence a source of insecurity. If a right-wing fanatic such as Stalin assumes power in the Soviet Union, how secure can we all feel given the tremendous stockpile of nuclear and other weaponry there?

Today, insecurity, like change, is one of the few *predictable* things. Eight of every ten jobs that will be filled by tomorrow's students after they graduate do not even exist today, so it's almost impossible to prepare for the future. New computer technology will become obsolete in two to three years. No one can keep up with the new (and frequently essential) information about jobs, health, communities, and a host of other personal and social issues. We are indeed living in a time when very little is secure. It is not surprising that so many security-oriented products, politicians, and organizations are making appeals to us on a daily basis.

Belonging Needs Once our security needs are met, at least in part (we know we will have a job in the future and that thugs will have problems robbing us), we become aware of needs on the third level: belonging, or association, needs. A number of options are open to us in meeting our need for association. We may choose to fulfill these needs in our immediate family. We all know of people who relate to no groups other than those at their job and in the family. This way of meeting belonging needs is the exception rather than the rule, however. Usually, individuals seek groups

FREEZE FRAME

It's this simple, dammit—I need an approach that taps the wellsprings of the human condition, and I need it by Friday!

FIGURE 6.6

The hidden persuaders identified by Packard are still with us though they may go by different names like "the wellsprings of the human condition." (*Freeze Frame* cartoon from *Advertising Age*, August 31, 1987. Copyright Crain Communications, Inc. Reprinted by permission of Crain Communications and Don Reilly.)

with which to fill this need. Suburbia is filled with persons who seem to have a strong need for belonging—they are the joiners of our society. They become members of dozens of groups such as the PTA, bowling leagues, churches, golf clubs, or service groups. Usually, we keep the number of groups we join small and, although we may be members of several organizations, we are active members in only a few. Regardless of how many groups we join or of how active we are in them, we meet our belonging needs only partially.

Like basic and security needs, the need to belong often interacts with these other needs and continues to reemerge throughout our lives. Also, what fulfills our belonging needs differs at various points of our lives. But the need to belong will always be with us. Persuaders know this and often make appeals promising a sense of belonging if you buy their product, vote for them, or, more frequently, join their group or cause. As persuadees we need to recognize when this need is being appealed to by persuaders so that we can critically evaluate their appeals.

Love or Esteem Needs Once we satisfy belonging needs, we will feel the emergence of needs in level four of Maslow's model: the needs for love or esteem. Once we are part of a group, we want to feel that the group — be it family, lodge, or bowling team — values us as a member. We want to feel wanted and valued as human beings. We are happy when our families understand and admire the things we do. The esteem need is also a re-emerging need. That is, if we find that we are needed and esteemed and loved by our family, our need for esteem does not fade away. Instead, its focus shifts. We want now to feel needed and loved by our co-workers, our boss, and our friends. The more we get of this kind of esteem, the less compelling the need becomes. However, it is never fully satisfied, and we try to seek other circumstances in which we can achieve status and rank. Many product appeals offer a kind of symbolic substitute for esteem. You will be held high in your fellow workers' eyes if you read the *Wall Street Journal*. Your spouse will adore you if you make that Betty Crocker cake. Your kids will love you if you take them to Disney World — all great Dads and Moms do that.

Cultural trends also influence our love or esteem needs. For example, during the 1980s, esteem or love came from *conspicuous consumption*, consumption engaged in for purposes of display. People could get esteem from their peers by wearing Calvin Klein's Obsession perfume at $175 an ounce, by belonging to an exclusive Manhattan dinner club, by owning an expensive import automobile, or by otherwise "showing off" to gain approval through "upscale" consumption. But, as noted earlier, several important things happened to change the way one satisfied esteem or love needs. One of them was the realization that AIDS was not confined to the homosexual population and that it would reach epidemic proportions. Several political and Wall Street scandals and several revelations about television evangelists showed that politicians, businesspeople, and preachers are also capable of sinning — all of which led to a renewed interest in ethics, as noted elsewhere in this book.

The nineties have begun on a different note. There seems to be communal concern for the environment. Young and old, producers and consumers, conservatives and liberals are pitching in in a variety of ways to clean up our air, land, and water resources. People seem to realize that working in community can help meet our love and esteem needs.[14]

Self-Actualization Needs Although Maslow initially put the need for self-actualization at the top of his pyramid, thereby implying that it would rarely emerge, he later came to believe that in a way the need to live up to one's potential is an integral part of everyone's life. At first, Maslow believed that individuals could live up to their potential only when all four of the lower needs were fulfilled. Once you were promoted to president of the bank, *then* you could begin to live up to your own potential.

In many ways, Maslow's initial ideas are accurate. It is hard for a young person on the way up to think about self-actualization, just as it is hard to meet love or esteem needs if you do not belong to some group that can give you love or esteem — a family, a fraternity, or a church, for example. Yet Maslow's later thinking about all these needs and their prepotency is valid, too. He came to see self-actualization as occurring through what he called "peak experiences" — events in which people can enjoy themselves, learn about themselves, or experience something they have only dreamed of before. Thus, the person who goes out into the Boundary Waters Canoe Area wilderness and learns to be self-reliant and not to fear isolation has enjoyed a peak, or self-actualizing, experience. The same might apply to people who learn something about themselves when they take their first job after high school or college and discover that they have abilities that are of value to a company or to fellow workers.

Again, cultural trends can affect the ways in which we seek to satisfy our self-actualization needs. Social critic T. J. Jackson Lears has noted that the search for ways of identifying one's self and one's potential came about when the United States shifted from being a culture of production to a culture of consumption. We shifted from secure farm living (typified by hard work, attending church, saving money, and having self-control) to an unsettling urban loneliness, a shift away from traditional values, and chaotic changes in our lifestyles. The result, Lears claims, was the search for a "therapeutic ethos," or an identity that would let individuals be at ease with themselves — that would permit them to self-actualize. To a large extent, this therapeutic ethos offered inner harmony, a reduction of feelings of emptiness, and a hope for self-realization through patterns of consumption.[15] As we approach a new century, what will be the means for achieving self-actualization — our own true potential? It is certain that there will be persuaders offering a variety of means for achieving this final prepotent need.

Maslow's pyramid can be used in many everyday persuasive situations. When we want to persuade a teacher that a certain grade or method of evaluation is unfair, we must analyze what kinds of needs the professor has. Is he or she likely to feel insecure? Is he or she in need of esteem? Is he or she trying to self-actualize? Or suppose you are trying to persuade your roommate to take a trip to Florida with you instead of working over the midterm vacation. You would want to know what kinds of needs would be fulfilled by the trip as opposed to what needs would be satisfied by earning money during the break. As you encounter various persuasive events and opportunities (public and interpersonal), apply Maslow's model to those involved. See whether it sheds light on the needs that people feel and that may motivate their actions. You may want to experiment with persuading another person using several levels of Maslow's model. If the person doesn't seem motivated by appeals to security, try appealing to basic or belonging needs. Clearly, the "Be All That You Can Be" campaign, which was so successful in gaining new recruits, wasn't aimed at the security needs of college students. Some ads run during the Vietnam War era, however, urged students to enlist to be eligible for special training that would keep them away from the front lines. That appeal was irrelevant to most college students in the 1980s, so

an appeal to a new need had to be employed — in this case, a self-actualization need.

Uses of the Needs Process Premise

In our search for the first premises that serve as springboards for persuasion in enthymemes, psychological processes show us promising possibilities in the area of human needs. These needs, whether identified by Packard's list or Maslow's pyramid or some other model, are strongly felt by audiences. Persuaders frequently tie other minor premises to them to allow audience members to complete the argument by drawing the conclusion. For example, feeling the need for job security, the college student decides to major in a field that holds the promise of job openings after graduation. It is only common sense. Yet what we call "common sense" is common only because so many of us have the same or similar needs.

We may wish to relabel our needs in terms other than those used by Maslow or Packard, but their categories serve as good general descriptions. We ought to consider the requests persuaders make of us from the perspective of our own needs.

As persuaders, we ought to examine the current needs of those we wish to influence. If we do that, not only are we more likely to succeed but we are also more likely to do our audience a service by giving them a means to satisfy their needs.

A good way to train yourself to evaluate appeals from this critical perspective — as persuadee or persuader — is to restate persuasive messages, such as television commercials, from the perspective of the Packard and Maslow models. In our search for first premises on which persuasion may be built, it is clear that human psychological and physiological needs are powerful motivators. As you will see, attitudes, the second type of process premise, operate in similar ways.

ATTITUDES: THE SECOND PROCESS PREMISE

When we surveyed the theoretical perspectives on persuasion, we looked at how various researchers explain attitudes using a variety of theories. One unifying element among these theories is the fact that attitudes can serve as the unstated major premises in persuasive enthymemes. Rokeach pointed out that individual beliefs range from those that are primitive and strongly held to those that are based on authority and are not as strongly held.[16] These beliefs sets cluster and form **attitudes**, which, according to Rokeach, fall into two categories: *attitudes toward objects or issues* and *attitudes toward situations*.

Both classes of attitudes can predispose us to action, but they can also confuse us, especially when they conflict with one another. Such conflict can be seen when parents protest the presence of AIDS-infected students in public schools. The parents' attitudes toward the object (the infected student) and their attitudes toward the situation (the possibility that their own children will be infected) may either conflict or converge. These attitudes, in turn, probably emerge from complex sets of opinions toward both object and situation: The parents may hold certain sympathetic opinions toward the innocent victim while at the same time holding certain negative opinions toward the situation — the epidemic proportions of sexually transmitted diseases (STDs) and the deadly outcome of the AIDS virus. A persuader on either side of this controversy would need to address both sets of opinions.

Opinions resemble beliefs but are far more fickle; as opinion polls demonstrate, opinions change rapidly and often dramatically. We all have opinions about politicians and what they say in a campaign and about what they do after taking office. These opinions can change, however, especially if a president makes a few key errors: a foolish statement, fighting Congress on a particular issue, or choosing to support a friend who turns out to be corrupt. The Gallup and Harris polls record such shifts of opinion on a regular basis. Remember, however, that opinions may not influence the behavior of persons who hold them. For instance, although our opinions about a president may slip toward the negative over a period of a few months, we may still vote for that person in the next election. This is not to say that opinions do not at all affect behavior — only that they sometimes exert a weak influence.[17]

Given a large enough change in opinion, however, we *may not* support a president in the next campaign; or, given enough small shifts in our opinions, we may change our overall attitude toward that president. We have an *attitude* toward smoking composed of many *opinions*: that it is costly; that it is unhealthy; that it is dirty; that it bothers others; that it destroys the body's supply of vitamin C, and so on. Philip Zimbardo, a prominent sociologist, notes that **attitudes** are "either mental readiness or implicit predispositions that exert some general and consistent influence on a fairly large class of evaluative responses."[18]

Notice that Zimbardo stresses the enduring quality of attitude shifts. There is even a school of advertising research known by the acronym DAGMAR.[19] The philosophy is that ad agencies ought to *D*efine *A*dvertising *G*oals for *M*easured *A*dvertising *R*esults. In other words, the goal of advertising may be only *attitudinal change* toward the company or product and not change in purchase behavior. It is hoped that if we have an improved image of a product — say Rice Chex — we will buy more of the product. Unfortunately, this attitude-behavior link has been difficult to demonstrate, perhaps because of the many intervening variables that might also affect consumer behavior. Simple awareness of a product's name, packaging, display location in the store, or the kind of background music being played may cause us to buy it. Other factors such as time of day or sex of purchaser may be the key. Even in carefully controlled experiments with many of these causes filtered out, attitude and behavior do not consistently link up. Researchers blame this on poor design in research studies or a weak measuring instrument.[20]

Thus, what we know about attitudes is not how or whether they determine actions but how they change and which of them are most likely to change. In his early studies, psychologist Carl Hovland found that attitudes that change usually are not ego-involving, are not central, and are based on previous experience or commitment of the people studied. Later research did make use of socially significant, ego-involved topics. (As we saw in Chapter 3, ego-involvement dramatically affects one's latitudes of acceptance and rejection.) Debate continues over which explanation of attitude and attitude change best explains human behavior and the responses of audiences to persuasion.

Another way to think about attitudes and their relationship to the persuasive process is to focus on their various functions, dimensions, or effects. Attitudes have a **cognitive function** or dimension: They are *learned* and hence become part of the storehouse of knowledge on which we take action.[21] Consider the destruction of the environment, for example. Our attitudes toward air and water pollution, recycling, and endangered species are all part of *what we know* about these issues.

Attitudes also have an **affective function**: They affect our emotions and feelings. In other words, attitudes toward recycling and air and water pollution affect *how we feel* about these issues.

Finally, and most important, attitudes have a **behavioral function**: They predispose us to take certain actions. Because we hold certain attitudes about air and water pollution, we do or do not buy gas guzzlers, we do or do not use detergents, and we do or do not recycle our garbage. In other words, the behavioral function of attitudes affects *what we do* about these issues. Unfortunately, it has been difficult to demonstrate this behavioral function, dimension, or effect very consistently. At times, attitude changes seem to predispose certain behaviors, but at other times the cause/effect relationship cannot be determined.

The work of Martin Fishbein and Icek Ajzen has added another concept to research on attitude and behavioral change.[22] This concept, labeled **behavioral intention**, relates to what one *intends* to do about an issue, regardless of what action one finally takes. Here, a fairly consistent set of results emerges: attitude change *does* seem to precede what people say they *intend* to do about the environment—as a result of attitude change, we *say* that we *intend* to recycle, that we *intend* to conserve water, or that we *intend* to use low-phosphate laundry detergents. This makes sense, for given any attitude toward or image of a politician, for example, there are several things a voter might do: vote for the candidate, stay home from the polls, donate money to the campaign, work for the opponent, and so on. Discovering overall attitude toward the politician does not tell us much about the probability of any of these behaviors. But when people describe what they intend to do, they have, in a sense, already symbolically enacted the behavior. Thus a person who displays a bumper sticker in favor of a certain candidate is stating a behavioral intention, and it is likely that this person will vote for that candidate. Politicians know this and urge potential voters to display buttons, bumper stickers, and signs, in order to guarantee their votes on election day.

There are several other dimensions to the attitude-change and subsequent behavior puzzle. One of these dimensions is the degree to which attitudes function as tools of interpersonal communication. In other words, do expressions of attitudes have more to do with fitting oneself into a comfortable position with those with whom we are interacting than they have to do with our ultimate behavior? For example, I have a hunting and fishing partner who is much more politically conservative than I am. When I express political attitudes or even opinions about political issues of the day to him, I am very careful about the exact words I use. His friendship is worth more to me than my need to express my attitudes bluntly. J. R. Eiser, a critic of much of the attitude research that has been conducted, puts it this way:

> One of the main shortcomings of many attitude theories is their emphasis on individualistic, intrapsychic factors to the relative neglect of the social and communicative context within which attitudes are acquired and expressed. Not only the expression but also the experience of attitude is shaped by how we have learnt to anticipate what we say and do. For this reason, attitude is both a subjective experience and a social product, and the expression of an attitude is a social act.[23]

In other words, we express attitudes in ways that help us get along with persons who are significant to us. As a result, there sometimes may be logical discrepancies between expressed attitudes and subsequent behavior.

Another approach is to explain attitudes as parts of larger concepts called "constructs," which we discussed briefly in Chapter 3. These constructs become increasingly complex as we age.[24] Our attitudes toward, say, religion are very different now from what they were when we were ten years old, and they are very different from what they will be ten years hence. The more complex our attitudes become, the less likely they are to be reliable predictors of our behavior, because many dimensions of a complex attitude conflict with one another.

Closely related to the constructivist approach is the perspective of theorists who focus on human information processing. They argue that you can't look at attitudes and behavior without also looking at what information in the persuasive message is processed by the audience, how it is stored, and how it is retrieved. When trying to look at this process, one of the first questions one must ask is: Can the audience comprehend this message? Once this is determined, perhaps by testing or interviewing, the next step is to determine how the message is stored in the audience members' long-term memory (sometimes referred to as LTM). It may be entirely new information to the audience, or it may fit with an entire network or several networks ("nets") of information already stored in the LTM. Take, for example, the "cents off" coupons appearing in newspapers, circulars, and magazines. As persuasive information, they fit with several memory networks in our minds: whether the product is one we use in our house or want to begin using, how often we would use it, and whether the value of the coupon is sufficient to justify taking the time to "clip" it. However, to someone else, coupons would mesh with a different net that might include the idea of getting coupons for food from the government, thus indicating a certain level of poverty. Research into how information is stored in LTM is in its infancy, but most theorists agree that it is usually stored in networks and in the form of key words, symbols, and relationships.

Joseph Cappella and Joseph Folger use an interesting example of a stored network based on the following sentences: "Gigolos are dispicable creatures. They deceive women and steal their money."[25] Here the concept of "gigolo" is linked with "creature" (modified by "despicable"), who then "steals" (objectified by "money"), and "deceives" (the object being "women"). If you drew

such a network, you would discover that the central concept/word is "gigolo," about which audiences have affective or emotional feelings that can be retrieved when the key concept is stated. This is one way "nets" can be built. Another organizing device for LTM may be *episodic* in nature. That is, we remember things that are presented to us in episodic or dramatic segments that then become integrated with LTM networks relating to one of numerous personal episode types such as stealing, being deceived, deceiving, winning over the odds, losing in spite of the odds, and others. If you can identify the episodic types that people have, these could serve as vital first premises in persuasive enthymemes. As we will see later, another theorist, Tony Schwartz, provides a model for resonating with or "evoking" such experiences from audiences.

At the behavior stage of the information-processing model (for example, voting, buying, joining, saluting, hitting, expressing one's view), the critical concepts or episodes are retrieved from the LTM and provide the persuadees with good "reasons" for taking action.

There are several other approaches to studying the message-attitude-behavior chain, each of which has its strengths and weaknesses. But all agree that attitudes have something to do with behavior and that attitudes can be altered via persuasive messages.[26] The presumption then is that the suggested behavior will ultimately follow.

What does all this mean to the persuadee who is in the business of listening critically in a world of doublespeak? What can we do to uncover persuaders' intentions and beliefs about the audience? One of the advantages of at least being aware of attitudes is that we can second-guess what image of us the persuader holds. For example, what kind of attitude construct, long-term memory, or episode is the customer presumed to have in the ad for the grandfather clock shown in Figure 6.7? The persuader obviously believes that members of the target market have high status needs, have strong attitudes about the importance of financial success, are somewhat snobbish, and cultivate taste. Are these the people who read *House and Garden*, the magazine in which the ad appeared? If you read the ad, would you be persuaded to go to look at the

If you have to ask the price you can't afford it.

On this Howard Miller clock, the famed cathedral chimes of Westminster, Winchester and St. Michael are reproduced by nine chromium-plated tubular bells. All are housed in a superb case 87 inches tall. A case made of oak and rare Carpathian elm burl veneers. This is set off by a brass and silver plated dial and ornaments of brass fretwork. A great lyre pendulum sedately measures every hour. If you crave the excellent—and have its price—ask for the President.

From the Howard Miller Golden Collection

FIGURE 6.7

The company (persuader) reveals its attitudes toward potential customers (persuadees) as well as assumptions about their attitudes, constructs, long-term memories, or episodic memories regarding such issues as spending, status, and quality. (Used by permission of Howard Miller Clock Company. All rights reserved.)

clock? How would the company advertise in another kind of magazine — say, *Playboy* or *Outdoor Life*? By seeking the attitudes that persuaders assume we have, we become more critical receivers. We can become conscious of our attitudes and can see how persuaders use them to get us to buy a product, vote for a person, donate to an organization, or support a cause.

CONSISTENCY: THE THIRD PROCESS PREMISE

In Chapter 3, we looked at several of the theories that explain human behavior in terms of people's need for balance, consistency, congruity, or consonance. These theories posit that human beings feel comfortable when the world lives up to or operates consistently with their perceptions of or predictions about events. When this consistency is not evident, people are predisposed to change either themselves or their interpretations of events to bring the world into a more balanced state. Knowing where and when receivers are likely to perceive inconsistencies, persuaders cast their messages to offer a means to return to consistency and thus comfort. Many cigarette ads, for instance, compare their brand with several others in terms of the amount of tar or nicotine they contain. More recently, other tobacco interests have promoted the use of snuff, now called "smokeless tobacco," as a doublespeak alternative that will let the smoker (receiver) ingest the nicotine without having to suffer the ill effects of inhaling smoke.

If it is true that humans seek out psychological equilibrium, it is valuable for us as receivers to try to identify what puts us into states of imbalance and makes us vulnerable to persuasion. Conversely, if it is true that psychological equilibrium is our goal, we ought to identify those situations or circumstances that make us feel comfortable and can be targeted for persuasion that reinforces this comfortable feeling. Pioneers in consistency theory research Charles Osgood and Percy Tannenbaum put it this way: "Changes in evaluation are always in the direction of increased congruity with the existing frame of reference."[27] As Eiser

points out, defining "the existing frame of reference" is a critical factor in predicting attitude shifts. One must identify the receiver's present frame of reference in order to create the kind of incongruity or inconsistency that will prompt feelings of psychological "dis-ease" that will then lead to movement along an attitude scale. According to Eiser, these "evaluative frames of reference . . . are more general than the specific objects of judgment being evaluated."[28] What are some of these frames of reference for groups of potential persuadees? In other words, what are some of the sources of dissonance and consonance? Both are important. Sources of dissonance are critical when persuaders want to change attitudes. Sources of consonance are important when persuaders want to strengthen or reinforce existing attitudes, perhaps eventually calling for action, much as speakers who use a unifying style do.

Sources of Dissonance

What kinds of situations or events cause you to feel a sense of imbalance? Some of them are unique to you, of course, but many of them are similar — even identical — for large groups of people. These are likely targets for persuaders because the predictable inconsistencies in life are potent first premises in persuasive arguments.

Loss of Group Prestige One way for persuaders to make us feel discomfort is to cause us to perceive a loss of **group prestige**. Something we had is now "going, going, gone," so to speak, or something we still have is in danger of being lost. In political persuasion, this might be our country's prestige as a great and powerful nation. Certainly that helps to explain why there is such concern when an American airplane and its passengers are hijacked by terrorists. We are apparently helpless to defend against terrorists who are so zealous that they are willing to sacrifice their lives in order to make a point. The feeling of loss of prestige and of the ability to defend ourselves was used by persuaders to justify a number of foreign policies: the deployment of U.S. Marines on ships offshore; the condemnation of Libya, which was thought to be a central planning and training ground for terrorists; and the formation of programs with other countries to infiltrate terrorist groups and annihilate them.

Economic Loss Another kind of fear frequently exploited by persuaders is the fear of **economic loss**. When we perceive that our economic value (measured in any terms you like — savings, property, salary) is in danger of being reduced, we feel psychic dissonance and insecurity. Persuaders can appeal to this fear to induce us to vote for politicians who promise to reduce inflation, budget deficits, or wasteful spending. Persuaders can sell us investment schemes to protect our savings, as recurring stories of investment frauds demonstrate. We can be induced to join organizations or causes to protect our economic well-being. In the mid-1980s, an allegedly nonprofit lobbying organization was set up to prevent Social Security benefits from being cut. It received millions of dollars in donations from retired persons who feared economic loss, but the records show that the organization spent next to nothing on lobbying efforts and merely gave out handsome salaries and plush expense accounts to its officers.

Loss of Personal Prestige Loss of **personal prestige** or self-respect can create another type of dissonance for persuaders to exploit. An ad for a series of motivational programs said, "If your child comes home with bad grades from grade school, refuses to practice the piano, watches too much television, and seems bored with school, then the responsible thing for a parent to do is to send the child to Chicago's Motivational Institute." In other words, parents could regain lost self-respect by being responsible and enrolling their child. We are all familiar with ads that warn that if people see dandruff on your collar in the elevator on Monday morning, your personal stock at work will drop out of sight. You can avoid losing prestige if you get yourself some Head and Shoulders shampoo before this happens to you. All of these appeals are aimed at the discomfort we feel when we are losing or are in danger of losing personal prestige. Other fears related to loss of prestige include fears about loss of youth, loss of health, or deteriorating appearance. You can name others. All such fears make us vulnerable to appeals related to our need for consistency.

Uncertainty of Prediction We also feel discomfort when we are unable to **predict** people's behavior or the course of events with any degree of certainty. This is why during periods following natural catastrophes the populace typically behaves irrationally. The world behaves unpredictably when hurricanes strike or when floods crest higher than they should, and this unpredictability carries over to the hours and days following the event. Only when the world has somewhat returned to order do the inhabitants of the disaster area begin to restore their own sense of being able to cope with and predict world events. A dramatic example of this followed the liberation of the prisoners from concentration camps after World War II. In his book *Man's Search for Meaning*, Victor Frankl recorded that some of the camp's inmates, on being liberated, found it impossible to reenter the world of normality.[29] They turned away from the open gates of the unpredictable, free world. They needed the predictability of the camp schedule and personnel in order to cope. We find the same reaction in much less vivid but more personalized examples whenever we change our environment: when we change schools, when we move to a new job, when we break up with our lover, when we join the army, and when we enter any number of new and unpredictable worlds. We are uncomfortable and want to find something familiar and predictable. This makes us vulnerable to all sorts of persuasion related to products, political philosophies, or religious or ideological movements.

A well-known and controversial religious cult — the Moonies — frequently persuaded college students to join the movement. The converts had to give up belongings, family, future plans, and friends. One of the group's tactics was to find a person who was uncertain and perhaps alone on campus and to invite him or her to a retreat for a weekend at a nearby camp or lodge. Here the uncertainty and unpredictability of campus life was used as a first premise in a persuasive campaign that promised the stability of the cult in exchange for zealous conversion. Moonies also were particularly successful at recruiting teenagers who had run away from home and who, presumably, felt particularly uncertain. Frequently the Moonie strategy was so successful that parents decided to "kidnap" their children from the group and have them "deprogrammed." Quacks frequently sell bogus cures for terminal diseases because victims and their families cannot live with the unpredictability of the disease and the resulting sense of helplessness, and also because they are facing loss of life or loved ones.

We are likely to see other products, ideas, and leaders promoted by targeting our sense of dissonance or inconsistency when things become unpredictable. Few of us can abide the lack of control we feel when we can't predict outcomes.

Sense of Guilt A final source of dissonance is **guilt**. Related to our fears of loss of self-respect or status, guilt springs from the potential disapproving judgments of a symbolic source outside ourselves — such as a deity, our parents, our peers, or world opinion. In late 1984, for example, American television reviewers got their first glimpse of the worst famine in Africa's history when a BBC news clip of masses of emaciated children was shown. One woman seeing the news clip said, "I just couldn't finish my dinner; I felt too guilty." She used her employer's sense of guilt to persuade it — a small British airline — to donate two planes and money to buy and ship tons of relief food and supplies to Ethiopia. Relief societies all reported donations pouring in after the news clip. The guilt here was not direct — people did not feel they had *caused* the famine, but rather that they would feel guilty if they failed to take action to alleviate suffering.

Such self-imposed and internalized feelings of dissonance can be explained in various ways. Freudian psychoanalysts would say that we are afraid of reprimands from our symbolic parents, incorporated in our conscience or super-ego. These fears lead to shame or self-hate, and guilt is a symptom of that shame. Transactional psychology offers a similar explanation for guilt: The *child* in

us fears a reprimand from the *parent* in us, which the *adult* in us handles by taking action to alleviate the feelings of guilt. A behavioral explanation might rely on a pattern of reinforcement, perhaps via praise or blame from others, which leads to guilt-removing acts such as donating to charitable causes.

In any case, this source of dissonance is frequently used in persuasion. Kenneth Burke, whom we met in Chapter 5, explains the process using a religious allegory. In the epilogue of his book *The Rhetoric of Religion*, Burke narrates an argument between God and the Devil about human motivation.[30] God explains that he will ultimately win out over the Devil, who has introduced sin into the world. His explanation hangs on the development of guilt as an inevitable result of sinning. This guilt will then have to be purged. The purgation will have to set things right with God, against whom the mortals have sinned, and the result of the purgation will be some sense of redemption. Of course we have seen this pattern repeated in various religions, sometimes involving burnt offerings to purge the sin, sometimes the sacrifice of animals or even humans. However, we ought not overlook more mundane examples of this sin-guilt-purgation-redemption chain. Politicians who urge us to return to the principles "that made this country great" are using the religious model. Our sin lies in disregarding those principles. Our guilt is the sense of dissonance we feel. Our purgation is whatever action is suggested to return us to the tried-and-true principles — prayer in the schools, the cessation of busing to correct racial imbalance in the classroom, or a constitutional amendment banning abortion on demand. When the legislation is passed, we will feel redeemed. Various ideological movements also use the religious approach. Advocates of the Equal Rights Amendment tapped societal guilt with claims that women were being paid fifty-nine cents for doing the same work for which men got a dollar. This inequality was the social sin that caused many people to feel a sense of guilt and to work for the passage of the amendment to purge the sin.

Certain products are marketed by developing a sense of guilt in potential customers and then offering them the opportunity to purge their sins by purchasing the product. Life insurance frequently is marketed this way. If you really care for your family, you will insure your spouse as well as yourself, claims a familiar insurance ad. Because the character in the ad didn't insure his wife, he and his children have to leave their wonderful home and move into a condo. He was insured, but Jane wasn't; Jane is the one who became ill, and now house and child care are so costly that the family's possessions and life-style will have to be sacrificed to make ends meet. If you haven't adequately insured both yourself and your spouse, you are committing a potentially tragic "sin," and you ought to feel some guilt about it. A way of purging the guilt is to purchase the insurance, which will redeem you. You can identify other examples in which this religious model is used to market products or services.

Undoubtedly there are other ways to use incongruity to get people to change their attitudes and behavior. As a receiver, you need to search for the tactics persuaders use to give you a sense of "disease" that you can relieve by buying their product, voting for their candidate, or supporting their claims.

Sources of Consonance

Another kind of appeal is made to give receivers a sense of consonance. This kind of appeal is made more frequently than those aimed at creating dissonance. The consonance-producing appeal is used to reinforce existing beliefs, attitudes, or behaviors and frequently to activate receivers. What are some of the means used to persuade us that because things are comfortable, predictable, or congruous, we can go ahead and buy, join, or vote in accord with the persuader's requests?

Reassurance of Security One of the ways that persuaders appeal to our need for equilibrium or balance is to reassure us that we are **secure**. As noted in both Maslow's and Packard's lists of needs, security needs are basic and can have several dimensions. We may need to be reassured that we are secure in our social interactions and that

reading *Time, Newsweek*, or *U.S. News and World Report* will make us interesting conversationalists. Or perhaps our "social security" will be assured if we use a certain deodorant, cosmetic, or shampoo. A good example of how this reassurance is offered by political persuaders is the use of the term "safety net" in campaigns to reduce domestic spending by cutting social programs such as food stamps or aid to certain groups of people covered by Social Security. The mental image we get of a "safety net" is that of circus performers walking a tightrope but feeling secure because the net is there to catch them if they fall. The campaigners claimed that, even if some individuals are cut off from benefits by the budget reductions, the truly needy will be covered by other federal or state programs. Thus voters could feel secure about not hurting the truly needy. At other times we see reassurance of security being used to justify increases in military spending or to support nuclear arms reductions. Sometimes we see ideological persuaders use this tactic as well. Religious leaders convince their followers that by remaining true to the faith, by participating in rituals, or maybe by increasing their donations they can avoid damnation.

Demonstration of Predictability A consonance-producing tactic related to reassurance of security is to demonstrate that the world operates in **predictable** ways. If we could predict when or where the next terrorist act is going to occur, we would just set up a police SWAT team to trap the terrorists. Following the crash of 1929, the largest crash in the history of the U.S. Stock Exchange, predictability went out the window and this uncertainty caused several other devastating drops in the value of the market. Only after it had bottomed out and people could see that the economy was somewhat stable were investment advisors able to demonstrate predictability to small investors, who then began once more to buy and sell.

Manufacturers also rely on the appeal to predictability: "You Can Be Sure If It's Westinghouse." Anytime we see warranties emphasized, we are probably being persuaded by a consonance-producing appeal regarding predictability. Ford

Goodbye Frustration,

Rats! Much too dark!

Oops! Forgot to focus!

Darn! Missed the shot!

Hello NEW Sure Shot!

"Once-in-a-lifetime" moments only happen once, so it's really frustrating when your pictures are out of focus. Or too light or too dark. Or maybe you missed a shot because life wouldn't stand still while you got your camera ready.

Now you can say "Goodbye Frustration" with the NEW Sure Shot from Canon. It's so automatic, it even loads itself! Sharpness, lighting—everything is set for you. Just press one button for perfect pictures every time.

A motor winds the film after each shot so you're always ready to shoot. Pop-up the built-in flash and indoor shooting is totally automatic, too. You can't lose the lens cap because it's also built-in, and you can't shoot if the lens cap's closed!

So say "Goodbye Frustration." Visit your Canon dealer and start shooting with the NEW Sure Shot today. When your pictures come back, the biggest smile will be on your face!

Auto Loading & Power Rewind
no more fumbling with film!

Auto Winding
you're always ready
to shoot!

Action Grip
designed for fast,
easy handling!

Pop-Up Flash
just touch a button for
indoor shooting!

Auto Focus
works instantly, keeps your
subjects sharp and clear!

Auto Exposure
keeps pictures bright under
all lighting conditions!

NEW **Canon**® SURE SHOT

*The Official 35mm Camera
of the 1984 Olympic Games*

*Contributor to the
U.S. Olympic Team*

SUPER SURE SHOT
Just as automatic with a fast f1.9 lens!

Canon U.S.A. Inc. One Canon Plaza, Lake Success, New York 11042 · 140 Industrial Drive, Elmhurst, Illinois 60126 · 6380 Peachtree Industrial Blvd., Norcross, Georgia 30071
123 Paularino Avenue East, Costa Mesa, California 92626 · 2035 Royal Lane, Suite 290, Dallas, Texas 75229 · Bldg. B-2, 1050 Ala Moana Blvd., Honolulu, Hawaii 96814 · Canon Canada, Inc. Ontario

Motor Company says "Car Repairs Guaranteed for life. . . . And it doesn't matter if you bought it new, or used. Or who you bought it from." The Canon Sure Shot camera ad shown in Figure 6.8 demonstrates another appeal to predictability. Note the unpredictable snapshots taken by other cameras at the top of the ad. Then look at the features that assure the amateur photographer of predictably good results: auto loading, auto winding, auto focus, and auto exposure. You can't make a mistake with Sure Shot: "perfect pictures every time."

Use of Rewards A third consonance-producing tactic is the use of **rewards**, or positive reinforcements. We dealt with learning theory briefly in Chapter 3, and you will remember that positive reinforcement increases the probability that a behavior will be repeated. Thus reinforcement tends to aim at getting people to act. We discussed the schedules of reinforcement that can be used to develop complex behavior chains. Persuaders often use positive and complimentary statements to flatter their audience and to thus reinforce the behavior for which they are offering the compliment. They may also compliment the audience to develop their own positive image or credibility. In one of his most famous books (which incidentally was scorned by many in the communication profession as being "too manipulative"), Dale Carnegie offered this advice to his readers:

Let's cease thinking about our accomplishments, our wants. Let's try to figure out the other man's good points. Then forget flattery. Give honest sincere appreciation. Be "hearty in your approbation and lavish in your praise," and people will cherish your words and treasure them and repeat them over a lifetime — repeat them years after you have forgotten them.[31]

Canon promises predictable results if you use this camera. (Used by permission of Canon U.S.A., Inc.)

As you can see, Carnegie had put his finger on ways to make one's audience feel good about themselves. This is a good approach to persuading audiences or, as Carnegie put it, *influencing people*.

Ads for products also frequently use the positive or complimentary pitch to prompt feelings of consonance and to reinforce behavior. For example, look at any travel section from a Sunday newspaper and you'll find numerous examples, such as the ad for a Midwest ski resort that advises the reader to "Go Ahead. This Year Give Yourself the Best Ski Vacation of Your Life — You Deserve It" or the American Express ad that promises "Our London. Now You Can Afford to be Penny Wise and Pound Foolish." These claims and others like them build feelings of psychological comfort in the readers, who now perceive that they deserve the ski vacation they have wanted or that they can now afford to go to London. These pitches and others are persuasive because they compliment the persuadees and convince them that they deserve something they thought was too extravagant or unreasonable. These promises reinforce prior behavior or activate new behaviors.

What are some examples of such persuasion in your world? Consider the ads you see on television or that you read in newspapers or magazines. Chances are you will begin to identify numerous examples of consonance-producing persuasion in your everyday life.

REVIEW AND CONCLUSION

In Part I, we investigated the definition, ethics, and theoretical foundations of persuasion, as well as one of the most important tools of persuasion: symbolic activity, especially as we encounter it in language. In Part II, we are searching for various kinds of unstated and nearly universally held major premises that can serve in persuasive enthymemes. One of these kinds of premises, the process premise, relates to appeals to the emotions and the will — to the psychological processes operating daily in each of us. One kind of process premise involves our needs and wants. We can see needs and wants operating in Maslow's hierarchy of needs model and in Packard's (sometimes Freudian) listing of human needs. There are other models of human need states as well. A second kind of process premise that can predispose us to action involves our attitudes and beliefs. If persuaders change our beliefs and attitudes about fuel efficiency, they predispose us to buy fuel-efficient autos, furnaces, and hot water heaters. If persuaders want us to continue voting for a certain party, they reinforce our existing beliefs and attitudes. Both of these persuasive types can be used with either attitudes toward objects/issues or with attitudes toward situations. It may be important for persuaders to reinforce or change our behavioral intentions—for example, to get us to put a bumper sticker on our car, so we will likely vote for their candidate. If persuaders can get us to clip a product coupon, their job is more than half done, for we already intend to buy the product when we clip the coupon. Finally, closely related to both attitudes and needs is the human desire for psychological consonance. We seek a world in which our predictions are verified, in which people we like approve of the same things we do, and in which our values and attitudes do not conflict with our behavior. If we feel a lack of balance, we actively seek ways to bring our world into congruity. If we perceive balance to exist, we experience ease and can be easily motivated to continue to act as we have been doing. Persuaders try to create imbalance if they want us to *change* our behavior and try to reinforce balance if they want us to *maintain* our behavior. Although each of us is unique, our need states, attitudinal clusterings, and desires for psychological balance are similar enough that persuaders can use these processes as first premises for large groups of people.

QUESTIONS FOR FURTHER THOUGHT

1. What is a process premise? Explain.
2. What is the difference between an attitude and a need? Give examples.

3. What does Maslow mean when he calls his hierarchy of needs "prepotent"?
4. Which needs described by Packard are the most ego-involving or personal in nature?
5. Give an example of the need for emotional security.
6. Give an example of how advertisers use the need for ego-gratification.
7. Give an example of the need for a sense of power.
8. What are three functions of an attitude?
9. What is the difference between an attitude and an opinion?
10. What is the difference between a behavior and a behavioral intention?
11. What are some sources of dissonance?
12. What are some sources of consonance?

NOTES

1. Winston S. Churchill, Speech on Dunkirk, House of Commons, June 4, 1940.
2. Vance Packard, *The Hidden Persuaders* (New York: Pocket Books, 1964).
3. *Ibid.*, p. 5.
4. *Ibid.*
5. *Ibid.*
6. David H. Freedman, "Why You Watch Some Commercials—Whether You Mean to or Not," *T.V. Guide*, February 20, 1988, p. 5.
7. Packard, *op. cit.*, pp. 61–70.
8. Robert Marquand, "Needed: Curriculum with Character," *Chicago Tribune*, January 24, 1988, Tempo section, p. 1.
9. Robert N. Bellah, Richard Madsen, William M. Sullivan, Ann Swidler, and Steven M. Tipton, *Habits of the Heart: Individualism and Commitment* (New York: Harper & Row, 1985), pp. 294–296.
10. Thomas Harris, *I'm O.K.—You're O.K.: A Practical Guide to Transactional Analysis* (New York: Pantheon Books, 1967).
11. Jesse Liesse Erickson and Judann Dagnoli, "Brand Fame Spreading: Line Extensions Are

Marketers' Lifelines," *Advertising Age*, February 22, 1988, pp. 3, 76.

12. Abraham H. Maslow, *Motivation and Personality* (New York: Harper & Row, 1954).

13. Alvin Toffler, *The Third Wave* (New York: Bantam Books, 1980).

14. Bill Barol, "The Eighties Are Over," *Newsweek*, January 4, 1988, pp. 42–43.

15. T. J. Jackson Lears, "From Salvation to Self-Realization: Advertising and the Therapeutic Roots of the Consumer Culture, 1880–1930," in *The Culture of Consumption: Critical Essays in American History, 1880–1980*, ed. Richard Wightman Fox and T. J. Jackson Lears (New York: Pantheon Books, 1983), pp. 3–37.

16. Milton Rokeach, *Beliefs, Attitudes, and Values: A Theory of Organization and Change* (San Francisco: Jossey-Bass, 1968); Milton Rokeach, *The Nature of Human Values* (New York: Free Press, 1973).

17. Charles Larson and Robert Sanders, "Faith, Mystery and Data: An Analysis of 'Scientific' Studies of Persuasion," *Quarterly Journal of Speech* 61:178–194, 1975.

18. Philip G. Zimbardo, Ebbe E. Ebbesen, and Christina Maslach, *Influencing Attitudes and Changing Behavior* (Reading, MA: Addison-Wesley, 1976). p. 20.

19. Russell H. Colley, *Defining Advertising Goals for Measured Advertising Results* (New York: Association of National Advertisers, 1961).

20. As quoted in Zimbardo, *op. cit.*, p. 92.

21. See for example, Sarah Trenholm, *Persuasion and Social Influence* (Englewood Cliffs, NJ: Prentice-Hall, 1989), pp. 8–9.

22. Martin Fishbein and Icek Ajzen, *Belief, Attitude, Intention and Behavior: An Introduction to Theory and Research* (Reading, MA: Addison-Wesley, 1975).

23. J. Richard Eiser, *The Expression of Attitude* (New York: Springer-Verlag, 1987), p. 2. For an earlier discussion of this concept in relation to persuasion, see Charles Larson and Robert Sanders, cited in Note 17.

24. Daniel J. O'Keefe, "The Relationship of Attitudes and Behavior: A Constructivist Analysis," in *Message-Attitude-Behavior: Theory, Methodology, and Application*, ed. Donald P. Cushman and Robert D. McPhee (New York: Academic Press, 1980).

25. Joseph N. Capella and Joseph P. Folger, "An Information-Processing Explanation of Attitude Behavior Inconsistency," in Cushman and McPhee, cited in Note 24.

26. See Donald P. Cushman and Robert D. McPhee, eds., *Message-Attitude-Behavior: Theory, Methodology, and Application* (New York: Academic Press, 1980).

27. Charles E. Osgood and Percy H. Tannenbaum, "The Principle of Congruity in the Prediction of Attitude Change," *Psychological Review* 62:43, 1955.

28. Eiser, *op. cit.*, pp. 27–31.

29. Victor Frankl, *Man's Search for Meaning: An Introduction to Logotherapy* (New York: Washington Square Press, 1962).

30. Kenneth Burke, *The Rhetoric of Religion: Studies in Logology* (Boston: Beacon Press, 1961). pp. 276–316.

31. Dale Carnegie, *How to Win Friends and Influence People* (New York: Simon & Schuster, 1952), p. 38.

CHAPTER

7

Content Premises in Persuasion

▼

Another kind of premise that can operate in an enthymeme is the content premise. **Content premises** rely on our rational and intellectual processes: content of messages is critically analyzed in the persuadee's mind to determine whether it is credible and meaningful in relation to the issue under consideration. Content premises rely on our ability to use our reasoning faculties to analyze evidence.

We all have learned certain logical patterns because we have encountered them repeatedly over time. Most of us believe, for example, that events have causes and that when certain things occur, other things invariably follow. Problems also have causes, and when these causes are removed, the problem seems to be eliminated. This particular pattern of rational and intellectual reasoning — called **cause-effect reasoning** — is a powerful first premise often used in persuasion. For example, evidence could be presented to prove that a certain baseball team's pitching staff had experienced many training camp and early season injuries. A logical "effect" of this "cause" would be that the team would end the season with a poor record. It would not be necessary to convince an audience that injuries lead to losses; it would be necessary only to list the various injuries and then conclude that a losing record was likely. This example shows that the cause-effect pattern can be a potent first premise. This pattern is a type of content premise that is frequently used by politicians and government officials, in the courts, in business, and even in consumer advertising to some degree. All first premises use assumptions already in the audience's mind as the implicit major premise in an enthymeme. Content premises rely on the patterns by which the *content* of messages is connected with what are believed to be accepted patterns of logical or rational thought. In other words, content premises "sell" because they are assumed to be logical.

WHAT IS CONTENT?

Suppose that you are confronted by an evangelist on campus who wants you to join his group as a new convert. He tells you that you must go to the informational meeting in the student center lounge at 7:00 P.M. tonight. You have three options: You can do as he asks, you can reject him out of hand, or you can ask him to provide good reasons for going to the meeting. The first two options are likely the results of some kind of emotional response you have to the speaker and the topic. You might hate "holier than thou" evangelists and thus reject the persuasion. You might be a true believer already and so warmly follow the advice. The last option, however, is the one that seeks further information. If you say, "Give me three good reasons," you would be asking for proof in the form of content premises — arguments or statements that would be convincing to most reasonable persons. The crusader could say, "Well, because you are in my philosophy of religion class, attending the meeting would be a good way to add to your knowledge about that subject. You may even get information useful in writing that term paper we have to do." This would be a good enough reason for many people to give the informational meeting a try. You might be a little more demanding and say to the persuader, "That's one good reason — two more to go." If the evangelist hoped to persuade you, he would have to come up with more information that would be reasonably acceptable.

The power of the content premise lies not in its ability to stir the emotions, to create psychic "disease," or to appeal to hidden needs. Rather, its power lies in eliciting a rational or logical response from or conclusion in the persuadee. Of course, what may be sufficient content persuasion for one person may not be sufficient for another. But whatever the level of proof an individual requires, content persuasion will rely on the nature of the evidence and reasoning presented in the argument, which fits either with a "widely accepted" proof level or the idiosyncratic proof requirements of various individuals.

WHAT IS PROOF?

Proof varies from *situation to situation*. What may "prove" a point to people in a weekly fraternity meeting may not "prove" the same point to a university administrator. Several books in the last three decades have tried to "prove" that President Kennedy's assassination was caused by a complex conspiracy. They successfully persuaded some people but failed with others. Thus, proof varies from *person to person* as well. The Bush administration tried to "prove" that cutting the capital gains tax would actually benefit the poor and middle classes. The proof worked for some people (especially the rich) but did not convince many others. Proof can thus vary from group to group. In general, though, we can say that proof consists of enough evidence that can be connected through reasoning to lead audience members to take the persuader's advice or to believe in what he or she says.

This is what Aristotle meant by *logos*, which we touched on in Chapters 1 and 3. He pointed out that because we are thinking and resasoning creatures, appeals to this logical side of our makeup could be persuasive. He even identified several "places" where persuasion seemed to focus when appealing to our logical sides. As you will recall from Chapter 3, Aristotle called the "places of argument" *topoi*, or topics, of argument and rational discourse. Sometimes, for instance, the topic might be some sort of precedent that the audience recognizes as the way things have always been done. The precedent sets a guide for the future, and, unless the audience is given numerous good reasons for breaking the precedent, it controls future instances of similar issues. For example, a precedent that you take for granted is that school, from the primary grades to high school, is typically a September-to-June affair. Why? From an economic standpoint, that calendar is foolish given the expense of heating school buildings during the winter months in most of the United States. However, we all know that there is a precedent for the September-to-June model. It was originally devised during the agrarian phase of our society, when young people's help was essential to get the crops planted, tended, and finally, harvested. The precedent still serves as our model even though the need for it is no longer critical and even though it is costly.

Most contemporary theorists agree that proof is composed of two factors: **reasoning** and **evi-**

dence. In the proper mix, these two will lead persuadees to adopt the changes a persuader advocates.

EVIDENCE AND REASONING

There are several ways to look at evidence and reasoning. By examining what persuaders do—how they operate—we can infer motives and discover what they are up to. For example, suppose I wished to persuade you that smoking causes lung cancer. The thrust of my message—the strategy of it, so to speak—is to create a cause-effect argument. I want to prove to you that a given effect—lung cancer—has a given cause—cigarette smoking. Along the way I might engage in a variety of tactics (for example, I might show slides of cancerous body cells, I might give vivid testimony of the pain and suffering involved in cancer deaths, or I might offer statistical correlations), but they would all be related to my general strategy or intention. These tactics are the source from which proof will ultimately emerge for you as persuadee; somewhere along the line, I will reach the threshold for you and will have "proved" to you that smoking causes lung cancer. This, of course, may convince you to stop smoking. In other situations, other elements will persuade you to stop—the key may not even be planned by a persuader but can still be the threshold for change.

Considering evidence and reasoning from the perspective of the theme of this text (that there is both permanence and change in the means of persuasion), we see that the nature of evidence and reasoning has remained quite stable. What has changed dramatically in the information age are the *kinds and amount of evidence*.

Before the advent of electronic media, modern advertising, and contemporary propaganda, audiences were accustomed to receiving very specific, verifiable evidence. For example, if you used a person's testimony to prove a point, it was critical to tell the audience why that person qualified as a good source of evidence. Audiences were suspicious of some kinds of evidence—analogies, for example. Today, however, we accept the testimony of Mike Ditka when he endorses an investment plan, even though he does not qualify as an expert on economics. And we frequently accept analogies as evidence: animated automobile tires depicted as having cat's claws to grip the road, for instance.

TYPES OF EVIDENCE

Generally, there are two broad forms of evidence: evidence that appeals to our emotions (which is usually dramatic in form) and evidence that appeals to our reasoning (which is usually logical or rational in form).

Different kinds of evidence, whether dramatic or rational, vary in strength or persuasive power, depending on the context in which they are used. In some situations, for instance, statistics are used to powerful effect; in others, pictorial evidence is relied on; and in yet others, retold or vicarious experience most effectively delivers the persuasive message of the content premise. In all of these instances, persuasion relies on the assumption that one can learn and act on the basis of information gained indirectly and vicariously.[1] Watching a child get burned may "persuade" another child to stay away from fire, for example. This is why stories that relate the experiences of others are such effective evidence and why they are favored as persuasive devices. Frequently, advertisers use testimonials from well-known people who endorse products. The advertisers assume that consumers will vicariously absorb the experience that the movie star or athlete relates and will buy the product.

But even when we do not learn by or become swayed by the experience of others, our own experience is usually enough to cause us to change. The Sioux Indians were aware of this. As a baby crawled close to the campfire, they did not pull it away with shouts of "Hot! Stay away, baby! Hot!" as we do in our culture. Instead, they watched the baby's progress very closely and allowed the baby to reach into the fire and touch a hot coal, burning itself mildly. Then they quickly pulled the baby away and treated the burn. The experience "persuaded" the child to be careful with fire. The fol-

lowing section explores these two forms of evidence in more detail.

Dramatic Evidence

Narratives People have always been fascinated by **narratives**, or stories. The myth, legend, and ballad — all types of narrative — frequently served as social glue in preliterate cultures, allowing people to pass on information by word of mouth from generation to generation. Although we live on the brink of the twenty-first century, the same fascination with narrative remains and is often more powerful than statistics, charts, or expert testimony in persuading others.

Evidence that is dramatic in nature invites and encourages vicarious experience on the part of persuadees in an attempt to persuade them to a certain course of action.[2] Such persuasion relies on the persuadees' ability to project themselves into the context or situation described by the persuader — to "feel" what others feel, to "live" the problem vicariously.

If we were to look at highly successful speeches of the past and present, we would undoubtedly find a great deal of emotional and dramatic evidence. The persuader presents a dramatic situation to the audience and then "invites" the listeners to use their imaginations to participate — to become actors themselves. There is no intellectualizing here. The audience's reaction is neither logical nor illogical. They merely respond to dramatic evidence. This type of evidence encourages persuadees to *co-create* proof with the persuader. The result is powerful, and probably long-lasting, persuasion.[3]

Several types of evidence lend themselves to the dramatic approach. For example, a good way to use dramatic evidence is through the narrative, or story. In his book *People of the Lie: The Hope for Healing Human Evil*, noted author and psychotherapist M. Scott Peck relates "The Case of Bobby and His Parents" in an attempt to prove that there is genuine evil in the world — something that the "science" of psychology has refused to research, leaving such matters to philosophers and theologians.[4] The narrative begins with a patient named Bobby, who was admitted to the hospital emergency room the night before for depression. The admitting physician's notes read:

> Bobby's older brother Stuart, 16, committed suicide this past June, shooting himself in the head with his .22 caliber rifle. Bobby initially seemed to handle his sibling's death rather well. But from the beginning of school in September, his academic performance has been poor. Once a "B" student, he is now failing all his courses. By Thanksgiving he had become obviously depressed. His parents, who seem very concerned, tried to talk to him, but he has become more and more uncommunicative, particularly since Christmas. Although there is no previous record of antisocial behavior, yesterday Bobby stole a car by himself and crashed it (he had never driven before), and was apprehended by the police. . . . Because of his age, he was released into his parents' custody, and they were advised to seek immediate psychiatric evaluation for him.[5]

Peck goes on to observe that although Bobby appeared to be a typical fifteen-year-old, he stared at the floor and kept picking at a small sore on the back of his hand — in fact, there were several such sores on both hands and forearms. When Peck asked Bobby if he felt nervous being in the hospital, he got no answer — "Bobby was really digging into that sore. Inwardly I winced at the damage he was doing to his flesh."[6] After reassuring Bobby that the hospital was a safe place to be, he tried to draw Bobby out in conversation. But nothing seemed to work, whether Peck tried talking about Bobby's parents, his theft of the car, school, even his relationship with his brother. Peck got "No reaction. Except that maybe he dug a little deeper into one of the sores on his forearm." Bobby admitted that he hurt his parents by stealing the car but couldn't identify any other specific instances. He only knew that he hurt them because they yelled at him. When asked what they yelled at him, he replied, "I don't know." "Bobby was feverishly picking at his sores now and . . . I felt it would be best if I steered my questions to more neutral subjects."[7] They discussed the family pet — a German shepherd whom Bobby took care of but didn't play with because she was his father's dog. Peck then turned the conversation to Christmas, asking what sorts of gifts Bobby had gotten:

BOBBY: "Nothing much."

PECK: "Your parents must have given you something. What did they give you?"

BOBBY: "A gun."

PECK: "A gun?" I repeated stupidly.

BOBBY: "Yes."

PECK: "What kind of a gun?" I asked slowly.

BOBBY: "A twenty-two."

PECK: "A twenty-two pistol."

BOBBY: "No, a twenty-two rifle."

PECK: "I understand that it was with a twenty-two rifle that your brother killed himself."

BOBBY: "Yes."

PECK: "Was that what you asked for for Christmas?"

BOBBY: "No."

PECK: "What did you ask for?"

BOBBY: "A tennis racket."

PECK: "But you got the gun instead?"

BOBBY: "Yes."

PECK: "How did you feel, getting the same kind of gun that your brother had?"

BOBBY: "It wasn't the same kind of gun."

PECK: I began to feel better. Maybe I was just confused. "I'm sorry, I thought they were the same kind of gun."

BOBBY: "It wasn't the same kind of gun. It was *the* gun."

PECK: "You mean it was your brother's gun?" I wanted to go home very badly now. "You mean your parents gave you your brother's gun for Christmas — the one he shot himself with?"

BOBBY: "Yes."

PECK: "How did it make you feel getting your brother's gun for Christmas?"

BOBBY: "I don't know."

PECK: I almost regretted the question: How could he know? How could he answer such a thing? "No, I don't expect you could know."[8]

Peck then brought the parents in for counseling. However, they either claimed (lied) or they really were unable to realize what message they had sent their remaining son by giving him his brother's gun. Bobby continued therapy until he was sent to live with a favorite aunt.

> By the time he was discharged to Helen's care, three weeks after his admission to the hospital, the sores on his arms and hands were only scars, and he was able to joke with the staff. Six months later I heard from Helen that he seemed to be doing well and that his grades had come up again. From his psychiatrist I heard that he had developed a trusting therapeutic relationship but was only barely beginning to approach facing the psychological reality of his parents and their treatment of him.[9]

When I first read this dramatic example, I literally gasped as I discovered that Bobby's parents had given him a gun for Christmas, and I was totally dumbstruck to learn that it was *the* gun. That Bobby's parents didn't understand what they had signaled to him or that they lied about it convinced me that some people are indeed evil. Bobby's essential humanity forced him to steal a car and crash it so that he could receive the kind of help he needed. His subconscious realized the wickedness of his parents' actions. Although the story was emotionally charged, you would be hard put to call it "illogical." In fact, it is probably totally logical to conclude that such neglect of other people is harmful, even though that conclusion is based on a single case. If the evidence is dramatic enough or emotional enough, persuadees will not ask for more. The case of Bobby and his parents is a narrative. Most of the great preachers, orators, and politicians have also been storytellers. They used the narrative skillfully. Often the narrative is used to capture an audience's attention and

to draw them into a topic. This effect is reinforced with other evidence, and more narratives might be worked in to keep us interested.

Once, during a trial in which he was trying to explain what "self-defense" meant, Abraham Lincoln used a narrative about a man who, while walking down a country road carrying a pitchfork, was attacked by a vicious dog, which he was finally forced to kill with the pitchfork.[10] Lincoln said that the dog's owner, a local farmer, had asked the man:

> "Why did you kill my dog?"
> "What made him try to bite me?" said the man.
> "But why didn't you go at him with the other end of the pitchfork?" asked the farmer.
> "Why didn't he come at me with the other end of the dog?" replied the man.

Lincoln demonstrated his notion of self-defense through the narrative: that the degree of permissible force in self-defense is determined by the degree of the attacker's aggressive force.

Chances are that you have heard speeches or sermons in which the story, or narrative, was skillfully used. Such speeches seem to have the most impact and are remembered the longest. The parables of the New Testament are easy to recall, whereas many of the other verses fade from our memory soon after we hear them. As Ralph G. Nichols, a professor of mine, once said, "The narrative will carry more persuasive freight than any other form of evidence."

Testimony Another type of dramatic evidence is **testimony**. Here, the persuader might read an eyewitness account aloud or simply recount his or her personal experience. If the issue being discussed is unemployment, persuadees might be swayed if they hear from out-of-work persons. The details of having to wait in line for one's unemployment check, the embarrassment of having to take government-surplus foodstuffs, and other experiences of the unemployed will probably have dramatic persuasive power. As receivers, we vicariously live through what the witness experienced when we hear direct testimony.

Although eyewitness testimony is potent, studies have shown that it is often unreliable and even incorrect. Psychologist Elizabeth F. Loftus discusses the many cases in which persons have been wrongfully imprisoned on the basis of eyewitness testimony.[11] She points out that the controversy over the accuracy of such evidence has created confusion in the courts and that many judges do not allow "experts" to testify on the reliability of eyewitness testimony because it might "confuse" the jury—whose job it is to evaluate what they hear. As the appellate court in *People vs. Plasencia* stated:

> The cornerstone of our system remains our belief in the wisdom and integrity of the jury system and the ability of 12 jurors to determine the accuracy of witnesses' testimony. The system has served us well.[12]

As Figure 7.1 illustrates, witnesses often see and hear what they want to see and hear, and often give testimony from their own idosyncratic points of view.

As receivers, we need to carefully examine the testimony used to persuade us. Ask questions such as: Was the witness in a position to see what is claimed? Could the witness be mistaken in any way? Does the witness have a bias that might cloud his or her testimony? Might the witness have a motive for giving the testimony? After all, we all know that those athletes, movie stars, and pop singers who claim to use such and such a product probably are offering their endorsement not because they like the product but because they are well paid for giving the testimony. As we will see in Chapter 12, testimony as a form of proof frequently is used by politicians to mislead receivers; it is a powerful and ancient persuasive device.

Anecdotes The anecdote is a related form of persuasion. **Anecdotes** usually depict a short narrative that makes a point in a hurry—maybe in only a sentence or two. For example, there is the anecdote of the optimist who was asked to describe his philosophy. He said, "That's simple. I'm nostalgic about the future." Anecdotes are often funny and

are frequently hypothetical, so they are quite different from actual testimony. The key thing about anecdotes is that unlike testimony, we rarely take them as truth. Instead, we tend to process anecdotes as if they are the exclamation points of persuasion. Lincoln was once trying a case in which the opposing attorney was rather long-winded. Lincoln used this anecdote to make that point to the judge and jury:

> My friend is peculiarly constructed. When he begins to speak, his brain stops working. He makes me think of a little old steamboat we had on the Sangamon River in the early days. It had a five-foot boiler and a seven-foot whistle, and everytime it whistled, it also stopped.[13]

Participative Evidence

There are several other ways in which persuaders can dramatize evidence. At an antismoking presentation, for instance, audiovisual materials can show cancerous lung tissue. The audience can **participate** by exhaling cigarette smoke through a clean white tissue and observing the nicotine stains left behind. Sometimes persuaders dramatize a point by using visual aids to demonstrate the problem and solution. One of my students spoke on the need to be aware when stress is building up and how to use jogging to reduce it. He displayed a large, deflated balloon that he said represented an average student at NIU. The "student" was inflated a little with the stress of settling into a new dorm room. Another puff of air was the stress of registration. More air went in for the first exams and fraternity rush. Soon the balloon was ready to pop. The speaker then called on his audience to release their stress through exercise. He ended the speech saying, "Or else do you know what could

FIGURE 7.1

Witnesses see events or persons from their own point of view. (Reprinted by permission of John Jonik from *Psychology Today*.)

happen?" Whereupon he popped the balloon with a pin. The audience's attention never strayed from the balloon or the point of the speech. This kind of dramatization is useful and persuasive. You will encounter many kinds of dramatizations as you process the many persuasive messages aimed at you each day. Learn to recognize them and to respond to them wisely.

Rational Evidence

Not all evidence is dramatic. Sometimes evidence appeals to our logical processes in nondramatic, intellectually oriented ways. For example, newspaper editorials frequently use evidence that appeals to the reader's logical processes. A good example comes from a series of editorials in the *Chicago Tribune* that promoted early-childhood education.[14] The lead sentence of the editorial made the major claim that "early childhood education is the surest way to break the chain of chronic poverty." The case was developed with supportive claims, such as:

> Early childhood education reduces the costs of welfare, special education, and the criminal justice system. . . . Early learning programs reduce the risks of mental malnutrition. . . . These children, then, [those going to preschools] need less special and remedial education. They are happier with themselves and their school environment. They get along better with teachers. . . . They are more likely to graduate from high school, get a job or go on to higher education. . . . They are less likely to get caught up in delinquency and crime.

The editorial then provided statistics gathered from a study of 123 children who had a high risk of failure. Fifty percent had had high-quality preschool education; the other 50 percent had had none. The students were followed for twenty years, and the researchers reported that those having had preschool had

> better grades and fewer failing marks. They were absent less from school. They needed

less special education. And they had a better attitude toward school than a group of similar youngsters who did not get the preschooling.

At age nineteen, the children with the preschool were:

> more likely to finish high school and to score average or above on competency tests. More of them had jobs or were involved in higher education. And they were less likely to have been arrested, to be on welfare, or to become pregnant.

The logical argument then went on to cite the savings resulting from preschool education and the resulting cut in remedial programs:

> It actually cost less to educate the children who got the preschooling . . . even when the expenses of the early classes [were] included. . . . Preschool cut the cost per student of each succeeding year in school by about 20 percent — about $800 per child every year in savings.
>
> In terms of reduced crime alone, taxpayers will save $3100 for every one of the youngsters who got the preschool training. . . . These are the direct costs and don't count the anguish, fear and suffering that criminals can inflict on victims. Nor does it attempt to measure the psychological benefits of a reduction in crime rate in a community. . . .
>
> Taxpayers have already saved seven times the cost of one year of preschool in the Ypsilanti project and 3½ times the tab for two years. And the savings resulting from reduced needs in welfare, from less crime, and from greater ability to earn will continue for the rest of the lives of these young people — even reach into the lives of the following generation.

Notice how these claims appeal to our logical processes. The writer knows that we receivers have a major premise in our heads about costs versus benefits. We desire that any idea, product, or program have benefits that justify the costs. Knowing that we have this internal premise, the writer makes claims of great benefits for the preschool idea. The writer also knows that we expect to see some sort of evidence to back up such claims and that we will probably respect this evidence if it is reported "scientifically." The twenty-year study of the high-risk children fits the bill for our evidence needs; we are persuaded.

There are no narratives in the editorial. There are no anecdotes. The only testimony was the report of the Ypsilanti project, which is not testimony from an eyewitness but rather is a statistical summary.

This appeal to our logical processes can be seen in other persuasive messages — in advertising, for example. A confident Lee Iacocca steps in front of the camera as cars swoosh past on the freeway in the background. He reminds the viewers that Chrysler was the first corporation to guarantee its automobile drivetrains for five years or 50,000 miles and that the industry finally followed suit. He then announces that Chrysler will set another service record by offering the same warranty for its trucks, and he challenges the industry to try to come up to Chrysler's standards once again. Granted, there are emotional aspects to the TV spot. There is also an appeal to our logical or rational processes. "Since Chrysler has a record of standing behind its products, it will stand behind them in the future" is the argument being made. Given our predisposition to use the past as a touchstone, as well as knowledge of the follow-through on the Chrysler warranty, we draw a conclusion that Chrysler trucks may be a better buy given the costs and benefits.

Look at Figure 7.2. The Campbell Soup Company knows that persons concerned with health and nutrition are aware of the much-publicized need for increasing the amount of fiber in the American diet. Most of the literature on this subject has recommended eating high-fiber foods such as whole wheat bread and bran cereals. However, many people don't like dry cereal, let alone dry bran cereals. Campbell's offers similar benefits but with different costs — you can get fiber by eating Manhandler soups such as Bean with Bacon or Split Pea with Ham.

As you can see from these examples, the appeal to logical processes relies on a reasoning pattern such as "the past is a guide to the future" or "the cost is less than the benefits." What are some other logical patterns that persuaders often use?

TYPES OF REASONING

Remember our definition of proof: enough evidence *connected with reasoning* to lead an audience to believe or act on a persuader's advice. We will now explore the second step in the process of logical persuasion: connecting the pieces of evidence by reasoning. Several patterns of reasoning seem to be deeply held in our culture. One school of research suggests that there is a linguistic explanation for reasoning. The premise is that the "deep structure" of our language (for example, *ed* endings indicate verbs, whereas *ly* endings indicate adverbs, and declarative sentences usually indicate actions that have a beginning, a middle, and an end) is accompanied by deep logical structures.[15] The possibility that this is so is perhaps most dramatically exhibited when people violate the accepted "deep structure" of logical reasoning and are hence labeled as "off the wall," "way out in left field," or just plain "crazy." Consider the following letter to the editor of a local newspaper regarding ways of removing nuisance deer from public parks in the area:

> Let's look at some hard facts:
> - It cost taxpayers $50,000 to shoot the deer at Ryerson Woods.
> - It would cost taxpayers $30,000 a year to shoot the deer at Rock Cut Park.
> - The Department of Conservation made $20,000 a year from hunting at Rock Cut.
> - Hunters already have won the right to hunt on public land in the Supreme Court.
> - Hunters pay millions of dollars annually to buy state parks.

Pretty good so far, even if you don't agree with the man's position. He has begun with what appears to be an inductive line of argument using "effect-to-cause" reasoning (that is, citing a set of effects and

MADE OF THE FINEST FIBER

If you're like most people who eat right, you probably give high fiber high priority.

And like most people, when you think of fiber, you probably automatically think of bran cereals.

Well, there's another good source of dietary fiber you should know about. Delicious Campbell's® Bean with Bacon Soup.

In fact, Campbell's has four soups that are high in fiber.

And you can see from the chart that follows exactly how each one measures up to bran cereals.

So now when you think of fiber, you don't have to think about having it just at breakfast.

Instead, you can do your body good any time during the day. With a hot, hearty bowl of one of these Campbell's Soups.

You just might feel better for it—right to the very fiber of your being.

FIBER IN A SUGGESTED SERVING			
CAMPBELL'S SOUP		BRAN CEREALS	
Bean with Bacon	9g	100% Brans	11g
Split Pea with Ham	6g	40% Brans	6g
Green Pea	5g	Raisin Brans	5g
Low Sodium Green Pea	7g	Others	5–10g
This comparison includes soluble and insoluble fiber			

CAMPBELL'S
SOUP IS GOOD FOOD

Campbell's has a full line of low sodium soups for those people who are on a salt-restricted diet or have a concern about sodium.

then concluding by identifying a probable cause). He shows the varying degrees of effectiveness of several alternate plans used in the past (his first three points), and then goes on to state a fact about the law relating to hunting on public lands. Finally, he makes a claim that hunters pay for state parks. This last point is a little unclear, but he probably means that state parks are at least partially funded by revenue from hunting licenses, the high federal and state taxes on guns and ammunition, and of course, the hunter's own property, sales, and income taxes. We anticipate that he is about to claim something like

> Therefore, hunters are positive persons and deserve to hunt in state parks, especially when their hunting helps to remove nuisance deer from these parks in economic and even revenue-producing ways.

The fact that we anticipate such a "logical" conclusion is probably evidence of at least one type of deep logical structure. Now notice what happens when our expectations are unmet in the conclusions the author actually draws from the five points noted above:

> If you were an animal, would you prefer to live ten years free, even if you died a slow death, or would you want to live it penned up, sleeping in your own manure? I think most Americans would want to be free. That's also the way God wanted it. That's why he said it is a good thing to be a hunter. For Jesus Christ is alive and well, but Bambi never was.[16]

The conclusion is whacky; it seems befuddled and barely related to the evidence. What do living free and dying slowly have to do with the argument? How does sleeping in one's own manure relate to the issue? Where did God say that it was good to be a hunter? What does the Jesus Christ versus

Bambi comparison mean? None of these conclusions flow from the evidence.

It is clear that the author's conclusion demonstrates several serious violations of the deep structural logical expectations held by most people; our preference for a line of reasoning has been violated. But what does this example have to do with our study of persuasion from the receiver's point of view? Remember, we are looking for content premises — logical patterns that serve as the first premises in enthymemes. The deep structural logical preferences serve in this way: We believe and act on what we perceive to be logical arguments presented to us by persuaders. As a result, it is useful for receivers to be aware of the logical patterns most people prefer and that are used by persuaders every day. Let us explore some of these logical "deep structures" in more detail.

Cause-to-Effect Reasoning

Cause-to-effect reasoning is powerful in our culture; even our language depends on it. For example, we rarely say "The ball was thrown and the window was broken," which is a passive-voice sentence. Instead we put the cause out front and let it create the effect. We say "Johnny threw the ball, which broke the window." This active-voice sentence tells us that Johnny *caused* the ball to go through the window, and that, in turn, the flying ball *caused* the window to break. This construction gives us much more information; this is an active-voice sentence. It tells us *by whom* or *what*.

Persuaders frequently use cause-to-effect reasoning to identify events, trends, or facts that have caused certain effects. They tell us that if a cause is present, we can expect certain effects to follow. If the effects are bad and we want to do something about them, we usually try to remove the cause.

Take the world of television advertising, for example. As Bob Garfield, staff writer for *Advertising Age*, claims, "Good commercials finally outnumber the bad ones on TV."[17] He noted some that operate from cause to effect. One of them is for the product Equalactin, which is claimed to "restore water balance in the intestines," supposedly working to aid in the diarrhea/constipation

FIGURE 7.2

This ad appeals to our logic. What rational arguments does it present? (Used by permission of the Campbell Soup Company.)

cycle. For some demographic reason, it is best to advertise such personal-care products early in the evening, but it is difficult to create tasteful and yet effective commercials for products such as Preparation H, Summer's Eve, or Tampax. As Garfield puts it, "The consequence is advertising either too disgusting to digest or couched so delicately as to be nearly meaningless."[18] Yet, he describes the Equalactin spot as "Sheer genius. Four stars." Instead of using humans in the ad, Equalactin uses animation, with the central "persons" in their ad being a human-looking tortoise and hare, which symbolize the twin discomforts of the irritable-bowel syndrome. The ad opens with the hare saying, "If you're like me with an irritable bowel, stressful days can mean diarrhea one day," (fade to tortoise) "constipation another," but with Equalactin in your system you can "feel like a human being again." Equalactin is the cause and relief is the result.

Effect-to-Cause Reasoning

Another type of reasoning that is less used (and sometimes flawed) is called **effect-to-cause reasoning**. Here, the persuader cites some known effects and tries to work back to the cause. For example, in the world of the television spot commercial, Bob Garfield also gave four stars to a spot for Stokely's Singles, microwaveable single-serving vegetables. "Moms don't like heating and reheating broccoli for their busy families' various dinner shifts. They hate trying to please four finicky palates with one frozen vegetable dish. And they despise the grimaces that greet their bowls of succotash."[19] Those are the effects. How to identify the cause, remove it, and substitute Stokely's Singles was the problem. If they did a "slice of life" ad, the family members would come off as ingrates who were lucky to be getting a meal at all. So they did an exaggerated "slice of life" using humor. "When mom dishes up the vegetables, Dad and the kids grimace outsize grimaces, Mom responds with an outlandish sneer and slings the whole bowl over her shoulder in disgust. The problem is real. The identification is immediate. The exaggeration is amusing. And the solution, lo and behold, is Stokely's."[20]

Reasoning from Symptoms

Persuaders sometimes identify a series of **symptoms** or signs and then try to conclude something from them. For example, politicians may cite how much worse things are now than they were when their opponent took office: unemployment is up, inflation is running wild, and recent polls show that people have lost faith in their ability to control their own destinies. The hope is that the voters will blame the incumbent opponent for the troubles.

Returning again to Garfield's four-star TV spots, we find reasoning from symptoms in an ad for South Carolina Federal bank. Their agency understood that "People pay no attention to disingenuous *ersatz* bankers. To persuade anybody that it is more human than the competition, a bank first must get their attention. Then it has to *act* more human." The usual bank ad relies on research to find out what people dislike about banking and then has some "bankerish-looking actor" claim that "Our bank is different because we value our customers."[21] And because the ads all look alike, consumers overlook them in the clutter of spots being aired during that segment. South Carolina Federal's approach was different. Instead of using humans, they used animals to react to the things consumers dislike about banking. One ad featured an orangutan in its opening shot. "How does your bank react when you ask for a home equity loan?" asks an offscreen wimpy voice. The orangutan yawns. Then the voice asks about bank hours: "Do they have all-day banking?" The orangutan shakes its head "No!" "Free checking?" The orangutan blows a raspberry at the camera. And so it goes, with the voice eliciting other symptoms of disliked bank practices followed by a humorous look or gesture by the orangutan until the final line: "Well, if we were you we'd bank with us."[22]

Criteria-to-Application Reasoning

Sometimes persuaders establish what appears to be a reasonable set of criteria for purchasing a product, voting for a candidate, or supporting a cause, and then offer their product, candidate, or cause as one that meets these criteria. For example, a well-known actor was featured on a Bell

System ad, following telephone deregulation. His pitch for using Bell established several criteria for good telephone service:

1. Reasonable rates and reliable service
2. Free information services for long-distance areas
3. Ability to handle calls to all parts of the country, not just those areas serviced by the system

The actor reminded viewers of the Bell System's past dependability and of its ability to reach anywhere in the country as well as foreign countries. Finally, after noting the free information service Bell provides, he offered viewers the "ten-dollar hour"; they could get sixty minutes of long-distance telephone time anywhere in the country for only $10 if they called a special number and made the request. Note that by setting up what appears to be a reasonable set of criteria initially, the persuader has already won half the battle. Receivers, having accepted the criteria, logically infer that Bell is a good choice when they get the reminders of past dependability, free information services, international dialing, and — the final hook — the ten-dollar hour. A competitor of AT&T claimed to charge 40 percent less for the same "ten-dollar hour."

Reasoning from Comparison or Analogy

Sometimes persuaders use **comparison** as their logical reason for some conclusion. In this form of reasoning, an example is analyzed and described and conclusions are then drawn about that example or situation. The persuader then compares the example with another situation, pointing out similarities and reasons why conclusions about the example apply to the present situation.

In 1985, for instance, both houses of Congress considered various ways to alter the U.S. tax code in order to simplify its complex rate structure and also to shift tax burdens from certain classes or groups to others. In the arguments, both pro and con, argument by comparison was a frequent logical appeal. Tables, charts, and graphs were used to compare how much individuals earning a cer-

tain annual salary paid under the old system with how much they would pay under the new one. Supposedly, voters who saw their position improved as compared to their position under the old system would lobby their congressional representatives and senators to vote for the new plan. We also frequently see argument by comparison in advertising: A product is compared with its competitors in terms of cost, effectiveness, safety, and so on. The big battle over the light beer market is largely an argument from comparison, with one brand claiming fewer calories and better taste than others. The same thing is seen in the ads for the low-tar and -nicotine cigarettes.

In the case of reasoning by **analogy**, something familiar is used to demonstrate something that is unfamiliar or complex. For example, suppose we wanted to compare the military fighting going on in Central America with the Vietnam War. We might point out that in both cases, guerilla warfare was the predominant mode of fighting and that government leaders were corrupt dictators. We also might point out that while the revolutionaries believed in socialism, they were not Communists. This would be a *literal* analogy. In other words, we are comparing a familiar past war (Vietnam) with an unfamiliar present (and possibly future) war in Panama or Nicaragua. Using a *figurative* analogy, we would compare a familiar but unrelated and simple thing to something that is unfamiliar and complex. For example, political races are often compared to horse races, by using such expressions as "front-runners," "early starters," "late comers," and "dark horses." Either of these persuasive means of comparison can simplify the issue or example being discussed.

Deductive Reasoning

A familiar form of appeal to logic is **deductive reasoning**, which can be defined as reasoning from the general to the specific. In a legislative body, a persuader might support a bill or a motion by saying something like "The legislation before us is desperately needed to prevent the state budget from going into a deficit situation." Then, the persuader goes on to provide the specifics. An editorial might begin, "Sycamore needs to pass this school referendum in order to save its extracurricular sports, its music and art programs, its newspaper, and its dramatics program" and then go on to describe the details. One of the problems with the deductive approach is that receivers who feel the least bit negative about the persuader's general point may "check out" and not pay attention to the specifics that are at the heart of the issue. Or the initial generalization may prompt rebuttal before the persuader has the opportunity to provide the details of the case.

Inductive Reasoning

Inductive reasoning gets the specifics out on the table before bringing up the generalized conclusion. For example, in the school-bond case the persuader might begin by saying, "Many of you know that it costs over $60,000 just to run the athletic program. The budget for the marching band was over $12,000 for travel, instruction, and uniforms. I was surprised to learn that it cost over $2000 just to pay the royalties for the spring musical. We have cut and cut until there is nothing left to cut. The last referendum increase was fourteen years ago—inflation has risen over 200 percent since then. Unless we pass this referendum, the district now faces elimination of these valuable extracurricular programs." With the specific evidence apparent, the generalization flows logically from it.

TESTS OF REASONING AND EVIDENCE

Of course, logical persuasion can be exploited by intentionally or unintentionally misusing either evidence or reasoning or perhaps by misusing both evidence *and* reasoning. Let's look at some examples of the misuse of evidence so that we can spot it when it occurs in interpersonal persuasion, political persuasion, advertising, and other persuasive arenas in our daily lives. We will also discuss the tests of evidence that we can apply in order to uncover the misuse.

The following examples of misuse of evidence and how to test evidence are not exhaustive. Rather they are offered as guidelines for the responsible and critical evaluation of the "logical" and even the "quasi-logical" persuasion aimed at you. You may want to look further into the use and misuse of logical appeals—reasoning and evidence.[23]

Use of Statistics

One of the mainstays of logical persuasion is the use of statistics. This is probably related to the highly technical and scientific world in which we live. We tend to believe statistics without questioning them. But several questions ought to be asked when statistical evidence is offered. First, is the sample from which the statistics are drawn a representative one? In other words, is the sample selected in any way that might bias the results? We need to know whether the statistic/sample is a reliable representation of reality. We might want to know how the sample was selected. From the phone directory? Not everyone has a telephone, some people have several, and others have unlisted phone numbers.

Another misuse of statistical evidence is using a single instance as an example of all instances. We frequently hear about the Defense Department being charged highly inflated prices for everyday items that you or I could pick up at the local K-mart for a fraction of the cost. One or two examples may lead us to believe that taxpayers are being gouged at every turn—that the $500 paid for a screwdriver is typical of the prices paid by our government. Frequently, however, this is not the case. Bids are made for various defense needs, and sometimes the high cost of one item is offset by a lower cost for other items—even a lower-than-cost price.

Another misuse of statistics is biased sampling, which occurs when a nonrepresentative portion of the population is sampled. Responses from a sample drawn from subscribers to *The National Rifleman* will be very different from one drawn from subscribers to *Horticulture* or *The Organic Gardener*.

The mode of presentation can also be employed to misuse or misrepresent statistics. For example, a minister on our campus spoke on gay rights and presented the graph in Figure 7.3 to demonstrate the degree to which homosexuality exists in the general population. The shaded portion indicates persons who have had at least one homosexual encounter. These range from persons who have had just one such encounter to those for whom all sexual encounters are homosexual. The unshaded portion of the graph indicates heterosexual persons. The highest estimates for homosexuality in the population range from 20 to 25 percent, but the graph suggests that the proportion is at least 50 percent. Thus it visually misrepresents the case and distorts the meaning of the statistics. What the graph fails to provide is information about the size of the sample in each segment. For all we know, the sample in the unshaded segments may be 1000, whereas the sample in the blackened part may be only 100. There are many other ways to distort statistics using graphic presentations of the numbers, so receivers need to be alert not only to what statistics really mean — for example, the way they were sampled and the type of measurement used — but also to the mode of presentation.

Use of Testimony

As noted earlier, one problem with the use of testimonials is that the person "testifying" may not be reporting accurate information. Also, seemingly insignificant shifts in wording can "lead" a witness to certain answers. And most of the time we don't have the opportunity to "cross examine" the person giving the testimonial. Instead, when we see or hear a person endorsing a product, a candidate, or an organization, we are forced to make up our mind right away as to whether the person is qualified to give the testimonial. Some of the questions you should raise in your own mind when testimonials are used to persuade you are:

1. Is the person giving the testimonial an authority on the subject, and if so, how reliable is he or she?

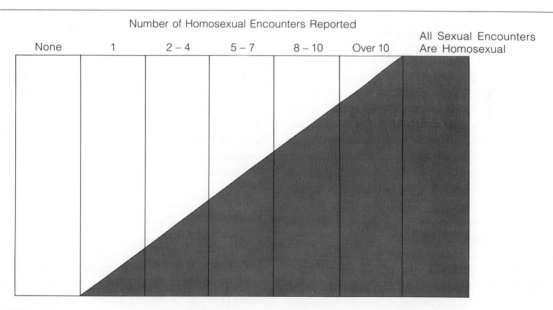

FIGURE 7.3

This graph is misleading because it implies that half the population is homosexual, whereas the statistics being represented are much lower than that.

2. Was the person giving the testimonial close enough to have witnessed the evidence he or she is testifying about?

3. Is it possible that the person giving the testimonial is biased for some reason or another, and if so, is the bias pro or con?

As persuadees, we need to be alert to the ways in which testimonials can be distorted or misused. We know that in many cases the testimonial is being given only because the sponsor has paid the person who is testifying — which is the case in most product-related testimonials. The only "law" about testimonials in product advertising is that the person testifying has to have used the product at least once. So the next time you see a sports personality endorsing a product, don't assume that he or she uses it on a daily basis. And try to determine the degree of authority the person has about the product and whether he or she might be biased or mistaken in some way — intentionally or unintentionally. When the bias is intentional, the ethical dimension comes into play.

Use of Comparisons and Analogies

The misuse of comparisons and analogies (sometimes labeled the fallacy of faulty comparison or faulty analogy)[24] is common in product advertising, and we will examine several examples of it in subsequent chapters. Here, let's look at nonproduct-oriented misuses of comparison or analogy. For example, politicians frequently compare the national budget to the budget necessities of the individual family. The family has to live within its resources, so for the comparison to be valid the government should live within *its* resources. Furthermore, individuals can't create money like governments can, they don't have to provide for national defense, and they don't have to build the roads they drive on. If they did, there would be no money left for the necessities of life. So comparing the government's budget to the individual family's budget is like "comparing apples to oranges," as the old saying goes.

The same thing applies to faulty analogies. For example, one father of a college freshman maintained that his college experience was analogous to that of his son: Since the father had gotten by on $5 a week spending money, the son should surely be able to make it on $10 a week. This faulty analogy has several dimensions: Inflation had quadrupled, not doubled in the years since the dad was in college; dormitories no longer provided clean towels and linens, so some of the spending money had to go to laundry costs; and athletic, theater, and concert tickets were no longer provided for a single low price but had to be purchased separately.

Figurative analogies can also be confusing. For example, it is misleading to compare a political campaign to a boxing match, with the incumbent delivering a "knockout punch" in the "late rounds," thus putting the challenger (who is a "real contender") "on the ropes" ready to be "decked" and "out cold" before the finish of "the match." Why is the analogy misleading? Whereas boxing matches are determined by a point system in which early rounds count as much as late rounds, in a campaign the final weeks and days are much more important than the early ones. Furthermore, boxing matches are determined by two judges and a referee, whereas elections are determined by an "audience" — the electorate. Granted, there are some similarities (for example, being "decked" and "losing"), but the analogy is misleading, taken in its entirety. It is obvious that persuadees need to examine comparisons and analogies to see whether they do indeed lead to a certain conclusion or whether there is some faulty comparison or analogy being used.

COMMON FALLACIES USED IN PERSUASION

Webster's defines the word *fallacy* as "deceptive appearance . . . a false or mistaken idea . . . an often plausible argument using false or invalid inference."[25] It is this last definition that concerns us here: believable arguments or premises that are based on invalid reasoning. In spite of the fact that these fallacies have been identified for centuries, they still pop up frequently in advertisements, political persuasion, interpersonal persuasion, and elsewhere. Briefly, here are the more common fallacies that we encounter almost daily.

Post Hoc Ergo Propter Hoc

This Latin phrase, commonly called the *post hoc* fallacy, translates to "after this, therefore because of this." As the translation implies, because one event follows another, the first event is assumed to be the cause of the second. We run into this fallacy almost daily in the world of advertising. For example, in a recent radio ad for *TV Guide*, a salesman for computer hardware is seated next to a French businessman on an airplane and describes how his firm could modify the Frenchman's computer system. The Frenchman wants to know about American television, so the salesman gives him a spare copy of *TV Guide* and makes a $30 million sale — all because of *TV Guide*.

In political persuasion, the *post hoc* fallacy often is used to blame the present state of affairs on the incumbent. For example, the reason the school system is out of money is that the new superintendent and his well-trained school board wasted all the money from the last referendum eight years ago on unneeded frills. Not necessarily so. At its present rate, inflation reduces the purchasing power of the dollar by half every seven to eight years. A humorous use of the *post hoc* fallacy can be seen in Dana Carvey's impersonation of President Bush on "Saturday Night Live." In one routine, Bush was featured standing in front of the torn-down Berlin Wall. "Before Bush, Wall," says Carvey, followed by "With Bush, No Wall."[26] "After this, therefore because of this?" Not always!

Ad Hominem

This Latin phrase, translated "against the man," means any attack against the personality whose purpose is to lead the audience to take certain actions just because of a character quirk or other flaw in a person of the opposite persuasion. This tactic frequently is used in political persuasion, which prompted the following letter to the editor in a recent election campaign:

> I am appalled at the selection of candidates for this year's election. No one is taking a stand on truly important issues. What am I hearing night after night on the news? Mudslinging, name-calling and back-stabbing! If a real crisis occurred, is this the tack these candidates would take? Pointing the finger elsewhere? Blaming everyone around them instead of shouldering some of the responsibility. . . .[27]

This tactic is not usually seen, read, or heard in advertising because products, not people, are being promoted. It is frequently used in ideological persuasion, where one leader attacks another. In the religious scandals of 1987 and 1988, it was hard to tell who was the worst sinner — adulterous Jimmy Bakker, his spendthrift wife Tammy Faye, or sexual voyeur Jimmy Swaggart — but it wasn't hard to hear the *ad hominem*. Whenever attacks are made on a person's character instead of on his or her stands on issues, be aware that the *ad hominem* strategy is at work. If persuaders have nothing substantive to debate, they frequently turn to attacking the personality of the opponent.

Ad Populum

As its name implies, the *ad populum* fallacy is persuasion that relies on whatever happens to be popular at that time. During the 1988 presidential primary campaigns, it became clear that the populism of the Reverend Jesse Jackson, a candidate for the Democratic nomination, was winning him delegates. As the trend continued, other potential nominees started to sound populist as well. As *Newsweek* pointed out:

> His [Jesse Jackson] rhetoric of resentment against "merger maniacs" and "corporate barracudas" became the basis of the newfound populism of Richard Gephardt, and, more recently, Albert Gore. His dovish foreign policy . . . has been echoed by Michael Dukakis.[28]

In advertising, we frequently see the *ad populum* fallacy being used to promote products. In the late 1980s, everybody of a certain age (including my teenage daughters) had to wear Guess jeans and Benneton sweatshirts and carry Esprit tote bags. In a different market segment, everyone had to have a Rolex watch and an expensive foreign car.

The Undistributed Middle

The fallacy of the undistributed middle is most easily seen when an argument is restated in the form of a syllogism with a major premise, a minor premise, and a conclusion. For example, consider the following:

> All members of the Tappa Kanna Bru fraternity are heavy drinkers. (major premise)
>
> "Gut" Malloy is a member of Tappa Kanna Bru. (minor premise)
>
> "Gut" Malloy must be a heavy drinker. (conclusion)

Obviously, there is something wrong here — we usually call it "guilt by association." Simply because "Gut" is a member of Tappa Kanna Bru doesn't *necessarily* mean that he is a heavy drinker.

Another kind of fallacy involving the undistributed middle is the following:

> Professors oppose class discussions. (major premise)
>
> Dr. Larson opposes class discussions. (minor premise)
>
> Dr. Larson must be a professor. (conclusion)

Just because Dr. Larson shares one characteristic of the group's thinking doesn't *necessarily* mean he is a group member.

As we will see later, no one actually runs around spouting syllogisms using the undistributed middle. But persuaders make claims that use the undistributed middle, and such claims are most easily recognized when put in the form of a syllogism.

The Straw Man Argument

In this fallacy, persuaders set up a weak, or "straw man," case that they know they can easily defeat. Then they represent this case as the position of the other side of the debate. Finally, they bring out their key evidence and reasoning and defeat the bogus case along with the opposition. The field of political persuasion is filled with this tactic. Candidate A says that candidate B's position on defense spending is thus and so, and then promptly shows how wrong the straw man position is by presenting impressive statistics, examples, and so on. Clearly, anyone holding to such a weak position shouldn't even be considered for public office. In the world of advertising, where it is usually considered bad strategy to mention your competition, we occasionally see, read, or hear a straw man case. A good example is a television ad in which the announcer says something like "Do you think this Chevy pickup truck can climb this tough mountain carrying a Dodge pickup on its back?" Then we see the Chevy climb the mountain with the Dodge on its back. Of course, if the Chevy couldn't do the job, they would never have aired the ad.

The straw man fallacy also is frequently used in ideological argument. Antiabortion advocates frequently argue that abortion is an inhuman way to practice birth control and should thus be outlawed. However, pro-choice advocates have never recommended abortion as a means of birth control; that claim is a straw man argument that will naturally be demolished by pro-life advocates. Or consider the controversial antiabortion films "The Silent Scream" or "Conceived in Liberty." The very titles seem to set up a straw man. In one scene, a fetus that is about to be aborted seems to be trying to desperately escape from a surgical instrument that has been inserted into the womb. The narrator, a medical doctor, uses powerful language to describe the struggle and the instrument. He relates what will happen when the fetus is removed, describing how its skull will be crushed by forceps. Naturally, the audience feels revulsion at the thought of the brutal crushing of the fetus. The natural response will be to reject abortion.

What the narrator does not tell the audience is that they are seeing a third-trimester abortion, which represents only about 10 percent of all abortions. Again, a straw man argument has been set up so that it can be easily defeated.

LOGICAL SYLLOGISMS

There are three major types of syllogisms that frequently form the foundations of content premise persuasion: conditional syllogisms, disjunctive syllogisms, and categorical syllogisms.

Conditional Syllogisms

Conditional syllogisms use "if A then B" reasoning. Like other syllogisms, they have a major premise, a minor premise, and a conclusion. The major premise states a condition or relationship that is presumed to exist in the world. Receivers are assumed to accept the existence of the condition or relationship in most cases. The following is a conditional syllogism in its classical form:

If you go to college, then you will succeed. (major premise)

You are going to college. (minor premise)

Therefore, you will succeed. (conclusion)

The first element in the major premise (If you go to college) is called the *antecedent*, and the second element (then you will succeed) is called the *consequent*. In affirming the antecedent, which is what we did in the minor premise by asserting that you are going to college, we can draw a *valid* conclusion that you will go to college.

I hope you are saying to yourself, "Hey! That's not necessarily the case." If so, you are making a distinction between **truth** and **validity**. The syllogism is not only invalid, it is also untrue. Validity depends on the general rules of reasoning and not on the truth of the premises. Advertisers know this and frequently make perfectly valid arguments using false premises. A good example is the statement on a package of Trilene fishing line: "If you

are seeking a world record, you should use one of the pound tests coded in the chart at the right." You can detect the *If . . . then . . .* format in the sentence. We all know that using the right line — Trilene — won't assure me of a world-record fish. In fact, I got the line as part of the prize for a record fish that I caught on generic line. But the advertiser uses the conditional form on the package, because receivers tend to accept it as logical and factual. In truth, no line can assure anyone of a world record.

Truth and validity are not the same in syllogistic persuasion. There are two valid forms of conclusion drawing with the conditional syllogism. First, you can affirm the *if* part of the major premise and conclude the *then* part of the major premise. A related but *invalid* procedure would be to deny the antecedent and conclude that the consequent has been denied. Note the following:

If we have a free market economy in Eastern Europe, *then* there won't be shortages or waiting lines.

The mechanisms for a free market economy have been introduced in Eastern Europe.

Therefore, there won't be shortages or waiting lines.

The reasoning here is invalid because there may be an *intervening cause*. In fact, there are several such intervening causes for the shortages and lines in Eastern Europe: poor distribution systems for getting the goods to market, hoarding, and a scarcity of hard currency. Some conditional syllogisms have the word "Only" in front of the antecedent, as shown below:

Only if we have a free market economy in Eastern Europe will the shortages or waiting lines disappear.

There is a free market economy in Eastern Europe.

Therefore, there are no shortages or waiting lines.

This makes the syllogism *valid* even if it is not necessarily true.

Another related but *invalid* procedure would be to deny the consequent and then deny the antecedent in the conclusion, as shown in the following:

If we have a free market economy in Eastern Europe, then there won't be shortages or waiting lines.

There hasn't been a decrease in shortages or lines.

Therefore, there is no free market economy in Eastern Europe.

Again, there could be intervening causes, such as those previously noted. Although invalid, this form of syllogism is frequently used in advertisements. A romance is "saved" by a certain mouthwash or shampoo, or a family feels more loving toward the mother because she decides to use a certain product in her cooking.

Thus, although a conditional syllogism may be perfectly valid in a logical sense, it may be untrue. Be alert to this trap. Persuaders may use a logically valid syllogism to camouflage untrue premises. Ask yourself whether the premises are true *and* whether the argument is valid.

As you have probably noticed, the conditional syllogism is similar to the cause-effect linkage described earlier.

Disjunctive Syllogisms

The disjunctive syllogism has as its basic form "either A is true or B is true." This is the major premise of a disjunctive syllogism and is usually accompanied by some set of proof or evidence that suggests the probable presence of A or B, or the probable absence of A or B. The conclusion is then drawn on the basis of these probabilities. In economically tight times, a school board might present voters with a disjunctive syllogism. They could threaten to do away with extracurricular activities unless the voters approve a certain referendum increasing property taxes, saying "Either you vote to increase property taxes or you lose the extracurricular activities." The voters then provide the minor premise of the syllogism through their vote. The strategy is often effective because the issue is so clear-cut. However, the strategy may backfire because it seems to be a threat. Refusing

to be bullied, the voters may reject the referendum, leaving the school board in trouble. The board can go ahead and cut the extras, thus angering the community and especially the students. Or they can seek other ways to lower costs, thus reducing their own credibility.

Most disjunctive syllogisms have another weakness. Few situations present a clear either–or, even in cases of life and death. A widely publicized case involved Karen Ann Quinlan, who was in a coma from which her doctors declared she would never recover. Her parents wanted to remove her life-support systems, or "pull the plug." After numerous court rulings on whether the young woman was legally alive or dead, a final ruling permitted the parents to disconnect the equipment. To everyone's astonishment, Karen continued breathing and lived without the machines for ten years. So even in such a concrete area as life or death there is no easy answer. Strict either–or logic cannot take into account other belief systems or more than two alternatives in a situation. Examine persuasion framed in the either–or mode to search for other alternatives or differing belief systems under which the disjunctive model would not work.

Categorical Syllogisms

Categorical syllogisms deal with parts and wholes. Those of you who have studied sets and set theory in mathematics are familiar with categorical reasoning. Both the major and the minor premises deal with membership or nonmembership in one of two categories or clusters. The conclusion relates the clusters of both premises into a new finding or result, as shown in the following:

All men are included in the class of mortal beings. (major premises)

Socrates is included in the class of men. (minor premise)

Therefore, Socrates is a mortal being. (conclusion)

Although this example is frequently used to demonstrate the categorical syllogism, it is not one that you will find many opportunities to use, and it is not likely to be brought up in any controversial arguments or debates. Its format, however, is frequently seen, read, or heard in various kinds of persuasion. Take, for example, the U.S. Marines' recruiting slogan: "We're looking for a few good men." The implied categorical syllogism is as follows:

All U.S. Marines are included in the class of good men. (major premise)

You are included in the class of good men. (minor premise)

Therefore, you are a U.S. Marine or should become one. (conclusion)

The categorical syllogism frequently is used as the underlying structure of persuasion that resembles "guilt (or sanctity) by association." Because you are a member of some category, it is assumed that you must be a member of another.

IBM recently used this technique when it ran a two-page public relations ad that featured two pairs of baby booties, one pink and one blue, and the question "Guess which one will grow up to be the engineer?" The ad went on to explain that boys are encouraged to excel in math and science, whereas girls are not, thus accounting for the discrepancy in the numbers of men and women engineers. IBM then pointed out that it has supported over ninety programs to strengthen women's skills in these areas and intended to continue such support. Two uses of the categorical syllogism can be seen here. First, there is one concerning engineers: "Persons encouraged to excel in math and science are likely to become engineers" (major premise); "Males are encouraged to excel in math and science" (minor premise); "Males are likely to become engineers" (conclusion). On another level, the ad says: "Good companies encourage women to excel" (major premise); "IBM encourages women to excel" (minor premise); "IBM is therefore a good company" (conclusion). If you are familiar with the use of Venn diagrams for testing validity, you might want to try testing these two intertwined categorical syllogisms. You will discover that although the first is valid (and probably true as well), the second is invalid. IBM uses the illusion of a logical syllogism to make its case. Be sure to check the validity of an argument couched in the categorical form.

THE TOULMIN FORMAT

Most of us do not encounter persuasion that is overtly syllogistic. Instead, the syllogism often is the underlying structure in persuasive arguments. British philosopher Stephen Toulmin developed a model that identifies the kind of logical persuasion we encounter in everyday events.[29] According to Toulmin, any argument aimed at our logical reasoning processes is divided into three basic parts: the claim, the data, and the warrant.

Basic Elements

First in Toulmin's model is the **claim**, the proposition that the persuader hopes will be believed, adopted, or followed. Claims usually need to be supported by evidence, or **data**, the second part of the model. Data give the receiver reasons for following the advice of the claim. However, sometimes the relationship between the claim and the data is not clear, so the persuader offers an explanation of the relationship; this Toulmin called the **warrant**. These three elements become clear as we examine persuasion at work.

Most colleges have a mechanism for students to appeal a grade if they believe it to be unfair. At NIU, the grade-appeals process describes three grounds on which a grade can be appealed and a set of steps that a student must follow when making an appeal. The grounds for the appeal are as follows:

1. The instructor radically departed from the course requisites as stated in class and in the class syllabus.
2. The instructor graded equivalent work from another student in a different way (that is, there was a double standard).
3. The instructor's grade was capriciously determined (that is, the grade was assigned on some basis other than actual course performance — age, race, sex, and so on).

Suppose a student is making an appeal on the first of the three grounds. The appeals committee will want to know to what degree the instructor departed from announced requisites of the class. The student making the appeal will have to show that the departure from announced requisites was unreasonable. The claim is, "Instructor X *radically* departed from the announced requisites of the class."

If you were sitting on the appeals board, how would you respond to this claim? It is clearly stated and the terms used fit with the requisites for an appeal. However, you do not know the details of the case. Perhaps you have taken a class from the instructor and know the teacher's habit of departing from announced requisites. If so, you might be inclined to accept the student's claim without further questioning. Although you realize that your own experience does not *prove* that the claim is true, it does increase the *probability* that it is. Or perhaps you have heard that this student tries every semester to boost his or her grades by appealing them. You might be inclined to reject the claim as just another of this student's attempts to beat the system. Although the claim may be true in this case, the student may have to suffer the penalty of "crying wolf." If, however, you have neither of these sets of information, you will probably ask for more data. In other words, you do not want to judge the case without knowing more. Thus, receivers have three options when responding to claims:

1. Accept the claim on its face. Usually this occurs when it is common knowledge that the claim is likely to be true ("The U.S. tax code has inequities").
2. Reject the claim outright. This occurs either when the claim is obviously false (as when the Flat Earth Society declares that "the Earth is a disk, not a globe"), or when the receiver is so biased against or distant from the message that he or she really doesn't process it ("The church is just a successful corporation," if said to a Catholic bishop).
3. Request data to demonstrate the claim.

In most cases, receivers choose the third option. In our example, you ask for evidence of "radical departure" from course requisites.

The student making the appeal might bring to the committee the course syllabus and show the required assignments. The student might also bring several statements by other students in the class, verifying that the instructor announced those requisites several times at the beginning of the class, only to add three more term papers. They might testify that the instructor altered grade weightings after the midterm exam because there was only a ten-point spread between an "A" and a "D." The student could bring his or her own papers and exams, and maybe those of other students in the class. As a member of the committee, what would you do now? Again, you have three options:

1. You can now accept the claim as supported by the data.
2. You can reject the claim as not being supported by the data.
3. You can request that the persuader explain why the data support the claim.

In many cases, one of the first two options is chosen. Receivers usually can tell when there are enough data to support the claim, or when there are clearly not enough. However, there are a substantial number of cases in which it is not clear whether the data support the claim. For example, in this case it seems reasonable to shift the weighting of grades on the midterm exam if the range was so narrow, which would leave the charge of "radical departure" from course requisites hanging on the evidence of the additional term-paper assignments. Let's suppose that you request an explanation of why the extra assignments and weighting shift add up to a "radical departure."

The student making the appeal must now demonstrate how the changes in course requisites are unreasonable. Suppose he or she comes up with the following argument:

There are four sections of this class, each taught by the same instructor. All took the same midterm, but only in our section was the range so narrow. All the sections should be curved together — otherwise the same work will be graded differently depending only on which section you are registered for. My section is also the only one that had the extra research papers, because of the midterm curve, so actually we were forced to do more work than other sections in order to get the same grade — again, simply because our section scored higher than the other three (we should have — we are the honors section).

By this time, you should be able to make a judgment; however, you still have the three options:

1. Accept the claim as supported by data, which are related through the warrant.
2. Reject the claim as unsupported by the data, given the warrant.
3. Request further clarification of the case.

Figure 7.4 shows the flow of the student's case. This case is typical of good, sound reasoning and in most cases would win the day. Only if there are minor points of interpretation (such as on the definition of "radical departure") or outside factors would the case need to be argued further. Chances are that any further argument would be on philosophical issues such as the degree to which an instructor has autonomy or the degree to which flexibility in course requisites is desirable. The discussion also might focus on the implications of the case; for example, would granting the claim mean that instructors can never discount an exam that doesn't have an acceptable curve?

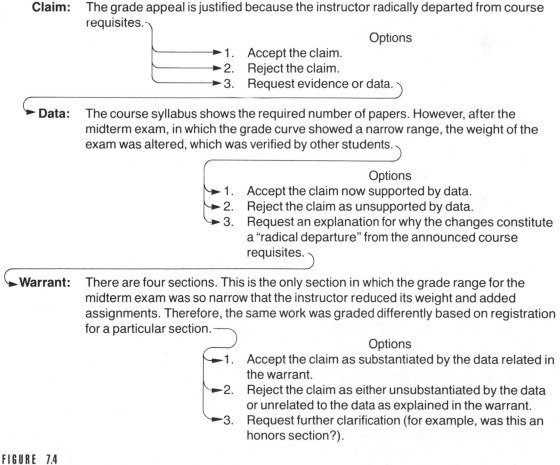

Claim: The grade appeal is justified because the instructor radically departed from course requisites.

Options
1. Accept the claim.
2. Reject the claim.
3. Request evidence or data.

Data: The course syllabus shows the required number of papers. However, after the midterm exam, in which the grade curve showed a narrow range, the weight of the exam was altered, which was verified by other students.

Options
1. Accept the claim now supported by data.
2. Reject the claim as unsupported by data.
3. Request an explanation for why the changes constitute a "radical departure" from the announced course requisites.

Warrant: There are four sections. This is the only section in which the grade range for the midterm exam was so narrow that the instructor reduced its weight and added assignments. Therefore, the same work was graded differently based on registration for a particular section.

Options
1. Accept the claim as substantiated by the data related in the warrant.
2. Reject the claim as either unsubstantiated by the data or unrelated to the data as explained in the warrant.
3. Request further clarification (for example, was this an honors section?).

FIGURE 7.4

An illustration of the Toulmin format.

Substantiating Elements

Toulmin's system has a number of secondary terms. For example, a claim may be modified by what is termed a **qualifier**. (Usually it is a simple qualifier—something like *"In most cases"* or *"Probably"* or *"It is likely that."*) The concession qualifies or limits the claim; it allows for the possibility that this is not an "Either A or B" argument. The claim is *probably* acceptable and true, but there is the *possibility* that another factor may enter in and affect the final outcome.

To continue our grade-appeals example, you might request the student to qualify the claim by adding "probably" or limiting the grounds of the appeal to this particular case by saying, "Given the *unique character* of this situation, Instructor X *may have* radically departed. . . ." Such qualifiers do not bind future grade-appeals committees to follow this precedent.

Another minor term in Toulmin's model is the **reservation**, a statement attached or related to the warrant that states the conditions under which the warrant is valid. It is stated in words like "unless" or "only if there is a reason to believe that." In our grade-appeals case, the committee may discover that when the honors program was established, more demanding course requisites were expected of students in honors classes. The reservation might evolve into something like "Therefore, it is unfair that the same work is graded differently based on registration for a particular section, *unless* a particular section is special in some way."

Notice that the reservation states the conditions under which the assumptions and philosophical bases of the argument operate. This aspect of the reservation is often overlooked by persuaders and persuadees alike; they assume that both parties begin from the same point, from the same frame of reference. Only when we begin at the same point or when we make allowances (such as reservations) for these differences can we really progress in any persuasive transaction. Coupled with the qualifier, the reservation allows for great flexibility in persuasion because both terms allow for dialogue; both provide the persuadee the opportunity to object or agree to part but not all of the per-

suasion. As persuaders, we need to include these elements of flexibility in our persuasion. As persuadees, we need to request them of the persuaders who are attempting to get us to take action.

Unfortunately, history is filled with examples in which legislation has been destructive because of the absence of qualifiers or reservations. The lack of a reservation in the 1964 Tonkin Gulf resolution gave the president unrestricted power to wage war, thereby eventually costing the United States thousands of lives in Vietnam. Much earlier, a gag rule in the U.S. Senate prevented discussion of the issue of slavery for nearly ten years while various territories were being added to the country, thereby necessitating continuous and informal negotiation and compromise. In the business world, the U.S. automobile industry must have had a long-standing premise about not building cars that got good gas mileage. There must have been a reservation missing from that premise, something like *"Unless* the public turns to foreign autos, we will make big autos as we always have done."

There is also another danger: having indefinite or vague qualifiers or reservations. For instance, the 1955 Supreme Court ruling on desegregation used the words "with all deliberate speed" to define the time frame for desegregation. As we all know, this problem is still with us in the form of conflict over busing, racial quotas, and so forth. Clearly, the phrase "all deliberate speed" has many possible meanings.

Advertisers are clever with the use of qualifiers (see Chapter 13). For example, the label on Cascade dishwasher detergent says that it will make your dishes "virtually spotless." Not spotless, but *virtually* spotless, and who can say whether one spot or three spots or twelve spots qualifies as being *"virtually* spotless"? So the persuadee needs to be aware of two problems connected with qualifiers or reservations. One is the absence of them, which can lock us in to one course of action or belief. The other is the too-vague qualifier, which may allow persuaders to wiggle out of any commitment to a product, action, person, or idea. It is far better to be specific about qualifiers, as in the energy-saving legislation of 1975 and 1976. This legislation allowed for something of a "fudge factor" on gasoline mileage but set specific mileage performance for specific dates. Persuaders may still try to interpret the qualifiers to their advantage, but it is much more difficult when specificity and details are given. Persuadees need to think twice when confronted with lack of details and lack of specificity in persuasive claims. If advertisers say that their tires will stop faster, we need to ask such questions as "Faster than what?" and "Under what conditions?" For all we know, they may be comparing the tires with wagon wheels or doughnuts.

The final element in Toulmin's system for showing the tactics of argument is called the **support**, or sometimes the *backing*, for the warrant. Toulmin observed that many issues hang on this element — that it justifies acceptance of a warrant. Suppose a persuadee does not consider a warrant to be true or doubts some part of it. The persuader must then provide proof that supports the reasoning expressed in the warrant. What we have then is a whole separate argument with a separate claim, data set, and warrant to support the original warrant. Essentially, persuaders claim that the warrant is acceptable because of the support. The backing is really data for this second claim. This same process of claim–data–warrant within claim–data–warrant can and often does go further — creating the complexity surrounding most controversial and philosophical issues.

We can now see that the tactics of persuasion are not usually parts of simple syllogisms. Instead of making statements such as "If A then B; A is true; therefore B is also true" or "Either A is true or B is true; B is false; therefore A must be true," most persuaders make claims that persuadees may respond to by (1) accepting them outright with no questions asked, (2) rejecting them outright, or (3) asking for proof. Persuaders then can provide data, which again can be accepted, rejected, or questioned. If the persuadee continues to request more, the persuader ultimately provides the warrant, or reason, for linking proof to request. Given enough time, three other elements may enter into the persuasive appeal: the qualifier, the reservation, and the backing.

Some of you might be wondering how persuadees ever get their input noticed and considered. After all, there are thirty or more people in most classes, and not everyone will get a chance to participate. And the problem is compounded as time goes on and as an audience gets larger, as in political campaigns. Although that is true, you must also remember that in another sense persuadees *always* provide input; they always are "heard" in some way. The persuader who knows anything about audiences must anticipate the kinds of questions persuadees *might* ask if they had the opportunity. Furthermore, if not satisfied with the completeness of the argument offered by the persuader, the persuadees may decide not to follow the suggested course of action, thus in essence asking for more proof, reasoning, qualification, backing, or reservation. Finally, the job of persuadees is to dissect persuasion, knowing *when* and *whether* to be persuaded. It doesn't matter whether persuaders are exposed to this analysis; they will eventually catch on if fewer and fewer persons buy or vote or give rewards. What *does* matter is that persuadees are aware, critical, and fairly sophisticated and systematic as they are exposed to persuasion. Toulmin's system for analyzing the tactics of persuasion provides us with a simple but discriminating tool that operates well with the kind of persuasion we are exposed to every day.

RESEARCH ON CONTENT PREMISES

Some researchers use the scientific method to determine the effects of evidence on receivers. In such studies, presumably typical persuadees (for example, several hundred college students) are given attitude tests. Then they are exposed to various degrees or types of persuasion and evidence (for example, emotional versus logical evidence, good delivery of evidence versus poor delivery of the same evidence). Following this, the subjects' attitudes are reevaluated. The results are compared, by statistical methods, with pretreatment scores to determine the effects of varying types or amounts of evidence. Early studies demonstrated that although the relationship between evidence and attitude change is elusive and sometimes even fickle, several patterns seem to be stable:

1. Evidence increases persuasive effects if the persuader is unknown or has low to moderate credibility.[30]
2. There seems to be little difference in the persuasive effects generated by emotional as opposed to logical evidence.[31]
3. Usually, some evidence is better than no evidence.[32]
4. "Reluctant" evidence (that given by people against themselves or their own interests) is no more effective than biased evidence or unbiased objective evidence.[33]
5. Good delivery can enhance the potency of evidence, but perhaps only when the sources are unknown or have low credibility, so that the delivery makes them and their evidence more believable and therefore more persuasive.[34]
6. Evidence can make persuasive changes more permanent.[35]
7. Evidence is most effective when the persuadee has not heard it before.[36]
8. The method of transmitting the evidence (live, on tape, and the like) seems to have no effect on evidence potency.[37]
9. People are likely to believe evidence that agrees with their own position more than evidence that does not.[38]
10. Highly dogmatic persons are more affected by evidence than are persons who are not so dogmatic.[39]

In 1983, communication scholars Rodney Reynolds and Michael Burgoon reviewed the relationships among belief processing, reasoning, and evidence. They determined that some of the previously fickle or negative findings could be interpreted from a different perspective, one that suggests that there is a positive relationship between datalike assertions and what appears to be attitude change. These patterns led them to make a series of propositions that support the evidence/persuasion relationship, especially in cases where other variables are present (for example, credibility of the speaker, the use of citations, mode of delivery, prior knowledge of evidence, and selection of the evidence). Reynolds and Burgoon made the following assertions:[40]

1. Using evidence produces more attitude change than not using evidence.
2. Using evidence produces more attitude change than using simple assertions.
3. Using irrelevant evidence from poorly qualified sources produces counter-to-advocated attitude change (in other words, produces the opposite effect) regardless of an advocate's credibility.
4. If advocates who have low to moderate credibility fail to use relevant evidence from qualified sources, the result may be counter-to-advocated attitude change.
5. If advocates fail to cite relevant evidence in a message that follows an opposing message that *does* cite evidence, their credibility will be lowered.
6. Citing evidence produces more attitude change when the evidence source and source qualifications are provided or when evidence is presented without a source citation than when evidence is presented with only a source identification.
7. If an advocate who has low to moderate credibility cites evidence clearly, the advocate's credibility and success in persuasion will increase.
8. Using evidence from highly credible sources will, over time, increase an advocate's credibility.
9. If an advocate cites evidence from less credible sources after, rather than before, other evidence, message acceptance will improve.
10. Poor delivery of evidence citations by advocates who have low to moderate credibility reduces persuasive effects.
11. Using evidence results in attitude change when receivers have no prior knowledge of the evidence.

12. Using evidence increases attitude change over time, regardless of the credibility of the advocate.

13. Using evidence results in attitude change over time only when receivers hold extreme attitudes on an issue.

14. The credibility of an advocate increases the evaluation of message attributes.

15. The clarity of evidence citations increases evaluations of the evidence and the advocate.

16. Highly dogmatic people select persuasive messages containing highly documented, rather than undocumented, evidence.

17. People tend to evaluate evidence from the perspective of their own attitudes, regardless of the quality of the evidence.

18. Evidence that is inconsistent with the major propositions being advanced is more difficult to detect than is irrelevant evidence or evidence from unqualified sources.

These propositions make sense, especially when applied to familiar persuasive events. For example, in the 1990 Iraqi invasion of Kuwait and the resulting economic sanctions and embargo, satellite photos served as *evidence* that the Iraqis were not withdrawing. This *evidence* increased public opinion in favor of the sanctions and embargo (proposition 1). Saddam Hussein's claim that historical evidence proved that Kuwait had always belonged to Iraq didn't convince anyone, and, in fact, may have reduced Hussein's credibility in the world community (proposition 3). U.S. evidence (satellite photos) showing that Hussein had moved rockets capable of carrying poison gas into Kuwait probably increased U.S. credibility and increased support for the sanctions (proposition 8). Each piece of new evidence cited by President Bush and showing Hussein's history of aggression seemed to increase public support of the President and his decision to send 40,000 troops in the first month of the crisis (proposition 11). Hussein claimed that

FIGURE 7.5

Saddam Hussein's credibility suffered during the 1990 Middle East crisis. Which of the principles or postulates concerning the use and effects of evidence might apply to this situation? (Reprinted by permission of UFS, Inc.)

the sanctions, troops, air power, and warships served only to prove what he had always thought: that the United States wanted to conquer the Arab world. This position, coupled with Hussein's earlier actions, was used as evidence that he had the potential to become another Hitler (both demonstrate proposition 17 at work).

In a review of the past fifty years of research on the effects of evidence on persuasion, communication scholar John C. Reinard identified, using Petty and Cacioppo's Elaboration Likelihood Model, a number of consistent trends.[41] If you recall, that model suggests that there are two information-processing modes in persuasion: the peripheral and the central processing paths. Persuasion in the peripheral path is typified by nonpersonally involving topics or issues. The audience is often swayed by variables other than the message or good evidence. For example, persuasion may be affected by variables such as the attractiveness of the source, how discrepant, or "far out," the message is from the audience's own position, and so on. In the central processing route, however, the persuadee is highly involved on a personal level with the issue or topic. You can persuade these persons only with compelling arguments that are well documented by evidence. Using the model, Reinard was able to identify the following trends:

1. Testimonials seem to be consistently persuasive as long as the source of the testimony is clearly documented.

2. Factual information such as reports of events or examples seem to be persuasive, but they can be affected by the mode of presentation. For example, on issues regarding policy ("The United States should stockpile petroleum for the next five years"), specific facts are more persuasive than general facts.

3. In spite of the almost reverent attitude that many people have toward statistical evidence, such evidence is not as persuasive as other factual evidence. Reinard speculates that this may be because statistics are not vivid or dramatic. However, when powerful, involving, and vivid examples are backed

up by statistics that show the examples to be typical, the examples become more powerful.

4. Consistent with McCroskey's findings, presenting audiences with evidence seems to "inoculate" or protect them against subsequent conterpersuasion.

5. Evidence seems to have long-term effectiveness when an issue is processed in the central path, but there is little long-term effectiveness when the issue is processed in the peripheral path.

6. A source's credibility has persuasive effects—that is, credible sources are more persuasive than less credible ones. This is one of the most consistent patterns identified by Reinard.

7. Evidence that reinforces the receiver's beliefs is more persuasive than evidence that does not reinforce the receiver's position.

8. Strong evidence is more persuasive than weak evidence, especially when an issue is personally involving to the receiver, who then uses the central processing path.

9. Novel evidence is more persuasive than evidence the audience already knows.

10. Unless a topic is personally involving, credibility seems to be more persuasive than evidence, but even credible sources can enhance their persuasiveness by using evidence.

11. Evidence consistently increases speaker credibility

12. Good delivery enhances the effectiveness of evidence unless the audience is distracted.

13. Evidence is most effective with highly intelligent receivers, those who are "hard-nosed about getting the facts."

14. People who are highly analytical are more likely to be persuaded by evidence, and intellectually sophisticated receivers prefer technically oriented evidence.

Reinard's overall conclusion is that evidence is persuasive, especially if we look at the past fifty years of research from the perspective of the Elaboration Likelihood Model. As with the Reynolds and Burgoon conclusions, the patterns Reinard identified (especially those related to the model), make real sense when we use them to analyze some "real world" persuasive examples, such as the Middle East crisis of 1990. General statistics regarding what percent of the world's oil supply comes from Iraq and Kuwait probably had less effect on public opinion than the vivid and dramatic examples of hostages being taken. The hostage examples probably were strengthened when statistics about the number of foreign nationals being detained in Iraq were used during news reports about the hostages. This is precisely what Reinard's trend 3 is all about. To Western eyes, Hussein lacked credibility at the outset of the crisis, and his credibility steadily deteriorated as time went on (a situation similar to the one described in trend 6). Satellite evidence of Iraqi troop movements probably had a strong effect, especially for persons who were personally involved in the crisis. Hussein's dramatic visits to some of the hostages and his "fatherly" petting of some of the children did not enhance his credibility in Western eyes. It probably did enhance his credibility in the Arab world, however, which fits with trends 10, 11, and 12. One could find many other real-world examples to demonstrate the validity of the Reinard findings.

In conclusion, several characteristics of the use of evidence in content premises in persuasion can be noted. First, evidence is probably most effective when it encourages audience participation. Earlier we noted that, in using emotionally oriented evidence, persuaders are most effective when they present audiences with a dramatic scene or setting and then ask the audience to empathize with the character acting within that setting. By participating with their imaginations, members of the audience co-create the proof. They incorporate the proof into their own frames of reference — the persuasion thus achieved is more permanent and potent. In using intellectually oriented evidence, effective persuaders present claims and perhaps data to support them. They hope that warrants will be provided by the audience, but even if listeners do not supply the necessary linkage and instead question the persuaders' conclusions, they are still

participating in their own persuasion when they begin to play the game (that is, co-create a proof with the persuaders).

A second characteristic that seems to help in using evidence for "logical" or content-oriented persuasion is to highlight the evidence — either as part of a narrative or in some form of analogy. The earliest form of human ritual and entertainment was the narrative as it was used in dances, tales, and myths. As noted earlier, the narrative is an extremely powerful form of evidence.

REVIEW AND CONCLUSION

Content premises do not necessarily rely as much on the internal states of persuaders as do process premises. Instead, they rely more on universally agreed on norms or rules.

Evidence tends to be either dramatically oriented or intellectually oriented. Users of dramatically oriented evidence may lead persuadees to a "logical" conclusion, drawn from a content premise, by creating a dramatic scene and then inviting the audience to join in the drama. Persuadees thus "prove" the validity of the premise to themselves. Users of intellectually oriented evidence, on the other hand, may lead their persuadees to "logical" conclusions by presenting them with a set of data in support of a certain claim or content premise. The persuadees provide the connection between these data and the claim in the form of a warrant.

Both types of evidence rely on a kind of self-persuasion on the part of the persuadee. Persuadees ought to participate in some way in their own persuasion, whether the evidence is intellectual or dramatic. Some of the most fascinating research done in persuasion has focused on self-persuasion. Much of this research is based on Leon Festinger's theory of dissonance, and studies usually ask persuadees to state arguments that are contrary to their own beliefs or attitudes (for example, why a dull experiment is interesting, why strange foods taste good, or why they might accept some group or idea that is counter to their beliefs). Having engaged in this kind of participation, the responders tend to change their beliefs in accord with the false or counterattitudinal message they advocated. Although this issue has been plagued with problems in research measurement and design, the findings have been fairly consistent: When we engage in self-persuasion, even if it runs counter to our own beliefs, the effect of the participation is powerful.

From a strategic point of view, the traditional syllogism usually forms the skeletal structure of an overall argument or content premise. Within this structure, the tactics or particular arguments or premises are represented by claims supported by data. Claims and data are linked by audiences through warrants.

Finally, of the types of evidence available to the persuader, several seem more important than others. First, probably, are those that support the three major linkages: cause-effect, symptoms, and congruency. Also, evidence that provides perspective for the audience is probably more effective than evidence that does not. We have focused on two particularly effective methods of providing this perspective: the use of analogy, which provides a comparative perspective, and the use of narrative, which has the same ability to provide a perspective within a dramatic frame of reference. Both are also "artistic" in the sense that neither merely presents information: Both depict evidence in dramatic or visual formats.

In sum, we are most effectively persuaded by our own experiences — real or imaginary. Successful persuaders try to shape content premises, their linkages, claims, data, and warrants in terms of the audience's experience. If they can invite audiences to participate in drawing conclusions or in the drama of the proof, audiences will share in their own persuasion, thus being affected by it.

QUESTIONS FOR FURTHER THOUGHT

1. What are the three types of syllogisms discussed in this chapter? Give examples of each from advertisements, political speeches, or some other source of persuasion.

2. Define *proof*. What constitutes adequate proof for you? Does it change from issue to issue? If so, in what ways?

3. Review some of the magazine commentary concerning a particular issue and attempt to identify the data that are offered. What kinds of evidence are they? Are they dramatic? If so, in what ways? If not, are they persuasive? Why or why not? What is the underlying syllogistic structure inherent in the discussions of the issue?

4. What is the difference between intellectually oriented evidence and emotionally oriented evidence? Give examples and explain how they differ.

5. Give examples from your own experience of (a) opinion, (b) attitudes, (c) beliefs, and (d) values that affect *behavior*. Give examples that do not affect behavior. Why is there a difference?

6. Why was "The Case of Bobby and His Parents" so persuasive? Was logic involved? Was the example an illogical one to prove the point Peck wanted to make?

7. What is the difference between a figurative and a literal analogy? Which is being used when a political campaign is compared to a horse race?

8. What are some of the ways in which statistics can be misused? Give examples.

9. What are some of the ways in which testimony can be misused? Give examples.

10. What is a *post hoc* fallacy? Give an example.

11. What is an *ad hominem* fallacy? Give an example.

NOTES

1. A good discussion of this premise (that we learn much of our knowledge vicariously) is presented in Mark Abrahamson, *Interpersonal Accommodation* (New York: Van Nostrand-Reinhold, 1966).

2. Several good discussions of the importance of the dramatic structure can be found in literature from various fields. For example, from the perspective

of literary criticism on the power of the dramatic to cause persuasive motivation, see Kenneth Burke, *A Grammar of Motives* (Berkeley: University of California Press, 1970); Robert F. Bales, *Personality and Interpersonal Behavior* (New York: Holt, Rinehart & Winston, 1970), especially Chapter 7, "Describing Fantasy Themes," pp. 136–155; Ernest G. Bormann, "Fantasy and Rhetorical Vision: The Rhetorical Criticism of Social Reality," *Quarterly Journal of Speech* 58:396–407, 1972.

3. Good examples of the use of dramatic invitations can be found in a number of recent speeches as well as in the history of public speaking. Some examples are Clarence Darrow's defense of joy killers Richard Loeb and Nathan Leopold, which "invites" the judge to join in the high drama of humanitarian change; and John F. Kennedy's Inaugural Address, which invites the listeners to do something for their country. Both speeches are often anthologized in histories of American Public Address.

4. M. Scott Peck, "The Case of Bobby and His Parents," in *People of the Lie: The Hope for Healing Human Evil* (New York: Simon and Schuster, 1983), pp. 47–59.

5. *Ibid.*, p. 48.

6. *Ibid.*

7. *Ibid.*, p. 50.

8. *Ibid.*, p. 52.

9. *Ibid.*, pp. 52–59.

10. Charles Moore, *A Short Life of Abraham Lincoln* (Chicago: Houghton Mifflin, 1909), p. 49.

11. Elizabeth F. Loftus, *Eyewitness Testimony* (Cambridge, MA: Harvard University Press, 1980).

12. Quoted in Elizabeth F. Loftus, "Eyewitnesses: Essential but Unreliable," *Psychology Today*, February 1984, p. 25.

13. Moore, *op. cit.*, p. 49.

14. "The Payoffs for Preschooling," *Chicago Tribune*, December 25, 1984, p. 10.

15. H. H. Clark, "Linguistic Processes in Deductive Reasoning," *Psychosocial Review* 76, 1969, pp. 387–404. See also Rodney Reynolds and Michael Burgoon, "Belief Processing, Reasoning and Evidence," *Communication Reviews and Communication*, 1983, pp. 83–104.

16. Barry Scott, "It's God's Way," *The Rockford Register Star*, November 8, 1989, editorial page.

17. Bob Garfield, "Ad Review: Good Commercials Finally Outnumber the Bad Ones on TV," *Advertising Age*, March 14, 1988, p. 86.

18. *Ibid.*

19. *Ibid.*

20. *Ibid.*

21. *Ibid.*

22. *Ibid.*

23. See, for example, Nicholas Capaldi, *The Art of Deception* (Buffalo, NY: Prometheus Books, 1975); Anthony Flew, *Thinking Straight* (Buffalo, NY: Prometheus Books, 1977); Howard Kahane, *Logic and Contemporary Rhetoric: The Use of Reason in Everyday Life*, 3rd ed. (Belmont, CA: Wadsworth, 1980); J. Vernon Jensen, *Argumentation: Reasoning in Communication* (New York: D. Van Nostrand, 1981); and Stephen W. Littlejohn and David M. Jabusch, *Persuasive Transactions* (Glenview, IL: Scott Foresman, 1987).

24. Kahane, *op. cit.*, p. 65.

25. *Webster's Ninth New Collegiate Dictionary* (Springfield, MA: Merriam Webster, 1987), p. 447.

26. Maureen Dowd, "Bush-speak," *The Chicago Tribune*, April 1, 1990, sec. 5, p. 3.

27. "The Mail," *Newsweek*, March 21, 1988, p. 4.

28. Jonathan Alter, Howard Fineman, and Sylvester Monroe, "Jackson's Message," *Newsweek*, March 21, 1988, p. 23.

29. Stephen Toulmin, *The Uses of Argument* (Cambridge, England: Cambridge University Press, 1969). See Chapter 3, "The Layout of Arguments," pp. 94–145.

30. See the discussion on evidence by James C. McCroskey, *Studies of the Effects of Evidence in Persuasive Communication*, Report SCRL, 4–67. (Speech Communication Research Laboratory, Michigan State University, 1967); Gerald R. Miller and John Baseheart, "Source Trustworthiness: Opinionated Statements, and Response to Persuasive Communication," *Speech Monographs* 36:1–7, 1969.

31. McCroskey, *op. cit.*

32. *Ibid.*; Robert S. Cathcart, "An Experimental Study of the Relative Effectiveness of Selected Means of Handling Evidence in Speeches of Advocacy," doctoral dissertation, Northwestern University, 1953.

33. William E. Arnold and James C. McCroskey, "The Credibility of Reluctant Testimony," *Central States Speech Journal* 18:97–103, 1967.

34. James C. McCroskey and R. Samuel Mehrley, "The Effects of Disorganization and Nonfluency on Attitude Change and Source Credibility," *Speech Monographs* 36:13–21, 1969.

35. McCroskey, *op. cit.*

36. *Ibid.*; Karl W. E. Anatol and Jerry E. Mandel, "Strategies of Resistance to Persuasion: New Subject Matter for the Teacher of Speech Communication," *Central States Speech Journal* 23:11–17, 1972.

37. McCroskey, *op. cit.*

38. Victor D. Wall, Jr., "Evidential Attitudes and Attitude Change," *Western Speech* 36: 115–123, 1972.

39. Gary Cronkhite and Emily Goetz, "Dogmatism, Persuasibility, and Attitude," *Journal of Communication* 21:342–352, 1971.

40. Rodney A. Reynolds and Michael Burgoon, "Belief Processing, Reasoning and Evidence," *Communication Yearbook*, vol. 7, 1983.

41. John C. Reinard, "The Empirical Study of the Persuasive Effects of Evidence: The Status After Fifty Years of Research," *Human Communication Research*, vol. 15, No. 1, Fall 1988, pp. 3–59.

CHAPTER 8

Cultural Premises in Persuasion

All of us are, in a sense, prisoners of our own culture, and as a result we often overlook patterns of behavior that influence how and by what means we are persuaded. Anyone who has visited another culture (even another Western culture) immediately becomes aware of significant cultural differences between his or her patterns of behavior and those of the foreign culture. Not only are values, languages, and customs different, but hundreds, even thousands, of little things differ from our familiar American ways. For example, only one-third of the world's people use our kind of flatware to eat. Another third eat with chopsticks, and the rest eat with their fingers. Even in England, differences are apparent. People wait at bus stops in neat, orderly lines, or queues. We Americans usually crowd around the bus door or the sale table at the department store.

If you happen to visit a formerly communist country in Eastern Europe, you will quickly understand the immense difference between "hard currency" and "soft currency"—even the hotel I stayed at in Prague refused to accept Czech currency. A thriving black market in currency is commonplace in the cities of Eastern Europe. A friend recently told me that taxis in Moscow will stop only if you hold up a pack of cigarettes; they don't want rubles. In Eastern European countries one always carries a shopping bag just in case one finds something available. In fact, the slang term for a shopping bag is a "perhaps." Such conditions make an incredible difference in a country's purchase patterns. You don't buy something there because you need it; you buy it because it happens to be available. This idea would never cross our minds back here in the United States, because we know full well that most items are in good supply.

Although many aspects of any given culture are permanent, cultures are also subject to constant change. In the United States, for example, the constant influx of different ethnic groups is reflected in a variety of ways. Evidence of new cultures begins to appear in supermarkets, for example. You will find soybean curd, bean sprouts, and wonton—products one had to go to Chinatown to get only a decade ago. You will find corn and flour tortillas in the freezer case and pita bread at the deli. You can buy a wok or futon at your department store. These minor cultural differences are, of course, only the tip of the iceberg. The important differences among cultures are values, beliefs, and patterns of behavior that are trained into us from early childhood through our language, the myths and tales we hear, and our observations of how those around us behave. Many of these values and beliefs are relatively permanent aspects of a culture, although over time they change in response to societal shifts.

This training, which we absorb from our culture and language, forms some of the premises we have been discussing. The cultural preferences we have, the cultural myths we believe in, and the cultural values we embrace are all missing premises in enthymemes that persuaders can construct. This kind of persuasion occurs at a low level of awareness; we often react subconsciously to various stimuli based on our cultural training. Consider the following instance of cultural patterning.

Suppose that you are a member of an Eskimo tribe called "People of the Deer," whose sole food supply is caribou. You kill enough animals in the spring to last the tribe until the fall, when again the animals migrate south following the food supply. The tribal custom is to kill and preserve these deer in a period of a week or two. The tribes are perhaps one hundred persons strong. Suppose that you have just finished your fall hunt and discover that you face a severe winter without having killed enough caribou to feed the tribe until the spring migration. Death is certain without sufficient supplies of meat and fat. You attend a tribal meeting called to consider the matter. What would you do?

In several persuasion classes, students brainstormed solutions to this problem and came up with the following suggestions in this approximate order:

1. Let's follow the deer and kill enough of them, and thus increase the supply.
2. Let's seek an alternative food supply—we can eat berries or fish or birds.
3. Let's send a band of the tribe to get help.
4. Let's ration food to make it last longer.
5. Let's eat all the parts of the caribou—skin, horns, everything—to increase the supply.

6. Let's send some of the people away to another place where food is more plentiful and thus decrease demand.

7. Let's kill some of our tribe to decrease demand.

8. Let's kill the most useless tribe members — the old first, and the very young next.

9. Let's resort to cannibalism; let's eat those we kill.

The most practical solutions emerged first, and then the ideas became increasingly desperate until someone suggested cannibalism. The actual People of the Deer *do nothing* — they eat the food at their regular rates, knowing full well that they will not live through the winter. Then they sit and wait for death. In fact, they even refuse the help of the Canadian government! The tribe simply does not enter into the problem-solving frame of mind typical of Western culture. They accept a situation and do nothing, whereas we try to find solutions for any problem, even though it may be insoluble. We are trained to *do something*. In our culture, persuaders succeed if they outline a problem and suggest solutions.

One of the problems of the Middle East crisis of 1990 was that there seemed to be no solutions available, yet diplomats and others scurried around dreaming up far-fetched compromises, offers, and counteroffers. Egypt's President Mubarak probably suggested the most realistic solution when he offered Iraq a bribe: some of Kuwait's oil and a cash settlement. Bribes are commonplace in the Arab world where *Baksheesh*, as it is called, is part and parcel of everyday life.

You can probably observe yourself and others, when faced with a problem, responding to this cultural pattern with an almost compulsive seeking for solutions of any kind. Unfortunately, this pattern can sometimes make us easy prey for unethical persuaders, or may shunt our efforts away from certain problems. People spent thousands of dollars on laetrile in the hope that it would cure cancer. Americans purchase vitamins, laxatives, analgesics, and sleeping pills in astonishing amounts.

The case of the People of the Deer reveals other cultural attributes that we have and that can be targeted by persuaders. Notice, for instance, that the early solutions emphasized positive and assertive steps. These always are suggested first, indicating an American cultural bias in favor of the pull-yourself-up-by-your-bootstraps approach.

Americans have always valued individualism and individual achievements. This country has always been a place where immigrants could come to make a new life *for and by themselves*. Persuaders market a whole host of products and services based on this "bootstraps" belief. And some political candidates promise a "New Day" for America, when each individual will have the opportunity to reach his or her full potential.

Another appeal to the value or potential of the individual and his or her ability to succeed is the many pyramid schemes for selling products. One example is AMWAY, which stands for "The American Way." Such schemes persuade individuals that they can go into business for themselves, not only by selling products to their friends and neighbors but by recruiting others to do the same and getting a percentage of the recruit's sales as well. The recruit presumably will recruit others, and you will get a percentage of what they sell, and so on down the line, until you have developed a wide and complex "network." Your success will be measured by your wealth and by the various symbols — awards, pins, jewelry, or whatever — that the company awards to show others in your network what you have achieved. At Mary Kay Cosmetics, for example, persons in the top levels in the pyramid get a pink Cadillac. Most recently, with the increasing number of television channels available via cable and/or satellite, there is even a self-help network that markets real-estate development tapes, books, and other materials that sell via direct-response television/telephone for several hundred dollars.

But there is a flip side to the determined individual, as Robert Bellah and his associates point out in *Habits of the Heart: Individualism and Commitment in American Life*. As you will recall from an earlier discussion of this book, Bellah and his colleagues did in-depth interviews with over 200 Americans from various walks of life, attempting to duplicate what Alexis de Tocqueville did in his book *Democracy in America*, written in the 1830s, in which he described central American values and mores as "habits of the heart." Key among them was the value of the individual. Bellah and his coauthors point out:

> The central problem of our book concerned the American individualism that Tocqueville described with a mixture of admiration and anxiety. It seems to us it is individualism and not equality, as Tocqueville thought, that has marched inexorably throughout our history. We are concerned that this individualism may have grown cancerous.[1]

What they mean by "cancerous" is that individualism has become "me-ism": emphasizing the individual at the cost of the community, thus drawing individuals inside themselves with little concern for others. As they note:

> American cultural traditions define personality, achievement and the purpose of human life in ways that leave the individual suspended in glorious but terrifying isolation.[2]

And others have echoed their theme. What we describe as yuppie values are those that Bellah and his associates see as the early signs of a cancerous individualism and that are closely tied to the early assertive and positive responses in the People of the Deer simulation.

The second pattern of responses in the People of the Deer example is much more community oriented. I call them the "Let's-make-the-best-of-what-we-have" solutions. These include suggesting that the tribe send for help, ration its food, and utilize all parts of the food supply. These solutions are not only problem-solving in approach, but they demonstrate a need for cooperation. Perhaps this need is more simply put in the collect for Labor Day in *The Episcopal Book of Common Prayer:* "So guide us in the work we do that we may do it not for the self alone, but for the common good."[3]

"Damn it, the eighties are over!"

FIGURE 8.1

During the eighties — the "me" decade — high value was placed on the individual through the individual's symbols of success or conspicuous consumption. Competition was fierce, and mammoth mergers put many persons out of work for the sake of an individual's success. Apparently these expressions of the value of the individual and the value of success are persistent American cultural values, but like other cultural values, they ebb and flow with the times. What has replaced the means for expressing these values in the 1990s? (Drawing by C. Barsotti; © 1988 The New Yorker Magazine, Inc. Reprinted by permission.)

It is this sense of community that seems missing in the late eighties and early nineties and that Bellah and his associates interpret as a potential symptom of a cancerous individualism. Although "networking" may make the individual successful, there isn't any sense of community in the networks we hear so much of recently.

I wonder what Bellah and his colleagues would think of the third and final cluster of solutions that emerged in the People of the Deer simulation. These include reducing demand by banishing some members of the tribe to another place, killing the old and the young to reduce demand, and finally cannibalism itself. I suspect they would infer that these were not just symptoms of a possible cancerous individualism but conclusive evidence of a deadly cultural malignancy.

How do we identify these patterns of cultural values? Where do they come from? How do persuaders appeal to them? Questions such as these are the focus of our search for cultural premises.

In order to see how these premises relate to persuasion in general, we look first at how we get them (cultural training and pressure). Then we look at kinds of cultural premises: (1) cultural images or myths and (2) the American value system. Bear in mind that a *value* is an idea of the good or the desirable that people use as a standard for judging means or to motivate others. Examples of values are honesty, justice, beauty, efficiency, safety, and progress. Because our value system is a major source of persuasive leverage, you may be interested in discovering how persuaders link proposals and arguments to our values.

CULTURAL AND SOCIETAL PRESSURE

Everyone has heard stories about the children of various Indian tribes who never cried because it was essential not to frighten off game. Anyone who has been around a newborn infant must doubt these stories. Children cry when they are lonely, hungry, or want exercise. How, then, did Indians train their children not to cry out?

During the first hour of life, whenever a Sioux baby cried, its mother clapped her hands over the child's mouth and nose. The hand was removed only if the child stopped crying or began to smother. If this was done within the first hour of life, the infant never again cried out loud. Of course, as the child grew, it saw a pattern repeated over and over again. Parents and the elders spoke of the power of silence. They valued quiet and stealth in stalking game. The Indian brave was tested and proved his courage by experiencing pain and not crying out. The most significant test was the Sun Dance, which has been outlawed for more than fifty years. A leather thong was sewn into the shoulder flesh of a brave. The brave would be tied to a totem pole at the center of a tribal circle. The test was to dance away from the pole until the pain of the thong forced him to fall (usually after several days of dancing). The fall usually tore out the thong from the shoulder. The brave was then a full-fledged warrior. Later he could do the Sun-Gazer's Dance. This involved dancing while staring directly into the sun. Sitting Bull is supposed to have done this for three days, after which he had a vision of the future massacre of Custer and his soldiers at the Little Big Horn.[4] Thus the pattern introduced at birth was seen at work throughout life.

In less dramatic terms, perhaps, each of us is trained in the ways of our culture. This training forms the core of our values, which then become rules for governing ourselves as we interact. We do not even notice that they are there. We respond instinctively to them. This training underlies each of the cultural premises we are going to study. It lurks beneath our surface thoughts and acts. Sophisticated persuaders appeal to these premises directly and cleverly. They can appeal to cultural and societal premises because they believe in them and expect that their audiences do also.

CULTURAL IMAGES AND MYTHS

Every culture has its own myths, and heroes who do things valued by the culture. For example, early Greek society developed a series of myths surrounding the sin of pride. Eventually, the myths became institutionalized in such Greek dramas as *Oedipus Rex*.

Parts of the myths related to physical acts, such as trying to control one's own destiny, that were discouraged. Greeks placed a high value on avoiding prideful action. They valued modesty. They elected leaders who were modest. We have similar beliefs. You probably know that the overly proud student is less likely to be elected to office or chosen as team captain than the more humble person. We view the antics of a pompous person with disfavor. We ridicule needless pride.

What are some of the cultural myths or legends or images underlying American culture and society, and how do persuaders use them? Can these images be changed? If so, how? Are they being changed at present, and if so, how? Stereotypes and proverbs are good indicators of cultural myths. Let us consider a few of these cultural myths.

Wisdom of the Rustic

One of the legends in American literature that has great persuasive appeal is that of the clever rustic. No matter how devious the opposition, the simple wisdom of the backwoods wins out. Numerous folk tales rely on this image. The Daniel Boone tales, the stories about the inventiveness of Paul Bunyan, and many Lincoln stories rely on the rustic image. We have faith in humble persons when we look for leaders. The small-town boy is chosen team captain. We believe in humble beginnings, and we believe that difficulty teaches even the most uneducated of us to be wise in a worldly way.

Politicians across American history have tried to emphasize their humble origins. In fact, many have manufactured myths about their rustic origins even to the point of constructing log cabins that they claimed as their birthplace, as did Benjamin Harrison, or "Tippecanoe." President Reagan emphasized his humble origin in Dixon, Illinois, and Jesse Jackson lets it be known that he was born in a three-room house without indoor plumbing.

If the politician cannot claim humble beginnings, then he or she must find some substitute for them—usually hardship or suffering. Thus we find patricians such as Franklin D. Roosevelt and John F. Kennedy using their physical handicaps or emotional suffering as symbolic substitutes for the hardship of the rustic beginning.

Products are frequently marketed using a rustic as the spokesperson—Will Helmsley of *Our House*, for instance, serves as a rustic endorsing the value of good old-fashioned Quaker Oats.

At the same time that we seem to value the simple, common-sense rustic, American culture tends to devalue the intellectual or the educated. Eighteenth-century French social observer Alexis de Tocqueville, in *Democracy in America*, described this distrust:

> The nearer the people are drawn to the common level of an equal and similar condition, the less prone does each man become to place implicit faith in a certain man or a certain class of men [intellectuals]. But his readiness to believe the multitude increases, and opinion is more than ever mistress of the world. Not only is common opinion the only guide which private judgment retains . . . it possesses a power infinitely beyond what it has elsewhere.[5]

Richard Hofstadter also wrote about this anti-intellectualism.[6] Persuaders often use this reverse side of our value in the wisdom of the rustic. The intellectual is often the brunt of jokes. Advertisers often have the rustic win out over the smart guy.

Possibility of Success

The Horatio Alger myth is based on several novels written by Alger in the nineteenth century. The protagonist of these novels was invariably a young man who, through hard work, sincerity, honesty, and a faith in the future, was able to make good. He might even rise to the top and own his own company, have a beautiful wife, live a fine life, and be able to do good for others. The myth has appeal and was particularly appealing to immigrants, the poor, and the downtrodden. They passed it on to their children, admonishing them to work hard and achieve success. In more recent times, the myth has been generalized to include women. One of the slogans on college campuses today is "Get a degree, get a job, and get ahead." That slogan is part of the Alger myth, which parents reinforce over and over, as the Sioux tribal elders reinforced the value of silence.

In a sense, this myth — that success will come to those who are honest and work hard — links up with the wisdom of the rustic myth. If you follow the advice of the common people and use common sense, with sincerity and hard work, you will be a success. It incorporates the values of hard work, sincerity, honesty, and law and order. Some persons claim that the myth was established to enslave the common people and to keep them on a treadmill. If you think that you have a chance to achieve success, you will not risk questioning authority figures. Instead, you will submit to them and try to gain power for yourself. Again, this myth was observed by Alexis de Tocqueville:

> No Americans are devoid of a yearning desire to rise; . . . All are constantly seeking to acquire property, power, and reputation. . . . What chiefly diverts the men of democracies from lofty ambition is not the scantiness of their fortunes, but the vehemence of the exertions they daily make to improve them. . . . The same observation is applicable to the sons of such men; they are born . . . their parents were humble; they have grown up amidst feelings and notions which they cannot afterwards easily get rid of; and it may be presumed that they will inherit the propensities of their father, as well as his wealth.[7]

You probably can see your parents and your relatives in this description. If Tocqueville was right, you may see yourself also. You are thus ready for persuasion that promises the possibility of success. Products (for example, computers) are marketed with the claim that they will result in success for the entire family, from Mom and Dad on down to the toddlers. Politicians promise a successful future to the voter who supports a common-sense approach to problems. This promise probably will continue to be a part of our political vision. After all, who would vote for a politician whose campaign promises don't offer a chance to improve ourselves? Only if the country is heading for some disaster will we listen to another pitch, and even then the cure had better be tied to a promise of better things to come. Expect to hear appeals made for the myth. Persuaders will offer success "just around the corner," if only you will follow them and not the false prophets. They will offer the "big break" and the chance to have a better life for you and your children. Whether it is a speed-reading course, a body-building machine, or a weight-loss club, the carrot is always the same — try and you will succeed.

Coming of a Messiah

A cultural myth that is related to the possibility of success is that of the coming of a messiah. Here the situational assumption is slightly different — the culture is near disaster or perhaps even already in the midst of an almost impossible mess, be it economic, religious, or political. It is a period of great uncertainty and pessimism; it is chaotic, confusing, and frightening. At such times, we expect to be rescued from the chaos and danger by some single great leader who projects a sense of confidence and who we believe can turn things around. Many leaders have served to fulfill this role. Lincoln emerges from obscurity to save the Union; despite his handicap, Franklin Delano Roosevelt saves the country from economic collapse; John F. Kennedy "rescues" the entire world for Democracy; and Ronald Reagan delivers the country from double-digit inflation and worldwide scorn. Similar figures in industry have also fulfilled the role. For instance, Lee Iacocca of Chrysler took over at the helm when the company was in trouble and promised and delivered relief. Although circumstances may change, Americans seem to be always waiting for another messiah to come down the road and save them from one big bad wolf or another.

What makes us receptive to the messianic? First, we are action oriented. As shown by the values expressed in the People of the Deer solutions, we seem to want our saviors to be doers, not thinkers. Second, our solutions had better not be too theoretical or intellectual — we prefer simple answers to the most complex problems. The messiah should also be vigorous, witty and charming, and not afraid to try the unknown or unproven.

Presence of Conspiracy

Another cultural premise operant in our culture is the belief that big problems don't have simple causes. Richard Hofstadter calls this belief the *paranoid style*.[8] This is the belief that when problems appear great, the only reasonable explanation is that a powerful group has conspired to cause them. This conspiracy argument has recurred throughout our history in the form of alleged Papist conspiracies, Masonic conspiracies, and populist conspiracies, among many others. President Roosevelt used the argument in connection with the Great Depression: Money interests and the great banking houses had caused the depression and should be "thrown out of the temple." The Cold War of the 1950s and 1960s sometimes was blamed on a conspiracy of Communist agents who had infiltrated various levels of government. In the 1980s, there was a recurring charge that "liberals" had conspired to ruin our economy and spoil our morals. If Hofstadter is right, we can expect to hear the conspiracy offered as an explanation for problems any time three factors are operating for the audience:

1. They have something of value to lose — they are in possession of some kind of power or property.
2. They see themselves in danger of losing some or all of this power or property or as already having lost some of it.
3. They see themselves as helpless to prevent the loss.

It is easy to see how these beliefs in a conspiracy could link up with a messiah: The messiah can defeat the evil conspirators and thus save the culture. Here lies one of the dangers of the conspiracy argument: It invites mass hysteria and charismatic leaders.[9] In times of trouble and confusion, we may see the rise of mass movements following leaders who are believed to be heroes or saviors.

Value of Challenge

Associated with the messiah or savior myth is another myth: the value of challenge. The myth is fairly simple and may parallel tribal tests of strength and character. It suggests that there is a kind of wisdom gained only through great challenge and testing. There is a rite of passage or initiation that gives one power, character, and knowledge.

You are probably now going through such a test in college. People say that going to college is a test of endurance more than training for a specific job. College graduation shows that you can meet a challenge and handle it, that you have matured, and that you have learned how to learn. Employers hire college graduates and then train them for a job after college. Boot camp offers another example of belief in the value of overcoming difficulty and in meeting challenges.

The concept of the Outward Bound program rests on the value of challenge myth. Somehow, it says, the most problematic children will be restored to good behavior if they get through a mountain-climbing expedition, a rafting trip down the Colorado River, or a wilderness canoe trip. Even corporate America recognizes this and often sends its executives on such Outward Bound experiences to shape them up.

Political persuaders frequently offer voters a dramatic challenge and paint their election as one of critical importance. Lincoln said his election would decide whether the nation could exist "half slave and half free." Roosevelt said that the coun-

FIGURE 8.2

The U.S. Army's "Be All You Can Be — in the Army" campaign exemplifies the persuasiveness of "the value of challenge" myth, especially for women in this advertisement. (Army photograph courtesy U.S. Government, as represented by the Secretary of the Army.)

try under his leadership would have "a rendezvous with destiny." John F. Kennedy said that with his election a torch had been passed to a new generation and the light from the torch would "light the world." Reagan offered a "new beginning."

In many cases, the value of challenge myth is presented as a rite of passage that underscores several cultural values that persuaders frequently use in their appeals. First, the myth suggests that there is something good about suffering or that nothing good was ever accomplished without pain. Second, the myth suggests that suffering begets maturity, humility, and wisdom — you learn and grow as you meet challenges and surmount them. Finally, the myth suggests that all great leaders have become great because they were tested and found equal to the challenge. Thus, defeats and failures can be explained away as tests that prepare you for the future. As you begin to catalog the persuasion aimed at you, you will find the value of challenge used frequently, whether for products, candidates, or ideologies.

Myth of the Eternal Return

Mircea Eliade, a professor of history at the Sorbonne, identified a historical myth that was persistent not only in Western culture but in other cultures as well. He called it the "myth of the eternal return."[10] He said that people reject concrete historical time and instead yearn for and often reenact a "periodical return to the mythical time of the beginning of things, to the 'Great Time.'"[11] American culture seems to embrace this myth, perhaps because our beginnings are so recent compared with those of other cultures. America was conceived with the perception that it was a "second Eden," a chance to start anew with no historical baggage to clutter up our purpose.

According to the myth of the eternal return, as Eliade explained it and as used by persuaders, there was a time when things were perfect and harmonious; things could be shaped or molded as they were meant to be. This time of creation is usually associated with a specific geographical "center," where things are assumed to have begun.

In the United States, this center is probably Philadelphia, where the Continental Congress signed the Declaration of Independence, or perhaps Washington, DC, where our great historical documents are enshrined in the National Archives. At the creation, there were heroes (George Washington, Benjamin Franklin, John Hancock, and so on). There were also villains (King George, the colonial governors, the British generals, and the redcoats). After suffering for some time, the heroes participated in some critical act that was redemptive — it released them from their former enslavement and permitted them to create the "Great Time" or the "Golden Age."

Included in the myth is the notion that society has lost sight of this archetypal beginning, and we must find our way back if we are to rid ourselves of the corruption, misplanning, and confusion that have been built up since then. This is usually done through reenactment of the original act in a ritual, usually held at the center where everything began. This periodic return to the origins of our beliefs reestablishes these values for us and is an act of redemption.

The rite freezes us in a mystical time that has power to transform us through the ritual. As Eliade notes:

> Time, too, like space is neither homogeneous nor continuous. On the one hand there are the intervals of a sacred time, the time of festivals (by far the greater part of which are periodical); on the other hand there is profane time, ordinary temporal duration. . . . *By its very nature sacred time is reversible* in the sense that properly speaking, it is *a primordial mythical time made present.*[12]

Our contemporary language reflects this belief in the cyclical nature of things and of the two types of time. For example, when we say "Everything that goes around, comes around," we mean "This will come back to haunt you," "What ye sow, so shall ye reap," or "History repeats itself." Although we have a reverence for certain "sacred" times — historical holidays, ritualistic meals (such as Thanksgiving, Christmas, Passover), and governmental rites (the Inaugural Address, the Oath of Office, the State of the Union address, among others) — we disdain persons who waste time, are just "passing the time," or are just "couch potatoes" living through "profane" time.

Commercial persuaders are aware of the importance of sacred time. They have special sales on historical holidays: a "Hatchet Days Sale" on Washington's birthday, an "Independence Day Sale" on the 4th of July, a "Pre-Christmas Sale" the day following Thanksgiving. And in recent years, some stores hold a "Super Bowl Sale" in mid-January.

Politicians are often skillful at challenging us to return to an earlier time — to reestablish and renew ourselves. Not only is this apparent in their speeches, but the inaugural ceremonies themselves are acts of renewal that promise to return to the untainted past. As noted earlier, Ronald Reagan promised "Together — A New Beginning."

In ideological campaigns and mass movements, the return and renewal theme is also persistent. Martin Luther King, Jr., used it in his "I Have a Dream" speech. Jesse Jackson used it throughout his 1984 and 1988 bids for the presidential nomination, and again to try to unite the party in his speeches at the Democratic conventions. We hear strains of the myth even in the pro-life, antiabortion movement: One leader of the pro-life movement said, "People are going to look back on this era the way they look back on Nazi Germany. They'll say 'Thank God there were a few sane people.'"[13] Moral majority leader Jerry Falwell said of abortion, "This criminal activity . . . sets us back to the Stone Age."[14] In this antiabortion case, the focus was not on sacred ground or creative acts but on the profane ground of the abortion clinics and symbolic acts such as bombing those clinics. One pro-lifer called the Christmas, 1984, bombings "a gift to Jesus on his birthday."[15]

Even in product ads we can detect appeals to the new beginnings or to the return and renewal myth. NEC Corporation says, "The new information age is built on the merging of computers and communication . . . you deserve no less. NEC,

the way it will be." The famous Virginia Slims "You've Come a Long Way, Baby" ads are based on a new beginning, which is contrasted with a tainted past. Mercedes-Benz reminds us that "This year, as for ninety-nine years, the automobiles of Mercedes-Benz are like no other cars in the world." In fact, one of the most frequent advertising appeals is a renewal idea: "New and Improved!"

This myth of the eternal return and the cyclical reenactments of the Golden Age — with its heroes, villains, and sacred and profane ground — is a powerful tool that persuaders use in a variety of circumstances. We must remember, however, that not all returns to the past are necessarily good and that the Golden Age may not have been so wonderful after all.

Reich's Cultural Myths

In his book *Tales of a New America*, Robert Reich discusses the problems facing us in the 1990s. He contends that the future appears chaotic for a variety of reasons: rapidly advancing technology, rising expectations for prosperity throughout the world, and a generalized confusion about where we are headed as a nation. Reich and his Harvard colleagues have identified what they call basic cultural parables for the United States. These parables convey:

> . . . lessons about the how and why of life through metaphor [which] may be a basic human trait, a universal charcteristic of our intermittently rational, deeply emotional, meaning-seeking species. . . . In America the vehicles of public myth include the biographies of famous citizens, popular fiction and music, feature stories on the evening news and gossip. . . . They anchor our political understandings. . . . What gives them force is their capacity to make sense of, and bring coherence to, common experience. The lessons ring true, even if the illustration is fanciful.[16]

Reich's concept of cultural parables closely resembles what we have been calling cultural myths, and his work often echoes what parts of this text have emphasized: Human beings are fascinated, perhaps even driven, by the power of the dramatic or the narrative.

Reich's myths are rooted in the vignette of a man named George, the son of immigrant parents who worked hard to provide a good home. George did well in school and worked long hours to bring home a few dollars for the family. He was good in sports, although he didn't have much time to participate. He never picked a fight, but on one occasion did step in to stop the town bully and banker's son, Albert Wade, from beating up on the smallest kid in class. He let Albert have the first swing and then decked him with a single punch. George went off to fight Nazism in Europe and saved his squad by single-handedly destroying a machine gun nest, but was too humble to wear or display the medal he received for heroism. After the war, he returned to his hometown, married his childhood sweetheart, and became successful in the construction business. He gave his spare time to good causes and lived modestly. George kept pretty much to himself until his old nemesis, Albert Wade, inherited his father's bank and began to squander the depositors' savings by making shaky loans to his buddies and buying himself into the office of mayor. The only person to stand up and challenge the corrupt election was George. Then Wade's bank refused to loan any money on houses built by George. In a showdown town meeting, one of Wade's corrupt councilmen finally couldn't take George's accusatory gaze and broke down, spilling the beans on Wade, who ended up in jail while George went back to his quiet and modest life. It is *the* American morality play, according to Reich.[17]

This brief story has been told over and over again in various versions, including Horatio Alger novels, films such as "It's a Wonderful Life," and "Big," and biographies of famous Americans. It contains Reich's four basic cultural parables, which are discussed next. As you read about these parables, note some of the similarities between the work of Reich and his colleagues and what we have been calling cultural myths.

The Mob at the Gates The basic idea in this parable is that America stands alone in the world as the last, best remaining hope for a good, moral, and affluent life in a world that is filled with perilous possibilities and awesome powers. This parable creates an "us" and "them" mentality, or mind set. The mob may be drug traffickers, illegal aliens, or something more abstract: the sinister Nazis; the ideological Communists, who tirelessly seek world domination; the populations of the Third World countries, who are jealous of us; foreign producers, who can provide goods at prices much lower than the American worker can produce them; secular humanists; minorities; and a host of other "mobs." The parable has at least two sides — a liberal or Democratic one and a conservative or Republican one. Both sides may defy the mob at the gates on one issue, such as foreign competition, but on the other issues the mob may be acceptable for one side and not for the other. Such a case might be the issue of illegal aliens, which the liberals see as far less dangerous than do the conservatives. The liberal reaction to this "mob" may be to help them become legitimate, productive citizens. The conservative sees them as an inherent danger to the economic community, as nothing more than potential welfare recipients.

Reich cites several events of central importance to our nation that rested on the mob at the gates parable. One example he gives is Franklin Roosevelt's "rotten apple" metaphor — several "rotten" nations could ruin the "whole barrel" of nations. Reich argues that the post–World War II "domino theory," in which nation after nation falls to the Communists, was also an appeal to the mob at the gates myth. Similar to this is John Kennedy's image of America holding back the communist threat by a "finger in the dike." More recently, we have seen this myth used by the leadership of the Soviet Union to convince the various republics of the U.S.S.R. not to break away from the union. The underlying lesson in all of these uses of the appeal to the mob at the gate is that "We must maintain vigilance, lest dark forces overrun us."[18]

Advertisers base many of their ads for products on this parable. Millions of germs are lying in wait to infect you, but if you use Listerine mouthwash, you'll knock 'em for a loop. The twin villains of summer heat and winter cold can ruin your car engine unless you protect it with Prestone anti-freeze and coolant. Hordes of mosquitoes will ruin your picnic unless you are vigilant enough to spray the area with long-lasting Raid insect fog.

The mob myth is a natural for ideological campaigns as well. For example, the secular humanists are ready to taint America's moral fiber with their approach to questions of morals, so it is absolutely essential to join the "moral majority." And of course politicians use the image in a variety of ways — sometimes the mob is the other party, or it could be the threat of uncontrolled terrorism or a runaway national debt.

The Triumphant Individual This parable has as its subject the humble guy or gal who works hard, takes risks but has faith in himself or herself and as a result eventually reaches or even exceeds goals of fame, honor, and financial success. It is the story of the self-made man or woman who demonstrates what hard work and determination combined with a gutsy approach to problems and a spunky style can do. Usually the individual is a loner, sometimes even a maverick who is willing to challenge the establishment and try to do something on a shoestring. A contemporary example is Steven Jobs, the inventor of the Apple computer and an officer of the company before leaving the corporation. Not only did Jobs begin building the Apple empire in his garage, but he went out and started over again when he left Apple to form NEXT. Like George in Reich's vignette, Jobs was self-reliant, hard-working, and believed in himself. Another example from the corporate world is Lee Iacocca, the maverick at Ford who bucked the odds and the office politics, fighting long and hard for a product he believed in and finally convincing the company to bring out its most successful product ever: the Mustang. After he was fired by Ford, Iacocca took over the nearly bankrupt Chrysler corporation and turned the company around, paying off a $1.2 billion government "bailout" loan early, innovating with front-wheel drive the mini-

van, and bringing back the convertible. This myth strikes the same chord as the wisdom of the rustic and the possibility of success myths discussed earlier.

We frequently see the triumphant individual in a variety of persuasive arenas. In politics, self-made men or women are the ones to put your money on — they made it this far on a gutsy attitude and a belief in themselves, and as a result, they will come out winners on election day as well.

The Benevolent Community The myth or parable of the benevolent community is the story of the essential goodness of people and their willingness to help out the other guy in time of need. An ad for the Miller beer company portrayed this myth in action. A small town in Wisconsin was struck by a tornado that demolished several homes and nearby farms. But the men and women of surrounding communities joined forces and within two weeks had nearly rebuilt all that had been destroyed. Of course, at the end of a hard day of raising walls and rafters, they enjoyed the camaraderie of the event by drinking the sponsor's product.

Reich finds roots for this parable in the Puritan pioneers and pilgrim heritage. He quotes John Winthrop's sermon "A Model of Christian Charity," which was delivered on board ship in 1630 just offshore of what was to become Salem, Massachusetts. Winthrop likened the new life they were about to begin to the Sermon on the Mount: "The new settlers would be 'as a City on a Hill' whose members would 'delight in each other' and be 'of the same body.'"[19] Three-hundred and fifty years later, Mario Cuomo, governor of New York, used the same "city on a hill" image at the 1984 Democratic National Convention. We find this cultural myth recurring throughout our history in the struggle for freedom from English domination, freeing the slaves, women's suffrage, the civil rights movement, and the pro-life demonstrations of recent times. Reich sees it reflected in Franklin Roosevelt's "New Deal," Harry Truman's "Square Deal," and Lyndon Johnson's "Great Society." Perhaps one could argue that Ronald Reagan's

"New Beginning" continued the chain, as did George Bush's "Kinder, Gentler Nation." As Reich notes, "The story celebrates America's tradition of civic improvement, philanthropy, and local boosterism."[20]

However, as noted earlier, this sense of community is extremely fragile and perhaps is even disappearing, as Robert Bellah and his colleagues have pointed out in *Habits of the Heart: Individualism and Commitment in American Life*. The possible reasons for this decay of community-mindedness include the escalating technology that fragments and isolates us, the "me-ism" of the yuppies, and the "graying of America" as the baby boomers — many of them your parents — reach mid-life. Nevertheless, the myth persists and has enough persuasive power to motivate people to oppose war in the Middle East, to join one of a variety of mass movements, and/or to purchase products that promise or are associated with a sense of community. We can be sure persuaders will continue to use the lesson of the benevolent community to market products, candidates, and ideologies.

Rot at the Top   This parable or myth has conspiratorial aspects and revolves around a number of subthemes: corruption, a lack of morals or ethics, decadence, and the malevolence of persons in high places. Like the presence of conspiracy myth mentioned earlier, it seems to follow a cyclical pattern, which Reich calls "The Cycles of Righteous Fulmination."[21] First we rely on the benevolence of the elite, and then we find them lacking in trust or good will, and we end up distrusting or unseating them. Reich traces the myth to the founding fathers' sensitivity to the abuse of power experienced under King George and his designees, the colonial governors and English soldiers. For this reason the founding fathers built the system of checks and balances, which each of us learns about in our government or civics classes. In spite of those protections, there exist abuses of power by elites who buy their power with money and favors (as did George's archenemy, Albert Wade) or whom power has made arrogant and corrupt.

Our history recounts numerous and varied types of rot at the top, but Reich believes that the myth usually has one of two targets — political corruption or economic exploitation. Politically, we have seen it in Teapot Dome, the McCarthyism of the fifties, Watergate in the seventies, and Irangate in the waning months of the Reagan administration, with over 100 former Reagan officials convicted of one crime or another. Economically, we often hear that big business has exploited the common man, Teddy Roosevelt was a "trust-buster" on behalf of the common man, and Franklin Roosevelt promised to "throw the money changers from the temple" in his first inaugural. Even President Dwight Eisenhower, a five-star general, warned us of "the military-industrial complex" in his farewell address. The economic stagnation of the late seventies was the fault of the big spenders in Congress, according to Jimmy Carter. And the late eighties had numerous Wall Street scandals based on insider trading by "stock market jackals" and "corporate barracudas," to use Jesse Jackson's term — all examples of rot at the top.

The lesson of the rot at the top myth is simple: "Power corrupts; privilege perverts."[22] And the power of this myth is considerable, especially in politics: When in doubt, "Vote the scoundrels out."

The "Man's Man" and the "Woman's Woman"

Another popular myth is that for a male to be a success, he must be a man's man. The schools, the family, and television tell children that important males are those who do macho things: compete in macho activities, use colognes with names like "Iron," are involved in sports, talk tough, and own guns, heavy-duty equipment and four-wheel-drive vehicles. They never show their emotions, and they die with their boots on.

On the other hand, ideal women are soft-spoken, kind, and nurturing. They may work, but they are also perfect wives and mothers, are immaculately groomed, and are vain. They love to gossip — especially about other women.

FIGURE 8.3

What will the "graying of America" mean for you? For your parents? For the economy? For the fading sense of community that we've discussed? (*Arlo and Janis* reprinted by permission of NEA, Inc.)

These myths, of course, affect the way we treat our children—valuing certain things they do and devaluing others. It is "unfeminine" for a woman to engage in any sport except tennis, golf, or swimming; it is "unmasculine" for any man to take up gourmet cooking, needlepoint, or flower gardening (vegetables are OK). Boys shouldn't cry. Girls always do. This myth of the distinctions between the sexes is obviously changing, however. High schools and colleges boast women's field hockey, basketball, and baseball teams. In many towns, you will find girls' softball leagues for seven-, eight-, and nine-year-olds. In fact, we now place great emphasis on athletic ability and health in both men and women. Female executives are featured in ads for hotels. Female pilots are shown using deodorant. At the same time, men are now expected to contribute their fair share of housework.

Old myths do not die easily, however, and we still see many examples of the stereotypical macho male and the "perfectly feminine" woman. Beer ads feature retired athletes engaged in a man's world, bragging to one another over beers. The sponsors for L'eggs pantyhose know that dancer Juliet Prowse still epitomizes femininity for many. One look at any current magazine will show advertisers pitching their products at people who must believe these images of men and women.

Although gender-bound, stereotypical representations of men and women are changing, these images still have persuasive power and are still used to advertise products, push candidates, and promote ideas. Despite reductions in gender differences in job and political candidacy and in gender-related language use, the old stereotypes are still potent persuaders. The major change in attitude toward gender-related issues has occurred in young, college-educated, upper-middle-class, nonminority populations. But the far greater proportion of our population still seems to buy into the man's man and woman's woman myths. We can expect to see ads for macho four-wheel-drive jeeps and super powerful chainsaws for as long as we continue to see ads for Maidenform bras, Hanes pantyhose, and Emeraude perfume, along with their advice: "Want Him to Be More of a Man? Try Being More of a Woman."

Persuaders will adapt as Americans shift their values regarding gender and other human characteristics, such as age, single parenthood, and economic status, but their persuasion will reflect the premises that the audience believes. Persuasion is

FIGURE 8.4

Here are examples of the myth of the "man's man" done tongue in cheek. (*Making It* copyright 1988 Keith Robinson. All rights reserved. Reprinted by permission of Universal Press Syndicate.)

more often a reflection of a culture's values than a shaper of them.

IMAGE (CHARISMA) OR ETHOS AS A CULTURAL PREMISE

Sometimes persuaders are successful because of their **image**, or **charisma**. We believe them because their presentations are so convincing and dynamic or because they have a reputation for being truthful or knowledgeable. As noted earlier, this kind of proof was recognized by Aristotle, as well as others. He called it *ethos*, or ethical proof. More recently, researchers have worked at identifying exactly what causes or creates high ethos in some persons and low ethos in others. One research technique is to have audiences rate various speakers on a variety of bipolar scales that have sets of opposing adjectives at either end.[23] Figure 8.5 shows a set of such scales.

The researchers used several hundred such pairs of terms and then tried to determine which traits seemed to typify speakers who were considered persuasive and believable. They discovered in repeated tests that the choices seemed to cluster around three traits or three dimensions of what came to be called **source credibility**. The first dimension was the *expertise* component of source credibility. In other words, highly credible sources were perceived as having knowledge and experience regarding the topic they addressed. This makes sense; we tend to put more store in the ideas and advice that come from experts than those that come from nonexperts. Whom would you listen to for advice on auto racing — the winner of the Indy 500 or the kid down the block who drag races on Friday nights? The clustering of items related to expertise was later verified by experiments in which a variety of groups listened to the same tape-recorded speaker giving the same speech. The speaker was introduced to some of the groups as an expert — say, the surgeon general. As we described, these groups believed the speaker much more than they did another introduced as a college senior.

In a 1969 study, researchers found that three believability factors emerged from audience-generated words describing credible sources. These factors were *safety, qualification*, and *dynamism*.[24] Qualification is similar to expertise.

This speaker is (mark scale at the spot you think fits best):

Fast	.....	.....	.....	.....	.....	Slow
Light	.....	.....	.....	.....	.....	Heavy
Powerful	.....	.....	.....	.....	.....	Weak
Open	.....	.....	.....	.....	.....	Closed
Truthful	.....	.....	.....	.....	.....	Untruthful
Sincere	.....	.....	.....	.....	.....	Insincere
Biased	.....	.....	.....	.....	.....	Unbiased
Graceful	.....	.....	.....	.....	.....	Clumsy
Dumb	.....	.....	.....	.....	.....	Smart
Unstable	.....	.....	.....	.....	.....	Stable

FIGURE 8.5

Audience rating scale for evaluating ethos.

This dimension has been identified under various conditions repeatedly since then, and seems to be one of the more stable factors in determining whether we believe someone.

Another dimension that recurs in studies of image is *trustworthiness* or *sincerity*. Over thirty years ago, researchers at Yale identified this factor in their studies, concluding that the credibility of any source is tied to "trust and confidence" attributes.[25] This dimension has reemerged in numerous studies over the years, although at times it may have been labeled "safety"[26] or "personal integrity."[27]

An interesting indicator of trustworthiness involves the biased source who testifies against his or her own self-interest or bias. This may give us a clue to what really is involved in the trust dimension. Communication researchers Herbert Kelman and Carl Hovland gave an interesting example.[28] They wanted to know who would be believed in the following situation: A message promoting the need for stiffer penalties for juvenile delinquents was attributed in one case to a juvenile court judge and in another case to a drug-pushing juvenile delinquent. The audience believed the judge because of his expertise in dealing with juvenile cases, but their belief in the delinquent came from their trust in testimony that obviously was against the speaker's bias.

Trust involves receivers analyzing a speaker's motives, or hidden agenda. A person's motivation is a key to his or her sincerity. The etymology of the word *sincerity* gives us some insights. It comes from the Latin *sincerus*, which literally means "without wax." This had a dual meaning in ancient times. The first meaning referred to the use of wax coatings as preservatives. To be without wax was to be fresh, pure, or unadulterated. The second meaning referred to a practice of unethical pillar carvers, who used wax to cover up their mistakes or to hide imperfections in the marble. Only after decades of weathering did the wax fall out to reveal the deception practiced by the long-gone carver. So a sincere person was the genuine article, that is, *without wax*, or uncamouflaged. This was the idea to which the *sincerity* dimension of the credibility scale related. Such words as *truthful* or *honest* or *genuine* differentiated the sincere speakers from the insincere. Perhaps the audiences believed speakers were sincere because the former maintained good eye contact or didn't shift back and forth on their feet or didn't have a tremor in their voices. Or maybe the respondent judged sincerity from the person's reputation.

Trustworthiness or sincerity is also a fairly stable factor in credibility, as has been demonstrated in many research studies. Although its effects vary from situation to situation, receivers believe persons they trust, whether because of the sources' reputation, their delivery, or their supposed motivation.

A final dimension of credibility that has been demonstrated through experimental research is not as easy to describe or define. This factor has been labeled *dynamism, compliance*, or *image* by various researchers; it is the degree to which the audience admires and identifies with the source's attractiveness, power or forcefulness, and energy. The following pairs of words have been linked in testing to the dynamism factor: *aggressive* as opposed to *meek*; *emphatic* as opposed to *hesitant*; *frank* as opposed to *reserved*; *bold* as opposed to *passive*; *energetic* as opposed to *tired*; and *fast* as opposed to *slow*.[29] This characteristic is clearly related to charisma, and although it is influenced by a speaker's attractiveness, unattractive persons can be charismatic or dynamic, too. Dynamic speakers don't necessarily move about or wave their arms to give off dynamism cues. They just seem to take up a lot of psychological space. They enter a room and people expect them to be in charge.

There are other dimensions of source credibility that could be investigated, and others already have been. We mentioned, for example, that a tall speaker is generally more likely to be believed than a short one. Timid or shy and reserved persons are likely to have low credibility, whereas authoritative and self-assured ones have high credibility. Bossy and egotistical persuaders lose credibility, whereas pleasant and warm persuaders do not. These and many other dimensions of source credibility interact and affect the three fundamental dimensions of trust — sincerity, expertise, and dynamism or potency.

For Bill Demby, the difference means getting another shot.

When Bill Demby was in Vietnam, he used to dream of coming home and playing a little basketball with the guys.

A dream that all but died when he lost both his legs to a Viet Cong rocket.

But then, a group of researchers discovered that a remarkable DuPont plastic could help make artificial limbs that were more resilient, more flexible, more like life itself.

Thanks to these efforts, Bill Demby is back. And some say, he hasn't lost a step.

At DuPont, we make the things that make a difference.

Better things for better living.
REG. U.S. PAT & TM OFF

FIGURE 8.6

This ad enhances DuPont's ethos by implying that the company is responsible for Bill Demby's "getting another shot" at life. (DuPont Company photograph. Used by permission of DuPont.)

These values are not shared by all cultures. In cultures where the bribe or "baksheesh" is the order of the day, people are admired for being *untrustworthy*. Haggling over prices in the bazaars and markets of other cultures is based on *insincer-ity*, not sincerity. Many cultures value the *undyn-amic* persuader who is cool and calm. In some cultures, a religious leader who perhaps lacks expertise in economics and diplomacy becomes the head of state, whereas the experts are rejected from government. Credibility or ethos is culturally dependent.

PRESENCE OF AN AMERICAN VALUE SYSTEM

The myths we have just examined are actually fantasy forms of deep and enduring values that most Americans hold. They are expressed in myths in order to simplify them. This makes them seem less lofty — more down-to-earth and ordinary. For example, Americans have a belief or value that all persons are to be treated equally and that in the eyes of God they *are* equal. This value has been debated for more than two centuries through such issues as slavery, women's suffrage, civil rights, desegregation, and affirmative action programs. The value is acted out or dramatized in the possibility of success myth. We see the myth acted out in television spots and portrayed in print ads. For example, a recent image ad for the DuPont Chemical Company featured a black man who was still able to play top-notch basketball even though he had lost both legs in Vietnam, thanks to the good folks at DuPont who sold the raw materials for making the artificial limbs that now enable him to be successful in the world of amateur sports. Of course, the film *Rocky* and its sequels depicted a man who rose from being an unknown boxer to being a champ, an ex-champ, and a champ once more. And almost every politician will claim to have come up the road of hard knocks.

One of the early speech-communication studies that explored values was conducted by Edward Steele and W. Charles Redding.[30] They looked at the communication of several political campaigns and tried to extract core and secondary values. These were the core values observed by Steele and Redding:

Puritan and pioneer morality. This value involves the willingness to cast the world into categories of foul and fair, good and evil, and so forth. Although we tend to think of this value as outdated, it has merely been reworded. The advocates and foes of present marijuana laws and of legal abortion both call on moral values such as just/unjust, right/wrong, and moral/immoral to make their cases.

Value of the individual. This value involves the ranking of the rights and welfare of the individual above those of government and as being important in other ways. This value seems to persist. All politicians claim to be interested in the individual. Cosmetics are made "especially for you." We praise the house decorating scheme that expresses individuality. Burger King lets you "Have It Your Way."

Achievement and success. This value entails the accumulation of power, status, wealth, and property. The late sixties and seventies was a time when young Americans seemed to reject this value, favoring communal living instead and refusing to dress up for school, church, or even job interviews, many of those same young people are now the upwardly mobile, achievement-oriented yuppies we hear so much about today. People today seem to evaluate others by symbols or emblems of success — whether BMWs or Mercedes-Benz's, Rolex watches, Mont Blanc pens, or even "success" pinky rings.

Persuaders frequently appeal to this need for achievement or success. Most of the military recruitment posters, advertisements, and slogans promise that by starting a career in the Army, Navy, Air Force, or Marines, one will be able to climb the ladder to success faster. If you read *The Wall Street Journal*, success and status will be yours. First impressions count, so be sure to "dress for success" by shopping at Neiman Marcus.

The achievement and success value, like the cultural myths, seems to wax and wane or ebb and flow with time. All of the self-help courses and pyramid schemes that we noted earlier will continue to be marketed, even when the values of achievement and success seem most dormant.

Change and progress. This value is typified by the belief that change (of almost any kind) will

"First impressions are very important during an interview Ms. Crawford, but frankly, I don't think Cher was your best possible choice."

FIGURE 8.7

The "dress for success" fad rests on which core American value? (Reprinted from *The Saturday Evening Post*, © 1990.)

lead to progress and that progress is inherently good for us. This is the appeal of any product that is either "new" or "new and improved." The product life-cycle theory almost dictates "change" and "progress" in the form of "improvement" to delay the eventual decline of product sales. From a legal point of view, the producer of a laundry product, for example, can claim that its product is new and improved merely by changing the color of the "beads of bleach" or by slightly altering the ratio of ingredients. Because we as a culture value change and progress, we go for new and im-

proved products like a trout goes for a red worm. This is not to say that all such products are bad—only that the appeal has great power. Indeed, many changes have led to progress that was good: the downsizing of the American automobile and the increase in its fuel efficiency, the development of new generations of home and business computers, the use of the dish antenna, and the development of the microchip. Some changes are not good, however. Take for example the "Tax Simplification Act of 1986," which not only did not simplify anything but confused even the most skilled tax accountants and baffled the average citizen. A bogus 1040 tax form was circulated the year following the act on which there were two lines — one to list all your income and the other telling you to send it in.

Ethical equality. This value expresses the belief that all persons ought to be treated equally. They should have an equal opportunity to get an education, to work and be paid a fair wage, to live where they choose, and to hold political office. We all know that although this value may be laudable, the reality is that not everyone is born equal, nor do they all have an equal opportunity for jobs, education, or decent housing. Nonetheless, attempts to create a situation of equality are a part of American history: emancipation of the slaves, women's suffrage, the civil rights movement, the women's liberation movement, affirmative action programs, and similar actions, which demonstrate that the value still carries persuasive potency.

Effort and optimism. This value expresses the belief that even the most unattainable goals can be reached if one works hard and "keeps smilin'." The myths of the triumphant individual and the possibility of success are examples of these values in action. Norman Vincent Peale's book *The Power of Positive Thinking* links optimism with religion and has been adopted by many as a map to their lives. Other optimistic self-help books and programs are further evidence of the ongoing belief in these values. And in today's business world, it is important to be a "striver" or a "self-starter." Folk wisdoms such as "Every cloud *must have* a silver lining," "If at first you don't succeed, try, try again," "Keep on the sunny side," "Lighten up," and "happy face" buttons serve as cultural metaphors of the value we place on effort and optimism.

Efficiency, practicality, and pragmatism. This value entails solution-oriented as opposed to ideologically oriented thinking. A key question often asked of any piece of legislation is "Will it work?" This value extends to other

parts of our lives, too. We want to know whether a microwave oven is energy efficient, practical, or handy. We want to know whether our schooling will lead to a job. In other words, we value what is quick, workable, and practical.

Even though these values were catalogued over thirty years ago, they still have a great deal of relevance. This, if nothing else, suggests their basic quality. The fact that political position has less to do with the strength of these values than with the method of enacting them seems to underscore the probability that these are core values for Americans. Our culture has been effective in instilling a set of values in all, or very nearly all, of its members; radicals, moderates, and reactionaries all believe in the same things but apply them differently. The power of a social system or culture to train its members is immense, even though the members do not often realize this as they react to the dictates deeply ingrained in them.

In the 1988 presidential primary campaigns, a student of mine found many of the same values articulated in similar if not identical ways to those presented here. For example, recurring words in George Bush's campaign were: *ambitious, striver, competitive, independence*, and *family*. At the other end of the political continuum, the speeches of Jesse Jackson were studded with words such as *working people, equality, coalitions, change, hope*, and *family*, and the televangelist candidate Pat Robertson used phrases such as *moral problem, faith in God, faith in individual initiative*, and *faith in freedom*, all of which reflect to some degree the values first identified by Steele and Redding thirty years ago.[31] Democratic nominee Michael Dukakis reinforced the pattern by frequently noting an optimism about the *future* through individual and national *strength*.

Does this mean that values remain essentially static and cannot be changed? Not necessarily. It means only that values are so deeply ingrained in a culture that its members often forget how strong these pressures are.

REVIEW AND CONCLUSION

By this time, you know that the world of the persuadee in an information age is not an easy one. There are so many things to be aware of: the persuader's self-revelation using language and stylistic choices, the internal or process premises operating within each of us, and the interactive rules for content premises. Now we have glimpsed societal and cultural predispositions for persuasion that also may act as premises in persuasive arguments. Persuaders, either because they have studied and analyzed our cultural predispositions or because they instinctively appeal to these values, rely on the societal training in the people they are trying to reach. On at least three separate levels, this training has an effect on each of us — in the cultural myths or images to which we respond, in the sets of values we consciously articulate, and in the nonverbal cues to which we react (artifacts, space, and touch, to mention a few).

QUESTIONS FOR FURTHER THOUGHT

1. What are the three types of culturally or socially learned predispositions for persuasion? Give examples of each from your own experience.

2. How does a culture or society train its members? Give examples from your own experience.

3. How do you rank the core values mentioned in this chapter? How do you put them into practice? Are there other values in your value system not mentioned here? What are they? Are they restatements of the core values? If so, how? If not, how do they differ?

4. Considering today's headlines, is there a mob at the gates present? Explain.

5. To what degree can you identify a benevolent community in your life? Explain.

6. In the award-winning film *Platoon*, there clearly is rot at the top being depicted. If you have seen the film, identify the critical moment when the "narrator" of the film discovers the "rot," and describe what he does about it.

NOTES

1. Robert N. Bellah, Richard Madsen, William M. Sullivan, Ann Swidler, and Steven M. Tipton, *Habits of the Heart: Individualism and Commitment in American Life* (New York: Harper & Row, 1985), p. vii.

2. *Ibid.*, p. 6

3. *Ibid.*, p. 66.

4. For a good discussion of the trials by pain used by the Sioux, read John Neihardt, *Black Elk Speaks* (Lincoln: University of Nebraska Press, 1961). Black Elk was second cousin to the great Sioux chief Crazy Horse, and was considered by the Oglala to be the last *Wichasha wakon*, or holy man. Shortly before Black Elk's death, John Neihardt, poet laureate of Nebraska, recorded his biography as translated by the old man's son. The Sioux's use of smothering to prevent crying is discussed in Maria Santos, *These Were the Sioux* (New York: Dell, 1961), p. 19.

5. Alexis de Tocqueville, *Democracy in America* (New York: Mentor Books, 1965), p. 148.

6. Richard Hofstadter, *Anti-Intellectualism in American Life* (New York: Alfred A. Knopf, 1963).

7. Tocqueville, *op. cit.*, pp. 156–158.

8. For a more complete discussion of the conspiracy argument, see Richard Hofstadter, *The Paranoid Style in American Politics and Other Essays* (New York: Vintage Books, 1967).

9. For a good discussion of the degree to which persons will follow charismatic leaders, see Eric Hoffer, *The True Believer* (New York: Harper & Row, 1951).

10. Mircea Eliade, *The Myth of the Eternal Return: Or Cosmos and History* (Princeton, NJ: Princeton University Press, 1971).

11. *Ibid.* See Chapter 3, "The Regeneration of Time."

12. Wendell C. Beane and William G. Doty, eds., *Myths, Rites, Symbols: A Mircea Eliade Reader* (New York: Harper Colophon Books, 1975), p. 33

13. "America's Abortion Dilemma," *Newsweek*, January 14, 1985, p. 20.

14. *Ibid.*, p. 22.

15. *Ibid.*, p. 23.

16. Robert Reich, *Tales of a New America* (New York: Times Books, 1987), p. 7.

17. *Ibid.*, pp. 2–4.

18. *Ibid.*, p. 9. See also Chapters 4–8.

19. Reich, *op. cit.*, p. 10. See also Chapters 13–16.

20. *Ibid.*, p. 11.

21. *Ibid.*, pp. 201–211.

22. *Ibid.*, p. 13. See also Chapters 17–19.

23. For a full description of the development of the semantic differential, the central measuring device for research on ethos, see Charles Osgood, George Suci, and Percy Tannenbaum, *The Measurement of Meaning* (Urbana: The University of Illinois Press, 1957).

24. David Berlo, J. Lemmert, and M. Davis, "Dimensions for Evaluating the Acceptability of Message Sources," *Public Opinion Quarterly* 33:563–576, 1969. See also James McCroskey and T. Young, "Ethos and Credibility: The Construct and Its Measurement After Three Decades," *Central States Speech Journal* 32:24–34, 1981.

25. Carl Hovland, Irving Janis, and H. Kelley, *Communication and Persuasion* (New Haven, CT: Yale University Press, 1953), p. 20.

26. Berlo et al., *op. cit.*

27. S. Baudhin and M. Davis, "Scales for the Measurement of *Ethos:* Another Attempt," *Speech Monographs* 39:296–301, 1972.

28. Herbert Kelman and Carl Hovland, "Reinstatement of the Communicator: Delayed Measurement of Opinion Changes," *Journal of Abnormal and Social Psychology* 48: 327–335, 1953.

29. For an excellent review of the research that uncovered the dynamism factor, see Robert N. Bostrom, *Persuasion* (Englewood Cliffs, NJ: Prentice-Hall, 1983), pp. 63–87.

30. Edward D. Steele and W. Charles Redding, "The American Value System: Premises for Persuasion," *Western Speech* 26:83–91, 1962.

31. Ann Larrette Chaney, "A Value Analysis: The 1988 Presidential Primaries," class paper for COMS 607, "Seminar in Persuasion," March 30, 1988.

CHAPTER

Nonverbal Messages in Persuasion

Videotapes of persons shopping in video-monitored stores during the devastating 1989 earthquake in San Francisco show that the first thing people did after checking the environmental symptoms of the earthquake — whether objects fell from shelves, or windows and walls cracked — was to check out the nonverbal behavior of the people around them. They looked for facial expressions, movement, and probably a host of other cues of impending danger. During the Middle East crisis of the early nineties, Iraqi strongman Saddam Hussein tried to win worldwide public approval for his actions by being photographed and televised talking with young Western children who were being "detained" (or held hostage) in Iraq. During his interviews he stroked the children, and, as a result, prompted worldwide criticism. Fictional hero Jason Bourne, in Robert Ludlum's bestseller *The Bourne Ultimatum*, is able to identify disguised assassin and terrorist "Carlos the Jackal" by the way the villain walks. Advertising researchers observe and record the dilation of the pupil and the eye's path as it surveys a print advertisement to determine the ad's effectiveness. And "Saturday Night Live" humorist Dana Carvey cleverly mimics the nonverbal gestures, facial expressions, and vocal qualities of George Bush in his hilarious impressions of the president. These are but a few of many examples of nonverbal communication that occur around us everyday. You and I produce and process hundreds — perhaps thousands — of nonverbal messages each day. In fact, researcher Albert Mehrabian once estimated that nonverbal communication accounts for over 80 percent of the meaning transferred between people.[1] Usually, these nonverbal messages are part and parcel of the appeals we process in our world of persuasion.

Nonverbal premises in persuasion resemble cultural premises in several ways: both are culturally taught to us, and both are consistent across and within cultures. A major difference between the two is that many nonverbal premises exist at a low level of awareness and aren't readily apparent. Neither are they carefully examined and analyzed. We may sense that a certain persuader seems disreputable and that it may have something to do

with his shifty eyes, but we don't analytically dissect our interaction to find out exactly what it is that causes us to distrust or why. One of the more valuable strategies persuadees can use to deal with the barrage of persuasion aimed at them is to sensitize themselves to some of the nonverbal factors that enter in anytime someone tries to persuade another. This sensitivity serves a dual purpose: It increases the amount of information on which to base decisions, and, more important, it provides "tip-offs" to the persuader's "hidden agenda" and ultimate goals. You see, most nonverbal communication occurs almost instinctively or automatically. It is hard to fake, and even when faked, the persuader's intent seems to "leak" through nonverbal channels.

NONVERBAL CHANNELS

There are several channels through which we can communicate nonverbal meaning. Communication researcher Dale G. Leathers identifies nine nonverbal channels in his book *Successful Nonverbal Communication: Principles and Applications*, including facial expression; eye behavior; bodily communication; proxemics (the use of space); personal appearance; vocalic factors such as voice stress, timbre, and volume; and, finally, tactile communication (the use of touch).[2] Mark Knapp identifies eight channels in his book *Nonverbal Communication in Human Interaction*: the environment (including architecture and furniture), proxemics and territoriality, physical appearance and dress, physical behavior and movement, touching, facial expression, eye behavior, and vocal cues.[3] Other researchers identify similar categories with some, such as Ekman and Friesen, focusing only on various aspects of facial communication.[4]

FIGURE 9.1

What kinds of meaning do you derive from this photograph? How is the meaning communicated? (Photo by AFP. Reprinted by permission of *Newsweek*.)

THE GULF CRISIS
Special Report

Newsweek.

September 3, 1990 : $2.50

HORROR SHOW
Saddam's Prisoners of War

Iraqi TV

Gender differences are the focus of study for some researchers,[5] whereas others study nonverbal cues of deception and the nonverbal behavior of liars.[6] We can't begin to examine all of these fascinating topics in a single chapter, but we can focus on some of them, especially those that affect persuasive messages in a variety of ways. For our purposes, let's use the categories suggested by Leathers as well as considering gender differences in nonverbal communication.

Facial Expression and Eye Behavior

The first nonverbal message channel identified by Leathers is **facial expression** (sometimes called "affect displays") and eye behavior. He claims that the face is "the most important source of nonverbal information."[7] Facial expression is familiar and readily noticed, and subtle nuances in facial expression can make a world of difference in perceived meaning. Such variables as the amount and rate of dilation of the pupil or one's eyeblink rate can communicate a great deal of information about one's attention, emotion, and interest.

Knapp notes that, correctly or not, people often use the face as a measure of personality, judging high foreheads to indicate intelligence, thin lips to indicate conscientiousness, a bulbous nose to indicate drunkenness, and close-together eyes to indicate low intelligence.[8]

LINCOLN-MERCURY DIVISION *Ford*
Buckle Up-Together We Can Save Lives.

GOLDEN
What a bear should be.

FIGURE 9.2

How do you "read" Jack Nicklaus's facial expression in this ad? Happy? Disgusted? (Reprinted by permission of Golden Bear International.)

Leathers identified ten general classes or categories of facial expression (and many more specific kinds of facial meaning), including disgust, happiness, interest, sadness, bewilderment, contempt, surprise, anger, determination, and fear. Among his more specific kinds of expressions, Leathers includes rage, amazement, terror, hate, arrogance, astonishment, stupidity, amusement, pensiveness and belligerence, to name a few.[9] Ekman and Friesen identify only six categories of facial expression on which they found universal researcher agreement, including happiness, sadness, surprise, fear, anger, and disgust.[10] Interestingly, they find that some of these facial expressions are consistent across cultures (for example, 95 percent to 100 percent agreement among American, Brazilian, Chilean, Argentinian, and Japanese subjects on the expression of happiness, but only 54 percent to 85 percent agreement on the expression of fear).[11] The key facial expressions used to convey meaning include the raising or drooping of the eyebrows, smiling or frowning, knitting or relaxing the forehead, closing or widening of the open eye (thus exposing more or less white), wrinkling the nose, pursing the lips, baring the teeth, and dropping of the jaw.[12]

Leathers identifies six functions that the eye serves.[13] One is the *attention function*, indicated by mutual gazing. We have probably noticed some persons who continually look over our shoulder while we are talking, as if they are looking for more interesting possibilities. Such eye behavior serves a *regulatory function*, by indicating when conversation is to begin or stop. When speakers look back at a person or audience, this is generally taken as a signal for them to take their turn talking. Eyes can also serve a *power function*, as when a leader stares at an audience. Persons who watched Adolf Hitler speaking to audiences often remarked on the power expressed in his eyes and by his stares. Eye behavior also serves an *affective function* by indicating positive and negative emotions. You probably know what your parents' eyes look like when they are angry or what the eyes of someone "in love" look like; both are examples of the eyes' affective function. Eyes are also used in

impression formation, as when persons communicate a winning image or a lack of self-esteem. Finally, Leathers notes the *persuasive function* of eye behavior. We rate speakers who maintain eye contact as credible, and we suspect those whose gaze is continually shifting about. If people avert their eyes when talking to us, we assume that they are either shy or are hiding something from us.[14]

Bodily Communication

Bodily nonverbal communication has several dimensions, including *kinesics*, or physical movements of the body, such as gestures, the way one holds one's body (tense or relaxed posture), and how one uses the body in given contexts. For example, Leathers reports that Nelson Rockefeller, a power seeker, had a set of stairs rigged to his office desk so that he could climb up on the desk when he wanted to command attention.[15] Powerful persuaders want to be physically or perceptually "above" their audience. They also demonstrate relaxed but erect posture, dynamic gestures, good eye contact, and a variation in speaking rate and inflection. Powerless persuaders behave more submissively and exhibit lots of body tension, little direct eye contact, "closed" postures (for example, legs and arms crossed), and few gestures.[16]

Knapp identifies several head movements that convey meaning: cocking of the head, tilting or nodding of the head, and the thrusting out of the jaw or the shaking of the head.[17] And of course there are other bodily movements that convey meaning: clenching one's fist, having one's arms akimbo on the waist, and standing in an "open" stance with legs spread apart. These bodily movements can indicate anger, intensity, and degree of commitment or dedication.

In some cases, gestures and bodily movements are emblematic — they stand for a particular meaning. For example, stroking the index finger while pointing it at someone is emblematic of "shame on you," crossed fingers indicate "good luck," and the hitchhiker's closed fist and extended thumb are emblematic of wanting a ride (although the same gesture means "gig 'em" to a student of Texas

A&M). You can probably add to this short list of emblematic gestures and bodily movements.

Proxemic Communication

Proxemic communication (or how one uses physical space) is the fourth category of nonverbal channels in Leathers' system. You have undoubtedly noticed how most people fall silent and don't look at one another when they are in crowded elevators, for example. Edward T. Hall identifies four kinds of space in his book *The Silent Language*:[18]

Public distance. This type of distance is often found in public speaking situations where speakers are fifteen to twenty-five or more feet from their audiences. Informal persuasion probably will not work in these circumstances. Persuaders who try to be informal in a formal situation meet with little success.

Social or formal distance. This type of distance is used in formal but nonpublic situations such as interviews or committee reports. The persuader in these situations, although formal in style, need not be oratorical. Formal distance ranges from about seven to twelve feet between persuader and persuadee. You would never become chummy in this kind of situation (regardless of whether you were persuader or persuadee), yet you would not deliver a "speech" either.

Personal or informal distance. This type of distance is used when two colleagues or friends are discussing a matter of mutual concern. A good example might be when you and your roommate are discussing this class or a problem you share. In these situations, communication is less structured than in the formal situation; both persuadee and persuader are more relaxed and interact often with one another, bringing up and questioning evidence or asking for clarification. Informal distance, in our culture, is about three-and-one-half to four feet—the eye-to-eye distance if you sit at the corner of a teacher's desk as opposed to the formal distance created when you sit across the desk.

Intimate distance. This is the distance people use when they mutter or lovingly whisper messages they do not want others to overhear. Persuasion may or may not occur in these instances; usually the message is one that will not be questioned by the receiver—he or she will nod in agreement, follow the suggestion given, or respond to the question asked. When two communicators are in this kind of close relation to one another, their aims are similar, in all probability. The distance ranges from six to eighteen inches.

How do persuaders use these distance boundaries? Are you and I vulnerable to persuasion using proxemics? The examples that surround us often escape our notice because proxemic communication is transmitted at such a low level of awareness. Take automobile sales as an example. When customers come into a new-car showroom, what would result if the salesperson rushed over to them and within personal or even intimate distance said something like, "What can I do for you folks today?" In all likelihood, the customers would retreat from the showroom or at least from the salesperson, saying something like "Well, we're just looking around." Clever sales representatives stay within public distance of the customer until they get an indication of interest or a signal from the customer that their help would be appreciated. Only then will the salesperson move into informal or even formal distance. The sale could easily be spoiled if the representative moved into intimate distance and said something like "Tell you what I can do for you today."

Look at the advertisements in any popular magazine and you will notice the use of proxemics as a persuasive device. The young adults who "Go For It" in the beer ads are having fun and enjoying one another in personal or intimate space. The upwardly mobile status-seekers in the Players cigarette ads who are in the personal or intimate space and who are having the fun are the ones smoking the Players.

Recently, people in the real-estate business became interested in the communicative power of the correct and strategic use of space. Industry publications discussed questions such as how close the

FIGURE 9.3

Which of Hall's four types of communication distance seems to be operating in this ad? Why do you suppose this distance was used? (Reprinted by permission of Hotel Intercontinental, Chicago.)

real-estate agent should be to the prospective buyer during a tour of a home or whether the agent should lead or follow the buyer. In many other contexts — offices, hospitals, banks, prisons, and factories — serious consideration is given to the use of space as a communicative device or as a communication facilitator. Try to be alert to the uses of space in your life. How have you arranged your room or apartment? Does the arrangement facilitate or deter communication? How do various people with whom you interact use their space? Do foreigners use space differently? You will soon discover how important this nonverbal channel of communication is to persuasion.

Physical Appearance

During a recent faculty externship at an advertising agency, I learned that the agency had just fired a female employee because of her appearance; they simply couldn't expose their clients to her unprofessional and sloppy appearance. And it is always easy to guess what's going on toward the middle of the spring semester when my students come to class "dressed up fit to kill": It is interview time on campus, and everyone knows that appearance sends a message to the interviewer. But **physical appearance** goes much further than just good grooming and proper attire, according to Leathers. For example, his sources maintain that large facial features — nose, ears, and lips — are generally considered unattractive.[19]

Knapp reports other interesting studies regarding physical appearance. For instance, firstborn females who are attractive tend to sit toward the front of the class and make more comments during class. They also tended to get better grades.[20] Attractive females are also more likely to persuade male audiences than unattractive females. You probably wonder what is meant by "attractiveness" in these cases. The research used the same female in both the attractive and unattractive conditions. In the unattractive condition, she wore loose-fitting clothing, had no makeup on, had messy hair, and appeared ungroomed.[21] Another element in physical appearance is bodily attractiveness, according to Leathers. His sources show

that slenderness is considered attractive in females, and waist and hip measurements correlate negatively with ratings of attractiveness (larger-waisted and hippier females are perceived as less attractive).[22] For males, broad shoulders, a well-muscled upper body, and a tapering upper trunk correlate positively with attractiveness ratings.[23] Leathers also found that one's self-image has a lot to do with ratings of attractiveness; if you feel good about yourself, you will probably engage in good grooming and keep your body in good physical condition.

Clothing and adornments such as jewelry also contribute to one's physical appearance. In the case of the dismissed ad agency employee, I learned that she tended to dress too casually for the workplace, and her clothing wasn't always clean or pressed. Her supervisor suggested that I advise students to dress at the level of their supervisor; one rarely makes a mistake by being too well-dressed or groomed. Jewelry also communicates. Think of the different evaluations you might make of a person wearing a Rolex as opposed to a Timex watch or the degree to which gold jewelry can attract your attention. East European businessmen appeared threadbare to me, and I wondered what was cuing that response. After some analysis I realized that none of them had a genuine leather attaché case, and the quality of their shoes rated below that of the specials at el cheapo discount stores.

Artifactual Communication

We humans are probably not so far removed from animals, but there are some differences. Although birds feather their nests with bits of string, straw, hair, and wood, they do it for purely functional reasons: to keep their nests intact and cozy. We humans feather our nests not only for these reasons but also for highly symbolic reasons. The best way of discovering how this happens is to look at your work area or at that of your roommate or spouse. It is not arranged only for work; people feather their nests with objects — **artifacts** — that symbolize their sense of self. Arrangement is also symbolic (certain kinds of people have messy desks,

Who says charm isn't hereditary? We've been helping it along for 172 years. And while change is inevitable, a tradition of quality is our legacy. And yours.

Grandfather, tuxedo from Brooks Brothers formal wear collection, from $495, and exclusive furnishings. *Grandson,* classic navy blazer, $95.

THE MAN IN THE BROOKS BROTHERS SUIT

Brooks Brothers

FIGURE 9.4

Clothing is used to communicate. What is the message being communicated in this ad? (Reprinted by permission of Brooks Brothers Clothing.)

whereas others have extremely neat desks, with each pencil sharpened and papers stacked in neat piles). Our culture has taught us to react in certain ways to the artifacts of others and how they are used. These patterns of responses form premises for persuasion.

A common type of artifactual cosmetology is revealed in the objects surrounding a persuader in a message situation (for example, in a public speech situation, the banners, the bunting, the use of flags, the insignias)—all contributing to the ultimate success (or failure) of the persuasive attempt. Another type of artifact is clothing. What people wear sends signals about what they are like (think of the differences between casual sports clothes and a tuxedo), what they believe or represent (for example, a priest's collar or an army officer's uniform).

Another type of artifact is exemplified in the personal objects surrounding a persuader. Consider how you feel when you go into a doctor's office that has diplomas on the wall—no art, no colorful posters, or any other kind of decoration—just diplomas. What cultural signal do you receive about the kind of person the doctor is likely to be? Compare that with the feeling you have as you enter a college professor's office that has posters or abstract art on the walls. The artifacts symbolize the kind of persuasion you will be likely to hear—in one case, professional, concrete, and probably prescriptive, and in the other, abstract and informal.

Large objects such as furniture also can give off signals. We can expect a certain kind of communication to occur when we are told to sit down at a table and the persuader sits at the opposite side. Persuaders who put a lectern between themselves and the audience will probably engage in a certain kind of communication—formal. If they step out from behind the lectern or walk around while talking, they may well be more informal. Types of furniture can also symbolize certain characteristics. What kinds of persuasion and what kinds of persons would you associate with French Provincial furniture? What kind of persuasion is likely to occur in a room with industrial metal furniture? What kind in a Danish Modern room? Or Early American?

These artifactual messages vary from culture to culture and even from subculture to subculture. Frequently, artifactual communication can make the difference between successful and unsuccessful persuasion. Try to identify the kinds of artifacts that are most persuasive to you. What kind of furniture, what kind of jewelry or accessory might be the added something that persuades you?

Vocalic Communication

Each of us has had the experience of answering the phone and not being quite able to figure out who is calling us. We listen carefully and ask innocuous questions until something the person says matches his or her vocal patterns, and then we recognize who it is and carry on as if we had known all along who was on the other end.

Leathers notes that there is a **semantics of sound** that affects how we respond to a persuader's message. Some of the factors he identifies include: volume or loudness, pitch, rate, vocal quality, clarity of articulation or pronunciation, regularity or intonation pattern, and how one uses silence.[24] These are the elements that make it possible for you to recognize the voice on the phone. More important, they are the vocalic factors that influence you to be or not to be persuaded by a given source, and they can indicate a lot about a persuader and his or her emotions, goals, and sincerity.

Monotonic persuaders bore the audience and deflect most of their persuasiveness. High-pitched voices indicate excitement; sometimes low-pitched but tense voices indicate anger. Rate of speech can indicate nervousness or confidence. Vocal quality can communicate a number of things: breathy voices in females, for example, communicate a stereotype of simplicity and shallowness, whereas breathy voices in males may indicate that the speaker is effeminate. Screeching or tense voices indicate stress and concern. Nasality, an undesirable vocalic feature, is often associated with being stuck up and maybe even sissified. Persons who articulate poorly and who mispronounce words generally lose some of their credibility and effectiveness.[25]

Knapp reports research that indicates that people can fairly reliably identify certain stereotypes from vocal cues. These include such characteristics as masculinity/femininity, age, enthusiasm/apathy, activeness/laziness, and good-looking/ugly. He also reports research that identifies the following correlations: breathiness in males indicates youth and an artistic nature; a thin voice in females indicated social, physical, and emotional insecurity; vocal flatness indicates sluggishness for both males and females; and nasality is associated with a number of undesirable traits in both males and females.[26] He also reports that most listeners are quite sensitive to vocal cues.

It is clear from the foregoing discussion that one feature of oral persuasion that receivers must pay attention to is the vocalic qualities of communication coming from the persuader.

Tactile Communication

Some of the more important nonverbal message carriers are the ways in which and the degree to which people **touch** one another. We know that infants genuinely *need* to be touched and cuddled. We also know that this need doesn't diminish as the child matures, but that in our culture the number, type, and duration of touches a child gets are greatly reduced as he or she matures. Children may substitute other kinds of touches for the maternal or paternal touches they received from their parents: socking a pal, shoving someone, holding hands with someone of the opposite sex, and so on.

We know that there are gender-related differences in the use of touch. Women are more likely to use touch to communicate than are men. In fact, the average woman touches someone else about twelve times per day, whereas the average male touches someone only eight times a day.[27] Touches by both males and females are more likely to be with a person of the opposite sex, which is the reverse of what occurs in some other cultures. Touching is perfectly acceptable between two men on a football field or between two grade-school chums or between a man and a woman.

In Western culture, touch between men generally is limited to shaking hands or back-slapping. Persuaders who are too "touchy" with persons around them (for example, with fellow candidates

for office, with other people on interview shows, or with other members of the board of directors) are likely to offend not only the person touched but also the persons observing the touch. Credibility can be drastically undermined if persuaders misread a relationship and respond inappropriately with touch.

Leathers makes the point that our society, for the most part, is a noncontact society, with touch being noticeably absent in public places, particularly between men. We probably would not accept the vice-president hugging and kissing the president on the president's return from abroad, yet that is perfectly acceptable in the Soviet Union and many other countries of the world. These norms for the use of touch, Leathers notes, usually relate to two general factors: the part of the body that is touched and the demographic characteristics of the interactants (age, gender, social class, race, and status).[28] He also reports that research shows the head, shoulders, and arms to be the most frequently touched parts of the body, with other parts of the body being more or less "off limits" to public touch, and that the use of touch is more frequent among minorities.[29] In terms of persuasion, research shows that persuaders who touch persuadees are the most successful persuaders.[30]

Touch seems to be a good way to convey special kinds of emotional persuasion such as empathy, warmth, and reassurance. I once worked with a group of firefighters in a communication training program. For this group, the only acceptable touch from another male was the handshake or backslap. I, however, wanted them to understand the importance of touch as a communicative device. A firefighter must sometimes calm frantic men, women, and children to get them out of a burning building. But the firefighters resisted rehearsing any kinds of touches. Not until we played a game in which one of the men was trapped and ordered to break out of a circle formed by the others linking arms and waists did the group begin to accept the idea of touching. The game gave them a culturally acceptable way to hold one another. Once past this initial barrier, we could talk about how touch could be used to calm people in crisis situations. The laying on of hands used in some religions is sometimes given credit for conversions; it is possible that touch is persuasive enough to prompt people to come forward and convert.

Sometimes touch is extremely important in facilitating certain kinds of communication. Terminal cancer patients, for example, need more touch than less ill patients, according to some experts. Touch helps to express sympathy when one attends a funeral service. Recent studies showed filmic evidence of the importance of touch. Strangers were asked to give information to a researcher who was being secretly filmed on a street corner. In half of the cases, the researcher lightly touched the stranger before saying, "Excuse me, but I'm sort of lost. Can you tell me where . . . ?" The researcher got much more information and even conversation when using the light touch. Observe the printed ads in magazines. Look at the kinds of touches used in them. You will discover that the persuasive potential of touch has many dimensions.

Some touches are taboo. Several taboo touches identified by researchers Stanley Jones and Elaine Yarborough are: (1) touching strangers; (2) touching that inflicts pain, as when someone touches someone else's sunburn; (3) touching that interferes with another's activities or conversation; (4) touching that moves others aside; (5) playful touching that is too aggressive, as in mock wrestling or pinching; and (6) what they call "double-whammy" touching, in which touch is used to emphasize a negative point (as in touching someone's belly when mentioning that they have put on weight).

As you continue to improve your abilities as a receiver, one of the nonverbal channels of communication that you will want to observe closely is the use of touch, whether it is the punctuation that emphasizes the first meeting one has with a stranger, the closing of a business deal, the empathic sensitivity one has for another, or the assurance that can help move people out of a dangerous situation.

CHRONEMICS: THE USE OF TIME

Although Leathers has not researched the nonverbal messages conveyed by how we use and observe time, there is good evidence to suggest that our use of time sends many signals about how we evaluate others. A saying in our culture goes, "Time is money — don't waste it!" Time can communicate many messages to others. Let's suppose that you have set a time and reserved a place for a meeting of a work group in one of your classes. Because you are arranging the meeting, you show up ten minutes early to make sure things will go well. You want to be sure that there are enough chairs and appropriate materials for the meeting. A few minutes before the meeting is to start, two members of the group arrive and begin to chat. Right on time, to the minute, comes another group member. Now only two people are missing. You probably will say something like "Let's wait a few minutes before starting — people might have had a hard time getting served at the cafeteria." After five minutes, one of your missing persons shows up and you start the meeting, promising the rest of the group that you will see to it that the missing member gets the information. Nearly a half hour after the meeting has started, the missing member arrives with no excuses for her lateness. What has each person communicated to you? In our culture, it is permissible to arrive at a meeting up to five or six minutes late, but arrive later than that and you'd better have a good excuse, such as a flat tire, a stalled elevator, or a speeding ticket. By coming late, you "persuade" the others that you really don't care much about the appointment, that you are a thoughtless person, and that you are probably a pretty arrogant prima donna. If, on the other hand, you are invited to a party, be sure to show up at least forty-five minutes late if it is a college party and at least twenty minutes late if it is, say, a business cocktail party. Only losers show up on time at parties. If you show up on time, the host and hostess may still be grooming themselves or putting the final touches on the place settings. If you really want to put people in their place, make sure they have to wait to get in to see you — a favorite trick of some college professors. On one campus, a student must wait at least five minutes for an "instructor," ten minutes for a "professor," and twenty minutes for a "Dr." before assuming there will be no class. So time is not only money; it is often also status. Most important, begin to observe how time works in your culture or subculture, and don't be surprised if it doesn't operate the same way in other cultures or even in subcultures within our culture.

GENDER DIFFERENCES IN NONVERBAL COMMUNICATION

Particularly in the past decade, researchers have investigated gender differences in nonverbal communication. Some of their findings involve nonverbal communication in one of the channels previously discussed. For example, in a 1989 study of attitudes toward the use of touch, researchers found that women are significantly more comfortable with touch than are men, and that such levels of "touch comfort" are signs of a greater level of socialization.[31] Based on her review of the literature, Brenda Major noted significant gender differences in how one touches others and in how one receives such touches, and found that these differences are exhibited very shortly after birth.[32] Whereas men tend to initiate touching in cross-gender encounters, they are less likely to initiate touch in same-gender encounters. Women, on the other hand, are less hung up about touching other women. Although touch often cues warmth and intimacy (especially among women), it can also communicate power or status relationships. Here, men tend to use touch more frequently, indicating that they perceive themselves to be superior.[33] Major also reported on gender differences in reactions to touch. If, for example, the toucher is of the same status as the touchee, women react more positively and men more negatively, particularly when the toucher is a woman. Major concludes that, overall, women tend to react more positively to touch than do males and that this probably stems from the fact that girls are touched more frequently from birth on and are perceived as being more fragile and passive than boys.

Porter and Geis wondered whether gender and nonverbal communication were related to who was most often perceived of as the leader in group situations.[34] They found that in both all-male and all-female groups, geographical position at the head of the table is the best predictor of leadership. In mixed-gender groups, males emerge as the leader if they sit in the leadership position, but the opposite is true for women.[35]

Ellyson, Dovidio, and Fehr investigated dominance in men and women as it relates to visual behavior.[36] They found that dominance is usually indicated by what they called "look/speak" rather than "look/listen" behavior (that is, attempting to dominate by speaking rather than listening when catching the eyes of others). Further, they found no gender-related factors; that is, if women use the "look/speak" strategy, they are just as likely to be evaluated as dominant as males who use the same strategy.

Judy Hall found that women have more expressive faces than men, and smile and laugh more often than men, especially when they are in all-female groups.[37] She speculates that smiling and laughing may be seen as unmasculine, and that this tends to discourage males from exhibiting these behaviors.

Regarding "gaze" and "gaze holding," Hall found that women tend to gaze more at other persons than do males, and that women are more uncomfortable than men when they cannot see the person being spoken to. They also seem to be gazed at more frequently than men (which makes perfect sense to me). Hall hints that gaze differences between males and females exist because females are perceived as having more warmth than males. Also, males avoid the gazes of other males to bypass the confrontational implications of such gazing.[38]

Regarding proxemics, Hall finds that men maintain greater distances from others when in conversation, and that women are approached more closely than men.[39] Women tend to face more directly toward the person with whom they are interacting.[40] When given the choice of sitting adjacent to or across from others, men tend to sit in the "across" position, whereas women prefer the "adjacent" position.[41] Finally, females are also more approachable than males, and Hall attributes this to real or perceived "warmth, affiliativeness, and/or size," rather than any perception of lower status, as is the case when gender is not a variable.[42] She also found that women initiated touching more than men. Hall speculates that this may be due to women's appreciation for being touched more, and that there may be gender-related differences for various kinds of touch (for example, where on the body, how emphatic the touch, and so on).[43]

Regarding body movement and position, Hall found a paucity of research on which to base many generalizations. However, it does appear that men are more relaxed than women; more physically expansive (for example, spreading arms and legs, leaning back in chairs with legs forward, and so on), and they are more restless (for example, fidgeting, playing with objects, and shifting the body in various ways).[44] Another difference is that whereas women tend to carry things in front of their chest, men carry things at their side.[45]

Hall finds several gender-related differences in the use of the voice in nonverbal ways. Men, for example, seem to be less fluent than women, make more verbal errors, and use more vocalized pauses such as "uh" or "um."[46] Women's voices tend to have higher pitches, even though their vocal mechanism permits them to use lower ones. At the same time, women's voices have more variability in pitch, are more musical, and more expressive than men's voices.[47] Women's voices are also softer than men's voices, and, on a global basis, women's voices are judged to be *more* positive, pleasant, honest, meek, respectful, delicate, enthusiastic, and anxious and *less* confident, domineering, and awkward. Male voices, on the other hand, tend to be demanding, blunt, dominant, forceful, and militant.[48]

Using an entirely different perspective and methodology, Jean Umiker-Sebeok studied women as they appear in magazine advertisements.[49] Among other things, she found that in ads showing women in a professional role (for example, wearing a doctor's smock and taking someone's blood pressure, or dressed in a suit at a business conference), their hair is always in place, they always wear makeup, their posture and gestures are feminine, and the ad's setting is usually "feminized" using houseplants, floral arrangements, organza curtains, or mirrors. Umiker-Sebeok notes that the end result is women who are dressed *for* someone — usually a man — and defined, in the words of Roland Barthes, as "entirely constituted by the gaze of man."[50]

Umiker-Sebeok's major findings relate to how women are depicted at each of five life stages: infancy and childhood, adolescence, young adulthood, middle age, and old age and senility.

Ads depict gender differences beginning in the toddler stage. Females are depicted as being interested in appearance; they are smaller than males appearing in the same ads; they are subordinate and passive; they are rounder; and they are emotional, displaying smiles, laughter, fear, surprise, innocence, and dismay.[51] In childhood, females are rarely depicted away from home in the "rat race" or in a natural wilderness, whereas boys frequently are. Shopping seems to be one of the few "away from home" settings in which female children appear, and then they are usually seen being helped by a kindly older male. They are rarely pictured in independent roles; rather, they usually are seen close to Mom and doing things in the kitchen, the laundry, or flower garden. Umiker-Sebeok speculates that these settings associate female children with productivity and fertility. Fathers and sons, on the other hand, are more frequently depicted outside the home enjoying some sort of competitive activity: sports, contests, or daring adventures.[52]

In adolescence, females are depicted in extremes, vacillating between independence and being protected, usually by Dad now. They might be seen in or away from the home, trying on roles and the accompanying "costumes." They seem to be in a second infancy, with soft, hairless complexions, pink cheeks, rounded body contours, and wide-eyes as they sleep, stroke themselves, or smile demurely at the camera while they lick or suck something. If they are associated with athletics, female adolescents are usually in an auxiliary role, such as that of cheerleader.[53]

In young adulthood, females are depicted as seeking independence along one of two "paths": the glamour and sophistication path or the wholesome, girl-next-door path. They will be shown as either young, beautiful, and narcissistic women or somewhat older but happy housewives, presumably caring for a family. If a young woman is on the glamourous and sophisticated path, she may choose an aggressive lifestyle (posing in an aggressive male stance, fists on hips, chin held high,

FIGURE 9.5

The "glamourous and sophisticated" female is
depicted here. (Reprinted by permission of Carson
Pirie Scott.)

FIGURE 9.8

This wholesome "girl next door" is "owned" and "protected" by her man in this photo from an ad by Aquascutum. (Reprinted by permission of the Aquascutum Shop.)

and staring at the camera, perhaps with one foot propped up with the knee at a right angle — a male phallic display posture). She might, however, appear appealing and alluring (for example, kneeling or sitting, head tilted to one side, and smiling). If she is seen on the job, her office is "feminized," as previously noted; she might be sitting on the edge of her desk or standing in a doorway or at the outline of buildings, which Freud thought symbolized the womb. If she opts for the wholesome role, she is depicted as a pretty doll in a shop window, presenting herself for her hubby's approval or involved in courtship. In this life stage, men look at women more often than women gaze at men. Women gaze off into the distance with their hair blown back, eyes closed, perhaps involved in a fantasy or daydream — often about a male — as in Chanel perfume ads. If pictured with a male, he is holding her hand, and she is generally being protected by the male to whom she "belongs." She is almost always positioned lower than the male:

seated while he stands, shorter, or lying down. In courtship, she is a highly polished object who is being "traded" from her father to her husband. As a bride, she is innocent, angelic, vulnerable, and childish as she is "given away" by her dad. The groom usually dresses and stands like dad during the exchange. The two most common honeymoon settings are the bathroom and the bedroom. In bathrooms, the groom is in the bath watching the bride disrobe, or bride and groom are sharing the tub. In the bedroom, the male reclines on the bed waiting for the bride, who stands nearby in a negligée that resembles a bridal gown.[54]

Umiker-Sebeok found that middle-aged females are depicted as awkward, bumbly, somewhat overweight, and sometimes comical. Usually the middle-aged female is unattractive, but if she is attractive, she is featured because she doesn't look her age. The middle-aged female is often shown caring for a pet — a substitute child — and is pictured in the home more often than away from

"He'll never wear out. He has no moving parts!"

FIGURE 9.7

Which stage of a woman's life is depicted here?
(Reprinted by permission of *Saturday Review*.)

FIGURE 9.8

Which socioeconomic class is shown here?
(Reproduced with the permission of Kraft General
Foods, Inc.)

it. Again, if she is away from home, she is often shopping. If the middle-aged female is upper-middle class, she will be more angular, thinner, and will probably wear glasses as she engages in some information-seeking activity such as talking on the telephone or reading. She might offer women advice about personal-hygiene products. If she is lower-middle class, she will be plumper, more submissive, serving homemade food, or offering advice about housekeeping duties such as cleaning, cooking, or the laundry. When she talks to hubby, she frequently is discussing health-related topics such as high-fiber or low-sodium diets. She is usually in a servant/master relationship with her husband.[55]

In old age and senility, both males and females undergo radical changes: their hair turns to silver and they "return to the earth" by moving from the city to the country, where they like sitting on the porch, walking in nature, or gardening. Machines (even cars) are rare. Everything is peaceful and stable. Grandma and Grandpa give instructions in cooking or whittling, tend to look like one another, and frequently fall asleep while babysitting the grandchildren. They represent the values of stability and the home.[56]

Thus, even our life stages are reflected by nonverbal cues, and we have become culturally trained to read these cues, even in advertisements. In fact the nonverbal cues in an ad may be more persuasive than the verbal messages in the ad.

DIALECT

Dialect, or one's pronunciation and usage, is culture-bound and often indicates one's socioeconomic or regional background. We learn dialect culturally. It can communicate many things about us and can affect our persuasion too. Many of my students come from Chicago or its suburbs — often from the South Side. They get angry with me when I tell some of them to stop "talking like steel-workers." They do not hear themselves saying "dis" for "this" and "dat" for "that" and "dem" for "them." Yet they will be discriminated against if they keep their dialect. At the same time, others

from the North Side and some suburbs have another dialect that may cause equal problems for them. They say "Dubbie" for "Debbie," "Shovie" for "Chevy," and "newahht" for "north." Of course, it would be easy to document the kind of discrimination that occurs when black or Spanish dialect is used. Be aware of your responses to various dialects, and see whether people respond to your dialect in certain ways. I still have a Minnesota dialect and get certain responses because of my frequent use of "Yup" and "You betcha." People start looking for hayseeds in my hair.

Communication professor Norman Heap suggested a way to look at the influence of dialect.[57] He observed that we tend to regard dialect as signaling educational background and communication context, resulting in a four-category system:

Formal context/educated speaker. This category is typified by proper pronunciation and usage, such as that used in the courtroom, in governmental bodies, and on TV news programs.

Informal context/educated speaker. This category includes proper pronunciation accompanied by slang usages, which signal the informal context. It includes localisms like my "You betcha" or profanity. Once this usage is exposed in formal contexts it is sometimes viewed as unacceptable, as was the case with the release of Nixon's taped conversations during the Watergate debacle.

Formal context/uneducated speaker. This category is marked by attempts at proper pronunciation and usage, such as might be heard when an uneducated person testifies in court or at some sort of governmental hearing. It is like the custodian saying at an elegant dinner party, "This spoon is entirely too large for my mouth," or like the student's letter from Chapter 4. The persuaders are trying *too hard* to sound correct.

Informal context/uneducated speaker. This category includes pronunciation and usage such as we might expect in steel mills: the "dese" and "dem" and "dose" pronuncia-

FIGURE 9.9

Which social class and life-style are depicted here? (Printed by permission of the Norman Rockwell

Family Trust. Copyright © 1943 the Norman Rockwell Family Trust.)

tions. These will vary from locale to locale, but usually are associated with blue-collar job settings or informal outings. Educated speakers can lose credibility by being too formal or correct in such settings. Imagine the college professor asking the salmon snagger during the fall run: "The salmon is an andronomous species, isn't it — I mean it atrophies after the spawning run, doesn't it?"

Thus, although people are entitled to use their own dialect, remember that dialect signals a variety of meanings, including one's background, regional origins, and the context that is presumably in effect.

USE OF NONVERBAL TACTICS

One thing receivers must keep in mind is that nonverbal message carriers can be manipulated by persuaders in a process that Erving Goffman called **impression management**.[58] This involves using powerful verbal and also nonverbal signals to convince the audience that the source is a certain kind of person. For example, noted defense attorney Clarence Darrow once tried a case in a town in Idaho where the cultural values were quite different from those in his native Chicago. Thus he chose to wear a plaid wool shirt in the courtroom and to speak with a slight Western accent. President Carter managed our impressions of him by wearing jeans and workshirts, cardigan sweaters, and other casual clothes in the White House. President Reagan used a different set of cues when he wore a blue business suit to the inaugural instead of the traditional tuxedo and top hat.

The use of clothing to communicate nonverbally in impression management is a popular topic in the corporate world. Jacqueline Murray, a clothing consultant to the Dayton Hudson Corporation, also pioneered Dayton Hudson's in-house personal shopping and wardrobe-planning services. In her book *The Power of Dress*, Murray provides a number of case studies to demonstrate the use of dress. For example, at Electronic Data Systems ("cowboy capitalist" H. Ross Perot's company) everyone

has a military look: clean-shaven face; shiny, black, plain-toed shoes; white shirts and dark suits; and army haircuts.[59]

Murray identifies three categories of dress: *corporate dress* (most often used by bankers, attorneys, and executives), *communication dress* (most often used by persons in sales, marketing, education, personnel, or new, high growth industries), and *creative dress* (used most frequently by interior decorators, commercial artists, people in advertising, some retailers, such as boutique owners, and entrepreneurs). Corporate dress is simple in line, shape, and design; tends to be tailored; features gray and blue colors for suits and off-white or light blue for shirts and blouses; and uses fabrics such as silks, herringbones, tweeds, and flannels in suits or dresses and plain cottons, wools, or linens in shirts and blouses. Communication dress features suits and dresses that are practical, relaxed, semitraditional, as well as blazers and sports coats. Communicators use a mix of colors for their blouses and shirts; are willing to wear stripes or relaxed prints; and choose fabrics such as knits, loose or bulky weaves, and fabrics preferred by the corporate types. Creative dress tends to be loose fitting, with elongated line and exaggerated design in both suits and dresses and blouses and shirts. The preferred colors in this category are striking, dramatic colors, as well as understated taupes, peaches, and basics. Although some may question Murray's conclusions, few would argue that dress is unimportant as a nonverbal channel of communication.

OTHER NONVERBAL MESSAGES

Eye movements and other movements of the head can also communicate. We are all aware of the negative impression we get of persons whose eyes are continuously moving or who "can't look you in the eye" for more than a brief moment. Completely different meaning can come about from what is called "gaze holding" or maintaining eye contact with another person. Usually this conveys sexual interest. Even the *rate* of eyeblinks can communicate. Vance Packard reports in *The Hidden*

Persuaders that grocery shoppers' eyeblinks slow down as they proceed up and down the aisles — to the point that they are almost mesmerized, approaching the early stages of hypnotism.

There are other movements and uses of the body that carry nonverbal meaning. Albert Scheflen, a researcher in the use of gestures during psychotherapy, found that when a psychiatrist uses what was later called "the bowl gesture," patients often open up and revealed more about themselves and their problems. We are familiar with the use of this gesture in persuasion: It is the logo for a large insurance company — that's right, "You're in good hands with Allstate."

People can use their bodies to invite or inhibit communication. Notice the two configurations in Figure 9.10. In triad A, the body positions of the three persons would *inhibit* a fourth person from joining in the conversation, whereas in triad B, the body positions *invite* participation. The use of the body to discourage communication or interaction could be called "blocking" behavior, and the use of the body to encourage communication or interaction could be called "inviting" behavior. Scheflen came to call these and other nonverbal invitations or blocks "quasi-courtship behavior" when he observed the behaviors in pairs of persons of opposite genders.

Related to the use of the body to block or invite communication is the use of objects such as furniture, piles of books on a library table, a podium, and so on, to either encourage or discourage communication. A curious example was related to me by a colleague. The incidence of violence on the New York City subway system increased radically a number of years ago when the folio newspaper then being published went on strike. Apparently, many persons had been using the newspaper to "block" themselves from fellow passengers by holding it up in front of their faces. When the paper was no longer available to discourage interaction, there were more opportunities for confrontation to occur, which resulted in the increase in violent interchanges.

There are additional uses of body movement in communication. For example, research shows that lifting or lowering one's chin at the ends of sentences serves as a signal that the person is intending to continue to speak or that he or she is done speaking and someone else can join in. And of course, we are all aware of the communicative power of head-nodding, winking, and various obscene gestures, which may vary in meaning from culture to culture.

As you begin to observe the nonverbal messages occurring around you, you will discover

Top View

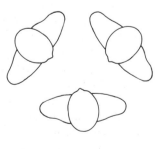

Triad A

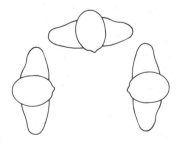

Triad B

FIGURE 9.10

Notice the difference between the body positions of the persons in each triad. Which is involved in "blocking" behavior?

an almost infinite number of potential nonverbal message carriers: the color of a room or of one's clothing; seating and furniture arrangements; who reaches for the check at a restaurant first; nervous gestures or twitches; volume, stress, and tone of verbal messages; breathiness when talking (which is supposed to indicate sexiness in women, but which may communicate something entirely different in males); the use of pauses; and curious habits, such as cracking one's knuckles or doodling, which may communicate subconscious intentions. Even the sense of smell seems to be an important carrier of information.

We are all aware of, for example, the person who uses too much cologne or aftershave lotion or someone who has body odor, but apparently we can detect more subtle odors as well. A real-estate agent I know asks persons who are trying to sell their homes to keep a loaf of raised bread dough in the refrigerator. When a potential buyer wants to be taken through the house, the agent phones ahead and tells the owner to put the bread in the oven. When the agent and potential buyer arrive forty-five minutes later, the smell of fresh bread lingers in the air. What might it communicate about the house? A similar tactic is to have a fire burning in the fireplace when a house is being shown to prospective buyers. In fact, there is some indication that each of us may have a dominant nostril in the same way that we have a dominant hand or eye and that we turn our dominant nostril slightly when we enter a new room, "smelling" if there is hostility, danger, or more comfortable "smells" coming from those in the room. I'm sure many of you have walked into a room and sensed a tension "in the air" as the phrase goes. This may be the olfactory channel of nonverbal communication at work.

REVIEW AND CONCLUSION

By this time, you know that the world of the persuadee in an information age is not an easy one. There are so many things to be aware of: the persuader's self-revelation using language and stylistic choices; the internal or process premises operating within each of us; the interactive rules

for content premises; and the world of nonverbal premises, which can be communicated by a variety of channels such as facial expression, eye behavior, and bodily communication (gestures and posture; proxemics, or the use of space; physical appearance and the use of artifacts; vocalic communication; tactile communication, or the use of touch; chronemics, or the use of time; gender and life-stage differences; dialect; and dress and other nonverbal communicators). These premises do not make receivers' tasks any easier, especially since these premises operate at particularly low levels of awareness and frequently are overlooked as we analyze persuasion. You will have to train yourself to be more sensitive to nonverbal elements in the persuasive process, not only so you can skillfully use these channels in your own communication, but, more important, so you can use a knowledge of nonverbal tactics to more accurately decode the real meaning of the messages aimed at you every day.

QUESTIONS FOR FURTHER THOUGHT

1. How often do you touch others? Try to increase the number of touches you use and observe the responses of others. Does the increase cause a different effect? If so, how?

2. With what artifacts do you surround yourself? What do they mean to you? (Some students have reported that the first thing they do after unpacking for dormitory living is to purchase "conversation pieces" or artifacts that symbolize themselves.) What about your roommate? What artifacts does he or she use? What do they symbolize about him or her? What about your family members' artifacts?

3. What is kinesics? Give some examples and explain how and what they communicate.

4. What is "blocking" behavior? Give examples from your everyday life.

5. What is the predominant dialect where you live? Are there any other dialects that you

can identify in your community? What effects do they have on people's attitudes and behaviors?

6. What are some of the facial expressions you find easiest to identify? Which are most difficult?

7. Which of your friends uses gestures most effectively? What does he or she do that makes the gestures so effective?

8. What are some examples of the ways physical appearance communicates in your world? What are some examples of how physical appearance identifies a contemporary musical artist or group?

9. Give examples of how chronemics operates in your life — on campus, in the dorm, in the classroom, and at home.

10. Identify some of the gender differences in nonverbal communication as they appear in contemporary advertising.

NOTES

1. Albert Mehrabian, *Silent Messages* (Belmont, CA: Wadsworth, 1971).

2. Dale G. Leathers, *Successful Nonverbal Communication: Principles and Applications* (New York: Macmillan, 1986).

3. Mark L. Knapp, *Nonverbal Communication in Human Interaction* (New York: Holt, Rinehart & Winston, 1978).

4. Paul Ekman and Wallace V. Friesen, *Unmasking the Face: A Guide to Recognizing Emotions from Facial Expression* (Englewood Cliffs, N.J.: Prentice-Hall, 1975).

5. Judith A. Hall, *Nonverbal Sex Differences: Communication Accuracy and Expressive Style* (Baltimore, Md.: Johns Hopkins University Press, 1984); and Clara Mayo and Nancy M. Henley, *Gender and Nonverbal Behavior* (New York: Springer-Verlag, 1981).

6. See, for example, Mark L. Knapp and Mark E. Comadena, "Telling It Like It Isn't: A Review of Theory and Research on Deceptive Communications," *Human Communication Research*, vol. 5, pp. 270–285; or Janice E. Hocking and Dale G.

Leathers, "Nonverbal Indicators of Deception: A New Theoretical Perspective," *Communication Monographs*, vol. 47, pp. 119–131.

7. Leathers, p. 19.

8. Knapp, p. 264.

9. Leathers, p. 30

10. *Ibid.*, p. 34.

11. Ekman and Friesen, p. 22.

12. *Ibid.*, p. 26.

13. *Ibid.*, pp. 37–46.

14. *Ibid.*, pp. 42–45.

15. *Ibid.*, p. 64.

16. *Ibid.*, p. 65.

17. Knapp, pp. 200–212.

18. Edward T. Hall, *The Silent Language* (Garden City, N.Y.: Doubleday, 1959); See also his *The Hidden Dimension* (Garden City, N.Y.: Doubleday, 1966).

19. Leathers, p. 92.

20. Knapp, pp. 153–154.

21. *Ibid.*, p. 155.

22. Leathers, pp. 93–94.

23. *Ibid.*, p. 94.

24. *Ibid.*, p. 115.

25. *Ibid.*, pp. 115–118.

26. Knapp, pp. 330–333.

27. Ronald Kotulak, "Researchers Decipher a Powerful 'Language,'" *The Chicago Tribune*, April 7, 1985, sec. 6, pp. 1 and 4.

28. Leathers, p. 136.

29. *Ibid.*, p. 137.

30. Kotulak, p. 1.

31. D. Fromme, W. Jaynes, D. Taylor, E. Hanold, J. Daniell, R. Rountree, and M. Frome, "Nonverbal Behavior and Attitude Towards Touch," *Journal of Nonverbal Behavior*, vol. 13, 1989, pp. 3–13.

32. Brenda Major, "Gender Patterns in Touching Behavior," in *Gender and Nonverbal Behavior*, Clara Mayo and Nancy Henley, eds. (New York: Springer-Verlag, 1984), pp. 15–37.

33. *Ibid.*, p. 24.

34. Natalie Porter and Florence Geis, "Women and Nonverbal Leadership Cues: When Seeing Is Not Believing," in Mayo and Henley, pp. 39–61.

35. *Ibid.*, p. 58.

36. Steve Ellyson, John Dovidio, and B. J. Fehr, "Visual Behavior and Dominance in Women and Men," in Mayo and Henley, pp. 63–79.

37. Judy A. Hall, *Nonverbal Sex Differences: Communication Accuracy and Expressive Style* (Baltimore, Md.: Johns Hopkins University Press, 1984).

38. *Ibid.*, p. 83.

39. *Ibid.*, p. 104.

40. *Ibid.*

41. *Ibid.*

42. *Ibid.*, pp. 100–102.

43. *Ibid.*, pp. 117–118.

44. *Ibid.*, pp. 120–123.

45. *Ibid.*, p. 125.

46. *Ibid.*, pp. 130–132.

47. *Ibid.*, p. 133.

48. *Ibid.*, pp. 134–135.

49. Jean Umiker-Sebeok, "The Seven Ages of Women: A View from American Magazine Advertisements," in Mayo and Henley, pp. 208–252.

50. *Ibid.*, p. 210. The Barthes quote is taken from Roland Barthes, *Mythologies* (London: Paladin Books, 1973).

51. *Ibid.*, pp. 212–213.

52. *Ibid.*, pp. 214–215.

53. *Ibid.*, pp. 218–225.

54. *Ibid.*, pp. 226–238.

55. *Ibid.*, pp. 238–244.

56. *Ibid.*, pp. 244–247.

57. Norman A. Heap, Trenton State College, private correspondence.

58. Erving Goffman, *The Presentation of Self in Everyday Life* (New York: Anchor Books, 1957).

59. All of Murray's observations are drawn from Jacqueline Murray, *The Power of Dress* (Minneapolis, MN: Semiotics Press, 1989).

III

APPLICATIONS OF PERSUASIVE PREMISES

In Part I, we examined some of the definitions of persuasion and the underlying theoretical foundations for persuasion with a special emphasis on language. We focused on receivers and noted how we could use a knowledge of persuasion to process critically the persuasion that bombards us every day. In Part II, we explored sources for the various premises that persuaders use to develop their pitches. These are the unstated but powerful first premises in the enthymeme, a form of argument in which persuadees provide a missing part (usually a major premise), thereby participating in their own persuasion.

In Part III, we will look at applications of these theories and audience-held premises in a variety of contexts. We will maintain the receiver focus, always asking how our analyses of these applications can assist us to make critical judgments about whether to buy, to elect, to join, to quit, to give, to believe in, or to support.

In Chapter 10, we will look at a familiar application—the persuasive campaign—a series of messages designed to lead receivers to specific ends. In Chapter 11, we will shift our focus to the source of persuasion and discuss how to become a persuader. In addition to helping you persuade others, what you learn can help you process critically the persuasive messages aimed at you. Knowing what kind of proof or organization a persuader is using will help you judge the validity of the message.

In Chapter 12, we will explore the most dominant channels for persuasive messages — the mass media. Mass-mediated messages range from the brief but influential TV or radio commercial to more extensive advertisements, speeches, documentaries, and news reports. We will discover that the media of our time may be the determining factor in deciding on what problems we, as a cul-

ture, concentrate. They may even be taking over the role of the family or parent in shaping our values. We will ask how these mass-media applications affect receivers.

In Chapter 13, we will explore the ways in which propaganda, foreign and domestic, operates to persuade us and to shape our opinions. In Chapter 14, we will investigate a particular form of persuasion — print and electronic advertisements — and how they have come to dominate contemporary American society.

∎

CHAPTER 10

The Persuasive Campaign or Movement

For many years the study of persuasion focused mainly on the public speech and the "single-shot" perspective on persuasion. That is, persuaders, researchers, students, and teachers overlooked the impact of artistically coordinated multiple messages that ultimately lead to product adoption, voting decisions, or support of various kinds of movements. This overlooked kind of persuasion — campaign or social movement persuasion — was not carefully examined by communication researchers until the late 1960s. In fact, the Political Communication Division of the International Communication Association wasn't established until the 1970s.

Political scientists had, for the most part, also ignored the communication dimensions of political campaigns with the possible exception of research on campaign financing. They remained focused on the nature and structure of government. Meanwhile, most of the research done on campaigns in advertising or marketing departments was proprietary — it belonged to the client — who naturally did not want to make it public or divulge it in any other way. And in advertising departments at colleges and universities, only a few persons each year received a Ph.D.; in fact, even today fewer than twenty institutions in the country offer a doctorate in advertising. Furthermore, this handful of experts could garner much higher salaries doing research for an agency or within a corporation or even on a "freelance" basis than they could earn at a research-oriented university. Only rather recently have we in communication devoted teaching and research efforts to the persuasive campaign. Yet it is probably the most prevalent form of persuasion today. Our purpose in Chapter 10 will be to look at three general types of persuasive campaigns: *product-oriented campaigns, person- or candidate-oriented campaigns,* and *idea or ideologically oriented campaigns.* We will also look at these types of campaign from several perspectives.

Of course, a single chapter can't possibly cover all there is to say about persuasive campaigns. All that can be hoped for is that you become more aware of campaign persuasion as you receive it and as you produce it. Yes, as we produce it, because as individuals we wage our own campaigns — for the purchase of a new appliance, for a desired change in the behavior of someone we know or love, on behalf of some organization we belong to, and on other public and personal issues.

The impact of advancing technology in computers and video (among other areas) on a campaigner's ability to convey powerfully persuasive messages cannot be underestimated. We can only imagine what a changed world we face in the 1990s. As we approach the year 2000, the number of campaigns will increase — and so will the sophistication of those campaigns. With satellite and cable television options increasing, costs for media time will drop, and market segmentation will become much easier to accomplish.[1] It will be critical to understand something about persuasive campaigns for products, persons/candidates, and ideas in order to avoid being completely taken in.

THE ROLE OF COMMUNICATION IN CAMPAIGNS

Campaigns and mass movements are classic examples of communication systems at work. The first **communication system** we discussed in this text was in Chapter 1, when we introduced the Shannon and Weaver SMCR model, including a feedback loop. This model is a good example of a communication system because it comprises a systematic and predictable flow of symbolic information, including a means of evaluating the success or failure of the attempted communication using feedback. All communication systems have some means of feedback or evaluation.

This systematic and predictable flow of persuasive information in campaigns includes all of the auditory and visual symbols that are either verbal or nonverbal: words printed on a sign, page, or screen; visual pictures, symbols, or scenes in an ad; auditory words; and auditory "pictures" created by music, words, sound effects, and silence. For example, a colleague in the Theater Arts department was once employed as a character voice in radio dramas during radio's early years. He recounted how auditory "pictures" were used. During an episode of "Nick Carter — Detective," the producer decided to "persuade" listeners that the

"I'd like to thank my mom, my dad, my kids and
most of all . . . my media consultant!"

FIGURE 10.1

Person-oriented campaigns—especially political
campaigns—rely heavily on sophisticated uses of
media. (Reprinted by permission of Bill Whitehead.)

scene was taking place at night. For the first time
in the history of radio, the sound of chirping crickets "created" an imaginary picture of night. In the
following days, almost every dramatic series re-
wrote its scripts to include a night scene dramatized by the sound of crickets.[2] An example of a
visual symbol within the systematic flow of campaign information occurred in 1990 with the introduction of a new automobile called the "Infinity."
The vehicle was never shown throughout the entire
campaign. Instead, the advertiser used various
visual symbols of the concept of infinity—a flock
of geese migrating south (as they have done for
thousands of years) or the rushing water in a
stream, accompanied by classical music. Then the
scene faded to the word "Infinity" printed on the
screen—nothing else. Understandably, the campaign created a lot of interest for the unveiling of
the first models. In both of these cases, the system-

atic flow and evaluation of persuasive information
had measurable effects on either the audience or
the environment. The computer provides a nice
analogy for this systematic feature of campaigns:
In a computer, the programmer plans what is to
take place. Then information is introduced or implemented. This input is dispersed and processed
and, finally, there is some kind of output, usually
in the form of new or reorganized information.

One way to think of this flow is to imagine
yourself moving into, passing through, and moving out of a huge block of "information bits" of
the campaign and coming into contact with some
but not all of them—for example, ads, news conferences, bumper stickers, direct-mail pieces, and
news programs featuring the product, candidate,
or idea. This happens to us many times daily with
numerous distinctly different campaigns. And if a
campaign is well designed, we will pass through it

several times, being exposed to different information bits each time. These information bits will differ from those our fellow consumers are exposed to during their passages.

The rule of thumb in advertising agencies is that it takes at least three exposures to move a consumer to action. The first exposure passes by almost unnoticed by the consumer. The second exposure alerts consumers to the existence of the product and triggers their unconscious memories of the first exposure. It also creates curiosity about the product. If it is well designed and properly timed, the third exposure either prompts a preexisting need for the product or creates a new need, both of which should lead to consumer action in the form of putting the product on a shopping list, cutting out a coupon or recipe, or going to the store for either a trial or a purchase of the product.

Notice that the successful campaign is not a case of "salesmanship in print," as it has sometimes been defined.[3] Campaigns don't sell; instead, they systematically prepare the consumer, the voter, or the joiner/donor for some kind of action: trying or buying a product, voting or working for a candidate, or joining or donating to a cause. We will explore this process at some length later.

THE ROLE OF GOALS, STRATEGIES, AND TACTICS IN CAMPAIGNS

Every campaign establishes persuasive goals or objectives for a product, person, or idea; articulates strategies for getting to the goals; and then develops and executes tactics to implement the strategy for marketing the product, supporting the candidate, or promoting the idea or ideology. A standard step in running any ad agency campaign is to establish explicit and measurable goals of persuasion such as increasing regional sales, changing a candidate's image, or converting nonparticipants or nondonors. These goals are then supplemented by campaign strategies and tactics. For example, the *campaign strategies* for a product campaign goal (to increase regional sales, for example) might be achieved by promoting new uses

and brand-switching for the product. This strategy could be implemented through the tactics of using television advertising to demonstrate new product uses and providing purchase incentives in the form of coupons.

In the case of a politician, the goal of gaining support for the candidate might be strategically accomplished by enhancing the candidate's name recognition and personal image using the tactics of billboard advertising and promoting personal appearances at public events.

The goal of converting a nondonor might be strategically handled by educating potential donors about the purposes of the ideology using the tactics of leaflets explaining the cause and holding rallies where people can donate time, money, or other resources.

CAMPAIGNS VERSUS "SINGLE-SHOT" PERSUASIVE MESSAGES

How do campaigns differ from other kinds of persuasion? Campaigns are not just a series of messages sent to audiences over time about the same product, candidate, or cause. Nor are they debates over a specific issue. Campaigns differ from single shots of persuasion or from "collections" of persuasive messages delivered over time in three major ways. They

1. systematically create "positions" in the audience's mind for the product, candidate, or idea.
2. are intentionally designed to develop over time. In other words, campaigns are composed of stages for getting the audience's attention, preparing the audience for action, and, finally, for calling the audience to action.
3. dramatize the product, candidate, idea or ideology for the audience, inviting receivers to participate in real or symbolic ways with the campaign and its goal.

Viewing a TV serial is like following movements or campaigns. Each daily drama leads to a conclusion of that episode, and each episode adds to the overall result of the campaign or movement.

Although the episodes can stand alone (each has its own beginning, middle, and end), they rely on one another to form a collage of messages that meld into one another until an entire image or picture of the campaign is perceived and stored in the minds of the consumer, voter, or joiner. By the end of the campaign, if it is well designed, large segments of the population will have been exposed to enough episodes that a similar image of the product, candidate, or idea emerges.

If you want to explore campaigns in more depth, you can read accounts of campaigns, participate in one, or perhaps even plan and conduct one. Discover how you are persuaded by campaigns. In identifying how we are affected and swayed by campaigns, we see trends we can use in our own campaigns. We may wish to object to a college or university policy. A campaign can help elect a member of the student senate who will work to change people's minds and actions. A campaign can even get parents' support for the purchase of a car or for the right to live your own life-style.

TYPES OF CAMPAIGNS

As noted earlier, three kinds of movements or campaigns predominate: (1) the *politically oriented* campaign for office, (2) the *product-oriented* advertising campaign, and (3) the *ideological*, or *cause-oriented*, campaign (sometimes called mass or social movements).

The first and last types of campaigns have many similarities. Frequently, well-known persons actually do represent an issue, a cause, or an ideology. The person-oriented political campaign, however, centers on the individual's name. The focus of such campaigns may be on electing *someone* to office, getting *someone* out of prison, or raising enough money to pay for *someone's* organ transplant. We have seen campaigns with slogans such as "Free Vigilante Goetz" (the man who shot four black youths in a New York City subway as they apparently tried to shake him down for five dollars). The slogan might feature a candidate's name — "Be Sure to Vote for John Countryman" — or it may feature a person needing financial support — "Dollars for Jimmy, Our County's Liver Transplant Candidate." In issue-oriented campaigns, on the other hand, the slogan or theme always features the cause before the person. For example, we give money to the Muscular Dystrophy fund, not to Danny Thomas. We want to enact a nuclear freeze, not elect its chief advocate. We support a certain course of action or embrace a certain belief. Leadership may shift throughout the idea campaign or may be shared by several subgroups or their spokespersons.[4] Despite these differences, there are remarkable similarities in the three kinds of campaigns, as we will see, and

FIGURE 10.2

Here, a person-oriented image campaign fails.
(Reprinted by permission of UFS, Inc.)

sometimes it is difficult to draw exact distinctions between them. A good example would be Jesse Jackson's presidential campaigns, in which he promoted the idea of establishing a "rainbow coalition" of the poor, minorities, and the underprivileged to influence government. Thus, within his political campaign there was also an idea-oriented subcampaign.

POSITIONING: SYSTEMATIC INFORMATION FLOW

All campaigns must establish a "position" in the marketplace — a "niche" or "creneau" in the words of Jack Trout and Al Ries.[5] A brand has to differentiate itself from other brands and from nonbranded or generic products. A candidate has to position himself or herself so as to be distinguishable from the opponent, usually through emphasizing different positions on issues and through projecting a different image (for example, the highly competent "all business" image or the empathic "human" image). An idea or ideology has to differentiate itself from other causes (for example, the United Fund has to emphasize the *range* of services it supports as opposed to the more narrowly targeted fund drive by the Arthritis Foundation, and the "pro-life" supporters must look and sound very different from the "pro-choice" advocates).

Positioning demonstrates the alternatives in purchasing, voting, and supporting. Positioning also gives the product, candidate, idea, or ideology a "niche" or a "creneau" in the audience's mind that results in "top of mind" awareness. The audience doesn't forget that the product, candidate, or cause exists; instead they attend to the related messages and ultimately take action in the form of purchasing, voting, or supporting. The following are some ways in which persuaders "position" their product, candidate, or cause.[6]

Being First

Products, candidates, or causes can position themselves as being the "first" in a given category. Chrysler was the first auto manufacturer to offer a 5-year, 50,000-mile warranty, and the competition had to follow suit with "me-too" offers. Senator Fogbound can say that she was first to tie property tax cuts to state lottery receipts. The National Organization for Women (NOW) can argue that it was the first group since the Suffragist movement to officially represent women on feminist issues.

Being Best

Another claim to a position in the market is that your product, candidate, idea, or ideology is the best option — the highest quality choice in the market, election, or cause. Butterball Turkey claims to be the juiciest, moistest, and hence the best turkey in the supermarket. Congressman Dimbrain can say that he has the best attendance record in Congress, has sponsored the most successful bills, has made the most visits back to the home district, and hence is the "best" candidate in the election. The Citizen's Utility Board (CUB) argues that it is the utility user's best advocate because it has the highest success rate for defeating utility price increases.

Being the Least Expensive

Emphasizing the low price of a product, the minimal "cost" in effort and/or money for supporting a candidate, or the reasonable "cost" (dues or work) involved in supporting an idea or ideology is another way to position a product, candidate, or cause. The Sears Discover Card can claim that it is the least expensive because it rebates 1 percent of all purchases; a candidate can serve hot dogs and baked beans at his or her fundraiser instead of a more expensive meal; and a campaign to rebuild a church's fifty-year-old pipe organ can claim that rebuilding is the least expensive way to restore high-quality music for services.

Being the Most Expensive

Since price is often the best indication of quality, another "niche" in a campaign is as the most expensive product, candidate, or cause. Visa Gold Card could claim that its annual fee and interest rate are the most expensive because the card is the most universally accepted form of credit. An underdog candidate might say that his or her campaign won't be easy: It will be the toughest and will require the most support in money and effort. A campaign to recycle instead of investing in a new landfill may be the most expensive method of disposing of waste, but it is also the most ecologically sound method.

What We're Not

Another means of positioning is to tell the consumer or audience what a product, candidate, or cause *is not*. For example, Seven-Up made a dramatic market recovery when it advertised its product as the Un-cola. More recently, Claussen claims that its pickles are *not cooked* and hence do not have a long shelf life, but they are the crispiest pickles on the market. The candidate for governor is *not* a tax-increase candidate. The pro-choice group is *not* in favor of reinstating the death penalty just because they favor offering abortions on demand.

Positioning by Gender

Many products and some candidates position themselves by appealing mainly to a specific sex. Eve and Virginia Slim cigarettes are "niched" for females, whereas Camels and Marlboros target males. When Walter Mondale selected Geraldine Ferraro as his vice-presidential running mate — the first woman ever nominated for national office — he was targeting that segment of the population that believed it was time for a woman vice-president. The grass-roots supporters of the Equal Rights Amendment to the Constitution are primarily women.

Positioning by Age

Some products, candidates, and causes are aimed only at certain cohorts (the term *cohort* refers to persons born in the same year, the same decade, or the same set of years — the baby boomers, for example, who were born between 1948 and 1964). Pepsi is positioned for younger cola drinkers,

whereas Coke is targeted for older cola drinkers. A candidate might portray herself as the "youth candidate," and MADD — Mothers Against Drunk Drivers — is supported by people of both genders who are old enough to be parents of children who have been or might be killed by a drunk driver.

Positioning by Benefit

Another way to position a persuasive campaign is to identify the unique features of the product, candidate, or ideology that will most appeal to the target market, voters, or adopters by promising them some kind of benefit. In 1990, Chrysler Corporation promoted a product feature (an air-bag cushion in the steering wheel) that promised a convincing benefit (the driver would be cushioned from injury in case of an accident). A candidate might persuade voters that he or she is the "No More New Taxes" candidate, thus offering voters a financial benefit for their vote. And the Citizen's Social Security Board might position its cause by promoting the "feature" of having paid lobbyists at the state legislature. This promises the potential joiner a possible financial "benefit" in the form of monthly payment increases tied to inflation.

Thus one important function served by persuasive campaigns is to position the product, candidate, idea, or ideology at the "top" of the audience's mind, where it holds their attention and becomes distinct from other brands, other candidates, or other causes vying for the receivers' attention and commitment.

DEVELOPMENTAL ASPECTS OF IDEOLOGICAL CAMPAIGNS

Ideological campaigns, sometimes called mass or social movements, differ from person-, product-, or idea-oriented campaigns in several ways. First, ideological campaigns are usually involved in "selling" political, social, economic, or religious dogma. Ideological campaigns don't urge their audiences to purchase, vote, donate money, or drive slower; instead they want some kind of change in

FIGURE 10.3

Here, Canadian Club is positioning by price. Notice the
words *premium* and *quality*. (Reprinted by permission
of Hiram Walker & Sons, Inc., Farmington Hills, MI.)

Here is an example of positioning by gender. (Used by permission of Jeff McElhaney.)

the political, social, economic, or religious system. In order to facilitate such change, ideological campaigns usually urge the audience to convert to a new belief system and to join and become active in the cause promoting the new belief system. Ideological campaigns resemble religious conversions in that the converts not only exchange their old belief system for the dogma of the cause but also become active advocates for the new belief system. The pro-choice campaign to keep abortion legal is one example; the countercampaign to outlaw abortion is another. Ideological campaigns seem to come and go in cycles, depending on the times. If things are bad — the economy is down, there is a war, there is a lot of crime, and so on — and there is a charismatic leader such as Adolf Hitler, Franklin Roosevelt, Winston Churchill, John Kennedy, Martin Luther King, Jr., Ronald Reagan, or perhaps Jesse Jackson, an idea campaign can develop. Unless both elements are present, however, the ideological campaign, be it political, religious, or economic, is unlikely to occur. Martin Luther King's SCLC (Southern Christian Leadership Conference) would not have been able to mount the great civil rights campaign without the hope for equal opportunities for minorities. Jesse Jackson's attempt to gain the Democratic presidential nomination in 1984 was unsuccessful in the face of an improving economy and greater perceived respect for the image of America by the rest of the world. However, in 1988, after the largest stock market crash in history and with the widening of the income gap between the poor (and even the middle class) and the wealthy, Jackson's campaign touched many people, and he attracted large numbers of white voters in traditionally conservative states such as Michigan and Illinois.

Whatever the cause of particular campaign successes, however, campaigns go through several clearly identifiable stages. These stages are developmental — that is, they lead from one to another. The first develops the foundation for the second, and so on. Missing one or more of the developmental stages can spell doom for the campaigner. Let us look briefly at the ideological campaign. It may be the most susceptible to failure if it lacks developmental stages.

Who Joins Them?

One theorist, Eric Hoffer, has pointed out that "true believers" who are followers of idea campaigns come from groups of disaffected people.[7] These are the undesirables, the minorities, the poor, the social or physical misfits, the students, the sinners, the bored, and the selfish. These people see the idea campaign as a way to move up from the bottom. Such people are most likely to be disaffected during tough times, which explains why the black power and student power movements developed. The Vietnam War threatened both groups through the military draft. It explains why the moral majority was able to affect elections at the same time that pornography was increasing, marriage was decreasing, divorce was increasing, and abortions were increasing. Who will be the disaffected groups to form the idea campaigns or mass movements of the 1990s?

What Motivates Them?

Hoffer reports that the followers of mass movements have several motivations for joining.[8] First, they see the movement as a way to lift themselves from their poverty, degradation, or difficulties. Usually, they have nothing to lose and everything to gain from joining the movement. A second motivation is that some of the potential joiners are bored with their present status and way of life. This explains why some people who have affluent lifestyles join ideological movements; it is a way for them to gain identity, to rebel, or to be excited. The movement is a game for them. A final motive for joiners of mass movements is the possibility of reversing some social or individual "sin" such as prejudice. This can be done in real or symbolic ways: We can execute tyrants or we can burn them in effigy.

Thus the "sin" of prejudice was battled in the civil rights movement, the "sin" of undeclared war in Vietnam spawned the antiwar movement, the "sin" of the Palestinian issue gave birth to several militant and terrorist movements, and the "sin" of ecological pollution of all kinds led to the environmental movements of the 1990s.

What Are Their Strategies: The Bowers and Ochs Model

In their book *The Rhetoric of Agitation and Control*, John Bowers and Donovan Ochs described several stages or strategies through which most ideological movements pass before ultimately failing or succeeding.[9] In the first stage, agitators **petition** the sources of power (the government, the school district), making demands that are constructed to just barely exceed the level that the power source can or will give up. This makes the power source appear unreasonable and assists the agitators in their second stage, which is called **promulgation**, or the marketing of the movement. Using handbills, leaflets, or rallies, the agitators develop their movement by informing outsiders of the unreasonableness of the power source. At this stage, the movement leaders hope to gain recruits and to get publicity that will attract even more recruits. If this stage is successful, the movement grows and moves into a third stage called **solidification**. Now the newly recruited members are educated and hyped up through rallies, protest songs (for example, *Solidarity Forever, We Shall Overcome*, and *We Shall Not Be Moved*), salutes (for example, the Nazi "Heil," or the "V" for victory and, later, for peace), or symbols (for example, the swastika, the picture of a fetus with the "forbidden" international traffic signal superimposed on it, or the logo of the nuclear freeze).

In stage four, with a now-committed and educated following, the movement leaders seek **polarization** of the uncommitted population. They do this by focusing on a *flag* issue or person. Past flag issues have been the use of napalm, the extinction of some species of fish, the development of a nuclear site, or the aborting of fetuses that could be kept alive with newly developed technology. Flag persons personify the issue. Past flag persons include TV evangelist Jimmy Swaggart, Iraqi strongman Saddam Hussein, and, in local politics, various mayors, councilpersons, senators, representatives, or any leader who is depicted as the root of the problem. A frequent tactic here is to use highly charged emotional language such as "pig" or "Uncle Tom." Polarization forces the onlookers to choose between "us" and "them."

In stage five, **nonviolent resistance** is used. Police all call in sick with the "blue flu." Students occupy a building, claiming that they have "liberated" it. There is a rent strike. There is an illegal march. These and other devices call attention to the mass movement and hopefully prompt some sort of response by the power source. Agitators may hope that the power sources will call out the army or police and that the press will cover this. Then agitators may claim repression or gestapo tactics. Usually this leads to some kind of public confrontation, or the sixth stage—**escalation**—which is intended to increase tension in the power sources. Perhaps threats are made—rumors of planted incendiary bombs or public displays of weapons. Perhaps some violent act occurs—for example, a strike with fights; a killing or kidnapping; or a symbolic bombing, such as the bombing of abortion clinics. If the forces in power try to repress the movement at this time, there usually is a split inside the movement between those who favor violence and those who favor nonviolence. Bowers and Ochs call this stage **Gandhi versus guerilla**. Usually, the nonviolent segment of the movement goes to the power source and argues that unless the power source gives in, the guerillas will take over. Depending on the outcome of this stage of the model, the final stage may or may not emerge. This last stage is **revolution**.

Especially in the last decade, we have seen the stages that Bowers and Ochs describe occur repeatedly in countries such as Nigeria, Iran, Poland, and, most recently, in Eastern Europe. In the United States, we have seen these stages in the civil rights, antiwar, and pro-life movements. These U.S. movements never reached the final stage of revolution.

PRODUCT CAMPAIGNS

The campaign to promote a product has been with us since the first snake-oil hawker loaded a wagon and headed for the boondocks. The goal then, as it is now, was to flimflam the gullible yokels out on the frontier. The hawker would usually come into town with much hoopla, leaflets, and ballyhoo.

Often the next stage of the campaign was some form of entertainment — an "Indian" show, magic, music, or oratory and dramatics. Once a sizable crowd was gathered, the huckster would begin to sell the product, using on-the-spot demonstrations, testimonials, and so forth. Frequently, listeners sampled the product. Finally, the flimflam artist talked about the need to be moving on and suggested that they had better take advantage of this offer right then and there. It was their last chance to get a bottle of the Formula X elixir to cure warts, baldness, hot flashes, and anything else that might ail anyone. Things have not changed that much, when you think about it.

Most of the sports and entertainment on TV is equivalent to the hoopla of the medicine show. Recently, this has been carried to the extreme in the "show-business" sport of professional wrestling. Promoters such as Ann Gunkel and Vince McMahon have hyped the sport so cleverly that, where once a sparse crowd of 2000 came to a wrestling show, 15,000 now appear. The medicine-show tactics involve using rock stars such as Cyndi Lauper (who has it bad for "Hulk" Hogan) to get audience attention. McMahon's "stable" of men and women wrestlers (including several midget wrestlers) totals 200. McMahon earns close to $100 million annually, and his best stars earn in the high six figures. One of them, "Junkyard Dog," wears a spiked collar into the ring, barks during the matches, and eats the dog biscuits that fans throw into the ring. The hoopla has drawn the young — punkers, rockers, and everyone in between.[10]

We see the same kind of promotional orgies on prime-time television. Right there, squeezed in between segments of *L.A. Law*, *The Cosby Show*, *Dynasty*, and *Thirtysomething*, we find pitches for the "snake oil" of the last years of the twentieth century: Big Macs, rug and room deodorizers, wine coolers, four-wheel-drive vehicles, whiter whites and brighter brights, gourmet meals in minutes, and various antiwrinkle potions promising a slowing of the aging process for the baby boomers approaching midlife.

Despite their differences, the three kinds of campaigns have many similarities in the kinds of communication strategies they use to sell their person, product, or idea. The persuadee who wants to be aware of the "snake oil" that is being pushed and who wants to spot doublespeak needs to be aware of these strategies. In the next section, we look at several such strategies. Those discussed are by no means all the communication strategies that could be cited; they are only representative ones.[11]

STAGES OF SUCCESSFUL CAMPAIGNS

One of the common characteristics of all three types of campaigns is that they are **developmental** — that is, they grow and change and adapt to audience responses and the emergence of new issues. They do not run on the same level or pitch throughout. They do not repeatedly pound away at the same bits of information. They do not always have the same strategy. You might think of a campaign as a fishing expedition in which the strategists try in various ways to get the attention of the "fish" — the audience. They use different methods or lures. If one method does not succeed after some use, they try another and perhaps another. As the mood of the audience develops, the mood of the message must also change. The whole thing must be planned so that each shift follows from what came before.

For instance, suppose you are hired to establish product X, a new kind of building material, in the public eye — to get across the idea that this is the greatest, most impressive development in construction since the steel beam. What would you do first? You would not blindly go about trying first this method and then that method. Instead, you would outline the major points you want to make about this new product. What kinds of people will buy it? What are their values and beliefs about construction? How can you reach them? Now suppose that your first advertising attempt fails — people are not that excited about the durability of the product. They are more impressed by its high cost. You will have to shift your strategy. You would never have discovered the discrepancy between what you thought was important (durability) and the actual key factor (cost) if you had not tried out your idea. The discovery will affect your next ads for the product. Campaign planners adapt to audience responses.

FIVE FUNCTIONAL STAGES OF DEVELOPMENT

Most campaigns pass through several, if not all, stages of a model described by researchers at Yale who were interested in following the development of national identity in the numerous Third World countries that emerged in Africa, Latin America, and the Middle East in the 1960s.[12] Although the model originally was used in this international political context, it is applicable to product, person, and idea campaigns in other contexts as well. The five functional stages noted by the researchers are: *identification* (including but not limited to name identification), *legitimacy, participation* (real and symbolic), *penetration*, and *distribution*.

Identification

One thing an emerging nation must develop is **identification**, not only internally but worldwide. The country may design identifying symbols (for example, flags, insignias, or anthems) to encourage citizen patriotism as well as recognition by the rest of the world. It must also develop some kind of *national policy*. Similar developments occur in campaigns for people, products, or ideas. Product promoters develop logos or emblems that identify a product visually. Examples are the winged foot of Mercury for Goodyear (Figure 10.5), the multicolored apple with a bite out of it for the Apple Computer, the lowercase "e" for the ecology movement, the pentagon encasing a star for Chrysler, and the golden arches with which we are all familiar.

Another device that helps identify a product is color coding. Here, the campaigner picks a color or colors and consistently uses them in packaging, in advertising, on letterhead, and perhaps in uniforms. United Parcel Service carriers wear dark-brown uniforms and their trucks are painted dark brown; candidates usually select some combination of red, white, and blue; camouflage and drab olive green are associated with the army; and Century 21 real-estate agents wear gold smocks. Further identification can be achieved by using the same typeface in all ads, signs, buttons, bumper stickers, and so on.

Slogans also help identification and frequently become part of our cultural heritage if they are catchy enough: "Folgers—The Mountain Grown Coffee"; "When You Care Enough to Send the Very Best"; "Try the Manhandlers"; "We Try Harder"; "It's the Real Thing"; and "Major Motion" are all examples. Finally, jingles, uniforms, salutes, and all sorts of campaign paraphernalia

FIGURE 10.5

Many devices are used to gain product, person, or idea identification in campaigns. Logos such as this one are one kind of device. Why is the winged foot of Mercury used? What does it communicate? Why put it between "GOOD" and "YEAR"? Answers to these questions help explain how product image or identification develops. (Used by permission of The Goodyear Tire and Rubber Company.)

(balloons, buttons, nail files, and so on) can help establish name and purpose identification. What are some means that candidates in your district have used for identification? How have new products established identification? What identification devices do idea campaigns use?

Legitimacy

The second functional stage entails the establishment of **legitimacy**. Candidates frequently achieve this by getting the party endorsement or by winning primary election battles. Legitimacy can be thought of as a power base. Candidates may choose to demonstrate how power works. They have rallies. A student hoping to live in an off-campus apartment gets legitimacy or power by taking a summer job that will cover the costs or by joining ranks with several fellow students to share costs. A student running for class president establishes legitimacy when group members begin to support him or her.

In political campaigns, incumbents have automatic legitimacy (unless they have bumbled and botched the job), so challengers have a major task. They must try to discredit and erode the legitimacy of the opposition and develop their own. Further, they may have to do this while running in primary elections against fellow political leaders who are also emphasizing the shortcomings of the incumbent. The mudslinging in a political campaign is usually an attempt to destroy another candidate's legitimacy. A challenger finds out that the incumbent gave government contracts to friends or used the office for self-advancement. The incumbent points out the nasty tactics of the challenger and shows his or her lack of experience in office. The real question is which candidate the voters will consider the most legitimate.

Products can demonstrate legitimacy in several ways. One way, of course, is to show that the product is effective. The patent-medicine show frequently used testimonials from persons who had been cured using the product. Testimonials are seen frequently today also. Arnold Palmer tells why a certain golf club helps his game, William "Refrigerator" Perry advertises soft drinks, and

trend-setters wear Calvin Klein jeans. Established endorsements can help products demonstrate legitimacy also — the Underwriter's Laboratory seal of approval is an example, as is the Good Housekeeping seal. Demonstrations on TV can create legitimacy by showing how efficiently Top Job cleans a filthy wall, how well the Volvo can carry a load, or how easily the "ram-tough" Dodge trucks plow over rough terrain.

In idea campaigns, large numbers of participants or amounts of money frequently are used to demonstrate legitimacy. Such tactics as newspaper ads with the names of known supporters who endorse the movement or who oppose what the campaign opposes (such as new tax rates) can establish legitimacy. A good way to establish legitimacy might be to get large numbers of people to show up at a council meeting or call in sick. In one high school, students who objected to the lunch program demonstrated the legitimacy of their movement. One day, several hundred students boycotted the lunches, leaving the school with tons of leftovers. The next day, all students bought the hot lunch, leaving the school short of supplies. The following day, everyone paid with a $5 bill, running the cashiers out of change. The next day, the students paid in pennies, creating havoc in the check-out lines as the cashiers counted each cent. By the fifth day, school officials negotiated with student representatives about the lunch program. The legitimacy of the complaint was demonstrated by the number of students uniting in nonviolent and effective tactics.

Participation

The legitimacy stage of campaigns frequently blends so smoothly with the **participation** stage that it is almost impossible to tell them apart. In the legitimacy stage, the participants are *known supporters*. In the participation stage, the leaders seek to involve previously *uncommitted persons*. There are many techniques for doing this. Some involve effort by participants, whereas others involve minimal or only symbolic involvement.

The distributors and users of products *participate* in the use and profit of the product. Coupon

She makes it look effortless.

Reflecting the thousands of hours she's practiced and honed her skills, until every muscle responds in unison

to the command for perfection. It is this dedication, this courage to face competition boldly and without compromise, that has inspired Phillips Petroleum to proudly sponsor United States Swimming since 1973.

And we'll be national sponsor for years to come. Because we believe that with every leap of grace and form, we are watching the future of our nation take shape.

PHILLIPS PETROLEUM COMPANY PHILLIPS 66

offers are made to product users who buy and use the product and get money or gifts. In some instances, stores are paid to allow some of their space to be used for special displays of certain soaps, wines, and so forth. The dealer may get an extra discount for pushing a certain product. Vikin Fjord vodka, for example, used an interesting device for getting reader participation in one of its print ads. It used the words "Vikin Fjord (pronounced 'Vee-kin-fee-yord')" with the correct pronunciation included in the ad to prompt participation. Other participation-producing devices are being developed continually.

Similarly, a movement may urge participation in real or symbolic ways. Women stopped doing housework in a one-day strike. The slogan of one such strike was "Don't Iron While the Strike Is Hot." In other situations, people may be asked to wear arm-bands or badges, to yell slogans at rallies, or to put signs on their lawns or on their bumpers. People running for student president may ask others to participate in their campaign by canvassing dormitory floors or student groups. For a Campus Crusade for Christ rally, many students were asked to distribute leaflets and urge others to attend. This kind of activity gets people involved in the campaign or movement and guarantees further active support. As previously mentioned, people who put bumper stickers on their cars will vote for the name on the sticker most of the time. Movements ask supporters to do something, even if it is only symbolic. Supporters can march, hold a vigil, or salute. The effects of this are to increase commitment to the cause.

Recent innovations to get audience or customer participation include "scratch and sniff" ads that get potential customers to "sample" a perfume, cologne, or room deodorizer. The age-old free sample or free trial also attempts to get customer participation with the product prior to purchase. The use of participation is a powerful persuader in

FIGURE 10.6

Phillips Petroleum establishes its legitimacy by sponsoring U.S. Olympic teams. (Reprinted by permission of the Phillips Petroleum Company.)

campaigns because by scratching and sniffing, by clipping the coupon, by wearing the candidate's buttons, or by taking the test drive, we have already symbolically purchased the product, voted for the candidate, or adopted the idea.

Penetration

The **penetration** stage can be thought of as the stage where a person, product, or idea has "made it" in the market; that is, has been successful enough to establish a meaningful share of the electorate, market, or constituency. In presidential politics, especially in the early primaries, a candidate doesn't have to win the most delegates to establish penetration.

For products, gaining a significant share of the market is enough to achieve the penetration stage. Crest and Gleem dominated the toothpaste market for years by offering fluoridation as a feature and decay prevention as the resulting product benefit. Then, in the 1970s, new toothpastes such as MaCleans, Pearl Drops, and others offered the benefits of whiteness and sexiness in place of decay prevention, thus segmenting and penetrating the market. This resulted in several other "me-too" toothpaste campaigns that offered the white and sexy benefits while both Gleem and Crest lost sales. Chrysler's innovations enabled it to penetrate the auto market — with front-wheel drive in 1980, the minivan in 1984, and the seven-year, 70,000-mile warranty in 1988. The share of the market that these innovations captured was significant enough to force the competition to follow suit; front-wheel-drive cars and minivans were being marketed by several manufacturers within a year or two. When you see a successful penetration stage in campaigns for products, you can be almost certain that the competition will begin to market their own versions of the newly dominating product.

In idea-oriented campaigns, penetration is achieved when those in power find that they are hearing about a campaign frequently enough or it is "costing" them so much (for example, legislators are barraged by mail or have to repeatedly answer questions about the campaign topic at

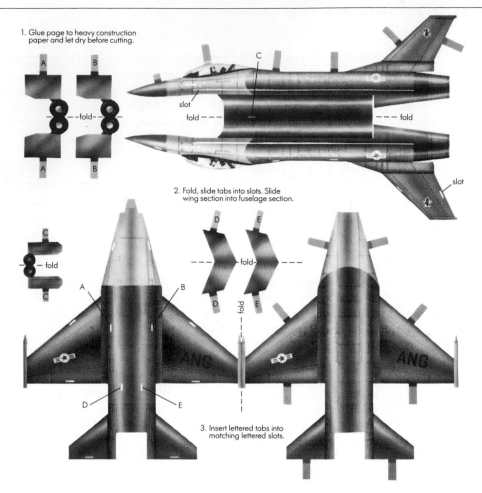

1. Glue page to heavy construction paper and let dry before cutting.

2. Fold, slide tabs into slots. Slide wing section into fuselage section.

3. Insert lettered tabs into matching lettered slots.

One of two ways to get your hands on an F-16.

If you think you're too young to fly, cut it out.

Fold. Assemble. And prepare for take-off.

While your paper airplane may not quite reach the speed of sound, use it as a reminder of just how fast the Air National Guard can help you get your future off the ground.

And we're not just talking about a military career. Air Guard training can prepare you for a civilian career in over 200 fields of technical expertise. Every-thing from meteorology to security. Tele-communications to computer technology.

We'll even pay part of your college tuition. What's more, you'll have the chance to take part in exciting adventures that can lead you around the world.

All you have to do is serve as little as two days a month and two weeks a year.

Want to learn more? Call your local recruiter. And find out if you're cut out for the Air National Guard.

Americans At Their Best.

FIGURE 10.7

This ad for the Air National Guard encourages real, not symbolic, participation.

(Courtesy Air National Guard.)

CHECK THE MIRROR. HAVE YOU BEEN TELLING YOURSELF A LITTLE WHITE LIE?

The mirror never lies. Are your teeth as white as they could be? If the mirror is saying "no," but you've been saying "yes," continue reading.

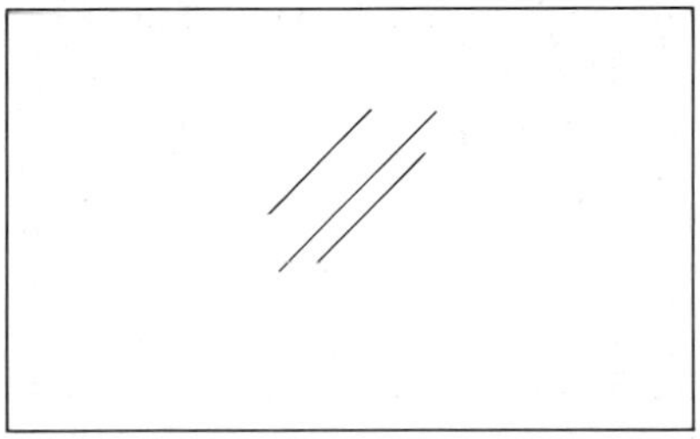

The truth is, your teeth could probably be whiter. Gleem's whitening formula was proven superior in laboratory tests to regular leading fluoride toothpastes. In fact, Gleem is unsurpassed in whitening even when compared to toothpastes designed to control tartar, protect sensitive teeth, or fight smoking or coffee stains. Which means if you're not using Gleem, your teeth might not be as white as they could be. And that would be a shame.

White teeth can do a lot for your smile. They can make it brighter. More confident. So one of your most attractive features will always look its best.

There's more to Gleem than a pretty smile. Part of getting teeth their whitest is keeping them their healthiest. That's why Gleem has fluoride to protect against cavities as it cleans.

See for yourself. If you're already brushing twice a day (and we hope you are), why not try Gleem? Then you can stop telling yourself that little white lie. Because every time you pass a mirror, you'll smile. **And every time you smile, you'll Gleem.**

FIGURE 10.8

Does this ad make use of real or symbolic participation? (The square in the middle represents a mirror.) (Used by permission of The Procter and Gamble Company.)

speeches or news conferences) that they must do something about it. They might pledge to vote for the antiabortion amendment, or they might agree to accept a delegation from a pro-ERA group, or they might agree to appear in a public debate with the campaign representatives. On the other hand, those in power may launch a countercampaign.

Distribution

In the fifth and final stage of development — **distribution** — the campaign or movement succeeds and becomes institutionalized. Having achieved the control they sought, the campaign or movement leaders must now live up to their promises in some way. They must signal the people that change is going to occur. The likely moves are the designation of subgroups of the campaign staff or the movement's leadership to positions of power with tasks to complete. These tasks fit with the promises made in the campaign and with the goals of the movement. This stage does not always occur in product campaigns. However, devices such as rebates, money-back coupons, and incentives to store owners are kinds of distribution that we see in product campaigns. In the case of an emerging nation, the distribution stage can be seen when the new government begins land reform, court reform, changes in the social structure, and other changes to show that power is now being divided and shared with the people, the faithful, the party, or the movement leaders.

In a highly developed campaign, the distribution stage may be specialized. For example, in states such as Illinois, where the patronage system is highly developed, any change in government officeholders will bring about a new distribution of government jobs, ranging from sanitation work to street-maintenance to egg-hatchery inspection. In product campaigns, handsome bonuses are frequently offered in the distribution stage as a reward to the sales force that displaced the competition.

One problem with idea-oriented campaigns and, to some degree, with political campaigns is that the persuaders don't always live up to their promises: The land isn't distributed, the jobs aren't given out, and the legislation isn't passed in the

form promised. The populace then becomes cynical about the movement or politicians. This is how many people come to believe that all politicians are crooks. As Cicero put it, "Politicians are not born; they are excreted."

OTHER DEVELOPMENTAL MODELS

We will now look at some other models that describe the stages campaigns must pass through before achieving full success.

The Communicative Functions Model

Communication researchers Judith Trent and Robert Friedenberg describe four stages in the political campaign that candidates must achieve if they are to be successful.[13] They call their model the **communicative functions** approach. In the first stage, the candidate lays a lot of groundwork by mapping out the district, organizing financial committees, developing contacts in key areas of the district, and so on. This process is usually accompanied or preceded by a formal announcement of candidacy. This stage is called the *surfacing*, or *winnowing*, stage. In this stage, the major campaign themes are tested and focused, the candidate's image is tested and promoted, and, with luck, adequate funds are raised. In presidential politics, this may begin for the out-of-power party as early as the day after losing the election and probably right after the midterm House and Senate elections for the incumbent.

In stage two of this model, the *primaries* serve to further narrow the field of candidates and to focus issues. More people get involved, as in the participation stage of the Yale model. These persons may pass out leaflets, attend rallies, sponsor fund-raisers, or perform some other overt activity that gets them involved.

In American politics, this stage is extremely expensive, even with the matching funds the government gives to candidates. Twenty million dollars would not be an unbelievable sum to spend in pursuing a presidential nomination. Of course, the costs are smaller with lower office, but even Senate primaries can cost several million dollars. This is a dangerous stage for candidates because they may make promises that they later can't fulfill, may reveal plans that later come back to haunt them, and may make mistakes or gaffes that can topple their candidacy.

During stage three — the *nomination* — the candidate is legitimized in front of the press and the corresponding media audience, and so are the party's platform and themes. The final stage — the *election* — is that eight-week period from Labor Day until election day when candidates wear themselves to a frazzle going from crowd to crowd saying basically the same thing over and over. Here, the use of the press is critical in both paid-for political promotions (billboards, signs, bumper stickers, buttons, TV ads, radio spots, newspaper ads, and so on) and unpaid-for media coverage (*Meet the Press* type programs, short blurbs on the evening news, and so on). Candidates must be covered by the press so that they get key items broadcast or quoted. They must purchase their TV and radio times carefully to get the messages to the target audience at the right time and in the right way. As we will see in Chapter 12, this use of media is sophisticated and complex.

The Social Movements Model

To analyze ideological campaigns or social movements, campaign scholars Stewart, Smith, and Denton provide another approach, which resembles the Bowers and Ochs model.[14] In their model of social movements, there are five stages: genesis, social unrest, enthusiastic mobilization, maintenance, and termination. In the *genesis* stage, the ideologues begin to preach about shortcomings or injustices in the status quo. These early prophets may go unheard for a long time, but finally like-minded zealots are drawn to them, and the first stage creates a hard core of devoted supporters. Then, usually, a dramatic event (such as a Supreme Court decision, an assassination, or martial law) catapults the issue into the public spotlight.

In the second stage — *social unrest* — growing numbers of people identify with the movement and feel displaced by the shortcomings described by the prophets, who now agitate these frustrated

people by identifying the devils and gods of the movement and its sacred and profane grounds and acts. This leads to the third stage — *enthusiastic mobilization* — in which the true believers of the movement begin to convert more and more people and begin to encounter opposition from those in power. These are active converts now, not merely persons who identify with the movement, as in the social unrest stage. They may engage in nonviolent or violent actions, but they rarely sit on the sidelines. Sometimes, competing organizations promoting similar ideals spring up, and there may be internal bickering and disagreements. The overall message of this stage is that there is a "we–they" world out there and "you" had better join "us" so "we" can take care of "you" and defeat "them."

In the *maintenance* stage, the movement adopts a lower profile as the media turn to other events and as some successes are perceived by converts. These successes may dull enthusiasm and siphon spirit from the movement, so it must bide its time until some crucial event or perhaps a charismatic spokesperson emerges to rekindle enthusiasm. In some cases, the movement achieves its goal(s), or it may merely wither and die in the *termination* stage. Perhaps supporters lose faith and patience, the movement may be outlawed or become outmoded, or its leaders may be co-opted by or assimilated into the establishment. As Stewart, Smith, and Denton stress, persuasion is adapted to the stages of a movement's development, so the movement's communication (persuasion) will be built on the needs perceived by its adherents.

The Diffusion of Innovation Model

Everett Rogers, a student of a process called **diffusion of innovation**, describes four stages through which consumers pass as they adopt new products or new brands of old products.[15] In stage one — *information and knowledge* — the consumer acquires information about the new product or brand. This sparks curiosity, as the consumer wonders whether the product will be satisfying or the new brand will be better. I recall hearing about a new product from McDonald's being test-marketed in the Chicago area — a sandwich called McRib that tasted like barbecued ribs. The person telling me about it was a swine producer who thought the product would offer a new market for his hogs. I then engaged in the second stage of the process — *persuasion*. I listened to ads for the McRib and talked to people who had eaten one and with students who worked at the McDonald's chain. They all offered persuasive messages, which I then used in a process of self-persuasion as I balanced my bias against fast foods with my curiosity about the new product. One day, returning famished from a fishing trip, I passed a McDonald's with a huge banner declaring, "McRib Is Here! Only 99¢ Today!" and I couldn't resist. I was in stage three of Rogers' model — *decision, adoption, and trial*. Here, the consumer is triggered into making the first purchase of the new product or brand, and that is why, in its initiation into the market, a product usually benefits from low prices or even free samples or trials.

Next, the consumer evaluates and reconsiders the product in the *confirmation or reevaluation* stage. In this stage, consumers gauge their experience of the product against their expectations of it. Does it measure up to what was promised? Did I find it useful? Was it better? Would I buy it again? I discovered that McRib didn't taste like ribs; instead, it was like pork sausage with barbecue sauce. It didn't measure up, so I decided not to buy another one.

Throughout your life, you will continually be exposed to new products, new brands, or "improved" versions of old brands. You will probably pass through the stages described by Rogers. Be aware of the process and observe yourself as your awareness and knowledge of the product develop, as you receive persuasion about it, as something triggers you to try it, and as you reevaluate it.

INVITATION TO THE DRAMA

We have already talked about a dramatic impulse in human beings. We see the world and identify its forces in ordered ways, and the most common form of ordering is the dramatic episode. It is interesting to observe in our own lives how often we tend to structure the world in episodes. We see

meals as having a "plot line." One way for a meal to progress is for it to start with a prayer. Certain foods such as salads are followed by other courses in a neat, orderly progression to an after-dinner liqueur with coffee. We see our workdays as divided into episodes: first-hour class, opening-the-mail time, lunch at the dorm, and so on. We see our weeks ordered the same way. Wednesday is called *hump day* because it is the halfway point. We see those around us as actors in the drama. Our parents may be villains and our friends may be heroes. Our fellow workers are classic stereotypes: the gossip, the bitter old-timer, the apple polisher, the good-natured fellow, the footloose-and-fancy-free jokester, and so on.

Recent research claims that the dramatic model may be the human imperative — that we cannot really understand an event, a circumstance, or a social unit until we process it as a narrative. This is certainly true of most campaigns, which rely on dramatic events, personalities, and interchanges. The modern campaign depends on its ability to create in its audience the sense of a momentous event or series of events that must be lived out or else the whole world and all people involved will suffer. Given such a drama, the movement or campaign succeeds to the degree that it can also invite the audience to participate in the drama in real or symbolic ways.

Let us look at the dramatic impulse. What is it that creates a sense of drama? How are dramatic elements used by persuaders? How do they occur? What effects do they have?

The first thing we need is a setting or **scene**, to use Burke's term (see Chapter 5), with dramatic potential. For instance, someone's backyard may have dramatic possibilities, but they are limited. A posh New York nightclub or an impressive apartment or perhaps a deserted junkyard all obviously have dramatic possibilities much broader than the backyard scene.

Given a dramatic scene, we now need the second element, **characters**. To keep it simple, let's limit ours to the good guys and their helpers and the bad guys and their helpers. We need to see our dramatic scene filled with opposing forces that are going to do battle. In a political campaign, these opposing forces may be the politicians of compassion and understanding versus the politicians of special interests. In many laundry products, the good character—enzymes or Mr. Clean—opposes the baddies of dirt and grime. Television commercials for STP motor oil have played out this bad guys/good guys theme in a familiar drama. A poor distressed auto engine is shown surrounded by four villains—dirt, heat, cold, and rust—dressed as attacking "Indians." They are spotted by four cans of STP, dressed as cavalry, coming over the brow of a hill. A bugler sounds the charge, and the cavalry gallop down onto the plateau and chase off the nasty villains to win the gratitude of the coy engine, which is now safe. In an idea campaign, the forces of good and evil may be personified or linked to certain groups.

The third element of the dramatic model that is common to movements and campaigns is **plot**.[16] Most plots are simple: The weak are exploited and a hero arises in their midst to lead them to liberty. Another variation may be the scenario in which members of a group are being enslaved or exploited. Through some event or other means, they become aware of their grievances and then try to overthrow the bad guys. The women's liberation movement used both of these plot lines, with men being the exploiters and women needing to take aggressive action to avoid slavery.

There are several common plots, examples of which are: the *overcoming of great odds*, the *quest* (for peace, for security, and so on), the *purgation* (throwing the rascals out), the *fatal flaw* (as with Wendy's hamburger ad line "Where's the Beef?"), and *outwitting the mastermind* (as in beating OPEC at its own game).

If the raw materials of the drama are at hand in the setting or situation, in the characters, and in the plot, the persuader uses these elements to invite the potential supporter of the movement or campaign to enter into the dramatic setting, to do battle with or to lend support to the characters of the drama, and to act out a part of the plot. Supporters of the movement or campaign then share in the victory. Their actions result in ego rewards, as they see payoff in election returns or as they see authority figures lose their tempers because

of wisecracks, comments, or chanting. In other words, the supporters' actions become part of the whole theme of the movement or campaign. They engage in the drama.

Many movements must fight off competing dramas or their own dramas never really take hold. At other times, movement or campaign leaders do not invite participation. Instead, they prefer to dwell on ideology by themselves or to reap praise for themselves.

Some dramas fail to be played out fully in the audience's minds because the campaigners choose to dwell on issues of philosophy. People want to see ideas acted out. They do not want to be preached to. For example, the American Indian movement (AIM) failed at first when it merely preached its ideas. It succeeded later by acting out demands: AIM members captured the entire Pine Ridge Indian Reservation in South Dakota. This setting had the needed drama; it was not far from the site of Custer's last stand, and it included the site of the massacre of Sioux women and children at Wounded Knee, South Dakota.

The antiabortion movement initially was unsuccessful when it preached religious ethics and the philosophy of human life along with its own definition of life. But it succeeded when it dramatized its points through such acts as the bombing of abortion clinics, publishing graphic photographs of aborted fetuses, and even producing a movie titled *The Silent Scream*, in which the audience could see a sonogram of a fetus apparently retreating from a probing abortion instrument. The narrator claimed that the fetus felt fear and anxiety as this alien force invaded the safety of the mother's womb. This dramatic presentation got the attention of many people, both pro- and antiabortion.

A second characteristic of movements and campaigns, then, is their tendency to succeed when they focus on the dramatic—when they act out their ideology instead of preaching it. When action invites the audience to the drama in real or symbolic ways, the movement becomes vital and attractive. It succeeds to the degree that it avoids overstatement and preachiness and to the degree that it can present historic dramas.

RHETORICAL VISIONS AND FANTASY THEME ANALYSIS

Not only are we drawn to the dramatic but we are likely to affiliate with other persons who share our dramatic preferences and avoid those who don't appreciate our dramatic tastes. In other words, every drama must have an audience that is unified in some way, and this unification or sharing of the meaning of the drama is powerful. For example, the film industry has produced several powerful, award-winning films depicting the Vietnam War. Such films have a large, built-in audience of Vietnam veterans and their families. Of course, there are some Vietnam veterans who do not want to even talk about the war let alone see a movie about it. But there are many for whom such films have a deep meaning and serve a unifying purpose: to give them a sense of community with other veterans and nonveterans who find the films appealing.

Throughout history there has been this development of a sense of community that revolves around dramas common to most of us.[17] These dramas, called **rhetorical visions**, are *values and beliefs that we share with one another through the use of the dramatic creation of social reality*. In terms of persuasion, it is obvious that, knowing the shared dramas of a certain group, a clever persuader can fashion convincing messages and entire persuasive campaigns that included parts of or even the complete dramas.

Symbolic Convergence Theory and Methodology

A theory of communication and a method for identifying these shared dramas have been developed by E. G. Bormann, a communication scholar at the University of Minnesota, and his students and colleagues. The theory is called **symbolic convergence theory**, and the methodology is called **fantasy theme analysis**.[18] They have been applied to small-group, interpersonal, and organizational communication, and, for our purposes, for doing audience analysis for product, idea, and political campaigns. When combined with focus-group interviews (a technique we will hear more about later) and a statistical technique called *Q-sort*

analysis, the theory and method have great power in analyzing the kinds of dramas to which specified groups of consumers and voters respond. In fact, when used properly, the method even provides copywriters with the exact language and images to use in advertising messages or the exact language and issues to focus on in political campaigns.

A basic premise of symbolic convergence theory is that reality is socially based and socially constructed. That is, the way each of us perceives the world is the result of our interactions with others and our adoption of and addition to the meanings of these interactions. Because we share our inputs and interpretations with others in our social group, we come to believe them even more devotedly than if we had been told what to believe from some authority. When this sharing occurs fully, we have a "symbolic convergence" of meaning.[19]

Bales's Categories and Dramatizing

The first clues to the power inherent in the social creation of realities came from the work of Robert F. Bales, a professor of sociology at Harvard. His initial interest was in identifying the kind of interactions that occurred in small, task-oriented groups, and he developed a system for categorizing such interactions. It was called the **interaction process analysis** instrument and consisted of six bipolar pairs of interactions. For instance, one pair was labeled "gives opinion" and "asks opinion," and another pair was labeled "creates tension" and "reduces tension." Bales noticed that in this last category, much of the tension reduction was being accomplished through the telling of stories in which the group seemed to participate, so he relabeled the category "dramatizes." He began to describe the way these stories or minidramas seemed to develop, or, as he called it, "chain out" in the group, resulting in what he came to call **fantasy themes**. At this point, Bales's work caught the attention of Bormann and later of Bormann's students and colleagues. They, too, had noticed the sharing of fantasies in small groups at Minnesota, and thought that the process of reality-building in small groups had a wider application. In a series of studies, Bormann and his followers identified the operation of symbolic convergence in presidential election campaigns. Using a variety of techniques, they discovered that "a number of communities of voters shared differing configurations of dramatizations and thus shared statistically different visions of the campaign."[20] These visions were later checked against actual voting behavior and were found to be reliable predictors of voter behavior. Bormann's students also found symbolic convergence occurring in diverse groups such as politicians, firemen, farm managers, and hog breeders.[21]

Rhetorical Visions and Market Segmentation

Bormann's next step was to shift the focus from politics to other kinds of campaigns — product campaigns, service campaigns, and idea campaigns — and to try adapting the fantasy theme methodology to various communication contexts such as hospitals, corporate settings, and so on. The result was that the power of the methodology seemed generalizable to these other contexts. In fact, depending on how one used the methodology, one could not only segment markets for specific products or ideas but could also generate the "rhetoric," or words, that would be most persuasive to the specific audiences.

At about the same time, a new term developed within the methodology. Bormann and his followers frequently saw the same or similar fantasy themes being developed — clusters of related dramas that they called **rhetorical visions**. These visions frequently were shared with similar market segments from a variety of geographic locales. Sometimes these clusters of fantasy themes could be used to tap into voters' or consumers' minds to discover what motivated them to buy this product instead of that or to vote for this candidate versus that or to follow a certain course of action as opposed to another.[22]

Two brief examples in which Bormann engaged relate to proposed campaigns to get people to quit using tobacco and to wear motorcycle helmets — both idea campaigns.[23]

Tobacco users were divided into three groups — male smokers, female smokers, and

males chewing tobacco or using snuff — and were interviewed about their tobacco use. The ultimate goal was to find a way to convince tobacco users to cut down or to cease tobacco use. It soon became clear that it would be nearly impossible to motivate groups of smokers to quit. Fear appeals had not worked, nor had limiting advertising to the print medium. So these groups were set aside, with the attention going to the tobacco chewers or snuff users. These individuals were interviewed in small focus groups about their tobacco use and about other values they seemed to share. The researchers discovered that, in addition to tobacco use patterns, this group shared an important set of fantasies that might be called the "smokeless tobacco" vision of the world. It included having a macho image and communicating it through wearing western clothes and cowboy boots, driving four-wheel-drive vehicles, drinking lots of beer, and picking up and seducing women using a method that included a common terminology — "beer goggles" or "beer goggling." This meant going to shopping malls and estimating how many beers it would take before a "smokeless" user would be willing to seduce various female passersby. This shared language provided a key that might persuade the smokeless tobacco users to quit. The idea was to create a campaign ad in which an attractive female — a two-beer specimen — was shown refusing to kiss or even be close to a smokeless user because chewing was so crude and made for horrible breath.

Motorcyclists also were divided into three groups based on their focus-group interview responses. One group rode motorcycles for practical reasons of economy, and another rode cycles because it gave them macho feelings to be speeding down the open road at 100 mph with their girlfriend holding onto them from behind. A third group, which Bormann called the "daredevils," rode cycles because they wanted to flirt with death. The researchers asked each group whether they would be willing to quit riding a cycle if they were to receive the most expensive automobile they could find. The pragmatic riders said yes for economic reasons and also proved to be good candidates for wearing helmets. The macho group also said yes but reported that they would then sell the car and use the money to buy bigger cycles. They proved to be poor candidates for wearing helmets because they felt it hid their faces from female motorists. The daredevils, having already "put one down" or knowing of someone who had, were willing to wear other protective gear — leather jackets, pants, gloves, and so forth. On the basis of these findings, the safety campaign could create various messages to appeal to at least two of the three groups of riders.

Fantasy Types in Political Campaigns

In terms of recent political campaigns, Bormann and his followers have found that although the candidates' rhetorical visions of America and their campaigns have varied considerably over the years, the vision held by the media has remained remarkably consistent, and several fantasy types have emerged that make up this vision.[24] According to the vision of political campaigns held by reporters, editorialists, photojournalists, and others in the media, political campaigns and candidates are pretty sleazy. As Bormann notes, "They portrayed a shoddy and disappointing state of affairs," with candidates rated somewhere along a continuum ranging from "uninteresting" to "despicable."[25] To those in the media, every candidate is measured against their vision of an ideal candidate — someone who is articulate on the issues and has no skeletons in the closet. Another part of the media's vision of the campaign is that it is their task to "dig out" the truth. In this digging process, apparently there are favorite themes or visions that appear again and again in the campaigns studied by Bormann and his colleagues. Let us examine a few of these fantasy types for political campaigns and then speculate about what sorts of themes might exist for product or idea campaigns.

One fantasy theme identified by Bormann is that of "the front-runner," the candidate who, according to the polls or because of incumbency, has the kind of legitimacy discussed earlier in the five-stage campaign model. This candidate is focused on by the media, which cover such issues as how far ahead he or she is, whether he or she is showing signs of stumbling, whether he or she can win the general election, is hiding something, is just stalking horses for other candidates, and a number of related issues. All of this makes interesting and dramatic narrative news — the kind that gets good ratings and hence commands higher advertising rates, thus justifying good bonuses or "perks" for intrepid reporters who are good at digging out the "truth."

Another fantasy theme is that of the baseball game, with the candidates being in "the early or final innings" or unable to "get to first base" with the electorate. Another theme makes use of boxing images, with candidates "being on the ropes" or delivering "knockout blows" to the opposition, who is "just a lightweight" and not a real "contender."

A fantasy theme that makes for good dramatic and narrative news in a campaign is the "gaffe" — the mistake or blunder. A sure sign that the gaffe is "chaining out" in the media and hence in the eyes of the public is when humorists, such as cartoonists, focus on the gaffe. Bormann gives an example from the 1988 presidential campaigns that drew on the "adultery gaffe" of Gary Hart. Hart had been asked by reporters whether he had ever committed adultery, and he waffled on his answer. In a Doonesbury cartoon strip, all the reporters who had ever committed adultery were asked to raise their hands. Only the pure ones — those who kept their hands down — would be permitted to cover the campaign.[26]

There is also the fantasy theme of the "Spin Doctor," a media expert attached to the candidate's campaign staff. The Spin Doctor's job is to see to it that the press gives the proper interpretation to the candidate's words and deeds. In the fantasy, the candidate tends to be a bumbler in need of propping up by "behind-the-scenes manipulators" who will put the perfect "spin" on his or her statements or actions.

In product-oriented advertising, the ad agency or an advertising huckster puts "spin" on the product using press releases about the product's introduction, by getting press coverage for giving the product away to some worthy group, and/or by emphasizing the product's astounding benefits.

"Roger Ailes was telling me the candidate was so wonderful, all I needed was to tell the plain truth about him—no spin at all. Then I woke up."

FIGURE 10.9

What are some examples of "spin" in product-oriented campaigns? In political campaigns? In ideological campaigns?

(Cartoon by Ed Fisher. © 1990 *Advertising Age*. Reprinted by permission of Ed Fisher.)

Bert Metter, chairman of J. Walter Thompson USA advertising agency and part-time columnist for *Advertising Age*, defines it this way:

> We are in the age of spin. The art and science of creating images is out of the closet. . . . As spin becomes more common . . . we've got to deliver more effectiveness. . . . The agencies with the answers will succeed. Others will have a lot of spinning to do.[27]

Naturally, this kind of spin-doctoring for products is bound to raise criticism from those who believe that the ad industry is responsible for conspicuous consumption and all of its accompanying ills: pollution, easy credit, and "keeping up with the Joneses."[28]

Although it is true that some useless products are passed off on some consumers via clever campaigns and that there are unethical individuals in the advertising industry, the situation is not as bad as some would have it appear. In fact, consumers are remarkably inattentive to the many product-oriented campaign messages. As University of Chicago sociologist Michael Schudson observes, most people do something else when the TV spots come on the air. In fact, 60 percent of them leave the room during a commercial. Only 9 percent can recall an ad they saw the night before without prompting and hinting, and even with such hinting, only 25 percent recall the ad. Ads, according to Schudson, are the background—the white noise—of the American household. Although they may be tasteless and may, like flatulence, be a repugnant kind of air pollution, research shows that ads go amazingly unnoticed by the average citizen, and most advertisers will tell you that their purpose is not to sell a product but to sell a *brand*.[29]

Advertising does work, and Schudson agrees, noting that price advertising is the most effective kind of advertising.[30] He goes on to argue that *because ads go so unnoticed and unattended to, is exactly wherein their power truly lies*: "[It is] precisely because people pay them so little heed that they do not call critical defenses into play. . . . Because, to put it simply, advertising is propaganda and everyone knows it."[31] Schudson's point is argued by a number of persons, frequently from a Marxist position, who say that although advertisements in product or idea campaigns may not be fraudulent in a legal sense, they are fraudulent in another way: They *imply* that an audience and the *supposed values* of that audience (for example, consumption) are indeed quite harmful to society as a whole. We might label this rhetorical vision the "culture of consumption" explanation of advertising and its effects. The originator of the term and cultural critic Christopher Lasch claims that in a consumer culture, advertising "manufactures a product of its own: the consumer, perpetually unsatisfied, restless, anxious and bored. Advertising serves not so much to advertise products as to promote consumption as a way of life."[32] The criticism of such a consumer culture in which human values are on the trash heap leads people like Schudson to observe that "people sacrifice people to accumulate wealth or that they sacrifice themselves to the pursuit of goods in order to accumulate people. . . . [They] are seen as philistines; acquisitive and upwardly mobile. . . . Character has degenerated and values have, in a sense, disappeared. . . . Narcissism runs wild, the unguilty desire for objects and experiences to 'pleasure' oneself runs free."[33] Consumers become more interested in the wrong characteristics of the goods they purchase, according to Schudson. They are interested "not in workmanship but convenience, not character but cheapness and portability, not aesthetic design but glitzy showiness, not *sub-*

stance . . . but *image*. . . . They do not love things too well but use them mindlessly instead of caring for them. Their attitude toward things of the world is profane rather than sacred."[34] As sociologist Daniel Bell puts it, "A consumption economy . . . finds its reality in appearances."[35]

So the vision of the "consumer culture" is often associated with or blamed on the persuasive advertising campaign on behalf of a product. What kind of vision may come from the persuasive campaign on behalf of an idea, a dogma, or an ideology?

Rhetorical Visions in Ideological Campaigns

Throughout American history, various populist movements have focused on such issues as the gold standard, the prices paid to farmers for their goods, the right to form a union and bargain collectively with management, the right to vote, abolition, and the prohibition of alcohol. These movements have always formed around "men [and women] of words," to use Eric Hoffer's term.[36] He points out that "mass movements do not usually rise until the prevailing order has been discredited. The discrediting is not an automatic result of blunders and abuses of those in power, but the deliberate work of men of words with a grievance."[37] One of the common fears in this country is that a talented persuader might be able to agitate the common man into a movement or perhaps even into revolution. The rhetorical vision that seems to emerge from this fear might be labeled "the demagogue takes over." We fear such takeovers because frequently they are highly emotional and can easily get out of control. If you look back to our earlier discussion of Hoffer's ideas and his identification of who joins such movements and what motivates them, it is easy to identify with those in power, or the "establishment," as it is sometimes called. Further, Hoffer identifies fanaticism as one characteristic of such leaders.

It is this fanatical zeal that most average citizens fear, because the "true believers" will say anything, believe anything, do anything, and sacrifice anything—even their own lives on occa-

Wordsmiths

FIGURE 10.10

These are the wordsmiths for the politically oriented campaign. How effective would they be for an idea-oriented campaign? Why? (Drawing by W. B. Park;

© 1988 The New Yorker Magazine, Inc. Reprinted by permission.)

sion — on behalf of the movement. The followers cease to be individuals, as Hoffer points out, and instead become melded into a powerful entity — the movement. It is the basis for the individuals' collective and individual identities.[38]

The "men [and women] of words" use several unifying devices to forge the collective power of the movement. Following from our earlier discussion of who joins mass movements — the dispossessed, misfits, those without hope — it is clear that the offer of change and of hope can be a means of developing unity among the followers. It is no accident that the leaders of mass movements of the

past promised their followers "a better tomorrow." This kind of ideological campaign rhetoric catches the imagination of the audience and can unify them in zealous action.

Unifying Devices Hoffer points out several unifying devices that seem to be characteristic of the ideological campaign. In many ways they are the reality links in the fantasies, which ultimately create the rhetorical visions of mass movements. These reality links have led to, for example, the abolition movement, the union movement, and the civil rights movement in their positive forms or to

Nazism, terrorism, and racism in their negative forms.

Hatred is a powerful unifying device. In fact, Hoffer says, "Hatred is the most accessible and comprehensive of all unifying agents. . . . Mass movements can rise and spread without belief in God, but never without a belief in a devil."[39] We know that Hitler used Jews as the hate device, and abolitionists used slaveholders. Today, Palestinian terrorists use Israel. Hoffer speculates that this unifying hatred frequently springs from self-contempt and guilt or feelings of impotency, ineffectiveness, and worthlessness. At the same time, the unified hatred removes individual guilt and permits the individuals to do things they would never do if they were acting on their own. As Hoffer notes, "When we lose our individual independence in the corporateness of a mass movement, we find a new freedom—freedom to hate, bully, lie, torture, murder, and betray without remorse or shame."[40] This helps explain the dementia of Nazism, racism, and terrorism. The same thing applies to the antiwar activists of the sixties and seventies, who often damaged property and verbally and physically abused persons representing "the establishment." Finally, our national guilt was raised to the point that the nation's conscience insisted on leaving Vietnam in defeat instead of victory.

Imitation is another unifying device in the ideological movement, according to Hoffer. It helps to make the fantasy seem more real when there is tangible evidence of the power of the movement. He says there must be a "diffusion of uniformity."[41] This accounts for the chanting of the crowd at a rally, the salutes frequently adopted by mass movements, the adoption of official uniforms in some movements, the use of bumper stickers or pins bearing a symbol of the movement, and numerous other real and symbolic means of imitation.

Persuasion and **coercion** also are unifying agents that help to spread and maintain the fantasy of the movement. What Hoffer refers to here is the kind of propaganda that is used within the movement to build emotion and develop loyalty in its membership. As Hoffer puts it, "Propaganda by itself succeeds mainly with the frustrated. Their throbbing fears, hopes, and passions crowd at the portals of their senses. . . . It is the music of their own souls they hear in the impassioned words of the propagandist."[42] Hitler could easily raise the emotions of the crowds with his anti-Semitism—they already hated Jews, though they did not dare articulate their hatred. In fact, Hitler said that if there were no Jews in Germany, the Nazis would have had to invent them. But with this persuasion there also must be a certain level of coercion. Paul Joseph Goebbels, the Nazi minister of propaganda, put it this way: "A sharp sword must always stand behind propaganda if it is to be really effective."[43] According to Hoffer, if fanaticism begets violence, then it is equally true that violence begets fanaticism or at least reinforces it.[44] Also, persuasion and coercion frequently result in a powerful need to proselytize, or "spread the word," to the uncommitted.

Leadership is a critical unifying element that can spark powerful fantasies in audiences' minds. They can visualize themselves doing great things and enacting noble and historical deeds through the leader. The circumstances must be ripe for such leadership to emerge, according to Hoffer. The potential converts must feel dissatisfied with things as they are and must be willing to dream of things as they might be. As Hoffer puts it, "Once the stage is set, the presence of an outstanding leader is indispensible."[45] It was Lenin who exploited the chaos in Russia in 1917, Hitler who used the bankruptcy of Germany in 1931, and Martin Luther King, Jr., who sparked the imagination of millions of nonviolent protesters in the 1960s.

Suspicion is another excellent unifying device in sparking fantasies in the audiences of mass-movement rhetoric. This fits with the cultural myth of the presence of conspiracy. If you suspect that someone may be planning to harm you, it is natural to turn to a movement for assistance. Hoffer asserts that it is the dissatisfaction with ourselves that leads us to identify the same sort of shortcomings in others. He notes, "We have seen that the acrid secretion of the frustrated mind . . .

acts yet as a marvelous slime to cement the embit-tered and disaffected into one compact whole. Sus-picion too is an ingredient of this acrid slime, and it too can act as a unifying agent."[46] Suspicion was certainly at the root of the antiwar movement of the sixties and seventies. And certainly the mass movements that overthrew governments in the communist countries of East Europe thrived on suspicion—some of it well founded.

Action is a final unifying agent in the ideologi-cal campaign, according to Hoffer. He notes how important a simple action like marching together can unify people, and how the Nazis recognized that "'Marching diverts men's thoughts. Marching kills thought. Marching makes an end of individ-uality.'"[47] Small wonder that so many mass move-ments have relied on the rally followed by a demonstration, many times in the form of a march. As Hoffer explains, "The frustrated see in action a cure for all that ails them. It brings self-forgetting and it gives them a sense of purpose and worth."[48] If the action is too successful, Hoffer says it may become an end in itself and spell the premature end of the movement, for entirely successful ac-tion builds self-confidence and restores individu-ality. Being successful is all the true believer desires—there is no longer a need for the ideol-ogy of the movement. When the rhetorical vision promised by the movement becomes objective reality, individual true believers quickly retire.[49]

Ideological Movements in the 1990s While studying Hoffer, Bormann, and others on the ide-ological movement, I have often wondered why such mass movements as civil rights, ERA, and antiwar movements seem to occur in cycles, and why we saw so few of them in this country in the 1980s. Arthur Schlesinger has made some inter-esting remarks regarding this pattern in his fore-word to the recent book *Robert Kennedy: In His Own Words*. Schlesinger's words fit with much that has already been said about the "me generation." He notes:

> American politics seem to flow in thirty-year cycles between times dominated by public

purpose and times dominated by private inter-est. The 1980s, like the 1950s and the 1920s, were a time where private action and private enterprise were deemed the best way to meet national problems. But private-interest eras do not go on forever. Rest replenishes the national energies; problems neglected demand remedy; *greed as the point of existence, seems inade-quate* [emphasis added]. After a time, people begin to ask not what their country can do for them but what they can do for their country."[50]

If Schlesinger is right, the 1990s will be a decade when fantasy themes and rhetorical visions will capture the interests, attention, and energies of "true believers," who will be drawn to ideological campaigns. And given the continually advancing technologies and the inexpensiveness with which one can develop and distribute campaign mes-sages, the ideological campaigns of the nineties will be much more sophisticated than those of the sixties and seventies. They will require an ethical and responsible audience.

OTHER COMMUNICATION CHARACTERISTICS OF CAMPAIGNS

There are several other characteristics of cam-paigns that relate to how they communicate—what messages they send overtly and what mes-sages they send covertly. We will now look briefly at some of these communication characteristics of the successful persuasive campaign.

Credibility

Successful campaigns usually communicate a sense of credibility about their product, person, or idea. We follow the advice of those in whom we have faith—those we feel we can believe. Credi-bility relates to a number of factors discussed ear-lier, such as *dynamism, trustworthiness*, and *expertise* or *competence*. Some candidates build

credibility by showing their expertise on some issue or another, whereas others focus on their dynamism or honesty. In one Senate campaign in
Illinois, a long-time incumbent who was physically attractive and dynamic was defeated by pro-
fessorial congressman Paul Simon, who wore a
bow tie. The incumbent was depicted as insincere
through ads that called him a "chameleon" while
emphasizing that Simon had always been consistent and was an expert on problems downstate. In
other states, rugged, active, macho types seemed
to win the day. Credibility — whether communicated through expertise, sincerity, or dynamism —
is essential to the successful campaign.

Climate of Opinion

Successful campaigns tie in with the prevailing
climate of opinion. Public opinion is a fickle thing
in our culture, and many critics have observed the
pendulum effect, wherein popular opinion moves
from one side of the political continuum to the
other. These shifting sands of public opinion are
critical to the successful persuader and need to be
identified and then worked into the campaign.

In product-oriented campaigns, we have seen
this many times. Seven-Up, for example, was
nearly bankrupt when it asked the J. Walter
Thompson ad agency to design an ad campaign.
The agency hooked Seven-Up into the then-
prevailing ideal of being different and nonconformist, launching the "Un-cola" campaign and
turning Seven-Up's fortunes around. We see a
similar thing in ads aimed at the "me generation,"
members of which are now reaching child-bearing
years. The ads stress being good to yourself and
being all you can be, even if you are going to
balance holding a job with raising a family and
with pursuing your private interest in sky diving.

With more people reaching their forties, the ad
planners have presumed a positive climate of opinion for people — particularly women — between
thirty-six and fifty-four years old (their numbers
will increase by 56 percent in the next decade or
so). Little wonder that ad pitches feature Candice
Bergen and Cybil Shepard, both of whom are in

their forties. As columnist Ellen Goodman noted,
"Those of us who failed to look like Brooke
Shields at seventeen can now fail to look like Victoria Principal at thirty-three, like Linda Evans at
forty-two, and Sophia Loren at fifty."[51] Clearly,
her observation underscores the ever-shifting climate of opinion.

Opinion Leaders

Successful campaigns seem to aim their messages
at opinion leaders. Studies done over thirty years
ago to discover how farmers adopted new farm
methods (contour plowing or crop rotation) found
an interesting phenomenon. Most farmers did not
respond to direct appeals from the Department of
Agriculture. Instead, they seemed to adopt the
new methods only after a highly respected farmer
or an opinion leader did. This pattern was labeled
the *two-step flow* theory of communication.[52] We
are most persuaded when an opinion leader does
something in response to what a persuader says.
Later studies demonstrated that this flow had many
levels, and the two-step notion was elaborated to a
multistep flow of information. The Successful
Farmers, who followed the lead of the Super Farmers, were leaders in turn to the Good Farmers,
who were opinion leaders to the OK Farmers.
Even OK Farmers were opinion leaders to the
Unsuccessful Farmers.

A problem that everyday campaigners may
have in using this third characteristic is the identification of opinion leaders. A little research will
usually help. How might you determine who the
opinion leaders are on your campus? In your town?
In other contexts?

Uniqueness

Successful campaigns make the ordinary seem unusual; the banal becomes unique. One TV ad depicts an ordinary homemaker fixing dinner for
hubby. She is busy at work on the salad, and it is a
pretty humdrum salad until . . . Chef's Delight!
As she opens the foil package, a symphony begins
to play. The lights dim as the camera cuts to an

elegantly set table. By candlelight, hubby pours the vintage wine from a towel-swathed bottle. In the final shot, he romantically eyes humdrum housewife, who now is a knockout. The clever persuader takes boring events or routines and makes them unique. The banal aspects of life are dressed up to become really special, and this shift draws our attention in potent ways. We enjoy the out-of-the-way, the special, the unique things in life. The persuader ties the product, candidate, or idea into such unique moments. Hundreds of times each day on TV, ads such as the one for the salad seasoning make many mundane things unique. Politicians make themselves unique through their actions. In our town, one rode a horse along the route of a proposed freeway. Another debated an empty chair when the opponent didn't show up for the debate. Mass movements also strive for uniqueness.

"OK-ness"

Successful campaigns have messages that make persuadees feel OK. Thomas Harris, in his book *I'm OK — You're OK*, noted that all humans want to feel OK but that most of us do not.[53] This un-OK feeling stems from the many years during childhood when we were not able to do the things needed to support ourselves. For instance, we were too little to drive or cook. This not-OK feeling is deeply recorded in our minds like a kind of tape recording, says Harris. It forces us to find ways to feel loved, content, witty, well liked, and so forth. The campaign offers rewards for taking action that will make you feel OK in a variety of ways. Women who suspect that they are becoming unattractive to their husbands are urged to feel OK about themselves by using certain cosmetics, perfumes, or hairsprays. Mothers are urged to feel OK about themselves by having a large supply of Bactine around when their kids skin their knees. Dads are warned not to be un-OK as they view a little boy watching his role-model dad smoke; the American Cancer Society then gives Dad an out by offering him a packet on how to quit and feel OK again. In another ad, Dad is advised that he

will move up to a penthouse suite of offices if he works late at night and drinks Johnny Walker Red Label scotch, the sign of an OK executive. The goal to link rewards or OK-ness to a persuader's advice is likely to aid in the success of a campaign. Persuadees need to observe when and how they are being made to feel not OK or when their not-OK state serves as an assumed premise for the persuader.

Internal States

Successful campaigns usually rely on information, experiences, or memories that are already inside persuadees rather than trying to teach the audience new information. This idea comes from Tony Schwartz's book *The Responsive Chord*.[54]

Schwartz has been a media consultant to several presidents and presidential nominees as well as to many state and local politicians. We will explore his theory in depth in Chapter 12. His basic idea is that campaigners should try to identify the internal state of the target audience: What are poignant memories or experiences for them? Then the campaigner determines how these can be prompted, or cued out. Schwartz advised several presidential nominees to advertise on Monday Night Football, when the audience is primed for a fight in reaction to the game; they would have just seen numerous murderous tackles, bone-crunching blocks, and similar fight-oriented events.

A good way to sell a drain cleaner is to show someone sticking her hands into a stopped-up sink full of greasy water filled with food bits, coffee grounds, and the like. Most people have had to do that at least once in their lives and so already have the feeling embedded in their experiential storehouse. Then someone pours in some Liquid Plumber, and we watch the sink drain out as the faucet pours out clean fresh water to wash away the muck. This is another great clean feeling to which those of us who have had to unclog sinks can relate. In this ad, the persuader *gets the meaning out of* the viewer. Contrast this ad with a commercial that might explain how traps in sinks get clogged with grease and hair. The ad then shows a cutaway of such a trap and goes on to explain that the grease can be cut by either an acid or an alkalyde. Because acids can damage plumbing, the announcer suggests that we use Drano, an alkaline-based product, to dissolve the grease and unclog the sink. The ad then shows that happening. This ad is busy trying to *get something into* the viewer.

As noted, there is no persuasion that does not involve self-persuasion. We must agree to be persuaded and then find good reasons for deciding. Many of these good reasons are already embedded in our subconscious and conscious memory. Clever persuaders identify these memories and draw them out, tying the product, candidate, or idea to the memories.

You will notice other communication patterns that seem to be associated with the successful campaign: timing, choice of theme musical score, and clever uses of colors in print and TV ads. Noting them is the most useful thing you can do, even if you don't verify them through some high-falutin' scientific system. You will be tuning your persuadee's ear to the kind of doublespeak that will be spewed at us in campaigns seeking new buyers, new voters, or new joiners.

REVIEW AND CONCLUSION

Person/candidate, product, and idea/ideology campaigns also demonstrate permanence and change. The formal and functional characteristics of campaigns that we have explored seem to persist over time, forming permanent patterns. The ever-shifting issues and increasingly sophisticated technologies of product testing, public-opinion polling, media production, and direct marketing are the elements of change. Among the recurring formal aspects of campaigns are:

1. a systematic flow of communication from the persuader to the audience and back to the persuader via a feedback loop — something that typifies all communication systems.
2. the establishment of formal goals, strategies, and tactics.

Among the recurring functional aspects of campaigns are:

1. the creation of a "position," "niche," or *"creneau"* in the audience's mind.
2. stages through which most campaigns must pass.
3. a participatory dramatization of the product, candidate, or idea/ideology. The audience is invited to participate in the campaign drama in real or symbolic ways.
4. the kinds of appeals that unify and recruit zealots for the mass movement.

Although particular positions, developmental stages, and dramatic invitations shift over time, the patterns of positioning, staging, and dramatic invitation persist. If Theodore Schlesinger's predictions are accurate, persuadees of the 1990s should be prepared to encounter numerous campaigns in the coming years, especially those of an ideological nature. We are beginning to see this already in the pro-life and pro-choice campaigns as well as in the environmental movement. You need to get ready to be a critical receiver who makes responsible decisions about which product to buy, which candidate to vote for, and which ideas or ideologies to endorse. These decisions are appropriate only after thorough analysis of the campaigns. Ask yourself how the campaign responds to feedback; what are its objectives, strategies, and tactics; how the campaign positions the product, person, or idea; what developmental stages emerge; and in what kind of drama you are being invited to participate. When you have answered these questions, you will be ready to make a responsible decision.

QUESTIONS FOR FURTHER THOUGHT

1. Define each of the developmental terms and identify examples of the first three stages in some magazine or newspaper campaign.
2. What stage of a campaign or movement is represented when we vote for or against a particular candidate or proposition? Why?

3. To determine what elements of the drama are successful in capturing audience attention, look at your local newspaper as well as at national news events and nationwide ads. Who are the heroes of the dramas? Who are the villains? Are there common plot lines? Values? Settings?

4. Give examples of successful campaigns in which you identify the six patterns. How do they differ from campaign to campaign? Are some better with one kind of campaign than others?

5. Identify a social movement that is either going on or seems to be developing. Use the Bowers and Ochs model and the Stewart, Smith, and Denton model to trace its development. Which most accurately describes what is happening?

6. Choose a campus or local campaign and try to identify some of the characteristics we discussed. Which are used most frequently? Are they effective? Explain.

7. Using Bormann's symbolic convergence theory, explain the same social movement identified in question 5. Which of the methodologies seems most message oriented? Which is most audience related?

8. Identify several "fantasy types" in a campaign for a product made popular in the 1980s. Are they similar to those for products of the 1990s?

9. Why does Schudson call advertising ". . . the uneasy persuasion"?

10. What are some of Hoffer's "unifying devices"? How have they worked in past campaigns? Where do they seem to be working now?

11. What are some ways now being used to position products you are presently using? Candidates presently running for office? Idea campaigns requesting your active or financial support? Mass movements presently seeking converts?

12. What appear to be the objectives, strategies, and tactics of present-day campaigns for products, persons, and ideas/ideologies?

NOTES

1. Don DeVale, President, The Valley Co., Inc., a division of Kidde Corporation, personal conversation.

2. Sidney Smith, Department of Theater Arts, N.I.U., personal conversation.

3. As quoted in Courtland L. Bovée and William F. Arens, *Contemporary Advertising*, 2nd ed. (Homewood, IL: Richard D. Irwin, Inc., 1986), p. 5.

4. A good discussion of the differences between the issue and the image of candidates for political office and what those differences imply is available in Dan F. Hahn and Ruth M. Gonchar, "Political Myth: The Image and the Issue," *Today's Speech* 20:57–65, 1972. Hahn and Gonchar conclude that the image may well be the best indicator of a candidate's future behavior. Issues change and fade, they maintain, but image indicates a pattern of behavior independent of issues. See also Judith S. Trent and Robert V. Friedenberg, *Political Campaign Communication: Principles and Practices* (New York: Praeger, 1983); Ruth Mandel, *In the Running: The New Woman Candidate* (New Haven, CT: Ticknor and Fields, 1981); Murray Edelman, *The Symbolic Uses of Politics* (Urbana: The University of Illinois Press, 1964); Robert E. Denton, *The Symbolic Dimension of the Presidency* (Prospect Heights, IL: Waveland Press, 1983); Thomas B. Patterson, *The Mass Media Election* (New York: Praeger, 1980).

5. Al Ries and Jack Trout, *Positioning: The Battle for Your Mind* (New York: McGraw-Hill, 1986).

6. *Ibid*.

7. Eric Hoffer, *The True Believer* (New York: Harper & Row, Perennial Book Edition, 1966), pp. 26–56.

8. *Ibid*.

9. John Bowers and Donovan Ochs, *The Rhetoric of Agitation and Control* (Reading, MA: Addison-Wesley, 1971).

10. "Rasslin' Redux: Funky New Players in a Theatre of the Absurd," *Newsweek*, March 11, 1985, pp. 84–85.

11. Some of the strategies arise out of communication research, others out of theory and research in other areas — history, for example — but all of them have been verified in numerous campaigns.

At Northern Illinois University, we have looked in depth at more than 800 different person, product, or idea campaigns. Not all of the strategies occur in each campaign, but those listed seem most prevalent.

12. Leonard Binder et al., *Crisis and Sequence in Political Development* (Princeton, NJ: Princeton University Press, 1971), especially Chapter 1. I wish to thank William Semlak for calling this source to my attention; Mr. Semlak used the suggestions offered by the volume to analyze the campaign of George McGovern (unpublished paper).

13. Judith S. Trent and Robert V. Friedenberg, *Political Campaign Communication* (New York: Praeger, 1983). See especially Chapter 2.

14. Charles J. Stewart, Craig Allen Smith, and Robert E. Denton, Jr., *Persuasion and Social Movements*, 2nd ed. (Prospect Heights, IL: Waveland Press, 1989). See especially Chapter 3.

15. Everett M. Rogers, *The Diffusion of Innovation* (New York: Free Press, 1962).

16. Many times these plots resemble or are identical to the cultural myths discussed in Chapter 7.

17. For an in-depth discussion of how such communities can develop, see Charles U. Larson and Christine Oravec, "*A Prairie Home Companion* and the Fabrication of Community," *Critical Studies in Mass Communication*, September 1987, pp. 221–244; and Charles U. Larson, "Fantasy Theme Analysis and the Evoked Rhetorical Vision of Lake Wobegon" (Paper delivered at the Speech Communication Association convention, November 1986), pp. 1–54.

18. For a fully developed discussion of the theory and methodology, see Ernest G. Bormann, *The Force of Fantasy* (Carbondale and Edwardsville: Southern Illinois University Press, 1985). I am grateful to Dr. Bormann for sharing a manuscript titled "Media Fantasies of Campaign 1988," which was delivered March 30, 1988, on the NIU campus and elsewhere and is now in submission to a national journal. It provided most of the history of the development of the theory and the methodology. I also wish to express my gratitude to Dr. Bormann for permitting me to sit in on his seminar during the summer of 1972 while I was a visiting professor at the University of Minnesota. It was then that the first stage of the theory development was occurring, and for a short while I was privileged to be among the "turtle racers" at Minnesota.

19. See, for example, David K. Rod, "Kenneth Burke and Suzanne Langer on Drama and Its Audience," *Quarterly Journal of Speech* 72:307–317, 1986; W. Lance Haynes, "Of That Which We Cannot Write: Some Notes on the Phenomenology of Media," *Quarterly Journal of Speech* 74:71–101, 1988; Walter R. Fisher, "Narration as a Human Communication Paradigm," *Communication Monographs* 51:1–22, 1986; Karen A. Foss and Stephen W. Littlejohn, "*The Day After*: Rhetorical Vision in an Iron Framework," *Critical Studies in Mass Communication* 3:317–336, 1986; and Janice Hocking Rushing, "Mythic Evolution of 'The New Frontier' in Mass Mediated Rhetoric," *Critical Studies in Mass Communication* 3:265–296, 1986.

20. Bormann, "Media Fantasies of Campaign 1988," p. 3.

21. For some good examples of how the methodology has been applied in a variety of contexts, see John F. Cragan and Donald C. Shields, *Applied Communication Research: A Dramatistic Approach* (Prospect Heights, IL: Waveland Press, 1981).

22. Ernest G. Bormann, "Recent Developments in Fantasy Theme Analysis," afternoon seminar delivered March 30, 1988, at NIU. Bormann, "Shared Media . . . " p. 3 (see Note 18).

23. *Ibid.*, pp. 6–7.

24. *Ibid.*, pp. 8–9. See also Dan Nimmo and James E. Combs, *Mediated Political Realities* (New York: Longman, 1983), Chapter 6, "Fantasies of the Arena: Popular Sports and Politics," pp. 124–140.

25. *Ibid.*, p. 15.

26. *Ibid.*, pp. 16–20. See also Nimmo and Combs, *op. cit.*, Chapter 7, "Elite Political Fantasies: Groupthink, Decisionmakers and Gatekeepers," and Chapter 8, "Pack Journalism: Group Mediation of Political News," pp. 142–182.

27. Bert Metter, "Advertising in the Age of Spin," *Advertising Age*, September 17, 1990, p. 36.

28. Good examples of this type of criticism of modern product-oriented campaigns are Richard Wrightman and T. J. Jackson Lears, eds., *The Culture of Consumption: Critical Essays in American History, 1880–1980* (New York: Pantheon Books, 1983); William Leiss, Stephen Kline, and Sut Jhally, *Social Communication in Advertising: Persons, Products and Images of Well-Being* (New York: Methuen, 1986); and Michael Schudson,

Advertising, The Uneasy Persuasion: Its Dubious Impact on American Society (New York: Basic Books, 1984).

29. Schudson, *op. cit.*, pp. 3–10.

30. *Ibid.*, Introduction, p. 11.

31. *Ibid.*, p. 4.

32. Christopher Lasch, *The Culture of Narcissism* (New York: W. W. Norton, 1978), p. 72. For similar views, see also James Coleman, *The Asymmetrical Society* (Syracuse: Syracuse University Press, 1982); the Wrightman and Lears book and the Leiss, Kline, and Jhally book, both cited in Note 28.

33. Schudson, *op. cit.*, p. 7.

34. *Ibid.*, p. 8.

35. Daniel Bell, *The Cultural Contradictions of Capitalism* (New York: Basic Books, 1976), p. 68.

36. Hoffer, *op. cit.*, Chapter 15, pp. 119–129.

37. *Ibid.*, p. 119.

38. *Ibid.*, pp. 60–72.

39. *Ibid.*, pp. 85–86.

40. *Ibid.*, p. 85.

41. *Ibid.*, p. 94.

42. *Ibid.*, p. 98.

43. *Ibid.*, pp. 98–99.

44. *Ibid.*, p. 99.

45. *Ibid.*, p. 104.

46. *Ibid.*, p. 114.

47. *Ibid.*, p. 112.

48. *Ibid.*

49. *Ibid.*, p. 113.

50. Edwin O. Guthman and Jeffrey Schulman, eds., *Robert Kennedy: In His Own Words* (New York: Bantam Books, 1988), Foreword.

51. "The Look of a Certain Age," *Newsweek*, January 28, 1985, p. 64.

52. An early reference to this phenomenon is found in P. E. Lazarsfeld, B. Bevelson, and H. Gaudet, *The People's Choice* (New York: Columbia University Press, 1948), which identified a two-step flow in the 1940 presidential election. Later elaboration to a multistep flow can be seen in J. N. Rosenau, *Public Opinion and Foreign Policy* (New York: Random House, 1961). See also Rogers, *op. cit.*

53. Thomas A. Harris, *I'm OK — You're OK: A Practical Guide to Transactional Analysis* (New York: Harper & Row, 1967).

54. Tony Schwartz, *The Responsive Chord* (New York: Anchor Press/Doubleday, 1973).

CHAPTER

Becoming a Persuader

▼

Until this point, *Persuasion: Reception and Responsibility* has focused on receiver skills: how to be a critical, responsible, and ethical consumer of persuasion. However, even the shyest person must become a persuader from time to time, whether interpersonally, with an instructor or parent; in small work groups, where one may have to convince other members to follow a plan; or in public contexts, where it may be necessary to make business presentations to one's boss or department, a speech to the city council, or persuasive statements to a congregation encouraging them to increase their giving. Luckily, the knowledge gained in our role as a persuadee can be applied to our occasional role as a persuader. We can use tactics of intensification and downplaying; we can make use of our feel for what makes persuasive language; we can mold our persuasion using process, content, cultural, and nonverbal premises; and we can apply our knowledge of what is ethical in persuasion. As a persuader, your first step in preparing your message is *knowing your audience.* Audience-held premises will be one of the things you want to know. A second stage in becoming a persuader is *shaping your message.* Here, considerations such as patterns of organization, kinds of proof, and styling of messages will be important. Finally, you must choose how to go about *delivering your message.* This will involve not only the physical characteristics of how you speak (eye contact, posture, and so on) but also choosing a channel through which to deliver the message, timing the message delivery, and so on. Finally, we will discuss some common persuasive tactics used by persuaders.

KNOWING YOUR AUDIENCE

It is easy to assert that you should know as much as possible about your persuadees, but it is not so easy to prescribe specific ways you can get to know your audience. One of the best ways is to *listen to them as they persuade.* As we have seen in the congruency, dissonance, and balance models discussed in Chapters 3 and 6, people want

the world to be congruous with their expectations and in line with their predictions. When they persuade, they use tactics that would be persuasive to them. I am most persuaded when the source uses narratives and examples. Skim back and see how often I use the narrative example to get you to take my advice. If you want to persuade me, fill your message with narratives and examples. Know your audience, observe them, listen to them, and analyze what they say and how they say it. When your parents try to persuade, how do they go about it? What values do they believe you or others should have? What kinds of evidence do they use? These questions can be most useful for persuading in an interpersonal context. Some people, for example, are most easily persuaded when they think that *they are the ones who came up with the idea for change.* It is best to give such persons several alternatives and let *them* make the choice. Then they "own" the idea or innovation and think of it as their brilliant contribution. I once used precisely this tactic to convince a potential client to hire me for my consulting services. I had prepared several alternative advertisements to those he was using, and I had several alternative approaches for the transition from the firm he was using to do his advertising. He appropriated the alternative he preferred, and it became *his* idea, which, of course, he enthusiastically supported. That's why this tactic works so well.

Demographics and Audience Analysis

When persuasion is aimed at larger audiences than occur in the interpersonal context, advertisers and marketing specialists use a method known as **demographics** to analyze their audience. In demographics, persuaders cluster groups of people by discovering their shared attributes—their likes, dislikes, habits, values, status, political ideologies, religious beliefs, and other characteristics that can help group people together. A good example of demographic clustering is in the magazine subscriptions people have. Various magazine, catalog, and periodical publishers do elaborate statistical analyses of their subscription lists. If you subscribe to *Outdoor Life, Field and Stream*, and *Sports Illustrated*, you are likely to be different from the person who subscribes to *Atlantic, Horticulture, Organic Gardening*, and *Bon Appétit*. Probably both of you are interested in the outdoors (the sports and gardening magazines indicate this) and would be good bets for catalogs featuring outdoor clothing. In all likelihood, only you are interested in hunting or fishing and would be a good candidate for a catalog of decoys or boats. Probably neither of you is interested in rock music and both of you would throw away a catalog on music video carts. The subscriptions you have are just one kind of information that can be used to cluster an audience demographically. Your affiliations (such as with church, fraternal, political, or community groups) are another, as are the credit cards you carry and the services you hire. All of these and more are used to cluster us into demographic groups. Through the census, the state driver's license department, returned warranty information, and many other sources, each of us has been identified as a member of a certain demographic cluster — as a good candidate for certain pitches.

Neither you nor I can do this kind of elaborate analysis of a potential audience, but we can do a lot even if we are limited in time and resources. For example, suppose you have been asked to make a presentation to a zoning board. You will want to find out who its members are and what they do for a living. Where they themselves live will be useful information. Their ages could also be a factor. Most important, get information about how your audience has acted in the past. What kinds of zoning restrictions have they strictly upheld? What kinds of alternatives have they allowed? Why? These are the kinds of questions that can help you analyze your audience. In some cases, you won't be able to find out these facts, and will be limited to more general information. You may be able to find out only who the members of the board are, where they live, and what party they represent.

What are some of the demographic factors to look at in preparing a formal persuasive presentation? The first step is to decide which factors will be significant for your audience. For example, in a presentation to a group of systems managers, I was able to find out that most of them worked in the insurance industry. I shaped my examples to fit the persuasive problems confronted by insurance people and asked questions related to insurance issues. Audience factors that can make a critical difference vary with the goal of the persuader. Age would be important if you were discussing "Tax Planning for Retirement," but it might not be so important if your topic was "Recycling" or "Dressing for Success." Gender will be important for some topics but not for others. The same thing goes for income, religion, or politics. Let us suppose that you have been asked to speak to an alumni group to convince them to support the building of new handball courts on campus. Which of the following will be among the factors you will want to explore about your audience?

1. *Average Age?* Will it matter if they are all over fifty or if they are all under thirty-five? Probably.

2. *Income?* Will it matter if they are well-to-do or just struggling along? Probably not so much, because it is the group's money that will be used and not personal income. However, handball is a costly sport. Most people have to rent a court. It will be good to tell about the value of handball for off-season times for members of the baseball team. The moves in handball are similar to those needed in fielding a baseball, so the court could serve several purposes, cutting the cost per user. You can sell your idea on more than one level here.

3. *Sex?* Are your alumni likely to be male or female, and does that matter? If 90 percent are male, then sex will matter.

4. *Religion?* Are Jews, Catholics, or Protestants more likely to favor handball? This factor is one you can ignore for the most part.

5. *Family Size?* Will it matter if your audience members have zero, two, or five children?

6. *Political Party?* Will it matter if they are Republican or Democrat? No, but if you had reason to believe they were Socialist, that might

FRANK AND ERNEST   by Bob Thaves

FIGURE 11.1

Frank knows his audience's preference for certain kinds
of words. (*Frank and Ernest* reprinted by permission of
NEA, Inc.)

make a difference. They might oppose handball as an elite sport identified with expensive
health clubs and spas.

7. *Type of Occupation?* If the audience members
are white-collar workers, they may be convinced by a solid set of statistics and a tightly
reasoned presentation done in a formal manner. The use of graphs, charts, and informational handouts may be helpful, and you
may want to let them have some time to think
it over.

And of course other demographic information
is available on particular audiences for a fee (such
as that from market research firms) or for free (for
example, from the census, your local chamber of
commerce, or the city directory).

Once you know the key demographic factors
for your group/topic/context, the next stage is to
explore them. The president of the alumni group
will be able to tell you about some of these. Membership lists will show you where alumni live,
which can cue you to income and age. Past actions—maybe even old yearbooks—can be useful
in finding out whether they prefer certain projects.
If they have turned down past requests from students, you need to know why. If they have not

funded athletic requests, you need to explore that,
too. Sometimes just talking to one or two typical
members of a group before you begin to persuade
can be helpful. Any characteristics they share as a
group can be useful in shaping your message for
that audience. Figure 11.1 shows an example of a
clever persuader who knows his receiver.

Determining Audience Needs

We touched on audience needs when we looked at
the kinds of premises people hold. Some are emotional, some are logical, some are cultural, and
some are nonverbal. Determining the motives
likely to persuade our target audiences will have to
be guesswork. We are not advertisers with sophisticated techniques for getting at the deep needs
many people have. Nonetheless, we can still do
some pretty sophisticated analysis on our alumni
group. We could focus on people's need for self-
confidence and try to sell our handball courts on
the basis that athletes are self-assured because they
do *something* well. Now the alumni can give others the same feeling by opening up the handball
option. Or we could talk about body image. We
need to keep in good shape in order to be healthy
in our minds—"and more than 50 percent of

hospital beds are filled by people who have mental problems." All these appeals and many others hook into key needs in today's world, if we judge by present advertising strategy.

All audiences have some sets of shared experiences. People my age can tell you exactly where and when they first heard of the murder of John F. Kennedy. It is an experience that can be used by a persuader dealing with people born before 1955. You can probably recall where you were when the space shuttle tragedy occurred. All parents know what it is like to fret over the first baby. An interesting example of such shared experiences and emotions for college students is the classic examination dream first identified by Freud.[1] Apparently it is common for college students to dream about showing up for a final examination only to be unable to recall anything about the class. In other variations, students cannot find the examination room or realize that they never studied for the exam or perhaps never even went to class or purchased the texts. College students probably also have similar dreams regarding registration, meeting a roommate at the dorm for the first time, and so on. All these stored visions can be persuasive building blocks.

Thus, in the process of audience analysis, we can also try to locate the key experiences that relate to our topic or goal. The next time you need to persuade someone, try to list the experiences he or she is likely to have had. Can some of these be tied into your message?

Another factor in audience analysis is also suggested by Tony Schwartz in his book *The Responsive Chord*.[2] Schwartz favors messages that are built for the time and place, when and where they will be heard. If you were an ad agent trying to send a message to people telling them to vote for someone, and you knew that they would hear it on Labor Day weekend, how would you design the message? You would want to plug into the picnic mood, the out-of-doors experience, and the family fun that people are having on that weekend. You might have the candidate talk about conservation for us and for our children or about the need to make it easy for friends to be together. Schwartz calls this the *task-oriented* approach to persuading. You can use it, too.

First ask yourself whether your goal fits with the audience's ability to follow your advice. If you are going to ask them to quit smoking, you'd better do it in such a way as to make it easy for them. Give them brochures that offer helpful hints on quitting. Advertisers ask what their market targets are going to be doing when they receive the message. So can you. The same thing applies to the state of mind of your persuadees — the alumni, the sales force, or the job interviewer. What is the likely mood for the alumni? They will be relaxed. They will remember old times. They might be bragging to former classmates. Take these things into account and design your message to do its task, using the good mood, nostalgia, and the feel of success. Remind them of the good feeling of competing with classmates on the athletic field and how that feeling served them in later years. Remind them of the new people they met. Then tell them that there is a chance to make that kind of feeling available to more students through the handball courts. Although you will be only guessing at the mood of your listeners in this stage, your guesses can be more than random-chance flings if you spend some time getting to know the audience.

Once we know something about our target group and how its members feel about our topic, we can shape the message, be it a speech, interview, ad, or rally cry. There are many steps in the shaping process. First we need to *organize* the message in the most useful way. People recall things that are well organized better than things that are helter-skelter.

FORMS OF ORGANIZATION

There are a number of ways to organize messages to make sure they are persuasive and easy to remember. We will look at five such formats here: the topic format, the space format, the chronological format, the stock issues format, and the motivated sequence format. In the first three of these formats, we will apply the following example: A student group on my campus wanted to bring a highly successful filmmaker and former student back to campus as a guest speaker. He commanded a large fee for an afternoon seminar, a preview of his upcoming film, and an evening speech on his career. He was, however, willing to donate his fee to the student group to be used for field trips, travel to national conferences, and funding for a career day. The persuasive presentation to the student government group could be organized in several ways.

Organization by Topic

The topical format is most useful when the message that you want to convey covers several topics or issues. In the guest-speaker example, such topics include

1. the fame and success of the former student as a reason to bring him to campus.
2. the kind of role model the speaker would provide.
3. the special offer of previewing the speaker's previously unreleased film.
4. the speaker's fee and the degree to which he is in demand on the speaking circuit.
5. the speaker's generosity in donating his fee to the student group.
6. the other benefits to be derived from the speaker's presence on campus: publicity for the school, the added programming made possible by his donation, and the career counseling he might be able to give to aspiring student filmmakers.

By presenting the six topics with supporting evidence, you give the student government a variety of good reasons to fund the speaker. The topic format is a good choice when presenting specific reasons for some suggested action.

Organization by Space

The spatial format is a good choice when we want to compare our topic to the larger picture. The spatial idea relates to the comparative size our topic has to the overall state of affairs. In the filmmaker example, we might compare the relative cost of this speaker to that of speakers invited by other departments and sponsored by the student government. Our speaker's fee might be only a quarter of that asked for by a similar student group

and for a much less well-known speaker. Furthermore, this speaker's fee represents only 5 percent of the total guest speaker budget for the semester, and our student group is only one of ten similar groups in the college. In the spatial format, we might draw several pie graphs. In one, we could visually depict our speaker's fee as one-fourth of the pie and label the other three-fourths "Other Speaker Fees." Another graph might show our requested 5 percent in comparison to the other available 95 percent. And a third graph might show our 5 percent share as only half of that allotted to the nine other student groups. In all of these examples, we would be using space as an organizing principle.

Organization by Chronology

Sometimes the essential message in a persuasive communication is best relayed to the audience by taking them through the issues in historical sequence, making use of the chronological organizational principle. In the case of our guest speaker, we might relate our speaker's career to the Speaker's Fee Committee as follows:

1. In 1975, the speaker became a major in our department.
2. Two years later he transferred to the USC film school, eventually graduating in film. But he still values the basics of filmmaking he learned while he was with us.
3. He made his first picture as an independent a year later.
4. It was released the next June, and as a minor summer hit recaptured the initial investment plus a small profit.
5. Later that year, the film got several "honorable mentions" at film festivals, and our speaker then signed a three-year contract to make at least one picture a year for one of the largest film studios.
6. In the next three years he turned out several small money-makers.
7. Then in 1982, he made his first blockbuster, which went on to win several Academy Awards.

8. Since then he has been independently turning
    out about one popular hit a year and is one of
    the best-known writer/producers in Holly-
    wood. His fee for the most recent speech to a
    college audience was considerably higher than
    the fee we are asking for.

Organization by Stock Issues

The stock-issues organizational format is most frequently seen in cases where a major policy change
is being considered. Its name refers to the fact that
there are several universal issues that need to be
addressed when major policy changes are considered. Since our "famous former student" example
doesn't involve a policy change, we will look at a
different example.

In the Broadway musical comedy *The Music
Man*, a professor Harold Hill sells an entire town
on a need for a boys' band complete with uniforms
(which he, by chance, happens to sell) on the flim-
siest of logical appeals. He points out numerous
symptoms of trouble in the town (kids are smoking, reading "dirty" books, cursing, dressing out-
rageously, and so on). He then concludes with
these words, "There's trouble, my friends, right
here in River City. I said trouble, and that starts
with T and that rhymes with P and that stands for
'Pool'!" He goes on to point out that with a band
to be busy with, the boys will make no more visits
to the pool hall where the bad habits are all
learned. In this example, an overkill of evidence
enables the persuader to short-circuit the reasoning process. Hill's "proof" relies on a rhyme
scheme—P rhymes with T; therefore pool means
trouble.

Hill is successful because he plays on the stock
issues expected when a policy such as starting and
supporting a city band is addressed. In a stock-
issues approach, two sides debate an issue. One
side wants change, and the other prefers the status
quo. In our law courts, the side wanting change is
the prosecution, and the side favoring the status
quo is the defense. In our legal system, you are
presumed innocent (the status quo) unless the
prosecution can show that you are guilty beyond
reasonable doubt (change). We say that the **burden of proof** rests with the prosecution, the side

that wants to change the status of the defendant.
The status quo is presumed to be wise or true until
proven otherwise. When you face persuasion that
involves some kind of policy change, ask yourself,
"Who has the burden of proof here?"

The side with the burden of proof must show
serious shortcomings with the status quo, usually
by indicating *symptoms* of a problem: an inflationary price spiral, increasing levels of pollution, falling wages, increased levels of nuclear weapons,
or reduced feelings of self-identity, for example.
These symptoms are then tied to a supposed cause
to create a cause-effect or problem-solution frame
of reference. The political persuader might tie the
inflation to deficit spending and say that reducing
the deficit will slow inflation, or tie the inflationary
spiral to increased costs in fossil energy. What
might be a proposed solution?

Once the persuader has presented an adequate
need for change, the focus of the argument shifts
to the necessity for some **plan of action** that we
can reasonably assume will somehow solve a problem. In other words, effective persuaders can't just
point out shortcomings in the status quo and leave
it at that. Neither can they offer a ludicrous plan of
action that obviously cannot solve the problem or
that has no possibility of being enacted. A critic
of the status quo can't offer to solve the federal
deficit problem by having the government print
$2,000,000,000,000 in unbacked paper money.
There is no possibility that such a plan could pass
Congress, and, further, it would create runaway
inflation. The critic might suggest that marijuana
be made legal and its manufacture and sale be
operated by the federal government, thus generat-
ing $30 billion in revenue. Or he or she might
suggest a national lottery, like the Irish Sweepstakes, which could generate another $20 billion
to be set aside for debt service and debt reduction.
This final plan might pass Congress and could ultimately retire the debt. Having shown a need for
change and a realistic plan for change, the persuader can now move to the stage of stock issues,
demonstrating that the need shown can be dealt
with through the suggested plan.

This third stage, the **plan-meets-need** stage,
involves demonstrating that the suggested plan
could be enacted, could generate the needed reve-

nues, and additionally, would not create other problems that would be worse than the status quo. Here, the side defending the status quo might bring up such issues as the possible side effects of marijuana legalization, such as increased use of the drug or increased drug-related automobile and other accidents. The critic of the status quo might point out the realistic nature of the plan and its supposed effects by presenting examples in which the plan has worked elsewhere, as when income is generated by legalized marijuana sales in Jamaica, and might go further and point out added benefits flowing from the plan, such as reduced costs for the criminal-justice system by not prosecuting and jailing marijuana users and dealers. This give-and-take is sometimes called *comparative advantages or comparative disadvantages*, and frequently the status quo may grant the presence of a need for change and move directly to this plan-meets-need stage, comparing a repaired status quo with the proposed plan or offering a totally different plan and then debating the comparative advantages and disadvantages of the two.

In any case, these stock issues must appear to be logical and able to get at the root of the problem and even to lead to practical solutions to vexing problems. We see stock issues frequently used as content premises in the world of politics and business, and in other policymaking forums. As a receiver, you should also be aware of the stock issues. Persuaders may assume that you will grant the need for change and then skip ahead to plan, or they may even move directly to advantages and disadvantages. Any time you are the target of persuasion focused on policy change, identify the side suggesting change and the side supporting the status quo.

As a persuader attempting to bring about a change in policy, you need to begin by addressing the need for a change. Like Harold Hill, you need to be specific about the "trouble" being caused by the status quo. *You* have the burden of proof. It is useful to start by citing symptoms of the problem. In your case, the problem won't be as simple as that faced by the citizens of River City, Iowa. You will have to research specific instances that demonstrate to the audience that they are suffering something, losing something of value, or are in

danger of losing it. Those symptoms can then usually be tied to a cause that, if removed and replaced, will solve the problem. Then you'll need to present a reasonable alternative to the status quo — the plan or the new policy. Finally, you'll have to show that "plan meets need." One way to do this is to show that the plan has been successful in another place. For example, if a national lottery such as the Irish Sweepstakes has been successful in helping to reduce deficits in other countries, using them as examples helps to prove that plan meets need.

At each stage of the stock-issues format, the persuader should expect some kind of rebuttal. In some cases the rebuttal is openly stated, as in a Congressional policy debate or a policy debate in your student government. If you are giving a speech covering all three stock issues — need, plan, and plan meets need — the supporters of the status quo may hold their rebuttals until the question-and-answer period. Successful persuaders anticipate such rebuttals and are ready to counter them in the question-and-answer period. They might also short-circuit anticipated rebuttals by presenting a two-sided message stating the anticipated rebuttals in the speech and answering them then and there.

The stock-issues format is useful for persuaders who are proposing a change in policy from the status quo. It is easy to remember the steps of the stock-issues format if you think of Harold Hill. After all, he was able to persuade the citizens of River City to fund a boys band for the town simply because the letter "t" (as in "trouble") rhymed with the letter "p" (as in "pool hall"), after he had made them aware of troublesome symptoms in the actions of the young people of the town.

Organization by Motivated Sequence

Another organizational pattern that resembles the stock-issues approach is the **motivated sequence format**, suggested by communication scholars Alan Monroe, Douglas Ehninger, and Bruce Gronbeck.[3] This format involves five steps and is often used by persuaders to get persuadees to attend to their message, to feel a need to follow the advice of the persuader, and, most important, to take action related to the advice. Thus the motivated sequence is a good pattern to use in sales, recruitment — say, for the armed forces or some organization — in politics, where the action step is the vote, and in many other instances.

The first step in the motivated sequence is the **attention step**. No persuader can be successful if the audience is uninterested in the persuasion, so capturing the attention of the audience is the first task. There are hundreds of ways to do this. A persuader might begin the message with a startling statistic, for instance: "Over 70 percent of the heart attacks today are related to the kind of person you are — type A or type B. Today you can decide for yourself what type you want to be."

The persuader might use a joke or humorous anecdote. We often hear this on the after-dinner-speech circuit and even in sermons. Another approach used by persuaders is to make an important announcement in the first few moments of the message. The president announces settlement of a strike or a new peace initiative in the Middle East.

Our old friend the narrative can also serve to capture audience attention, as can visual aids (for example, a giant mock-up of a speeding ticket for a speech on auto safety, or a graph or chart of some kind). All these tactics are useful in getting the audience's attention. Avoid the frequently used (and usually ineffective) rhetorical question, such as "How many of you in this room have ever wondered what causes pollution?" Rhetorical questions rarely get attention — they frequently bore the audience.

The second part of the motivated sequence is to convince the audience that it is losing something, is about to lose something, or could be gaining something but isn't. This is the **need step**. We might show this unfulfilled need by using some statistics: "Half of you will contract some form of cancer in your lifetime." We might use a real or hypothetical case to show the need:

Most of us will be in debt to some degree by the time we graduate from college. It may take us years to repay that debt, and it will be difficult during those early lean years of our careers when most of us will be working hard to pay for homes, perhaps children, and many of

the other things to which we have become accustomed and have not had to pay for on a regular basis. How would you like to come out of college with a different kind of situation — one in which you graduated with a sizable net worth? William Jones began investing in mobile homes for alternative student housing when he was a sophomore. In three years, he has built a net worth over $50,000 — just by investing a small part of his student loan each year. And he has lived rent-free in one of the mobile units while completing his degree. You can follow his example and not only graduate but end up with a nest egg.

This need step could easily be tied to the attention-getting step (for example, use a "reward poster" that offers a $50,000 nest egg on graduation for enterprising students), thus creating a smooth flow from step to step for the audience.

Steps three and four are the **visualization** and **satisfaction steps**. In them, the persuader gives examples, data, testimony, or some other form of proof to induce the audience to visualize either what life will be like for them if they follow the persuader's advice (if they go ahead and invest part of their student loan in mobile homes for student housing) or what life will be like if they don't (what it will be like to have root-canal work because you didn't use dental floss). Following this visualization step, the persuader then offers some way to satisfy the positive need or to avoid some negative consequences.

Sometimes, though not usually, these steps are reversed. In the alternative version, the persuader offers the satisfaction of the need first, then induces the audience to visualize what it will be like to have the need taken care of in some way. For example, I might explain the details of the mobile-home investment scheme first, then discuss what you might be able to do with the $50,000 profit on graduation.

Finally, the persuader needs to give a definite, specific, and realistic **action step**. It probably will do no good to ask audience members to alter their attitudes on the topic. Attitudes are fickle, as we have seen, and, furthermore, it is hard to know whether an audience has changed. It is far better to give the audience specific things it can do to avoid tooth decay, save energy, make wise investments, or earn good grades. In one research study, people given a booklet with specific action steps to cut electric consumption registered less use of electricity on their meters in the following two weeks than did those not given the specific action steps.[4] One action step (which is probably ineffective) frequently used in student speeches is to suggest that the audience write to their representatives in government—something unfortunately, that few people actually do.[5] It would be good, therefore, to have a petition on hand that the student audience could sign as it leaves, or you could announce the phone number of the legislator's local office. Better yet, have the phone number duplicated so audience members can take it with them. (Phoning is as easy as writing a letter and more effective.)

In effective persuasion, it is essential to give persuadees a realistic action step, whether it is signing a sales contract, phoning a representative, or boycotting a nonunion food market. Build such steps into your persuasive attempts at sales, recruitment, and so on, and you will find your percentage of success increasing dramatically.

A related model for making a persuasive appeal is called the **AIDA approach** (AIDA is an acronym that stands for *Attention, Interest, Desire,* and *Action*).[6] In this model, as in the motivated sequence, the first step is to capture the audience's *attention* using any of the tactics cited earlier. In the second step of the AIDA model, the persuader's goal is to heighten the audience's interest in his or her topic or proposal. This might be done using a satisfaction or a visualization process, as in the motivated sequence, but other techniques might be used. For example, the persuader might tell how many persons have already tried the product or used the new procedure and found it to be useful, or the persuader might point out unforeseen problems with continuing the present practice.

In my proposal to the conservative banker, I plan to remind him that by doing business with someone close to home instead of with a Chicago-based agency, he will be able to react more quickly to market changes (such as offers made by the competition) and that by hiring my services, he

will be spending the agency-fee portion of his annual advertising budget in his own hometown—something I think he would prefer doing.

Sometimes visual aids can be effective in increasing audience attention. Another of my clients is a large beef-cattle feedlot that is being underused owing to previous poor management. New management wants to interest potential users of the feedlot in its many benefits: a low death/loss rate, proximity to a source of free starch and oils (which cuts the overall cost to fatten the cattle), professional management, ease of getting one's investment in the cattle financed, and other benefits. A short slide/sound show could be used to raise the interest level in prospective feedlot users after having captured their attention in a variety of ways: advertising, brochures, free investment seminars held in a host of small towns nearby, and booths at beef-cattle trade shows.

Once attention and interest have been gained, the next task for the persuader using the AIDA model is to create *desire* in the persuadee to purchase the product or service, to vote for the candidate, or to follow the persuader's advice. There are several ways to create such desire. In product-related persuasion, it usually is done by providing some product benefit or product promise. For example, in 1990, Chrysler advertised a safety feature that was standard in their cars: the built-in air bag. The obvious benefit of this feature was that it could save one's life in an accident. By mentioning research that proved how well the bag cushioned the driver's body, Chrysler created desire for the product in the audience. In their action step, they asked the customer to go to their nearest Chrysler dealer to learn more about the air bag and for a test drive.

Communications professor Hugh Rank, whom we met in Chapter 1 through his intensify/downplay model, has offered a simple four-part model for creating desire.[7] Although it can be used in promoting products, it also can be used in a variety of other persuasive situations. The persuader can use four kinds of desire-stimulating tactics with this model (see Figure 11.2). First, the persuader can promise the audience security or protection by demonstrating that his or her advice will allow the audience "to keep a 'good'" they already have but

To Keep a "Good" (Protection)	To Get Rid of "a Bad" (Relief)
To Get a "Good" (Acquisition)	To Avoid a "Bad" (Prevention)

FIGURE 11.2

Rank's model for ways to create desire in audiences.

might be in danger of losing. Crest and other fluoridated toothpastes, for example, promise that regular use of their toothpaste will help keep your teeth free from decay — you keep a "good." Politicians frequently point out all of the funding they have brought to their districts. They then claim that their reelection means keeping this "good."

A second set of desire-stimulating tactics relates to "bad" or uncomfortable symptoms or feelings. Persuaders who use these tactics promise that by following their advice one can either "get rid of a 'bad'" or experience "relief" from a symptom or feeling. Hand in hand with getting relief is the promise that by following the persuader's advice, one can "avoid a 'bad'" feeling or symptom. Rank calls these two approaches the "relief" and "prevention" appeals. Advertisers often promise that products can prevent embarrassment in a variety of forms: bad breath, body odor, dandruff, athlete's foot, and even "jock itch." Or they promise that by using their products you can get relief from headaches, heartburn, flyaway hair, or acne. Again, these negative tactics, or "scare and sell" approaches, can be used in nonproduct persuasion. For example, a persuader can promise that by passing the school bond referendum we can "avoid" losing the athletics and music programs and other extracurricular activities. Other persuaders can promise that by voting for a certain candidate the audience can get "relief" from corruption in government, de-

fense spending, and inflation. You probably will discover ways to use any or all of these desire-creating tactics when you are asked or choose to become a persuader.

The last stage in the AIDA model is to present the audience with a clear and effective *action* step, as was the case in the motivated sequence. Action steps can be prompted by stressing concepts such as timeliness (for example, "Deadline is March 15" or "24-hour sale!") or limited supplies or opportunities (for instance, "While supplies last!" or "This may be your last chance to . . ."). Action steps also can be prompted by using the competition or opposition as foils. For example, the persuader promoting passage of a school bond referendum may appeal for donations "to pay for the kind of advertising that the people opposing the referendum have been running." The manager can appeal to employees to adopt a new technology (robotics, computerized typesetting, superconductors, or whatever) in order to beat the competition or to avoid being beaten by the competition (for example, foreign-built automobiles). And there are other ways to stimulate action on the part of audiences. Usually they depend not only on the vigor with which they are presented but on the quality of the reasoning and evidence persuaders use.

FORMS OF PROOF

We want good reasons for changing our attitudes and beliefs, and the proof requisites for taking action steps are even more demanding. Even if we are sure the change that is advocated is a good one, we still need proof to motivate us to act. Usually this proof comes in the form of data or evidence, which we discussed in Chapter 7. There we looked at proof from the receiver's perspective. Here let's look at the forms of proof available to persuaders and discuss how they can be used to prompt audiences to change attitudes or take action.

Statistical Evidence

Sometimes the most effective support is statistical. For instance, car buyers are interested in gas mileage. They will be more persuaded by the Environmental Protection Agency (EPA) figures than by reassurances from the sales staff that the car is a real gas saver. Statistics are most useful when they are simple and easy to understand. When persuaders decide to use statistics, they need to make them clear. They need to provide a reference point for the numbers. If you are warning persuadees about the increasing national debt, make it clear and real to them. Tell them that the interest on the debt amounts to $1800 per year for every man, woman, and child in the country.

Narratives and Anecdotes

We have noted the power of drama, stories, and jokes. The narrative makes examples come alive. It makes them easy to recall and relate to. The persuader who tells of a person rising from rags to riches will have more success than one who relies on statistics alone.

Testimony

We are suspicious of people who try to convince us of a certain idea if it is based only on their own feelings or brainstorms. This is why the testimony of another person is so useful. Even if the person testifying is unqualified, the testimonial still has influence. Of course, it is much better to have an expert witness to the wisdom or folly of the idea, person, or product. Even better is testimony of a hostile or reluctant witness.

Visual Evidence

We have noted how useful it is for an audience to see or experience evidence. This is why visual aids are used in sales work. If you have ever walked into a department store where a salesperson was showing a veg-o-matic or pasta machine, you know the power of visual data.

Of course, actual demonstrations of a product are not always feasible in a public speech or persuasive presentation, but persuaders can develop various kinds of visual evidence to help the audience understand the problem. We have mentioned graphs and charts, which can show trends, the way money is being spent, or some other fact. They should be large enough so everyone can see them. They should be simple. Complex charts will confuse the audience. It is useless to hold up a postage stamp in a speech on "The Rewards of Stamp Collecting." An enlarged photograph of a stamp would be better. Pictures can make a point too. A student advocating a trip to Jamaica sponsored by the student association effectively used travel posters, large pictures of Jamaican cuisine, easily seen cutouts from magazines depicting sandy beaches, and other pictures of tropical life to motivate her audience. And you can create excellent visual aids using computer graphics and videotape.

Keep the visual evidence unobtrusive. It may be better to use drawings of how to fend off an attacking dog than to bring your dog to class and have it pretend to attack you. One student who did this was embarrassed when his dog relieved itself instead of attacking on command.

Comparison and Contrast

Sometimes it is hard to see a problem in perspective. We see the issue from a single viewpoint and cannot judge it accurately. So it is wise to provide something with which to compare or contrast your point. Comparisons should help the audience see the difference between two sides of the issue or between two cases. It doesn't help them much to know that OPEC decided to increase production by 550,000 barrels per day. It will be more meaningful to add that this is an increase of 20 percent over previous production levels. Make your comparisons and contrasts meaningful by elaborating on them and by explaining the *relative difference* in the things being compared.

Analogy

We discussed the analogy as a form of proof and noted that although it can be effective, there is a risk involved in using analogies—particularly figurative ones—because they can be turned around on the persuader. Analogies must be chosen carefully. Consider the following figurative analogy used by Abraham Lincoln in a speech about extending slavery into the territories. In it, he compares the institution of slavery to a serpent:

> If I saw a venomous snake crawling in the road, any man would say I might seize the nearest stick and kill it; but if I found that snake in bed with my children, that would be another question. I might hurt the children more than the snake, and it might bite them. Much more if I found it in bed with my neighbor's children, and I had bound myself by a solemn compact not to meddle with his children under any circumstances. It would become me to let that particular mode of getting rid of the gentleman alone. But if there was a bed newly made up, to which the children were to be taken, and it was proposed to take a batch of young snakes and put them there with them, I take it no man would say there was any question how I ought to decide. That is just the case. The new Territories are the newly made bed to which our children are to go, and it lies with the nation to say whether they shall have snakes mixed up with them or not.[8]

Lincoln's analogy works persuasively, but it could be turned around on him. Couldn't an opponent argue that venomous snakes prosper only in the proper climate? You can't take a tropical snake and transplant it to Minnesota. Slavery can exist only in places where the economy, landscape, habitat, and so on are suitable for growing cotton. The new territories aren't suited for cotton, so slavery, like the viper, can't flourish. Therefore, insisting on forbidding slavery in the territories merely agitates the citizenry for no good reason. This is the danger in using even well-designed analogies. They can be easily turned around to prove different or even opposing points.

BUILDING YOUR CREDIBILITY

All the evidence in the world, organized perfectly and delivered well, will not persuade if listeners do not trust the speaker. This happens time after time in politics. Presidents all suffer from a credibility gap. We see it in the world of sports when coaches and players come out of long meetings over salary or during trades. They *say* that everyone's happy, but we know better. You do not fight over your future and come away without any bad feelings. Surely, in many product appeals, credibility suffers. It is hard to believe that we can have an instant change in personality, social life, and sex appeal by using a certain hair dye or aftershave lotion. We accept some of this "incredibility" as part of the game, but in matters such as persuading the boss to give us a promotion or parents to let us marry before graduation, credibility is a key factor. What makes some people credible while others are not? How can we build our own credibility before and during persuasion? Let us look further at some answers to these questions.

Remember that we discussed the idea of credibility in Chapters 3 and 9 using Aristotle's ideas about the reputation of the speaker, the speaker's delivery during the speech, and perhaps the audience's response to the speaker's image or charisma. In more modern times, this translated into several dimensions of credibility—reputation was roughly equated with the known *expertise* of the speaker. To whom a speech is attributed is important. For example, when an identical speech was attributed to experts in some cases and to novices in others, the speech attributed to an expert was always more persuasive than was the novice version.

Delivery and charisma are related to sincerity and dynamism. Audiences often don't believe speakers who cannot maintain eye contact. Tall speakers have more persuasive potential than do short ones. Speakers whose delivery is animated are able to persuade more effectively than those who are frozen at the podium. Exciting language usually helps make the speech more persuasive. A well-groomed speaker probably will be more persuasive than one whose clothes have that slept-in look: The interpersonal persuader who is disheveled will have more difficulty persuading others than the persuader who is neat, bathed, and mouthwashed. You would think that most of these points would be obvious, yet they are overlooked daily by sales reps, politicians, spouses, teachers, students, and parents. Here are some examples from everyday life in which the elements of credibility can be and are used.

Trust

We trust people for many reasons. We trust them because they have been trustworthy in the past. We trust them because they give off trustworthy cues: direct eye contact, a calm voice, and so forth. We trust them because we know it would not be in their self-interest to betray us. A good example of this might be airplane hijackers, who trust the passengers and crew not to gang up on them—to do so would endanger all their lives. Usually, it is the first two kinds of trust we wish to communicate. We tell employers that they can trust us because we have been constant in the past. We tell voters to support us because we have been faithful to campaign pledges in the past. Or we tell customers that they can trust Listerine antiseptic because it has been around since Grandma's time.

We also try to give off trust cues. We look at our persuadees directly. We try to sound sincere, even if we are not (although this isn't always effective—our nonverbal messages "leak" that we are lying). Persuaders who want to have a trust relationship with the audience need to remind that audience of their past record for trust. They need to refer to times when it would have been easy to break trust. Sometimes this can be worked into the persuasive speech or interpersonal exchange early. We might remind our boss that there have been many times when she was out of town and we could have slacked off but didn't. We might point out to our boyfriend or girlfriend that there have been plenty of opportunities to go out with other people without him or her knowing about it, but we didn't do it. Or we might remind our parents that there have been many opportunities to party it up, but instead we studied. We also encourage trust during speeches or interpersonal encounters. We look receivers in the eye and have relaxed posture. We speak with a sure voice and avoid nervous mannerisms. All these devices and others help build credibility.

Expertise

How do we know whether someone is a true expert on a topic or job? Mostly we look for past success at a task. If a person was a good treasurer for the Luther League, he or she will probably be a good treasurer for the student council. Sales representatives who did well in the Midwest should also do well in the more complex East. A person who has had experience in many areas of the company—shipping, sales, and so on—is much more credible to workers than the person who has had experience in only one area. If a person has served on the budget committee of the student association, we assume that his or her advice on how to request funding is believable.

Even if we do not have direct expertise on a given topic, we can borrow it by referring to known experts in our presentation. It is always useful to refer to your sources' background so the receivers will be able to judge the credibility of their testimony.

Some people believe that you can create credibility by giving off competence cues. John T. Molloy, clothing researcher, has written several books and a syndicated column dealing with how one's clothes can give off messages that say "I am competent and in charge," or "I am a threat."[9] Molloy says that the color of our clothing communicates, too. To project a power, or "take-charge," image, one should wear three shades of blue. To project sincerity and warmth, browns are the key. The subtleties involved are complex, but speakers should consider what they wear as an element in the expertise they communicate. Of course, there are other nonverbal signals that can further develop your credibility. Finally, you can signal expertise by being well prepared, by demonstrating that you know about the topic (constantly referring to or reading a manuscript of the speech shows that you are unfamiliar with the topic), and by being willing to engage in question/answer sessions when you have finished speaking.

Dynamism

The dynamism factor of credibility is elusive and even mysterious. It is sometimes related to physical appearance. The taller candidate wins more often. Attractive people hold attention better. This kind of dynamism, sometimes labeled *charisma*, probably cannot be developed much. However, other factors are in your control. Many people who aren't particularly attractive are nonetheless persuasive and dynamic. Hitler, for instance, was neither particularly attractive nor tall. Yet we know that he was an incredibly dynamic and spellbinding speaker, often holding his audience in an almost hypnotic trance. Dynamic speakers seem to take up a lot of psychic space—they have "stage presence"—which calls attention to them when they stand up or speak out. There are several strategies each of us can use to project a dynamic image. One is to speak with authority. Use your voice with good projection and volume, and choose words that indicate certainty. Posture and appearance also can signal dynamism, as can gestures, facial expression, and eye contact.

Politicians frequently associate with charismatic people such as Robert Redford, Paul Newman, or Jane Fonda in an attempt to "borrow" some of the guest's image. Often these same politicians pursue physically active life-styles—they play tennis or touch football, they ski or jog. All such activities help communicate a sense of dynamism.

STYLING YOUR MESSAGE

Receivers are more likely to be persuaded by stylish speech and exciting language choices than by dull speech, even if it is accurate and factual. How can you as a persuader develop style in your presentations?

Variety in Word Choice

Anyone can improve his or her vocabulary. Don't just run to the *thesaurus* to find synonyms. Try to rewrite ads, speeches, or slogans using word variety to make them livelier, flashier, sexier, more dramatic, or more humorous. Develop an interest in puns and other word games. Children can be your best coaches here; pay attention to how they play with words. Notice how children's educational television shows, such as *Sesame Street*, deal with vocabulary.

There are many vocabulary-building plans on the market; one has batches of little cards with the new words defined and used in a sentence on them. Study the eloquence of other people. Read some of the great inaugural addresses of our presidents; analyze some of the great speeches of history. Pay attention to the language used in government news releases or in speeches by politicians. Finally, study uses of humor. In many cases, humor is based on word ambiguity or "double meanings." Using appropriate, accurate words conveys that you know your subject and will increase your credibility. The intellectual humor of puns and word games helps you get the attention and friendship of your audience.

Figures of Speech

You can enhance your style by using proper figures of speech at the right time. Metaphors and similes can help your audience visualize a point. The audience ties information to the metaphorical structure and later recall is easy and accurate.

Alliteration or assonance also can liven style. Alliteration is repetition of consonant sounds; assonance is repetition of vowel sounds. Both create a kind of internal rhythm in the message, which makes it easier to recall. We see this device used in advertising frequently to aid in brand name recall. Satin cigarettes are "smooth, slender, and sensuous," and the Parker pen is "wrought from pure silver and writes like pure silk." Assonance can be seen in "A portable phone system? Gee! No, GTE." Both devices can improve your style.

Vividness

Choose vivid words to catch your audience's interest. Although vividness can be overdone, it is more frequently overlooked in favor of dull, uninteresting, and tedious language or jargon. Which of the following is most vivid?[10]

Your article on the homeless-shelter initiative in Washington brought deserved attention to an important issue.

Activists are expressing great concern about adequate shelter for people who in some cases weren't all that concerned themselves when they abandoned the roof over their heads.

Now compare these:

I'm offended by your representation of lutefisk. It is *not* rubbery!

Lutefisk may be "a rubbery and repulsive ethnic dish" to the socially deprived, but to the properly initiated it is the nearest thing to ambrosia this Earth has ever produced.

Vivid and colorful language helps make a persuasive presentation memorable and effective.

Conciseness

Avoid being overly wordy. Be as economical with your words as possible. Go over your presentation and pretend you are paying fifty cents per word to send it. Then see how much excess baggage you can cut. Often, a straightforward statement is most effective.

It is also useful to state your point in a short introductory declaration. Elaborate on it later when and if necessary. Once when Lincoln was trying to justify a pardon he was granting to a deserter, he said, "I think the boy can do us more good aboveground than underground," thus stating his case concisely.[11] He could have elaborated on the unnecessary waste of executing a young man, but his concise statement did the job eloquently.

You don't have to say everything in one sentence; you have an entire speech. Make your major point as a concise assertion or frame it in a provoking question. Then follow up with elaboration. If you try to say everything in the opening sentence, you will confuse your audience.

Parallel Structure

In a speech about the "me decade," the persuader noted that the Roaring Twenties were typified by self-interest, materialistic pursuits, and pleasurable experiences. It was not until the stock market crash of 1929 that the pleasure seekers were brought to their senses. The crash was followed by the deepest depression our country has ever known, the persuader went on, and that hardship created a concern for others and a sense of community that drew people together. The persuader then pointed out how the stock market crash of 1987 — a much larger crash in terms of percentage of loss than that of 1929 — perhaps brought the pleasure-seeking "me generation" to a renewed sense of concern for others and for the need for community. This time, however, the community was not achieved through economic hardship but through the realization that the United States was potentially facing its worst epidemic — AIDS — and that it was rapidly becoming the largest debtor nation in the world, a dangerous situation needing united effort to reverse. The persuader was using parallel examples intended to clarify complex issues and problems to the audience.

Parallel structure also involves using parallel sentences or assertions. For example, the following three sentences say similar things but have different structures:

The income you earn will depend on the kind and amount of education you have, even in a sales job.

Your initiative and willingness to put in the extra effort can lead to promotions and handsome commissions.

People know that lucky breaks can make or break your future remuneration, especially in sales work.

They can be restated in parallel ways for more effect as follows:

Your income will depend on your educational background.

It will depend on initiative and extra effort.

It will depend on lucky breaks.

Or they can be worked into a single sentence with parallel elements:

In sales work, earnings are related to the triad of education and knowledge, initiative and extra effort, and those all-important lucky breaks.

Imagery

Imagery is related to our senses, experiences, and impressions. You may not be able to bring the smell, taste, touch, sight, or sound of an object to the audience, but you can use words that conjure up memories of a "tall, cool, glass of chilled beer dripping with beads of perspiration" or of that "fragrant smell of Mom's pot roast, ready to fall apart, with its juices making a savory gravy that starts your mouth watering." Think about the sensory experiences your audience has had that you can evoke. Try stating your points so that they appeal to the senses. A good way to develop this skill is to take a given product and try to restate its appeals in terms of the various senses. For instance, Campbell's soups are "Mmm, Mmm, Good." How can they be described using the other senses? As one salesperson put it, "Don't sell the steak; sell the sizzle."

Humor

The effective use of humor in persuasion is an obvious stylistic asset. How can you develop humorous examples, comparisons, anecdotes, and stories? People who regularly engage in public speaking usually have a ready supply of humorous material with which to stud their speeches. Most of them don't come by the ability to use humor naturally; they develop it as they work up other materials for their speeches. You may be the kind of person who can never remember a story or joke. If so, keep a file of stories you read or hear. Somehow, writing down a story or joke or even its punchline on an index card for your humor file rivets it in your memory. When you need the anecdote, the file will trigger your memory, and you will be able to relate those to-the-point humorous examples. Some places to find humorous examples and anecdotes are *Reader's Digest* (browse in it while you're waiting at a doctor's office); collections of stories or jokes (you will be amazed when you go to the library and see how many and varied these are); television and radio shows such as *Saturday Night Live*, the *Arsenio Hall Show,* or *Johnny Carson*; your daily newspaper (especially the comics); and people who frequently tell jokes (bartenders, barbers, and others). Get yourself a supply of humorous material to improve your style; it will make your persuasion easier to remember and more effective.

DELIVERING YOUR MESSAGE

Usually we think of delivery as a source factor — that is, something that only the source itself can affect. To some degree, this is true. However, there are several other factors that can affect the message, such as the selection of the appropriate channel through which to convey the message and the means of audience involvement. Persuaders often overlook these. In the following consideration of delivery, we will look both at those things that the source does during delivery and at those that are not tied to delivery.

The Persuader

Among the factors that a persuader can adjust before and during delivery are posture, eye contact, body movement and gesture, articulation, and vocal quality. Other factors that are under the speaker's control are the use of visual aids and other nonverbal signals.

Posture We all have seen persuaders who are so nervous about their speeches that they cannot stop pacing back and forth. When they do stop, they stand so ramrod stiff that it looks as if they might freeze into statues. At the other extreme, we have seen speakers who are so relaxed that they do not seem to care at all about their messages. They slouch lazily across a podium or slide down into their chairs during a meeting. They rarely look up, and you wonder whether they will nod off in the middle of a sentence. It is clear that posture can signal the audience that you are either too relaxed or too nervous. The ideal posture lies somewhere in between. Be alert and erect. Your shoulders should not be tensed, but neither should they slump. Show no visible signs of nervousness or tension. (I wiggle my toes, but no one can see that.) Overall, the message should be one of confidence. Try to observe persuaders in differing contexts: interviews, speeches, arguments, and so on. You will see that the effective ones avoid both the nervous and the "nearly asleep" extremes.

Eye Contact There is some truth to the folk wisdom that a person cannot lie to you and also look you straight in the eyes. This is true most of the time for most people. We are more believable if we maintain eye contact with our audience. We need not look at everyone, but we need to look at various areas in the audience. Politicians know this and use devices such as teleprompters to enable them to read a speech and appear to be looking around at the same time. In a one-on-one context, establish repeated eye contact with your persuadee. Politicians make sure to look directly into the TV camera and hence to have apparent eye contact with each viewer. In a meeting, establish eye contact with many people, or maybe even everyone, at the meeting.

Body Movement and Gesture We can move during a speech, if the movement is not likely to distract. We can likewise gesture during a speech. During a meeting, we can gesture or pound the table for effect. In an interview, we might include gestures or facial expressions. Frequently, persuaders are overly simplistic and indicate their three major points by holding up first one, then two, and finally three fingers as they say, "For my first major point. . . . For my second major point . . . ," and so on.

It is a mistake to overrehearse gestures, body movements, and facial expressions. These nonverbal elements in delivery must appear natural or they have a negative effect. Each of you uses gestures every day without thinking about them. Let that same unconscious and natural impulse guide you in your use of gestures in formal presentations or in interpersonal exchanges. Nothing is less persuasive than a stilted phrase or gesture; nothing can add more to your message than a natural gesture, movement, or facial expression. If you expect your audience to laugh at a certain point and then practice smiling or laughing with them, you could

be surprised when they don't do the expected; your solitary cackle will only make the audience embarrassed for you. The naturally prompted gesture is the most effective.[12]

Articulation and Vocal Quality Everyone has heard people who have speech defects or who pronounce words or sounds incorrectly. What is the result of these kinds of errors? Mostly, we focus on the error and not on the message. In other words, the mistake distracts us from the message. Successful persuaders listen carefully to themselves and work on articulation. Listening to ourselves on tape pinpoints our own careless articulation and can help us focus on our vocal quality. If you know the phonetic alphabet, another good idea is to transcribe your articulation from a tape. Your mistakes will become crystal clear. Vocal quality—a nasal-sounding, wheezy, breathy, or pitched-too-high voice—can be improved by using some of these methods as well. If you are interested in persuading others, spend some time working on your voice and your articulation.

The Channel

In a campaign I once studied, the candidate put much of his money into billboard space. I was surprised because I assumed that in a TV age, the major advertising expenditure would be for TV. The reason for the apparent mistake relates to the communication-channel factor. The candidate's district was large, stretching nearly half the length of the state. No single TV channel reached all of the district. To use TV would mean paying a triple load to get a single message across. However, since the district was large, all residents had to drive to do shopping, business, or farming. Thus the billboard was the channel that could touch nearly all voters in the district.

During his tenure in office, President Reagan frequently used radio to broadcast speeches during the day, even though presidential use of radio was considered a thing of the past by the 1980s. Why? Well, first, Reagan was a superb radio communicator, having started in show business as a radio announcer. Second, many people listen to the radio while they are doing something else — driving, ironing, reading, mowing the lawn, washing dishes, or exercising. They also usually do these things during the daylight hours, so by choosing the relatively inexpensive medium of radio, Reagan was able to reach people he otherwise might not have.

The same care that goes into selecting the channel for conveying a candidate's persuasion should go into your choice of media for your persuasion, formal and informal. Schwartz's notion of task-oriented persuasion is critical here.[13] Ask yourself what is the best way to inform your boss that you will look for another job if you don't get a raise or promotion. The grapevine might be best. Or maybe a straightforward memo will do the job. Maybe giving her name as a reference so she will get an out-of-the-blue inquiry will be best. Start by listing all the potential channels that could be used to send your message. Then try to match these with your audience. If your boss likes to talk on the phone, calling would be best. If your boss likes to have things in writing, then maybe a memo or letter would be most effective.

The Audience

Sometimes persuaders can encourage audience participation, which can increase audience energy and activity. In the 1988 primary campaign speeches, Jesse Jackson frequently encouraged audience participation. He would say "I am somebody!" and the crowd would repeat his statement. He would say "Down with dope!" and the audience would respond "Up with hope!"

Get your audience involved by asking direct questions and calling them by name if possible. Audiences feel more familiar with speakers who use this approach than they do with speakers they think don't know or give a hoot about them. You can also get audience involvement by leaving sentences incomplete and letting the audience supply examples. For instance, you might say, "There are three or four things I can think of to save energy — installing storm windows, caulking, weather-stripping windows and doors, and letting your clothes dryer vent into the house. And there

are others, such as . . ." One speaker gets audience involvement right away by asking the audience to stand up before he even begins his speech. He then asks them to become aware of the muscles they are using in their feet, ankles, calves, and thighs at that moment and ties this awareness to his topic — the need to develop communication awareness on the job. W. Clement Stone (who originated the idea of positive mental attitude, or PMA) used to ask his audience to stand and shout the words "Yes, I can" several times. Be creative and daring and get your audience involved.

One word of caution: Don't distribute any reading material until the end of the speech. Audiences start reading right away, and the speaker loses their attention and interest. Hand out such materials at the end of your presentation, or, if you must distribute them first, remain silent for a moment to give people time to read and digest the material. More than one sale has been lost because the salesperson went right on talking while the customer was reading the specifications sheet on the product being sold.

SOME COMMON TACTICS OF PERSUASION

Successful persuaders spend time finding out what the audience already believes, and then they use various tactics to tie their points to audience beliefs. What follows are some *tactics* for doing this. Tactics are the working tools that put strategy into action. These tactics are by no means the only ones you can use; you can add to this list as you try new techniques of persuasion in your own life.[14]

The Yes-Yes Technique

A common tactic used in sales and other persuasive appeals is called **yes-yes**. The source attempts to get the target group or person to respond "yes" to some parts of the appeal, holding the key request until last. Having agreed to most parts of the appeal, the target person is somewhat tied into saying yes to the key and final request. For example, suppose that you were trying to sell a lawn service. The service provides yearly fertilization, raking, and weedkilling. You might ask the home-owner, "You would like to have a beautiful lawn, wouldn't you?" The answer is going to be yes; all homeowners want nice lawns. Then you ask, "And you'd like the weeds removed?" Another yes is likely. You might follow up with, "And wouldn't it be nice if these things could be effort free, huh?" A yes answer is likely again. Now that the home-owner has accepted all your points in favor of the service, it is nearly impossible to respond with a no answer to the final question. So you ask, "Then you'd like to be one of our lucky customers?" By accepting the yes pattern, the buyer is more in-clined to fall into agreement with your final re-quest. The same technique is useful in a meeting, where a persuader gets the group members to agree with all but the final point in favor of the change in work schedules, for instance. They agree that flexibility is good, that more free time for workers is good, and so on. They are almost bound by the need to be consistent to agree that the change is a good one. A politician might ask whether we want to lower unemployment rates, whether we want to stop high fuel imports, and whether we want to cut inflation. It follows then that we may be inclined to favor the politi-cian's plan of action to combat the weakness in the status quo.

Persuaders use the yes-yes technique to lead their target group or person through stages to a final yes answer to the request for purchases, change, or votes.

Don't Ask If, Ask Which

Suppose you run a small company and want to ask an elderly department head to take early retire-ment. This is a common problem in all organiza-tions. Now suppose your persuadee is evasive: He is not available when you phone, he finds excuses to avoid conferences, and he refuses to discuss a retirement date. You need to get some kind of ac-tion. So you use the **don't-ask-if, ask-which** tech-nique, in which you ask the person to make a choice. There is no option other than the ones given. In the retirement situation, you say, "I need

to have a meeting with you. Is Tuesday or Wednes-day better?" There is no room for an answer such as "I don't want to meet at all." The person can try to shift ground by saying, "Neither of those is good." This can be met easily with the same tac-tic. You ask, "Which day this week is good then?" You will eventually nail down a definite day. You can follow with "Your office or mine?" or "Two o'clock or three?" and thus force the action. Once the meeting is set, the tactic can go on as you ask whether June or July would be a good time to retire. There may be need for an interim step, such as "Have you thought about retirement or is that something you haven't considered?" This sets the stage for your suggestion.

Salespersons often use this tactic, asking, "Which suit is best on you — the brown or the blue?" They follow with "Would you like a match-ing shirt and tie or just the suit for now?" Politi-cians ask, "Do you want a party hack or myself to lead this great state?" TV and print ads often ask, "Which wax will you buy — the more effective Pledge or the lemon-oil brand X?"

Although the don't-ask-if, ask-which tactic can be manipulative, it has the value of forcing action when buyers, voters, or others are stubborn and try to avoid making decisions.

Answering a Question with a Question

A tactic that some people use to throw you off guard is to respond to a request by asking a ques-tion. For example, they say, "Why do you think I would like to do that?" or "What gave you that idea?" or a similar response. We are expecting them to come to the point, to make a statement that relates to the discussion or the request. This throws us off pace and leaves us speechless for a moment. Then the initiative is gone.

The tactic of responding with another question is useful because it usually catches other people off guard and gives you time to think. Even ask-ing them to repeat themselves or to elaborate can have these effects. Suppose someone asks you to "roast" a friend. You are taken aback by the re-quest and want to say no on first impulse. But perhaps it would be better to think it over. Maybe you could handle the "roast" better than anyone else. You can answer the question with a question by saying, "When do you have to know whether I can make it?" This puts the ball back in the other's court and lets you make your decision without going into elaborate explanations, which may just bore the person. People who question you sometimes are trying to discredit or annoy you. Turn the tables — answer with another question.

Getting Partial Commitment

Evangelists often close their pitches by asking members in the tent or auditorium to bow their heads and close their eyes for prayer. This gets a **partial commitment** from all the audience. The preacher then asks the Lord to enter the hearts of all and asks those who want God to come into their lives to raise their hands or to stand up. This is a second act by which people commit to part of the request. The final request may then be "Those of you with your hands up come to the front and be saved." The tactic is seen elsewhere, too. A sales pitch may include asking whether you can afford to give up one pack of cigarettes a week to help put the Great Books series into your home. This willingness to commit oneself to a part of the deal can be continued until the sale is made.

Of course, other kinds of commitment are used to persuade. Ads offer a free sample of the product. You try it and have taken the first step in the purchase process. You get a free taste of cheese or sausage or yogurt in the supermarket, and you are more likely to commit yourself to buying the product. A politician asks you to sign a petition to put his or her name on the ballot. The act is a form of commitment to that politician.

The tactic resembles the yes-yes technique but uses *acts* instead of *words* to lead the persuadee to the final request. Persuaders can use it with neutral or negative audiences.

Ask More, So They Settle for Less

Ask more, so they settle for less involves setting a price or level in people's minds that is higher than

what they really want; when the persuader backs off, the buyers or voters think they are getting a special offer. For example, suppose I bring in a set of test scores to my class and write on the chalkboard the curve that the computer suggests. Now I distribute the answer sheets; students moan because the curve is so high. Then I say that because I am so kind I am making my own curve. I write a lower curve on the board. Students cheer and sigh with relief. Then I tell them that the one-to-three-point essay can be added on without changing the curve. I set a high expectation. Then I back off from that high level and although my curve may be stringent, compared with the machine curve, it is like a gift from Santa Claus. Government officials often use this tactic when they ask for more appropriations than they expect to get. The whole sales field is built on the notion of setting prices that you can mark down.

Persuaders can use this tactic when they have a product or goal that is hard to sell. Better to ask for more than your audience will stand for, so that, in compromising, you will persuade.

Planting

The device called **planting** is related to imagery, discussed earlier as an element in style. Planting uses one of the five senses to open a channel to a memory. We want the target group or person to recall our product, idea, or candidate. Memory responds best, it seems, to messages that have sense data as raw material. Restaurant ads often appeal to several senses, not just the sense of taste. They describe the "crisp and crunchy garden salad." The words *crisp* and *crunchy* appeal to the sense of touch. The restaurant may offer "sizzling hot steaks seared on a grill," thus appealing to the customers sense of hearing. Describing the "thick red tomato sauce" appeals to the sense of sight, just as the words "a steaming fragrance of garlic and spices" appeal to the sense of smell. In a classic case of using the sense of touch, Mr. Whipple of Charmin toilet tissue fame is regularly caught squeezing a pack of Charmin when he thinks no one is looking. An ad for an automobile may have someone slam the door shut so the audience hears the solid "thunk' and mentally compares it with the rattles of their own five-year-old car. Try to tie your persuasion to one of the five senses and you'll find that the audience will remember your message.

Getting an IOU

Sometimes called the *swap* or *trade-off* tactic, the technique of **getting an IOU** aims to get your listeners to feel that they owe you something. For instance, the insurance rep spends several hours doing a complex assets-and-debts analysis for a buyer. The goal is to prove to the buyer that he or she needs more insurance. The sales rep then spends more hours explaining the figures to the husband and wife, perhaps taking them out to lunch or dinner. By the end of all the special treatment, the couple may feel that they really *ought* to buy something, even though they may not need it or cannot afford it. They need to cancel out the obligation — the IOU — that was built by the salesperson's effort.

Persuaders find this tactic useful when it is hard to make a first contact with buyers, voters, or joiners. You can place your audience in your debt by giving them free gifts, samples, or offers of help. The old adage "there's no such thing as a free lunch" is a pretty good warning in our doublespeak world.

REVIEW AND CONCLUSION

We all have to persuade at some point. To be effective, we must plan how our format will affect the message. We must develop our forms of support and think about which would be most useful. We must control factors in delivery. We need to use source factors, such as posture, eye contact, and dress. Channel factors are subject to our control. Receiver factors can be used to get the target group involved in its own persuasion. As you are called on to persuade, use these skills in preparing. Rely on the audience analysis that the receiver-oriented approach teaches — listen to your audience. Get messages out of them, not into them.

QUESTIONS FOR FURTHER THOUGHT

1. Where does humor fit into the persuasion process? Give examples of sources who use humor. Does it relate to the audience? How?

2. What demographic clusters can you identify for the people in your class? In your dorm? In your club? Elsewhere?

3. What is a task-oriented message? Give examples from ads in which persuaders have used this technique effectively. Give other examples from ads in which they have failed.

4. What are the forms of organization? How do they differ from the forms of support? What might be other ways to organize a message?

5. What are the factors in credibility? Give examples of people who have them. Find ads that rely on each factor. Describe the person and the ad in terms of the factors.

6. What is AIDA and how does it differ from the motivated sequence?

7. What are Rank's desire-building tactics? How do they work?

8. How can a persuader get his or her audience more involved? What are some examples you have seen or heard recently?

NOTES

1. Bob Greene, "Exam Dream Never Fails to Panic," *Chicago Tribune*, October 19, 1982, sec. 1, p. 15.

2. Tony Schwartz, *The Responsive Chord* (Garden City, NY: Anchor Press/Doubleday, 1973), pp. 40, 88–91, 100–105.

3. Douglas Ehninger et al., *Principles and Types of Speech Communication*, 9th ed. (Chicago: Scott, Foresman, © 1982. Used by permission.)

4. S. J. Kantola, G. J. Syme, and N. A. Campbell, "Creating Conflict to Conserve Energy," *Psychology Today*, February 1985, p. 14.

5. In research I conducted in 1980, legislators in Illinois unanimously confirmed this. The most important and effective ways to communicate with them are via personal visits, letters, or phone calls. Resolutions or petitions are virtually ignored.

6. I am indebted to Professor Charles Parker of North Carolina State University for calling the AIDA model to my attention.

7. Hugh Rank, *The Pitch* (Park Forest South, IL: The Counter-Propaganda Press, 1982).

8. Charles W. Moores, *A Short Life of Abraham Lincoln* (Chicago: Houghton Mifflin, 1909), pp. 71–72.

9. John T. Molloy, *Dress For Success* and *The Woman's Dress For Success Book* (Chicago: Reardon and Walsh, 1977).

10. "Letters," *Newsweek*, February 11, 1985, p. 9.

11. Paul Selby, *Lincoln's Life Story and Speeches* (Chicago: Thompson and Thomas, 1902), p. 218.

12. Albert E. Scheflen, "The Significance of Posture in Communication Systems," *Psychiatry* 27: 316–331, 1964.

13. Tony Schwartz, *The Responsive Chord* (Garden City: Anchor Books, 1973).

14. These and many other tactics are mentioned in texts and books of advice for persuaders. For example, see the following, which mentions many of the tactics noted here: Clyde J. Faries, "Teaching Rhetorical Criticism: It's Our Responsibility," *Journal of the Illinois Speech and Theatre Association* 33:7–15, 1977. See also Ernest G. Bormann et al., *Interpersonal Communication in the Modern Organization* (Englewood Cliffs, NJ: Prentice-Hall, 1969), pp. 233–241. See also William S. Howell and Ernest G. Bormann, *The Process of Presentational Speaking*, 2nd ed. (New York: Harper & Row, 1988).

Chapter 12

Modern Media and Persuasion

There have been four major communication innovations in the history of humankind, each tied to the development of a new medium for communicating with one another. Each innovation/medium shaped and changed the world and the destiny of humanity forever after. And each allowed humans to see the world in vastly different ways and to interact with one another more efficiently and with varying degrees of permanence. These innovations are the spoken word, the written word, the printed word, and the electronic word.

MEDIA INNOVATIONS

The Spoken Word

While we were still only *hominoids*, or humanlike creatures, grunts and gestures were our only means of communicating.[1] Over thousands of years, we developed the first communication innovation in human history: the power to speak and to symbolize. This permitted humanity to gather into groups or tribes. Speech also allowed us to develop labor specialization, rituals and religions, and a history, even if it was embodied only in myths, ballads, and legends.

We sense the immense power of this development in the reverence with which the spoken word is held in most religions and in our everyday lives. For example, in the Book of Genesis, the story of the Creation indicates that with each creative act, God *spoke*. *Speaking* was the catalyst for the creation of night and day; earth and seas; fishes, animals, and birds; and ultimately man and woman. Later in the Old Testament, God again *speaks* to various characters: Jacob, Moses, and David. In the New Testament, almost all of Christ's miracles are brought about by His *speaking* some words, and Christ is also referred to as the "Word made flesh." In our daily social life, this religious attitude toward the spoken word continues. We must be sworn in to *testify*, or to *speak* to the court. At baptisms, the child's name must be *spoken*. At weddings, the vows must be *said*. The judge must *speak* the sentence before the defendant can be

taken to jail. Even at death, we *speak* words of absolution and commit the body to the grave using the *spoken* word.

The spoken word permitted humans to become *social animals* and to work together for the common good. It allowed one generation to pass down the history of the tribal society in the form of myths or legends. It allowed the society to pass information down from generation to generation. That allowed progress to occur: The wheel didn't have to be reinvented in each generation. In a sense, the development of the spoken word led to the recognition of *information* that could be shared by everyone. In oral/aural cultures, such as the American Indian tribes, information or knowledge is most frequently and fully held by the old. Thus, age is valued and honored. And because wisdom or knowledge increases with age, the older one becomes, the more important he or she is to the tribe. Among the Oglala Sioux, it was the custom to give every newly married couple an "Old One," perhaps a relative, to live in the couple's tepee to do the simple chores of tending the fire, comforting the babies, and being available for advice when asked. Not only did this help the young couple but it provided the Old One with a home.[2] There were no "bag ladies" among the Sioux.

The spoken word still exists, of course, but not in the same way it did in an oral/aural world, as Father Walter J. Ong, S.J., has pointed out.[3] In the oral/aural culture and even after, the spoken word was an experience—an event. It occupied time, not space. It was ephemeral; the beginning of the word was gone before the end of the same word was uttered. Its only permanence was in the human mind and memory, and it could be reexperienced only by reuttering it. The spoken word had magical qualities, which still exist today.

The Written Word

The next major communication innovation was the development of the phonetic alphabet, an alphabet tied to *speech sounds*, and not an ideographic one tied to vision. It had equally profound effects. With the alphabet, one could collect knowledge and store it. Advances of various kinds could be based on these stored records of what others had tried to do and how. The written word allowed us to develop complex legal systems and to assign or deed land and other possessions. That led to the centralization of power. Knowledge was power, and it was obtained and held by those who controlled the written word: kings, emperors, popes, and conquerors.

In ancient Greece and Rome, few people could read or write, and only the rich could afford to hire scribes. Thus information came to be thought of as *individual property* that could be "owned" and not shared with others. The great libraries were the repositories of these societies' knowledge and information. But they weren't "lending libraries" as we know them—that would have to wait until Benjamin Franklin invented them in the eighteenth century. These libraries were private, so not everyone had access to the knowledge or information. Without access to it, the average person remained ignorant of much of society's knowledge and thus remained at the bottom of the social order as soldiers, peasants, or slaves.

Not long after writing made the "ownership" of knowledge possible, the concept of ownership was applied to other property—land, cattle, horses, jewelry, buildings, and so on. Such ownership could be officially recorded in deeds to property, for example, which made the lawyer, or official interpreter of the deed, a necessary evil. No such concept existed in the oral/aural culture of the Sioux, for example. As a result, the American Indian had no concept of land ownership. The Sioux "Nation" existed only in the tribe's mind, as a collection of beliefs, knowledge, and rituals. This accounts for much of the misunderstanding associated with the land treaties of our history. To the white man, they represented the legal contracts through which land ownership was transferred. To the Indians, the treaties were "worthless scraps of paper."[4]

Ong points out that whereas the spoken word took up time, the written word took up *space* and was not ephemeral—it lasted across generations—making us more likely to rely on written records for the "last word" on an issue. Indeed, the written word came to be thought of as more trustworthy than the spoken word. Even if they couldn't read, people wanted to see things "in writing" before they would believe them.

Ownership of knowledge as property also made knowledge a key ingredient for establishing and maintaining power. The written word allowed powerful persons to develop "nations" over which they ruled. It is no accident that the Romans attacked and destroyed the great Greek library at Alexandria. Without its permanent store of knowledge and information, the Greeks were vulnerable and ultimately defeated.

Yet the word as an experience persisted in societies where writing was invented. As Ong points out:

> Ancient Hebrews and Christians knew not only the spoken word but the alphabet as well. . . . But for them and all men of early times, the word, even when written, was much closer to the spoken word than it normally is for twentieth-century technological man. Today we have often to labor to regain the awareness that the word is still always at root the spoken word. Early man had no such problem: he felt the word, even when written, as primarily an event in sound.[5]

So the word remained an experiential phenomenon, even when it was written *down* and looked *up*.[6] And it was to continue to be so perceived until the next great communication innovation, the printed word, came along.

The Printed Word

The third major communication innovation was the invention of printing, in the late 1400s. The effects of spreading the power of the written word to the common people were immense. Within a short time, the release of this power led to the Renaissance. Because information could be spread and shared, science developed rapidly. Scientists could read about one another's work and build on what others had done. Such knowledge was no longer limited to clerics, although religion itself was greatly affected by the printing press. Before the printing press, few people outside the church could read or write. Books were expensive and not always perfectly accurate because they had to be copied by hand, one at a time. Knowledge was power, and it was held mainly by the church. But when you could cheaply and accurately reproduce the Bible and other books, pamphlets, and tracts, this power became diffused. The Reformation, like the Renaissance, was the inevitable outcome of this diffusion of knowledge and thus power. If no one could read, what good would it have done for Martin Luther to nail up his ninety-five *Theses* on the door of the church in Wittenburg? Because people could read and because the printing press was available, his objections were duplicated and spread to many people. They agreed or disagreed, and finally many decided to start their own churches. The process continued with various factions fragmenting off, forming different Protestant sects.

Governments weren't immune to this diffusion of knowledge either, and soon most of them set up a censorship policy to help them control information and thus maintain power—an early form of propaganda. Not until John Peter Zenger, a German printer in the American Colonies, was tried for printing a tract that criticized the British Colonial governor did the notion of *freedom of the press* gain credibility. Curiously, Zenger was not tried for *writing* the criticism but for *printing* it. The British government held all printers responsible for what they published, in effect making every printer an unofficial censor. Zenger may never even have read the seditious pamphlet.

We have a similar anomaly in our present-day copyright laws regarding photocopying. These laws hold the person who runs the photocopier responsible for seeing to it that no copyright has been infringed. This means that the office worker is responsible for seeing to it that the boss has obtained permission to copy a certain work or that only a single copy will be made. Of course, the law is broken every day, and it is probably impossible to enforce. The government can't possibly monitor the photocopying of books and articles, musical scores, photographs, or even currency. New copyright laws are being designed to handle the increasing technology of our times, but developments such as videotape recorders and home computers make designing the proper legislation a nightmare. An example is the case of Tom Tcimpidis, a home-computer user, who started a modem-accessed "bulletin board" in 1980 for various computer users to access and trade information. An anonymous member of the network listed an AT&T credit-card access code, encouraging members of the network to "enjoy" it. Pacific Bell served Tcimpidis with a search warrant and charged him with fraud. This example underscores the problems in designing copyright laws in the face of ever-increasing technological development.[7]

Like the power of the spoken word, the power of the printed word has diminished to some degree. Although the number of newspapers published in the United States has risen since the advent of television, readership of newspapers and news magazines is down. In fact, some sources estimate that the average amount of time a person devotes to reading the newspaper is now only about eight minutes per day.[8]

So the printed word gave us the Reformation, the Renaissance, and their many effects: the "New Science," because scientists could share the results of experiments in learned societies; the "New Art," because artists did not need to devote their energies to religious subjects alone; and the "New Music," because musical scores could be printed accurately and cheaply and exchanged among composers, who learned from one another's works. But most important, in terms of persuasion, the printed word gave us *literacy*, which was to greatly influence the way we formulated and shared our thoughts and ideas. It led to a conception of humans as unique because they could think and reason and write down their thoughts and logic. Logic became the password of literacy, and the emotions of experience were demoted. The emotional mob was "that way" because they were "illiterate," not because they were excited by the experience of hearing the voice of the agitator.

Literacy led to great discoveries and inventions in Europe and in America. As noted earlier, Benjamin Franklin invented the "lending library"—a remarkably generous concept when you think of it. He also invented the postal service, the fire department, bifocals, central heating, the lightning rod, the rocking chair, the *Saturday Evening Post*, and a host of other inventions. In fact, he held over 5000 patents during his lifetime. It is probably no accident that Franklin's background was as a printer's apprentice.

Literacy opened the remarkable door of opportunity for Franklin and for many others, but it also enslaved us to some degree. We had to set aside a certain number of years of our lives to "learn" all the things that literacy had led to, and as a result we had to invent "childhood" — that time when a person gets an education. Naturally the length of childhood has had to be expanded several times as the amount of knowledge to be learned increased. Today, we know that we can never be able to read all there is to read on any subject, no matter how infinitesimal, so we talk of "lifelong learning" and frantically try to read as much as we can, falling further and further behind all the while.

The Electronic Word

The electronic word began in 1844 with the first demonstration of the telegraph. Now, new advances were made almost daily. The telegraph used electrical impulses that were turned on and off by the telegrapher's key to symbolize the various letters and spaces, thus allowing words to be sent as a series of dots and dashes. Then, in 1876, came the telephone, which transformed the spoken word into electronic impulses. Shortly thereafter came the radio, or wireless telegraph, which transformed written and later spoken words into electronically produced sound waves. We looked briefly at the changes brought by the electronic word when we discussed technological determinism in Chapter 3. As noted there, we are only dimly aware of the influence of these electronic words — the telegraph, radio, and telephone — but it is possible to get a glimmering of their effect with a hundred-year perspective. For example, the telegraph greatly sped up the communication process. Instead of relying on the Pony Express to get a message across the country (which took ten days), people could telegraph the message in minutes.

In commerce, we still have the futures market in commodities, as noted in Chapter 3, and some people think that being a telegrapher also gave insights about the value of time to Thomas Edison, Andrew Carnegie, and other industrialists.[9] A cliché we still hear, "time is money," possibly arose from the realization that, with modern electronic communication, minutes and even seconds could make a large profit-or-loss difference in the trade of stock or some commodity. Time could also make a critical difference in the cost of manufacturing products. Time-study engineers still search for ways to cut wasted movements in factories and offices, thereby reducing production costs and increasing profit and competitiveness.

Of course, there exist other versions of the electronic word — videotape, home computers, video games, and more. Each of these innovations has the same potential for creating changes similar to those that followed the invention of the printing press. More important, most of them have occurred only recently. The changes they are bringing about are probably unnoticed by us. The changes are there, however, and the critical consumer of persuasion should be alert to the ways the electronic word influences us and our culture. Some people are concerned that these media will adversely affect us. For example, many critics are worried that the home computer will drive Western culture inward, making us unable to interact with others on an interpersonal level. People regularly complain about the way society is becoming depersonalized by electronic technology such as the computer. Likewise, many people are concerned about the amount of television being watched each day by the average American child — and adult. We worry about the effects of television violence. We wonder whether America's youth may go prematurely deaf because of the volume used on stereo sets and radios. Surely it is necessary for us as receivers of persuasive messages to take a close look at the use of modern media in persuasion.

The most common kind of persuasion that we receive is advertising — in TV and radio spot commercials and in print ads. As noted before, most college freshmen have seen more than 22,000 hours of TV programming.[10] We live in a world in which media messages literally surround us — on billboards and in newsletters, magazines, catalogs, and a host of other mass media. As critical receivers, we need to be alert to ways in which advertisers use the power of the media to achieve their goals.

Because we are devoting an entire chapter to the topic of advertising at the request of many users of this book, the present chapter is devoted mainly to other aspects of modern mass media and persuasion.

Researchers have only started to study the processes by which we receive and use media in our lives. Results are either speculative or sketchy. One thing is clear, however: The mass media are the most effective channels to persuade people. Mass media persuade us to buy products, to vote, and to take up causes. Why is this? One reason may be that there is no real feedback in mass message systems (you cannot question, applaud, or respond), so certain ploys work that will not work in an open arena.

Another reason that modern mass media, particularly electronic media such as radio, television, video games, and the personal computer, are able to persuade so effectively is that they are inherently experiential in nature. That is, in the same way that spoken words are fleeting, electronic signals or images are heard or seen for only an instant, and then disappear from the screen or speaker never to be recalled unless we have "saved" them on an audio- or videotape or a computer disc. These electronic signals are "experienced" more than they are logically thought out, reasoned with, or subjected to tests of proof.[11] For example, one can't ask whether Bill Cosby in his role as Cliff Huxtable is true or false. He is neither, and he is both. What happens to him this week is now over and done with (until it is "reexperienced" in reruns). Our experience with this week's episode is not necessarily logical. In fact, it is more likely to be emotional. The same holds true of many other electronic media messages: Like the spoken word, they are events meant to be experienced before being recorded or analyzed. Future technological developments suggest that such messages will become even more experiential—perhaps not as experiential as the "Feelies" of Aldous Huxley's *Brave New World*, where one *really* "experienced" the movie—but they will definitely appeal

to the emotions and senses in highly experiential ways.[12]

To give you a notion of how this is going to happen and what some of its potential effects might be, consider *The Media Lab: Inventing the Future at M.I.T.* by Stewart Brand.[13] Brand's book describes some of the developments at the Media Lab at M.I.T. that occurred while he was there on sabbatical.

The $45 million lab was established and funded by the leading corporations in three communication fields: the print industry, the film/video/audio industry, and the computer industry. Each corporation and industry realized that phenomenal changes in communication technology were imminent and that to develop them most effectively and prudently was far beyond the financial and research capabilities of any single corporation or industry. So they pooled their resources and sought out the brightest and best media researchers, technicians, engineers, and theorists in various communication fields and asked them to literally "invent the future" in the various communications industries.

The Media Lab's director, Nicholas Negroponte, knew that the three industries were already beginning to converge, as shown in Figure 12.1. Some examples of this convergence include print that is computer typeset and enhanced visually by video technology; video graphics that are computer generated and produced; electronic mail, FAX, digital audio; recent print ads that incorporate appropriate electronic music; and 3-D IMAX theaters, to name but a few.[14]

Negroponte foresees a much broader convergence of the three technologies, which will look more like Figure 12.2 by the year 2000. The predicted kinds of changes exceed our wildest dreams. Perhaps the ballyhoo on the jacket of Brand's book says it best:

The rapidly converging technologies of recording, broadcasting, film, and publishing are in the process of redefining the entire field of communications media. New media are being created which can transform the human abilities to express, to learn, to communicate. At the Media Lab are telephones that can chat

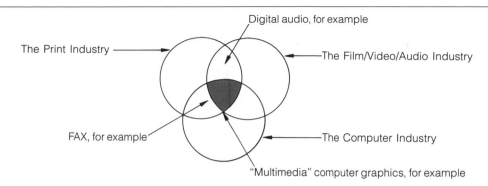

FIGURE 12.1

The convergence of the print, film/video/audio, and computer industries and technology at the present time.

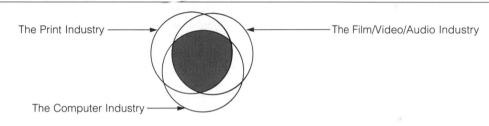

FIGURE 12.2

The convergence of the print, film/video/audio, and computer industries and technology in the year 2000.

with your friends, disembodied faces of real people that gesture and converse, interactive video discs, life-size holograms in midair, television sets that combine the networks and assemble programs that reflect each viewer's interests and glimpses of computerized "virtual reality."[15]

It is awesome to consider these and other possibilities. A brief example demonstrates the immensity of these changes:

Negroponte bases all of his plans on the growing computer intelligence of the TV set itself. ". . . twenty years from now your TV set will probably have 50 megabytes of random access memory and run at 40 to 50 MIPS [Millions of Information Pieces Per Second]. It'll basically be a Cray computer." (The Cray is at present the world's most powerful supercomputer and costs a cool $15 million.) "It will not be receiving pictures. It will be receiving data, and *it* makes the pictures."[16]

It is not our intent here to survey and hypothesize over these future developments, but it is our purpose to try to understand how they will affect us and to prepare for the ways in which these new mass media will try to persuade us. Here, the work of two important media theorists can help us understand the experiential nature of the present level of technology and prepare ourselves for the developments we will encounter in the next decade.

SCHWARTZ'S PERSPECTIVES ON MEDIA USE

We mentioned Tony Schwartz earlier.[17] The ideas found in his book *The Responsive Chord* have been used by sources ranging from a presidential media staff to hundreds of firms and ad agencies selling everything from baby powder to bottles of booze. Schwartz offers two competing models for explaining the way media work to persuade: the evoked recall, or resonance, model and the transportation, or teaching, model. Schwartz favors the first approach and offers reasons why.

The **evoked recall**, or **resonance** model, rests on the idea that it is better to get a message out of receivers than to try to put one into them. In other words, it relies on the set of experiences and memories that people have stored inside themselves. The basic tactic in getting these data out is to cue them in some way. Using this approach, persuaders might want to think of the problems people have with, say, a stalled car. Sometimes a stall occurs when we are most rushed. The stall is sometimes a result of some minor bit of repair that we neglected. Maybe it was ice in the gas line or a dirty air filter. Knowing that the potential buyer of the product—an AAA membership—has been through at least one stall, the source can build a message around the feelings you have when your car stalls. Actors in an ad can show frustration. They can signal the anxiety you felt when you knew that the stall would make you late. The music or score can heighten the feelings. The voice-over at the end can say soothingly, "When you've got to be there, triple A gets you there."

Schwartz observes that most experiential meaning is not cued symbolically because it is not stored as a symbol. Instead, it is stored as a feeling—a sense of ease or dis-ease. The best way to cue these feelings out is drama; the source acts out the feeling in the listener's head. Many times, the cueing is done by music, color, sound effects,

the actors' facial expressions or tone of voice, the acoustics, or some other nonverbal message.

What are some stored experiences and emotions that are common to large numbers of people and that media can prompt out of us? We discussed some of them earlier. The examination dream mentioned in Chapter 11 is one example; the frustration over the clogged sink is another; and car trouble is another. Any event or situation to which people respond with "Isn't that the way it always is" or "Every time I hear that I want to . . ." or "Boy, are you touching a nerve there" or "You're getting awfully close to home" is a common experience that resonates with large numbers of people. Mass-media persuaders, especially advertisers, have identified many of these resonating experiences and use the media to cue them out of you and me. As you examine the media persuasion aimed at you in magazine ads, TV and radio spots, and billboards, try to identify the common experiences being aimed at.

You probably won't find these experiential or emotional roots for media persuasion in the *verbal script*, for the latter most often contains the logical and discursive part of the message. The messages that tug at the heartstrings instead of the mind probably will be elsewhere. One place is in the *auditory script*, which goes beyond verbal symbols. This would involve such things as the musical score, the lyrics of the jingle, the sound effects, and maybe even the subliminal cues. Another place where common experiences might be identified is in the *visual script*—the images, editing, montages, camera movement, use of lenses, and other visual effects such as computer graphics. Each of these media "languages" can be critical in plucking a responsive chord.

The Verbal Script

Of course, Schwartz's idea runs counter to what many ad agencies believe. It is also counter to much of the theory about persuasion that emphasizes being specific, logical, and clever with words. That view looks only at the verbal script, which *is* the message. When ad agencies test their ads, they do just that. They ask people to look at

FRANK AND ERNEST ®by Bob Thaves

FIGURE 12.3

An evoked recollection of a stored experience is like a déjà vu experience — it is neither true nor false. It just exists. (*Frank and Ernest* reprinted by permission of NEA, Inc.)

ads and then to respond by recalling the words, numbers, and names that are in the ad. Rarely are viewers asked about their feelings or about the characters in the ads. It is often a quirk of fate that brings out such data, as in the case of the people who resented their suitcase because it survived a plane crash.

The Auditory Script

The TV spot is more than just its verbal script. It includes a sound script — things you hear that are not words. For instance, the good feelings we have about keg parties can be cued out by the sounds of a keg being tapped. As we hear the thunk of the tap being punched through the cork, the spin of the wing nut bolting down the tap, and the gurgle of the first mug being filled, the good times come back. Then it is fairly easy to add words: "We've got beer in a can that's as good as beer from a keg — Burpo Draft in the new aluminum can." The can is shaped like a barrel or keg to reinforce the good feelings most people have about past keg parties. The "language" of sound — sizzles, pops, grinds, klunks, plops, and buzzes — can sometimes cue powerful, unconscious, emotional feelings.

This type of auditory-script message can be reinforced by the musical score and sound effects and can also prompt feelings and emotions.[18] The same thing happens in spot ads. A recent example is a TV spot for Pepsi-Cola. An entrepreneur drives his mobile snack stand onto the beach. A subdued musical score is playing. He turns on his loudspeaker system and opens a bottle of Pepsi in front of the microphone. We see the crowd at the beach perk up and become interested. The young entrepreneur then slowly pours the Pepsi into a glass just in front of the mike, letting the fizzling sounds carry over the loudspeaker. The crowd gets to its feet and begins to move toward the snack stand. The young hero opens the stand to begin selling Pepsi to an eager and thirsty crowd. By the end of the ad, the viewers have had the experience of being thirsty cued out of their collective storehouses of experiences in the same way that a small cue can prompt what we call a déjà vu experience. Now, there is nothing necessarily logical about the ad or the response it cues out of the viewers, nor is the ad particularly true or false in any way. It simply "is."

The same kinds of experiences can be cued out in an entertainment program, a radio spot ad, or a "talking" or "singing" print ad such as those used

FRANK AND ERNEST ©by Bob Thaves

FIGURE 12.4

Clever editing can alter the sight script in very persuasive ways. (*Frank and Ernest* reprinted by permission of NEA, Inc.)

during the Christmas season. They all rely on stored experiential memories associated with a particular sound cue — a sound effect, a musical score, or the timbre of the announcer's voice. In fact, some of the scores for jingles have been so effective that they have become popular songs. For instance, the Coca-Cola jingle "I'd Like to Buy the World a Coke" was transformed into a popular song titled "I'd Like to Teach the World to Sing."

The Sight Script

The sight script is also an important source of cues. The keg-shaped beer can is a good example, as is the packing of certain cleaners in drum-shaped bottles to give the feeling of heavy-duty power. There are other ways the sight script can cue feelings out of us. Camera angle often has a cueing value. A low angle that looks up to a leader distorts size somewhat and "says" that this person is one to be looked up to — a cut above most people. A wide-angle shot with crowds of people thronging to see a leader and shouting salutes sends the message that this is a great leader of a great movement. Hitler used this technique in the famous Nazi propaganda film *Triumph of the Will*. It was outlawed in Germany for many years after World War II because of its power to raise emotions and feelings.

Close-up or zoom-in shots of people convey that we need to get a closer look, to find out what kind of stuff they are made of and what sort of people they are.[19] Editing can call out feelings that can then be used to persuade. Many news films of battle situations depend on clever editing to build a sense of action. They use quick cuts from one action shot to another. Tanks shoot across the screen. Then we cut to planes diving. Then we cut to troops running across a field firing all the way, and so on. The quick cut makes the viewer feel that there is a lot of effective action. It looks like the good guys are making raceway progress across the land of the bad guys. Or a camera can pan from left to right in a slow revelation of the immensity of a crowd. Frequently, when there are few people in a crowd, the camera hides the fact by dollying (moving or rolling forward) up to the backs of the last row of spectators, thus giving the illusion of a crowded room when actually there are many empty seats. If film producers want to show the sparsity of a crowd for a certain politician, however, they can take a shot from behind the speaker that pans the empty seats.

A quick cut can be used to build excitement and give a sense of speed. For example, we might use a snowmobile leaping across the screen and cutting through a huge snowdrift. Then the view is quickly cut to downhill racers carving their way

FIGURE 12.5

Here is the ad for *Ms.* magazine that prompted the angry letter to the editors of *Advertising Age*. Is the ad true or false? Is it realistic or unrealistic? To whom was the ad probably targeted? What do you think would be Tony Schwartz's response to the ad, to our semiotic analysis of it in Chapter 5, and to the letter to the editors? (Used by permission.)

through a tough slalom course, and we end with a final quick cut to ice-boat racers zooming across a frozen lake. Only at the end would we have to include some verbal script such as "Warm Up Winter This Year. Come to the Winter Wonderland of Lake Geneva" and close with an attractive couple nuzzling one another in front of the fireplace in the after-ski lounge. The visual script does most of the work here. It builds the excitement and prompts out the experiential memories from the audience's subconscious. The verbal script merely tells the viewer where the memories can be brought to life.

Other aspects of the sight script continue the job of getting messages out of us. Many newscasts

convey a newsroom atmosphere. The teletype's clatter, people rush around the set carrying pieces of paper meant to be news flashes, and so on. The network anchorpersons are then superimposed on the set from another studio, giving the visual impression that they are in the middle of the hustle and bustle. You get the impression that you won't miss any news if you stay tuned to that channel. The background shots for political candidates can signal sophisticated nuances of meaning. If the candidate is standing in front of the Lincoln Memorial with the president, we may conclude that he or she is devoted to issues of equality and justice and that he or she is probably a member of the president's party.

Props, jewelry, furniture, art works, costumes, and other visible effects are part of the sight script too. Look at the ad for *Ms.* magazine that we semiotically analyzed in Chapter 5 for the various signifiers and their signifieds (Figure 12.5). There, each visual element added more layers of meaning. They suggested that the new *Ms.* reader was a sophisticated and very attractive woman, approaching middle age, who was well dressed, bejeweled, a world traveler, and a mother. She used cosmetics, carried cash, and drove an Audi, all the while being sentimental but open to new technologies. These elements were all part of the sight script. Were they true or false? One reader had some strong feelings about the ad, which she put in a letter to the editors of *Advertising Age* magazine, where the ad appeared:

> [The] ad on behalf of *Ms.* magazine is one of the most unrealistic, off-target ads I've seen in a long time, and probably succeeds in irritating, if not aggravating, the very reader it was targeted at.
>
> No woman of any note, especially one who's "made it to the top" would ever carry around most of the objects "falling" out of her pocket. . . . Guys gimme a break: A passport? A champagne cork? A $100 bill? Not to mention "cute" kid drawings, credit cards and pills or breath mints. Why do you think women carry purses? . . . Women are lucky to find velvet pants with pockets in the first place.
>
> . . . My second objection is that any woman

worth her gender and deserving of making it to the top would never find herself in this "falling out of pockets" position in the first place even if she DID have stuff in her pockets. Any reader of *Ms.* magazine would have been prepared and removed this stuff before becoming comfy in an upside-down mode.[20]

It is clear from the tone of the letter and from several phrases in it that the author assumes that the intended targets of the ad are the readers of *Ms.* magazine (for example, "any woman worth her gender" and "any reader of *Ms.*"). The criticisms she raises in her letter would probably be accurate if that was the intended target. However, the target was *potential advertisers* in *Ms.* magazine. *Ms.* magazine had been sold to the same company that publishes *Sassy* magazine. They tried to reposition *Ms.* by shifting its image from a magazine for ardent feminists to one for successful, upscale women in their middle years—the baby boomers, the yuppies, and the muppies ("mature urban professionals"). They hoped to get airlines to advertise in the new *Ms.* magazine, hence the passport. They wanted cosmetics companies to advertise, hence the lipstick. They wanted computer companies to advertise, hence the solar calculator. They wanted companies that marketed sentimental products to advertise, hence the champagne cork and the florist's card with her husband's name on it. And there are numerous other potential advertisers the ad was trying to reach. Of course the ad was unrealistic; it was intended to be that way in order to be explicit about the readership of the NEW *Ms.* magazine. The strategy failed, however, and the new *Ms.* went bankrupt. It is now being published as a newsletter with no advertising.

Thus the most real, most true advertisements are those that *resonate* most closely with the experiences in the audience, and the title of Schwartz's book *The Responsive Chord* reflects that relationship between the audience and the persuasive message, whether the message is the advertisements, the articles printed in magazines, or programs heard on radio or seen on TV. The degree to which they resonate with the experiences

stored in the conscious or unconscious minds of the audience predicts their success or failure. In fact, Schwartz says that the issue of truth is irrelevant in examining the programming or the advertising of electronic media. I suspect that he would say much the same thing about many of the print ads we see in contemporary magazines and newspapers. In a sense, they have become more like the video medium in the past decade. Today we see ads with little or no copy that present a potential dramatic script that could be brought to life on a television screen. Take, for example, the Chivas ad in Figure 12.6. The visual script is effective because it resonates with the experiences of many parents of young children. My spouse and I used to answer the question "How do you like being parents for the first time?" with what we thought was the perfect metaphor: "It's like being thrown into a cement wall at 100 mph." Our escape was to hire a babysitter and play in a tennis league on Friday nights. The couple in the Chivas ad are treating themselves to the best restaurant dinner, the finest scotch whisky, and probably a night of lovemaking. The plot, characters, and setting are in the visual script, and it is a drama with which many consumers can identify. In other words, the script resonates with the experience(s) consumers have stored in their conscious or unconscious minds. The persuader's task is to identify such common experiences and then to design print or electronic messages that will help the audience recall the experience while they also mention the product, candidate, or organization seeking support.

What if the audience doesn't have such a stored experience? Schwartz recommends "planting" the experience in ads early in the campaign. For example, show macho guys in whitewater rafts being bounced up and down and getting doused with water until they reach a slack pool, paddle to the shore, and open their cooler to enjoy a cold can of Schlitz—the official beer of the Olympics. Even someone who has never whitewater rafted now has the experience planted in his or her mind. The next step is to reinforce that experience in print ads, focusing on the final scene, and with shorter television and perhaps radio ads. Then, at the point of purchase, voting, or joining, some cue

Sometimes life begins
when the babysitter arrives.

What are you saving the Chivas for?

FIGURE 12.6

Despite the fact that only a select number of critical words are used, this ad presents a visual script that is very clear. What is the script? What is the plot? What will happen after dinner? (Courtesy of Joseph E. Seagram & Sons, Inc.)

is used to prompt the recall. It may be the shape of the product's packaging; it may be the candidate's name on the ballot; or it may be the organization's logo on a billboard or package.

McLUHAN'S PERSPECTIVE ON MEDIA USE

Marshall McLuhan, whom we discussed in Chapter 3, was another theorist who studied media use in our times. His ideas in many ways are like those of Schwartz. In fact, the two were friends and often drew on one another for examples and insights. McLuhan believed that we relate to media in two ways.[21] First, every medium is an extension of one of our senses or body parts. Second, media can change our way of thinking about our world, as when the telegraph gave people the idea that they could communicate quickly across long distances. The invention of the wireless helped bring David Sarnoff, former president of NBC, to power. As a young man, he was broadcasting from high atop a hotel on the night the *Titanic* struck an iceberg and slowly sank. He heard her distress message and contacted her, serving as a key liaison between people aboard the ship and their families, business associates, and attorneys. Essential directions about where wills were located, what to buy and sell, and so on were exchanged through Sarnoff.

Television led to the eyewitness coverage of events, to quiz shows and quiz show scandals, to the Muppets (TV's equivalent of Walt Disney's world of animation), and to the two-minute drill in football. The home computer has led to myriad changes in the way we look at our lives. McLuhan, a technological determinist, believed that the technology available at any given time determines the future direction of a culture. Because media are a kind of technology, it is logical that McLuhan believed that *the medium is the message*.

One of the ways in which media tend to affect the way we look at our lives, according to McLuhan, is by their *form* or *fidelity*. Some media signals come to us in a complete, high-fidelity form. Others come to us in an incomplete, or low-fidelity, form. High-fidelity forms require little of

us in assembling the signals into complete messages. Low-fidelity forms require us to use our senses and to convert incomplete signals into complete messages. The telegraph would be such an incomplete, low-fidelity form or signal, whereas the radio would be less so. The same message sent via the two forms would be different, according to McLuhan. The high-fidelity form, by requiring little participation, would result in *little physiological* or *sensory involvement*. The low-fidelity form, requiring much participation, would result in *high physiological* or *sensory participation*. McLuhan called the high-fidelity, or complete, message signals "hot" and the low-fidelity, or incomplete, ones "cool" (see Table 12.1).

Hot Media

As previously noted, "hot" refers to media and messages that have high fidelity or definition. These media are easy to perceive. Their images are well drawn or recorded. We do not have to work to get the image or the sound. It is like the difference between the old wind-up phonograph that scratched out the sounds of the 1920s and the laser disc sound that makes you feel as if you are right in the middle of an orchestra. The laser-disc set-up is hot because it has high fidelity or definition. It is easy to perceive. Hot messages have the same quality. A good example might be the advertiser who comes on during the late movie and tries the hard sell about three rooms of carpeting for only $599.99. The message is distinct and comes through crystal clear. Or consider the hot politician who comes on strong and does not pull any punches but blurts out his message in simple words. In 1985, Patrick Buchanan, the noted conservative columnist, said that those people who bombed abortion clinics were "freedom fighters." Naturally, that remark was inflammatory and drew much fire. Buchanan is the kind of persuader, Schwartz said, who would blow out audience fuses because he was too hot.

Another example of a "hot" persuader on a "cool" medium is Geraldo Rivera, who regularly invites controversial guests to his show and then prompts the audience to get into verbal combat with them, and vice versa. Geraldo sits on the

Medium	Source of Information	Definition	Participation	Type of Medium
Television	Lighted dots	Low	High	Cool
Books	Completed letters	High	Low	Hot
Cartoons	Dots on paper	Low	High	Cool
Photographs	Image on film	High	Low	Hot
Telephone	Low-fidelity sound wave	Low	High	Cool
Movie	Moving image on film	High	Low	Hot
Telegraph	Dots and dashes in sound	Low	High	Cool
Digital audio	High-fidelity sound wave	High	Low	Hot

TABLE 12.1

Hot and cool media

sideline fanning the flames with his commentary. In contrast, Johnny Carson is a cool spokesperson on a cool medium, and the audience is less "fired up" by his program format, style, and guests.

Cool Media

Cool media have low fidelity or definition. We have to work to process these messages. On TV, for example, at any given instant only half of the lines of resolution are lit. We have to put together these "half-images" we see on TV, just as we have to imagine a lot of sound quality into the wind-up Victrola. Low-fidelity sounds come out of a telephone. What kinds of messages are best for these media? McLuhan said that cool media breed cool messages, or messages that are vague and ill defined. He saw the politician of the TV-dominated future as abstract, fuzzy, shaggy around the edges. There is no need for this type to say everything at gut level. Instead, the candidate lets the voter fill in or put together a meaning or image. If McLuhan was right, we should have seen a growth in image politics since the theory was first presented in 1964. That is exactly what happened. The politicians who seem to catch on are those with an easy-going approach. They are abstract to the voter, not distinct. Likewise we ought to be seeing more TV commercials that rely less on words or scripts than on giving a mood or feeling to which viewers can add to or subtract from to get a final meaning. Think of the many commercials that do this through the use of music or sets or lighting. We

hear the sounds of a Broadway-musical love ballad. Then we see a well-dressed man and woman slowly walking down the stairs at the opera house. The man asks the doorman to signal for his car. Up drives a Volkswagen Golf. Only then do we hear the voice-over tell us that the Volkswagen Golf is in good taste anywhere. And we fill in or add to the message we have received. So cool media are low in fidelity or signal quality and high in audience participation and, as a result, in audience involvement. The participation is usually physiological — we must use our senses to "complete" the message. The message itself may be insipid and not worth processing, but the interaction between the signal and the receiver may be very high.

McLuhan also said that we are spending an increasing portion of our days involved with cool compared to hot media. We know, for example, that the television set is on about seven hours a day in the average American home. It may not be watched all that time but its presence is making itself known. Many workers spend nearly eight hours a day in front of a computer terminal and screen. Of those who don't, the report is that a great portion of their workdays is spent on the telephone, another cool medium. And many homes have video recorders and computers, which also involve family members with the cool medium of television.

McLuhan predicted that this great increase in the use of cool media and the corresponding increase in audience participation, coupled with satellite transmission of television, radio, and telephone signals, will lead to a "Global Village" in which everyone is interested in everyone else's business. That prediction has also come true. It is here that McLuhan and Schwartz overlap and enhance one another. The involving and participatory trend, coupled with the notion of identifying experiences that can be prompted by mini-cues that allow people to add their own meanings to the words, pictures, or sounds they see and hear, add up to a powerful set of tools in the hands of creative and insightful persuaders, be they advertisers, television programmers, editors, newspersons, athletes, or actors.

MEYROWITZ'S PERSPECTIVE ON MEDIA USE

Joshua Meyrowitz's book *No Sense of Place: The Impact of Electronic Media on Social Behavior* presents another perspective on the power of persuasion in modern media, particularly the electronic media.[22] Operating from a sociological point of view, Meyrowitz claims that electronic media, especially television, have had great effects on our social behavior. His claim is not of the "TV Violence Causes Street Violence" type, but rather that from electronic media we learn expected patterns of behavior for specific *situations* we may have to face and that these lessons are blurring many of the distinctions we relied on in the past to determine a variety of socially acceptable patterns. Furthermore, Meyrowitz claims that

> one common theme that connects many recent and diverse phenomena is a change in America's "sense of place." The phrase is an intricate — though very serious — pun. It is intricate because "sense" and the word "place" have two meanings each: "sense" referring to perception and logic; "place" meaning both social position and physical location. The pun is serious because each of these four meanings represents a significant concept in the theory. Indeed, their interrelatedness forms the foundations of the two basic prem-

ises presented here: (1) that social roles (i.e., social "place") can be understood only in terms of social situations, which, until recently, have been tied to physical place and (2) that the logic of situational behaviors has much to do with patterns of information flow, that is, much to do with the human senses and their technological extensions.[23]

Now, of course, Meyrowitz's and my own sense of place are probably very different from yours inasmuch as I didn't see television until I was eleven or twelve, and he may remember seeing his first television broadcast. Meyrowitz uses a situational approach drawn from the work of sociologist Erving Goffman. Goffman used a dramatistic model not unlike that of Kenneth Burke, which we discussed in Chapter 5. Goffman talks of a *backstage* area of life (where we "rehearse" for certain situations we expect to encounter) and an *onstage* area of life (where we present our "rehearsed" roles). Meyrowitz's example for explaining these two is the alterations that probably occur in the behavior of waiters as they move from the dining room (onstage) to the kitchen (backstage). Goffman also speaks of a middle region, or *sidestage*, where the audience is permitted to observe parts of both the backstage and the onstage areas. Here the sense of place/situation begins to blur and may force the development of what he calls the *deep back* area and the *forefront* area. These emerge as "performers" become increasingly isolated from or intimately involved with the audience.[24] A forefront area in today's television programming can be seen when an actor interacts with the audience by speaking to the camera as if it is the audience, perhaps saying something like "It's probably time for a commercial now" in the middle of a dramatic episode. A deep back area might never be seen — say, the actual meetings between heads of state.

What has all of this to do with modern electronic media and their effects on our social behavior? And further, how do those effects relate to persuasion? Meyrowitz says that situations and the roles that go with them fall into three broad categories: (1) affiliation roles or group identity, (2) transition or "becoming" roles, and (3) authority or hierarchical roles. When new media are developed, people's access to these three types of roles changes. For example, in a literate culture dominated by a print technology such as we had until the 1950s, illiterate individuals did not have access to certain group identities, such as the Rotary Club. They were blocked from certain transition or "becoming" roles, such as graduations, and may never have access to authority roles, such as being promoted on the job. However, when new media such as our contemporary electronic media come into play, access to group identity, transition, and authority roles may be drastically altered, because electronic media do not always require a great level of literacy in order to be used by the average individual. In fact, literacy rates are falling.

The Blurring of Social Place

This increase in accessibility to situational roles results in a blurring of situations or "places," and a "leveling" effect among populations begins to occur. For example, compare the level of literacy required to make good conversation in an era dominated by print to the level of literacy needed when electronic media are in use. Most Americans report that they get most of their news from television and that they find it to be most trustworthy.[25] Yet one doesn't need to be literate to understand the news as it is presented on television. And the amount of news covered on television would amount to about two columns of print in the *New York Times*.[26] So the amount and "difficulty" of access to the news becomes remarkably equivalent across the population, regardless of one's social or educational "class." Meyrowitz's insightful example of this situation involves historian Theodore Roszak's critique of McLuhan's focus on media versus messages. Roszak claimed such an interest reminded him of a quote from Jean Harlow when asked what she wanted for her birthday — "Don't buy me a book. I gotta book" — which suggests a certain level of illiteracy. But it would make perfect sense if she had said, "Don't buy me a television set. I gotta television set."[27] And although it takes years to learn to read well enough to under-

stand complex material — the work of undersea biology, for instance — it takes no time to learn of it from a television documentary. In comparison to reading and writing, says Meyrowitz, "television viewing involves an access code that is barely a code at all."[28] And although television doesn't provide "reality," it *appears* to be more real than a book does.

Modern electronic media thus have the effect of leveling social classes by making basic information (which has been equated with power since the invention of writing) available and understandable for the literate and the illiterate; the rich and the poor; and the technological, industrial First World and the less developed Third World. As a result, it is increasingly difficult to know our "place" in society.

The Blurring of Physical Place

The loss of sense of place can be seen in the ads put out by AT&T to promote their rates on overseas phone calls. The blurring of place in these ads is a blurring of physical, not social, place. The scenes usually involve a parent and a child who are continents apart. They are able to bridge this physical space by making a ten-minute phone call to their loved one. In a sense, they are "together" for those ten minutes, and thus physical place is blurred.

A more bizarre example of the blurring of place occurs when persons "attend" and "speak" at their own funeral service using audio- or videotape recordings. Videotaped wills are also becoming more popular. Imagine trying to contest such a will.[29]

In the process of writing this sixth edition, I will develop several important relationships with people I will probably never meet in person. While writing the fourth edition, one such relationship developed with a woman named Vicki. We worked closely together over the phone on various stages of the manuscript, and I put her on "hold" to receive the news of my father-in-law's fatal heart attack. Vicki sent a sympathy card even though she had never met me. Again, physical place and social place were in a sense wiped out.

Parasocial Relationships

This alteration in the sense of place leads to what Meyrowitz calls "parasocial" relationships with fictional persons we are not physically close enough to to develop a relationship with. My spouse liked Lacey better than Cagney. We both like Roxanne but not Arnie Becker all the time, and we almost always hate Douglas. During his first five years on the air, Dr. Marcus Welby received over 250,000 letters asking for medical advice.[30] We also form parasocial relationships with real media figures such as Oprah Winfrey, Johnny Carson, and Geraldo Rivera. Meyrowitz notes that these parasocial relationships have led to a new type of murder—the parasocially motivated murder. Mark David Chapman, for example, knew so much about his victim, John Lennon, that at times, he thought he actually was Lennon.[31]

Another change in our sense of social place has come about by the leveling of the types of images that enter our home. Ghetto residents see and hear the same programs as sophisticated suburbanites. Minorities sense the unfair disparities between themselves and the majority; they began to make demands in the 1960s that would have been unheard of in the 1950s and earlier. Social consciousness may have been fostered by media consciousness.

Introduction to the "Backstage"

The new media also can permit us to enter "backstage" areas. The Watergate tapes demonstrated what can happen when the backstage becomes public, as did George Bush's "private" off-the-air comment that "Dan Rather . . . makes Leslie Stahl look like a pussy."

They also can change politics and politicians. Over twenty years ago, McLuhan predicted that politics would shortly become entertainment and that we would have to go to the right casting agencies to find personalities with "presidential timber." Enter Ronald Reagan. It seems, as Meyrowitz points out, that today's authorities have to "look and sound good" even if they can't read, write, or reason very well. The appeal from authority has always been one of the prime tools of clever persuaders. Now, the new media may have changed what authority actually is. Remember that power and authority were always in the hands of those who controlled information. Television, telephones, and computers allow many more people access to more and more of this information/power in corporations, educational institutions, research facilities, government, and in many other places. Also, computer hackers can destroy information/power by infiltrating a data set with a "virus" that can confuse and/or destroy the data set and all other data sets to which it is exposed. And remember the predictions about increasing sophistication made by the director of the Media Lab at M.I.T. Certainly the first resignation of a U.S. President—our ultimate power symbol—was the result of the new media.

Even your sense of individuality or place in your social world is being altered by the new media. Did you ever wonder how you got on so many mailing lists? Your federal government, through the census, placed you on some. Your state government placed you on others by selling the information on your driver's license and on any other licenses you purchased to mailing-list brokers. Your town or city government placed you on other lists by selling the information it has about you. And most ironic, you placed yourself on some lists by filling out questionnaires such as those accompanying warranties. Soon you can expect to be getting as many telephone sales pitches as you presently get mail-order pitches. Privacy may have to be protected in a variety of new ways if we are to maintain a sense of place in the future.

The Blurring of Generational Place

Another shift in our sense of place relates to the generation gap. Once age was an obvious marker for a person's place in society. Now, with the sharing of the same or at least similar information pools, there is a blurring of the difference between childhood and adulthood. Meyrowitz gives an interesting example of this blurring: manner of dress. He points out that many adults dress up like "'big children' in jeans, Mickey Mouse or Superman T-shirts and sneakers" while children dress in designer dresses or designer jeans and use designer perfumes.[32] On television, children frequently are pictured as more sensitive and intelligent than their adult counterparts. Many children are far more computer literate than are their parents. The music videos that teenagers watch are often more violent and explicitly pornographic than many X-rated films, and the lyrics of many youth songs are very explicit about the previously taboo topic of sex. Remember, childhood may have been "invented" because of the printing press and the resulting need for literacy — a time to learn to read and write. All ages watch TV.

Meyrowitz concludes that the past three decades have witnessed immense social change owing to the rise of electronic communication — particularly television. These changes, as we have seen, are as multifaceted as they are immense. He predicts a new social order that will thrive on information, much of which is not gleaned through reading or reasoning but through seeing, hearing, and experiencing. We may be "reentering the tribal world," as McLuhan once put it.[33] We will become "hunters and gatherers in an Information Age."[34] Our prey will be information and its resulting power. If this all sounds extremely deterministic, consider Meyrowitz's closing words:

> Ultimately, the most deterministic perspective may be unwittingly embraced by those who refuse to apply our greatest freedom — human reason and human analysis — to the social factors that influence behavior. We do not retain free choice simply because we refuse to see and study those things that constrain our action. Indeed we often give up the potential of additional freedom to control our lives by choosing not to see how the environments we shape can in turn work to reshape us.[35]

Our lost sense of place is a loss to which persuaders can appeal in powerful ways. It is also related to the lost sense of community and public commitment that we discussed earlier and that was verified and elaborated upon in *Habits of the Heart: Individualism and Commitment in American Life* by Robert N. Bellah and his colleagues. If Meyrowitz and Bellah et al. are correct, we are facing a time not only of great technological change (as documented and predicted in *The Media Lab* by

Stewart Brand) but one of great social change and challenge. It will be imperative that each of us be acutely aware of the power the mass media have to bring about change and to influence us. If the mass media have the power to change as many things as Meyrowitz identifies, then they also have the power to unify us and motivate us to reach humane and community-oriented goals. Let us explore a few ways in which the mass media are already doing this.

AGENDA SETTING BY THE MEDIA

Emphasis and Selection

One explanation of how mass media persuade is called the **agenda-setting function** of mass media.[36] According to the theory, the public agenda — the kinds of issues people discuss, think, and worry about (and sometimes ultimately press for legislation about) — is powerfully shaped and directed by what the news media choose to publicize. As theorists put it, mass media do not tell us what to think; they tell us what to think about. Each day, many more items of news than can be printed or broadcast come in over the newswires, from reporters, in press releases, and so on. Some of these items are selected for publication or broadcast, and this selection process sets the public agenda. Sometimes the decision is made by broadcast news producers and directors or newspaper editors, but more and more it is being made by network newscasters and programmers. The late-night news show "Nightline" got its start in 1980 because news programming staffs at the network decided to do a special news program on the American hostages in the embassy in Tehran, Iran. Following the release of the hostages, the program was kept on because of its ratings. Later it proved central in setting the agenda on topics such as the fall of the Berlin Wall, the breakup of Eastern Europe, the 1990 Iraqi invasion of Kuwait, Operation Desert Storm, and other current events.

From a slightly different perspective, the National Coalition on Television Violence claims that the media have put violent acts on the public agenda, thus leading to increased concern about violence on TV.[37] The Coalition says that by the time children are fifteen years old, they have seen about 24,000 shootings on television and that even on the morning cartoon shows there are violent acts — 8000 per year are viewed by the average four-year-old. The Coalition claims that there is more violence during one day's average prime-time television than most police ever see. Does this make people commit violent acts? Some researchers make that argument, but that is not the point from an agenda-setting perspective. Rather, they emphasize that displaying so much violence makes people think and talk about violence, even though they may never see or hear a gun fired in anger. As columnist Bob Greene put it:

> Television has won — it has become the dominant picture of how we see ourselves. And as long as it insists on deciding that gunfire qualifies as entertainment, it is guaranteeing that we will see ourselves in the most depressing possible light.[38]

Violence predominates in other news media as well. Remember, we are not being told what to think but what to think about. It is not surprising, given the dominance of violent programming, that there are many elderly inner-city citizens with numerous deadbolt and safety-chain locks on their doors, or that, even in small towns, people in coffee shops, taverns, bowling alleys, and churches are talking about rising crime rates and warning their children about the "danger stranger" problem. (We are not claiming that it is foolish for them to do so — only that they are more likely to worry about violence when they see it emphasized by the mass media.)[39]

Further, willingness of the mass media to exploit important social issues as well as sensationalistic anomalies seems to be increasing. For example, Phil Donahue's "shows" focus on such issues as genetic engineering, AIDS, and infidelity, or Geraldo Rivera "interviews" Charles Manson, Siamese twins, male strippers, and a woman who wants to marry serial murderer John Wayne Gacey. Do such programs and their print media companion pieces (such as *The National En-quirer* — the "newspaper" with the world's largest circulation) help us shape the future? Do they encourage a sense of place or a sense of community in the audience? How much effect do they have on who governs or what our domestic and foreign policy should be? These are all important questions that we need to address, especially when we consider how our personal and national agendas are set for us by the mass media, largely by groups or individuals referred to as "gatekeepers."

Gatekeepers

Closely related to the agenda-setting function theory is the idea of a **gatekeeper**, the decision maker who selects a certain story to put on the evening news broadcast or in the newspaper. Gatekeepers hold great power in determining the public agenda, and their decisions can have ripple effects. In the mid-1980s, one gatekeeper decided to feature a story about a day-care center in California where employees had reportedly sexually abused the children. Within days, similar reports were cropping up in other cities, and soon news weeklies were focusing on the topic of sexual abuse of children. This was followed by special stories on child abuse in Sunday newspaper supplements, family magazines, and *Psychology Today*. We don't know much about gatekeepers except that they are editors, news directors in radio and television stations, and magazine publishers. What they choose not to tell us may be as important as what they select for our viewing, listening, or reading.

How do gatekeepers make programming decisions and by what criteria? Not much is known about this process, but there are some hints of how and why the decisions are made. Meyrowitz refers to one criterion called LOP, or "Least Objectionable Programming." This means that "the key is to design a program that is least likely to be turned *off*, rather than a program viewers will actively seek out."[40] Some media critics note that while media advertisements purportedly *sell products* to viewers, the economic design of mass media is to *sell audiences* to advertisers. In terms of television, for example, we tend to think of programs as "products" for which we pay a price — we have to watch ads from the program's sponsors. In reality we are the products, and we are being sold to the advertisers.[41] Therefore, the goal is to design programming that will capture and "hold" the attention of the largest number of people or of a certain segment of people, such as upscale spenders.

Recently, CBS, finding itself at the bottom of the ratings, determined that henceforth the "news" programming had to make a profit. The news division at CBS had been a sacred cow since the days of Edward R. Murrow, but that went out the window when ratings dropped and profits entered the picture. Perhaps this explains the ever-increasing incidence of what has come to be called "fluff journalism" (for example, a report of a raincoat being worn by a dog in a Kansas City downpour).

Another criterion for deciding what is to be broadcast on television is whether or not a piece can be delivered as a 20-to-30-second "news

Berry's World

"You're talking in 30-second bites again."

FIGURE 12.7

The 30-second news bite is one criterion that affects gatekeepers' decisions as to what is newsworthy and what is not. As this cartoon implies, the news bite may even be affecting our conversational styles. (*Berry's World* reprinted by permission of NEA, Inc.)

bite," defined by Jamieson and Campbell as a piece of news less than 35 seconds long, delivered by a credible source in an energetic way.[42] Meyrowitz explains that viewers actually may prefer short "bites" because they report whether anything important has happened that day. For example, if the first story or bite in the broadcast is not earth-shattering, then it hasn't been an important day insofar as news is concerned. On the other hand, if the first story is of a crisis nature, viewers know that there will be an in-depth follow-up.

Newspapers, since they generally provide us with yesterday's news, very frequently follow the gatekeeping decisions of television. They run stories on what the television news programmer determined was important the day before. News weeklies are caught in the same bind, presenting last week news in this week's issue. However, both the newspaper and the news weekly have the space to do in-depth coverage of the issues placed on the public agenda by the electronic media. Unfortunately, as pointed out previously, people spend little time with the newspaper and other print media (eight minutes per day), relying instead on the 20- to-30-second bites they get on TV.

Another criterion used to determine which story gets broadcast and subsequently printed is the expressiveness or dramatic quality of both the video and the audio elements in the message.[43] It is "newsworthy" to get the instantaneous reactions of a mother who has just heard that her son has been kidnapped. A mike is shoved under her chin and the camera zooms up to her face and supposedly the audience "experiences" how she must feel at that moment. At least that's what seems to drive the ratings. McLuhan once observed of newspapers that the only good news in them nowadays is advertising and PR, and that it took an awful lot of bad news to sell all that good news.

As critical receivers of persuasion, we need to diversify our reading, listening, and viewing of news and information to expose ourselves to as many divergent sources as possible. Too often we select a favorite news source and neglect the others. It is especially insightful to listen to the news as reported on public television or public radio. There the leverage of sponsors, profits, and management is not so intense and the reporting is less influenced by outside pressures. Try adding *Morning Edition* and *All Things Considered* to your radio selections and *Washington Week in Review* or the *MacNeil/Lehrer News Hour* to your TV viewing (they are also on public radio). Above all, don't let one medium — such as TV — so dominate your awareness of the world that you overlook other sources of news and information. Even if you watch as much TV as the student in Figure 12.8, delve into other sources such as radio, books, periodicals, and newspapers. Widen the range of the agenda being set for you. With *several* sources telling you what to think about, you may be able to decide more wisely what to think.

ROLE MODELING AND THE MEDIA

In earlier times, people learned to model themselves after those with whom they worked or lived. Girls learned to be homemakers by watching their mothers. Boys learned to be farmers by watching their fathers and the other farmers in the community. Today, the media exert a much more potent force on role modeling than does the world around.

In many contexts we are forced to adopt various roles, patterns of acting and talking that signal many meanings to people around us. For example, when we act like a stuffy teacher, that sends messages to students that lead them to treat us as stuffy. We come on as the hale, hearty, extrovert type, and people expect us to have good jokes, to be easy to talk with, and so on. These roles shift from place to place and time to time. I do not often swear in church, but I am quite good at it on a canoe trip. You act the humble student when you are trying to get the teacher to let you do extra-credit work to make up for your low grade on the midterm test.

We adopt such roles in two ways. First, we may take on a certain role because the scene or setting

Berry's World

"Seventeen years ago, he was just a BABY. Now, he's watched more than 15,000 HOURS OF TV."

© 1984 by NEA, Inc.

FIGURE 12.8

The hours we spend watching TV strongly influence our agenda. Note also that the average seventeen-year-old now may have watched 20,000 or more hours. (*Berry's World* reprinted by permission of NEA, Inc.)

demands it of us. For example, certain roles are called for at funerals, whereas others are called for at weddings. These are **assigned roles**. A president may suffer a personal tragedy but should not show its effects too obviously in public. The scene assigns a president the role of leader, and shows of emotion are not called for in leaders. At other times, the setting may demand a role that we do not accept, and we choose another role. For example, a pro-football player should be tough and burly. He should make a show of proving that he is "all man." Big, tough, burly he-men don't hurt, and they don't cry. The football-field scene assigns this role. However, suppose that players know that a teammate is dying of some disease. Now the tough guys show emotion and cry at the end of the final game of the stricken player's final season. These actions come from roles dictated by the players, not the scene. These are **assumed roles**. They are taken on at the will of the role player and often run counter to the demands of the scene. Again and again throughout our lives, we choose between these two options—the assumed and assigned roles. We have varying degrees of success and failure in playing roles, and we learn from them.

How do we learn which roles are called for and which are not? Here is where mass media come in. Ask yourself what a working mother is like. Your responses may come from watching your own working mother, but they will also come from characters in ads or in situation comedies or in other TV and radio programs. You read newspaper or magazine stories featuring working mothers and your role model grows.

This is why the critics of the mass media are so concerned about programs, ads, and other messages that feature sex or violence. When Suzanne Somers was first featured on the sitcom *Three's Company*, she skyrocketed to fame. But women's groups objected to the featuring of her body in almost every episode of the series, arguing that the female public was being persuaded that the way to be successful in love and on the job was by using one's body. Eventually, this led to outcries and even product boycotts against "jiggly" programming. More recently, series such as *L.A. Law*, *The Golden Girls*, and *Cheers* have provided more realistic alternatives to jiggly programming using other role models. Successful women don't always have to be beautiful, shapely, and ready to tumble into the sack (although they still are in many series). Successful men don't always have to be aggressive and macho, or look like Tom Selleck.

When the cartoon sitcom "The Simpsons" first debuted on evening prime time, many parents were outraged and forbade their children to watch it. Why? After all, it was all in good fun, and the barrage of Simpson paraphernalia (t-shirts, signs, lunchboxes, stickers, and so on) on the market was good evidence of the program's popularity. Communication researcher Mary Larson has observed that objections were related to the role models depicted by the Simpson family members. For example, Bart is an underachiever who has an "attitude problem," which means that he is disrespectful of parents and authority figures. He also uses smart aleck slang words and phrases such as "dude" and "Don't have a cow!" Mother Marge Simpson yells at her kids and sometimes uses earthy language: "Get your butts down here; we're going to be late for church!" Larson believes that these objections are related to the possible role models children may get from the Simpson family.[44]

NEWS MANIPULATION AND PERSUASION

In his book *Don't Blame the People*, Robert Cirino observes that the role of the news industry is to do business with business.[45] After all, the media stand to profit from the success of their clients and customers. Does news manipulation really occur or are people such as Cirino supersensitive and paranoid about the power of the networks, the wire services, and the major newspapers and newsmagazines? Any answer to that question leads to debate between those who espouse a free press and free speech and those who denounce the profit system. A better way to react to the question is to say, "There may be cover-up, shading, and other ways to shape the news." If there are, persuadees ought to acquaint themselves with the possible tactics that can make or unmake news. That will allow us an extra safeguard against possible "hidden persuasion" in news programs. Let us look at some of these tactics and at our news system.

The three major wire services to which we are exposed in mass-media news programs or reports are United Press International (UPI), the Associated Press (AP), and Reuters. These three services supply most of the news we hear and read. Go through your daily newspaper and see how many stories are run from each service. In a way, we are all getting the same news. There is nothing wrong with that, as long as the news is accurate and as long as the key news items get printed or broadcast. This is the problem. The key items are not always the ones on the front page, as we noted with agenda setting. The problem is more severe with broadcast news. The evening news on TV contains only about twenty-two minutes of news. Furthermore, the messages are sent through the aural/oral channel. We speak and listen at speeds much slower than those used for reading. The speech speed on broadcast news is about 125 words per minute, or about 3000 total words of news, weather, sports, and perhaps an occasional editorial comment. The average 400-words-per-minute reader could cover that in print in only seven to eight minutes. As noted before, you will miss a lot of important information if you rely on only the electronic media for news.

Furthermore, even this truncated version of news has been diluted by the pressure of the ratings. The news as "show business" began with male and later female anchors, and continued with slick news teams who wore coordinated blazers, blouses, and ties or scarfs. According to Ron Powers, the end result was a market-oriented "people" news that catered to audiences instead of educating or informing them. As he noted:

> People did not want complicated, disturbing newscasts any more. . . . People were sick of unpleasant news. The new "mood of the country" . . . was no longer "issue-oriented" but "people-oriented." The very term "Pee-pull" to denote a news genre became oracular; it was spoken in hushed italics; it bore the tintinnabulation of cash register bells.[46]

The result is a news *program*, not a news *broadcast*. The news is manipulated, selected, shaped, and massaged to attract the largest share of the audience—to please the most and offend the fewest.

Powers's observations are shared by many in the news industry. Barbara Matusow notes in her book *The Evening Stars*, "The triumph of the Anchor is, in fact, the logical outgrowth of a system almost totally unfettered by any consideration except the need to maximize profits."[47] Her account of the struggle to land Dan Rather as the CBS anchor to replace retiring Walter Cronkite makes the point clearly. After lots of bumping and shoving between CBS management, Rather, and other networks, Rather was offered the anchor spot for a fee of approximately $25 million, spread over ten years, plus other perks. Matusow quotes Roone Arledge of ABC news, which was competing for Rather's services, as saying, "It's hard to put a value on

Dan Rather. If he . . . brings viewers to the 'World News Tonight' how much he is worth over ten years is incalculable."[48]

When you are trying to gain a certain segment of the market, the temptation is to manipulate the news, to make it more interesting, sexier, more sensational, and more entertaining. Your tactics are limitless, and bias is bound to creep in. As Edward R. Murrow, the first electronic news star, put it:

> One of the basic troubles with radio and television news is that both instruments have grown up as an incompatible combination of show business, advertising and news. Each of the three is a rather bizarre and demanding profession, and when you get all three under one roof, the dust never settles.[49]

The show-business aspect of electronic news distorts the news just as surely as yellow journalism distorted print news. Our job as receivers is to determine how this distortion takes place. Here are some ways news can be manipulated.

Ignoring

One way gatekeepers distort the news is by simply ignoring it. Mark Lane's book *Rush to Judgment*, investigating a possible conspiracy in John F. Kennedy's assassination, went unnoticed for fifteen months before he finally found a publisher for it.[50] More recently, the danger of building materials containing asbestos was largely ignored until one school district in Virginia finally brought suit. Asbestos without a lawsuit apparently wasn't an interesting story—people would not listen or watch for very long, and ratings would drop. The news specials commemorating the fortieth anniversary of the liberation of the Nazi death camps frequently noted that war criminals were thought to be still at large. Their existence had been ignored for forty years by the U.S. government. Finally, the coverage of their continued freedom forced the U.S. government to join forces with other agencies that were trying to find and punish the remaining war criminals.

Favoring the Sponsor

Because every commercial news program has sponsors, there is the strong possibility that news reporters and editors will soft-pedal any negative news about their own sponsors. Good examples are the difficulty Ralph Nader had in publicizing the lack of safety of the Corvair, the number of years it took to get broadcasters to refuse advertising from cigarette manufacturers, and the campaign against drinking and driving that mass media supported to keep beer and wine ads from being banned. It is always wise to ask who the sponsor is for a newscast. Getting your news from several sources may help you avoid sponsor-favoring editing.

The Pseudoevent

Although there is an overabundance of news each day, not all of it is interesting or entertaining, so frequently news reporters are drawn to highly dramatic or bizarre events. Daniel Boorstin called these "pseudoevents." In other words, they are "planned news." It really isn't news that the new models of automobiles were unveiled, but the event is heralded on all the media. The same thing occurs with the announcement of stock dividends, contract settlements, or grand openings. Reporting them may not be news coverage, but rather a hybrid somewhere between public relations and hard news. Various mass movements use pseudoevents to draw media attention to their cause by holding marches, rallies, or vigils, or even using violent tactics such as bombings, lootings, or other dramatic events.

Bias: Verbal and Nonverbal

We have previously noted several kinds of bias, such as gatekeeping and ignoring; there are numerous others. A skillful interviewer can make an interviewee seem to be quite different from his or her real self. Mike Wallace is an expert at drawing out the interviewee in selective ways. Further editing can heighten the bias. If we want to make the point that a candidate is controversial, we can put an audio-track of booing on a video-track of cheering and have our announcer say that the candidate faces opposition from left and right. We might superimpose two or more conflicting images: angry farmers and grain dealers; college students and college loan officers; homemakers and supermarket owners; starving children and people wasting food or gorging themselves. We can select who is featured on the documentary, choosing only pro or only con advocates. The reporter can say that so-and-so refused to comment on the issue, thus making it seem that so-and-so must be guilty.

Finally, news can be biased by simply taking things out of context or by misquoting a source. As Black Muslim leader Malcolm X put it, "I don't care what points I made . . . it practically never gets printed the way I said it."[51]

We can't possibly look at and listen to all the print and electronic news available on TV and radio or in print. What we can do is diversify our exposure, not relying on any one medium (as so many people do with television) or on any one network, newspaper, or magazine. Vary the networks you watch, read different news weeklies on a regular basis, and read several newspapers.

REVIEW AND CONCLUSION

We mentioned the statistic that the average eighteen-year-old American has seen 22,000 hours of television and hundreds of thousands of commercials. Remember that TV is just one media channel being used for persuasion. Most of us are affected by billboard persuasion. Films persuade us; magazines and newspapers frequently persuade us through their ads and stories and editorials and cartoons. Labels, bumper stickers, t-shirts, and other paraphernalia seem to be used increasingly for persuading. Although, on the average, Americans buy less than one-third of a book per person per year (we don't know whether they are ever read), books may sometimes persuade us.[52]

All in all, we live in a highly persuasive, media-rich environment. We cannot hope to provide you with enough tools to filter out all the messages, and maybe that would not be good anyway. You need to be persuaded about some things, and media persuasion is sometimes the best way to get information about your choices. One thing that we all can do, however, to protect ourselves from all persuasive attempts made by the media is to begin to look beyond the surface meanings in media messages. Look for the responsive chords that are being plucked and decide whether the messages that elicit them are hot or cool. Look for the agenda items that are being set up. Also, consider the immense changes we are facing because of the development of new communications media at M.I.T. Try to determine the ways in which media, especially electronic media, affect the many aspects of human interaction and behavior pointed out by Meyrowitz and others.

QUESTIONS FOR FURTHER THOUGHT

1. Which of your values or experiences are premises that could be evoked by persuaders and then tied to their product, idea, or candidate? Think of favorite experiences you have had that could be tied to a product. Recall some unpleasant experiences that could be used.
2. What is a hot medium? Give an example. Why is it *hot*? What kinds of messages seem to go best with a hot medium?
3. What does Schwartz mean by "evoked recall"? Give several examples.
4. What are some similarities between the primitive oral/aural cultures and the electronic culture in which we now live?
5. Why is information associated with power? Give examples.
6. How was the concept of "ownership" associated with the development of writing?
7. What were some of the things that resulted from the development of print?
8. How did literacy free us and also "enslave" us?

9. What are some of the developments at the Media Lab at M.I.T.? How will they affect us in the future?
10. According to Schwartz, are symbols used to store the experiences we have?
11. What "mistake" did the writer of the letter to the editors of *Advertising Age* make about the target audience of the *Ms.* magazine ad?
12. Which media type — hot or cool — dominates our times?
13. Why is the phrase "no sense of place" a double pun?
14. Give examples of shifting senses of place.
15. Give examples of the criteria gatekeepers may be using to determine what will be put on the evening TV news.
16. What is the agenda-setting function of mass media?

NOTES

1. In the early stages of critique and review for the fifth edition of this book, one of the reviewers pointed to an apparent inconsistency in this section: using the word *hominoids* (which suggests a belief in Darwinian evolution) in the same section that I quote from the Book of Genesis (which suggests a belief in "creationism"). I am in sympathy with the man who owned a factory that made meat grinders. He had heard endless debate in his church as to whether the creation should be taught to the children as a mythic representation of evolution guided by the Deity or whether to remain strictly tied to the words of the Bible. Late in the debate, he requested the floor to express his opinion. "As most of you know," he said, "I own a small factory that makes meat grinders. There are sixteen parts to these meat grinders, and they have to be assembled in exactly the correct order. Otherwise the meat grinder won't work at all. I can train a worker to do this correctly in an hour or so. Now I have heard this argument that the universe tumbled along for millions of years while mankind slowly evolved from the slime. Well, maybe those folks are right. I only know that you could put those sixteen parts for my meat grinders in a

bushel basket and shake the damned thing for a *trillion years*, and you'd never come out with a meat grinder that worked!''

2. Maria Sandoz, *These Were the Sioux* (New York: Dell, 1961), pp. 79–80.

3. See Ong's *The Presence of the Word* (New Haven, CT: Yale University Press, 1967), *Interfaces of the Word* (Ithaca, NY: Cornell University Press, 1977), and *Orality and Literacy: The Technologizing of the Word* (London: Methuen, 1982).

4. Sandoz, *op. cit.*, pp. 82–83.

5. Ong, *The Presence of the Word*, p. ix.

6. It is interesting that the use of the directions "down" and "up" to describe writing and reading is common to many languages.

7. Peggy Watt, "Use a Modem — Go to Jail," *Profiles*, February 1985, p. 28.

8. Promotional packet, WAUR radio, Aurora, IL, 1986.

9. James Carey, "The Telegraph and Its Effects," lecture delivered at Northern Illinois University, Spring, 1982.

10. David Burmeister, "The Language of Deceit," in *Language and Public Policy*, ed. Hugh Rank (Urbana, IL: National Council of Teachers of English, 1974), p. 40.

11. For an especially insightful discussion of the return to the experiential mode of persuasion, see W. Lance Haynes, "Of That Which We Cannot Write: Some Notes on the Phenomenology of Media," *The Quarterly Journal of Speech*:71–101, 1988.

12. In Huxley's novel of the future, movies and television are replaced by "Feelies," or booths where one could go to "experience" the movie by being "wired" to a set of sensors that would permit the viewer to feel every physical and psychological pleasure and/or pain the characters on the screen were portraying. You could "experience" being shot, eating the gourmet meal, drinking the fine wine, sailing the sloop, racing the motorcycle, skydiving on a perfect day, have orgasm with the star or starlet (depending on your preference), and so on.

13. Stewart Brand, *The Media Lab: Inventing the Future at M.I.T.* (New York: Viking Penguin, 1987).

14. Gregory Solomon, "Through the Looking Glass," *American Film*, September 1990, p. 50.

15. Brand, book jacket, inside cover.

16. *Ibid.*, pp. 77–78.

17. Tony Schwartz, *The Responsive Chord* (Garden City, NY: Anchor Press/Doubleday, 1973). See also Tony Schwartz, *Media: The Second God* (New York: Random House, 1981).

18. *Ibid.*

19. A more complete discussion of how to criticize these elements is found in Charles U. Larson, "Media Metaphors: Two Perspectives for the Rhetorical Criticism of TV Commercials," *Central States Speech Journal* 33:533–546, 1982.

20. Victoria Benes Victory, Director of Marketing, Quik Wok, Inc., "Pocket Veto," *Advertising Age*, April 25, 1988, p. 20.

21. For a full discussion of these ideas, see Marshall McLuhan, *Understanding Media: The Extensions of Man* (New York: Signet Books, 1964).

22. Joshua Meyrowitz, *No Sense of Place: The Impact of Electronic Media on Social Behavior* (New York: Oxford University Press, 1985).

23. *Ibid.*, p. 308.

24. *Ibid.*, pp. 28–33, 46–51.

25. *Ibid.*, p. 89.

26. *Ibid.*, p. 90.

27. *Ibid.*, p. 83.

28. *Ibid.*, p. 75.

29. *Ibid.*, p. 106.

30. *Ibid.*, p. 119.

31. *Ibid.*, p. 121.

32. *Ibid.*, p. 227.

33. "This Is Marshall McLuhan: The Medium Is the Message," CRM/McGraw-Hill Films, 1967.

34. Meyrowitz, *op.cit.*, pp. 307–329.

35. *Ibid.*, p. 329.

36. Maxwell McCombs and Donald Shaw, "The Agenda Setting Function of Mass Media," *Public Opinion Quarterly* 36:176–187, 1972.

37. Bob Greene, "Less Violence Would Be a Big Hit on TV," *Chicago Tribune*, January 15, 1985, sec. 2, p. 1.

38. *Ibid.*

39. Based on research on the effects of heavy doses of television violence, George Gerbner, dean of the school of communications at the University of Pennsylvania, concludes that those who watch the

most television are more likely to buy guns, watch-dogs, and new locks for their homes. "There are six to eight acts of violence per hour in prime time and two 'entertaining murders' per night. . . . Weekend children's programming includes an incredible 25 acts of violence per hour." "T. V. Message Hitting Home," *Chicago Tribune*, February 2, 1987, sec. 5, p. 20.

40. Meyrowitz, *op. cit.*, p. 73.

41. *Ibid*. See also Erik Barnouw, *The Sponsor: Notes on a Modern Potentate* (New York: Oxford University Press, 1978); Todd Gitlin, *Inside Prime Time* (New York: Pantheon, 1983); Herbert Gans, *Deciding What's News* (New York: Pantheon, 1983); and Edward Jay Epstein, *News from Nowhere* (New York: Vintage Books, 1974).

42. Kathleen Jamieson and Karlyn Kohrs Campbell, *The Interplay of Influence* (Belmont, CA: Wadsworth, 1983), p. 96.

43. Meyrowitz, *op. cit.*, p. 90.

44. Richard Ramhoff, "Bart's Not as Bad as He Seems: 'Simpson's as Positive as other Family Sitcoms' Researcher Says." *Rockford Register Star*, October 18, 1990, sec. C, p. 1.

45. Robert Cirino, *Don't Blame the People* (Los Angeles: Diversity Press, 1971).

46. Ron Powers, *The News-Casters: The News Business as Show Business* (New York: St. Martin's Press, 1978), p. 1.

47. Barbara Matusow, *The Evening Stars: The Making of a Network News Anchor* (New York: Ballantine Books, 1983), p. 40.

48. *Ibid.*, p. 1.

49. *Ibid.*, p. 304.

50. Cirino, *op. cit.*, p. 284.

51. Cirino, *op. cit.*, p. 147.

52. Schwartz, *The Responsive Chord*, p. 6.

The Techniques of Propaganda

For a number of years, the idea of studying propaganda in a communications class seemed somewhat archaic. Aside from in wartime, which was often typified by heavy-handed propagandistic techniques, the study of propaganda seemed like wasted effort. There were a few who cheered the addition of this propaganda chapter a decade ago, but many thought it a waste of time to cover such a seemingly antiquated topic in contemporary times. At about that same time, however, a new focus in propaganda emerged, and the communication discipline began to investigate ideological communication in its various forms.

Since that time, we have had dramatic witness to the powers of modern propaganda, which brought about the fall of the Shah of Iran and of Ferdinand Marcos of the Philippines. In our own country, the Reagan administration used propaganda to dismantle long-standing liberal programs in social welfare. Propaganda was also used to justify the invasion of Grenada — a miniscule Caribbean Island — to "protect American interests in the area." Throughout the 1980s, Mikhail Gorbachev used propaganda to promote a new ideology — perestroika — reversing the 75-year-old ideology of Leninist/Marxist communism. At the same time, American propaganda was used to paint the USSR as an "Evil Empire." Modern propaganda was used to legitimize the invasions of El Salvador and Panama by U.S.-supported rebels and even American troops. In 1989, propaganda forced the South African government to free Nelson Mandela, a leader of the African National Congress (ANC), and begin to reverse the long-standing practice of apartheid, the policy of institutionalized segregation and discrimination. In 1989, propaganda was central in toppling the socialist states of Eastern Europe, setting them on the path to free-market systems, which will, in turn, propagate their own economic ideologies. More recently, sophisticated and massive propaganda warfare on both sides was used to justify as well as condemn the Iraqi invasion of Kuwait. Propaganda united the United Nations Security Council to pass numerous condemnations of the invasion and, more important, a blockade of Iraq supported by both the United States and the Soviet Union — something unthinkable in 1983. In related action, skillful propaganda was used to legitimize the deployment of hundreds of thousands of American military personnel to Saudi Arabia to oppose and finally to reverse the Iraqi invasion.

As you can see, far from being a rickety and antiquated concept, propaganda is alive, well, and quite active in this last decade of the twentieth century. As receivers, we need to recognize propaganda when we encounter it and respond accordingly. This chapter outlines the dimensions of modern propaganda and offers some tools for recognizing and responding to it.

WHAT PROPAGANDA ISN'T

What do you think of when you hear the word propaganda? How would you differentiate it from the word persuasion? How does it differ from the word coercion? How about the words education or culture or advertising? Some people would say that they are all one and the same — that virtually everything involving communication is in some way propagandistic. The problem with defining propaganda as "everything" is that it gets you nowhere. It doesn't allow you to say the words "I love you" or "I'm sorry" or "I think I understand, but please go over it once more for me" without spreading propaganda, which has a negative connotation in most people's minds.

The word propaganda comes from the Latin propagare, which means "to spread or grow" much as the word propagate (which comes from the same Latin root) indicates growth or spread. It was originally instituted formally by Pope Gregory XV in the Congregatio de Propaganda Fide in the seventeenth century to define and organize the church's missionary efforts to spread the faith and Christianize the world. It was a noble cause to be a true and successful propagandist in 1623.

Webster's Ninth New Collegiate Dictionary defines propaganda as "ideas, facts, or allegations spread deliberately to further one's cause or to damage an opposing cause."[1] Three key words in this definition help us to distinguish propaganda from other kinds of communication. The most important is the word *cause*, which implies some sort of dogma or ideology that one is trying to propagate, whether religious dogma, political dogma, economic dogma, vegetarian dogma, antivivisectionist dogma, pro-life dogma, pro-choice dogma, or a host of other "causes" that people hope to promote. This helps us rule out many kinds of communication that aren't dogmatic or related to a cause. The second most important word in the definition is *deliberately*, because it helps us rule out a great many kinds of communication in which we don't intend to spread any cause and in which we are simply trying to discover information or to express our feelings. The third most important word in the definition is *spread*, which carries with it the idea of affecting many persons with communication about the cause. This helps us distinguish propaganda from instances in which we are trying to affect only a few other persons — our family, our dorm floor, our fraternity or sorority — or when we are trying to affect only one other person — our neighbor, our friend, our parent, our spouse, or our child. So, for a start, the *deliberate spreading of a cause* is a good way to think of propaganda.

Now what about all those negative connotations that pop up when the word *propaganda* is mentioned? Where did all that negativity come from? Well, some of it comes from the overzealousness of certain religious propagandists who come knocking on our doors or who grab us by the arm and ask us whether we have been reborn. Some of it comes from deep-seated prejudices about race, gender, social class, or ethnicity. But most of the negativity associated with the word *propaganda* stems from wartime propaganda used by "us" and "them" in this century. And much of the paranoia about propaganda comes about because of the tremendous communication power made possible by current and future technologies. As Garth Jowatt and Victoria O'Donnell note in their book *Propaganda and Persuasion*:

> The late nineteenth and early twentieth centuries were periods of great expansion of propaganda activities. The growth of the mass media and improvements in transportation led to the development of mass audiences. . . . Each of the mass media — print, movies, radio and then television — contributed its unique qualities to new techniques of propaganda. Radio, in particular, brought into existence the possibility of continuous international propaganda, whereas television has increased the problem of "cultural imperialism," where one nation's culture is imposed upon another nation.[2]

Let's look at what some people who have studied modern propaganda say and then try to formulate a working definition that can distinguish propaganda from other kinds of persuasion.

Views of Modern Propaganda

Modern propaganda began with the development of the modern media of communication (see Chapter 12 for more on this point). With the advent of the loudspeaker, radio, film, and later television, persuaders and demagogues learned to turn these media to their advantage. In America, people such as Huey Long, Father Coughlin, and Franklin Roosevelt used these new media to gain the support of millions. Elsewhere, Francisco Franco in Spain, Adolf Hitler in Germany, and Joseph Stalin in the Soviet Union were among those who used the new technology to great advantage. Scholars and social critics soon became concerned about the influence of propaganda coupled with electronic media.

Early investigators tried to define propaganda. For example, L. W. Doob, a world-famous sociologist in the middle of this century, said that the use of **suggestion** is the key. If suggestion is used "then this process may be called propaganda, regardless of whether or not the propagandist intends to exercise control." On the other hand, Doob said that if the same result would have occurred with or without the use of suggestion "then this process may be called education regardless of the intention of the educator."[3] Perhaps what you are doing in your persuasion class right now is propaganda.

J. Driencourt, a French student of political science, defined propaganda this way: "Propaganda is everything."[4] Of course, that isn't very helpful in distinguishing propaganda from other communication forms. To Joseph Goebbels, the Nazi Minister of Propaganda, it had to be covert: "Propaganda becomes ineffective the moment we are aware of it."[5]

J. A. C. Brown, a British scholar interested in propaganda, emphasized several critical points as he developed a definition. First, he said propaganda is a "scheme for propagating a doctrine or practice for influencing the emotional attitudes."[6] So, not all communication is propaganda — it must propose a doctrine, a dogma, or an ideology aimed at people's emotional state, not their rational state. Under this definition, most advertising is not propagandistic *unless* it promotes an ideology. (Some would argue that advertising does promote an ideology: conspicuous consumption.) Under Brown's definition, most religious communication would be considered propagandistic because it espouses a dogma and makes use of emotional, not logical, appeals. Under this definition, most governmental communication would be considered propaganda, since it promotes the ideologies of democracy and capitalism.

J. A. C. Brown adds another stipulation to distinguish propaganda from argumentation. He says that in propaganda, the "answers are determined in advance."[7] All propaganda attempts to change people's minds, but not all mind changing is propaganda; if there is an honest interchange of argument, or group discussions without hidden agendas, that is not propaganda. A court trial is not propaganda either — it espouses no dogma, and the final outcome isn't predetermined. Legislative debate over policy issues may use some of the techniques of propaganda, but as a whole, it is not propaganda, for the outcome isn't known in advance.

Propaganda is always *against* something at the same time that it is *for* something else — it isn't propaganda if there are no alternatives.[8] There can be propaganda by censorship also. Brown points out that it wouldn't have been propaganda to teach that the Earth is the center of the solar system in pre-Copernican times, but it would have been propaganda to suppress, censor, or conceal the ideas of Copernicus or Galileo, as was done until

1822.[9] Propaganda nearly always conceals something: the purpose of the propagandist, the means used to achieve the purpose, and so on. The distinction between education and propaganda is this: "The former tells people *how* to think; the latter tells them *what* to think."[10] However, according to the *Soviet Political Dictionary* of the 1960s, propaganda and education are equivalent: Propaganda is "the intensive elucidation of the writings of Marx, Engels, Lenin and Stalin and of the history of the Bolshevik Party and its tasks."[11] Doesn't that sound like education? Brown points out how this blurring could be carried out even in such "bias-free" subjects as mathematics. He reported the research of one social scientist who found that in a widely used American math textbook there were over 600 problems that focused on such "capitalistic" concepts as rent, interest, and investments.[12] Yet you and I would be unlikely to think that the math book was propagandistic. Finally, propaganda has to be "part of a deliberate scheme for indoctrination."[13]

Other people (including Ellul, whose theory we will examine later) maintain that nearly everything in a technocracy is propaganda: It is the combined rules, ordinances, administrative directives, patterns of living and learning, and social graces of the modern political state. It also is an automatic extension of a technological society, and may be covert (as in Goebbel's view) or overt.[14] In other words, much of the contemporary technocratic culture is propaganda.

A Definition

To distinguish propaganda from other kinds of persuasion, we need a definition that will allow us to identify the critical differences between, for example, propaganda and debate or propaganda and advertising. If we defined everything as propaganda, it would be both easy and impossible to identify it.

For our purposes, propaganda is first and foremost **ideological**. It tries to sell a *belief system* or *dogma.* Propaganda can be religious, political, or economic. Second, propaganda **uses some form of mass communication** to sell ideology. Speeches; documentary programs on films, TV, and radio broadcasts; posters; billboards; mass mailings; and so on all could be used in the propaganda process. Postage stamps, coins, paper currency, music, art, and drama have all been used for propaganda. Third, one or some combination of the following must be **concealed from the target audience**:[15]

1. The **source** of the communication
2. The source's **goal**
3. The **other side** of the story — various perspectives
4. The **techniques** being used by the source in sending the message
5. The **results** of the propaganda if successful

Finally, propaganda **aims at uniformity** in the *beliefs, attitudes,* and *behaviors* of its receivers.

Using this definition, we can see that not all advertisements are propaganda: They usually are not ideological and we usually know the source and the goal. However, some advertisements *are* propaganda. In an obvious case, an ad for an "Awareness Weekend" sponsored by an organization having the acronym CARP (which is actually the Unification Church of Reverend Moon) was clearly propaganda: It espoused a dogma, it used some form of mass communication, and information such as the source, the other side of the story, the techniques to be used (for example, sleep deprivation), and the probable results (being "converted") were all concealed. Finally, it certainly aimed at uniformity of behavior.

Triumph of the Will, a classic German propaganda film, clearly tried to sell an ideology in its depiction of the 1936 Nazi party rallies. It used visual techniques to give the impression of vastness. Powerful symbols such as flags, flames, the swastika, and legions of brown shirts were shown, and, throughout it all, the figure of Hitler dominated the film from his dramatic arrival through the clouds on a silvery plane to his fiery speeches. As he watched the thousands of party faithful, he stood above it all as the ultimate leader, *Der Führer*. These techniques persuaded the naive audiences who saw the film. It revealed neither the other side of the story nor the results if the audience followed the advice of the film and became

party members. An equally political film, *All the President's Men*, which tells the story of the unraveling of the Watergate scandal as seen through the eyes of the two reporters who first uncovered the story, probably is not propaganda. The only dogma it even implies is the value of a free press and the power of investigative reporting when done diligently. It doesn't advise the audience to take any actions or to join any party or believe any ideology. We know in advance the source and goal (and probably the outcome) of the film. The warning on cigarette packs isn't propaganda either, because it isn't ideological, whereas the hand-painted billboard reading "The Day of Judgment is at Hand! Prepare to Meet Thy God!" does express an ideology and probably is propaganda.

Thus, not all communication we get via the mass media is propaganda, using our definition. You can identify messages that clearly are propaganda or that border on being propaganda. Being able to identify propaganda, as Goebbels noted, reduces its effectiveness and perhaps even makes it harmless. Knowing *what* propaganda is, is only a part of the story; we also need to know *how* the propagandist works. What tactics are used and how can we identify them?

THE TACTICS OF PROPAGANDA

From the early concern over propaganda and its power to move entire nations in World Wars I and II up to the present, people have made numerous attempts to identify the tactics propagandists use. The Institute for Propaganda Analysis identified certain devices, and many teachers taught these devices.[16] In fact, some of you may be familiar with them. They are a good place to begin the study of the tactics of propaganda.

Plain Folks

The "**plain folks**" tactic is used by propagandists to convince the audience that the public figures or groups they represent are not well trained, shrewd, and manipulative but are just "plain folks" like you and me. Politicians are using this device when they put on bib overalls and clodhopper boots and wipe their brow with a red bandanna while talking with a back-country drawl. Sometimes the technique is as simple as using common language to appeal to the audience. It might employ plain, everyday actions such as washing one's own car, splitting wood, or sewing one's own clothes. The device uses pretense to create identification between source and receiver. Such sources are not plain folks at all. Instead, they are trying to manipulate the audience into following their call through a false feeling of kinship.

Testimonial

The **testimonial** is a familiar device in today's world; we see it used daily in both print and electronic media. A well-known and supposedly expert source gives testimony about the usefulness of a certain product, the honesty of a certain person, or the wisdom of a certain course of action. Sally Struthers tells us how good it felt for her to adopt a child through Save the Children Federation. A person who was held hostage by a terrorist group holds a press conference and tells how well he or she was treated by the terrorists and presents the group's aims.

In all of these examples, the audience cannot tell whether the people giving the testimony are actually reliable sources of information. Perhaps they have been hired to give the testimony because of their celebrity status. Or they might be dupes of some government. Furthermore, we do not know for certain what the goal of the source is. Is Sally Struthers actually interested in the adopt-a-child program? Is the program a front for some religious group? Did the hostage become converted to the terrorists' ideology? (This sometimes happens.) Has the hostage been duped by the group? Also, what will be the outcome if we follow the advice of the testimonials? These are but a few of the concealed elements in these testimonials. Of course, there are also many testimonials that do not promote any particular ideology or dogma: Martina Navratilova says she uses a certain racquet, or a famous athlete claims he uses a particular brand of aftershave lotion. Neither of these

qualifies as propaganda using our definition, although both are probably effective advertising.

Bandwagon

Propagandists, like some advertisers, try to convince the audience that it is *almost* too late to take advantage of the offer, to join the organization, to follow the fad, to vote for the candidate, to be contemporary — to get on the **bandwagon**. The history of the word *bandwagon* gives us a clue to the basic intent behind the appeal. When the circus came to town in the nineteenth century, part of the razzmatazz used to attract customers was the circus parade along the village main street. The parade gave the population glimpses of what they could expect if they bought tickets to the show. The first wagon in the parade was always the bandwagon. The circus musicians would toot and hoot loudly to get attention and draw a crowd. Reference to the bandwagon became synonymous with being a leader — a person who was "out in front" of an idea or a fashion. Suppose you receive a pitch such as "Only three more days left to support our cause. Sign the petition now! Help us stop the utility rate increases! Commonwealth Edison is a monopoly! Send a message to the legislature! The people's rights before the rights of capitalistic corporations!" Those phrases are tip-offs. The time limit and the stress on joining "the people" suggest that everyone is getting on the "bandwagon" — don't miss out.

Card Stacking

Building an overwhelming case on one side of an issue while concealing another, perhaps equally persuasive, side is called **card stacking**. Of course, few persuaders try to *tell both* sides of a story, but responsible persuaders at least suggest that there *are* other sides. In fact, we frequently see advertisers, for example, comparing their products with the competition in taste tests, mileage comparisons, tar/nicotine statistics, stopping power for tires, or starting power for batteries. In card stacking, this is not done. Instead, the other side may not even be recognized, or it may be downplayed or possibly denigrated. Thus the audience gets only one version of the story.

Transfer

The propaganda technique called **transfer** is similar to Rank's "association" tactic for intensification. For example, a politician is placed in front of the U.S. Capitol Building, and the aura of the U.S. government and historic Washington, D.C., is transferred to the candidate. The transfer implies that the candidate is a patriot who will follow in the footsteps of the great leaders of the past. Transfer also resembles an endorsement or a testimonial in that the credibility of the endorser transfers to the product. In international politics, to Hitler we compared Saddam Hussein: Hitler's negative aspects transferred to the dictator. In Illinois, calling a politician a "machine democrat" links him or her with Chicago and transfers the negativity of the Chicago machine to the candidate. On the other hand, calling the candidate a "downstate" politician dissociates him or her from the Chicago machine and transfers the positive aspects of small-town Illinois to the candidate. To destroy credibility, the opposition is linked to an undesirable action, person, or organization. The candidate is linked to big business, lobbyists, the CIA, or organized crime, and any negative loading for these groups transfers to the candidate and ruins his or her credibility.

Glittering Generalities

Abstract language, highly charged with emotion and cultural values, is used by propagandists because of its power. Such words seem to "glitter" with high purpose and energy that can short-circuit people's reasoning process and make them jump to conclusions. Words such as *justice, freedom, dignity, equality, patriot, integrity,* and *wisdom* are actually not very specific, yet they pluck at powerful emotions in audiences. Who hasn't heard some political speaker introducing a candidate who is "*dedicated* to the continuance of *justice* for all in this great nation of ours; who has worked *diligently* for our *freedom* and *dignity*,

fighting for *equality*. My friends, I give you a *patriot* of great *integrity* and *wisdom* — Senator Fogbound!" Later, of course, the voters may discover that Fogbound drinks too much, slips off to the strip joints on D Street, and has been videotaped taking bribes.

The **glittering generalities** of the advertising world are only slightly less emotional and vague. Some examples are *heavy duty, youthful, vitality, jumbo, old-fashioned, homemade,* and *glamorous*. No one has ever heard of a *light-duty* battery or a *medium-duty* vacuum cleaner, just as no one has ever heard of a *small* or *medium* shrimp — they come in only three sizes: *colossal, mammoth,* and *jumbo*. Leaf through any popular magazine and you will find hundreds of glittering generalities like these. Of course, in these cases the glittering generalities aren't being used to market an ideology or dogma, so, under our definition, they don't qualify as propaganda.

Name Calling

The other side of glittering generalities is **name calling**: using words that have high negative loadings to smear another person or group. For example, we might call a certain religious group "a bunch of zealous, fanatical Jesus freaks" to make the group seem on the fringe and unpredictable or wild-eyed. During World War II, Germans were called *huns, krauts,* or *heinies* and Japanese were called *Japs* or *nips*; during the Korean and Vietnamese wars, the enemy were called *gooks, slants, slopes,* or *Charlies*. Why? These names reduced the enemy to the level of brutes with low intelligence and apelike behavior.

Contemporary Devices of Analysis

With the advances of research done on the formation and alteration of attitudes, theorists took a new look at propaganda during the 1960s and 1970s. J. A. C. Brown, whom we met earlier in this chapter, took a look at propaganda from this more modern perspective. He identified several prerequisites for propaganda and the stages through which propaganda passes. Brown, somewhat surprisingly, held that, to be truly effective, propaganda had to tell the truth. However, this "truth" is interpreted to the propagandist's advantage, and he or she usually doesn't tell the whole truth but selects which elements of "truth" to publicize and which to conceal. Brown quotes an official of the British Broadcasting Corporation (BBC) commenting on British propaganda in the war:

> Do not say anything which you do not believe to correspond with the facts as known to you; and secondly do not say anything to one country, or audience, which is or looks inconsistent with what you are saying to any other country or audience.[17]

This makes perfect sense in terms of our old friend credibility. If you use lies and are caught, you destroy your credibility. However, if you interpret the truth to your own advantage, only your interpretation can be questioned. We know that during World War II many persons in occupied Europe and even Germany itself listened to the BBC because it was the most credible source of news. There was a Nazi news service, but it had been caught lying too many times, and the public distrusted it.

Brown also described the stages through which propaganda passes. In the **prepropaganda stage**, propagandists want to make their messages stand out among all of the other competing messages. The propagandist may spend time distributing leaflets, knocking on doors, or displaying posters. The purpose of this stage is to catch the audience's *attention* by appealing to the powerful emotions already in the audience: hatred, jealousy, envy, love, fear, hope, guilt, and so on. Frequently, this is done by creating *guilt* feelings in the audience. Hitler repeatedly told his audiences that it was Germans who had *betrayed* Germany at the end of World War I. Guilt is most powerfully called up in the audience using *suggestion*. For example, if the audience feels respect for authority, the propagandist can suggest that failure to support the authorities will make them feel guilty. On the other hand, if they resent authority, the propagandist can suggest that they are guilty if they fail to speak out

against authority. Note that it is the *interpretation* of the situation that is altered, not the *facts*.[18]

After drawing the audience's attention and interest, the propagandist creates *emotional tension*. Perhaps the audience is told that it has been kept from some opportunity or that its legal rights have been trampled or that its heritage has been stained. The powerful emotional tension that is developed is *identified* with some enemy — usually an **outgroup** such as the Jews in Nazi Germany, "camel jockeys" in Iraq, the Redcoats in colonial times, or "niggers" or "honkies" in America. This outgroup is identified in a number of ways:[19]

1. *Stereotyping*. Using powerful descriptive language, the outgroup is characterized with negative attributes and qualities. Thus, in propaganda the Jew is conniving, exploitative, clannish, and cheap. The black is lazy, dull, and interested only in mating. The Irish are drunkards, are dumb, and have criminal instincts. Of course there are, no doubt, some Jews, blacks, and Irish who have some of those characteristics and even some who have all of them, but the propagandist asserts that *all* Jews, blacks, or Irish have *all* these qualities.

2. *Substitution of names*. Again using powerful language, the propagandist substitutes unfavorable names for neutral ones. For example, the Jew becomes a *kike*, a *sheeny*, or a *hymie*; the black becomes a *nigger*, a *spook*, or a *coon*; and the Irish become *micks, lace-curtain Irish*, or *shanty Irish*. Words such as *rednecks, capitalist pig, dirty Communist*, or *diaper heads* also can be used.

3. *Repetition*. Propaganda tells the same tale over and over again using similar language, examples, and references. Goebbels thought that the masses would believe anything if you told the "big lie" enough times. We see this approach used frequently in slogans and jingles.

4. *Pinpointing the enemy*. Here, specific members of the outgroup are selected as representing the worst aspects of the stereotype: Jewish

bankers or pawnshop owners; black rapists, pimps, or whores; Irish drunks, cops, or mobsters. These are especially powerful if they fit with the preexisting patterns in the audience's experience, thus explaining why using the Jew as an enemy scapegoat worked so well in Europe, where there existed a long pattern of anti-Semitism, and why blacks are so frequently used as scapegoats here in America.

With the emotional tension built up and identified with an outgroup that has been properly denigrated and dehumanized, the propagandist can then impel the audience to action by giving them a way to relieve their tension. This almost always involves the real or symbolic destruction of the outgroup. Real destruction can involve torture, killing, and even genocide. In symbolic destruction, the outgroup is stigmatized in some way. The outgroup is segregated physically (having to step down into the gutter instead of walking on the sidewalk, or going to the back of the bus). They must wear some sign of negative caste (a yellow Star of David, a sign labeling them a traitor, or some other negative tattoo). Their businesses may be boycotted, and their homes, places of worship, and even their bodies may be violated in some way. The tension thus is relieved through the real or symbolic destruction.

Brown explains this process in terms of Freud's ego-defense mechanisms. The symbolic killing may involve *projection*, characterizing the outgroup as having one's own weaknesses or sins. (Hitler's bullies often beat and killed homosexuals as perverted examples of society; many people suspect that the bullies themselves were secret homosexuals.) The outgroup may be the victim of *compensation*, making up for a frustrated drive by finding a substitute goal (for example, if you fail in business, you become a successful villain, and thus villainy compensates for failure). *Conformity* and *identification* permit large numbers of persons to follow a charismatic leader because they believe he or she is their voice and is like them. This sanctions whatever the leader decides to do and permits the "big lie" to succeed (for example, Hit-

ler, Stalin, and Hussein purged their own closest colleagues in the name of the movement).[20]

Finally, propaganda is most likely to emerge in the *modern state*, in which the individual is isolated (as you may now feel if you are on a large campus), unknown, and helpless to control his or her own destiny.[21] The supporters of many propagandistic mass movements are the uneducated or the unemployed—those who are helpless to get a good job or decent housing and hence find the movement attractive because it promises change. Feelings of loneliness are removed by becoming a member of a group. The group offers individuals substitute identification and value. Furthermore, a group, and especially a crowd, is likely to behave more emotionally than any single individual. *Mob psychology* can take over, and violent acts (lynchings, gang rapes, stonings, riots, and so on) are committed in the hysteria. Further, the guilt is shared by the group, and no one individual need feel remorse.[22] As Brown says, "Each society has its own kind of circus and hopes that after the performance is ended, the participants will return less reluctantly to their dull round of daily life."[23] Propaganda hawks the tickets to the circus.

JACQUES ELLUL'S PERSPECTIVE

A common feeling in the final decades of the twentieth century seems to be that everything is out of control—the machine is about to go smash. We are all familiar with the incredible mountains of information—more than we can handle—available to us on a variety of fronts. We know only too well the insignificance of our individual efforts to reduce the deficit, enforce a nuclear freeze, help the poor, or *really* make a difference. We all realize that change is occurring so fast that it is impossible to keep up. It is like a dream I have. My shoes are made of lead, and they stick to the ground. I can't catch the departing train, no matter how hard I try to run. These feelings are apparently common for persons living in highly sophisticated technological societies. Jacques Ellul, a French sociopolitician and theologian, has discussed these feelings and their causes using a concept he calls

la technique. La technique includes all the rules, ordinances, patterns of behavior, forms to be filled out, directions, values, administrative orders, and so on, that characterize any modern bureaucracy. Then add all the technology that is necessary for efficiently carrying out the orders. In other words, la technique is the modern political **technocracy**. As Ellul says:

> The first great fact which emerges from our civilization is that today everything has become means. There is no longer an end; we do not know whither we are going. We have forgotten our collective ends and we possess great means: we set huge machines in motion in order to arrive nowhere.[24]

La technique has at least three aspects: First there are **economic techniques** (investment, capital, profit, loss, inflation, deflation, taxes, welfare, and budgeting, to name a few). Then there are **political techniques** (laws, electoral processes, the courts, organizations, government, administrators, and so on). Finally, there are **human techniques** (advertising, public opinion polling, attitude testing, evangelism, time study, and demographics are a few examples). Each of these aspects of la technique is interrelated and is essential to the others, and each is typical of the modern technocracy in which we live.

How different this view of propaganda is when compared with earlier views — even ones as contemporary and well conceived as J. A. C. Brown's. Here, propaganda is frightening not because of its use of deceptive gimmicks or the immense power of modern media but because it is so immense and at the same time so apparently benign. It is not something *they* do; it is rather something *we* do. Each of us experience it every day from childhood on, and we probably approve of it. This makes it all the more difficult for us to identify, evaluate, and accept or reject. Furthermore, the technology binge we are on seems endless — no one can turn it off. One of Ellul's critics said that facing la technique is like saying, "The kitchen has burned, and the intellectuals keep writing cookbooks; the boats have sunk, and the people on the life rafts still worry about time schedules."[25]

Propaganda and Technology

Ellul's description of propaganda comes closer to what Jowett and O'Donnell describe as "The New Audience" influenced by "The Emergence of Mass Society," which seems to devour and believe everything "The New Media" tells them is true.[26] They trace this depersonalizing process beginning with the penny press of the 1830s. During the Civil War, media were used by the North and the South to propagandize against one another. Following the war, the print medium was repeatedly used for propaganda — the sinking of the battleship *Maine* and the resulting Spanish American War is a good example.[27]

Particularly interesting are the ways in which the technology of film was used for propaganda purposes from its earliest years.[28] A few of the titles of propaganda films during these early years give one a feel for how they might have appeared. *Tearing Down the Spanish Flag*, produced during the Spanish-American War, was nothing more than a flagpole flying the Spanish flag, whereupon it was torn down and the American flag was raised in its stead, which had "sensational" effects on the audiences.[29] During World War I, films such as *The Kaiser, The Beast of Berlin*, and *Battle Cry of Peace* (1915) showed Germans attacking and demolishing New York City. Of course, the most famous propaganda film of the early years was the Russian-produced *Potemkin* (1925), which justified the Russian Revolution to the Russian people, most of whom couldn't read but all of whom could look at a movie screen and see the brutality of the Czar and his troops.

In the years between the world wars, Hollywood dominated the movie screens around the world — a precursor of the "cultural imperialism" noted previously. My father's decision to come to America in 1929 was probably partially influenced by his vision of America and its tremendous economic opportunities as seen on movie screens. The Depression was the stick and the filmic images of the 1920s were the carrot. Also, the new wave of immigration that began at the turn of the century and continued until the Great Depression provided an eager audience for whatever American filmmakers could produce. Immigrants were illiterate but could still watch the screen. This example recalls Meyrowitz's observations about literacy and television: Media with simple access codes can be powerful in influencing people who have minimal or no literacy.

With the rise of nazism in Germany, the Soviet film industry turned out large numbers of anti-Fascist propaganda films. Not until 1939 did Hollywood produce its first anti-Fascist propaganda film, *Confessions of a Nazi Spy*, and until the United States entered the war in late 1941, the "propaganda" films were mainly recruiting devices, such as *Devil Dogs of the Air* and *Here Comes the Navy*. And even after getting into the war, less than a third of the films produced actually dealt with the war.[30] Jowett and O'Donnell note of this period that "American films were most successful when they stressed positive themes particularly as they depicted normal life on the homefront or the inner strength of the ordinary fighting men."[31]

Radio, developing side-by-side with film, was recognized early on as a potential propaganda medium. Lenin described it as a "newspaper without paper . . . and without boundaries" and directed its development to communicate Communist ideology to the illiterate peasants at home and in other countries. By 1922, Moscow had the most powerful radio station in the world, broadcasting its propaganda in a variety of languages.[32] The Fascist governments of Germany and Italy soon broadcast in a variety of languages aimed at North and South America, Africa, and Asia. Radio Tokyo began propaganda broadcasting in 1936.[33] During World War II, the BBC was the major broadcaster of Allied propaganda. Presently more than eighty nations broadcast some kind of radio propaganda (for example, the Voice of America, Radio Moscow, the BBC, Radio Peking, and All Asia Service out of Sri Lanka).[34] Radio as an economical and efficient propaganda technology has great impact in Third World countries, where it is not uncommon to see a peasant listening to a walkman while plowing the land with oxen.

Although television has not been frequently used for direct propaganda, its impact in the area

of "cultural imperialism" has been immense. Most Third World programming comes from the United States, Great Britain, and West Germany. Each year the United States alone sells 150,000 hours of programming to other countries, conveying American values, fashions, and capitalist ideology. The programming area that is most propagandistic is news reporting, which has raised the issue of the "free flow" of information between the First World and developing nations.[35] Here is where the Third World becomes distorted. We see pictures of famines, revolutions, fanatical dictators, and conflict, instead of stories about positive developments. We naturally come to believe that the negative situations are the entire "Third World story."

One of the most potentially exploitable communication technologies is the 8 mm videotape/camcorder. In many countries, American films are outlawed. However, copies can be smuggled in easily, dubbed onto multiple tapes, and thus begins a flourishing underground trade in these "forbidden" films. In the late 1980s, for example, an X-rated video called *Playboy Lovers* was brought into the Philippines. Most of the pornography had been erased and replaced by a documentary on the assassination of opposition leader Benigno Aquino. The tape was duplicated many times over and was seen by large numbers of people, thus helping to shape their attitudes toward the Marcos regime.[36] The X-rated video became an "envelope" for anti-Marcos propaganda, which eventually led to the revolution and expulsion of the dictator. A similar "enveloping" was used in Iran before the fall of the Shah: Tapes of speeches by the Ayatollah Khomeini were smuggled into Iran, duplicated many times over, and passed along from person to person involved in the movement to overthrow the Shah.

During the overthrow of many communist governments in Eastern Europe and in the "minirevolutions" that splintered the USSR, television stations were primary targets of the revolutionaries. Control of the means of communication was critical to seizing political power in these countries. Then, too, with the inexpensive costs of renting satellite space for transponder transmission, even a relatively small and not very well-funded group of terrorists, religious sects, and so on, can broadcast messages to their country that would be very difficult to jam.[37] As Jowatt and O'Donnell note, "Television's potential as a propaganda medium has yet to be fully realized in modern society."[38]

This brief history of examples of how technological developments lead to increased and more efficient propaganda underscores what Ellul is saying.

What can you and I do about a propaganda having the dimensions of la technique? More important, what can we *realistically* do? Ellul describes la technique as "an indispensible condition for the development of technical progress and the establishment of a technological civilization" and says it "has become an inescapable necessity for everyone."[39]

A brief example of the dilemma may help. One of the major myths put forward by la technique is that *progress* is good — it is desirable to improve our products, our processes, our bodies, our minds, our lot in life, and a host of other things — and progress is seen as improvement. You and I have no future without progress, for if there were no progress, there would be no jobs, no way to clean a polluted environment, no challenges, no possibility to discover cures for diseases, and no chance to improve our fortunes. That piece of propaganda is essential to you and me. Frankly, I can't live without it. I couldn't feed my family without it, and my children aren't prepared for a life without it. At the same time, I know I should do something about the myth of progress — accept it, reject it, or something. Most of us find ways to anesthetize our dependency (and la technique frequently supplies them): television, narcotics, family, alcohol, pleasure, the "me generation," careers, sex, and the cult of the self are all ways.

Ellul emphasizes, however, that just because la technique is necessary doesn't mean it is therefore good and to be fostered. Rather,

> necessity never establishes legitimacy; the world of necessity is a world of weakness, a world that denies man. To say that a phenomenon is *necessary* means, for me, that it denies man; its necessity is proof of its power, not proof of its excellence. However, confronted by a necessity, man must become *aware* of it if he is to master it. . . . Only when he realizes his delusion will he experience the beginning of genuine freedom — in the act of realization itself.[40]

Can we do this? Can we step back from our hectic culture and at least identify the many myths that keep us twitching? Ellul seems to think so; he says the probable alternative is a life in which

> man will be fully adapted to this technological society, when he will end by obeying with enthusiasm, convinced of the excellence of what he is forced to do, the constraint of the organization will no longer . . . be a constraint, and the police will have nothing to do.[41]

Let us look at the propaganda of la technique and seek to discover its characteristics, its tactics, and its methods in hopes of recognizing its permeation of modern society.

Basic Propaganda Devices

All propaganda, according to Ellul, relies to some degree on one of two basic psychological devices, the **conditioned reflex** (or the automatic, knee-jerk response) and the **myth**. "Let's put it to a vote!" might stimulate a conditioned response. Stereotypes such as that of the prissy English, or the impatient and emotional Italian, or the authority-driven German, or the inscrutable Oriental might also be used to evoke conditioned responses. By a "myth," Ellul means "an all-encompassing image: a sort of vision of desirable objectives . . . [which] pushes a man to action precisely because it includes all he feels is good, just, and true."[42] Examples he notes are the myth of race and the myth of productivity.

According to Ellul, both the conditioned reflex and the myth are part of a *prepropaganda phase* in which people are prepared for action by being conditioned into accepting the values of a culture. When the time comes for action, the leader or the "establishment" can prompt a reflex response by appealing to people's mythic beliefs. For example, our American culture treasures the myth of democracy, which says that the wisdom of the people, when operating in a democratic fashion, is the best and will prevail. This myth explains our overwhelmingly positive reactions to the student demonstrations in Tienanmen Square as well as to the collapse of Leninist-Marxism across East Europe during 1989 and thereafter. The assumption was (and perhaps still is) that democracy, coupled with a free marketplace, would reverse the economic and political slavery experienced by these countries since the end of World War II. Events seem to demonstrate that the answer isn't nearly that simplistic, yet our trust in the myth of democracy continues to lead us to recommend democracy as the "best" political system for other countries.

Another myth of la technique is that of *pragmatism*: what is most efficient is best. This myth is aimed at bringing people into conformity by facing them with the questions "Will it work?" "Is it practical?" "Is it efficient?" As long as we buy the legitimacy of the questions, we are conforming with the propaganda of la technique. What does such conformity imply? What can we do about efficiency-related issues when we disagree? An interesting example, which was the focus of several films during the mid-1980s, is the inefficiency of the family farm. In *Country*, a young family tried to make it on a family farm in the 1980s and found themselves facing the question of efficiency. In *Places in the Heart*, the theme was the same but the setting was the 1930s in dustbowl Texas. Both films emphasized the efficiency issue. If you were sold on efficiency, then you had to help the bureaucracy foreclose on the loans and dispose of the belongings by bidding at auctions, or you at least had to look the other way. However, in both films la technique was blunted by individual action and by rephrasing the questions implied by the myth of pragmatism.

In *Country*, for example, instead of asking of the family farm, "Will it work?" the heroine, Jewel Ivy, asks "Is it a healthy way to bring up children? Is it a humane way to relate to other people?" Her questions turn the myth of efficiency on its head and ultimately lead the local administrator of the Farm Home Administration to quit his job rather than pursue the myth of efficiency to

foreclose on the Ivy farm. La technique seems to work its will over the Ivys, nevertheless, when a bureaucrat from Washington supervises an auction of the Ivy belongings, machinery, and tools. However, a critical restatement of the questions Jewel has been asking throughout the story is made by her son as he bids all his savings on his grandfather's horse harnesses — the ultimate symbol of inefficiency in modern farming. This act spurs the rest of the crowd to recognize that it has been duped by the myth of efficiency. They refuse to cooperate in the auction and bid ridiculously low prices — seven cents for a combine, a dime for a tractor, and so on. The bureaucrat tries to reassert the myth by threatening to haul the belongings to another county to auction them. Jewel points out that "When you try to auction off this land and get no bids, you can't take *it* to another God-damned county!" La technique loses. As long as people responded with a conditioned reflex to what they had been taught about efficiency and pragmatism in the prepropaganda phase, la technique was the obvious victor. But once the questions had been rephrased to focus on *people* instead of *production*, la technique was relatively toothless. The technocracy of the federal government had to reverse its position and aid farm families in refinancing their debts.

The same questions could be asked about the many other myths we embrace: the myth of progress, the myth of pleasure, the myth of production, the myth of the individual, the myth of status, the myth of success, and others. Are they humane? Healthy? Rewarding? These are the kinds of questions Ellul wants us to ask once we have identified the propaganda of la technique, which, you will remember, is the first step in liberating oneself. How can we identify these myths and this propaganda?

Eight Characteristics of Modern Propaganda

Ellul's theories of propaganda were analyzed by Clifford Christians and Michael Real.[43] On the basis of their analysis, Ellul's work can be seen as revolving around eight central ideas that help identify the propaganda of la technique.

1. Propaganda is always associated with industrialized societies in which la technique (or the quest for ever more efficiency through technology) supersedes human social interaction. Thus a "communications expert" may simply be a salesperson for complex telephone set-ups and may know nothing about the human interaction that is the essence of communication.

2. Propaganda is not a set of tricks but is an ongoing, ever-present, interrelated system of methods, technologies, or "techniques" that pervade modern society and become increasingly dominant as the society becomes increasingly totalitarian (centrally controlled).

3. Propaganda inevitably occurs in societies in which people are depersonalized and unknowingly forced into *masses* while at the same time isolated as individuals. They derive their identity from the mass, which is united through propaganda. You may be an isolated individual on a large college campus, but you get identity from groups of varying sizes: From your college or university — "He's a Yale-ie." From your class and dormitory — "She's a Grant Tower sophomore." From your political affiliations — "He's president of the Young Republicans." From religious ties — "She's Jewish." And so forth. From Ellul's perspective, propaganda works because American society strives for individualism while technology and other forces create *mass* audiences, *mass* media, *mass* movements, and other masses in which individualism is submerged.

4. The purpose of modern propaganda is not to agitate the masses to action but to integrate them into society. This is done through peer pressure, social norms, and collective standards — usually expressed by a leader. For example, if you are a good American, you will urge Congress to cut the budget to stop inflation. Or, if you believe in free public education, you will approve this school referendum. Or, if you believe in the standards of fair play, you will think that American auto manufacturers cannot compete with foreign automakers and will endorse trade quotas.

5. Present-day international propaganda tends to come from "propaganda blocs" such as the United States, China, the Arabs, the Israelis, the USSR, and the Third World. Propaganda intended for internal consumption to calm, not agitate, the masses can come from governments, corporations, political parties, or religions.

6. Propaganda in a highly technological society is *totalitarian*. Everything is infused with some element of a propagandistic message designed to promote uniformity of *action* and *behavior* rather than uniformity of *belief* or *dogma*. For example, the words "In God We Trust" on our money tell us and others that we picture our nation as righteous and religious. The American bald eagle frequently seen on our money depicts our society as saying "hands off" while remaining ready to fight. The great heroes of our history are pictured on our money. Other propaganda sources are similar devices. Totalitarian propaganda also infuses our social interactions. We find flags in church, pledges of allegiance at the Lions Club, patriotic songs sung at school and church, and mealtime prayers in many homes. If you search further, you will find many traces of Ellul's totalitarian propaganda.

7. Among the effects of contemporary propaganda are isolation of the individual, stereotyping of public opinion, and simplistic answers to social questions. For example, American propaganda offers insecure people clear-cut solutions to complex problems (for example, "make the people on welfare go get a job"). It might also provide surrogate heroes or friends to the lonely or weak.

8. Once we consider the mass media, propaganda in Ellul's terms is everywhere. The entertainment shows on TV promote the values of our society. They teach our young how to grow up and how to behave as adults. News programs report the accomplishments of our society and identify its weaknesses and its

enemies — criminals, other countries, or our own shortcomings. Our art and music — even antipatriotic and nonpolitical art and music — identify our cultural values and beliefs. These things are expressed even when producers of the message do not intentionally engage in propaganda. In fact, this book, which asks you to be a conscientious receiver of persuasion, would be but another example of propaganda if seen through Ellul's eyes.

Other Ways to Detect Modern Propaganda

In a study of the lying done by members of the Nixon administration during Watergate, author Robert Rasberry used Ellul's work on la technique to analyze deceit.[44] He noted several characteristics of la technique and the external and internal characteristics of its propaganda. Knowing them may help you identify modern propaganda in action:

1. *Rationality.* La technique exists in the ultimate system — the contemporary technocracy — so it thrives on rational processes. Prime among them is the development of layers of self-proliferating administration or bureaucracy. Any time you find a lot of bureaucracy, la technique probably is present. Much of the propaganda generated by the layers is self-serving (it serves to justify itself). Long-winded goal statements and definitions of roles, duties, and procedures are other tip-offs.

2. *Artificiality.* La technique is not naturally occurring and is a human artifact, so it creates an artificial world. Thus, such phenomena as "image politics" are produced by la technique. The emphasis is on appearance, not on substance. This would apply to areas other than politics: education (a "prestige" school is thought to be better than a public one); advertising (how you appear, not what you are, is what counts); foreign policy ("we" must not appear to be weaker than "they"); religion (especially the kinds that play on image, hype, or

mass media); and others. Whenever things seem plastic, look for la technique at work.

3. *Automatism.* This is the tendency to reduce choice on the part of the citizen and to let technology make the decision. Ellul uses the heart transplant as an example, although now the artificial heart might make the point more strongly. Once the technology for it existed, it had to be tried whether it was a good idea or not. We are helpless to decide in such cases. In a less controversial example of automatism, there is no realistic choice nowadays about whether to learn to use computers. Even if you resist, you still have to use them to get your check okayed for cashing at the market, to get some moola from Mr. Money, or to do many of the daily tasks of life into which this technology has inexorably crept.

4. *Self-augmentation.* This means that technology increases geometrically. "Technology creates more technology" is a way of saying that la technique is self-augmenting. For example, the first computers were the size of buildings. They designed other computers that were the size of rooms, which in turn designed others the size of cabinets, which designed others the size of television sets, which designed others the size of typewriters, and so on. This characteristic reduces human choice, because whatever you choose is automatically obsolete before you choose it. In fact, it was probably obsolete before it was engineered.

5. *Monism.* This is the unity that characterizes a particular technique across many different settings. For example, the techniques of modern advertising are constant: Products, politicians, religions, and even mass movements are marketed nearly identically. When various techniques used in one area of human life begin to resemble those in another in disturbing ways (for example, when political advertising uses the techniques of product advertising), la technique is probably at work.

6. *Universality.* Technical developments are universal around the globe and affect humans in universal ways. The Third World peasant

plowing behind the musk ox hears the same music, news, and propaganda as the First World technician. Even the most personal aspects of our lives are invaded by technology: birth, death, emotions, and feelings. We no longer have a technological country but a technological world. We share many of the same experiences via media.

Unhappy Boston! see thy Sons deplore,
Thy hallow'd Walks besmear'd with guiltless Gore:
While faithless P—n and his savage Bands,
With murd'rous Rancour stretch their bloody Hands;
Like fierce Barbarians grinning o'er their Prey,
Approve the Carnage, and enjoy the Day.

If scalding drops from Rage from Anguish Wrung,
If speechless Sorrows lab'ring for a Tongue,
Or if a weeping World can ought appease
The plaintive Ghosts of Victims such as these;
The Patriot's copious Tears for each are shed,
A glorious Tribute which embalms the Dead.

But know, Fate summons to tha' awful Goal,
Where Justice strips the Murd'rer of his Soul:
Should venal C—ts the scandal of the Land,
Snatch the relentless Villain from her Hand,
Keen Execrations on this Plate inscrib'd,
Shall reach a Judge who never can be brib'd.

Engrav'd Printed & Sold by PAUL REVERE BOSTON

FIGURE 13.1

Here is an early use of propaganda: a depiction of the Boston Massacre engraved, printed, and sold by Paul Revere. It tells only one side of the story, and Revere's goal is not clear. (Used by permission of The New York Historical Society, New York City.)

7. *Autonomy*. Technology has no law but its own. It is independent of morality, ordinances, laws, or litigation. Its only law is efficiency.

Internal and External Characteristics of Propaganda

Rasberry also offers some symptoms of the propaganda that we are exposed to by the modern technocracy. Knowing these symptoms may awaken you to its pervasiveness. Following is a list of the **internal characteristics** of propaganda.

1. *It knows the psychological terrain*. This is close to what Tony Schwartz said in *The Responsive Chord*, discussed earlier. Modern propaganda begins and ends with what is already in the citizenry's belief system, prejudices, or stereotypes. When you feel most justified in taking some action (voting in a certain way or believing in something), you are probably being appealed to by a propaganda that knows your psychological territory.

2. *It is aligned with prevailing social currents*. This resembles the propaganda device called bandwagon but is far more sophisticated. Here we deal with the underlying ground rules of our society: "Don't be old-fashioned," "Strive," "Try harder," "Do your best," "Don't lie," "Be all you can be," and "Work within the system" are all examples. The slogans aimed at how we direct our lives are part and parcel of modern propaganda.

3. *It is timely*. Ellul pointed out the fixation modern society has with the news. We are driven by the need to be current: We study current events, and we feel lost when we are out of touch with the news. Thus, propaganda is best when it is newsworthy (hence the pseudoevent). Religion, business, politics, and education are examples of institutions that make their propaganda effective by becoming news.

4. *It is aimed at the undecided citizen*. The concerned but as-yet-undecided person is the prime target of contemporary propaganda. This links up with the ideas of timeliness and agenda setting. People who are current and informed are in the process of moving toward a decision and can be appealed to easily.

Rasberry's **external characteristics** resemble the definition with which we began this chapter. They are those characteristics about propaganda messages that we can point to directly.[45] The **internal characteristics** might not be so observable.

1. *Propaganda addresses both the individual and the masses*. Rasberry notes that "propaganda stops when simple one-to-one dialogue begins," because individuals have too much resistance to it. It would be impossible to aim propaganda at a large mass of people on a one-to-one basis. Instead, propaganda treats groups, crowds, or the masses *as if they are individuals*. It appeals to those common characteristics that unite the crowd and that make individuals identify with that crowd. Mass-media appeals to patriotism framed as appeals to individuals can reach large numbers of people. Ellul, noting this aspect of propaganda, says:

   > Each one must feel individualized, each must have the impression that he is being looked at and that he is being addressed personally. Only then will he respond and cease to be anonymous although in reality remaining anonymous.[46]

2. *Propaganda uses every means of communication — it is totalitarian*. Because each medium attracts different audiences at different times and may make receivers respond in differing ways, propaganda uses all of them. However, television has become central. It can be especially effective as a medium of propaganda because people place more trust in it than in any other medium for their news, and nearly every American home has a TV and uses it several hours each day. We know how mass media — particularly TV — can shape public opinion. But the icons and the images we share via TV will recur in other media: radio, newspapers, magazines, postage stamps, and more. Growing levels of illiteracy promise to make television the central feature of contemporary life.

3. *The message must be continuous and lasting.* As Ellul points out:

> Propaganda . . . must not leave any gaps, but must fill the citizen's whole day and all his days; lasting in that it must function over a very long period of time.[47]

The repetition of a particular propaganda myth — say, the myth of progress — develops a deeply embedded and long-lasting belief in the myth. The productivity myth develops in layers, beginning in the home, where the child knows that both parents produce goods or services not only for the child directly but also for society. The child soon learns that he or she also must be productive in the home. Later, at school, daily assignments reinforce the productivity model, and household chores emphasize it too. The first part-time job and paycheck continue the layering, as do graduation and the first full-time job. This slow process creates a belief in the propaganda myth of productivity that is extremely durable.

4. *Propaganda messages provoke action.* Contrary to earlier models of propaganda, which focused on shifting attitudes or opinions, Ellul's propaganda aims at changes in behavior. As Ellul notes:

> It is no longer to change adherence to a doctrine, but to make the individual cling irrationally to a process of action. It is no longer to lead to a choice, but to loosen the reflexes. . . . Only action is of concern.[48]

Saluting, singing, applauding, signing petitions, consumption, wearing uniforms, and displaying posters or signs are all examples of actions propaganda can provoke. Ellul says propaganda aims at *orthopraxy* (*ortho* means straight or true, *praxis* means doing or action) instead of *orthodoxy* (*doxa* means opinion). So even if your opinion is that the myth of the individual is hocus pocus, you will still act *as if* you believed it, if propaganda has been effective. In other words, you will voice your ideas (knowing that they won't be heard). You will continue to vote (knowing that your vote

won't make a difference). You will continue to express your unique individuality in taste, lifestyle, and religious belief (knowing that these are not unique to you at all). Propaganda pulls us into action, and, having acted in accord with its directions (even though they may run counter to our beliefs), we are hooked.

What Can We Do?

If all of this sounds negative and depressing, don't be surprised. It is. In fact, one of the recurring criticisms of Ellul's work is that it offers so little hope and that it is nihilistic. Ellul's own words often prompt such criticism:

> The individual is in a dilemma: either he decides to safeguard his freedom of choice . . . thereby entering into competition with a power against which there is no efficacious defense and before which he must suffer defeat; or he decides to accept a technical necessity, in which case he will himself be the victor, but only by submitting irreparably to technical slavery. In effect, he has no choice.[49]

However, a closer reading of Ellul's work and that of his critics reveals a position that is not totally hopeless. First, Ellul says that the act of recognizing something as propaganda liberates us to some degree, even though we still have to live in the technocracy. Second, Ellul sees hope in the existence of groups and subcultures in society, which negate to some degree the effects of la technique. They (for example, the ecology movement) provide alternative perspectives that are perhaps more humane and that call various propaganda myths into question. Jewel Ivy in *Country* provides us with another possibility — rephrasing the propaganda myths in more humane and individual-oriented ways. Through her rephrasing, the cost-consciousness of the bureaucracy was shifted to the people-consciousness of the family and community. Try rephrasing the myths of success, of productivity, of the individual, or of pleasure. Is success healthy? Does it produce humane family relations? What does it do to communities? Is individual success a threat to other people? Asking this type of question will not destroy the myth, but it will allow you to recognize and de-fang it to some degree.

Ellul sees the solution in a three-step process.[50] In stage one, we *recognize* the existence and dangers of la technique in its many forms: bureaucracy, isolation of the individual, and its various myths. Ellul asks for a "desacralization" of technology and for "ruthless honesty" in facing the problems of la technique. He hopes that intellectuals will be the guards who will sound the alarm. This phase also involves resisting standardization, whether brought on us by the media, government, economics, or some other force. Perhaps what you have been doing throughout your study of this chapter is leaning toward stage one.

Stage two of Ellul's solution is the *transformation* of the self into a nontechnological human. This doesn't involve seizing power in some sort of coup. Rather it requires identifying ways in which an individual's life can be changed. Ellul suggests disengagement from the technological aspects of modern life to a "life of rectitude" and examination of one's own ethics.[51] I'm not sure myself what that means; Ellul isn't entirely clear about it. However, it seems to me that, having identified ways in which we are influenced by the propaganda of la technique, the best means of disengaging ourselves is to reject as much technology as possible. Instead, look for humane activities in place of technologically oriented ones. Try to discover who you are when you have removed technology and its propaganda from your life as much as possible. Do without some technology for a time. Discuss the problem with others who share your perceptions. Try to avoid total reliance on electronic media and read printed media as well.

In any case, Ellul is certain that realization of the dangers of la technique, coupled with disengagement from technology, will lead to stage three — the *action* stage. Here Ellul advocates "creative nonconformity . . . spontaneous movement . . . and tangible acts which *ipso facto* circumvent the sociotechnological order."[52] He is not prescriptive about specific actions and instead advocates a "passion to play" or a return to festivals and rituals that emphasize humane values such as

the individual and social life.[53] One way to think about these actions is to study the nonviolent acts of many of the mass movements in recent history, in which individuals in groups or alone made symbolic statements. Answering election exit polls falsely could be a symbolic act. Returning all the postage-paid envelopes from mass mailings empty and marked "special delivery" could be another. The school lunchroom demonstration mentioned in Chapter 10 was one such nonviolent, nonconformist symbolic act. Ellul says that the liberated individual can be extremely creative in his or her resistance to the technological state. Clifford Christians, one of Ellul's critics, puts it this way: "One label for Ellul's strategy is a conscious exclusion of all physical and psychological violence."[54]

Even Ellul recognizes that stage three is extremely difficult and potentially dangerous. For our purposes, realization, reflection, and then avoidance of technological nonnecessities may suffice. Asking humane questions of technological institutions seems to be the most promising action we can take. At least it has the potential of raising the consciousness of others in regard to the dangers of la technique.

REVIEW AND CONCLUSION

Our interest in propaganda and its uses usually comes to the fore during times of war or national crisis. It is then that we see the one-sided, monolithic, blatant use of propaganda. When we are not faced with war or national crisis, our interest in propaganda diminishes. We become more concerned with the events of the day and with our personal problems. Yet, as we have seen, the absence of war does not mean the absence of propaganda. A major difficulty arises in identifying just what propaganda is, in determining its sources and intent, and in determining how and why it affects us.

It is useful to stop and observe the communications going on around us with the concept of propaganda in mind. Do these messages try to indoctrinate us? Are ideological issues being pressed on us? Who is the source? What is the source's intent or goal? Is there another side to the story that is being concealed? Are techniques such as subliminal messages being employed without our knowledge? If we follow the advice being transmitted to us, what will happen? All these questions and others can help us to process responsibly the propaganda aimed at us.

It is clear that even if Ellul overstates his case, his theory is useful. It jars us. It forces us to look deeper—to take a second and even a third look at many of the things that are happening around us. In those second or third looks, we often can identify propaganda that we might otherwise have overlooked.

QUESTIONS FOR FURTHER THOUGHT

1. Where in your world is the value of efficiency espoused? Look at advertisements, editorials, campaigns, and so on.

2. Look back at the cultural-values discussion in Chapter 8. Are any of these values being urged on you? If so, can you identify the source of the urging?

3. Are you being persuaded through a technique of which you are only dimly aware (for example, telemarketing)? If so, what is it?

4. What is the plain folks device? Identify its use in several examples of persuasion.

5. What is the glittering generalities device? Identify uses of it.

6. What is the transfer device? Identify uses of it.

7. What is card stacking? Identify uses of it.

8. In what ways do you agree and disagree with Jacques Ellul's ideas on propaganda?

9. Which medium discussed by Jowatt and O'Donnell is the most underused for propaganda purposes? Which has the most potential?

10. What can we expect in the future regarding propaganda, la technique, and the develop-

ments going on at the Media Lab at M.I.T. (see Chapter 12)?

NOTES

1. *Webster's Ninth New Collegiate Dictionary* (Springfield, MA: Merriam-Webster Inc., 1987), p. 942.

2. Garth S. Jowatt and Victoria O'Donnell, *Propaganda and Persuasion* (Beverly Hills, CA: Sage Publications Inc., 1986), p. 63.

3. Leonard W. Doob, *Propaganda—Its Psychology and Techniques* (New York: 1935) as quoted in Robert Taylor, *Film Propaganda* (New York: Barnes and Noble, 1979), p. 20.

4. *Ibid.*, p. 19.

5. *Ibid.*, p. 23.

6. J. A. C. Brown, *Techniques of Persuasion: From Propaganda to Brainwashing* (Baltimore, MD: Penguin Books, 1963), p. 12.

7. *Ibid.*

8. *Ibid.*, p. 13.

9. *Ibid.*, pp. 13–16; see especially p. 16.

10. *Ibid.*, p. 21.

11. *Ibid.*

12. *Ibid.*, p. 22.

13. *Ibid.*

14. Jacques Ellul, *Propaganda: The Formation of Men's Attitudes* (New York: Vintage Books, 1973). See also Clifford G. Christians and Jay M. Van Hook, *Jacques Ellul: Interpretive Essays* (Champaign, IL: University of Illinois Press, 1981); see especially Chapter 6.

15. Taylor, *op. cit.*, p. 23.

16. Clyde R. Miller, "How to Detect Propaganda," in *Propaganda Analysis* (New York: Institute for Propaganda Analysis, 1937).

17. Brown, *op. cit.*, p. 94.

18. *Ibid.*; see especially Chapters 1 and 3.

19. *Ibid.*, pp. 27–29.

20. *Ibid.*, pp. 68–73.

21. *Ibid.*, pp. 32–36, 68, and 24.

22. You might find it instructive to read Shirley Jackson's short story "The Lottery," in *Fifty Great Short Stories*, ed. Milton Crane (New York: Bantam Books, 1962).

23. Brown, *op. cit.*, p. 73.

24. Jacques Ellul, "The Presence of the Kingdom," in *Jacques Ellul: Interpretive Essays*, eds. Clifford Christians and Jay M. Van Hook (Champaign, IL: University of Illinois Press, 1981), p. 21.

25. Jowatt and O'Donnell, Chapter 3.

26. *Ibid.*, pp. 69, 70.

27. *Ibid.*, pp. 72–82.

28. *Ibid.*, p. 73.

29. *Ibid.*, p. 74.

30. *Ibid.*, pp. 76–79.

31. *Ibid.*, p. 83.

32. *Ibid.*, pp. 84, 85.

33. *Ibid.*, p. 87.

34. *Ibid.*, pp. 92, 93.

35. *Ibid.*

36. *Ibid.*

37. *Ibid.*, p. 95.

38. *Ibid.*

39. Jacques Ellul, *Propaganda: The Formation of Men's Attitudes* (New York: Vintage Books, 1973), pp. x–xv.

40. *Ibid.*, pp. xv and xvi.

41. *Ibid.*, p. xviii.

42. *Ibid.*, pp. 30–32.

43. Clifford Christians and Michael Real, "Jacques Ellul's Contributions to Critical Media Theory," *Journal of Communication* 29:83–93, 1979. See also Christians and Van Hook, *op. cit.*, Chapters 6 and 8.

44. Robert Rasberry, *The Technique of Political Lying* (Washington, DC: The University Press of America, 1981).

45. *Ibid.*, pp. 7–81.

46. Ellul, *Propaganda*, p. 8.

47. *Ibid.*, p. 17.

48. *Ibid.*, p. 25.

49. Jacques Ellul, *The Technological Society*, trans. John Wilkinson (New York: Knopf and Sons, 1979), p. 84.

50. For an excellent synopsis of Ellul's views on solution, see Clifford G. Christians, "Ellul on Solutions: An Alternative but No Prophesy," in Christians and Van Hook, *op. cit.*, pp. 147–173.

51. *Ibid.*, pp. 151–153.

52. *Ibid.*, p. 154.

53. *Ibid.*, p. 155.

54. *Ibid.*

The Use of Persuasive Premises in Advertising

The most dominant, and perhaps the most effective, forms of persuasion in contemporary culture are print and electronic advertising. Although we may feel smug about not running out and buying every product we learn about from advertisements, product ads still have a dramatic impact on us. They shape not only our purchasing behavior but other behaviors as well (for example, becoming aware of a product's existence, developing attitudes toward products, and even making changes in our values and preferred life-styles). The field of advertising has a long and frequently sordid history, but it is also a fascinating area of persuasion to study. I hope that this chapter will provide insights into how you and your culture behave in response to and because of advertising. To give you an idea of how much impact advertising has on Western consumers (particularly those in the United States) and thus how it helps shape our culture, consider the following:

1. The average expenditure on advertising in the United States exceeds $400 per person per year.[1] This includes all kinds of print and electronic advertising. It doesn't sound like so much, does it — a little more than a dollar a day?

2. The average American is exposed to over 1700 advertising messages every day. Again, this includes all kinds of advertising. Now that's more impressive! It gives us a feel for what the word *clutter* means to persons in the advertising industry, and it explains why it is so hard to "break through the clutter."

3. Compare this quantity of and expenditure on advertising with that of the rest of the world. The average expenditure on advertising in the rest of the world (including such Western democracies as Canada, Great Britain, Mexico, and all of Western Europe, where advertising expenditures are also great) is only *$17 per person per year*. That's about $.32 per week, or $.04 per day.[2]

No wonder foreigners consider our advertising to be a reflection of our culture and easily come to the conclusion that we Americans are clearly the most compulsive, selfish, and greedy consumers of goods and services in the world.

ADVERTISING AND CULTURE

As we analyze "The World's Second Oldest Profession," as advertising has been referred to by some of its critics, you will find yourself evaluating our culture in various ways too. Keep in mind, however, that no matter where you look in human history, there have been sellers and promoters of one kind or another, whether in a barter society in the South Pacific Islands, in the middle of our own revolutionary war 200 years ago, in Czarist Russia, in Leninist-Marxist Russia, and even in today's emerging free-market Russia. Of course, advertising is most evident in contemporary American life. And the selling and promoting usually involved some kind of advertising, so we Americans aren't unique in the use of advertising. We are only highly effective in producing and consuming it. Some of it ranks as pop art and is extremely creative and even entertaining. Some of it isn't even good enough to rank as schlock.

The real lesson to learn from studying the persuasive appeals of advertising is how they affect human society and our behavior and whether none, all, or even just *some* of those effects are bad or good, ethical or unethical for humankind in general and for you in particular. A final value in studying advertising is that it can help each of us understand ourselves as consumers.

As you read this chapter, remember that the advertising industry is continually updating its research, production, and dissemination techniques in attempts to "get through the clutter" and to persuade us. Advertising agencies spend a lot of money making certain that what they produce will be as effective as possible, so even though it is entertaining, remember that it is also persuasive.

Also keep in mind that any discussion of the topic is really an interpretation of events as seen through the eyes of the beholder. Thus, historians see advertisements as social indicators of the times in which they were created. Marxist critics see advertisements as tools of the upper classes used to exploit the lower classes by encouraging them to conspicuously consume products they really don't need. Advertising executives see ads as better or worse than or more or less effective than those of the competition. My perspective is both as a teacher of persuasion (especially as seen in advertising principles) and as a practitioner of various advertising techniques in the real world. But throughout my perspective there is a greater concern for consumers as they face the cluttered world of advertising in their lives. If this chapter is at all worthwhile, you should come away from it as a much more critical, insightful, and selective consumer of today's barrage of advertising appeals.

ADVERTISING OR MARKETING? THE CASE FOR POSITIONING

One issue that comes up concerning advertising is: Which comes first, the product/service/idea/candidate or the advertisements to promote them? Most contemporary professionals in the field agree that advertising is a *tool of marketing*. In other words, you don't come up with a product and then try to sell it to consumers through advertising messages. Rather, the successful marketer begins with the minds of consumers and tries to identify potentially unmet needs. If one or more is discovered, then a product is either designed to fill the need or an existing product is "redefined" to fill the need. As noted in Chapter 11, this approach of beginning with the consumer was made popular by the work of Al Ries and Jack Trout. In their articles, speeches, and best-selling book, they deal with the idea of **positioning**—finding a *creneau*, or niche, in the minds of consumers that a given product might fill.[3] For example, Taster's Choice is positioned as the "freeze-dried" instant coffee, thereby preempting that position for other brands. My university is positioned as the "closest," though not the "most prestigious" or "best-party" public university for students living in the greater Chicago area. Chrysler is positioned as the "most innovative" auto maker because it brought out the following innovations in the 1980s: front-wheel drive, consumer rebates, the extended warranty,

the minivan, the convertible, and the air-bag safety device. Once a position is established for a product, advertising is used to prepare the customer for trial and purchase. It lays the groundwork for sales by increasing product or **brand awareness** (for example, repeating slogans or jingles), by communicating and/or improving the **product image or personality** (for example, Chrysler's innovative image), and by making an **offer** that will move the consumer to the point of purchase (for example, a one-month time limit on "guaranteed rebates"). Once the consumer is at the grocery store, the auto dealership, or the clothing store, the sales staff try to close the deal using various methods of sales promotion.

Problems of an Overcommunicated Society

One of Ries and Trout's main contentions is that we live in an overcommunicated society. They claim that the usual defense consumers have in our overcommunicated society is to develop an "oversimplified mind," by which they mean a mind that largely ignores most of the information to which it is exposed.[4] Most people select products they think are appropriate for their purposes and then generally stick with those products. We call this *brand loyalty*. Brand loyalty makes it easier to live in an overcommunicated society, because you never have to change your mind, and you can easily ignore the ads for competing brands in that product category. As Michael Schudson notes in his book *Advertising, The Uneasy Persuasion*, advertisers defend themselves from the criticism that they sell products that people don't really need by claiming that their aim is "not to change people's product choices but to change their brand choices. Advertising . . . is a competitive war against commercial rivals for a share of a market."[5]

In order to break through the defense of having an audience with an oversimplified mind, advertisers need to find something that is already in the audience's mind and then "retie the cords" of what is in the audience's mind to their products. In this way, they are very close to Tony Schwartz's evoked recall model, which "gets messages out of audiences, not into them." Ries and Trout suggest that the best way to do this is to use an "oversimplified message."[6] To demonstrate this point, they report the results of a recent survey of name recognition among supermarket shoppers, which showed that only 44 percent of the shoppers knew George Bush. At the same time, 93 percent of them easily recognized Mr. Clean and what he could promise (an oversimplified message).[7]

The overcommunication problem is extended by what Ries and Trout call the *media explosion*, which we looked at in Chapter 12: TV, cable, satellites, AM and FM radio, morning and evening daily newspapers, news weeklies, magazines, catalogs, direct mail, billboards, bus signs, and so on. Even the human body carries trademarks: Calvin Klein, Gucci, Benetton, Guess, and other product names.

The Product Explosion

Besides the overcommunication problem and the media explosion, we also have what Ries and Trout call the *product explosion*. For example, the average supermarket contains 12,000 products or brands, and in Europe, there are super-supermarkets (or hypermarkets) that contain over 60,000 or more products or brands from which to choose.[8] To further complicate the situation, each year 25,000 new trademarks are registered at the U.S. Patent Office, with "hundreds of thousands of products and brands being sold without trademarks."[9]

More products coming on the market results in more advertising. Ries and Trout call this the *advertising explosion*—a problem not only in the sheer increase in the volume of advertising but in the many new types of users being forced to turn to advertising, among them professionals (lawyers, dentists, and doctors) and institutions (hospitals, nonprofit organizations, and governments).

Breaking Through the Clutter

How do advertisers break through the triple whammy of increased media, products, and advertisements? In other words, how do they "break through the clutter"? The techniques of position-

ing provide one way to break through clutter. We encountered some of these in Chapter 10, which covered market segmentation in persuasive campaigns. "Being first" helped products such as Jello, Kleenex, and Xerox break the clutter. These products have become "imprinted" in consumers' minds to the extent that the brand names are almost generic for gelatin desserts, facial tissue, and photocopying, respectively. As Ries and Trout note, "You build brand loyalty in a supermarket in the same way you build mate loyalty in a marriage. You get there first and then be careful not to give them a reason to switch."[10] Not only were Apple personal computers the *first* in the PC market but they also were first at being "user friendly." This realization let them get the jump on IBM and others in creating software that was easy to use, thus giving consumers the best reason to remain loyal to Apple. A friend of mine who is a computer expert was describing this phenomenon to me, remarking that the Macintosh is "ten times easier to use than any other PC on the market and almost as powerful as a mainframe computer."[11] Apple was first and then gave their users many reasons to remain brand loyal. With their new, enhanced capability, there will be even greater reasons for remaining brand loyal to Apple.

But what if you're not first in the market? Then positioning becomes even more important. In earlier advertising eras—the *product benefit era* of the USP (or "Unique Selling Proposition"), innovated by Rosser Reeves, and the *product image era*, innovated by David Ogilvy—the competition wasn't nearly as fierce as it is in the 1990s. With more and more "me too!" products on the market, neither product benefits nor product images could beat the competition. Products have to be unique in the marketplace, and usually advertisers rely on simple but distinctive copy to communicate uniqueness. The poetry of product benefit or product image ad copy doesn't seem to work anymore. For example, according to Ries and Trout, Michelob beer advertising used copy that was unlike the poetic sloganeering of the image era. Instead it was "as poetic as a stop sign. And just as effective. 'First class is Michelob.'"[12] That slogan positioned Michelob as "unique" in the market—a premium-priced beer actually produced in Amer-

FIGURE 14.1

One of the major problems for advertisers today is what Ries and Trout call the *advertising explosion*, by which they mean the increased volume of advertising but also the new advertising "vehicles," or places where advertising can occur. (*Freeze Frame* cartoon from *Advertising Age*, April 25, 1988. Copyright Crain Communications, Inc. Reprinted by permission of Crain Communications and Sidney Harris.)

ica, which is something that is becoming rarer and rarer, as Figure 14.3 demonstrates.

Beck's did a similar thing to Lowenbräu with the slogan "You've tasted the German beer that's the most popular in America. Now taste the German beer that's the most popular in Germany." Ries and Trout contend that this slogan forced Lowenbräu to switch from selling itself as a German beer to selling itself as a domestic brand with a German formula.[13] There are a variety of techniques that make a product seem to be the only brand in the product category with a certain benefit. You are exposed to these kinds of pitches every day. For example, which coffee is "mountain

Mother's Helper.

Any way you slice 'em,
California avocados work miracles
in your kitchen.
For instance. They get along beautifully
with omelettes. They're sensational in any salad.
And they're a slice of heaven on a BLT.
Delicious, velvety smooth California avocados are full of surprises.
Ounce per ounce, they have more potassium than a banana. And they're
cholesterol-free.
So next time you need help in the kitchen, put a California avocado to
work. They make cooking so easy, all you have to do is take the credit.

California
AVOCADOS
Ripe with possibilities and no cholesterol.

FIGURE 14.2

A product benefit ad.

FIGURE 14.3

One niche in many markets today may be designated "American made," because so many types of products are being produced elsewhere. Inventory your own closet and see what percentage of your clothing is "Made in the USA." (© 1986, Washington Post Writers Group. Reprinted by permission.)

grown"? If you said "Folgers," you are wrong—all of them come from beans that were grown in the mountains, but Folgers preempted that product claim, thus carving out its unique niche in the coffee market. It would be advertising suicide to say, for example, "Maxwell House is mountain grown too." Instead, other brands of coffee need to find different niches.

And there aren't many niches in a given product category. Research shows that the average person can recall only seven (plus or minus two) instances of products in any given category.[14] So if the competitors are firmly entrenched in the audience's mind, what can be done? One possibility is to go up against one of them with *comparative advertis-*

ing. Ries and Trout give an example of this approach in the Avis Rent-a-Car campaign, whose slogan was "Avis is only number 2 in rent-a-cars, so why go with us? We try harder."[15] After thirteen years of losing money, Avis made $1.2 million the first year after admitting to being second, $2.6 million the second year, and $5 million the third year before being acquired by ITT, who ditched

FIGURE 14.4

How did this nonpoetic, hard-hitting product ad by Rapala break through the clutter? (Reprinted by permission of Normark Corp.)

Granted.There Are Some Similarities
Between Other Fishing Lures And A Rapala.

This year, we crafted the 100 millionth Rapala. It was attached to a testing rod and
pulled by hand through a tank to inspect and perfect its swimming action. For over
50 years, only Rapala has taken the time to hand tune and tank test every
lure. Only Rapala. Which is why we have no equal among our many imitators.

Rapala. Celebrating 100 Million Hand-Tuned, Tank-Tested Lures.

Rapala
Normark

© 1989 Normark Corp.

the number-2 idea and promptly began losing money.

One way a product can break clutter is to tell consumers what it "is not" that makes it unique. In 1968, Seven-Up was near bankruptcy when it shifted its advertising business to the J. Walter Thompson agency. JWT came up with one of the most successful "Tell 'em what you're not" campaigns in history with the "invention" of the word *un-cola*, which the agency then used in very creative ways. For example, the Seven-Up delivery trucks were labeled "The Man from Un-cola," which played on a popular TV series *The Man from U.N.C.L.E.* And there were a series of ads in various languages in which the only word most viewers could understand was "un-cola." The campaign positioned Seven-Up third in the soft-drink market right behind Coca-Cola and Pepsi-Cola. The only way to come up with an unconventional idea such as "un-cola" is to get into the consumer's mind: "You won't find an 'un-cola' idea inside a Seven-Up can. You find it inside the cola drinker's head."[16]

Another approach is to take advantage of one's existing image or reputation. For example, Arm and Hammer is known for producing baking soda, but did you know that it also makes and sells sodium bicarbonates to cattle raisers? Arm and Hammer took advantage of its already established reputation to market a new product — cattle feed supplements — in a very competitive marketplace. This is called *line extension*. Another example is the success that National Cash Register (NCR) has had in entering the highly competitive computer field, so heavily dominated by IBM. NCR played on its cash register reputation and focused on computerizing its cash registers, designing them not only for recording transactions but, through the brand-scanning devices, for inventory recording and inventory control. So, relying on one's strength and reputation can be an effective means of breaking clutter.

Many "me too" products claim to be "better." The problem is that it's hard to prove, let alone convince the consumer, that a product is better. A company may waste inordinate amounts of *time* and *money* trying to increase demonstrable prod-

uct quality, thus allowing the competition to catch up and out-advertise and out-sell the new "me too" product. This happened when Volkswagen broke into the U.S. compact-car market, finding what Ries and Trout call the "size *creneau*," because there were few compact cars available in the American market at the time.[17] Their campaign slogan, the two simple words "think small," permitted them to preempt the "small" niche in consumers' minds. American automakers countered by making smaller cars than they had been making, but none were as small or successful as the VW beetle. Not until the Japanese compacts entered the market was Volkswagen troubled.

Price can be another clutter breaker.[18] A product can find a lower-priced niche, such as that filled by the Yugo, or it can find a high-priced one like that of Mont Blanc pens, Rolex wrist watches, and BMWs. Another example of a high-priced niche is in the frozen turkey market. The most expensive frozen turkey is the widest-selling national brand: Butterball. It's true that Butterball has a distinct name advantage over its nearest competitors (Norbest, Honeysuckle, Land O' Lakes, and Armour), but it's also an expensive brand of turkey. However, Butterball turns its name and price into advantages by using advertising to "get into the consumer's head" and thus break the clutter. In their advertising, a young newlywed woman is worrying about having Thanksgiving at her house for the first time. She wonders whether her turkey will be as juicy as her mother-in-law's. Maybe it will be too dry, and she will be a failure as a cook in front of her husband and his whole family. Her fears convince her to buy a Butterball turkey and not take a chance. Interestingly, Butterball turkey purchasers spend twenty-two more minutes in the supermarket than purchasers of other brands, and they tend to buy

FIGURE 14.5

This product image ad breaks through the clutter using a copy-heavy strategy to tell Rolex's product story. The comparison between Rolex watches and Purdey shotguns relies on both the price and quality niches. (Reprinted by permission of Rolex Watch U.S.A., Inc.)

The Purdey firearm. Created by James Purdey and Sons, the fabled London firm that has been gunmaker to the royal family since Queen Victoria's reign.

Today, the company's impeccable traditions are scrupulously maintained under the direction of The Honourable Richard Beaumont, son of the Second Viscount Allendale.

For more than 170 years, Purdey has produced sporting guns so distinctive, no two are exactly alike. The barrel of one cannot be interchanged with the stock of any other.

Purdey and Rolex: The most refined expressions of their respective arts.

So meticulous is their construction, only 70 are produced in a year. So artful is

Hand-engraving is a hallmark of Purdey guns.

their workmanship, every one is signed by the craftsman who made it. And so enduring is their precision, Purdey guns are traditionally passed down from generation to generation.

Under Richard Beaumont's chairmanship, the most rigid traditions of bespoke gunmaking prevail. Every part of

every Purdey is custom-made. Distances between the owner's eye, cheek, shoulder and trigger finger are calibrated. The measurements are designed into the stock to ensure that each gun is precisely fitted to its owner.

Richard Beaumont is a man who maintains standards of craftsmanship that speak

Purdey utilizes the finest craftsmen in the world.

of a more civilized time. Which makes his choice of a Rolex understandable.

ROLEX

higher-priced products for the rest of the meal. Because these higher-priced items have a better profit margin, the supermarket manager is more than willing to give Butterball large, prime freezer space.[19]

Other clutter breakers are gender and age. The largest-selling perfume is not Arpege or Chanel No. 5 but Charlie—the first perfume to advertise using a masculine name. Examples of products occupying the age niche are Geritol and high-fiber foods. Distribution and packaging can break clutter, too. L'eggs was the first hosiery to be distributed in supermarkets, and its packaging gave it a unique position in the market.[20] Hosiery is usually packaged in a thin square envelope with a window in it to show the consumer the shade of the hose. There are high labor costs involved in folding the hose around a cardboard sheet inside the envelope. L'eggs hosiery, on the other hand, can simply be "stuffed" into the container, thus eliminating this labor cost and bringing the price down. And the egg-shaped container is not only visually unique but also has appeal for secondary uses, such as for storage of small items, as toys, and for various crafts.[21]

Advertisers can also break through clutter by repositioning an existing brand (for example, changing Cheerios from a "child" product to an "adult" product by stressing its high-fiber content).[22] Finally, clutter can be broken by choosing the right name and/or slogan for the product.[23] A powerful bathroom cleaner named "The Works" fits with the idea of trying the ultimate—"give it the works!" The Butterball brand name is another good example, as is "Taster's Choice" freeze-dried coffee. Compare the clutter-breaking abilities of various brand slogans. What, for example, is Buick's slogan? It's not very memorable: "Buick Builds It Better." For comparative purposes, try to recall Pontiac's slogan. If you are like most people, you will remember Pontiac's slogan ("We Build Excitement!"), because it is easier to remember—it cuts through the clutter.

All of these examples of clutter-breaking techniques grow out of various kinds of advertising research that permit the advertiser to get into your head and resonate with your needs. Let's explore some research of this kind.

GETTING INTO THE CONSUMER'S HEAD: ADVERTISING RESEARCH

Three general approaches to advertising or marketing research are dominant: the use of *demographics* (which we discussed in Chapter 11), the use of *psychographics*, and the use of *sociographics*. Sometimes they are used alone; sometimes two of them may be used in conjunction with one another; and sometimes all three may be used. There are also a variety of ways of conducting these kinds of research, including using census data, surveys and questionnaires; focus-group interviews (which we briefly explored in Chapter 10); a pupilometer, which measures the dilation of the pupil of the eye as it scans a printed ad; the tachistoscope, which gives viewers "mini-glimpses" at ads, after which they are asked to recall the visuals and copy; galvanic skin response, which measures electric resistance sweat in the palm of the hand when a person gets excited; heartbeat rates; and others too numerous to mention. All of these techniques have the same purpose: to identify the consumer's "hot buttons" and "cold buttons," to use the lingo of the trade. In the words of former advertising executive Terry Gallonoy in his book *Down the Tube: Or Making Television Commercials Is Such a Dog-Eat-Dog Business, It's No Wonder They're Called Spots*, the successful commercials have to "make people shut up or stop eating or freeze on the way to the bathroom. . . . 'Stop the lady with the full bladder for just one full minute' is the order of the day."[24]

Demographics

Demographics are used in the study of groups of consumers, or *market segments*, on the basis of some quantifiable variable or variables, including annual income, religious affiliation, political preferences, age, family size, gender, purchase patterns, or any combination of demographic factors. Based on these statistics, the advertisers design ads that feature certain kinds of characters or have certain settings, props, and so on. One recently identified pattern is the growing number of "DINK" families ("Double-Income, No-Kids" couples) us-

"WOW! We're DINKS — a double-income, no-kids couple!"

FIGURE 14.6

Demographics identified this growing market segment, which has two subgroups — yuppies and the parents of yuppies. Advertisers need to appeal to each subgroup in very different ways. (*Berry's World* reprinted by permission of NEA, Inc.)

ing two demographic variables — number of persons working in the household and family size. DINKs divide into two subgroups: those who intentionally have no children and who are largely self-indulgent (the yuppie segment of the baby boomers), and those whose children have left home and are now independent of their parents for living expenses, tuition, and so on (formerly called "empty nesters" before Mom decided to go back to work). This second group is sometimes called "muppies," or "mature urban professionals" — the parents of yuppies, in other words. Quite obviously, an advertiser needs to appeal to these two subgroups in very different ways, using very different characters, settings, music, props, and so on.

The muppie segment is increasing at the rate of 5500 persons per day, which adds up to over two million new consumers a year. Here are some other demographics on this market segment: There are about 157 women for every 102 men in this age group; the average age of the group is increasing;

they have a 76.8-year average life expectancy; their rate of divorce is increasing at three times the national rate.[25] Knowing this kind of data can indicate where, how, and when advertisers should appeal to this market segment. For instance, persons in this segment tend to get up earlier in the day and to retire earlier at night—perhaps just after the evening news. They have more discretionary income available than they did when their children were living at home, but they spend a good amount of it on children and especially grandchildren. They are concerned about health issues and are exercising more and more. They travel more than the average person does. About half of them live in seven states—California and New York with over two million each and Florida, Illinois, Michigan, Ohio, and Pennsylvania.

Now, you play advertising executive with these data and tell when, where, and how you would appeal to the muppie market segment. Your product is a nationwide travel network that permits older persons to travel in groups at special low rates during the off season. Would you advertise in *Modern Maturity Magazine*, or would you make your appeal during local evening news shows, which have a much smaller "reach" or population that could potentially see or hear the message? Or would you use direct mail to persons over 65 in the seven major states? Whom would you pick to be your spokesperson? Eddie Albert? Angela Lansbury? Yogi Berra? Bart Starr? John Forsythe? These and a host of other questions would rise out of the demographic identification of muppie DINKs.

Other demographic data may be used to break through the clutter too. Consider the implications of the following sets of demographic data generated from the graduation classes of 1960 and 1965 at New Trier High School near Chicago. Both classes could include persons like your parents, but the five-year gap between them accounts for remarkable differences. Both groups are now in their forties—midlife—but members of the class of 1960 were children of the fifties, whereas members of the class of 1965 were children of the sixties. These data have important implications for advertisers hoping to market identical products to these two sets of consumers.[26] First consider the

class of 1960. Twenty-nine percent of the women and 49 percent of the men are self-employed; 12 percent of the women and 14 percent of the men reported that they are millionaires; 28 percent of the women and 7 percent of the men reported annual incomes of under $10,000; both men and women have about 2.1 children; about 45 percent of both genders claim Republican leanings, whereas 65 percent of females and 60 percent of males had Republican parents; 80 percent of women and 65 percent of men reported themselves as either "moderate," "liberal," or "very liberal"; 36 percent of women and 25 percent of men have been sterilized; 55 percent of women and 58 percent of men reported having tried marijuana; and 3 percent of women and 7 percent of men reported having problems with alcohol.[27]

Several important events occurred in the early 1960s that undoubtedly affected members of the class of 1965 more than members of the class of 1960. For example, the United States mounted a botched attack and invasion of Cuba. Later, in 1962, the United States almost went to war with Russia over ballistic missiles in Cuba. Richard Nixon announced he was leaving politics forever. The civil rights movement burgeoned and peaked with the 1963 March on Washington and the "I Have a Dream" speech by Martin Luther King, Jr. President John F. Kennedy was assassinated, and Lyndon Johnson won the presidency in the 1964 campaign by appealing to fears of nuclear war and the race issue. By 1965, large numbers of American troops were being sent to Vietnam, and the student-activist years were in full swing; "drugs became penny candy,"[28] and the attitudes and values of the "counterculture" invaded everything from music to art and from politics to sex.

Today, the annual income for men from the class of 1965 ranges from $10,000 to $750,000, with an average of about $70,000. Seventy-eight percent of the women say that they are *not* full-time homemakers. Over 52 percent of households are based on two incomes. Those respondents who entered the family business reported making an average annual income of $84,000, whereas those who avoided the family business reported making $144,000. The divorce rate for men in the class of 1965 was only 14 percent—down from 24 percent for the men of the class of 1960. Regarding sexual attitudes and behavior, 56 percent of women from the class of 1965 thought that a woman should be a virgin until marriage — down from 74 percent for the class of 1960. Twenty-four percent of women and 12 percent of men from the class of 1965 have had only one sexual partner. Today, over 75 percent of them believe that premarital sex is OK. About 7 percent of the class has had some homosexual or lesbian experience. In terms of drugs, 76 percent of men and 68 percent of women from the class of 1965 have tried marijuana, and 28 percent of men and 22 percent of women have used cocaine. Forty-six percent of men and 23 percent of women label themselves Republicans. Five years earlier, 45 percent of the women of the class of 1960 called themselves Republicans. Eighty-one percent of men in the class of 1965 are "pro-choice," 72 percent of the class of 1965 opposed the Vietnam war, and almost 40 percent demonstrated against it. Those numbers are quite different from those of the class of 1960: Only 43 percent reported having opposed the war, and only 13.5 percent demonstrated against it.

Now suppose your product is Christian Brothers brandy. What, where, and how would you appeal to the class of 1960 market segment? Here's what Christian Brothers actually did: They ran a full-page ad in upscale, slick magazines. Most of the ad was taken up by a picture of Chuck Berry dressed all in orange — orange shoes, socks, pants, shirt, and vest — and he held an orange guitar. The ad's caption read: "C. B. in orange — With a little C. B. brandy and orange juice, Johnny be very good indeed."[29] Assuming that the class of 1960 from New Trier High School is the target, can you explain the rationale behind the use of the color orange, the use of Chuck Berry, and the caption? Another example of an ad pitched at this market segment was Lincoln and Mercury's use of a *Big Chill* effect in an ad with a Beatles sound-alike recording of "Help." This worked to "break through ad clutter and forge emotional links with baby boomers."[30]

If you wanted to market the same product to the class of 1965, what would you do differently? Maybe you would use a different musician in your ad — perhaps Bob Dylan, who wrote several anti-war songs, or perhaps a female singer would be effective. Maybe your ad would focus on living the up-scale life that would make Christian Brothers brandy the "in" thing to serve. Perhaps you would depict a two-income home at the cocktail hour. There are a host of other factors that could make a difference with one segment and not the other. As you can see, even the dullest demographic facts can lead advertisers to target you as part of the market segment they want to reach with their messages.

Psychographics

Psychographics is the study of consumers' lifestyles. It provides quantitative data as to how consumers spend their time, in what kinds of activities they engage, what their interests are, and what their opinions are on any given set of issues regarding a product or product category. One common term used in psychographic research is AIO, or "Activities, Interests, and Opinions." Some examples of activities are work, social events, vacations, hobbies, entertainment, club membership, community activities, shopping, and attending sporting events. Interests include the family and home, one's achievements, recreation, fashion, technology, food, and media. Opinions can be held about oneself, social and political issues, business and economics, religion and culture, education, and the future. A psychographic study is done by having large numbers of persons respond to lengthy questionnaires about activities, interests, and opinions that relate to a particular product. From these answers, the advertiser infers what the respondents' life-styles are like and how they are likely to respond to the product. In some cases, the results may dictate points to be used in the ad copy — and even specific language to be used.

The items in psychographic questionnaires may be general or specific. For example, a study could be conducted to determine what type of consumer would be most likely to bring a malpractice suit against a physician. Items in the questionnaire would be something like:

I have a great deal of confidence in my own doctor.

Many physicians are out of date.
Physicians are overpaid.
Malpractice is hard to prove.
You are your own best doctor.

Responses may range from "strongly agree" to "strongly disagree." Trends in responses are then correlated to persons actually bringing malpractice suits.

In a case directly related to product advertising, persons strongly agreeing with the following items are probably highly likely to use Listerine mouthwash rather than Listermint mouthwash and are more likely to use mouthwash in general:

I do not feel clean without a daily bath.
Everyone should use a deodorant.
A house should be dusted three times a week.
Odors in the house embarrass me.
The kind of dirt you can't see is worse than the kind you can see.
I am a very neat person.
Dirty dishes should be washed after every meal.
It is very important for people to wash their hands before eating each meal.
I use one or more household disinfectants.[31]

You can imagine several effective advertisements that could be developed just by knowing that Listerine users respond this way to cleanliness. Appeals could be made to the germ-killing and antiseptic qualities in the product. You could justify Listerine's bad taste by intimating that "clean doesn't mean 'good tasting' in mouthwashes" and go on to point out that "flavored mouthwashes" compromise cleanliness for the sake of taste.

So, knowing about the activities, interests, and opinions of consumers provides advertisers with critical psychographic data about their potential customers. Keep in mind that no matter how ineffective you think a given national print or electronic advertisement is, it probably had to pass rigorous research tests before ever going on the air or into print.

Another psychographic model widely used in advertising and marketing is known as VALS ("Values And Life-Styles"), developed by Arnold Mitchell at SRI (Stanford Research Institute).[32]

Mitchell describes three general life-styles and then breaks them down into subcategories having certain values, demographics, and buying patterns.[33] The three general categories are: persons who are *need driven*, persons who are *outer directed*, and persons who are *inner directed*.

Need-Driven Consumers These consumers are living on the edge of or in the midst of poverty. They represent only 11 percent of the population, and advertisers do not often target them because need-driven consumers have little discretionary income. They are forced to use most, if not all, of their income to buy the minimum essentials.

There are two subcategories of need-driven consumers — survivors (4 percent) and sustainers (7 percent). *Survivors* struggle to provide the daily necessities of life, tend to mistrust people and products, and are usually social misfits. They live in slums, have low educational backgrounds and poverty-level incomes, and most likely are members of a racial or ethnic minority. As you would expect, survivors' buying patterns are dominated by price and immediate needs.

Sustainers are a little better off. They are very concerned with security and safety; they really want to get ahead and think they can because of their "street savvy." Like survivors, they have low educational backgrounds and low income levels, but they may live in the country as well as the city and aren't necessarily members of minority groups. Although price is important to sustainers, they also want warranties and are cautious. But their desire to get ahead may make them targets for get-rich-quick schemes such as pyramid marketing (for example Amway) or lottery tickets.

Outer-Directed Consumers This category makes up 67 percent of the marketplace and is an important target for advertisers. Outer-directed consumers are divided into three subcategories. *Belongers* (35 percent) are very conventional and traditional. They usually do not experiment with new products or services and conform to traditional patterns. They tend to be blue-collar workers with low to middle educational levels. They are family oriented, focusing on products with domestic appeal. Belongers are also nostalgic and are good targets for direct-response television ads for "Great Music of the 50s" or "Patsy Cline's Greatest Hits" and other nostalgic products and slogans ("Bread like Grandma used to make"). They are affected by fads, too.

Emulators (10 percent) are upwardly mobile and ambitious persons who are status conscious and competitive. Sometimes they try to project a macho image. They have good incomes, tend to be young, and tend to live in urban areas. They have traditionally been males, but that is changing as more and more women enter the workplace, as the ad in Figure 14.7 shows. Emulators are into "conspicuous consumption" and purchase "in" products that represent popular fashion. They are good targets for the newest styles in clothing, automobiles, and leisure activities (health clubs, racquetball, cross-country skiing, and so on).

Achievers (22 percent) have "made it" in today's world. They are interested in efficiency, leadership, achievement, success, fame, comfort, and conspicuous consumption. They have excellent incomes and high degrees of education. They live in suburbs and "trendy" parts of large cities. They tend to be leaders in politics, business, and community activities. Achievers' buying patterns reflect their success—they always buy top-of-the-line products. They are willing to try "new" products and are good targets for luxury items such as Rolex watches, BMWs, "success rings," and spun-aluminum briefcases. They tend to be like Arnie Becker of *L.A. Law*—not always very likable.

Inner-Directed Consumers These consumers represent a small but distinctive slice of the market (22 percent) and are divided into four distinct subcategories. *I-am-me* consumers (5 percent) are very individualistic and reject traditional possessions or ways of behaving. They are experimental and impulsive, and tend to be dramatic and volatile. I-am-me's come from affluent backgrounds, even though they themselves may not have much discretionary income. Many are students or are just starting on the occupational ladder. Their buying patterns are more related to "taste" than high price—just the opposite of emulators and achievers. In fact, I-am-me's may be "far out" as consumers and go for faddish items.

As their name implies, *experientials* (7 percent) want to have many and varied experiences. They participate in many activities; are introspective and frequently artistic. They may have high or low incomes depending on their decisions about living standards. They have good educations and are likely to have families and be under 40 years of age. Experientials' buying habits focus on vigorous outdoor sports—mountain climbing, backpacking, wilderness camping, whitewater canoeing, and rafting. They are also into "do-it-yourself" projects if they relate to making a home. Experiential consumers would be good targets for products from L. L. Bean, hot-air balloon or glider rides, and advertising for the arts.

Societally conscious consumers are into simple living and have great concern over environmental issues. They have a strong sense of societal responsibility and are likely to join the Sierra Club, Greenpeace, the nuclear freeze movement, or Salmon Unlimited. They are interested in smallness of scale and inner growth. They are mainly white and have excellent educations but bimodal incomes (that is, they cluster around the low and high ends of the income scale). These consumers are as likely to live in cities and towns as in villages or the country. Their buying habits have a conservation emphasis, focusing on simplicity and frugality. They would be good targets for energy-saving devices, cars that get high mileage, solar heating, recycling aluminum cans, and the human potential movement. They might be interested in organic gardening, canning food, and freezing home-grown garden produce.

Integrated consumers (2 percent) feel good about themselves and their niche in life. They are tolerant and have a sense of psychological maturity. They are also self-actualizers who take a world view on products and issues, so they would be concerned with the issue of acid rain and might boycott certain products that pollute. They have good to excellent incomes but are bimodal in age. Like societally conscious consumers, their residential pattern is variable. Their occupations are diverse. They want to express themselves and do so in their buying habits, focusing on the

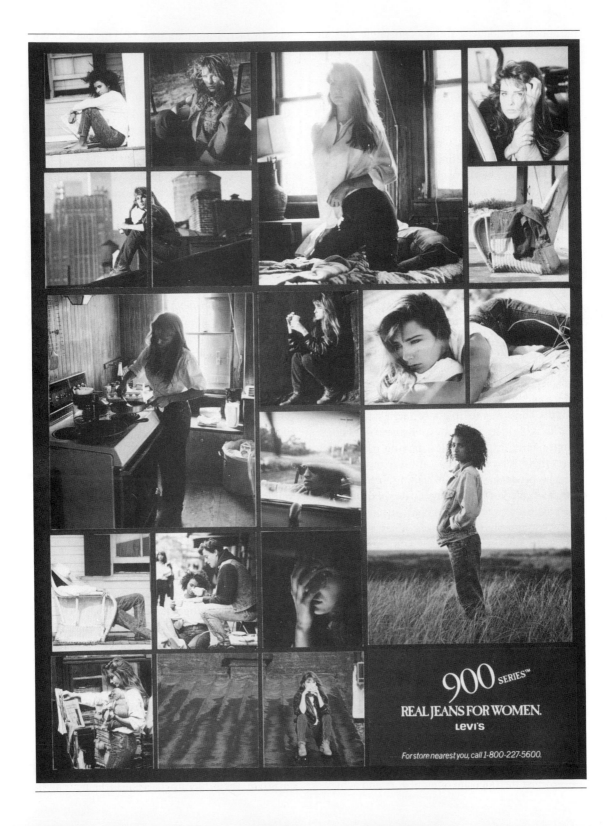

FIGURE 14.8

I-am-me's resent being labeled and want to be individualistic. They are also volatile and dramatic, as this cartoon shows. They usually are "early" baby boomers (born between 1946 and 1955). (*Arlo and Janis* reproduced by permission of NEA, Inc.)

uniqueness of the product in the marketplace. They would be good targets for products that allow for self-expression (for example, pottery throwing). They might also be interested in restoring historic homes, refinishing antiques, or collecting unique things. They are also esthetically inclined and might be good targets for "artistic" products (statuary, art, music, drama, and so on). Integrated consumers are usually "early" baby boomers, that is, born between 1946 and 1955. This market segment is growing rapidly, whereas the numbers of need-driven consumers are declining and the numbers of outer-directed consumers are remaining stable.

VALS is but one kind of psychographic research model or system. All such devices try to "get into the consumer's head" in order to strategically develop salable products and to design advertisements that will move consumers to take sales-related action (for example, product trial, coupon clipping, or going to the point of purchase). As critical consumers of persuasion, we

FIGURE 14.7

Although emulators tend to be male, this is changing as more and more women enter the workplace. (Used by permission of Levi Strauss & Co.)

need to be alert to the degree to which advertisers have psychographically designed ads aimed at us or our market segment.

Sociographics

Sociographics is the study of how, why, and where people gather. Its basic assumption is that "birds of a feather flock together"; that is, people choose to live with or near persons whom they find to be similar to themselves. It is like the combination of geographics (where people live) and demographics (the clusterings of variables). Research in sociographics is done by sampling persons from a given zip code that resembles the kind of neighborhood to which the advertiser believes the product will appeal. Then the ad researchers bring the subjects together to answer a survey that relates to the product and its competitors. Finally, the subjects are put into small groups known as *focus groups*. A leader directs them to discuss the product, its competitors, advantages, disadvantages, and their attitudes toward it.

The researchers then analyze the data and look for patterns in the survey responses and in the focus groups' use of language. They look for recurring words, phrases, or images. These results are then turned over to the ad agency's creative staff, who design messages around the consumer-

"NO, MISS BUCKNER, a FOCUS GROUP is
NOTHING LiKe aN eNCOUNTeR GROUP!"

FIGURE 14.9

Focus groups are used to elicit attitudes toward a product/candidate/issue and to develop actual ad copy. (*Freeze Frame* cartoon from *Advertising Age*, March 7, 1988. Copyright Crain Communications, Inc. Reprinted by permission of Crain Communications and Bill Whitehead.)

generated copy points. Sometimes they even use the exact language of the participants for the ad copy.

Some market research companies compile demographics about a variety of "typical" neighborhoods and sell these data to persons who then can confirm and add to their knowledge about the demographics of a target community. For example, the ACORN ("A Classification of Residential Neighborhoods") system identifies forty-four different residential types and then categorizes subsets of each. Market segment A2, for instance, is composed of "newer suburbs, professionals,

middle-aged families," and the demographics are "similar to A1's but with slightly younger families. Middle-aged and older white families. Children are in their teens." The housing in A2 is "newer than in A1, but still has extremely high values. Almost exclusively single family, owner occupied." The life-style and marketing implications are as follows:

Households in market segment A2 are second only to A1 in terms of investments, leisure activities, and travel. They are heavy spenders on their children, home furnishings, and clothing. They are the heaviest consumers of imported wines and mixed drinks. They drive expensive cars which are sportier than those of A1 households; the second car tends to be a mid-size American car, sometimes a station wagon. They are high on fitness and travel to warm climates.

Knowing this about a market segment tells the advertisers which of its products can most likely be marketed to the segment.

Demographics also show media-use patterns, what parts of the day are devoted to which media, radio format preferences, and so on. All of these data fall into place in designing the ads using sophisticated research techniques. Think how much research goes into ads that are nationally broadcast or printed. Persuaders who use demographics know a great deal about us and our consumer behavior. Nothing — well, almost nothing — in a national ad is accidental. It is all based on highly sophisticated "audience analysis."

FROM RESEARCH TO COPY: THE LANGUAGES OF ADVERTISING

Once the research department has done its job, the results are brought to the agency's creative staff for conversion into attention-getting and "memorable" ad copy. It must not only be believable but should also "sell" the product in the midst of a sea of other ads that clutter print and airwaves. Here is where our interest in persuasion should be greatest. If you have been fine-tuning your ability to analyze persuasive appeals of various types, and if you have become more aware of the nuances of meaning that both verbal and nonverbal communication can carry, then you should be able to get a sense of what copywriters are doing to us each and every day.

John O'Toole, former chairman of the board at Foote, Cone, and Belding (the eighth largest ad agency in the world) makes some interesting observations about reaching the audience in believable ways in his book *The Trouble with Advertising*. He recounts the experience of Albert Lasker, one of the great copywriters of all time and one of the founders of the Lord and Thomas agency. Lasker was handed a note one day in 1904 that said,

> I am downstairs in the saloon, and I can tell you what advertising is. I know that you don't know. It will mean much to me to have you know what it is and it will mean much to you. If you wish to know what advertising is, send the word "yes" down by messenger. John E. Kennedy[34]

Lasker thought he knew what advertising was — it was what N. W. Ayer had defined it as: "Keeping your name before the public." Lasker assumed Kennedy to be a madman, but he was tired of Ayer's limiting concept, so he sent down for Kennedy. They spent an hour in his office and then went to the saloon downstairs, where they stayed till midnight. What Kennedy had said to Lasker led to Kennedy being hired on-the-spot for $28,000 a year — a remarkable salary for 1904. Two years later, he was making $75,000 a year. What had he told Lasker? "Advertising is salesmanship in print."[35]

That statement and philosophy changed the nature of advertising from having an informational function to having a persuasive function, and O'Toole credits Kennedy's definition with bringing reason and logic into advertising planning. More important, it brought the consumer into advertising planning. The same concept applies to ad planning, copywriting, and final production and dissemination of the ad message: The consumer is at the center of the process.

O'Toole believes that the only kind of language — verbal and nonverbal — that can effectively persuade in an advertisement is that which is targeted at the consumer *as an individual and not just one of the masses*. At Foote, Cone, and Belding, the first task for a new product or account is to develop a "personal profile" of the consumer. The consumer is considered a unique individual with whom the client carries on an interpersonal dialogue using advertising as the means of communicating. To quote O'Toole on this: "Advertising works best when it most closely approximates a dialogue between two human beings."[36] He also says, "Regarding the other party as a person rather than as people . . . making that person know you recognize him as an individual rather than as a face in the crowd is going to cause him to respond more positively to you."[37]

O'Toole gives several examples of this kind of personal language and copy, including: "Aren't you glad you use Dial? Don't you wish everyone did?" This slogan addresses the consumer much more personally than the one for another deodorant: "Get off the can. Get on the stick." Or take the Sears DieHard battery ad copy that follows a demonstration of the battery in action: "The DieHard. Starts your car when most other batteries won't." What about "You're not getting older; You're getting better"? Finally, consider the copy for a farm implement — International Harvester's rotary cultivator: "Clean up your middles. Condition your soil. Mulch your beds. All at 14 acres an hour."[38] These copy lines are aimed at an individual, not at just another cipher in the masses. They fulfill Fairfax Cone's memo to O'Toole: "Let us make every advertisement that we make *personal*. Let us aim it at just *one* person, just as we would in face-to-face contact."[39]

That kind of ad copy gets what O'Toole calls "the nod of agreement." This phrase is close to what Schwartz means by resonance: Consumers recognize some part of themselves and/or their experiences in the words and/or visuals of the ad. The nod of agreement is part of what O'Toole calls "the implicit contract" between advertiser and consumer. Although the contract is unwritten, it is clearly understood by even the most naive consumer. The implied contract is simply that advertisers will try to promote a product but won't tell you about their competitors. The competition is already doing that. They will try to present their product in its best light, but they won't mislead you, lie to you, or bore you.

In return for the opportunity to promote their product, advertisers subsidize programs, journalism, documentaries, the news, music, sports events, entertainment, and more. Sometimes we are fooled and purchase a product that is not all it has been "puffed up" to be. In that case, we may return the product or never buy it again, and we can warn other consumers not to buy the product. O'Toole admits that there have been misleading and even outright false advertisements across the years, but he is quick to point out that consumers soon identify those ads and then ignore them.[40]

O'Toole contends that "American consumers are the canniest of creatures. . . . And they are powerful [because of] . . . their refusal to repurchase."[41] That is why 80 percent of the new products brought out on the market in any given year *fail*.

Although O'Toole's assurances are sincere, consumers should still be aware of some of the kinds of appeals advertisers make that do not actually "lie" or that are not obviously "fraudulent," but that "bend" the truth without actually fracturing it. Several of the more interesting, useful, and lively discussions of the topic of "misleading" advertising are found in the work done by Carl Wrighter and Hugh Rank.

LANGUAGE USE IN ADVERTISING: WRIGHTER'S MODEL

We have been looking at how advertisers use words in media messages. We know that symbols are the basic raw material of persuasion, and we know that words are central carriers of symbolic meaning. So we need to look at how clever persuaders can use words and at how these work in ad messages. Carl Wrighter, a former adman, in his book *I Can Sell You Anything*, focuses on some of the key words that he thinks are used to deceive us.[42] He calls them *weasel words* because they allow persuaders to seem to say something without ever really saying it. These words let sources weasel their way out of a promise. These are key tip-offs to the kind of pitch we need to guard against. Weasel words are most frequently seen in print, as opposed to electronic, media. When these tactics are used in a TV commercial, for instance, the sound and sight scripts demonstrate the claim, whereas the words themselves have less impact.

"Helps"

The word *helps* is a clever one. It seems to offer aid or perhaps even a cure. We hear that Listerine mouthwash *helps* prevent colds. Even if you get a cold, it *helps* you feel better right away. What is the promise here? Can you expect that you will feel better in a few days if you use Listerine? If you did, could you say your improvement resulted from the *help* Listerine gave? These questions point up the problem with a word such as *helps*. We need to be alert to this often-used weasel word.

"Like"

Another weasel word used in ads is *like*. For instance, there on the printed page is a famous tennis star telling us that driving a Honda Prelude is *like* driving one of those expensive European cars — but for pennies per day and a lot less in overall costs. Or the house brand is *like* the expensive name brands — "we just don't advertise."

You can easily see the deception that can be floated with a word that has as many loopholes as *like*. Cindy Crawford is supposed to be *like* young women all over the world. Soap operas claim to be *like* real life.

Perhaps this is the key to many of the words we see and hear. They are loaded with escape hatches. Think of the many promises that are given with the word *like*. A prepared food tastes just *like* homemade. A jug wine tastes *like* the expensive French wines. A facial cream acts *like* "a thousand busy fingers massaging your face." Geritol will make you feel *like* you are a kid again. A BMW hugs the road *like* a cat.

"Virtually"

The weasel word *virtually* resembles *like*, except that it seems to promise even more. The new cotton chamois shirts are *virtually* indestructible. Leatherette feels *virtually like* cowhide. Cascade leaves your dishes and glassware *virtually* spotless. The promise seems so specific. There is only a tiny loophole. But that loophole widens as much as is needed when the customer says that the leatherette wore out after several months or when we find a few spots here and there on the dishes and stemware. If the product did what is claimed, the word *virtually* would not be needed. The same thing applies to the politicians who ask for support for programs that will *virtually* wipe out discrimination.

"As Much As"

The weasel phrase *as much as* tells you *the most* you can expect from a product. Many thought that the policy of publishing Environmental Protection Agency (EPA) mileage estimates in every auto ad would assure honesty. The estimates were what you could expect under best conditions — perfect roads, good weather, fine-tuning of the engine, and so forth. You were promised *as much as* 38 miles per gallon in city driving in a Dodge Colt, but you were not *promised* 38 miles per gallon.

A politician promises to cut taxes by *as much as* 20 percent. We find that this applies to few people. The newscast states that there will be *as much as* ten inches of snow. All these uses of *as much as* aim to maximize the drama of the promise or event to get us to fall for the flimflam.

"Stronger," "Faster," or "Better": The Dangling Comparison

"Anacin fights pain *better* than ordinary aspirin." The promise of that claim lies in the comparison being made. What we are *not* told is *how much* better or better *in what ways*. The makers of Anacin might answer, "One-tenth of one percent better." They could say "better because it contains caffeine." However, they persuade us because the message limits our options. We can compare Anacin only with all other *ordinary* aspirin products. We now have a choice between two: Anacin and another. So the weaseling has two effects: It intensifies the advantages of one brand. At the same time, it limits the options that we consider.

"Everyone says that we have a *better* system of government." In what ways? Compared with what? These are the questions to ask. Entertainment programs imply that it is *better* to be sexy, rich, into sports, and so on. Why? In what ways? Compared with what?

Wrighter gives other weasel words in his book. A good way to find them is to search for words that sound like promises. They often have loopholes: "feels like . . ." or "it is almost . . ." or "can be effective in . . ." or "easier than . . . ," and many others. Sometimes the "faster," "stronger," or "easier" message is only implied, as we see two cars trying to stop on wet pavement, but the one with the Uniroyal radials stops *faster* than the other. In this case we have the dangling comparison. We really don't know what is being compared with what. We need to ask questions such as, "Under what conditions is Product X better, stronger, faster, or safer?" to dig out the key information that will help us make our purchase decisions.

DECEPTIVE CLAIMS IN ADVERTISING

Another kind of deception to which we are exposed in ads is found in claims. Clever sources use claims to attract our attention and to prompt us to buy products, to vote for candidates, or to adopt certain practices. Let us look at several kinds of claims.[43]

The Irrelevant Claim

Some persuaders use ad messages to make claims that sound impressive but are irrelevant if you look at them closely.

You are exposed to such claims whenever you turn on your TV, open a magazine, or tune in your radio. The basic tactic is to make a truthful claim that has little to do with the purpose of the product, plan for change, or idea. Then that claim is dramatized in such a way that the people link the claim with the product, candidate, or movement.

J&B scotch claims to be "rare" and "natural." Why would you want "rare" scotch? What is "natural" about J&B? Are other scotch whiskeys unnatural? If you can't find an answer, chances are you have identified an irrelevant claim.

The Question Claim

Wrighter notes a kind of claim we often see beamed at us through the media: the claim that is hidden by a question. "If you can't trust Prestone, who can you trust?" "Why not buy the original?" "Why not send the very best?" "Would a bunch of guys really go at it this hard just for a Michelob?" "Why not catch a lunker — with Stren monofilament?" are all examples of the question

claim. Notice that the product advantage is only implied. Trusting one's antifreeze is OK, but the question implies that dependability is to be found *only* in Prestone. But we know that other brands of antifreeze are also dependable. Why buy the original? It may be overpriced. Maybe the Michelob is just an afterthought. Will using Stren guarantee that I'll catch a lunker? When you see or hear a question claim, the best response is another question.

The Advantage Claim

Wrighter noted the type of claim that seems to offer some advantage for a product or idea. Mother's noodles claim to be made with 100 percent semolina wheat — so are all the other brands. If you compare the levels of vitamins in several types of breakfast cereal, you will discover that they are all about the same. Most of the protein comes from the milk you add and not from the cereal. Thus there is no advantage in Corn Chex's claim that it is "fortified with six important vitamins and minerals." These are advantages that aren't.

Politicians often claim to have come from humble beginnings, and this is supposed to be an advantage. It may be a real disadvantage from one perspective: People who had humble beginnings may be insecure. They probably had to compete for everyday things, which may limit their educational sophistication, sense of diplomacy, social skills, and ability to communicate with leaders in higher social strata.

Whenever we are faced with a person, product, or idea that claims some significant advantage, we need to ask whether the advantage is real; whether it is exclusive to that person, product, or idea; and whether certain disadvantages might not accompany it.

The Hazy Claim

The hazy claim confuses the buyer or voter. If persuaders can confuse you, you will follow their advice just to be on the safe side. Consider the ad for Dannon yogurt shown in Figure 14.10. It confuses the reader by implying that yogurt eaters live longer. As you read more of the ad copy, you see

Dannon Yogurt may not help you live as long as Soviet Georgians. But it couldn't hurt.

Bagrat Topagua, age 89.

His mother.

There are two curious things about the people of Soviet Georgia. A large part of their diet is yogurt. And a large number of them live to be well over 100.

Of course, many factors affect longevity, and we are not saying Dannon Yogurt will help you live longer. But we will say that all-natural Dannon is high in nutrients, low in fat, reasonable in calories. And quite satisfying at lunch or as a snack.

Another thing about Dannon. It contains active yogurt cultures (many pre-mixed or Swiss style brands don't). They make yogurt one of the easiest foods to digest and have been credited with other healthful benefits.

Which is why we've been advising this: If you don't always eat right, Dannon Yogurt is the right thing to eat.

By the way, Bagrat Topagua thought Dannon was "dzelian kargia." Which means he loved it.

Dannon Milk Products, 22-11 38th Ave. Long Island City, N.Y. 11101.

FIGURE 14.10

The hazy claims about longevity and yogurt may confuse the persuadee enough to try the product, just to be on the safe side. (Used by permission of Dannon Milk Products.)

that the only health claim Dannon can make is that its yogurt, unlike some others (how many? which brands? so what?), has active cultures. The consumer does not know whether it is good to eat Dannon yogurt, yogurt of any kind, or no yogurt. Out of this confusion, Dannon persuades through its slogan: "If you don't always eat right, Dannon yogurt is the right thing to eat." We ought to ask, "Why is it right?" "Who says?" and "With what proof?" when a hazy claim appears.

Again, we can see hazy claims widely used in the world of politics. For example, a politician says that she supports the economic policies of free trade and protective tariffs. These policies, however, are 180 degrees apart, so the result for voters is confusion. If voters watch images, the problem becomes worse. What does it prove when a politician kisses babies or plays baseball or talks about the price of pork? These activities do not tell us much about an elected official's ability to construct policies on education, leisure time, or farm prices. They are likely to confuse the voter and draw attention away from the issues.

The Magic Claim

Wrighter calls this the *mysterious* claim because it refers to a mysterious ingredient or device that makes a better product. I prefer the idea of magic instead.

Noxzema, for example, has a product called "Acne 12," which is claimed to contain a magic, secret ingredient that dermatologists prescribe most. Oxy-Clean contains "a powerful yet gentle medication no ordinary cleanser has." If the manufacturer had a real secret ingredient, they would not tell about it. So if there is turtle oil in a face cream, the oil might be a good binder and not a wrinkle fighter.

Many other kinds of claims are made through the mass media. Wrighter's book points out several. You will discover others as you begin to evaluate advertising messages you receive. The important thing is to maintain a critical attitude. Ask key questions of the claim.

Hugh Rank, who originated the intensify/downplay model discussed in Chapter 1, has out-

lined a five-stage quiz that consumers of persuasion can use to analyze ads, in particular radio or TV spots. Rank's quiz can be useful in analyzing print ads as well as political speeches and pitches that ideological persuaders throw at us. Rank's "30-Second Spot Quiz" is shown in Figure 14.11. Use this quiz to analyze radio and TV spots as well as print ads and other "pitches" aimed at you.

CHANGES IN OUR WORLD: IMPLICATIONS FOR ADVERTISING

Since I began writing the various editions of this book, a number of societal changes have occurred that have had enormous effects on the way we behave as consumers and how critics of persuasion — especially advertising persuasion — have come to look at this field. Consider a few trends. More families now rely on two incomes per household than in 1973, when the first edition was published. This trend has led to many new products. For example: Campbell's "Soup for One" is a single-sized serving of the product, just as Stokely's Singles are servings of vegetables for one person. Who are the targets of such products? Widows and widowers? Single persons? Divorced persons? To some extent yes, but research demonstrated to Campbell's that the eating habits of Americans were in a rapid state of change. Because of the two-income family pattern, meals were not the traditional "family around the dinner table" anymore. Dad was off to his late meeting while Mom was not yet home from her job; Bobby had to ride his bike to soccer practice, and his older sister Susie had to rehearse for the high school play. The perfect solution was to give both Bobby and Susie their choice of a sandwich and their favorite "Soup for One."

FIGURE 14.11

The 30-Second Spot Quiz by Hugh Rank. (Used by permission of Hugh Rank.)

the
30-SECOND SPOT quiz

Based on *The Pitch* © 1982 by Hugh Rank

How to Analyze Ads:
Use this 1-2-3-4-5 sequence of questions, (see next page) to focus on the *"skeleton"* underneath the *"surface variations"* of radio and TV commercials, newspaper and magazine ads.

Recognize that a 30-second-spot TV ad is a **synthesis,** the end product of a complex process in which scores of people (writers, researchers, psychologists, artists, actors, camera crews, etc.) may have spent months putting together the details. TV commercials are often the best *compositions* of our age, skillful combinations of purposeful words and images. Be patient and systematic: **analysis** takes time to sort out all of the things going on at once. **We perceive** these things *simultaneously,* but we must discuss them *sequentially.* Use this 1-2-3-4-5 pattern of "the pitch" as a sequence to start your analysis.

Recognize "surface variations": in 30 seconds, a TV spot may have 40 quick-cut scenes of "good times" (happy people, sports fun, drinking cola); or 1 slow "tracking" scene of an old-fashioned sleighride through the woods, ending at "home" with "Season's Greetings" from an aerospace corporation; or a three-scene drama: a problem suffered by some "friend," a product/solution recommended by a trusted "authority," and a final grateful smile from the relieved sufferer. But, the structure underneath is basically the same.

Recognize our own involvement in a mutual transaction. Persuaders are *benefit-promisers,* but we are *benefit-seekers.* Most ads relate to simple "trade-offs" of mutual benefits: consumers get a pleasure, producers get a profit. However, investigate issues relating to any non-consumer ad; these are paid presentations of only one side of an issue, often involving more than a simple purchase transaction.

Understand that advertising is basically persuasion, not information nor education, *And not coercion!* Many important moral and ethical issues (concerning intent and consequences, priorities, individual and social effects, truth and deception, legal and regulatory problems) are related. The more we know about the basic techniques of persuasion, the better able we are not only to cope with the multiple persuaders in our society, but also to consider these ethical issues.

What ATTENTION-GETTING techniques are used?

Anything unusual? Unexpected? Noticeable? Interesting? Related to:
- **senses:** motions, colors, lights, sounds, music, visuals (e.g., computer graphics, slow-motion)
- **emotions:** any associations *(see list below):* sex, scenery, exciting action, fun, family, pets.
- **thought:** news, lists, displays, claims, advice, questions, stories, demonstrations, contest.
(*Popular TV* **programs** *function as* attention-getters *to "deliver the audience" to advertisers.)*

What CONFIDENCE-BUILDING techniques are used?

- Do you *recognize, know* (from earlier repetition) the **brand name? company? symbol? package?**
- Do you *already know, like,* and *trust* the **"presenters":** the endorsers, actors, models?
- Are these "presenters" **AUTHORITY FIGURES** (expert, wise, protective, caring,)? Or, are they **FRIEND FIGURES** (someone you like, like to be, "on your side"; incl. "cute" cartoons) ?
- What key **words** are used? (*Trust, sincere,* etc.) **Nonverbals?** *(smiles, voice tones, sincere look)*
- In **mail** ads, are computer-written *"personalized"* touches used? On **telephone:** tapes? scripts?

What DESIRE-STIMULATING techniques are used?

(Main part of ad)

Consider (a) **"target audience"** as (b) **benefit-seeking;** and persuaders benefit-promising strategies as focused on (c) **product claims,** or, (d) **"added values"** associated with product.
- a. **Who is the "target audience"?** Are *you?* (If *not,* as part of an unintended audience, are you *uninterested* or *hostile* toward the ad?)
- b. **What's the primary motive of that audience's benefit-seeking?** Use chart at right. Most ads are simple acquisition (*lower left*). Often, such motives co-exist, but one may be dominant. Ads which intensify a **problem,** (that is, a "bad" already hated or feared; *the opposite, or the absence of,* "goods") and then offer the product as a **solution,** are here called **"scare-and-sell"** ads. (*right side*).

To keep a "good" (protection)	To get rid of a "bad" (relief)
To get a "good" (acquisition)	To avoid a "bad" (prevention)

FIGURE 14.11

(continued)

☐ c. **What kinds of product claims are emphasized?** *(use these 12 categories)* what key words, images? Any *measurable* claims? Or are they *subjective opinions, generalized* praise words ("puffery")?

SUPERIORITY *("best")*   STABILITY *("classic")*
QUANTITY *("most")*   RELIABILITY *("solid")*
EFFICIENCY *("works")*   SIMPLICITY *("easy")*
BEAUTY *("lovely")*   UTILITY *("practical")*
SCARCITY *("rare")*   RAPIDITY *("fast")*
NOVELTY *("new")*   SAFETY *("safe")*

☐ d. **Are any "added values" implied or suggested?** Are there words or images which associate the product with some "good" already loved or desired by the intended audience? With such common human needs/wants/desires as in these 24 categories:

"basic" needs: **"territory" needs:**
FOOD *("tasty)*   NEIGHBORHOOD *("hometown")*
ACTIVITY *("exciting")*   NATION *("country")*
SURROUNDINGS *("comfort")*   NATURE *("earth")*
SEX *("alluring")*
HEALTH *("healthy")*   **love & belonging needs:**
SECURITY *("protect")*   INTIMACY *("lover")*
ECONOMY *("save")*   FAMILY *("Mom" "kids")*
                                      GROUPS *("team")*

"certitude" needs:
RELIGION *("right")*   **"growth" needs:**
SCIENCE *("research")*   ESTEEM *("respected")*
BEST PEOPLE *("elite")*   PLAY *("fun")*
MOST PEOPLE *("popular")*   GENEROSITY *("gift")*
AVERAGE PEOPLE *("typical")*   CREATIVITY *("creative")*
                                      CURIOUSITY *("discover")*
                                      COMPLETION *("success")*

  ## Are there URGENCY-STRESSING techniques used?

(Not all ads: but always check.)

☐ If an urgency appeal: What words? *(e.g. Hurry, Rush, Deadline, Sale Ends, Offer Expires, Now.)*
☐ If **no** urgency: is this **"soft sell"** part of a *repetitive, long-term ad campaign* for standard item?

 ## What RESPONSE-SEEKING techniques are used?

Persuaders always seek some kind of response!)

☐ *Are there specific triggering* words used? (Buy, Get, Do, Call, Act, Join, Smoke, Drink, Taste, etc.)
☐ Is there a **specific response** sought? (Most ads: to buy something)
☐ If **not:** is it **conditioning** ("public relations" or "image building") to make us **"feel good"** about the company, to get favorable public opinion on *its* side (against any government regulations, taxes)?

Based on *The Pitch* © 1982 by Hugh Rank   (Teachers may photocopy for classroom use.)

FIGURE 14.11

(continued)

Observe. Understand. Judge. (In *that* sequence!)Observe closely what is explicitly said and shown; consider carefully what may be implied, suggested either by verbal or nonverbal means.

Anticipate Incoming Information. Have some way to sort, some place to store. If you know common patterns, you can pick up cues from bits and fragments, recognize the situation, know the probable options, infer the rest, and even note the omissions. Some persuaders use these techniques (and some observers analyze them) consciously and systematically; others, intuitively and haphazardly.

Categorize, but don't "pigeonhole." Things may be in many categories at the same time. "Clusters" and "mixes" are common. Observers often disagree.

Seek "dominant impressions," but relate them to the whole. You can't analyze *everything*. Focus on what seems (*to you*) the most *noticeable, interesting,* or *significant* elements (e.g. an intense "urgency" appeal, a very strong "authority" figure). By relating these to the whole context of "the pitch," your analysis can be *systematic, yet flexible,* appropriate to the situation.

Translate "indirect" messages. Much communication is *indirect,* through metaphoric language, allusions, rhetorical questions, irony, nonverbals (gestures, facial expressions, tone of voice), etc. Millions of specific concrete ways of communicating something can be grouped in the general abstract categories listed here as "product claims" (3c) and "common needs" (3d). Visuals imply.

Train yourself by first analyzing those ads which explicitly use the full sequence of "the pitch," including "urgency-stressing" and a specific "response-seeking." Always check for this full sequence; when it does not appear, consider what may have been omitted: *assumed* or *implied.* "Soft sell" ads and corporate "image-building" ads are harder to analyze: *less is said, more is implied.*

Practice. Analysis is a skill which can be learned, but needs to be practiced. Take notes. Use print ads. Videotape, if possible; replay in slow motion. No one can "see" or "understand" everything during the actual 30 seconds while watching a TV spot. At best, we pick up a few impressions. Use the pattern of "the pitch" to organize your analysis and aid your memory. Such organization helps to avoid randomness and simple subjectivity.

> **Are ads worth all of this attention?** Ads may not be, but *your mind is* . If we can better learn how to analyze things, to recognize patterns, to sort out incoming information, to see the parts, the processes, the structure, the relationships within things so common in our everyday environment, then it's worth the effort.

Professor Hugh Rank Governors State University Park Forest South, Illinois

FIGURE 14.11

(*continued*)

Another change has been the introduction of 1-800 dialing, which makes it much easier to purchase through catalogs or with direct marketing on television. For two-income families, time is a commodity that has to be "spent" carefully, and mail-order purchasing for oneself or for gifts for others saves time. As a result we have seen an explosion in cataloging — *they save time*. So does eating out, and as a result fast- and specialty-food establishments have proliferated. The average American eats out more than 50 percent of the time.

Retail square footage has increased by about 70 percent in the last decade while disposable consumer income has grown by only about 14 percent in that same time period.[44] This has led to a very competitive marketplace, especially given the amount of disposable income being used for catalog and other direct-marketed products. We now have "pre-Christmas sales" as well as the traditional "post-Christmas sales." The number of large discount chains has increased as well, which has important implications for advertising. For one thing, the amount of advertising will increase because one of the ways to try to beat the competition is to out-advertise them. There will be more sales promotions — coupons, rebates, sweepstakes, celebrities at point of purchase, shelf-talkers, product demonstrations, displays, and so on — a persuasion closely related to advertising. A new video-equipped grocery cart is being tested in several markets by Information Resources, Inc., whose chairman says that whereas most "in-store selling techniques are aimed at selling something without providing any benefits to the consumers, Videocart makes shopping more informative and fun for consumers."[45] The local supermarket's satellite dish antenna receives a new product's advertisement, which replaces the old ad on the store manager's computer. This new ad is transmitted to the shelf space where the product is on display. When a cart passes the transmitter, it triggers the coffee ad on the screen, which is part of the cart. At the checkout counter, the cash register/computer tells which ads triggered a purchase and what path the cart took through the store. In short, there will be more "clutter" for advertisers to try to "break through" and for us to try to sift through.

From an academic point of view, it has finally been recognized that television is a topic worthy of study and criticism and that even the lowly TV spot is a kind of "rhetoric" that needs to be critically analyzed instead of being dismissed out of hand.[46] One resource that is helpful in analyzing the languages of advertising is *The Language of Advertising* by Torben Vestergaard and Kim Schroder.[47] Although the authors are Danish and use only print examples of advertising that are mainly British, some of their ideas are intriguing and, I think, useful in the critical processing of the verbal and nonverbal messages carried in the many advertisements to which we are exposed. Let's explore some of these ideas.

Vestergaard and Schroder begin from a point of view akin to one we have already discussed: Marxism. They point out that advertising is senseless unless goods are sufficiently overproduced so that sellers need to "beat the competition." They note the shift in the United States and other Western democracies from a culture of production to a culture of consumption and of the marketing of goods that people really don't "need." They distinguish between our *material* needs (food, clothing, shelter, and so on) and our *social* needs (for instance, a sense of belonging, self-identity, security, status) and note that material needs and social status are frequently communicated through habits of consumption. In other words, the purchased objects have become *semanticized*, to use the words of Roland Barthes. The kind of clothing, cars, audio equipment, and so on, that we buy has a "meaning" to others with whom we socialize. This permits advertisers to exploit our needs for group affiliation, self-identification, and status.[48]

Vestergaard and Schroder go on to define advertising as a "text" that is meant to be "read" in all its verbal and nonverbal nuances (recall the many "meanings" in the objects falling out of the woman's pockets in the *Ms.* magazine ad). The advertising text has three dimensions:

1. It exists in a particular communication situation.

2. It is a structured unit and has texture.

3. It communicates meaning.

Perhaps the most difficult dimension to understand is the idea of a text having structure and texture. Vestergaard and Schroder provide helpful examples. Take the sentence "The bill is large." It is somewhat ambiguous, because you could be referring to the amount owed or possibly to the size of the sheet of paper on which it is written. Therefore, it lacks structure or *coherence*. But if the sentence is written "The bill is large, but it need not be paid," then we make perfect "sense" of it, and behind the "sense" lies much coherence and meaning:

"The bill is large"	This is unpleasant, because it means that we shall have to pay a large amount of money.
"but"	Nevertheless there is no need to worry for

"it need not be paid."[49]

So sometimes structure is tied to coherence. At other times it may be tied to the information content of the ad. As an example of sentence structure, Vestergaard and Schroder cite this copy from an ad in *Cosmopolitan*:

"An automatic applicator gently smooths on soft creme or high-shine colour, for a smooth silky finish that lasts. And lasts."

and

". . . colours that look lastingly tempting. Longer."[50]

Here, we have two sentence fragments — "And lasts" and "Longer" — which could have as easily been included in the sentences that precede them. Why split them up? Because the advertiser has cut two sense-making units into four, thus encouraging the reader to focus on the product benefits four times instead of two. The advertiser wants to make as many product-benefit claims as possible in a given space, or time, and wrenching sentence in-

dependency can give them four shots at you instead of two.

Now consider how specific words can structure meaning:

"Which of these continental quilt patterns will suit your bedroom best?"

versus

"All of these continental quilt patterns will suit your bedroom."

versus

"One of these continental quilt patterns will suit your bedroom better than the others."

The first version, which appeared in *Reader's Digest*, would be the most effective according to Vestergaard and Schroder, because it presupposes the other two versions.[51] In other words, reading the first sentence makes you decide which quilt pattern is best, and that automatically makes you accept that one or all would be best.

Another technique that can give an ad structure or texture is the drama implied in many ads. Vestergaard and Schroder use the work of A. J. Griemas and his pairs of terms, which are used to describe a fundamental drama in folk tales and myths:[52]

subject — object
helper — opponent
giver — receiver

An example of how this model can be used in analyzing the verbal and nonverbal languages of an ad is shown in an ad for Avon. The visual, or nonverbal, part takes up the upper two-thirds of the page. It shows a mature woman standing behind a younger woman who is trying to put on makeup. The headline reads, "I enjoy helping other women to look good," and the copy then goes on to explain that by being an Avon representative, you can bring all of the wonderful Avon products into customers' homes. Furthermore, Avon products have a "no quibble guarantee."[53]

The "subject" is the young woman, and her "opponent" is her uncertainty. The "helper" — the Avon representative — solves this problem by bringing a "giver" — Avon products — to her door. The "receiver" is thus "rescued" from the opponent by the product.

Vestergaard and Schroder point out several other concepts that contribute to the structure and texture of advertisements. The important thing is to try to take the ad apart, bit by bit, verbally and nonverbally, and see what it is *really* saying and how it works — "deconstruct" the ad, in other words.

They go on to point out the traditional task of the ad copywriter as having five steps:[54]

1. Attract attention.
2. Arouse interest.
3. Stimulate desire.
4. Create conviction.
5. Get action.

Attracting Attention

The easiest way to attract attention is by putting the product's name next to a visual of the product. Far more effective is to also describe a product benefit. For example, the sentence "At last, an entirely **NEW** collection of beautiful underwear and lingerie" is next to a model wearing some of the lingerie. She is standing next to a starburst balloon that has the words "**NEW** Glamourwear Catalog" in it. The words "At last" imply that there has never before been such a large collection available. The word **NEW**, boldfaced and in caps, ties into the exploding balloon, thus attracting attention and creating unity of appeal in the ad.

Another way to attract attention is to ask a question of the reader/viewer: "Why don't you come back to Folgers?" Or use the word *when* as in "When the day is done, have a cold one — Coors, the Rocky Mountain reward." Naming the user also captures attention: "Contact lens users — Now you can have all day comfort with Comfordrops."

Naming the consumer is even more effective when coupled with some kind of flattering statement about the user: "For the outdoorsman who has everything; give him a Schrade Knife." Other ways of attracting attention are the use of puns, metaphors, parallelism, or rhymes. For example, "Cutex Strongnail with nylon for long, strong, beautiful nails" is the headline beneath a beautiful female hand holding a long, durable, 16-penny carpenter's nail. The pun is visual as well as verbal.

Creating Interest, Desire, and Conviction

Vestergaard and Schroder also say that a good way to get audience attention and then to create interest is to ask a question that the reader or viewer probably cannot answer. This provokes curiosity and usually leads the audience to interact with the advertisement in some way: reading the copy, looking at the visuals, or even physically interacting with it (scratch 'n sniff, for example).

One example of this tactic is to ask a question that leads to a true/false "quiz" that the reader is supposed to answer. For example, the headline of a full-page, four-color ad by General Motors Parts asks, "Do you know where your next fender is coming from?" The readers most likely have to answer "No, why should I?" which leads them to the ad copy to satisfy their curiosity: "America's body shops are being flooded with imitation parts. Look-alike doors. Copycat hoods. Imitation bumpers, grilles, fenders and more. . . . These not-so-exact replicas seldom measure up to General Motors original specifications. . . . Insist on genuine GM parts."[55] This ad copy is designed not only to answer the attention-getting headline but also to create interest, desire, and conviction in the reader/viewer by pointing out product benefits or by presenting the *unique selling proposition* (USP), mentioned earlier. Again, notice the use of sentence fragments — "Look-alike doors" and "Copycat hoods" — to give the advertiser extra "shots" at the reader.

A problem in today's crowded marketplace is that most products are "me too" imitations of the original, and most of the USPs tend to be esthetic. All dog food, for instance, looks pretty much alike — either like pebbles if it is dry or like glop if it is canned. But look at what Gaines Burger did. In the first place, its name sounds and the product looks like hamburger — the all-American favorite food. Of course, its redness is not natural — it comes from an additive. It won't hurt your dog, but it will cause you to make a link with a past experience: buying fresh red hamburger (which is also not naturally red).

Another tactic used for creating interest, desire, and conviction is to stress the "high quality" of the product if it is a "me too" product. High quality is a slippery thing to prove, which is why the word is used so often in ads. If an advertiser says their product is the lowest-priced in town, that can be verified as true or false, which is why you do not often see that statement. Instead, advertisers more frequently say that they will "meet or beat" any price. But if they say the product has the best quality for the price, they are not likely to be called on to prove their claim. We all know that quality is not "job 1" at Ford — productivity and resulting profit are the real job 1.

One way to stress quality is to use a well-known celebrity (who is somehow connected with the product) to offer a testimonial on the product's quality.[56] Another approach is to appeal to the reverence we hold toward anything scientific by including some scientific-sounding ingredient such as "Platformate," "retsyn," or "DZM-21." An advertiser can also make a "scientific" claim: "The pain reliever recommended by a majority of doctors and hospitals" is one example. Or the spokesperson might be dressed in a laboratory coat and standing in a lab with microscopes, test tubes, and so on, in the background. This "scientist" then tells about the product benefits.

A final way to gain interest, desire, and conviction is to give the advertised product credibility by claiming that it is compatible with a greater goal such as cleaning up the environment in some way. For example, some paper bags have the store's name and logo printed on them and make the claim that the bags are "100 percent biodegradable" or "made from 100 percent recycled paper." In fact, most, if not all, paper bags are biodegradable and are made from recycled paper.

Getting Action

Any salesperson will tell you that the critical and usually the hardest thing to do is to "close" the sale — in other words, to get action. "Buy now" would seem to be the most direct call to action, but Vestergaard and Schroder found the word *buy* in only two advertisements in their analysis of the ten magazine issues on which their book is based.[57] However, there are other ways to say "buy now" without using the word *buy*. For example, "act now," "phone now," and "send now" say the same thing as "buy now" but avoid the negative connotations of the word *buy*. Other urgency-stressing words and phrases can be the call to action: "While supplies last," "Offer Good until . . . ," "24-hour sale," and so on. These are what Vestergaard and Schroder call *directive language*.[58] They found that 32 percent of the ads they studied used one form or another of this type of language. Directive language falls into three categories:

1. *The imperative clause, which composes 65 percent of directive language, and which gives an order*. "Get some today" is one example. My favorite is related to a fishing lure supposedly in short supply — the Shadrap. The ad copy for it read: "The Rapala company was only able to send 125,000 Shadraps to the U.S. — If you see one, grab it!"

2. *Other less directive and more suggestive language to encourage the reader or viewer to buy*. This approach made up another 12 percent of the sample. An example is the "negated interrogative" as in "Isn't it time you tried Dial?" A softer version of this is "Why not try Dial?" Even less directive is "Dial is worth a try." And in the weakest version, the directions are not directly attributed to the reader or viewer but to a reference group: "For people who believe a deodorant bath

soap should also be gentle on the skin, there's Dial with lanolin."

3. *Directive language that invites the reader or viewer to send for details, use the trial sample, or remember the product.* It represents about 23 percent of the sample. Sometimes these appeals are designed to get a sale, but more frequently, they are used to create "qualified leads" that can be followed up by a telephone call and/or a visit by the salesforce. If a person sends in for a free pamphlet on energy saving, for example, he or she is probably a good prospect ("qualified lead") for storm windows, aluminum siding, and energy-efficient furnaces. This lead-generating purpose is usually used for high-priced, durable goods.

Although only two of the ads investigated by Vestergaard and Schroder used the word *buy*, only twenty other verbs made up nearly 78 percent of the directive or suggestive appeals. They were:

try, ask for, take, send for, call/make, come on, hurry, come/see/give/remember/discover, serve/introduce, choose/look for.[59]

Gender and Age in Ad Copy

Vestergaard and Schroder also note that market segments can be targeted by verbal and nonverbal (visual) language. In an example using two almost identical ads for "Simplicity" pads by Kotex, they note that the ads' language and visuals are used to target younger and older women's market segments. In the "older woman" ad (titled "Boat Trip"), a woman, her husband, and their two children are going on a boat trip. She is in shorts and is the "caretaker" of her family, as shown in a scene where she provides them with a picnic lunch, soda pop, and so on, from the cooler. The ad copy reads, "There was so much to see on our boat trip, we stayed longer than I planned, but I felt safe all day. I'm glad I switched." There is a picture of the product next to the woman. In the "younger woman" ad (titled "First Flat"), the visual layout is similar, but here, it is moving day, and people are carrying boxes and furniture up

some stairs. In other shots, some people are going through cartons while others are stacking things on shelves. The ad copy reads, "Moving into my first flat was great. We had such fun. Sorting things took ages. Everyone stayed longer than I planned. Still I felt safe and secure. I'm glad I switched." The phrase "my first flat" clearly targets the younger women's segment, whereas the emphasis on family in the "Boat Trip" targets the older women's segment. In both cases, Vestergaard and Schroder maintain that the product is *semanticized* and that a process of *signification* is taking place — that is, objects or products come to signify a given lifestyle and a given set of values.[60]

Vestergaard and Schroder note that gender is used in ads, not only to target a market segment but also to work as an ideological device to define what a man or a woman ideally is in one or more subsets of the masculine or feminine roles.[61] Their argument strongly resembles one made earlier in the sections titled "The Man's Man" and "The Woman's Woman," and their examples are enlightening. They compared the number of ads for certain product types in single issues of three magazines: *Cosmopolitan, Woman* (a British publication), and *Playboy*. For example, *Cosmo* carried twenty-six hygiene-oriented ads for products such as deodorants, shampoos, toothpaste, sanitary napkins, and so on, whereas *Woman* carried ten and *Playboy* had three. However, in the food and detergent product category, *Woman* had thirty-one ads, *Cosmopolitan* had five, and *Playboy* had none. The results of the ad count for beer and spirits are not surprising: *Cosmopolitan* carried three; *Woman* carried none; and *Playboy* had twenty-five. In the technologically oriented product category (photography, radios, calculators, and similar items), *Playboy* carried thirty-eight ads, whereas *Woman* carried none and *Cosmopolitan* had only two.

What do these figures suggest? First, that there are at least two segments in the women's market and, second, that certain product types have definite gender-related associations. The *Woman* readers get a picture of the woman's role as a homemaker who has the responsibility for meals, home maintenance, and so forth. Though she should still be attractive, this is not the focus of her life. The *Cosmopolitan* woman, on the other hand, is concerned with the feminine "ideal" of beauty—and how to achieve it.

Men are also concerned with their appearance, but the products they use are for improving appearance (clothing, for example), whereas the feminine "ideal" *rejects* the natural features of women's bodies—hair, eyes, skin, teeth, nails, and so on.[62] In a pair of ads for Close-Up toothpaste, the ad targeting women has the headline "Your perfume turns him on. Will your breath turn him off?" and the toothpaste is on a dressing table surrounded by a lot of perfume bottles. The male-targeted ad has the same copy but its headline reads "You keep your body fresh. But is your breath a little stale?" The setting is a bathroom counter with shaving paraphernalia. Both ads close with the caption "Close-Up—Because life is full of them."

Within the women's market, Vestergaard and Schroder found several subsets or "ideologies" being expressed in the advertisements they analyzed. For instance, "the ideal of domesticity" features what a good Mom does—throws birthday parties, has Pillsbury refrigerated chocolate chip cookies on hand, depends on Kool Aid, and looks attractive when her husband comes home. A product named "Radox Herbal Bath Oil" depicts a worn-out woman surrounded by a jumble of toys. The ad promises: "We could make you a joy to come home to."[63]

Another subset of the women's market is called "the strait jacket of the beauty ideal." This ideal depicts women as having to be in constant competition with other women for the approval of their spouse, boss, lover(s), and other men they encounter. The copy for a product named "Aqua-maid" demonstrates this ideal: "Don't let motherhood spoil your bustline. . . . Thousands of women have used Aqua-maid to keep their bustlines firm and youthful—why don't you join them?"[64] Here, the woman is an object to be admired by men and critiqued by other women. This "gossip" motivation for the beauty ideal uses pitches such as,

"Will they talk about your unwanted hair behind your back?"

More recently, another subset of women has been appealed to through "the independent woman ideal." In 1982, *Cosmopolitan* decided to address this market. Their ads were populated by women working in offices in fashionable and rather formal clothing, supposedly to give them a more assertive image. The ad copy frequently gave these women a logical and investigative approach to decision making and then tied that image to the product. "I trust the facts" reads the headline for such an ad, "But first I check them out. It's the only way to feel confident when you're working against time and have important decisions to make." The rest of the copy goes on to give the reader the facts on the product—Tampax.[65]

Men who are featured in ads directed at women are either admirers, macho, or fathers and family men. An ad for British Gas stresses that both the husband and the wife made the decision to buy a gas stove. The male model in the ad appears to be kind, gentle, and intellectual, and it is clear from the ad copy that he knows about cooking. More frequently, however, men are depicted as "sexual animals" who want women to be either seductees or servants. Consider the names of some after-shave lotions: Brut, Iron, English Leather, Chaps, and Musk. And then there are such male-oriented slogans as: a martini you can have "before and after sailing, golf, riding. Before and after . . . just about after anything," and you are advised to "make every day your Brut day," to "carry a big stick," and to "give it your best shot."[66] An ad for Singapore Airlines reads, "Gentle hostess in your sarong kebaya . . . Singapore girl you're a great way to fly," demonstrating the servant role for women, whereas English Leather is "the civilized way to roar, . . . Earthy. Primitive. Fiercely masculine."[67]

The other approach to the macho male is through various kinds of heavy-duty (never "light-duty" or "moderate-duty") equipment used in male-dominated activities such as fishing, hunting, polo, lacrosse, handball, or rugby. An ad for the Rapala fillet knife is a good example of this kind of appeal. The Rapala fillet knife has "more guts than any knife in the world." Of course the word "guts" is the key macho signifier. This kind of macho male drives a four-wheel-drive vehicle, doesn't smoke a "low tar" cigarette, wouldn't mess with a "lite" beer, and buys his clothes from Eddie Bauer, with the exception of his cowboy boots.

Another male ideal is that of the assertive, logical, and cool decision maker. He owns a certain kind of automobile, drinks martinis or scotch (usually either Dewar's or Chivas). He smokes a particular cigarette; uses a special aftershave; plays golf, tennis, or polo on Sunday afternoons; and always reads *The Wall Street Journal*.

Vestergaard and Schroder also discuss how verbal and nonverbal language is used in class appeals to make positive or negative ideological appeals about the dominant system, the subordinate system, and the radical system.[68] And they address other ideological appeals to "youth and leisure"[69] and various psychological aspects of contemporary life — loneliness, insecurity, tension, distrust of the present economic system and "up-tight" moral conventions. You may want to examine these issues or others, and you will find that examples of them are all around us.[70]

SUBLIMINAL PERSUASION AND ADVERTISING

Subliminal persuasion is a controversial topic.[71] In this means of persuading, the message is either so brief or so disguised that it is not consciously processed by the receivers. For example, the soundtrack of the film *Jaws* had shrieks recorded at the precise points where the filmmakers expected real screams from the viewers. The subliminal cue or recorded scream triggered screams in the theater audiences. Of course, people who saw the show told their friends about how many people in the audience screamed during the film, thus advertising it better than any newspaper, radio, or TV ad could ever do. In other instances, hazy messages are included in films, photos, and soundtracks.

These enter our subconscious and may prompt us to action.

Subliminal persuasion has been tested in various situations. In one of its early trials, "buy popcorn" was momentarily inserted in several frames of a movie. Audiences stormed the popcorn stand when the supply was sold out. The message registered in the viewer's subconscious and created a compulsion to buy popcorn. Finally, the frustrated viewer *had* to act. At another time, viewers were exposed to a hidden message to call a certain phone number. The lines were supposedly busy for days, and callers reported that they felt compelled to call that number even though they did not even know what it was for. The technique seemed to be so powerful that it was barred from use by the radio and television industry following pressure from the Federal Communications Commission.[72] However, this did not forbid the use of subliminal messages in print and film media. In 1972, a corporation marketing movies to airlines announced that it would be selling spots for subliminal ads. Over a dozen commercial research firms in Chicago and New York offer services in producing subliminal messages to advertisers.[73] Subliminal messages were used in the film *The Exorcist*, leading to a personal injury lawsuit against Warner Brothers over an alleged accident during a screening, which was attributed to a subliminally embedded message.[74] Subliminal researcher Hal Becker used auditory subliminal messages to treat a number of psychological problems. Becker argued that subliminal persuasion could be used nationwide to reduce alcoholism, drug abuse, dangerous driving, and various phobias. He also recommended using subliminal messages to discourage shoplifting in stores by mixing messages about honesty and getting caught if you shoplift with the piped-in music.[75] The CIA has had a long and continuing interest in how subliminal communication might be used in intelligence work, especially in espionage and counterespionage.[76]

Wilson Bryan Key, an advertising researcher and college professor, decided to look at the possibility that messages could be "embedded" into the visuals used in magazine advertising. He was struck by the need to touch up by airbrush in certain magazine advertisements. For example, Key notes that most liquor ads need airbrushing because the ice cubes in the glasses melt under the hot lights needed for magazine-quality photos. As long as the persuaders were airbrushing in the ice cubes, Key reasoned, why wouldn't they consider airbrushing in a subtle message such as the words *buy* or *good*? The persuader needs to get maximum effect for the advertising dollar. We know that basic human needs are the most motivating and that themes of sex and combat are central in most people's fantasy worlds.

Operating from those premises, Key believed that it was likely that ad designers would try to embed sexual messages into ads to arouse readers. He tested his hypothesis with a Gilbey's gin ad in which the word *sex* seemed to be airbrushed into the ice cubes and in which other parts of the layout continued the seduction theme. He thought he detected phallic symbols, reflections that depicted various stages in seduction, and so on. Now, these vague airbrushed words and symbols might all have been in Key's head, so he tested 1000 people by showing them the ad and asking them to put into words the feelings they had while looking at the ad. None of the 1000 was told what to look for, and none had heard of or knew of subliminal techniques. Although 38 percent did not respond at all, the remaining 62 percent reported that the ad made them feel "sensual," "aroused," "romantic," "sexy," and even "horny" in several cases.[77] It is possible that this finding was accidental, but Key reports having replicated the test with several ads with similar results. It is also possible that the advertiser does not consciously put subliminal messages into the ads — that they are accidental. I suppose it really does not matter as long as there are receiver effects.

The point of persuasion is to get people to change their behavior or beliefs. We assume that any changes ought to be in source-intended ways, but the effect can be accidental and not related to the source. Of course, if the advertisers really were trying to persuade by manipulating the subconscious, that would raise some ethical issues, as we saw in Chapter 2. However, if an advertising agency did use subliminal techniques, they would probably deny it, as many agencies have done since the publication of Key's book. So whether or not the messages are there as a strategy of the source, the message has effects that correlate with Key's hypothesis that symbolic embeds (usually sexually oriented) affect audiences. Key advises us to become critical receivers by looking beyond the surface message in any ad and searching for elements in the background, in the lighting, in the potential symbolic messages. This will alert you to an ad's hidden meaning and may train you as an "embed spotter." He says that the ad copy, layout, and characters should tip you off to any potential embeds. Whether or not you see the embedded sex symbols, you can get cued to possible subliminal persuasion by looking at ads more critically and by trying to determine what they suggest without saying.

Consider the two perfume ads in Figures 14.12 and 14.13. The first ad is called "The Promise Made." The second is called "The Promise Kept." Use Key's technique to see whether you find any subtle messages here. First, note the actual words that are included in the ad. Then see whether they may imply dual meanings. If so, search for visual clues in the ad that would substantiate the implied meaning. Observe what has changed between "The Promise Made" and "The Promise Kept." The champagne bottle is empty, the phone is off the hook, the fire has died down, the woman's shoes are on the dais, the flowers on the left seem to have bloomed in the heat, and the woman's earrings are off, as is her stole.

In the early 1980s, the "dancing" logo of the Danskin Company was "hidden" in each of its ads, much as *Playboy* "hides" its rabbit motif on each *Playboy* cover. Subliminal persuasion devices are being marketed as aids in self-improvement, as seen in Figure 14.14.

A more important issue is whether subliminal messages can be effective in persuasion. The president of the American Psychological Association's Division of Consumer Psychology says,

FIGURE 14.12

What kind of promise is being made? (Courtesy Lanvin
Parfums Co., New York.)

FIGURE 14.13

What differences imply that the promise was kept?
(Courtesy Lanvin Parfums Co., New York.)

FIGURE 14.14

Subliminal behavior modification is now a multibillion-dollar business, with many users testifying to its effectiveness. (*Arlo and Janis* reprinted by permission of NEA, Inc.)

"Absolutely. . . . The controversy has always been over *changing* people's attitudes. That you can't do. What you can do is *trigger* a prior attitude or predisposition" (emphasis added).[78] Note how familiar to us that statement is — the most effective persuasion uses information already in the audience. Effective persuaders get messages out of their audiences, not into them.

There are several sides to the subliminal persuasion controversy. The ad people say they never use the stuff, and people such as Key say that our world is loaded with subliminal seducers. Interested observers also differ. Some say that Key is like the man who responded with "sex" in a Rorschach test to every inkblot presented by the psychiatrist. When accused of being preoccupied with sex, the patient countered that it was the doctor who collected all the "dirty" pictures. My position is that if it is possible to persuade through subliminal messages — sexual or otherwise — then someone is probably doing it.

I am not alone in my belief. A University of Utah professor of chemistry and president of Innovations Consulting, Inc., has tested the use of subliminal suggestion during sleep and recently advised Oak Ridge, Tennessee, nuclear scientists that they could use the method to increase productivity and creativity. Subliminal tapes have become a multibillion-dollar business, with many users being "true believers" in the method.[79] In another case, Dallas radio station KMEZ AM-FM regularly broadcast subliminal messages to "stop smoking" as part of the American Cancer Society's "Great American Smokeout" after checking it out with the FCC. The FCC doesn't consider paid announcements containing subliminals exactly illegal but as "against the public interest." In the Dallas case, however, the message was considered a socially desirable message.[80]

Of course certain ads that use sex aren't at all subliminal about their messages. The Calvin Klein ads for Obsession for men are good examples. Others border on the subliminal: The message is hazy but clear enough to give you the idea the advertiser wants you to get. A good example is the campaign to promote Travel Fox sneakers. With a tiny budget and facing competition such as Nike and Reebok, the company hired a Swedish agency, Hall & Cederquist, which created ads for Travel Fox sneakers that had very few words in them — only that the shoes were made of leather. The visuals showed various permutations of a man and woman wearing the shoes and in various "positions" just sexually distinguishable. One has them in the "missionary" position. Another ad has the woman's bare buttocks placed firmly on the man's

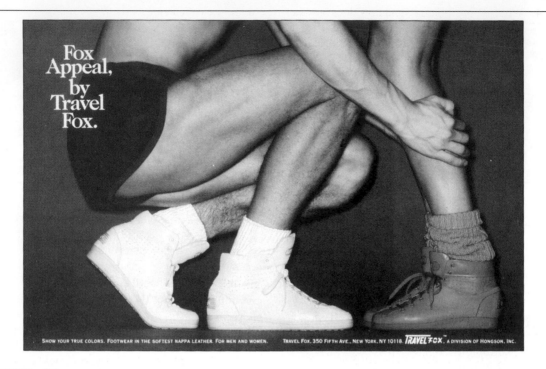

FIGURE 14.15

In this ad for Travel Fox sneakers, the words *Fox* and *appeal* tell you what is going on as we see a man and woman obviously in a sexual position. (Used by permission of Hall & Cederquist Advertising, Inc.)

shoulders. And the one shown in Figure 14.15 clearly shows the man and woman in a suggestive position. Sales in the New York test market tripled in a year.[81]

every day in advertising. This chapter has been only an attempt at showing you the tip of the tip of the iceberg. We need to keep in mind the idea that advertising is really just a map, not the territory.

REVIEW AND CONCLUSION

There is a great deal of controversy on the issue of the use of sex in advertising, especially the use of subliminal sexual images, but also on the more explicit use of sexual appeals. As one critic put it, "Cut the copy, crank up the copulation."[82] As persuadees, we need to take that second look before tumbling for the product just because it promises us a more abundant and varied sex life.

It takes many books to even begin to cover the various kinds of persuasion we are exposed to

QUESTIONS FOR FURTHER THOUGHT

1. How much money is spent for advertising in the United States on a per-person basis compared to that spent in other countries?

2. Why might advertising reflect the values and norms of a culture?

3. What might a Marxist critic say about the purpose of advertising?

4. What is "positioning" and how does it relate to the *creneau*?

5. What are some of the problems of an "over-communicated society"?

6. What is the "product explosion" and how does it affect us?

7. What does "breaking through the clutter" mean?

8. Why is "American made" an example of positioning?

9. What product features can serve as *creneaus*?

10. Explain the difference between demographics, sociographics, and psychographics.

11. What is the "muppie" market segment?

12. What is a DINK?

13. What is the VALS system, and how does it work?

14. What are "focus groups," and what is their purpose?

15. What is the ACORN system, and how does it work?

16. What are some of the "languages" of advertising? Give examples.

17. How does advertising research lead to advertising copy? Give examples.

18. What are "weasel words"? Give examples.

19. What are some deceptive claims? Give examples.

20. What is meant when we say that a product has become "semanticized"? Give examples.

NOTES

1. Al Ries and Jack Trout, *Positioning: The Battle for Your Mind* (New York: McGraw-Hill, 1986), p. 6.

2. *Ibid.*

3. *Ibid.*, pp. 5–9.

4. *Ibid.*, p. 6.

5. Michael Schudson, *Advertising, The Uneasy Persuasion: Its Dubious Impact on American Society* (New York: Basic Books, 1984), p. 9.

6. Ries and Trout, *op. cit.*, p. 7.

7. *Ibid.*

8. *Ibid.*, p. 14.

9. *Ibid.*

10. *Ibid.*, p. 21.

11. Personal conversation with Don Devale, President, The Valley Company, a Division of Kidde, Inc.

12. Ries and Trout, *op. cit.*, p. 26.

13. *Ibid.*, p. 27.

14. *Ibid.*, p. 30.

15. *Ibid.*, p. 33.

16. *Ibid.*, p. 34.

17. *Ibid.*, p. 54.

18. *Ibid.*, p. 54.

19. Charmaine Dollas, "Butterball Turkeys: An Examination of Advertising Theory and Practice," Master's "starred paper," Department of Journalism, Northern Illinois University, Fall 1986.

20. Ries and Trout, *op. cit.*, p. 58.

21. Charmaine Dollas, "A Description of Packaging Design as a Medium of Communication," Master's "starred paper," Department of Journalism, Northern Illinois University, Fall 1986, pp. 12–14.

22. Ries and Trout, *op. cit.*, Chapter 8.

23. *Ibid.*, Chapter 9.

24. Terry Gallonoy, *Down the Tube: Or Making Television Commercials Is Such a Dog-Eat-Dog Business, It's No Wonder They're Called Spots* (Chicago: Henry Regenery Company, 1970), p. 3.

25. "Happy 65th Birthday to 5,500 Americans — Daily," *Chicago Tribune*, April 20, 1988, sec. 8, "Silver Years," p. 10.

26. John McDonough, "Poll Probes the Status of New Trier's '60 Class," *Chicago Tribune*, September 21, 1986, sec. 2, p. 7.

27. John McDonough, "Class Picture," *Chicago Tribune Magazine*, November 11, 1990, pp. 14–18.

28. *Ibid.*, p. 15.

29. Bob Greene, "Wooing Boomers in Brilliant Orange," *Chicago Tribune*, date unknown.

30. *Advertising Age*, September 21, 1987, p. 68.

31. Michael L. Rothchild, *Advertising: From Fundamentals to Strategies* (Lexington, MA: D. C. Heath, 1987), pp. 55–56.

32. Arnold Mitchell, *Nine American Lifestyles: Who We Are and Where We Are Going* (New York: Macmillan, 1983).

33. James F. Engel, Roger D. Blackwell, and Paul W. Miniard, *Consumer Behavior*, 5th ed. (Chicago: The Dryden Press, 1986), pp. 256–257.

34. John O'Toole, *The Trouble with Advertising* (New York: Times Books, Random House, 1985), p. 9.

35. *Ibid.*, p. 10.

36. *Ibid.*, p. 122.

37. *Ibid.*, pp. 110–111.

38. *Ibid.*, pp. 96–97.

39. *Ibid.*, p. 86.

40. *Ibid.*, p. 24.

41. *Ibid.*, p. 21.

42. Carl Wrighter, *I Can Sell You Anything* (New York: Ballantine Books, 1972).

43. *Ibid.*, Chapter 3, "A Baker's Dirty Dozen of Claims," pp. 41–76.

44. Personal conversation with Ted Spiegel of *Spiegel's Catalog* at The Professor's Institute of the Direct Marketing Association, June 6, 1986.

45. Charles Storch, "Humble Grocery Cart Now a Video Ad Vehicle," *Chicago Tribune*, May 1, 1988, Tempo section, pp. 1, 5.

46. For examples of this trend toward treating ads as "rhetoric" or persuasion worthy of critical analysis, see Judith Williamson, *Decoding Advertisements: Meaning and Ideology in Advertising* (London: Marion Boyars, 1977); Neil Postman, *Amusing Ourselves to Death: Public Discourse in the Age of Show Business* (New York: Penguin Books, 1987); Edwin Diamond and Stephen Bates, *The Spot: The Rise of Political Advertising on Television* (Cambridge: M.I.T. Press, 1984); William Leiss, Stephen Kline, and Sut Jhally, *Social Communication in Advertising: Persons, Products, and Images of Well-Being* (New York: Methuen, 1986); Lynda Lee Kaid, Dan Nimmo, and Keith R. Sanders, eds., *New Perspectives on Political Advertising* (Carbondale and Edwardsville: Southern Illinois Press, 1986); and W. Lance Haynes, "Of That Which We Cannot Write: Some Notes on the Phenomenology of Media," *Quarterly Journal of Speech*, February 1988, pp. 71–101.

47. Torben Vestergaard and Kim Schroder, *The Language of Advertising* (London: Basil Blackwell, 1985).

48. *Ibid.*, pp. 5–6.

49. *Ibid.*, p. 15.

50. *Ibid.*, pp. 18–19.

51. *Ibid.*, p. 23.

52. *Ibid.*, p. 27.

53. *Ibid.*, p. 45.

54. *Ibid.*, p. 50.

55. *Newsweek*, May 23, 1988, p. 31.

56. Vestergaard and Schroder, *op. cit.*, p. 66.

57. *Ibid.*, p. 67.

58. *Ibid.*, pp. 67–70.

59. *Ibid.*, p. 68.

60. *Ibid.*, p. 73.

61. *Ibid.*, pp. 73–109.

62. *Ibid.*, p. 74.

63. *Ibid.*, p. 80.

64. *Ibid.*, p. 81.

65. *Ibid.*, pp. 90–91.

66. *Ibid.*, p. 104.

67. *Ibid.*, p. 104.

68. *Ibid.*, pp. 110–116.

69. *Ibid.*, pp. 122–124.

70. *Ibid.*, pp. 124–139.

71. For an especially interesting discussion, see Olivia Goodkin and Maureen Ann Phillips, "The Subconscious Taken Captive: A Social, Ethical and Legal Analysis of Subliminal Communication Technology," *Southern California Law Review* 54:1077–1140, 1983.

72. *Ibid.*, p. 1083.

73. *Ibid.*

74. *Ibid.*, pp. 1083–1084.

75. *Ibid.*, pp. 1084–1086. See also Lander, "In Through the Out Door," *Omni*, February 1981, p. 45; Hal Becker and N. Glanzer, "Subliminal Communication: Advances in Audiovisual Engineering Applications for Behavior Therapy and Education," in *Proceedings of the 1978 Institute of Electrical and Electronics Engineers: Region 3* (Atlanta, 1978).

76. Goodkin and Phillips, *op. cit.*, p. 1084; "The CIA's Subliminal Seduction," *High Times*, February 1980, p. 96.

77. Wilson Bryan Key, *Subliminal Seduction: Ad Media's Manipulation of a Not So Innocent America* (New York: Signet Books, 1973), p. 4. The book also has several sample ads in which Key claims to have identified "embeds." Key has added to his claims in two subsequent books, *Media Sexploita-*

tion (New York: Signet Books, 1977) and *The Clambake Orgy* (New York: Signet Books, 1980).

78. Lander, *op. cit.*, p. 48. See also Goodkin and Phillips, *op. cit.*, pp. 1089–1091; they conclude that the technique has significant effect on behavior.

79. "Success Through Subconscious: Subliminal Tapes Help People Improve, Consultant Says," *Chicago Tribune*, October 1, 1987, sec. 1A, p. 28.

80. "Subliminals Used to Fight Smoking," *DeKalb Daily Chronicle*, November 18, 1987, p. 11.

81. Andrew Sullivan, "The New Raunchiness of American Advertising: Flogging Underwear," *The New Republic*, January 27, 1988, p. 24.

82. Sullivan, *op. cit.*, p. 24.

EPILOGUE

One recurring phenomenon I have noted as I revised *Persuasion: Reception and Responsibility* over the years is the continually accelerating rate of change in a gamut of arenas. Change is fascinating—even if it leads to chaos, confusion, or even violence. Consider just a few of the changes that have occurred since the fifth edition of this book was published in 1989, three short years ago. The cold war that so dominated American foreign policy for over forty years is apparently over. Leninist-Marxism seems utterly bankrupt, and the Soviet Bloc is disintegrating and faces immense changes in the 1990s—changes that will affect Americans as well. The Japanese are in the process of acquiring the world. The 1980s—the decade of greed—has been supplanted by a new concern for the environment. The baby boomers who put an end to the Vietnam War now face sending their own children to war elsewhere in the world. The nineties will see the graying of America as the same boomers who rejected American society in favor of the counterculture and who evolved from yippies to yuppies now face midlife as muppies. They are returning to church in droves as they seek the meaning of life; 80 percent of them consider themselves religious.[1] We still haven't come to grips with the national debt, the energy crisis, AIDS, terrorism, or the waning of American influence in the rest of the world. As all of these changes unfold, the number of persuasive messages confronting us continues to mushroom, and not only are the messages more numerous, they are infinitely more sophisticated.

Many of the themes emphasized in the preceding fourteen chapters of this book seem to foretell a bleak world for receivers in the twenty-first century: a loss of individual identity for most of us, deterioration of a sense of community in American culture, and an increasing volume of and sophistication in the development and distribution of persuasive messages. Robert Bellah and his colleagues, in *Habits of the Heart: Individualism and Commitment in American Life*, describe our predicament this way:

> But we have never faced a situation that called our deepest assumptions so radically into question. Our problems today are not just political. They are moral and have to do with the meaning of life. . . . we are beginning to understand that our common life requires more than an exclusive concern for material accumulation.
>
> Perhaps life is not a race whose only goal is being foremost. Perhaps the truth lies in what most of the world outside the modern West has always believed. That . . . work that is intrinsically rewarding is better for human beings than work that is only extrinsically rewarded. Perhaps enduring commitment to those we love and civic friendship toward our fellow citizens are preferable to restless competition and anxious self-defense. . . .
>
> We have imagined ourselves as a special creation, set apart from other humans. In the late twentieth century, we see that our poverty is as absolute as the poorest of nations. We have attempted to deny the human condition in our quest for power after power. It would be well for us to rejoin the human race.[2]

Perhaps these words are overly critical of contemporary American culture and too pessimistic about the future. But it seems that the 1990s bode ill for us. With such challenges to face, isn't it more important than ever that we train ourselves to be truly *responsible* receivers of persuasion? I think so, and my feelings are reinforced by communication researcher and professor Rod Hart of the University of Texas at Austin. He describes the dramatic appeal he makes to his students each term:

> On the first day of class, I observe to my students that all persuaders ask to borrow just a

bit of their minds, just for a little while. . . . I tell my students that my course will return their minds to them. I tell them that the cups-full of themselves they willingly loan out to teachers and preachers and cheerleaders in the bleachers can lead to an empty cupboard. I tell them that if they keep giving portions of them-selves away that there will be nothing left when they need themselves most — when confused, when frightened, when pressured for a decision. I tell them that persuasion is a science that moves by increments, that it happens most powerfully when it least seems to happen at all. . . . I try to instill a kind of arrogant humility in my students, a mindset that gives them the courage to disassemble rhetoric but also the wisdom never to underestimate it. . . . the persuasion course is the most important course they will take in college.[3]

As you conclude this course, I hope you will *not* conclude your practice of the reception skills discussed here. I hope you will try to expand your skills and your ability to critically "disassemble rhetoric" and get at its obvious and hidden meanings. I hope you will recognize the complexities of the world we live in and the many persuasive messages we receive. I trust your instinctive suspicion of persuasive appeals. Together with Professor Hart, I ". . . trust, mostly, in the critical mind's wondrous capacity to call a spade a spade and a rhetoric a rhetoric, to depuff puffery and to make mortals of gods, and to maintain a tenacious resolve that we shall not all fall, lemminglike into the sea."[4]

NOTES

1. "A Time to Seek," *Newsweek*, December 17, 1990, pp. 50–55.
2. Robert N. Bellah, Richard Madsen, William Sullivan, Ann Swidler, and Steven M. Tipton, *Habits of the Heart: Individualism and Commitment in American Life* (New York: Harper & Row, 1985), pp. 295–296.
3. Roderick P. Hart, "Teaching the Undergraduate Persuasion Course: Why?" in J. Daly, G. Friedrich, and A. Vangelisti (Eds.), *Teaching Communication* (Hillsdale, NJ: Lawrence Erlbaum, 1990).
4. *Ibid.*

INDEX